ANCIENT ISRAEL

FOURTH EDITION

ANCIENT ISRAEL

From Abraham to the Roman Destruction of the Temple

FOURTH EDITION

EDITED BY
JOHN MERRILL AND
HERSHEL SHANKS

BIBLICAL ARCHAEOLOGY SOCIETY
WASHINGTON, DC

© 2021 by Biblical Archaeology Society

PUBLISHED BY
Biblical Archaeology Society
4710 41st Street, NW
Washington, DC 20016
www.biblicalarchaeology.org

Printed in the United States of America

All rights reserved under International and
Pan-American Copyright Conventions.
First edition 1988. Second edition 1999. Third edition 2010.

Library of Congress Cataloging-in-Publication Data

NAMES:
Merrill, John, editor. | Shanks, Hershel, editor.

TITLE:
Ancient Israel : from Abraham to the Roman destruction of the
Temple / edited by John Merrill and Hershel Shanks.—4th ed.

DESCRIPTION:
Washington, DC: Biblical Archaeology Society, [2021] | Includes
bibliographical references and index.

IDENTIFIERS:
LCCN 2021933277 | ISBN 9781880317235 (hardback) | ISBN
9781880317273 (paperback) | ISBN 9781880317303 (PDF) | ISBN
9781880317402 (EPUB)

SUBJECTS:
Jews—History—To 70 A.D.

CLASSIFICATION:
LCC DS121.A53 2021 (print)
LCC DS121.A53 (ebook)
DDC 933—dc22

LC record available at https://lccn.loc.gov/2021933277

Design by AURAS Design, Inc.

Image credits are noted in the back of the book.

COVER PHOTO:
A section of the original wall surrounding the City of David.

This Fourth Edition of Ancient Israel *is dedicated to the memory of Hershel Shanks.*

Hershel was a person of penetrating intellect who made the sometimes arcane field of biblical archaeology accessible to legions of non-specialist readers. This present volume expands on the solid foundation that Hershel and his many expert contributors built upon in previous editions.

It is said that immortality resides in the succession of human memories, with the insights gained in one lifetime being passed on to the generations that follow. *Ancient Israel* is part of his worthy legacy.

Contents

Illustrations

FIGURES

MAPS

COLOR PLATES

TABLES AND CHARTS

The Contributors

ANDREA M. BERLIN is the James R. Wiseman Chair in Classical Archaeology at Boston University. She has been excavating in the eastern Mediterranean for more than 30 years, working on projects from Troy in Turkey to Coptos in southern Egypt to Paestum, in Italy. Her specialty is the Near East from the time of Alexander the Great through the Roman era, with a focus on the realities of daily life, and the intersection of politics and cultural change in antiquity. Recent publications include "Land/Homeland, Story/History: the Social Landscapes of the Southern Levant from Alexander to Augustus," in *The Cambridge Social Archaeology of the Levant from Prehistory to the Present* (Cambridge Univ. Press, 2018) and *Spear-Won Land: Sardis, from the King's Peace to the Peace of Apamea*, coedited with Paul Kosmin (Univ. of Wisconsin Press, 2019).

MANFRED BIETAK studied Egyptology and Prehistory at University of Vienna (PhD 1964). He directed excavations in Sayala/Nubia (1961–1965), Tell el-Dab'a (1966–2011; discovery of Avaris, Hyksos capital), Thebes (1969–1978), and Bubastis (2013–2015). Bietak is Founder/Director of the Austrian Archaeological Institute Cairo (1973–2009); Chair-Prof., University Vienna (1989–2009); Director, Vienna Institute of Archaeological Science (2003–2011); Chairman, Commission of Egypt and the Levant, Austrian Academy of Sciences (1993–2013); Director, Special Research Programme SCIEM 2000 (FWF), at Austrian Academy of Sciences (1999–2011); and PI of the ERC Advanced Grant "The Hyksos Enigma" (2016–2020). He was a visiting professor at Collège de France (1997, 2006), Harvard (2004). Member of the Austrian, the American, the Royal Swedish, the British, Gothenburg, dei Lincei, and Polish academies, of Institut de France (AIBL), Institut d'Égypte, and German Archaeological Institute, and an Honorary Member of AIA. Bietak has (co)authored 17 monographs and more than 250 articles. He is the Editor-in-Chief of *Egypt and the Levant* (vols. 1–30) and has edited 80 monographs in the fields of Egyptology and Mediterranean Archaeology.

JENNIE EBELING is Associate Professor of Archaeology at the University of Evansville in Indiana and codirector of the Jezreel Expedition in Israel. Her research specialties include ancient food and drink technology and women in Canaan and ancient Israel, and religion and cult in the Bronze and Iron Age Levant. Her publications include *Women's Lives in Biblical Times* (2010) and the edited volumes *The Old Testament in Archaeology and History* (2017; with J.E. Wright, M. Elliott, and P.V.M. Flesher), *Household Archaeology in Ancient Israel and Beyond* (2011; with A. Yasur-Landau and L. Mazow), and *New Approaches to Old Stones: Recent Studies of Ground Stone Artifacts* (2008; with Y.M. Rowan). She is a frequent presenter at BAS Bible & Archaeology Fests and was a scholar-in-residence at BAS's St. Olaf Lecture Seminar program in 2016 and 2019.

MELODY D. KNOWLES is Associate Professor of Old Testament and Vice President of Academic Affairs at Virginia Theological Seminary. Her research areas include Yahwistic religion, ancient women's religious practices, and Jerusalem in the Persian period. In addition to chairing the sections on Book of Psalms as well as Chronicles-Ezra-Nehemiah for the Society of Biblical Literature, she has participated in excavations at Beth-Shemesh and Tel Miqne.

ANDRÉ LEMAIRE is Professor of Hebrew and Aramaic philology and epigraphy in the department of Historical and Philological Sciences at the École Pratique des Hautes Études at the Sorbonne in Paris. He has worked for more than 35 years in the fields of Northwest Semitic epigraphy, archaeology, ancient Hebrew literature and history and has published more than ten books and 400 articles on those subjects. In addition, he has participated in excavations at Lachish, Tel Keisan, Yarmouth and other sites in Israel.

JOHN MERRILL holds bachelor's and master's degrees from Harvard University. He is a former Chairman and current Trustee of the Biblical Archaeology Society, as well as a Contributing Editor of *Biblical Archaeology Review*. He has sponsored and participated in numerous archaeological investigations of ancient Israel, with emphasis on the Hasmonean, Herodian, and Roman periods. He has published two books dealing with these historical periods—*Sons of Light* and *The Pharisee Enigma*.

ERIC M. MEYERS is the Bernice and Morton Lerner Emeritus Professor of Religious and Jewish Studies at Duke University. He founded the Center for Jewish Studies at Duke, in 1972. His specialties include biblical studies and archaeology. He has directed or co-directed digs in Israel and Italy for more than forty years and has authored hundreds of articles, reviews, and reports, as well as 15 books. With his wife, Carol Meyers, he co-authored commentaries on Haggai and Zechariah for the Anchor Bible Series. He served as editor-in-chief of the monumental *Oxford Encyclopedia of Archaeology in the Near East* (1997). His most recent excavations (at Sepphoris) were fully published in 2018 by Penn State University Press under the Eisenbrauns imprint. Meyers also served for three terms as President of ASOR (The American Schools/Society of Overseas Research).

GARY A. RENDSBURG serves as the Blanche and Irving Laurie Professor of Jewish History and holds the rank of Distinguished Professor in the Department of Jewish Studies at Rutgers University. His teaching and research focus on ancient Israel, the history of the Hebrew language, and medieval Hebrew manuscripts. Rendsburg is the author of seven books and about 180 articles. His most recent book is *How the Bible Is Written* (Hendrickson, 2019), with attention to the use of language to create literature. In addition, he has produced two programs for the Great Courses series, one on the Book of Genesis and one on the Dead Sea Scrolls. During his career, Prof. Rendsburg has served as visiting professor or visiting researcher at the University of Oxford, the University of Cambridge, the University of Sydney, Hebrew University, UCLA, Colgate University, and the University of Pennsylvania.

Acknowledgments

NO PUBLICATION OF THE COMPLEXITY AND SCOPE of *Ancient Israel* could be completed without the efforts of a highly capable supporting cast. The editors wish to acknowledge, in particular, *BAR*'s Associate Editor, Marek Dospěl, who managed the Herculean task of pulling all the diverse material together, conducting the copy edit, and overseeing the subsequent flow of editorial work. BAS staff members Heather Metzger and Margaret Warker contributed to the overall production, including especially images, copyrights, and printing arrangements. Connie Binder compiled the index, and Evelyn Bence read the page proofs. Robert Sugar and his team at AURAS Design created design and layout of the book. And of course, all of this work was performed under the watchful eye of BAS's President and Publisher, Susan Laden.

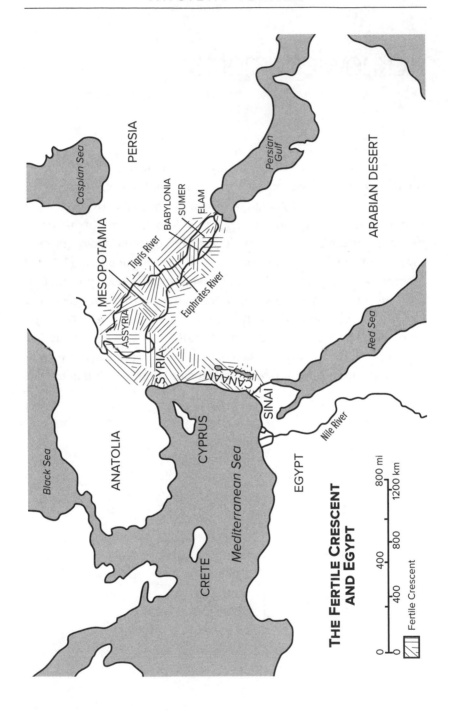

THE FERTILE CRESCENT AND EGYPT

Fertile Crescent

ANCIENT ISRAEL AND ENVIRONS

Mediterranean Sea

Sidon
Tyre
PHOENICIA
Lebanon Mtns.
Anti-Lebanon Mtns.
Damascus
THE KING'S HIGHWAY
Dan
Lake Huleh
Hazor
BASHAN
HAURAN
Acco
Highlands of Galilee
Sea of Galilee
Wadi Yarmuk
Carmel Mtns.
Dor
Mt. Tabor
Megiddo
Jezreel Valley
GILEAD
Taanach
Ibleam
Beth-Shean
Ramoth-gilead
Mt. Gilboa
Jabesh-gilead
Hepher
Samaria
Tirzah
Shechem
Mt. Ebal
Wadi Jabbok
Mt. Gerizim
Succoth
Plain of Sharon
Qasile
Joppa
Aphek
Shiloh
Highlands of Samaria
AMMON
Rabbah
Bethel
VIA MARIS
Gezer
Jericho
Jordan River
Gibeon
Jerusalem
Mt. Nebo
Heshbon
Ashdod
Ekron
Beth-Shemesh
Bethlehem
Ashkelon
Gath
Philistine Plain
Lachish
Hebron
Dibon
Gaza
SHEPHELAH
Ein Gedi
Wadi Arnon
Dead Sea
Gerar
MOAB
Arad
Beersheba
Kir-Hareseth
VIA MARIS
NEGEV
Wadi Zered
ARABAH
EDOM
THE KING'S HIGHWAY

Kadesh-Barnea

0   10   20   30   40 mi
0 10 20 30 40 50 60 km

— · — · — trade route

Petra

Abbreviations

AB	*The Anchor Bible*
ABD	*Anchor Bible Dictionary*
ABR	*Australian Biblical Review*
ADPV	Abhandlungen des Deutschen Palästina-Vereins
Ag. Ap.	Flavius Josephus, *Against Apion*
Anabasis	Xenophon, *Anabasis*
ANET	James B. Pritchard, ed., *Ancient Near Eastern Texts*, 3rd ed. (Princeton: Princeton Univ. Press, 1969)
Ant.	Flavius Josephus, *Antiquities of the Jews*
AOAT	Alter Orient und Altes Testament
ASOR	American Society of Overseas Research
BA	*The Biblical Archaeologist*
BAR	*Biblical Archaeology Review*
BAS	Biblical Archaeology Society
BASOR	*Bulletin of the American Schools of Oriental Research*
BETL	Bibliotheca Ephemeridum theologicarum Lovaniensium
BN	*Biblische Notizen*
BR	*Bible Review*
BT	Babylonian Talmud, or Bavli
BWA(N)T	Beiträge zur Wissenschaft vom Alten und Neuen Testament
BZAW	Beiheft zur Zeitschrift für die alttestamentliche Wissenschaft
CAT	Manfried Dietrich, Oswald Loretz, and Joaquín Sanmartín, eds., *The Cuneiform Alphabetic Texts from Ugarit, Ras Ibn Hani and Other Places* (Münster: Ugarit-Verlag, 1995).
CBQ	*Catholic Biblical Quarterly*
CD	Cairo Damascus Document
CHANE	Culture and History of the Ancient Near East
COS	*The Context of Scripture*, 4 vols., ed. William W. Hallo and K. Lawson Younger Jr. (Leiden: Brill, 1997–2016)
Cyropaedia	Xenophon, *Cyropaedia*
EA	El-Amarna Tablets
FAT	Forschungen zum Alten Testament
Good Person	Philo, *That Every Good Person Is Free*
HBAI	*Hebrew Bible and Ancient Israel*
HTR	*Harvard Theological Review*
Hypothetica	Philo, *Hypothetica*
IAA	Israel Antiquities Authority
IEJ	*Israel Exploration Journal*
IES	Israel Exploration Society
JAA	*Journal of Anthropological Archaeology*
JANER	*Journal of the Ancient Near Eastern Religions*
JANES	*Journal of the Ancient Near Eastern Society*
JAOS	*Journal of the American Oriental Society*
JBL	*Journal of Biblical Literature*
JCS	*Journal of Cuneiform Studies*
JEA	*Journal of Egyptian Archaeology*
JESHO	*Journal of the Economic and Social History of the Orient*
JJS	*Journal of Jewish Studies*
JNES	*Journal of Near Eastern Studies*
JPS	Jewish Publication Society
JSJ	*Journal for the Study of Judaism*
JSOT	*Journal for the Study of the Old Testament*
JSOTSup	Journal for the Study of the Old Testament, Supplement
JT	Jerusalem Talmud, or Yerushalmi (Palestinian Talmud)
J.W.	Flavius Josephus, *The Jewish War*
LHBOTS	The Library of Hebrew Bible/Old Testament Studies
Life	Flavius Josephus, *The Life*
Loeb	Loeb Classical Library (Cambridge, MA: Harvard Univ. Press)

LXX	Septuagint
NEA	Near Eastern Archaeology
NEAEHL	The New Encyclopedia of Archaeological Excavations in the Holy Land, 5 vols., ed. E. Stern (Jerusalem: IES; Carta, 1993–2008)
NRSV	New Revised Standard Version
OBO	Orbis Biblicus et Orientalis
OLA	Orientalia Lovaniensia Analecta
PEQ	Palestinian Exploration Quarterly
R.	Rabbi
RA	Revue d'Assyriologie et d'archéologie orientale
RB	Revue Biblique
SBL	Society of Biblical Literature
SWBAS	Social World of Biblical Antiquity Series
TA	Tel Aviv: Journal of the Institute of Archaeology of Tel Aviv University
TynB	Tyndale Bulletin
UCLA	University of California–Los Angeles
UF	Ugarit-Forschungen
VT	Vetus Testamentum
VTSup	Vetus Testamentum, Supplements
WAWSup	Writings from the Ancient World Supplement
WUNT	Wissenschaftliche Untersuchungen zum Neuen Testament
ZABR	Zeitschrif für altorientalische und biblische Rechtsgeschichte
ZAW	Zeitschrift für die alttestamentliche Wissenschaft
ZDPV	Zeitschrift des Deutschen Palästina-Vereins

Introduction

ANCIENT ISRAEL WAS FIRST CONCEIVED some 35 years ago by Hershel Shanks, the inimitable editor of *Biblical Archaeology Review*. Originally published in 1988, the book has been revised and updated approximately every ten years. This volume represents the fourth edition.

The distinctive attributes of *Ancient Israel* that were enumerated by Hershel in 1988 remain largely applicable today. It is compact, covering the more than a millennium of history beginning with the ancestral narratives and ending with the cataclysmic destruction of the Jerusalem Temple, all in a space of 420-odd pages of text, pictures, charts, and images. Its contents have been composed by, or derived from the work of, leading scholars in the field and reflect recent developments in scholarly understanding and archaeological discoveries.

Throughout its various iterations, *Ancient Israel* has been aimed at readers who are taking their first look at the history of ancient Israel—whether they are students, members of adult study groups, or simply the intellectually curious of all ages. The book is more than an introductory course, however. It is also an invaluable reference source, to which readers can return again and again to refresh themselves on the many complex facets of Israel's remarkable history. Moreover, each chapter is loaded with citations from supporting scholarly investigations and archaeological findings that will guide readers who wish to undertake a more intensive study program.

In the several decades that have passed since *Ancient Israel's* initial publication, it is inevitable that many of the work's original contributors—all "giants in the field," as Hershel liked to say—have not been available to provide revisions of their own work. In those cases, the editors have used various devices to update the material, while preserving as much of the original as possible. Some revisions have been performed by assistants to the original authors; for other chapters, new authors have been recruited; as a last resort, revisions have been performed by the editors themselves, although always with considerable input from experts. The details of all of these layers of authorship and revision have been carefully set forth by Hershel in his introductions to previous editions, so I will not repeat them here, but instead will focus on the process by which the fourth edition has been created.

First, we are pleased and privileged that two of our earlier contributors are still with us—André Lemaire, author of chapter 4 (*The Early Monarchy*), and Eric Meyers, author of chapter 6 (*Exile and Return*). In chapter 5 (*Israel and Judah in Iron Age II*), Melody Knowles has updated key passages to integrate new scholarly thinking and archaeology while preserving much of the earlier work of Kyle McCarter. Gary Rendsburg, who consulted extensively in the preparation of the third edition, has now taken over two chapters in their entirety—chapter 1 (*The Ancestral Narratives*), and chapter 3 (*The Emergence of Israel in the Land of Canaan*). In addition, Professor Rendsburg has collaborated with the noted Egyptologist, Manfred Bietak, in the composing of chapter 2 (*Egypt and the Exodus*).

Chapter 7 (*Judea in the Hellenistic Period*) and chapter 8 (*The Era of Roman Domination*) were originally authored, respectively, by Lee Levine and Shaye Cohen, neither of whom was available for the present undertaking. Discovering that his powers of persuasion had been exhausted by unsuccessful efforts to secure alternate contributors, your editor as a last resort tasked himself to make the appropriate revisions. In both cases, the sense of the original versions was painstakingly preserved, with full credit given to the original authors in the text and notes. Readers familiar with those earlier texts will note that some of the cultural material has been condensed to make room for more pure history. *Ancient Israel* is, after all, first and foremost a work of history, and the precise sequencing of events, as well as the clear identification of the relevant historical figures, seemed useful to understanding what transpired and why in these very turbulent periods of Israel's history. Moreover, the revisions to these chapters were not undertaken without significant expert assistance, including especially Andrea Berlin's careful reading of and numerous insights added to chapter 7, with the customary disclaimer that any errors or omissions are entirely the responsibility of the editor.

Jennie Ebeling's much appreciated contributions appear throughout the book, highlighting the important role of women in Israel's history, which has too often been overlooked in earlier scholarship due to the (at least outwardly) patriarchal nature of Israel's social order.

In sum, the fourth edition contains a great deal of fresh and updated information. It should be emphasized, however, that much of the core material originally created under the guidance of Hershel Shanks still remains.

Ancient Israel is aimed at the nonspecialist reader approaching the history of Israel for the first time. In this context, my own introduction to the book may be instructive. In 1986, I discovered in my late father's library, an inscribed copy of Albert Schweitzer's seminal work *The Quest of the Historical Jesus*.* The concept of Jesus as an actual historical figure intrigued me, but reading Schweitzer's book only served to deepen the mystery surrounding this subject and launched me on a decades-long program of research. One thing became clear early on: one could not possibly understand Jesus as a historical figure without first immersing oneself not only in the actual historical period in which Jesus lived, but also in the less-known (outside scholarly circles) history that preceded it. *Ancient Israel* was my first introduction to that history; I have turned to it repeatedly as a reference source, even though it is now joined by more than 400 volumes on related topics in my personal library. I sincerely hope this fourth edition will prove as useful to the new generation of readers as the previous editions have to me.

John Merrill
September 2020
Stanardsville, Virginia

---

* Translated by W. Montgomery, 3rd ed. (London: Adam and Charles Black, 1956). My father, a physician and Harvard Medical School Professor, had visited Schweitzer's hospital in Lambarene, French West Africa, shortly before Schweitzer's death in 1965.

1

The Ancestral Narratives

GARY A. RENDSBURG

ACCORDING TO THE BIBLICAL TRADITION, the people of ancient Israel traced their ancestry back to the three patriarchs: Abraham, Isaac, and Jacob. The name of the third of these, Jacob, was changed to Israel (Genesis 32:28-29; 35:10), and thus he becomes the eponymous ancestor of the people of Israel. Jacob/Israel, in turn, had twelve sons (Reuben, Simeon, Levi, Judah, etc.), each of whom becomes the eponymous ancestor of one of the twelve Israelite tribes.[1]

Origins

From the vantage point of modern history and historiography, clearly, the entire population of a nation does not spring from the offspring of one man. But such was the biblical tradition, which created an idealized account of the nation's origins, and which no doubt played a major role in the creation of a national consciousness. Since other biblical sources and archaeological evidence show that the people of Israel had diverse origins (see chap. 3), the narrative of the Book of Genesis (along with the rest of the Torah and the Book of Joshua) serves to unify the entirety of the nation. Regardless of whether one could trace one's ancestry back to the patriarchs or not, *all of Israel* was seen to be descended from Jacob/Israel, and, in turn, from Isaac and Abraham.[2]

1

The major part of the Book of Genesis (esp. chaps. 12–50), accordingly, narrates the story of a family: the three generations of the patriarchs and their primary wives. The key individuals, thus, are the following: Abraham and his primary wife, Sarah; Isaac and his wife Rebekah; Jacob and his two primary wives, Rachel and Leah. Then follows the generation of Jacob's twelve sons and one daughter, with the most prominent figures of Joseph and Judah, and with Reuben, Simeon, Levi, Benjamin, and Dinah also playing key roles. The narrative in the Book of Genesis, accordingly, is mainly a family affair.

At a distance of more than 3,000 years, it is difficult enough to find the people of Israel in the historical documentation (see chaps. 2–3); *a fortiori*, it is well-nigh impossible to find a single family or even more so a single individual within that family in the historical record. As such, any quest to identify the geographical and chronological horizons of the ancestral narratives must rely almost solely on the biblical material itself. Once such has been accorded, we then can seek background material from the wider ancient Near East. But first a word is due about the term "ancestral narratives" used within the title of this chapter, which in the previous editions was called "The Patriarchal Age."

The Term "Ancestral Narratives"

Throughout much of the 20th century, scholars believed that they could pinpoint the actual time period when the patriarchs lived, hence the term "patriarchal age," with emphasis on the second word. The focus typically was on the men alone, hence the emphasis on the first word. Today, scholars are less optimistic about situating the Genesis narratives in a particular historical context dated to a particular epoch, and there is now a recognition of the gender bias in the word "patriarchal." Accordingly, instead of attempting to determine the historical era of the patriarchs, scholars are much more likely to focus on the narratives themselves and what they may teach us about ancient Israel. They are also aware of the prominent role that the female characters play. After all, the story is about a family, and wives and mothers and daughters are central to the character and functioning of any family. Hence "The Ancestral Narratives" instead of "The Patriarchal Age" in the title of this chapter, even if, by necessity, we will use the latter term occasionally.

Matriarchs in a Patriarchal Society

The name of this chapter in previous editions ("The Patriarchal Age") did not do justice to the central role of women in the stories about Israel's ancestors. Even a random perusal of the Bible will discover women who are the antithesis of what we might expect from a patriarchal society. Biblical female protagonists are not passive, demure, timid, or submissive but rather bold and assertive, in which they differ significantly from the treatment of women in contemporaneous Near Eastern literature.

Why the difference, one might ask. It is because these female figures—although often not Israelites themselves—symbolically represent the newly emergent nation of Israel. That is, Israel was a small and relatively power-less nation, struggling to exist on the margins of more powerful, established empires like Egypt and Assyria. Lacking natural gifts and physical prowess, the Israelites could only survive through daring and determination. And this is how the women in the biblical stories are portrayed—from Yael, who killed the enemy general with a tent peg, to Rahab, whose courage was instrumental in Joshua's entry into Canaan.

Countless other examples are cited in Rendsburg's engaging article (see n. 23), which readers are invited to investigate further in the BAS online library. —ED.

In light of all that is stated here, many scholars view the quest to establish the putative time and place of Abraham and Sarah and the ensuing generations to be a "pursuit of the wind."[3] We understand this scholarly position, but in a book titled *Ancient Israel*, in which the reader may expect to find at least some discussion on the topic, we believe that the quest may be undertaken, even should be undertaken, albeit cautiously and judiciously.

From Where Did Abraham Come?

Fortunately, the Bible provides sufficient clues for an answer to the question of Abraham's origin. In Genesis 11:28, we learn that the family of Terah (father of Abraham[4]) originates in the city of Ur of the Chaldees (Heb. *'ur kaśdim*). In verse 31, we read, "And Terah took Abram his son, and Lot the son of Haran, the son of his son, and Sarai his daughter-in-law, the wife of Abram his son; and they went out with them from Ur of the Chaldees to go to the land of Canaan, and they came unto Harran, and they dwelt there." From this passage we learn that a journey from Ur of the Chaldees to Canaan would pass through Harran. Another important clue is offered in Joshua 24:2–3, where we learn that the ancestors of Israel lived "beyond the Euphrates," until God took Abraham from "beyond the Euphrates."[5]

These data points allow us to conclude that Abraham came from the city of Ur in northern Mesopotamia, that is, modern-day Urfa in southern Turkey. Local Jewish, Christian, and Muslim tradition holds that the city is the birthplace of Abraham, and there is no reason to question this belief, since it matches well with the information provided by the Bible.[6] Most likely, this city is the one mentioned as Ura in cuneiform tablets from Ugarit (14th–13th centuries), where it is associated with the Hittite realm.[7]

Many readers will have read elsewhere that Ur of the Chaldees is the great city of Ur in southern Mesopotamia, located at modern Tell el-Muqayyar in southern Iraq. There are several problems with this identification. First, the city flourished during the late third and early second millennium, which is too early for the date of Abraham. Second, Ur was a great metropolis of the Sumerians, of whom there is little or no mention in the Bible. Finally, the geography is all wrong, because the Ur in southern Iraq is not "beyond the Euphrates" but rather on the western banks of the river; and a journey from this Ur to Canaan would not take one via Harran.[8]

Although the identification of the birthplace of Abraham with Ur of Sumer in southern Iraq is standard teaching—present in almost all introductory textbooks of the Bible and the ancient Near East—it is wrong.[9] There is simply nothing to connect Abraham with the city. So how and why was the identification made? Leonard Woolley, who excavated the site during the years 1922–1934, uncovered one of the largest cities of the ancient world, replete with the great ziggurat, tens of thousands of cuneiform tablets, and the world's oldest law code, that of Ur-Nammu, king of Sumer (r. 2047–2030). Woolley simply assumed that Abraham must have come from only as great a city as Ur of Sumer.[10]

How, then, does one explain the latter part of the expression "Ur of the Chaldees"? The Chaldeans were indeed resident in southern

Mesopotamia during the first millennium B.C.E., making the terms Babylonia and Chaldea virtually interchangeable during the seventh and sixth centuries B.C.E. (see chaps. 5–6). But we know that the Chaldeans were not native to the land, to which they most likely had migrated from the northern reaches of Mesopotamia. The best evidence comes from the Greek historian Xenophon, who mentions the Chaldeans as a warlike people blocking the way to Armenia (*Anabasis* 4.3.4), and as neighbors of the Armenians but at war with them (*Cyropaedia* 3.1.34). Xenophon further mentions the Chaldeans in connection with the Carduchi (i.e., the ancient Kurds) (*Anabasis* 5.5.17). To this day, the name "Chaldeans" lives on within the Christian community of the region.

It is further noteworthy that the names of Terah's father (Nahor) and grandfather (Serug) are the names of cities in the general region of modern Urfa. While the precise location in upper Mesopotamia of Naḫur as known from Akkadian sources remains unknown, Serug— well known from later Syriac sources and called Suruç in modern Turkish—lies 29 miles (46 km) southwest of Urfa. In sum, everything points to a northern Mesopotamian location for Ur of the Chaldees.

The Bible refers to this region generally as Aram Naharaim, meaning "Aram of the Two Rivers" (Genesis 24:10, etc.). The biblical tradition of "a wandering Aramean was my father" (Deuteronomy 26:5)—referencing either Abraham or Jacob in the terse retelling of Israel's history—similarly situates the ancestral origins in northern Mesopotamia.

Nevertheless, there most likely is a connection between the great city of Ur of Sumer in the south and Ur of the Chaldees in the north. While we have no direct evidence to substantiate the claim, presumably northern Ur was established as a colony of the metropolis in the south. This would explain the expression *'ur kaśdim*, "Ur of the Chaldees." The great Ur required no further appellation, but one of its outposts did. In a similar manner, we must specify "London, Ontario" when referring to the New World outpost of the great city of England.

When Did Abraham Live?

Chronology of Abraham's (purported) life is another thorny question. Scholars have proposed a range of about seven centuries in which to situate the first patriarch: anywhere from c. 2100 to c. 1400, with the more recent date being the one best supported by the evidence.

Genesis 14 tells a story of the war between four invading kings from the north and east and the local five kings of the Dead Sea region (including those of the cities of Sodom and Gomorrah). The four invading kings are Amraphel of Shinar, Arioch of Ellasar, Chedorlaomer of Elam, and Tidal of Goiim. One would hope that at least one of these royal figures could be identified in the historical documentation from Mesopotamian sources, but such is not the case. Of the place names, Shinar most likely is the Hebrew version of Sumer; Elam is to the east of the Tigris River, in modern-day Iran; while Ellasar and Goiim are unknown. But we know of no king of Sumer or southern Mesopotamia by the name of Amraphel nor a king of Elam by the name of Chedorlaomer. The name Tidal, which is the Semitic way of writing the Hittite royal name Tudḫalia, was borne by four individual kings, who reigned during the years 1430–1230. Oddly, Tidal in the Bible is not associated with the Hittites but the enigmatic term Goiim (Hebrew *goyim*), which means simply "nations". Moreover, we have no record of any invasion by any of the Tudḫalias as far distant as southern Canaan, in the region of the Dead Sea. So while Genesis 14 may have some potential in the quest to situate Abraham chronologically, in the end, there is nothing within the chapter that allows one to pin down a specific date.

In similar fashion, we have no knowledge of any of the local kings mentioned in the Book of Genesis. This includes the five defending kings in Genesis 14; Melchizedek king of Salem (also Genesis 14); Abimelech king of Gerar (Genesis 20 and 26); Hamor king of Shechem (Genesis 34); and the long list of Edomite kings (Genesis 36). And while two pharaohs are mentioned in Genesis—one contemporary with Abraham (Genesis 12) and one with Joseph (Genesis 39–50)— only the title "pharaoh" or the phrase "king of Egypt" is used, with no name given in either instance.[11] One potential clue is the phrase "land of Ra'amses" (Genesis 47:11) as the designation for the eastern Delta, a term which could have arisen only with the reigns of the first two pharaohs bearing that name: Ramesses I (r. 1301–1300) and Ramesses II (r. 1290–1224)—unless the reference is an anachronism.

Years vs. Genealogies

In reaching back to as early as 2100 B.C.E., or even 1800, scholars have relied too heavily on the years provided in the Bible. The ages of the patriarchs presented in the Bible are clearly exaggerated and apparently evoke some sort of numerical symbolism:[12]

Abraham: $175 = 5^2 \times 7$ (Genesis 25:7)

Isaac: $180 = 6^2 \times 5$ (Genesis 35:28)

Jacob: $147 = 7^2 \times 3$ (Genesis 47:28)

Although the significance of these numbers eludes us, they presumably meant something to the author and to at least the informed portion of his reading audience. To be sure, these figures and others like them (e.g., Abraham was 100 years old at the birth of Isaac [Genesis 21:5]) behoove the modern reader not to rely on them as a chronological guide.

A much better guide is the approximate span of time that can be calculated based on the genealogies in the Bible.[13] Note, for example, the following lineage in Exodus 6:16–20: Abraham – Isaac – Jacob – Levi – Kohath – Amram – Moses. The date and nature of the Exodus are still debated, but almost all scholars agree that c. 1200 offers the most likely background of the biblical account. Accepting 1200 and estimating 30 years per generation,[14] we can calculate back in the following manner (using 1230 for Moses, since he already was older at the time of the Exodus):

1230: Moses	1350: Jacob
1260: Amram	1380: Isaac
1290: Kohath	1410: Abraham
1320: Levi	

Dating Abraham to c. 1400 places "the patriarchal age" in the Late Bronze Age (c. 1550–c. 1150).[15]

A Possible Middle Bronze Age Setting

Those who date "the patriarchal age" to the Middle Bronze Age (c. 2000–c. 1550), rely on the years expressed in the Bible, not on the genealogies. Their approach must postulate that many generations have been omitted from the biblical account and/or have been telescoped in the genealogies. Both ancient Near Eastern documentation and modern Bedouin cultural parallels, however, inform us that the genealogies are a much more accurate guide to a relative chronology than the time spans calculated by given years. For example, Nabonidus king of Babylon (r. 556–539) asserts that Naram-Sin, king of Akkad (r. c. 2254 –c. 2218), ruled 3,200 years before his time,[16] when we know that the distance separating the two rulers is c. 1,700 years. On the contemporary side, one may observe very accurate genealogical reckoning among the Bedouin, reaching back seven or even ten generations.[17]

Those who look to the Middle Bronze Age for the background of the Genesis narrative and/or Israel's origins often point to cultural and linguistic parallels forthcoming from Mari, a major city on the Euphrates in eastern Syria that flourished between c. 1850 and 1750.[18] One Mari text refers to the burial of precious metal belonging to the gods, which may remind us of Jacob burying jewelry near Shechem (Genesis 35:4). And the Akkadian word *merḫu(m)*, "high official, royal agent," attested in the Mari documents, is cognate to Hebrew *mere'*, which describes the position held by Ahuzzath, adviser to Abimelech king of Gerar (Genesis 26:26). In general, one observes the coexistence of urbanites (at Mari itself) and pastoralists (on the steppe land), a setting which calls to mind the patriarchs with their flocks near urban centers.[19]

While these and other parallels are intriguing, dating "the patriarchal age" to the Middle Bronze Age still faces the difficulty of the internal biblical data, especially the genealogical information. A reasonable way to resolve the issue is to assume that the social patterns, cultural markers, and linguistic items reflected in the Mari documents persisted in the general region of northern Mesopotamia (and elsewhere) into the Late Bronze Age (and perhaps later still).

The Late Bronze Age Setting

While placing Abraham in northern Mesopotamia (the general region of modern-day south-central Turkey) in c. 1400 B.C.E., we cannot make claims about a historical personage *per se*, for there is no extra-biblical documentation for said person, his wife, and others in his circle. Instead, we should understand Abraham as a figure—perhaps historical, perhaps legendary—representing for the Israelites the beginnings of their religious, cultural, and national identity.[20] And if not Abraham, then certainly Jacob, whose name was changed to Israel, in his role as eponymous ancestor. Furthermore, the ancestral narratives are not historical documents but rather literary creations told in the most vivid manner.[21]

We are not at a dead end, though. Once we have properly understood the geographical and chronological setting of the Genesis narratives, we are in a position to say more about the social, legal, and cultural norms reflected therein. Two Late Bronze Age sites are particularly helpful: Ugarit and Nuzi. Ugarit flourished in northern coastal Syria (reflecting the world of greater Canaan) between 1400 and 1200. The most relevant material from the site are two literary works: the Epic of Kirta and the Epic of Aqhat (the former a legendary king, the latter the son of the legendary king Dan'el), with significant parallels to the Genesis narratives.[22] Nuzi, in modern-day northern Iraq (reflecting Hurrian culture), has yielded approximately 6,000 cuneiform tablets with documentary texts dated to the 14th century B.C.E. The documents detail the legal, social, and economic life of the city, thus providing parallels to customs reflected in the Book of Genesis.

Ugaritic Parallels

The Patriarchal narratives of the Book of Genesis are dominated by two literary motifs: the childless hero with a barren wife; and the younger son. The first motif occurs with Abraham and Sarah (much of chaps. 15–21), Isaac and Rebekah (25:21), and Rachel (29:31; 30:22). Later in the Bible, the barren woman motif occurs with the wife of Manoah (Judges 13) and with Hannah (1 Samuel 1). The younger son motif appears in Genesis through setting aside primogeniture in each successive generation, so that the younger Isaac supersedes the firstborn Ishmael, Jacob supersedes Esau, Joseph supersedes his brothers, Perez supersedes Zerah, and Ephraim supersedes Manasseh. This motif is perhaps foreshadowed with God's favoring Abel over his elder brother Cain (Genesis 4) and is further reflected in the Book of Exodus, where Moses becomes the leader of the Israelites, with the firstborn Aaron holding second position (see

Exodus 7:7). The motif surfaces yet again in the case of David, whose last-born status is explicitly noted (1 Samuel 16:1–13), and then once more in the next generation, with Solomon (1 Kings 1–2).

These two motifs are part of the epic tradition of ancient Canaan, as can be observed in Ugaritic literature. The theme of the childless hero dominates the Epic of Aqhat, with the key couplet repeated throughout, with reference to Dan'el: "Who has no son like his brothers, and (no) offspring like his kinsmen" (*CAT* 1.17 I 18–19; with parallels at I 42–43, II 14–15).

At the opening of the Epic of Kirta, the hero loses all of his children, while his wife, Ḥuray, has departed (was taken from Kirta). The hero's desire, accordingly, is for new offspring (*CAT* 1.14 II 4–5) and for his wife to be restored to him (*CAT* 1.14 III 38–40). As the story continues, we learn of the return of Ḥuray to Kirta and the subsequent birth of seven sons and an eighth child, a daughter (*CAT* 1.15 II–III 25). Strikingly, either the god El or the hero Kirta (more likely the former) declares "the youngest of them I make to be firstborn" (*CAT* 1.15 III 16).

If all of this sounds familiar, it is because—as we have just seen—the same motifs occur in Genesis. The childless heroes Dan'el and Kirta find their echoes in Abraham and Isaac. And the raising of the youngest to firstborn status resonates in the stories of Isaac, Jacob, Joseph, Perez, and Ephraim. Interestingly, while Ugaritic lore focuses on the male childless heroes, the Bible stories highlight the female protagonists. In all five biblical cases, the stories are crafted with the reader's attention drawn to the barren woman: Sarah, Rebekah, Rachel, the wife of Manoah, and Hannah. This shift in focus bespeaks Israel's desire to identify with the lowly. Israel saw itself not as a heroic male or a firstborn son but rather as a barren woman and/or as a younger or youngest son without an inherited birthright. Israel is not Egypt or Assyria or Babylonia—nations of old with abundant water, natural resources, political clout, military might, and more—but rather a new nation, a younger nation, which flourishes only through a combination of pluck and divine intervention, as Yahweh guides and protects her.[23]

We observed above that a portion of the Kirta Epic is devoted to the hero's need to recover his wife, Ḥuray, for she had been taken into the foreign palace of King Pebel of Udum (*CAT* 1.14 III 38–40, VI 22–25). This motif resonates in the Book of Genesis: Abraham needs to reclaim Sarah from two foreign palaces, that of the Pharaoh (Genesis 12) and that of Abimelech king of Gerar (Genesis 20); while Isaac must do the same with Rebekah, as she, too, is taken by Abimelech king of Gerar (Genesis 26). The Dinah episode (Genesis 34) provides a variation on this theme: Dinah is the daughter rather than the wife of the hero, but the need to rescue her from a foreign palace animates the story.

In the two cases of Sarah and Rebekah, no military action was necessary, unlike in the Dinah episode. This latter story parallels Kirta's need to amass an army and to march on Udum in order to reclaim his wife. Unfortunately, this part of the text did not survive, but it appears that in the end King Pebel acquiesced to Kirta's demand for the return of his wife Ḥuray. To broaden our horizon further still, all these tales share the major theme of the *Iliad*, where Helen of Troy, the abducted wife of King Menelaus of Sparta, is reclaimed through what is known as the Trojan War.[24]

Nuzi Parallels

As we have seen, the Ugaritic texts are important for the literary parallels to the ancestral narratives. By contrast, the importance of the Nuzi documents lies in their portrayal of the legal, social, and economic life of the Late Bronze Age. Although we have many law collections from the ancient Near East (most famously, Hammurabi's Code),[25] the Nuzi documents—ranging from marriage contracts to court records to real estate transactions—constitute the single most important window into "real life" responses to "real life" conditions.[26]

One legal text among the Nuzi documents is particularly relevant to two different aspects of the Genesis narrative.[27] The tablet informs us that a man named Shurihil adopts a younger man named Shennima as his son and rightful heir, and that Shennima must serve Shurihil for all the days of his life—unless, however, Shurihil fathers a natural-born son, who then would become chief heir, with Shennima reduced to secondary position. In a case such as this, presumably Shennima came from a less well-to-do family, so that his servitude to Shurihil was a form of investment: he would serve the many years and eventually would inherit from Shurihil.

Although the Bible does not provide us with the legal underpinnings of the relationship between Abraham and his servant Eliezer, we reconstruct a situation parallel to the one that underlies the Nuzi document. We know from Genesis 15:2–3 that Eliezer is both chief servant to Abraham and his heir. And while the biblical account does not refer to adoption (here or elsewhere), this remains the best possible explanation of the legal relationship between the two individuals. Without a natural-born son, one must assume that Abraham had adopted Eliezer as his son, for how else could he refer to him as his heir? As the story continues, however, God informs Abraham that it is not Eliezer who will inherit, but rather a biological son to be born (v. 4). This follows the legal custom attested at Nuzi, whereby a natural-born son outranks the adopted son.[28]

The second half of the same cuneiform tablet provides information about the marriage of Shennima to a woman named Kelim-ninu. The contract includes the following stipulation: "If Kelim-ninu bears (children), Shennima shall not take another wife. But if Kelim-ninu does not bear, Kelim-ninu shall take a Lullu-woman as wife for Shennima."[29] The final clause is meant to assure that Shennima can father an heir, if his wife is unable to bear a child. Note that it is the responsibility of the wife to supply her husband with a second wife, here called a "Lullu-woman," meaning a servant woman.[30]

The scenario envisioned in this marriage contract is played out in the story of Abraham, Sarah, and Hagar. When Sarah is unable to conceive, she takes the first step and presents Hagar to Abraham (Genesis 16:1–2)—apparently because it was her legal responsibility to do so, as in the Nuzi document. As the story unfolds, Hagar indeed bears a child, Ishmael (16:15), though in the ensuing chapters the focus returns to Sarah, with the promise by God to Abraham that Sarah also will bear a child (17–18).

In sum, a single Nuzi document provides information relevant to the two solutions of childlessness: a man either may adopt a son or may take a second wife. Both avenues are realized in the Abraham story, with Eliezer serving as Abraham's adopted son (Genesis 15:2–3), and with Hagar serving as Abraham's second wife (Genesis 16:3).

LEARN MORE

Who Wrote Down the Stories of the Patriarchs and When?

The patriarchal characters and stories in Genesis are some of the most compelling in the entire Bible, yet they are among the most difficult to identify historically or archaeologically. But even though no material or textual evidence of Abraham, Isaac, Jacob, or Joseph has ever been found, many early-20th-century archaeologists, led by William F. Albright, the pioneer of American "biblical archaeology," were convinced that material and textual discoveries proved that the patriarchs were best understood and had in fact lived during the first half of the second millennium B.C.E. Yet, as historian and textual scholar Maynard Maidman makes clear in his insightful *BAR* article "Abraham, Isaac & Jacob Meet Newton, Darwin & Wellhausen" (May/June 2006), the Albrightian formulation of the patriarchal period had been undone by a kind of "archaeology" of the biblical text undertaken by German biblical scholar Julius Wellhausen over a half-century earlier.

Wellhausen's so-called "documentary hypothesis," brilliantly summarized and defended by biblical scholar Richard Elliott Friedman in his *Bible Review* article "Taking the Biblical Text Apart" (Fall 2005), proposed that the patriarchal stories in Genesis (along with the rest of the books of the Torah, or the Five Books of Moses) consisted basically of four separate textual strands, or schools of authors, who wrote at different times and in different contexts during the Israelite monarchy of the first half of the first millennium B.C.E. (i.e., the Iron Age), or shortly thereafter. These four authorial strands, which may also include much earlier traditions, are identified by scholars as the J (or Jahwist) source, the E (or Elohist) source, the P (or Priestly) source, and the D (or Deuteronomist) source, all of which give their own spin to the patriarchal narratives. As such, the written stories of the patriarchs—wherever and whenever the oral traditions of Israel's ancestors originated—reflect primarily the Iron Age Israelite context, in which they were first compiled and edited. Rendsburg in this chapter has taken a different approach (see below). –ED.

Because the Nuzi archive is unique in providing documentation about family law in "real life" situations, one cannot know whether the legal system reflected there was operative also in earlier and/or later times and whether it was common amongst other peoples or only the Hurrians of northern Mesopotamia.[31] Regardless, it is rather striking that the ancestral narratives include episodes that come to life against the backdrop of legal practices from the Hurrian realm of the 14th century B.C.E.[32]

Does all of this mean that Abraham and Sarah are to be dated to this time period? Northern Mesopotamia in c. 1400 does, indeed, provide the best historical and geographical context for the ancestral narratives. Yet all we can do is to understand Abraham as a figure—perhaps historical, perhaps legendary—who represented for the Israelites the beginnings of their religious, cultural, and national identity.

When Were the Ancestral Narratives Written?

Notwithstanding all that has been said so far, the ancestral narratives remain first and foremost literature. It is apposite to ask, accordingly, when might these stories have coalesced into the form presented in the Book of Genesis? As is often the case regarding the earlier biblical material, there is no consensus. From a linguistic standpoint, there can be no doubt that the ancestral narratives date to the time of the monarchy (c. 1000–586), during the heyday of Standard Biblical Hebrew, that is, before the Exile (586–538) and the subsequent rise of Late Biblical Hebrew during the Persian period (fifth–fourth centuries). The only question is: are we able to determine a time for the creation of the ancestral narratives that is more specific than the four-century time span noted above (c. 1000–586)? Our answer is yes, with an eye to the tenth century B.C.E.

It was during this period that the twelve tribes coalesced into a single United Monarchy under David and Solomon (see chap. 4). The new polity required a national narrative to unite the tribes and thus were born the ancestral narratives. This will explain why many of the literary themes and motifs in Genesis reappear in the Book of Samuel and why they reflect the reality of the tenth century.

For the former observation, note that both Rachel and Michal use *teraphim* to deceive their fathers in order to protect their husbands (Genesis 31; 1 Samuel 19); that a female character named Tamar is abused by a male lead, only to be vindicated at a sheep-shearing festival (Genesis 38; 2 Samuel 13); that the wife of Judah is called *bat šua'*, "daughter of Shua" (Genesis 38:12), while the most famous of David's wives is Bathsheba (2 Samuel 11–12), called *bat šua'* in 1 Chronicles 3:5;

and, finally, that both Reuben and Absalom sleep with their fathers' concubine(s) (Genesis 35:22; 2 Samuel 16:22). These parallels are too close and too many to be coincidental.[33]

As for the reflections of the tenth century, note that God promises Abraham, "and kings will come-forth from you" (Genesis 17:6), and then again, regarding Sarah, "kings of peoples will be from her" (Genesis 17:16), in which we may see reflections of the new reality of monarchy in the tenth century. More specifically, monarchy is associated with Judah: "And the staff shall not depart from Judah, nor the ruler from between his legs, until tribute comes to him, and his is the obedience of peoples" (Genesis 49:10), reflecting the tribal affiliation of David and Solomon. Note also that the boundaries of the land of Canaan promised to Abraham in Genesis 15:18 ("this land, from the river of Egypt to the great river, the Euphrates River") accord with the description of Solomon's realm (1 Kings 5:1). Finally, it is significant that Abraham's tithing to Melchizedek king of Salem (= Jerusalem) and priest to El Elyon (Genesis 14:20) adumbrates the centrality of Solomon's Temple in Jerusalem (1 Kings 6–8). Once again, the parallels cannot be coincidental, but must bear greater significance.[34]

One may conclude that the ancestral narratives were the product of the tenth century B.C.E.[35] As such, we may liken the Book of Genesis to other literary productions which refract the past through the present and the present through the past. Shakespeare's *Histories*, for example, describe the lives of earlier monarchs while reflecting attitudes and conditions during the reign of Elizabeth I; Arthur Miller's *The Crucible* narrates the Salem witch trials of the 1690s but simultaneously signals the McCarthyism of the 1950s. In the same way, the ancestral narratives likely contain both a kernel of history and epic or legendary elements interleaved by the brilliant literati responsible for the canonical version.

The further back one goes in the history of ancient Israel, the harder it becomes to reconstruct that history. Notwithstanding that underlying reality, this chapter has attempted to present a plausible scenario for the background of Abraham and his circle and for the stories told about them.

2

Egypt and the Exodus

**MANFRED BIETAK
AND GARY A. RENDSBURG**

THE STORY OF THE ISRAELITES IN AND OUT OF EGYPT may be divided into three main sections: the migration to Egypt, also called the Eisodus; the slavery in Egypt; and the Exodus from Egypt.[1]

THE MIGRATION TO EGYPT

The Beni Hasan Tomb Painting

For much of ancient Egyptian history, Semitic-speaking peoples from the Sinai and the Levant immigrated to Egypt and settled in the eastern Delta.[2] Numerous documents (one crucial one to be cited and analyzed below) speak to this point, though, in line with the saying that "a picture is worth a thousand words," pride of place still belongs to the famous Beni Hasan tomb painting (see images on the next page). The artwork appears on the north wall of Tomb 3 at Beni Hasan (c. 165 mi south of Cairo), dated to year 5 of the reign of Sesostris II, that is, 1895 B.C.E., during the 12th Dynasty of the Middle Kingdom.[3] The painting depicts a group of people, identified as 'Amu of Shu—the former a generic term for Asiatics, the latter presumably a specific location unknown to us. It is not impossible, however, that the generic word *'ꜣmw* ('Amu) is the Semitic word *'am(m)*, "people," attested espe-cially in Hebrew and Aramaic.[4]

THE PROCESSION OF ASIATICS from the third register (from the top) of the north wall in the tomb of Khnumhotep at Beni Hasan, Egypt.

ASIATICS IN DETAIL. Two segments of the third register of the north wall in the tomb of Khnumhotep at Beni Hasan. The arrivals present themselves to the Egyptian desert authorities under the mayor and overseer Khnumhotep, hence the presence of this visual representation in the deceased's tomb.

The image, from the tomb of Khnumhotep II, mayor of the town of Menat-Khufu and overseer of the Eastern Desert, portrays a caravan of Canaanites arriving as immigrants. They signal peaceful intentions, as expressed especially by the man playing the lyre. They carry weapons typical of the Levantine Middle Bronze Age (bow, quiver, spears, duckbill axe) and therefore are free people. In stark contrast to their status, however, the inscription above their heads classifies them as bound prisoners, which is the way that the Egyptians traditionally saw foreigners. Most significantly, the group arrives as an extended family unit, even if only fifteen individuals (eight men, four women, and three children) are depicted. Directly above the first two individuals (i.e., the ones on the right), the Egyptian hieroglyphics record that 37 'Amu (people) arrived (see image below), suggesting something akin to a large family unit.

These 'Amu people have a mushroom-shaped coiffure, typical for Middle Bronze Age Asiatics, they wear colorful dresses, and they have relatively fair skin. As they traverse the desert, they wear sandals, and the women and a boy even wear shoes of leather, while the Egyptians are depicted as barefooted. Only the chief of the caravan and his deputy have taken off the sandals as a sign of respect as they enter the space of the Egyptian dignitary. The men are bearded, per the Asiatic custom, in contrast to the clean-shaven Egyptian men seen elsewhere on this tomb painting and indeed throughout ancient Egyptian art. The newcomers bring as presents for the Egyptians the highly coveted galena (*kohl*) from the Red Sea shore, used as mascara for the eyes, and tamed desert animals, such as an ibex and a dorcas gazelle. Bellows mounted on the donkeys signify that they may be migrant smiths offering their services to the Egyptians, besides their possible ability in handling weapons as future soldiers.

CAPTIONED ASIATICS. The "caption" in the scene depicting the procession of Asiatics in the tomb of Khnumhotep at Beni Hasan (see images on the previous page) reads: 'Amu 37. The classifiers in the inscription include a throwstick for the category of foreign people, and a bound captive in contrast to the representation of the group which carries weapons freely.

The event or process portrayed here is far too early to have any direct relationship with the arrival of the Israelites in Egypt (which occurred centuries later), but various aspects of the painting evoke the biblical story, nonetheless.

In sum, in the minds of many scholars, the Beni Hasan tomb painting permits us to see not the Israelites *per se* but what the Israelites may have looked like when they too arrived in Egypt centuries later.

The Anastasi Papyri Collection

The collection known as the Anastasi Papyri is a group of nine hieratic papyri, dated to the Ramesside period, sold by the great collector Giovanni Anastasi to the British Museum in 1839.* These documents are collections of model letters and scribal exercises, assembled onto individual longer papyrus scrolls, which in turn served in the training of scribes. No one doubts, however, that the texts describe real-life events, of the type that scribes in the Egyptian governmental bureaucracy would write on a regular basis. It seems that, inter alia, original letters were used as exemplars to train apprentice scribes for their future tasks (see especially P.Anastasi VI). As far as one can tell, the papyri were found in Memphis or Saqqara, but as we shall see, many of the events described took place in the general region of the eastern Delta.

The papyri were published in facsimile edition soon after their purchase, within the series *Select Papyri in the Hieratic Character from the Collections of the British Museum* (London: W. Nicol, 1841–1860), under the supervision of Samuel Birch. Half a century later, the longest of the texts, P.Anastasi I, the so-called Satirical Letter, was presented afresh, in hieroglyphic transcription and English translation, by Alan H. Gardiner, *Egyptian Hieratic Texts* (Leipzig: J. C. Hinrichs, 1911).**

Several decades further on, the definitive edition of Anastasi Papyri (nos. II–VI) was published in hieroglyphic transcription: Alan H. Gardiner, *Late-Egyptian Miscellanies*, Bibliotheca Aegyptiaca 7 (Brussels: Fondation égyptologique Reine Élisabeth, 1937). And then Gardiner's student Ricardo Caminos produced an English translation of the documents, with detailed annotations: *Late-Egyptian Miscellanies*, Brown Egyptological Studies I (Oxford: Oxford Univ. Press, 1954).

One of the documents not published by Gardiner was P.Anastasi VIII, which fortunately received a fine edition by Sarah I. Groll, "The Egyptian Background of the Exodus and the Crossing of the Reed Sea: A New Reading of Papyrus Anastasi VIII," in Irene Shirun-Grumach, ed., *Jerusalem Studies in Egyptology*, Ägypten und Altes Testament 40 (Wiesbaden: Harrassowitz, 1998), 173–92.

Two additional papyri, which appear to be part of the same original collection, were sold to the Rijksmuseum van Oudheden (Leiden), and thus are

---

*For the general outline of Giovanni Anastasi's remarkable life, see Warren R. Dawson, "Anastasi, Sallier, and Harris and Their Papyri," *JEA* 35 (1949), 158–66, esp. 158–60.

** For the most up-to-date detailed study of this text, see Hans-Werner Fischer-Elfert, *Die satirische Streitschrift des Papyrus Anastasi I: Übersetzung und Kommentar*, Ägyptologische Abhandlungen 44 (Wiesbaden: Harrassowitz, 1986).

referred to as P.Leiden 348 and P.Leiden 349.

Finally, note that all of these texts are also to be found in the monumental achievements of K.A. Kitchen, *Ramesside Inscriptions: Historical and Biographical*, 8 vols. (Oxford: Blackwell, 1969–1990); K.A. Kitchen, *Ramesside Inscriptions Translated and Annotated: Translations*, 7 vols. (Oxford: Blackwell; Chichester: Wiley-Blackwell, 1993–2014); and K.A. Kitchen and Benedict G. Davies, *Ramesside Inscriptions Translated and Annotated: Notes and Comments*, 4 vols. (to date) (Oxford: Blackwell; Chichester: Wiley-Blackwell, 1993–2014).

Taken as a whole, the Anastasi Papyri are exceedingly important for the subject under consideration here. As we proceed, accordingly, the reader will note our repeated references to these documents, with striking parallels to the Eisodus, the Exodus, and more. –M.B. AND G.A.R.

The Joseph Story

The story of the Israelites' arrival in Egypt is narrated in Genesis 37–50, with the focus on the family of Jacob the patriarch (see chap. 1), and with special attention to his son Joseph. Through a series of both random and fortuitous events, Joseph rose to a position comparable to that of vizier, second in command to the Pharaoh (Genesis 41). In reaching this station, Joseph was thoroughly acculturated to Egyptian society: he shaved (Genesis 41:14); he was dressed as an Egyptian nobleman, with fine linen, a signet ring, and a gold chain about his neck (Genesis 41:42); he gained an Egyptian name, Zaphenath-paneah (Genesis 41:45), which translates to "the god has spoken, the one of life"; and he married the daughter of an Egyptian priest to the sun-god Ra located in On = Heliopolis (Genesis 41:45).

Joseph's acculturation to Egyptian society is seen also at the end of his life story, indeed, in the final verse of the Book of Genesis: Joseph dies at the age of 110 years (Genesis 50:26), the ideal lifespan in Egyptian literature;[5] and then he is embalmed and placed in a coffin (per the Egyptian practice of mummification).[6]

Thus, Joseph was in a position of power to assist his family members when they journeyed to Egypt in search of grain, in order to sustain themselves during one of the periodic droughts and resultant grain shortages that can strike the land of Canaan. Obviously, we strip the story of much of its pathos here (see esp. Genesis 44:18–45:15), but the basic outline remains.

The Report of a Frontier Official (P.Anastasi VI)

An exceedingly close parallel to the biblical Eisodus occurs in P.Anastasi VI: 4.11–5.5, dated to the reign of Seti II (r. 1214–1208 B.C.E.).[7] The document is an official letter from a frontier official to his superior, in which we read the following:

> Another message to my lord: We have finished admitting the Shasu tribes of Edom at the fortress of Merneptah Hotep-hir-ma'at, l.p.h., which is in Tjeku, to the lakes of Per-Atum of Merneptah Hotep-hir-ma'at, which are in Tjeku, to keep them alive and to keep their flocks alive, through the great *k3* ("spirit") of Pharaoh, l.p.h., the good sun in every land, in year 8, epagomenal day [Birth-of] Seth.[8]

Edom, of course, refers to the country to the south of what is later Israel, in the mountainous region spanning modern-day southern Israel and southern Jordan (i.e., on both sides of the Aravah valley). The term Shasu is the Egyptian word for nomads, Bedouin, pastoralists, and the like.[9] Most scholars argue, quite cogently, that P.Anastasi VI provides an exceedingly close parallel to the biblical story. In both accounts, a group of people from the general region of Edom traverses the Sinai, with their flocks, in order to sustain themselves. In both cases, the Egyptians permit the émigrés to settle in fringe zones of the eastern Delta. More specifically, in both instances, the newcomers are resident in the region of Per-Atum, that is, Pithom in Exodus 1:11 (see map below).

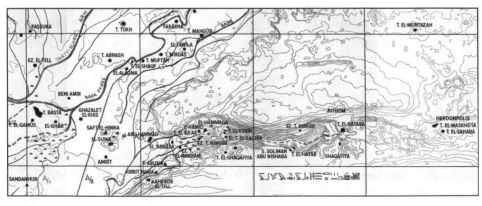

THE WADI TUMILAT, most likely the land of Goshen, with the Lake of Pithom.

In addition, P.Anastasi VI mentions Tjeku, to be identified with the Wadi Tumilat, presumably the place named Succoth in the Bible. While this toponym is not mentioned in the Eisodus account, it is mentioned in the Exodus account (Exodus 12:37; 13:20; Numbers 33:5–6). The word itself, Hebrew *sukkot*, means "booths built of foliage," of the type still seen today in the general area (see image below). The fact that the Egyptians called the Wadi Tumilat by this name indicates the extent to which Semitic-speaking peoples had settled the region, living, it appears, in these make-shift dwellings.

HUTS CONSTRUCTED FROM REEDS, daubed with mud, photographed in 2004 several kilometers north of Tell el-Borg in the eastern Nile Delta.

While not directly related to the present enterprise, we also note that the word for "lakes" in the afore-cited report by the frontier official is not the native Egyptian word for such bodies of water, but rather the Semitic word *brkt* (cf. Hebrew *bereka*; Arabic *birka*) rendered into hieroglyphics.[10] As with the word "booths" above, the use of this Semitic word for "lakes" in P.Anastasi VI points to a sizable Semitic presence in the eastern Delta and the Wadi Tumilat.

There are still other Semitic words associated with places in the Wadi Tumilat region to be found in Ramesside-period texts. Below we shall have occasion to discuss P.Anastasi V, in which occurs the expression *sgr n tkw* "the enclosure of Tjeku," with the former word equaling Semitic *seger*, "enclosure, fortified compound."[11] Finally, we call attention here to the geophysical or geographical term *gsm*, which appears in P.Anastasi IV, line 1b:2, in connection with a lake that makes waves.[12] Sarah Groll tentatively identified the name *gsm* with the biblical toponym Goshen (Genesis 45:10; Exodus 8:18, etc.). Given the textual mention of a lake and the proven existence in antiquity of a large lake (11 miles long) in the western half of the Wadi Tumilat, we suggest the Wadi Tumilat as the location of the biblical Goshen.[13]

The cumulative linguistic evidence of these Semitic words and toponyms in the Wadi Tumilat region, used even by Egyptian scribes (see image below), argues for the presence of a Semitic-speaking population in the area during the Ramesside period. All of this, in turn, speaks very strongly for locating the land of Goshen in this frontier region of Egypt.[14]

𓏏𓎡𓅱𓈖	ṯkw	סכות ?
	b-r-k-t	ברכת
	s-g-r	סגר
	g-s-m	גשם

SEMITIC TOPONYMS from the Ramesside-era inscriptions relating to the Wadi Tumilat, with classifiers highlighted here in gray.

The Shasu of Edom: Proto-Israelites?

In light of these points, we repeat the statement made above: most scholars consider P.Anastasi VI to be an exceedingly close parallel to the biblical story. While we concur with this overall appraisal, we also would like to propose a core question: could the reference to the Shasu of Edom in this text refer not to the Edomites *per se* but rather the early Israelites? Now, most scholars would date the Eisodus before the reign of Seti II (r. 1214–1208 B.C.E.), but in light of the chronology proposed herein (see below), one may consider P.Anastasi VI to refer to a segment of the Israelites. The argument goes as follows.

First, as we learn from the Bible, the terms Se'ir and Edom are essentially synonymous (see Genesis 32:4; 36:8–9; 36:21; Numbers 24:18; Judges 5:4; Ezekiel 35:15): the former is used for the geographical region, while the latter is used for the people who inhabit the land.

Secondly, Egyptian topographical lists from Soleb and 'Amarah (both in Nubia), dated to the New Kingdom period, collocate regions known as *tꜣ šꜣsw ya-h-wa*, "the land of the Shasu of Yahweh," and *tꜣ š3św śa-ʿ-r-ir*, "the land of the Shasu of Seʿir."[15] The former, of course, is the name of the God of Israel, though in the present instance it is more likely to be understood as a toponym. As an aside, we note that either the divine name existed first, from which the toponym was derived; or the toponym existed first, from which the divine name was derived.[16]

Thirdly, the Bible identifies the homeland of Yahweh as Edom/Seʿir (Deuteronomy 33:2; Judges 5:4) or more generally with Sinai (Deuteronomy 33:2; Psalms 68:9) and Teman (meaning "southland," in Hebrew) (Habakkuk 3:3).

Finally, the closeness of Edom and Israel is reflected in the foundational stories of the Bible through the twin-ness of the respective progenitors, Esau and Jacob. By contrast, other neighbors (Moab, Ammon, Aram, etc.) are more distantly related.

All of this is to say: quite possibly the Shasu of Edom mentioned in P.Anastasi VI are not Edomites *per se*, for there is a good possibility that they were early Israelites or at least a closely related group of people. From the eyes of the Egyptians, the two peoples may not have been distinguishable.[17] Alternatively, we may posit that the "gene pool" of people in the region of the far southern Levant had not quite been settled yet, with Edomites, Israelites, Midianites, Kenites, and the like all intermingled and interconnected. These groups—all to be considered Shasu nomads—repeatedly traversed the Sinai and settled in the eastern Delta and Wadi Tumilat in periods of drought, apparently welcomed by the Egyptians either for altruistic reasons (to keep them alive) and/or as a potential labor force to be exploited (see below). As such, P.Anastasi VI may reflect the period when the ethnogenesis of Israel was in progress, not quite finalized, and hence the Egyptian scribe referred to the people as Shasu of Edom. On the famous mention of Israel as a people in the Merneptah Stele, see our analysis of this passage further below.

Regardless of whether the Shasu of Edom arriving in Per-Atum, as mentioned in P.Anastasi VI, were Edomites or Israelites, the basic picture is confirmed: Semites from the general region of the southern Levant would traverse the Sinai and would be allowed to enter Egypt, including "through the great *k3* ("spirit") of Pharaoh" (i.e., with his blessing), per the report of the frontier official.

The key phrase "to keep them alive and to keep their flocks

alive" used by the scribe of P.Anastasi VI may be situated in a larger historical and geographic context, spanning the period of Ramesses II, Merneptah, Seti II (during whose reigns the Anastasi Papyri are dated), and their successors. As we know from other evidence—both textual and archaeological—the latter half of the 13th century B.C.E. was characterized by a general shortage of grain, doubtless brought on by climate-change issues, which in fact contributed greatly to the decline of Late Bronze Age civilization throughout the Eastern Mediterranean (including the Aegean).[18]

Two Hittite texts are especially germane. In one, Queen Puduḫepa (c. 1240 B.C.E.) writes to Ramesses II, "I have no grain in my lands." In another, from approximately the same date, we learn of a Hittite mission to Egypt to obtain wheat and barley and to arrange for its transport back to Ḫatti.[19] From a few decades later, Merneptah declaims the following on the great inscription on the walls of the Karnak Temple: "I caused grain to be taken in ships, to keep alive that land of Ḫatti."[20]

Finally, scientific analysis of pollen counts derived from core drilling in the Sea of Galilee indicates that the driest period throughout the span of thousands of years occurred during the years 1250–1100 B.C.E.[21] The biblical account of the Israelites traveling to Egypt in search of grain either should be situated in this historical context and/or constitutes a clear memory of these conditions.

In addition, soon after the arrival of the Shasu of Edom as recorded in P.Anastasi VI, we learn about Bay, a powerful vizier/chancellor of Near Eastern origin, who served under both Seti II (r. 1214–1208) and Siptah (r. 1206–1198). Bay's name appears on various monuments throughout Egypt, including on a statue in the Bull Cemetery of On (i.e., Heliopolis).[22] This singular figure even received the unprecedented privilege of having his tomb in the royal cemetery in the Valley of the Kings (KV 13), on the west bank of the Nile opposite Thebes.

Notwithstanding some differences between the career of Bay and the career of Joseph, the former could be seen as a model for the latter as recorded in the Bible. One key difference is that Bay was executed by Siptah,[23] even though the vizier/chancellor had helped this pharaoh gain the throne. This incident may have been forgotten in the Israelite tradition, and/or an echo thereof may appear in the famous description of the Pharaoh "who knew not Joseph" (Exodus 1:8). Regardless, the similarities are striking, from the general notion of a high-ranking vizier of Western Asiatic origin to the specific connection to the city of On (see Genesis 41:45). We would not claim that chancellor Bay was Joseph, but someone like him may have served as the model for the portrayal of Joseph in the Bible.[24]

THE SLAVERY IN EGYPT

Corvée Labor

According to the biblical tradition, at some point after their arrival in Egypt, the Israelite population was reduced to slavery, or better, corvée labor (see Exodus 1:13–14).

When we use the word "slavery," especially within an American context, one thinks of individual humans owning other individual humans. Such existed in ancient Egypt,[25] but the so-called slavery of the Bible is better identified as corvée labor. In a corvée system, a workforce is organized for specific projects from among the available people, which could include both locals and foreigners. One may wish to call this system "state slavery," as the workforce was beholden to the state. Note further that the Hebrew word *'ebed* means "slave, servant, worker, laborer, etc.,"[26] without the distinctions available in English, so that "corvée laborer" is the most probable connotation within the context of the Exodus narrative.

The Egyptians used the corvée system for large construction projects, and such is implied in the Bible as well. The system involved foremen to organize the workforce, their Egyptian taskmasters, and the quota of work to be done each day or each week.[27] See especially Exodus 5:14–15, with the reference to the Israelite foremen, who on the one hand supervise the Israelite workers, and who on the other hand must answer to the Egyptian taskmasters and ultimately to Pharaoh.

Pithom and Ra'amses

According to the biblical tradition, the main work was associated with building projects in the cities of Pithom (i.e., Per-Atum)[28] and Ra'amses (see Exodus 1:11).[29] Are we able to identify the precise location of these two cities beyond the general region of the eastern Delta? The answer is yes, and now with great confidence. After decades of debate,[30] the consensus now is to identify Pithom with Tell er-Retaba[31] (see image below) and Ra'amses[32] with Qantir/Tell ed-Dab'a.[33]

SLAYING OF A SHASU NOMAD. On a limestone relief from the left pylon of the temple of Atum at Tell er-Retaba, Wadi Tumilat. Ramesses II is killing an Asiatic man with a mace and is receiving the sickle sword from the god Atum. The short kilt and the bandaged upper body suggest the man is a Shasu nomad. (For the Shasu dress, see Walter Wreszinski, *Atlas zur altägyptischen Kulturgeschichte*, vol. 2 [Leipzig: J.C. Hinrichs, 1923], pls. 34 and 39.) The missing prototypical cap or turban of the Shasu could be explained by the iconic representation of the king, grabbing his foe at a curl of his hair. This relief proves that the temple of Atum, hence, Pi-Atum (biblical Pithom), was situated at Tell er-Retaba in the Wadi Tumilat—one of the two major infiltration tracks for the Shasu, the other one being along the Way of Horus (to the north, closer to the Mediterranean coast).

We also should note that Qantir/Pi-Ramesse was abandoned c. 1100 B.C.E., when the easternmost branch of the Nile silted up, so that Ra'amses no longer could serve as a harbor. In its stead, a new city arose, Tanis, 14 miles to the north. Remarkably, the religious architecture of Tanis was constructed largely of stones transported from Qantir/Pi-Ramesse rather than from newly quarried stones. This will explain why scholars in the past were misled and therefore identified Tanis with the city of Ra'amses mentioned in Exodus 1:11. At the time of the Israelite presence in Egypt, the city of Ra'amses was clearly located at Qantir.

That said, the geographical shift has a resonance in the Bible. Some centuries later, when the author of Psalm 78 wrote a poetic account of the experience in Egypt, he referred to the area where Yahweh performed miracles for his people as "the fields of Zoan" (78:12, 43). The form Zoan, Heb. ṣo'an, is the exact equivalent of Egyptian ḏ'n.t (Tanis). Remarkably, the original location of Ra'amses was forgotten; the city simply had "moved" to Tanis![34]

As to the specific task of the Israelite laborers, we have considerable evidence for brickmaking in ancient Egypt, especially during the 19th Dynasty (1301–1198 B.C.E.).[35] P.Anastasi III (verso) 1.2–3.3, dated to the reign of Merneptah (r. 1224–1214 B.C.E.), includes a ledger of sorts recording various building works, including the making of bricks.[36] P.Anastasi IV 12.6 = P. Anastasi V 3.1, dated to the time of Seti II (r. 1214–1208 B.C.E.), includes the complaint, "there are no men to mould bricks, and there is no straw in the district,"[37] calling to mind Exodus 5:16. Unfortunately, though, we are given no location for these brickmaking tasks.

We also may assume an increase in brick production in the Wadi Tumilat during the reign of Ramesses III, who constructed both the big fortress at Tell er-Retaba and the smaller one at Kom Qulzoum near Suez.[38] This activity certainly resulted in recruiting workmen from the local population who were, to a large extent, immigrants from the southern Levant, such as the Shasu of Edom in P.Anastasi VI. This is precisely the latter part of the assumed period of the sojourn of the (proto-)Israelites in Egypt (see further below).

The most detailed and elaborate record of brickmaking is the Louvre Leather Roll, dated to year 5 of Ramesses II, with various entries listed by a taskmaster. A sample entry reads: "Yupa son of Urhiya, (target) 2,000 bricks: 660 arrived, 410 arrived, 560 arrived / total 1,630 / deficit 370."[39]

In addition, we possess a short notice about construction work specifically at Pi-Ramesse, to wit, P.Leiden 348 (verso), 6.6–7, dated to the reign of Ramesses II (r. 1290–1224). The relevant section includes the following bureaucratic order: "Issue grain to the men of the army and (to) the 'Apiru who are drawing stone for the great pylon of the [...] of Ramesses."[40] Practically the same sentence occurs in P.Leiden 349, 14–15: "Issue grain to the men of the army and (to) the 'Apiru who are drawing stone (?) ..." In the former text, we cannot be certain that the project is underway in Pi-Ramesse, especially with the broken text just before the royal name, but such seems likely. In the latter text, we have even less information, due to the damaged papyrus.

The 'Apiru referred to in this construction project have been the subject of widespread discussion. The term appears in Egyptian texts throughout the second millennium B.C.E., though with a special concentration of references during the New Kingdom;[41] and it also appears in Babylonian cuneiform texts, as Ḫabiru. Scholars of the past sought to connect the 'Apiru/Ḫabiru to the term "Hebrews" (Heb. 'ibrim). While some ultimate connection cannot be discarded, given the range of dates and places recorded for the 'Apiru/Ḫabiru, it is clear that not all these people can be Hebrews in any way, shape, or form. In fact, the term 'Apiru/Ḫabiru is not to be seen as an ethnic designation at all, but rather refers to people living on the social margins. The wide range of Egyptian and Babylonian texts refer to them as marauders, mercenaries, militiamen, and the like (always in some inferior status), plus, as we have seen above, they were enlisted in state service.[42]

So, while we should resist the temptation to identify the 'Apiru busy at work in P.Leiden 348 with the Hebrews/Israelites—note also that the former are working with stone, while the latter manufactured bricks—we nonetheless gain some insight into how the Egyptians employed the socially marginal in their seemingly incessant construction projects, especially during the 19th Dynasty.[43]

Four-Room Houses at Medinet Habu

One additional piece of possible evidence for (proto-)Israelites in Egypt is worth citing here, even though it brings us to a totally different part of the country. We refer here to the presence of two four-room houses—one fully excavated, the other partially excavated— in Medinet Habu on the west bank of the Nile opposite Thebes (modern-day Luxor). These houses were found by an archaeological team of the University of Chicago during the 1930s,[44] though their significance was not appreciated until decades later.[45] The two relatively poorly constructed houses in wattle and daub served as shelters for workmen who were given the task to dismantle the temple of

Aya and Horemheb (end of 18th Dynasty) in order to obtain building material for the nearby temple of Ramesses IV (r. 1164–1156).

As the four-room house is considered by many scholars to be a vital cultural marker of the Israelites,[46] one is surprised to find four-room houses as far south as Medinet Habu. Such discoveries in the eastern Delta would not be surprising, given the evidence for the presence of Semites from greater Canaan in the region—but in Upper Egypt? And yet, upon further investigation, we may propose such Semites, perhaps specifically Israelites, in the area of Thebes as well, along the following lines.

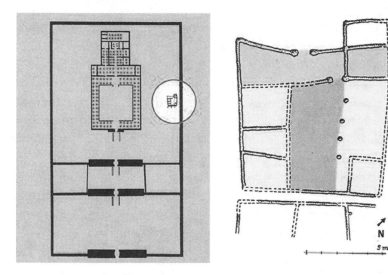

FOUR-ROOM HOUSE AT MEDINET HABU. Left: floor plan of the temple of Aya and Horemheb, with the circle indicating the location of the four-room houses. Right: floor plan of the four-room houses, one fully excavated, one partially excavated.

The building activity of Ramesses IV must have been initiated early in his short reign (r. 1164–1156). We must look, therefore, at the military activity of his predecessor, Ramesses III (r. 1195–1164). Most famously, this pharaoh defeated the Sea Peoples coalition led by the Philistines and their allies (see further below), but he also defeated the Shasu of Seʿir in a separate encounter. P.Harris I includes the following report (col. 76, lines 9–11):[47]

> I destroyed (the people) of Seʿir among the Shasu tribes; I razed their tents.[48] Their people, their property, and their

cattle as well, without number, I pinioned and carried away in
captivity, as the tribute of Egypt. I gave them to the Ennead
of the gods, as slaves for their houses (i.e., temples).

The key point here is that the defeated Shasu of Se'ir were taken
captive and were given to the temples as slaves. No doubt they were
put to work in the ever-ongoing construction projects. Based on what
we wrote above regarding the Shasu of Edom mentioned in P.Anastasi
VI, including the fact that Edom and Se'ir are virtually interchangeable designations, we propose here the possibility or probability that
amongst the Shasu of Se'ir mentioned in P.Harris I may have been the
Israelites or proto-Israelites.

All of this would explain the presence of four-room houses
within or adjacent to the temple compound at Medinet Habu under
construction during the reign of Ramesses IV. Two further points
are noteworthy: First, P.Harris I does not refer to the Philistine and
other Sea Peoples captives in the service of the temples, rather they
were taken to strongholds and made to serve in the Egyptian army;
second, the Philistines did not use the four-room house layout as
their domiciles.[49]

To our mind, accordingly, the builders of the four-room houses
in Medinet Habu originated from a population that shared the same
cultural background as the early Israelites, whose ethnogenesis may
not have been finalized by this time but certainly was under way.

Summary Statement

Summing up the evidence of the eastern Delta and Western Thebes,
we conclude that early Israelites most likely were in Egypt during
the late Ramesside period. The largest group were pastoralists at
the edge of Egypt in the Wadi Tumilat, presumably the area that the
Bible refers to as Goshen (Genesis 45:10). Another group may have
lived relatively nearby, in the "land of Ra'amses" (Genesis 47:11), that
is, most likely the land around the royal residence in Pi-Ramesse.[50]
In time, these settled groups were conscripted for corvée labor
works, especially when larger building projects, such as the one at
Tell er-Retaba in Wadi Tumilat, demanded a substantial increase of
workforce.

EGYPT AND THE EXODUS

LEARN MORE

The Song of the Sea: Israel's Earliest Memory

Like the patriarchal stories of Genesis, the events of Israel's Exodus from
Egypt are extremely difficult to locate in history. But as historian and biblical
scholar Baruch Halpern argues in the pages of *BAR* ("Eyewitness Testimony,"
September/October 2003), close examination of the biblical text reveals that
a small but extremely significant portion of the Exodus story—the defeat
of Pharaoh's army in the waters of the Red Sea—may have actually been
composed within living memory of the event itself.

Immediately following the long narrative account of the miraculous parting
and crossing of the Red Sea (Exodus 14), the Bible reports that Moses leads
the Israelites in a victory hymn celebrating Yahweh's crushing defeat of
Pharaoh's army (Exodus 15:1–18). The hymn, often called the Song of the
Sea, is thought to be one of the oldest pieces of Hebrew poetry preserved in
the Bible. As Halpern explains, such passages are marked by certain linguistic
and grammatical features that clearly distinguish them from later Hebrew texts
composed during the period of the Israelite monarchy or the Exilic period. In
the case of the Song of the Sea, these textual considerations, and the historical
and cultural context presented in the hymn, suggest that it was first composed
between 1125 and 1000 B.C.E., perhaps only a generation or two after the
miraculous defeat of the Egyptians had occurred. –ED.

The rebuilding of palaces and the construction of temples in
Pi-Ramesse continued throughout the 19th and the 20th Dynasties,
and these projects could be achieved only by additional workmen.
Others were captives, used as temple slaves in construction projects.
As we have only the evidence of the four-room houses at Medinet Habu
for our target group, which we suspect to be proto-Israelites, apparently
some among them were transported to Upper Egypt as well.

The Bible remembers only the former group, whose experiences formed the core of the Israelite mnemohistory.[51] Obviously, the
evidence from ancient Egypt is scant, at best. If the Shasu pastoralists mentioned in P.Anastasi VI were Israelites, presumably they joined
earlier immigrants of the same stock who already were present in the
land, perhaps going back to the time of Ramesses II (r. 1290–1224) or
even earlier. It would be quite remarkable if our single piece of evidence
(i.e., P.Anastasi VI) testifies to the earliest of these people to arrive in

33

Egypt. The preservation and/or discovery of documentary evidence from the ancient world is always random. Regardless, it was the experience of the Israelites in Pithom and Ra'amses that formed the core narrative of the Bible.

The Merneptah Stele

Into the above mix we also must add the Merneptah Stele, which contains the only direct reference to Israel in all of ancient Egypt documentation, and the oldest reference to Israel in all of the ancient Near East. In fact, since the Merneptah Stele dates to year 5 of this pharaoh's reign, which equates to c. 1220, and since the earliest biblical texts (Exodus 15; Judges 5, etc.) date to c. 1100,[52] the mention of "Israel" in the Merneptah Stele is the earliest record of this people.

The Merneptah Stele is a monumental inscription, about 10 feet high, found by Sir W. M. Flinders Petrie in 1896 at the mortuary temple of Merneptah on the west bank of the Nile opposite Luxor/Thebes.[53] The main part of the text details Merneptah's war against the Libyans to the west. Near the end of the inscription, however, the scribe turns his attention to Merneptah's campaign in the other direction, toward Canaan to the northeast. The relevant lines read as follows:[54]

> All the rulers are prostrate, saying: "peace,"[55]
> not one among the Nine Bows dares raise his head.
> Plundered is Tehenu (Libya), Ḫatti is at peace,
> carried off is Canaan with every evil.
> Brought away is Ashkelon, taken is Gezer,
> Yeno'am is reduced to non-existence;
> Israel is laid waste, having no seed,
> Ḫurru is become widowed because of Nile-land.
> All lands together are (now) at peace,
> and everyone who roamed about has been subdued,
> by the king of Upper and Lower Egypt, Baienre Meriamun,
> Son of Re, Merneptah, given life like Re daily.

Israel is mentioned here within a series of places associated with the land of Canaan, but there is one crucial difference: All of the toponyms in the inscription occur with the foreign-land classifier: ᨏᨏ. Israel, by contrast, appears with the people classifier: 𓀀. In the eyes of the scribe, Canaan, Ashkelon, Gezer, Yenoʻam, and Ḫurru were places that one could locate on the map. Israel, however, was not a foreign land but rather a recognizable people, presumably without a land.

Most scholars argue that the people-classifier signifies the people of Israel not yet settled, presumably somewhere in the Transjordan. This assumption is based on the geography reflected in the inscription, which proceeds from southwest to northeast, with Ashkelon on the Mediterranean coast, Gezer inland, and Yenoʻam to the east of the Sea of Galilee (though its precise location is not known) (see map on page 36).[56] By extension, Israel would be located in the northern Transjordan, that is, the land of Bashan, to use the biblical designation (Numbers 21:33; 32:33).

Alternatively, with somewhat less regard to the geographical argument just presented, other scholars suggest that the inscription may refer to early Israelite elements present in the central hill country.[57] A relevant passage may occur in P.Anastasi I (the so-called Satirical Letter), col. 23, line 7, which refers to Shasu lurking in the area (lit. "hiding under the bushes").[58]

Most scholars continue the argument as follows: if "Israel" in the Merneptah Stele refers to the people somewhere in the general region of Canaan (either Transjordan or Cisjordan), then the Exodus (however it is envisioned) must have occurred earlier than 1220 B.C.E., either within the first few years of Merneptah's reign or during the long reign of his father and predecessor, Ramesses II. According to this view, the reference to Israel as "a people without a land" evokes the latter portions of the Wandering period (described in the latter half of the Book of Numbers, with rehearsal in Deuteronomy 2–3), and/or the earliest arrival of the Israelites in either Transjordan or Cisjordan. The Exodus would then have occurred prior to this date.

To our mind, however, dating the Exodus prior to 1220 B.C.E. is too early. We shall return to this issue below: for the nonce, let us simply recall that the reigns of Ramesses II and Merneptah propel Egypt to the height of its imperial power. It is therefore difficult to imagine the Exodus (however it is conceived) occurring during this period of firm pharaonic control.

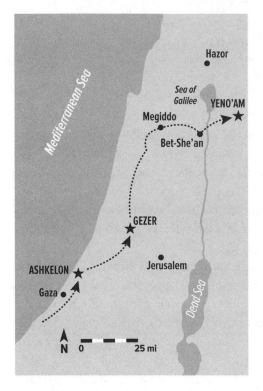

THE ROUTE OF MERNEPTAH'S ARMY in Canaan and the conquered cities (marked by stars) mentioned in the Merneptah Stele.

We would rather propose that "Israel" in the Merneptah Stele refers to Israelite elements that remained in the general region of Canaan and never took part in the Eisodus and residency in Egypt. Moreover, we would not wish to attempt to pinpoint this "Israel" on the map—in the land of Bashan, for example. As argued above, Israel developed out of the general Shasu population. It is hard to imagine that the totality thereof immigrated to Egypt. No doubt certain elements remained on the desert fringe in the southern Levant or were to be found in the rural mountainous areas, and most likely these are the people encountered by Merneptah's army.

In fact, one such component may be the tribe of Asher, which may be referred to in P.Anastasi I, col. 23, line 6 (*isr*), in the region of Megiddo—precisely where one would expect to find this group, according to the geographical information provided in the Bible.[59] In fact, this passage occurs immediately before the mention of the Shasu "hiding under the bushes." Now, it is true that this region places us in the western Galilee, far from the desert fringe, though one should keep in mind that the sedentarization of nomads and semi-nomads often brings them to the sown not immediately adjacent to their original steppe land and desert fringe.[60]

One also may wish to postulate that such groups of semi-nomads, who later became part of early Israel, were present in the rural areas between the fortified settlements in Canaan already during the Late Bronze Age.[61] Although originally different pastoralist groups were involved, the ethnogenesis of Israel was perhaps finalized only by the political process which led to the United Monarchy and brought together diverse tribes. These tribes may have been related to each other in some fashion, but they had not yet coalesced into the ethnos or entity called later by the term Israel.[62]

History is always more complicated than the simple narrative. The Bible narrates its tale, but it constitutes only the main tale, the one most told and retold, the one most remembered amongst others—until it became *the* narrative of the people of Israel.

Egyptian Motifs in the Book of Exodus

The goal of the present volume keeps us focused on the history of the period, and thus our attention remains on the historical evidence (textual, archaeological, etc.). It is worth noting, however, that the biblical account as just described is fully conversant with themes and motifs present in Egyptian magical and literary texts, including the following: the baby in the bulrushes (Exodus 2:3); the staff that turns into a reptile, whether snake (Exodus 4:3) or crocodile (Exodus 7:10); the elevation of Moses to the level of deity (Exodus 4:16; 7:1); the water of the Nile turning into blood (Exodus 7:19); the plague of darkness (Exodus 10:15); the killing of the first-born (Exodus 12:29); the splitting of the sea (Exodus 14:21); death by drowning (Exodus 14:28; 15:4); and more.[63]

These literary echoes indicate that the Israelite author (and presumably the educated portion of his audience) were well acquainted with Egyptian culture and religion.[64] This does not necessarily guarantee the historicity of the account recorded in Exodus 1–15, but it is a noteworthy observation nonetheless.

THE EXODUS

Epic Traditions in the Book of Exodus

At some point in time, the Israelites resident in Egypt were able to leave, traverse the Sinai region, travel through Transjordan, and settle in the central hill country of the land of Canaan (for this last stage, see chap. 3). The biblical account is filled with epic traditions: the episode commences with the ritual act of the sacrificing of lambs (Exodus 12:21–28); all Israel leaves as a collective unit at a single moment; the number of adult males in the group is given as 600,000 (both Exodus 12:37); and the narrative even takes time to mention the baking of bread for the journey (Exodus 12:39).

Such an account is to be compared to the Ugaritic Epic of Kirta, in which all of these elements are present. When Kirta, the legendary king of Canaanite lore, departs on a military expedition against Edom, the epic poem includes the following scenes: Kirta sacrifices a lamb to commence the proceedings, he prepares bread for the journey, and an enormous army of 3,000,000 men goes forth.[65] But beneath this epic treatment, one may plausibly infer a historical kernel.

P.Anastasi V—Another Report of a Frontier Official

We have noted the constant flow of Semites into Egypt (see esp. P.Anastasi VI); just as likely there was a flow of Semites out of Egypt, even if we have less evidence for such travels and migrations.[66]

One such text, even if it does not allow for the ethnic or national identification of the individuals leaving Egypt, is another report of a frontier official, included in P.Anastasi V, dated to the reign of Seti II (r. 1214–1208), once again with reference to Tjeku. In this well-known text, two slaves have escaped Egypt into the desert. The relevant section reads as follows:[67]

> Another matter, to wit: I was sent forth from the broad halls of the palace, life, prosperity, health, in the 3rd month of the 3rd season, day 9, at evening time, following after two slaves. Now when I reached the enclosure of Tjeku on the 3rd month of the 3rd season, day 10, they told me that to the south they were saying that they [i.e. the slaves] had passed by on the 3rd month of the 3rd season, day 10. When I reached the fortress, they told me that the scout (?) had come from the desert stating that they had passed the walled place north of Migdol of Seti Merneptah, life, prosperity, health, beloved like Seth. When my letter reaches you, write to me about all that has happened to them. Who found their

tracks? Which watch found their tracks? What people are after them? Write to me about all that has happened to them and how many people you sent out after them.

Once more there are parallels between an Egyptian document and the biblical account. Regardless of the manner in which the Torah presents Israel's history, it is noteworthy that the account includes an Egyptian force sent to pursue escaped slaves (see Exodus 14: 5–9). The above document informs us that this was perfectly natural, in fact, even when only two slaves escaped.

Moreover, the route of the two escaped slaves is significant. The two sites mentioned are Tjeku and Migdol. The former, as we saw above, is equivalent to the Hebrew term *sukkot*, that is, Succoth in English Bible translations, the very site mentioned as the Israelites' point of departure (Exodus 12:37; 13:20). Migdol is also mentioned in the biblical account (Exodus 14:2), even if we cannot locate the site precisely. Note further that the term is simply a variant pronunciation of the common Hebrew noun *migdal*, "tower" (as in the Tower of Babel story in Genesis 11).[68] Most likely, Migdol refers to one of the fortresses in the chain of such sites constructed by the Egyptian administration to supervise the eastern approaches to Egypt,[69] memory of which was kept alive by the Israelites as a component of the Exodus tradition.

Of all the toponyms in the general area of the eastern Delta and the Wadi Tumilat, it is rather striking that both the Book of Exodus and P.Anastasi V should mention both Succoth and Migdol in connection with escaping slaves. The evidence strongly suggests that the Israelites were using a route well traveled by fugitive slaves, somewhat akin to the "underground railroad" of American history.

The Sea of Reeds

According to the biblical account, the Exodus route brought the Israelites to the *yam suf*, "Sea of Reeds" (Exodus 13:18),[70] a term which appears commonly in Egyptian texts in the form *p3 twf*[71] and is most likely to be identified with the region of Lake Ballah and its marshlands.[72] Once again, the epic tradition takes command, as the Bible narrates the miraculous splitting of the sea and the drowning of the Egyptians. In addition, the account evokes Egyptian motifs: for in Egyptian lore, magicians were able to part the waters; in Egyptian religion, death by drowning was considered a noble death.

The splitting of waters occurs in two literary texts.[73] The first is the Demotic tale "Setne Khamwas and Na-nefer-ka-ptaḥ," known as "Setne I," set during the reign of Ramesses II, though composed in the Ptolemaic period (P.Cairo 30646). It contains the following line about the great magician Na-nefer-ka-ptaḥ, "He cast sand before him, and a gap formed in the river."[74]

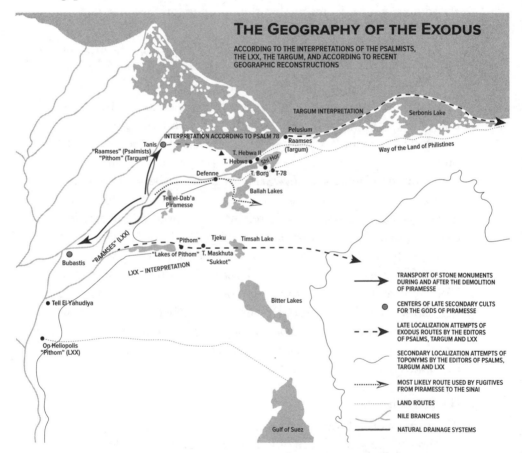

THE GEOGRAPHY OF THE EXODUS

ACCORDING TO THE INTERPRETATIONS OF THE PSALMISTS, THE LXX, THE TARGUM, AND ACCORDING TO RECENT GEOGRAPHIC RECONSTRUCTIONS

TARGUM INTERPRETATION

Serbonis Lake

Pelusium

INTERPRETATION ACCORDING TO PSALM 78

Raamses (Targum)

Tanis

"Raamses" (Psalmists)
"Pithom" (Targum)

Way of the Land of Philistines

T. Hebwa II

T. Hebwa

Shi Hor

Defenne

T. Borg

T-78

Ballah Lakes

Tell el-Dab'a
Piramesse

Tjeku

Timsah Lake

"Pithom"

"Lakes of Pithom"

T. Maskhuta

Bubastis

"Sukkot"

"RAAMSES" (LXX)

LXX – INTERPRETATION

Tell El Yahudiya

Bitter Lakes

On Heliopolis
"Pithom" (LXX)

Gulf of Suez

TRANSPORT OF STONE MONUMENTS DURING AND AFTER THE DEMOLITION OF PIRAMESSE

CENTERS OF LATE SECONDARY CULTS FOR THE GODS OF PIRAMESSE

LATE LOCALIZATION ATTEMPTS OF EXODUS ROUTES BY THE EDITORS OF PSALMS, TARGUM AND LXX

SECONDARY LOCALIZATION ATTEMPTS OF TOPONYMS BY THE EDITORS OF PSALMS, TARGUM AND LXX

MOST LIKELY ROUTE USED BY FUGITIVES FROM PIRAMESSE TO THE SINAI

LAND ROUTES

NILE BRANCHES

NATURAL DRAINAGE SYSTEMS

CITIES OF RA'AMSES AND PITHOM, AND RECONSTRUCTIONS OF EXODUS ROUTES IN THE COURSE OF TIME. The most likely route leads from Pi-Ramesse through the Ballah Lakes.

More famously, in The Boating Party story, the third of the five tales collected in P.Westcar (P.Berlin 3033), set during the reign of Khufu (4th Dynasty), though composed in the 13th Dynasty or the

Second Intermediate Period,[75] the great magician Djadja-em-ankh performs as follows:[76]

> He placed one side of the lake's water upon the other; and he found the pendant lying on a shard. He brought it and gave it to its owner. Now the water that had been twelve cubits deep across (lit. "on its back") had become twenty-four cubits when it was turned back. Then he said his say of magic and returned the waters of the lake to their place.

The drowning motif appears especially in New Kingdom texts and artwork (see image on next page for an example),[77] though it receives the clearest exposition in the words of Herodotus, *Histories*, book 2, section 90:[78]

> When anyone, be he Egyptian or stranger, is known to have been carried off by a crocodile or drowned by the river itself, such an one must by all means be embalmed and tended as fairly as may be and buried in a sacred coffin by the townsmen of the place where he is cast up; nor may any of his kinsfolk or his friends touch him, but his body is deemed something more than human, and is handled and buried by the priests of the Nile themselves.

From the evidence presented here, one gains the impression that the biblical author wishes to assert the following: okay, Egyptians, you think that magicians can part waters, and you think that death by drowning is a noble demise—we'll arrange it for you! And with that event, narrated in prose in Exodus 14 and recounted in poetry in Exodus 15, the departure of the Israelites from Egypt was complete. Never, from this point onward, through the end of the Torah, would the Israelites encounter the Egyptians again.

The Date of the Exodus

The next question to ask, one which continues to exercise scholars, is the following: assuming some historicity to the biblical account, when did the Exodus possibly occur? The dominant opinion in biblical scholarship is that the Exodus occurred sometime during the 13th century B.C.E. The single piece of evidence most commonly cited is the

Merneptah Stele, which most scholars interpret to mean that Israel already had departed Egypt by the year c. 1220 B.C.E. (see above). As we have suggested, however, this understanding of the inscription is by no means the only possible one.

First, during the 13th century B.C.E., Egypt was at the height of its power: the long reign of Ramesses II (r. 1290–1224) and that of his son and successor, Merneptah (r. 1224–1214), were characterized by great stability, military victories over Nubia and Libya, massive construction projects, and in particular control over the land of Canaan. However one conceives of the Exodus, the period of these two 19th Dynasty pharaohs seems to be the least likely time for the events of the Bible to unfold.

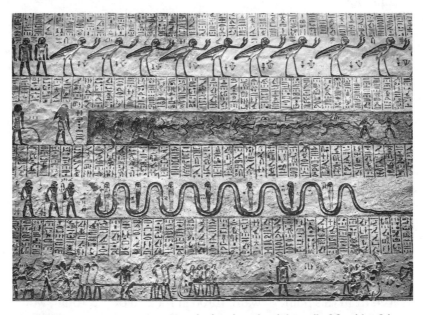

A SCENE FROM AMDUAT 10TH HOUR depicted on the right wall of Corridor G in the tomb of Ramesses VI (KV-9), featuring the drowned ones (second register from the top).

Secondly, as we shall see in the next chapter, the Israelites do not emerge in the land of Canaan until sometime later in the 12th century B.C.E. Moreover, Egyptian control over the land of Canaan not only continued into this time period but even increased considerably. Egyptian officials were stationed at Gaza and Deir el-Balaḥ in the southern coastal plain; at Lachish, Tell eš-Šari'a (perhaps Ziklag), Tell el-Far'ah (south), and perhaps Bet Shemesh in the southern inland territory; and at Megiddo and (most prominently) Bet She'an in the north.[79] In addition, Egyptian mining in the Timna Valley continued throughout the 19th Dynasty and into the reign of Ramesses VI in the 20th Dynasty (perhaps with a brief interruption during the transition between the two dynasties).[80]

And yet, according to the Bible, once the Israelites departed from the Sea of Reeds, they never again encountered Egyptians, including in the books of Numbers, Joshua, and Judges. Had the Israelites left Egypt at some point in the 13th century (per the standard approach), with an arrival in the land of Canaan sometime thereafter, it is hard to imagine that they would not have encountered Egyptian troops somewhere along the way. Various peoples are encountered—Midianites, Amalekites, Edomites, Moabites, Ammonites, and Canaanites—but not Egyptians.[81]

Let us look more closely at one particular city, Lachish in the territory of Judah. The excavations at the site reveal that Stratum VI, dated to the 12th century, was still governed by the Egyptians. This is confirmed by two finds: a heavy bronze city gate fitting bearing the name of Ramesses III (r. 1195–1164) and a scarab bearing the name of Ramesses IV (r. 1164–1156).[82] Stratum VI then was totally destroyed by fire, in c. 1150, and the site was abandoned for about two centuries.[83]

While the archaeological data do not (and typically cannot) inform us *who* was responsible for the destruction, the geography, chronology, and the account in Joshua 10:31–32 make the Israelites a prime candidate.[84] It is true that Joshua 10 does not mention the burning of Lachish by the Israelites, but the text reports that Joshua besieged the city, conquered it, and slaughtered the population (see v. 32 esp.). The archaeological record revealed a severe destruction with bodies still buried in the ruins.[85] If there is any historical validity to the biblical account, the Israelite attack on Lachish could not have occurred until *after* the Egyptian presence at the city had receded, c. 1150 B.C.E.

In short, the picture that emerges from the archaeological record compels us to focus on the late 12th century for the emergence of Israel in the land of Canaan, and by extension the early or mid-12th century for the Exodus from Egypt.

Exodus Scenario 1: The Turmoil at the End of the 19th Dynasty

One ideal historical scenario for the Exodus would be during the major turmoil that characterizes the transition between the end of the 19th Dynasty (1198 B.C.E.) and the rise of Sethnakht (r. 1198–1195), a general, a usurper, and the founder of the 20th Dynasty. The prime sources are the Elephantine Stele, erected by Sethnakht, and P.Harris I, concerning events during the reign of Sethnakht and his son Ramesses III (r. 1195–1164).

The chaos during the year c. 1198 B.C.E. is described succinctly in the Elephantine Stele: "this land had been in confusion, because (?) the Nile-land has lapsed into forgetting God."[86] The full account is not totally clear, but the text does mention how the enemies of Sethnakht tried to win Western Asiatic people (*šttyw*) over to their side with silver and gold, though eventually said people needed to flee and leave the payment behind. Now, it is true that in the Bible the Israelites leave Egypt with silver and gold (Exodus 3:22; 11:2; 12:35), and so the plotlines do not align. But one wonders if the Bible does not incorporate an echo of the feature described in the Elephantine Stele.

The relevant section of P.Harris I describes the chaos that precedes the establishment of the 20th Dynasty as follows:[87]

> The land of Egypt was cast aside, with every man in his (own standard of) right.[88] They had no chief spokesman for many years. ... The land of Egypt was officials and mayors,[89] one slaying his fellow, both exalted and lowly. Other times came afterwards in empty years. Irsu the Ḫurru was with them, he made himself prince. He set the entire land as tributary before him. One joined his companion that their property might be plundered. They treated the gods like the people, and no offerings were presented in the temples.

Attention is drawn to Irsu,[90] described as a Ḫurru, that is, someone from the Levant, who gained control over Egypt for a brief period, until Sethnakht was able to establish himself as pharaoh and the founder of the 20th Dynasty. Unfortunately, this is our only reference to the intriguing figure of Irsu, but the events surrounding his brief career could serve as the backdrop for the Exodus.[91]

Exodus Scenario 2: The Sea Peoples Invasion During the Reign of Ramesses III

A second possible historical scenario occurs during the reign of the son and successor to Sethnakht, namely, Ramesses III (r. 1195–1164). This pharaoh was engaged in warfare at both the western and eastern boundaries of the country, with the biggest threat stemming from the invasion of the Sea Peoples, dated to year 8 of his reign, hence, c. 1188 B.C.E. As the Medinet Habu inscriptions and the P.Harris I text testify,[92] the attack by the Sea Peoples, led by the Philistines and their allies, once again threw Egypt into great turmoil.

The texts imply that the action took place at the mouth of the easternmost branch of the Nile River in the northeastern Delta region and perhaps along the Sinai coast, with the Sea Peoples both attacking by sea via ships and traveling over land on ox-drawn carts carrying women and children.[93] Although Egypt emerged victorious, so that the Sea Peoples returned to the coast of Canaan (Philistines in the southern coast plain, Tjeker at Dor, etc.), the invasion attempt inflicted great damages upon Egypt. These events eventually would weaken the country to the point that the Egyptian army and administration would need to withdraw from the land of Canaan around 1150 B.C.E., as described above (see also map on p. 46). This invasion attempt prompted Ramesses III to rebuild the fortress at Tell er-Retaba and to construct small fortresses at strategic points such as the one at Kom el-Qulzoum near Suez (as noted above).[94] This activity certainly caused recruitment of and strong stress on the population in these border regions.

We see these events as a propitious time for the Israelites to have departed from Egypt. A further clue is provided by Exodus 13:17: "And it was, when Pharaoh sent-forth the people, and God did not lead them by way of the land of the Philistines, though it was closer, for God said, 'Lest the people reconsider when they see war and return to Egypt'." If we take this verse at face value, it tells us that at the very time the Israelites may have left Egypt there was military conflict along the coastal route, referred to here as the "way of the land of the Philistines." Or more generally, the Israelites may have left Egypt after the Sea Peoples invasion, under whatever circumstances, and still sought to avoid the array of forts and movements of armies along the "way of the land of the Philistines."

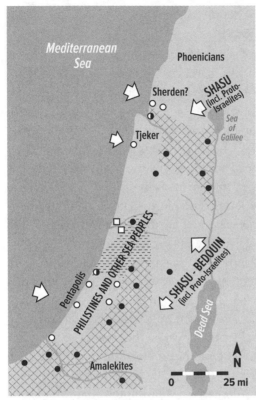

Mediterranean
Sea

Phoenicians

Sherden?

SHASU (incl. Proto-Israelites)

Sea of Galilee

Tjeker

PHILISTINES AND OTHER SEA PEOPLES

Pentapolis

SHASU - BEDOUIN (incl. Proto-Israelites)

Dead Sea

Amalekites

N

0   25 mi

REST OF THE EGYPTIAN PROVINCE CANAAN AFTER THE
INCURSION OF SEA PEOPLES IN THE REIGN OF RAMESSES

● 20th Dynasty Sites with
Egyptian Inscriptions

○ Towns of the Pentapolis,
and Dor, Akko, T. Keisan

◑ 20th Dynasty Sites
Dated by Artifacts

□ Important Later Towns
of the Philistines

⇨ Early Bridgeheads of
the Sea Peoples

⬲ Rest of the Egyptian
Province Canaan

THE EGYPTIAN PROVINCE of Canaan after the Sea Peoples incursion during the reign of Ramesses III.

It also may be possible to incorporate Amos 9:7 into this discussion. The verse reads as follows: "Did I not bring Israel up from the land of Egypt, and the Philistines from Caphtor, and Aram from Qir?" Might this verse imply that all three movements were more or less coeval with one another? Unfortunately, since we do not know where Qir is located,[95] and thus cannot say more about Aramean origins, including when the Aramean migration may have occurred, the question cannot be answered. Yet the posited contemporaneity of the named movements is suggestive. To be sure, the Philistines' migration from Caphtor (i.e., Crete specifically or the Aegean more generally) and the Israelite settlement in Canaan were more or less contemporary with one another.

In sum, the background of the Exodus is to be found in either of the two scenarios presented here, relatively early in the 12th century B.C.E., during the reigns of the first two pharaohs of the 20th Dynasty. In such case, the mention of "Israel" in the Merneptah Stele must refer to Israelite elements that did not participate in the Bible's main narrative (Eisodus, Slavery, Exodus).

Biblical Genealogies

There is a third line of evidence that we can admit here as well. The genealogies recorded in the Bible reveal a remarkable internal consistency, and thus to our mind they may be utilized to reconstruct the relative chronology of events narrated in the Bible.[96] In order to establish the date of the Exodus, for example, one seeks a genealogy from a known fixed point and then works back in time until one reaches the Exodus. Unfortunately (though not surprisingly), there is only one such genealogy in the Bible, namely, the genealogy of King David. We say "not surprisingly," because comparative sociological research has demonstrated that royal lineages are transmitted with greater depth than the genealogies of non-royals.[97]

The genealogy of David recorded in Ruth 4:18–22 and 1 Chronicles 2:5–15 is as follows: Nahshon – Salmon – Boaz – Obed – Jesse – David. Since, per scholarly consensus, David can be dated to c. 1000 B.C.E.,[98] and Nahshon lived five generations earlier, all we need to do is to determine the proper coefficient to be multiplied by these five generations. While most scholars use the average of 25 years per generation, exhaustive research by David Henige, based on a survey of 737 known genealogies in world history, demonstrates that the average age per generation is actually 30 years.[99] But that figure is only the calculated average: 217 of the 737 dynasties have a range of 30 to 34 years per generation, and 87 of them have a range of 35 to 39 years.

Working back from David at c. 1000 B.C.E., we therefore reach Nahshon at c. 1150 B.C.E. (i.e., 5 generations = 150 years). Nahshon is an important figure in our calculations, because he is mentioned on two occasions as a member of the Exodus and Wandering generation: in Exodus 6:23 as the brother-in-law of Aaron, and in Numbers 1:7 as the leader of the tribe of Judah. True, this calculation brings us only to the middle of the 12th century, and not to the early decades thereof, per what we suggested above. But if we use one of the higher figures based on Henige's research—say, 35 years per generation, which is well within the range of possibility—then the Davidic lineage reaches to 1175 B.C.E. In short, if the genealogy of David recorded in the Bible is to be accorded any credibility, it clearly favors a 12th-century date for the Exodus, as opposed to earlier dates proposed by other scholars.

Unfortunately, the genealogy of David is the only one in the Bible that can be used for the purposes of dating the Exodus. In theory, we would benefit from similar genealogies from others in David's circle, or from the approximate era, but no others are available. The lineage of Saul (presented in 1 Samuel 9:1) is promising, but each of his ancestors listed there is mentioned only here, and not earlier in the Bible: Aphiah – Becorath – Zeror – Abiel – Kish – Saul. It would be helpful if Aphiah or Becorath appeared in the Exodus-Wilderness narratives, but they do not.[100]

1 Kings 6:1

An oft-cited verse for fixing the date of the Exodus is 1 Kings 6:1: "And it was, in the four hundred and eightieth year of the Israelites' going-out from the land of Egypt, in the fourth year, in the month of Ziv, that is, the second month, in the reign of Solomon over Israel; and he built the House to the Lord." This seems to give us a clear chronology. If we can fix the date of Solomon's construction of the Temple, or more generally of his reign, and work back 480 years, one would reach the date of the Exodus.

Of course, the calculus is not that simple. We are able to date Solomon's reign with confidence to c. 965–930 B.C.E.[101] Since the construction of the Temple was begun during the fourth year of Solomon's reign and was completed seven years later (1 Kings 6:38), we can date the construction project to the years c. 961–954. If we use the year 960 B.C.E. for the purposes of our calculations, and the Exodus transpired 480 years earlier (1 Kings 6:1), we arrive to c. 1440 B.C.E.

But there are two problems with this approach. First, and most obviously, a 15th-century date for the Exodus leads to the question: where were the Israelites before they first emerged in the historical and archaeological record? Within Egypt, as we have seen throughout this chapter, references to Israel, the Shasu of Edom/Se'ir, the cities mentioned in the Bible (Pithom and Ra'amses), and more, along with the four-room houses at Medinet Habu, all congregate in the late Ramesside period (late 13th and 12th centuries). Within Canaan, the evidence from the central hill country reveals the emergence of Israel during the 12th century. A 15th-century date for the Exodus, as presupposed by a literal acceptance of 1 Kings 6:1, raises more questions than it answers.

Secondly, one cannot take at face value the years presented in the early biblical books. The numbers used are always greatly exaggerated and, at times, they are imbued with symbolism (even if the exact nature of that symbolism eludes us).

The use of round numbers, especially exaggerated ones and multiples of 40, is characteristic of the epic tradition. Examples include: God's words to Abram that his ancestors would be strangers in a foreign land for 400 years (Genesis 15:13); the 40 years of the wandering (Deuteronomy 29:4); Moses's age of 80 at his first appearance before Pharaoh (Exodus 7:7); his death at the age of 120 (Deuteronomy 34:7); the various instances of 40 and 80 in the Book of Judges (3:11; 3:30; 5:31; etc.);[102] and the 40-year reigns of both David and Solomon (2 Samuel 5:4; 1 Kings 11:42).[103]

This same use of exaggerated numbers using multiples of 40 is attested in ancient Near Eastern literature. For example, Nabonidus, king of Babylon (r. 556–539 B.C.E.), asserted that Naram-Sin, king of Akkad (r. c. 2254–c. 2218) ruled 3,200 years earlier,[104] when we know that the distance separating the two rulers is c. 1,700 years. This is all part of the epic storytelling style of the ancient world, which we have discussed above.[105]

All of this is simply to say that no historical reconstruction should be based on the 480-year time span mentioned in 1 Kings 6:1. Over time, and especially during the period of the kingdoms of Israel and Judah, accurate records were kept by royal chancelleries, so that the years provided in the canonical Book of Kings (at least from 1 Kings 12 onward), which in turn derive from the Annals of the Kings of Israel (1 Kings 14:19, etc.) and the Annals of the Kings of Judah (1 Kings 14:29, etc.), are most reliable.[106] However, this same accuracy does not apply to the round, exaggerated numbers used in the early biblical tradition.[107]

In recognition of the nonhistorical nature of the 480-year figure in 1 Kings 6:1, some scholars have attempted to interpret the number as symbolic of 12 generations × 40 years (as representative of a single generation in ancient Israelite lore). Yet this too fails, for there are neither 480 years nor twelve generations separating the Exodus from the construction of the Temple. As we saw above, the genealogy from Nahshon to David spans only five generations, so that the genealogy from Nahshon to Solomon spans only six generations.

Conclusions

As we have argued herein, the background for the Eisodus, Slavery, and Exodus is the Ramesside period, or to be more specific, the time period of the late 19th Dynasty and the first half of the 20th Dynasty, that is, c. 1250–c. 1150 B.C.E. All of the Egyptian material we have cited falls into this time period, as summarized here:

1. P.Anastasi VI, dated to the reign of Seti II (r. 1214–1208), with reference to the Shasu of Edom being admitted into Egypt and being allowed to settle in Per-Atum (= Pithom).

2. P.Anastasi III, dated to the reign of Merneptah (r. 1224–1214), P.Anastasi V, dated to the reign of Seti II (r. 1214–1208), and the Louvre Leather Roll, dated to the 19th Dynasty generally, all with reference to brickmaking, including the lack of straw—even if the specific identify of the workers is not disclosed.

3. P.Leiden 348, dated to the reign of Ramesses II (r. 1290–1224), with reference to the ʿApiru constructing the city of Pi-Ramesse (see also the more fragmentary version in P.Leiden 349).

4. The four-room houses at Medinet Habu, dated to the time of Ramesses IV (r. 1164–1156).

5. P.Harris I, detailing the achievements of Ramesses III (r. 1195–1164), with reference to the capture of Shasu of Seʿir and their assignment to work in the temples.

6. The famous reference to "Israel" in the Merneptah Stele, however it may be interpreted and to whatever "Israel" it may refer.

7. P.Anastasi V, dated to the reign of Seti II (r. 1214–1208), with reference to two slaves escaping via Migdol.

8. The Elephantine Stele, erected by Sethnakht (r. 1198–1195), with reference to the overall chaos at the end of the 19th Dynasty.

9. Another section of P.Harris I (see above, no. 5), with additional description of the overall chaos at the end of the 19th Dynasty.

10. The Medinet Habu and P.Harris accounts describing the Sea Peoples invasion during year 8 of the reign of Ramesses III (c. 1188).

We add to this mix a point intimated above, but not stated explicitly. As Sarah Groll noted, while some of the toponyms discussed herein occur in later Egyptian texts, only in the documents of this time period does one find the collocation of Per-Atum (Pithom), Pi-Ramesse (Ra'amses), Tjeku (Succoth), Migdol, *pꜣ-twf* (Sea of Reeds), and most likely Goshen.[108] Pi-Ramesse, for example, only reappears after a long absence in the third century B.C.E.

How, then, do we reconstruct what actually happened, and how do we correlate the history with the biblical narrative? We assume that groups of (proto-)Israelites and related tribes—among them the Shasu of Edom/Se'ir mentioned in Egyptian texts—entered Egypt in various stages and by various means during the Ramesside period. Some of these arrived as family units, with their flocks, per P.Anastasi VI, dated to the reign of Seti II. Some were brought to Egypt as captives, as indicated by P.Harris I during the reign of Ramesses III. Most were exploited as a ready labor force in the eastern Delta, constructing Per-Atum (Pithom) and Pi-Ramesse (Ra'amses), in line with Exodus 1:11. Some lived much farther south, including at Thebes. Still others did not participate in the Eisodus and sojourn in Egypt at all, but rather remained in the general region of Canaan, where they were encountered by Merneptah's troops and are referenced as "Israel" in the Merneptah Stele.

As we attempt to read the biblical tradition of the Exodus against the historical framework of Ramesside Egypt, somewhere within this mix, we may assume that one group of Israelites took advantage of the general turmoil during the transition period between the 19th and 20th Dynasties (c. 1198) and/or during or after the Sea Peoples invasion dated to year 8 of the reign of Ramesses III (c. 1188). They escaped into the desert, wandered the Sinai, and eventually settled in the central hill country of Canaan.[109] As we noted above, according to the biblical tradition, no Egyptian troops or authorities were encountered after the Sea of Reeds event, a point that speaks in favor of the arrival of the Israelites in Canaan after the Egyptians had retreated from the province.

In general, the sojourn in Egypt was not very long. Turning to the evidence of the biblical genealogies—with special attention to the lineage of Moses (Levi–Kohath–Amram–Moses; see Exodus 6:16–20),[110] we see that this lineage indicates that the total amount of time in Egypt could not have been very long. According to the biblical tradition, Levi and his son Kohath are among those who immigrated to Egypt (Genesis 46:11), while the latter's grandson Moses already is leaving Egypt.

Once more, we need to dismiss the actual years presented in the Bible. God informs Abraham that his descendants will be enslaved for 400 years in a foreign land (Genesis 15:13), and then the text states that the Israelites were resident in Egypt for 430 years (Exodus 12:40–41).[111] More importantly, we stress the other statement made by God to Abraham, "And the fourth generation shall return here" (Genesis 15:16), which is precisely what occurred (see above, e.g., for the Moses lineage).

We therefore posit that the biblical tradition arose out of the various movements (into and out of Egypt, as noted above), presumably at different times and under different circumstances. As we noted earlier, history is always more complicated than a single episode or a single account, but the tradition frequently memorializes, commemorates, and indeed celebrates only one main narrative. Such is what occurred in ancient Israel: the story is stylized as the descent to Egypt by a single extended family, Jacob and his children; the slavery of the main group engaged in brickmaking for the building of Pithom and Ra'amses; the miraculous hand of God bringing plagues against Egypt; and, finally, the Exodus from Egypt of the core group, which would traverse the Sinai and settle in Canaan.

What happened to others who arrived in Egypt and were not necessarily related to Jacob? The tradition is silent. What happened to the potential Israelite groups doing enforced labor in Upper Egypt, that is, those who lived in the four-room houses? The tradition is silent. What happened to Israelite elements that may never have experienced Egypt at all? The tradition is silent. And presumably so much more of the history of the Israelites during this crucial time period in their development is unknown. For the narrative coalesced around a single aspect of the history, and the rest is lost in the mists of time.[112]

A well-known analogy from American history presents itself.[113] The Mayflower event was a singular journey, which (after some stops and starts) left Plymouth, England, on September 6, 1620, and which arrived at present-day Cape Cod, Massachusetts, on November 9, 1620. This event was eventually integrated into the American national epic, but there were earlier journeys, including those that led to the establishments of the Roanoke Colony (1585) and the Jamestown settlement (1607), and of course numerous later voyages, including the arrival of others on a second ship named Mayflower in 1629, 1630, 1633, 1634, and 1639. Add to this the arrival of people from other European countries, most importantly the Dutch settlement of the Hudson Valley during the years 1609–1624, and we begin to see the emergence of the American nation.

Naturally, the history of America is more complex, as it includes the diversity of native Americans, Spanish colonization in Florida (starting already in 1565), Africans brought to these shores against their will (commencing in 1619), French colonization in Louisiana (starting in 1699), and more. But of all the Atlantic crossings, the one remembered and still celebrated by the vast majority of Americans as Thanksgiving Day is the Mayflower event.

And so it was in ancient Israel. Almost undoubtedly, numerous eisodi and exodi occurred. In fact, the geography of the region speaks in favor of this view, for the environment of both the city of Pi-Ramesse and the Wadi Tumilat implies different Exodus tracks, which cannot be united into a single sortie.[114] Or to put this cleverly, per the felicitous expression coined by Abraham Malamat, we rather should recall Moses's words to Pharaoh as "Let My People Go and Go and Go and Go."[115] However, in an effort to create a unified national epic, most likely with the goal of unifying disparate tribes, the tradition recalls only a single Eisodus and more importantly a single triumphant, dramatic Exodus.

The latter would be celebrated for generations during the combined festivals of Pesaḥ and Matzot, spring holidays associated with the lambing of the flocks and the start of the barley harvest, respectively. The meaning of the word *Pesaḥ* remains an enigma, notwithstanding its usual English translation as "Passover."[116] The latter word, *Matzot*, means "unleavened bread," still consumed during the week of Passover by Jews around the world. The two main components of the ancient Israelite economy were animal husbandry and crop production, with each segment of the population able to participate in one of these spring festivals. Eventually, they were combined into a single holiday, and then more importantly their agricultural origins were overlaid with the historical commemoration of the Exodus from Egypt.

Through this process, the Exodus from Egypt became the single unifying factor in ancient Israel, and the single event most mentioned in all the Bible, throughout all its genres (prose, poetry, prophecy, etc.).

400-YEAR STELE. Erected originally in the Egyptian capital city of Avaris to honor Pharaoh Seti I, this epigraphic document is now in the Egyptian Museum, Cairo.

THE HYKSOS (AN EXCURSUS)

Many readers of this chapter may have read elsewhere[117] that some connections existed between the Hyksos and the Israelites. In light of everything that we have written above, we deny any possible relationship, with one small qualification (see below).[118]

But first, who were the Hyksos? The term derives from the Egyptian term *ḥqꜣw ḫꜣswt*, "rulers of foreign lands," though it has come down to us in the Greek form via the historians Manetho and Josephus. The term is used in Egyptian texts to refer mainly to Near Eastern rulers who established themselves in northern Egypt in c. 1640 B.C.E., as the 15th Dynasty. Their capital was at Avaris (today, Tell ed-Dabʻa) in the eastern Delta, and they ruled until c. 1530 B.C.E.

The Hyksos rule rested on the considerable number of immigrants in the eastern Nile Delta, who arrived mainly from the northern Levant during the second part of the 12th Dynasty and during the 13th Dynasty (c. 1850–1700 B.C.E.), and who served the pharaohs of this period in different capacities. The inhabitants of Avaris, which was an important harbor town, were most probably responsible for expeditions and trade by sea, but they also offered military service and most likely participated in the expeditions to the turquoise and copper mines on the Sinai, during the second part of the 12th Dynasty (c. 1900–1800 B.C.E.). In a period of decline during the late 13th Dynasty, Avaris remained a booming trade center and therefore had the power to establish itself as an independent small kingdom in the northeastern Delta c. 1720 B.C.E., thereby constituting the 14th Dynasty ruled by kings of western Asiatic origin.

This dynasty seems to have been toppled c. 1640 B.C.E. by another group of Asiatic powerholders who established themselves as the "Hyksos," the 15th Dynasty. They were able to control the northern part of Egypt, and for some time even Upper Egypt, in a kind of vassal system. During this period, the south of Egypt was ruled by the 16th and 17th Dynasties, centered in Thebes. Together the 14th–17th Dynasties comprise what Egyptologists call the Second Intermediate Period.

The 14th and the 15th Dynasties introduced Canaanite religion and built temples of Near Eastern architecture in Avaris, such as a Broad-Room Temple for the Syrian storm-god and a Bent-Axis Temple for his consort, either Astarte or Asherah.[119] The presence of Canaanite religion in the eastern Delta became so firmly rooted that it was respected even after the former vassal dynasty under Pharaoh Ahmose conquered Avaris and established the 18th Dynasty. The Hyksos population was most likely largely dispersed throughout the country, but Canaanite cults continued in Avaris in unbroken succession until the 19th Dynasty, which adopted the Syrian storm-god Baal Zephon in the guise of the Egyptian storm-god Seth as their dynastic ancestor.[120] This move was intended to provide a certain legitimacy to the Ramesside 19th Dynasty of non-royal origin.

The era of the introduction of the cult of the storm-god was commemorated in the 400-Year Stele (see image on p. 54), originally positioned in front of the temple of the storm-god Seth of Avaris in the time of Ramesses II. The 400-year event itself, however, most likely had taken place already under the last king of the 18th Dynasty, Horemheb (r. 1315–1301 B.C.E.), who, being without heir, promoted his aged comrade-in-arms Pa-Ramesses (later Ramesses I [r. 1301–1300 B.C.E.]) and his son Seti I (r. 1300–1290 B.C.E.) to be his successors. Therefore, they appear also on the stela of Ramesses II, which seems to be a replacement of an older stela, commissioned under Horemheb.

The commemorative stela may concomitantly celebrate the return of the Egyptian capital to the general region of Avaris (after its long establishment in Thebes throughout the 18th Dynasty). According to their titles, the real founders of the 19th Dynasty seem to have originated from the eastern Delta and may have adopted some of the heritage of the Hyksos, especially the devotion to the local god Seth-Baal.[121] Note that the names of Ramesside pharaohs Seti I and Seti II (father and grandson of Ramesses II, respectively) mean "the one belonging to Seth."

How was the heritage of the Hyksos remembered more than a thousand years later? In the third century B.C.E., during the Ptolemaic period, Manetho, an Egyptian priest, wrote a history of Egypt in Greek, known as the *Aegyptiaca*, now lost to us. Significant portions of his work, however, were cited by Josephus, the Jewish historian of the first century C.E., who also wrote in Greek,[122] and by scattered later church fathers. Within the work is an extensive king list, with the kings divided into numbered dynasties—the system still employed today, so that Egyptologists remain in Manetho's debt until the present day.

While sometimes it is difficult to distinguish between the original Manetho statements, on the one hand, and Josephus's own statements, on the other—since the former are quoted and embedded in the latter—Manetho appears to refer to two different Exodus versions. In the one version, a group of 480,000 Hyksos, also called by him "shepherd kings," leave Egypt and travel to Jerusalem. In the other version, an Egyptian priest called Osarseph leads 80,000 lepers to rebel against Egypt, he commits all manner of sacrilege against the Egyptian deities, and at the end of the story he changes his name to Moses. Scholars have detected a hint of anti-Jewish sentiments in Manetho's second version especially (note the association with lepers), which is why Josephus was more inclined to favor the first version (*Ag. Ap.* 1.26–31).

Josephus's acceptance of the Hyksos–Israelite connection, as posited by Manetho, has at times been renewed in modern scholarship. Not that many scholars would date the Exodus to the removal of the Hyksos from Egypt, c. 1530 B.C.E., but many would associate the Joseph story with the rise of the Hyksos and the 15th Dynasty rule. The logic is: this would be the most likely time for a Semite from the land of Canaan (read: Joseph) to rise to a high level of power in Egypt, second in command only to the Pharaoh (Genesis 41:39–44).

As we have seen, however, the chronology is all wrong. The biblical narrative focuses on the 19th and 20th Dynasties, not the Second Intermediate Period. That said, there may be one glimmer of a connection, namely, the relationship between the 400-Year Stele and the use of 400-year time spans in the Bible.

As we saw above, the Israelites reckoned their sojourn in Egypt as 400 years (Genesis 15:13) and their overall residency in the country as 430 years (Exodus 12:40–41). Is there a connection between the two?

The best one can say is that the Israelites who recorded the historical narrative that emerged as the books of Genesis and Exodus understood their connection to the eastern Delta, and thus they may have appropriated in some fashion the figure of 400 years—perhaps in an honest way, or perhaps in a somewhat defiant way, with a meaning no longer obvious to us.

Here it is important to note that the Hyksos did not disappear after they were dethroned and the 15th Dynasty came to an end. The notion that they left Egypt, either by force or on their accord, after all, is mentioned for the first time only by Manetho at a distance of about 1,250 years. Most likely, the Hyksos-people simply remained in the eastern Delta region, where they blended in with all the other Semites who arrived on a regular basis in later centuries.[123] Possibly, some of the latter-day Hyksos-people left Egypt along with the Israelites, per the Bible's reference to the 'erev rav, "mixed multitude" (Exodus 12:38), which went forth with the Israelites.[124]

As such, the Israelites may have felt some modicum of connection to the Hyksos, but it would be a very distant glimmer. At an even greater distance, the *longue durée* of a Semitic population living in Egypt may explain Josephus's identifying the Hyksos with the Jews of yore.

All said, though: there can be real no connection between the Hyksos and the Israelites of the Exodus story. In addition to the chronological issue, there are also geographical and historical considerations. The palaces and temples of the Hyksos, as revealed through the decades-long excavations at Tell ed-Dab'a (ancient Avaris) are similar in architectural style to buildings in northern Syria and Mesopotamia; while the origin of the Israelites, as we have emphasized herein, are to be found amongst the Shasu Bedouin folk who roamed the far southern Levant (including Edom/Se'ir).

Furthermore, we note that the population under Hyksos rule was an urban and urbane society, characterized by trade, especially by sea, and by the importation of horses and chariots into Egypt. As indicated, they even experienced the glory of controlling the Delta and the northern part of the Nile Valley for more than 100 years. These historical facts stand in complete opposition to the traditions of the Israelites, characterized by their simple lifestyle, the herding of sheep and goats, and most important of all the experience of oppression in Egypt (with the singular exception of Joseph).

3

The Emergence of Israel in the Land of Canaan

GARY A. RENDSBURG

DURING THE 12TH CENTURY B.C.E., A NEW PEOPLE appeared in the central hill country of Canaan. Almost undoubtedly, these newcomers were the Israelites as attested in the Bible. To examine this subject, we begin with the archaeological evidence, after which we will turn to the biblical material, especially the books of Joshua and Judges.

The Archaeological Evidence

During the Late Bronze Age (1500–1175 B.C.E.), which immediately preceded the biblical period, the central hill country was relatively open terrain. Extensive archaeological surveys of the region—from the Jezreel Valley in the north to the Beersheva Basin in the south—have identified only about 30 settlements dating to this period. However, in the immediately following Iron Age I (1175–1000 B.C.E.), the number of settlements within the same geographical area rose dramatically, to about 250.[1] This expansion cannot be due to natural population growth, but must rather indicate the arrival of a new people in the region.

It is not only the number of sites that is relevant here but also the distinctive configuration of many of these settlements, especially of the earlier and smaller ones. Beginning in the 12th century, the landscape becomes dotted with settlements arranged in elliptical patterns: the houses are aligned solely along the perimeter of the ellipse while the interior of the site remains open, thereby creating a central courtyard (see plans below).

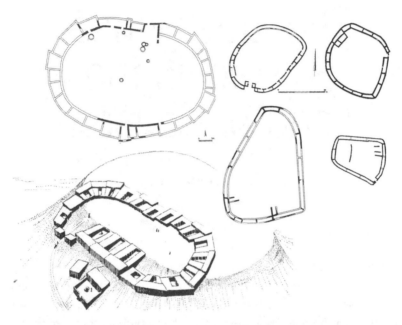

SITE PLANS OF SELECTED Iron Age I elliptical courtyard sites (clockwise from top left): 'Izbet Sartah, Ein Qadeis, Atar Haro'a, Ketef Shivta, Rahba, and Beersheba.

This layout strikingly resembles the manner in which the desert-dwelling Bedouin of our own era fashion their encampments—that is, with the tents erected side-by-side along the perimeter, leaving the interior as an enclosed space for the sheep and goats. In the nighttime only a few shepherds on guard duty, along with their sheepdogs, are required to ensure the safety of the flocks; in the daytime the sheep and goats are led out of the enclosure to graze in the surrounding countryside (see next page).

BEDOUIN TENT ENCAMPMENTS from the first half of the 20th century.

From this parallel we may posit that the people responsible for the Iron Age I courtyard or elliptical sites were former pastoral nomads or, better, semi-nomads who over time became more sedentary. As they transitioned from their nomadic ways to a more settled way of life, they did not leapfrog from Bedouin-style encampments to full-fledged villages. Instead, when they began to construct more permanent domiciles, these newcomers to the central hill country organized their structures according to their customary elliptical site plan. These early Iron Age I settlements served the same practical purpose—that is, protection of livestock—but the dwellings changed from tents made of animal skins (which were portable) to simple houses constructed of stone.[2]

"To Your Tents, O Israel!"

The picture outlined here dovetails nicely with the depiction of the Israelites in the Bible. The issue of their historicity aside, the books of Exodus and Numbers portray the Israelites as a desert people wandering from place to place and living in tents, before they settled in the land of Canaan. Indeed, a key phrase in Biblical Hebrew makes this point abundantly clear: the functional equivalent to the English expression "go home" is "to your tents." Note the following passages:[3]

"To your tents" phrase in the Bible

1. Judges 7:8	"and all the rest of Israel, he sent each-man to his tents" —with reference to Gideon's selection of his elite troops
2. Judges 19:9	"and you may arise-early tomorrow for your journey, and you may go to your tent" —the instructions of the concubine's father, after bidding his daughter and son-in-law to spend the night with him
3. Judges 20:8	"we will not go, each-man to his tent, and we will not turn, each-man to his house" —with reference to the decision by the Israelites to remain and to attack Gibeah of Benjamin
4. 1 Samuel 4:10	"and Israel was defeated, and they fled, each-man to his tents" —upon the defeat inflicted by the Philistines
5. 2 Samuel 18:18	"and all Israel had fled, each-man to his tents" —with reference to Absalom's supporters
6. 2 Samuel 19:9	"now Israel had fled, each-man to his tents" —upon the conclusion of David's mourning for Absalom
7. 2 Samuel 20:1	"each-man to his tents, O Israel" —spoken by Sheba, in his attempt to have the people defect from David
8. 2 Samuel 20:22	"and they dispersed from the city, each-man to his tents" —upon the end of the siege of Abel Beth Maacah
9. 1 Kings 8:66 (~ **2 Chronicles 7:10**)	"and they [i.e., the people] went to their tents" —upon the conclusion of Solomon's ceremony for the dedication of the Temple
10. 1 Kings 12:16 (= **2 Chronicles 10:16**)	"to your tents, O Israel!" —spoken by the people of northern Israel, when they realize that there is no purpose in following Rehoboam
11. 1 Kings 12:16 (= **2 Chronicles 10:16**)	"and Israel went (each-man) to his tents" —the Israelites return to their homes, in light of the above
12. 2 Kings 14:12 (= **2 Chronicles 25:22**)	"and they fled, each-man to his tents" —with reference to the Judahites, routed by Israel, during the reign of Amaziah

It could be argued that in the first four passages above, some or many Israelites still were living in tents. But for the remainder of the passages, this clearly is not the case. The approximate time frame for these episodes is c. 980 B.C.E. (5: David and Absalom) through

c. 780 B.C.E. (12: Amaziah), by which point the Israelites had abandoned their tents completely and were living in true houses built of stone, as revealed in the archaeological record.[4] And yet, tent imagery persists in the language, especially when used as a functional semantic equivalency for "go home" or "they went home" or "they fled home."

The endurance of this idiom bespeaks a people who once upon a time lived in tents. A good modern analogy is the enduring use of the word "horse" within such English idioms as "hold your horses"; "stop horsing around"; or "a dark-horse candidate."[5] These expressions reveal a people (to wit, Britons and Americans) for whom the horse was once an essential part of their cultural repertoire. Such is no longer the case, yet the word "horse" continues to inform the contemporary English language. Such was the case, arguably, with the word "tent" in ancient Hebrew. By the tenth century, most Israelites no longer lived in portable dwellings suitable for desert and desert-fringe lifestyle, and yet the word "tent" is well preserved in the key idiom examined above.

The Southern Homeland of Yahweh

The origins of the people of Israel in the desert or desert-fringe region to the south of the arable portions of Canaan may be demonstrated in another way as well. As is well known, archaic biblical poetry repeatedly associates Yahweh, the God of Israel, with the general region of the Southland, using a variety of geographical terms, including Sinai, Se'ir, Edom, Paran, and Teman in these passages:

> YHWH, from Sinai he came forth,
> And shined upon them from Se'ir.
> He appeared from Mount Paran,
> And approached from Rivevot-Qodesh.
> (DEUTERONOMY 33:2)

> YHWH, when you came forth from Se'ir,
> When you marched forth from the highland of Edom.
> (JUDGES 5:4)

> God comes from Teman,
> And the Holy-one from Mount Paran.
> (HABAKKUK 3:3)

> O God, when you went out before your people,
> when you marched through the wasteland, Selah.
> The earth trembled, indeed, the sky poured,
> because of God, the one of Sinai;
> because of God, the God of Israel.
> (PSALM 68:8–9)

As Yahweh became more associated with Zion and Jerusalem (see, for example, Psalms 9:12; 48:3; 74:2; 102:17; 135:21; Isaiah 4:5; 8:18; 24:23), the linkage between the God of Israel and the Southland would eventually recede if not disappear altogether. But the passages listed above serve as a strong reminder whence Israel (and its deity) emerged.

The Shasu Connection

Given the above evidence, the Israelites most likely are to be related to the Shasu of Egyptian texts, where this catch-all term refers to nomads, Bedouin, desert denizens, and the like. In fact, Egyptian topographical lists from Soleb (dated to the reign of Amenhotep III [14th century]) and Amara (dated to the reign of Ramesses II [13th century]),[6] mention a region known as *t3 š3św yhw*, "the land of the Shasu of Yahweh." The people referred to here are likely to have some connection to either the proto-Israelites or early fellow travelers (see chap. 2 herein).

Characteristic Features of the Early Israelites in the Central Hill Country

As stated at the outset of this chapter, the Israelites of the general Southland (i.e., the large desert that stretches across modern-day Sinai, southern Israel, and southern Jordan) sometime in the 12th century surrendered their pastoral nomadic ways and settled in the sown of the central hill country.[7] This explains the burgeoning of settlements in the area during Iron Age I (1175–1000 B.C.E.), as well as the distinctive shape of the rather simple elliptical courtyard sites. To be sure, many of the elliptical sites existed for only a short period, perhaps even less than a century (e.g., Ai, Raddana, and 'Izbet Sartah), at which point the newly sedentarized people coalesced into neighboring villages, which in turn grew in size during the second half of the Iron Age I and into the Iron Age II (e.g., Bethel and Tell en-Nasbeh [Mizpah]).

SHASU NOMAD. The Shasu people appear repeatedly in Egyptian texts of the Late Bronze Age as pastoral-nomads from the Southland and Transjordan and often show up in Egyptian art as bounded prisoners with bag-shaped headdresses, as in this colorful faience tile found at the Rameside temple in Medinet Habu, near Luxor.

Among the most characteristic features of these people and their lifestyle is the near total absence of pig bones in the archaeological record. At the same time period, one observes considerable pork consumption amongst the neighboring Philistines.[8] A glance at the map reveals the dearth of pig bones at sites stretching from Tel Masos and Beersheba in the south to Ai, Raddana, Shiloh, and Mt. Ebal in the central hill country (see map next page). This feature plots perfectly onto the area of Israelite settlement as evidenced in the archaeological record discussed above and in the biblical account. It is also noteworthy that the Bible's stories, especially in the books of Joshua, Judges, and Samuel, play out mainly in this area, for example: Joshua 7–10 (Ai, Bethel, Gibeon), Judges 3 (Ehud of Benjamin), Judges 6–9 (Gideon and Abimelech in and around Shechem), Judges 19–21 (Gibeah in Benjamin), 1 Samuel 1–3 (Shiloh), 1 Samuel 6 (Beth-Shemesh), etc.

Most striking is the difference in the number of pig bones found at very proximate cities, with the Israelites of Beth-Shemesh abstaining from pork consumption and the Philistines in nearby Gath, Ekron, and Timnah including considerable amounts of pig in their diet. The lack of pig bones at the early Israelite sites must be credited to the fact that the pig is the single most widely consumed animal prohibited according to the dietary laws of the Torah (Leviticus 11:7; Deuteronomy 14:8).[9]

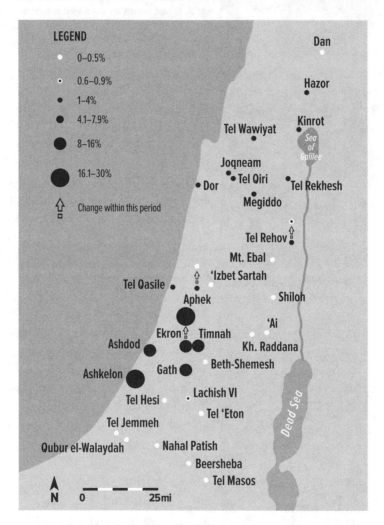

PORK CONSUMPTION in selected Iron Age I sites.

The main feature of domestic architecture in the villages was the four-room house, which begins in the Iron Age I and becomes ubiquitous in the Iron Age II. The same basic floorplan repeats at Israelite sites throughout the region (see photo on the next page and the plans on page 69[10]).[11]

ISRAELITE FOUR-ROOM HOUSE at ʿIzbet Sartah.

The four-room house was well suited to the needs of self-sustaining communities subsisting on a mixed economy based mainly on the cultivation of crops, animal husbandry, and small-scale craft production. Although the archaeological remains in and around Iron Age I houses vary, textual sources and ethnographic data from the Middle East make it possible to reconstruct some of the specific activities that took place in domestic spaces. On the ground floor, one of the long side rooms apparently could be used as a stable or corral (see Deuteronomy 22:1–3), as suggested by flagstone paving and other evidence. The other long rooms often feature permanent installations (ovens and storage pits) and contain grinding stones, ceramic vessels, and food remains, thereby attesting to the use of the space for food preparation, consumption, and storage. The broad room at the rear also was multifunctional, and the presence of large storage jars in some houses suggests that these spaces, too, were used for food storage. The upper story and roof spaces were used for sleeping and many other activities. If we assume (based on anthropological parallels) that 10 square meters of roofed space was required for each person, it is estimated that several Iron Age I houses excavated at Ai and Raddana could have housed between four and eight family members, along with other individuals perhaps.[12] One may deduce that this living arrangement constitutes the Hebrew term *bēt'ab*, "house of the father" (see, e.g., 2 Samuel 19:29), that is, the basic kinship unit comprised of several nuclear families, presumably descended from the same male individual.[13]

The commonest of all household activities was the grinding of grain into flour and the baking of bread. Relevant objects found in excavations include (as mentioned above) grinding stones and clay ovens, found either on the ground floor of the four-room house or in the courtyard space outside the house. From numerous passages in the Bible and from models of women working at these tasks found in Egyptian tombs, we know that bread production was an important task fulfilled by the women of the household.[14]

Scholars estimate that the daily per capita adult consumption of flour was about 500 grams, and about half that amount for children. A family of two adults and four children thus would require about 2 kg of flour each day, which would require about 2.5 hours of grinding. If a mother and older daughter worked together, as seems likely, it was about 1.5 hours of grinding[15] each day, day after day—hence our English expression "the daily grind."

In addition to the daily production of bread, women were responsible for the textile and clothing needs of the household (see esp. Proverbs 31:19–24)[16]—so much so that the spindle served as the symbol of feminine-ness, not only in Israel, but throughout the ancient Near East and the eastern Mediterranean.[17] Excavations frequently reveal spindle whorls used to spin thread from wool and flax, and loom weights hung on horizontal looms used to weave clothing and other textiles.

During the 12th and 11th centuries, one also finds new technologies being introduced in the central hill country, including terraced farming (typical of mountain people around the world), silos for grain storage, and cisterns for the collection of rainwater. While all three of these elements may be found sporadically in other places and/or at an earlier time, the convergence of all three in the central hill country at this specific time period speaks to an emerging population in the region, one which we may identify as the Israelites.[18]

Another important feature of the early Israelite sites is the plethora of simple unpainted pottery, in stark contrast to the ornately decorated pottery found especially in the neighboring Philistine sites. One need only compare the assemblage from a classic central hill country site, such as Shiloh (see p. 71), with the assemblage from Gath, a major Philistine city (see p. 72). Included in the former grouping are the collared-rim jars (so named because of their distinctive "collars"), found in greatest abundance throughout the central hill country.[19]

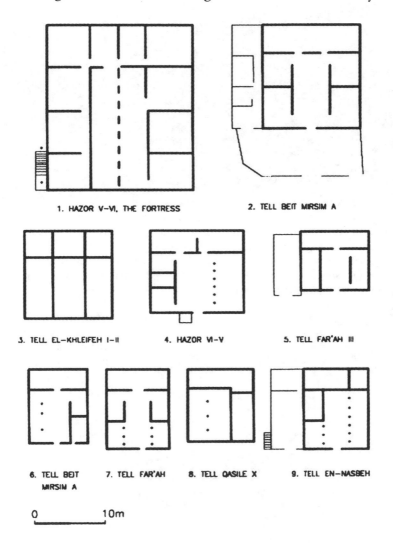

1. HAZOR V–VI, THE FORTRESS   2. TELL BEIT MIRSIM A

3. TELL EL–KHLEIFEH I–II   4. HAZOR VI–V   5. TELL FAR'AH III

6. TELL BEIT MIRSIM A   7. TELL FAR'AH   8. TELL QASILE X   9. TELL EN–NASBEH

0   10m

FLOORPLANS of selected four-room houses through ancient Israel.

TERRACED HILLSIDES IN THE JUDEAN HILL COUNTRY, NOT FAR FROM JERUSALEM.
No longer in use today (since modern Israel includes the coastal plain and the lush Jezreel Valley), these terraces nonetheless bespeak the Israelites of old. They were formed by intense labor, hewn from the limestone bedrock, out of necessity by the earliest Israelite settlers in the central hill country, 12th–11th centuries B.C.E., for the growing of crops.

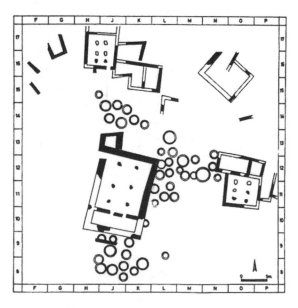

ʿIZBET SARTAH.
Line-drawing of an 11th-century B.C.E. four-room house (along with other nearby houses) at ʿIzbet Sartah, surrounded by several dozen grain silos.

SHILOH POTTERY ASSEMBLAGE. Note the plain, undecorated vessels, including collared-rim jars, bowls, and kraters, all typical of Iron Age I central hill country settlements.

The Egalitarian Ethos

From the foregoing archaeological evidence, a clear picture emerges. As Avraham Faust has stressed, the people who inhabited the central hill country—let us call them Israelites—were guided by an egalitarian ethos.[20] No one has a larger home than his or her neighbor; rather, each four-room house is more or less the same size. In this early period of biblical history, there are no governor's mansions or other large homes. Outside the homes, the silos and cisterns are approximately the same size (see plan on p. 70). No one has fancier pottery than his or her neighbor; rather, simple unpainted vessels dominate wherever one looks. Not mentioned until this point, but equally relevant, is the total absence of elaborate tombs in the Iron Age I central hill country villages. Instead, the dead were buried in simple fashion—mainly in nearby caves, person after person, family after family, generation after generation.

The lifestyle portrayed here harmonizes well with the egalitarian ethos that permeates the Bible, especially during the early biblical period. Naturally, there are priests and tribal leaders, and yes, slavery is countenanced, but a true social stratification, with a hierarchical figure or group dominating social, political, and economic realms, is not to be found in the Torah and other relevant books.[21] It would be hard, if not impossible, to imagine a biblical author writing as Aristotle did: "From the hour of their birth, some are marked out for subjection, others for rule" (*Politics* 1.5). Such was the manner throughout the ancient world (from Egypt to Mesopotamia), where the social and political elite dominated every aspect of daily life—except in ancient Israel.

TELL EṢ-ṢAFI (Gath) pottery assemblage.

In fact, as the Torah states on several occasions, there is a single law not only for all Israelites but also for the strangers who reside in their midst (Exodus 12:49; Numbers 15:16; 15:29). This approach explains why earliest Israel did not have a king (in addition to the theological reason, namely, that only Yahweh was king). Moreover, when human kingship was proposed, Samuel's denunciation of the proposal has less to do with the theological standpoint than it does with the distinctly undesirable prospect of an elite figure who would dominate the people's social and economic fortunes (1 Samuel 8). This egalitarian worldview unfolded most prominently in the biblical prophets of the eighth and seventh centuries B.C.E., but the very essence of this ideology is seen throughout the Bible, especially in the Torah and in early biblical narratives.

Midway Summary

To summarize up to this point: Early Israel emerged in the central hill country of Canaan during the Iron Age I period (1175–1000), when a core group of formerly pastoral (semi-)nomads underwent the process of sedentarization. They lived in simple elliptical sites reminiscent of Bedouin encampments; eventually they concentrated themselves in villages; and their lifestyle was characterized by simple homes, simple pottery, simple burials, and an egalitarian ethos.

Alternative Views

The picture offered here constitutes the most optimal reconstruction of what transpired during the 12th–11th centuries B.C.E. regarding the emergence of Israel in the land of Canaan. But other scholars have proposed different scenarios.[22] Throughout much of the 20th century, the conquest model held sway, due mainly to the outsized influence of its leading proponent, W. F. Albright.[23] Hardly anyone today, however, would countenance this view, since, as we have seen, the central hill country was large open terrain, with a very small population prior to the arrival of the Israelites.

An alternative approach, generally known as the "peaceful settlement" or "peaceful infiltration" model, was developed by Albrecht Alt.[24] The reconstruction offered in the present essay aligns closely with the work of Alt. The fact that Alt worked in an era long before the accumulation of data used in our analysis makes his groundbreaking research even more remarkable.[25]

A third model was developed by George Mendenhall and Norman Gottwald (working independently of one another, and with some differences between the two). According to their view, the Israelites were not outsiders who immigrated to the land of Canaan but rather were Canaanite peasants who revolted against their (largely urban) overlords to establish a new path and a new way of life. The knowledgeable reader rightly may see in this model (especially in the version espoused by Gottwald) a Marxist view of history, which holds that historical processes and outcomes are driven largely by socio-economic factors.

In general, neither of these two scholars worked with the archae-ological data, though recently William Dever, renowned expert in archaeological fieldwork, has supported their model, in whole or in part. In Dever's view, the material culture of the Israelites is sufficiently similar to that of the Canaanites to support the notion of a Canaanite origin for the people of Israel. Thus, for example, the pottery traditions of the hill-country settlements in Iron Age I are the same as those of the Canaanite areas of the coastal plains. In Dever's own words: "Early Israelites look ceramically just like Canaanites."[26] Naturally, not everyone agrees, for, as Israel Finkelstein has written, "Although it is possible to point to a certain degree of continuity in a few types, the ceramic assemblage of the Israelite Settlement types, taken as a whole, stand in sharp contrast to the repertoire of the Canaanite centers."[27]

Where does all this leave us? To be sure, the conquest model is contradicted by the mass of evidence (or, better perhaps, lack thereof). The third, autochthonous model may relate to certain non-Israelite elements which in time became part of Israel (see below), but it is controverted as the sole explanation for the origins of the Israelites by the converging lines of evidence discussed above. As we have seen, "core Israel" (as we may call this entity) emerged from Shasu Bedouin-style nomadic or semi-nomadic society, with roots in the southland, as the people entered the land of Canaan from the outside. Thus, the "peaceful infiltration" or "peaceful settlement" model, originated by Alt, is the one which has stood the test of time and which coheres best with the reconstruction offered here.

The Books of Joshua and Judges

The picture outlined thus far is based mainly on the archaeological evidence. Let us turn now to the biblical text, with especial attention to the books of Joshua and Judges. It is important to note that these two books present divergent views concerning the arrival of the Israelites in the land of Canaan. The more famous account is that of the Book of Joshua. According to that version, the following occurred: upon the death of Moses, Joshua assumed the leadership of the people of Israel (chaps. 1–5); a unified conquest of the land ensued (chaps. 6–12); and then the land of Canaan was apportioned to the individual tribes (chaps. 13–19). According to Judges 1:1–3, however, a different scenario unfolded:

And it was, after the death of Joshua, and the children of Israel enquired of YHWH, saying, "Who shall first go up for us unto the Canaanites to fight against them?" And YHWH said, "Judah shall go up; behold I have given the land into his hand." And Judah said to Simeon his brother, "Go up with me, unto my allotment, and let us fight the Canaanites, and I too will go with you, to your allotment"; and Simeon went with him.

LEARN MORE

The Origins of the Israelites

Who were the ancient Israelites and where did they come from? Archaeologists and historians have long grappled with these problematic questions, but two scholars, writing in the pages of *BAR*, have pointed the way toward new understandings of these complex phenomena.

In his article "Inside, Outside" (November/December 2008), historian, linguist, and biblical geographer Anson Rainey proposes that the early Israelites did not emerge out of Canaanite society, as is so often argued, but actually entered Canaan from the lands east of the Jordan River, exactly as the Bible claims. Not only do Israelite ceramic and architectural traditions—like the collared-rim pithos and the four-room house—conform to styles that appear in Transjordan as well, but the ancient Hebrew language itself seems to share a great deal more in common with eastern dialects like Moabite and Aramaic than with the Canaanite and Phoenician languages of the Levantine littoral.

But even if the Israelites did originate in the East, how do we explain their emergence as a single people, a people who saw themselves as unified and ethnically distinct from their Canaanite, Philistine, and even Transjordanian neighbors? In his path-breaking article, "How Did Israel Become a People?" (November/December 2009), archaeologist Avraham Faust uses archaeological, historical, and anthropological evidence to show that Israelite identity formed in opposition to the cultural, dietary, and religious customs of neighboring groups, particularly the urban Canaanites and the pork-eating Philistines.

However the Israelites originated, by the mid-12th century B.C.E., they had begun to settle in small farming communities in the hill country, where they evidenced an egalitarian ethos that set them apart culturally, economically, and ethnically from the Canaanite populations around them. –ED.

The differences between these two versions are manifold: 1) in Joshua, the eponymous character leads the conquest of Canaan; in Judges, the conquest does not begin until after the death of Joshua; 2) in Joshua, the nation acts as a unified whole; in Judges, individual tribes or two tribes together (as here, Judah and Simeon) conquer portions of the land; 3) in Joshua, the land was conquered and then apportioned to the tribes; in Judges, the land is apportioned to the tribes, and then the conquest commences, again, tribe by tribe. While the Joshua story is the one better known, almost undoubtedly the Judges version is closer to the historical reality.

Most importantly, in our tracing the contours of the Israelite settlement (and not conquest!) in the land, there is no room for a national military campaign. As we saw, the central hill country was essentially open terrain, so to put this in other terms, there was no conquest because there was no one to conquer! The account in Judges 1, accordingly, is more reasonable, with individual tribes moving into their allotted territories to set up shop, no longer as semi-nomads but rather as part of the settled population of the central hill country. The narrative begins with Judah (and Simeon), who are then followed by other individual tribes settling their allotments: Benjamin in 1:21, house of Joseph in 1:22, Manasseh in 1:27, Ephraim in 1:29, Zebulun in 1:30, Asher in 1:31–32, and Naphtali in 1:33—even if, in most of these cases, the text describes the areas not conquered within the individual tribal allotments. That point notwithstanding, the Book of Judges presents the individual tribes as acting on their own, in contradistinction to the national conquest account presented in the Book of Joshua.

As the Book of Judges proceeds to the stories of the individual judges, once again we see single tribes acting on their own, with a particular judge, or leader, serving either his tribe only or a few adjoining tribes (chap. 3: Othniel of Judah, Ehud of Benjamin; chaps. 4–5: Barak of Naphtali and Zebulun; chaps. 6–8: Gideon of Manasseh; etc.). The picture that emerges is one of a loose confederation of tribes, without a single leader uniting all Israel. And while these stories typically reflect the tribes already settled in their territories, as opposed to entering the land, they may relate to the latter process as well.

From the linguistic perspective, it is important to note that the

Book of Judges is written in an older register than the Book of Joshua.[28] One will then assume that Judges represents the more "original" account within the collective memory of ancient Israel. Some of these tales may go back to the pre-monarchic period, while the Song of Deborah in Judges 5 is amongst the oldest compositions in the Bible, dated to c. 1100 B.C.E. (see below).

At a later time, a different version of events was created, based on the notion of the entire nation acting in unison under a single leader, Joshua. With the movement to kingship, well established from c. 1000 B.C.E. onward, quite possibly a later Israelite writer felt the need to create an alternative narrative, with a single leader at the helm (à la a king), and thus was born the Book of Joshua.

A More Complicated Picture

Thus far we have presented the main narrative of the Bible, confirmed by archaeological evidence, to wit: the Israelites emerged when a group (or diverse groups) of Shasu Bedouin types settled the sown in the central hill country. But life (and history) is never that simple. Consider, for example, the formation of modern Great Britain: The core population was Celtic, but successive waves of Romans, Angles, Saxons, Vikings, and Normans created what emerged as England (and Wales and Scotland) in the Middle Ages and early modern period. Or consider the United States: the country emerged mainly from the migration of Britons to the New World in the 17th and 18th centuries, though with significant populations from other countries as well (Dutch in the New York and New Jersey region, Spaniards in Florida, French in Louisiana, etc.), not to mention large numbers of Africans transported to America against their will to serve as slaves. To this mixture were added— in the late 19th and early 20th centuries—significant numbers of central and eastern European immigrants, as well as Asians (mainly Chinese and Japanese). And all of these various immigrant groups are but an overlay to the native population, present in the land for thousands of years. So it is with ancient Israel as well. And while we may not be able to detail its emergence from diverse origins in the same manner as can be done for England and the U.S., we do have ample evidence to suggest a parallel picture, roughly speaking.

Dan, Asher, and Gad

The first piece of evidence concerns the tribe of Asher as mentioned in P.Anastasi I, which is dated by most authorities to the reign of Ramesses II (r. 1290–1224). This document contains a satirical letter of the master scribe Hori addressed to a scribe named Amenemopet, in which the former chastises the latter for his ignorance regarding the topography of Canaan.[29] In the course of his "tour" of the land, Hori mentions Reḥob and Megiddo and then states: "Your name becomes like (that of) *q-ḏ-r-d-y*, the chief of *i-s-r*, when the (bear?/hyena?) found him in the *b-k-i-*tree" (col. 23, line 6–7).[30] The full intent of this satirical line may elude us, but its main import is the mention of the place named *i-s-r*, almost undoubtedly Asher, precisely in the location where one would expect to find it.[31]

First, the tribal allotment of Asher as described in Joshua 19:24–31 is found in this very area, which includes (apparently) two cities named Reḥob (19: 28, 30). Second, the tree written as *b-k-i* recalls the biblical phrase in Psalm 84:7 *'emeq hab-bākā'*, "valley of the baka-tree" (thus the traditional interpretation), a northern locale, perhaps to be associated with the city of Baka, located in the Galilee and mentioned by Josephus (*J.W.* 3.39).

Incidentally, the same place name (*i-s-r*) is mentioned in a second Egyptian inscription, as a territory conquered by Seti I (r. 1300–1290), somewhere in the land of Canaan, though no greater specificity can be determined.[32]

Now, if an entity named Asher was resident in Canaan (more specifically the Galilee) during the time of Seti I and Ramesses II, almost undoubtedly it could not have participated in the events experienced by the desert component of the nation that would emerge as Israel. This is a crucial piece of information, for it allows us to suppose that other elements of the people of Israel were similarly resident in Canaan during this time period (more on this issue below). We can only speculate what must have transpired, but the following scenario suggests itself. The desert folk entered the land of Canaan, and in time elements within Canaan came to align themselves with the newly arrived and newly settled people. What factors would have led to such an alignment we cannot determine. Most likely they were socioeconomic and/ or military (e.g., mutual defense considerations), but one cannot rule out the religious factor. Possibly Israel's unique worship of a single deity who manifests himself in human history and who protects the underprivileged resounded with others in the region.

A second tribe of Israel whose nondesert origins can be traced is Dan. During the reign of Ramesses III (1195–1164), specifically in his year 8 (i.e., 1187 B.C.E.), Egypt was threatened by an invasion of Sea Peoples, a confederation of Aegean and Mediterranean entities that crossed the sea in an attempt to invade Egypt (see chap. 2). The alliance included the following peoples: Peleset, Dananu, Shardanu, Meshwesh, and Tjeker. As the inscriptions at Medinet Habu (funerary temple of Ramesses III) reveal, the full strength of the Egyptian army and especially its naval forces were required to repel the Sea Peoples invasion.[33] What happened to these people after they were defeated somewhere along the coast of the Egyptian Delta? The best answer is that they migrated northeasterly and settled along the coast of southern and central Canaan.

We shall now consider three of the Sea Peoples listed at Medinet Habu: Peleset, Dananu, and Tjeker. The first group are clearly the Philistines, who settled in the southern coastal region of Canaan and established the pentapolis of Gaza, Ashdod, Ashkelon, Gath, and Ekron (the first three on the coast, the other two inland). The Tjeker are known from the slightly later Egyptian literary work the Tale of Wenamun (11th century B.C.E.) to have settled in Dor, in the central coastal region. The Dananu, called in one instance by the shorter form Danu,[34] are to be identified with the tribe of Dan, whose original allotment was a small enclave on the coastal plain, precisely where one would expect it—between the Philistines to the south and the Tjeker/Dor to the north (Joshua 19:40–46).

The biblical tradition confirms the Aegean origins of the Philistines, who repeatedly are connected with Caphtor, a term which refers either to the Aegean generally or to the island of Crete specifically (Jeremiah 47:4; Amos 9:7; see also Genesis 10:14; Deuteronomy 2:23). As to the Dan(an)u, most likely they are to be connected with the Danaoi of Homeric tradition; also related, perhaps, are Adana in Cilicia and the Danunians of that region, both mentioned in the Azitawada inscription from Karatepe, which is to say, the Dan(an)u group may have dispersed throughout the Eastern Mediterranean.

More than the geography is required to connect the Dan(an)u of the Sea Peoples and the tribe of Dan of ancient Israel, of course. The following additional lines of evidence converge to argue in favor of the proposed identification. First, as observed above, the original territory ascribed to Dan in Joshua 19:40-46 is on the coast adjacent to Philistine territory. Second, the statement in Judges 5:17 ("and Dan, why do you dwell in ships?") connects the tribe to a maritime lifestyle. Third, the greatest of Danite heroes, Samson, has intimate relations with the Philistines (Judges 14–16). Fourth, Genesis 49:16 ("Dan shall judge his people like one of the tribes of Israel") implies that until this point Dan was not a tribe of Israel but was in the process of joining the tribal league. Fifth, notwithstanding the allotment granted Dan in the Book of Joshua, Judges 18:1 states that "the Danite tribe was seeking for itself a land-grant in which to dwell, because a land-grant had not fallen to it until this day among the tribes of Israel." Sixth, and finally, of all the tribes of Israel, Dan has the least developed genealogy. In fact, Genesis 46:23, Numbers 26:42, and 1 Chronicles 7:12 each record only one name (either Hushim or Shuham). Moreover, while 1 Chronicles 7:12 is a very late source, one is struck by the notation of Hushim son of Aher, with the latter word meaning "another" and standing for the tribe of Dan.[35]

We can conclude that Dan originates with the Sea Peoples Dan(an)u group, which reached the land of Canaan by sea at approximately the same time that the main Israelite group reached Canaan by land.[36] The various Sea Peoples entities shared a common experience (maritime voyage, attack on Egypt, etc.), but once they settled on the coast of Canaan, at least two of them, it appears, traversed different paths. For whereas the Philistines in time became the archenemy of the Israelites, the Danites elected to join the Israelite coalition. As with Asher above, we cannot determine for what reasons Dan chose this course. It might have been the common enemy, the Philistines, that led Dan to join Israel. While the Philistines and the Dan(an)u may have been allies during the Sea Peoples attack against Egypt, such cordial relations may have ended once this common enterprise ceased. From Genesis 49:16, Judges 18:1, and the evidence of genealogies (or lack thereof), it would appear that Dan was the last of the tribes to join what eventually became the twelve tribes of Israel.

In sum, we may posit that the tribes of Dan and Asher did not participate in the Bible's main narrative of the Eisodus/Slavery/Exodus/Wandering, equivalent to our understanding of "core Israel" as Bedouin nomads or semi-nomads who emerged from the desert fringe to settle the sown. The one entity (Asher) appears always to have been present in the land; the other (Dan) arrived by sea at about the same time (12th century B.C.E.) as "core Israel" transitioned from a nomadic lifestyle to the sedentary way of life. It may not be a coincidence that the tribes of Dan and Asher are among the handmaiden tribes in the Torah's account. Dan is the son of Bilhah, handmaiden of Rachel (Genesis 30:5–6), and Asher is the son of Zilpah, handmaiden of Leah (Genesis 30:12–13). It is quite possible that the biblical tradition retains an accurate recollection of the primary tribes of Leah and Rachel as "original" Israel, and of the tribes descended from Bilhah, Zilpah, and Leah secondarily (see Genesis 30:17–20) as secondary entities, who associated themselves with Israel at a later time.

In the primary, Leah and Rachel group, one finds Reuben, Simeon, Levi, Judah, Joseph, and Benjamin. Levi is distinguished for sacerdotal duty, and Joseph splits into two tribes, Ephraim and Manasseh. Plot these tribes on the map and one finds them in precisely the area described at the outset of this chapter, from just south of the Jezreel Valley in the north to the Beersheba Basin in the south, with the addition of Reuben in southern Transjordan. The six tribes belonging to the second set (Dan, Asher, Zebulun, Issachar, Naphtali, and Gad) lie outside this central area: Dan is along the coast; Asher is in the hinterland of Phoenicia, in the Western Galilee; the next three are in Galilee proper, north of the Jezreel Valley; and Gad is located in Transjordanian Gilead.

Some scholars also have drawn attention to Mesha Stele, line 10, "the men of Gad had dwelt in the land of Ataroth since ancient times" (*me-'olam*), implying that this tribe was indigenous to the region of Gilead.[37] Should this assumption be correct, then we have yet another tribe which did not participate in the grand narrative of the early books of the Bible. Note, moreover, that Gad is another "handmaid" tribe, with Gad born to Zilpah (Genesis 30:10–11).

Even within "core Israel," however, there were "foreign" elements linked with the Israelites. The best evidence derives from

Judges 1:16, regarding the Kenites, another desert group mentioned in the Bible on several occasions: "and the Kenites ... went up from the City of Palms [sc. presumably Jericho] with the Judahites, to the wilderness of Judah which is in the Negev of Arad; and they went and they settled among the people." Note also that the Judahite hero Caleb son of Jephunneh (Numbers 13:6) is called a Kenizzite in Joshua 14:6 and 14:14, which elsewhere is listed among the foreign nations in the region (Genesis 15:19). To further complicate matters, the Judahite judge Othniel is introduced in Judges 3:9 as Othniel son of Kenaz, the younger brother of Caleb. All of this indicates that the various desert groups would realign from time to time: Kenites and Kenizzites could be non-Israelites or non-Judahites at one time, and then connected to Judah at another time.[38]

Let us further recall the Jebusites of Jerusalem in Judges 1:21: "and the Jebusites dwelt with the Benjaminites in Jerusalem until this day." About a century later, when David conquered Jerusalem and established the city as his capital, the population was not killed but rather was assimilated into Israel. This point would be remembered centuries later when the prophet Ezekiel addressed Jerusalem with the words, "Your origin and your birthplace are from the land of the Canaanites; your father is an Amorite, and your mother is a Hittite" (Ezekiel 16:3).[39]

In sum, the ancestry (or better, ancestries) of the population of what emerged as Israel in the historical record is a much more complicated one than the main narrative may suggest. To be sure, the notion that the entire nation descends from the biological offspring of a single person (Jacob/Israel) and that all the people immigrated to Egypt, then wandered the Sinai, and then all at once entered the land is an idealized construct.

Reuben and Simeon

Two tribes from "core Israel" merit specific consideration, namely, Reuben and Simeon, who descended from the first- and second-born sons of Jacob/Israel, respectively. Reuben is the southernmost tribe in Transjordan, while Simeon is the southernmost tribe in Cisjordan. That is to say, the two tribes which remained closest to the desert fringe region geographically are the ones accorded first- and second-born status in the national narrative.

The last we hear of Reuben within the grand narrative of Genesis through Kings is in Judges 5:16, where, quite tellingly, the tribe is associated with its flocks and sheepfolds.[40]

Simeon disappears even earlier, in Judges 1, though already in this episode the tribe's individual identity is waning, as its destiny is allied with that of Judah. In the Book of Joshua, there is a unique, character-revealing statement about Simeon. While all the tribes gain "cities and their settlements," including Simeon (Joshua 19:7),[41] only with respect to Simeon do we read an additional statement with the word "'settlements": "and all the settlements that surround these cities" (Joshua 19:8). This implies that the lifestyle of the Simeonites was more connected with unwalled, non-urban settlements (Heb. ḥaṣerim) than that of other tribes.[42]

This is all rather obvious, since the territories of Reuben and Simeon are on the desert fringe, with no large cities. Consequently, the lifestyle of these two tribes was more connected to their flocks, sheepfolds, and unwalled settlements. And then the Bible loses track of Reuben and Simeon—not because they disappeared necessarily, but because the focus of the biblical material (prose, poetry, prophecy, etc.) becomes more and more focused on kingship, Jerusalem, and Temple.[43]

But the Bible never lost track of the first-born and second-born status of Reuben and Simeon, respectively. These tribesmen retained their pastoral ways, even as most Israelites became more and more urbanized, and thus their eponymous ancestors are accorded first and second position in the Jacob cycle (and in later rehearsals thereof, including 1 Chronicles 2:1–2).

The Book of Joshua

After this long excursion into the nature and background of the individual twelve tribes, let us now return to the narratives in the books of Joshua and Judges. As intimated above, the Book of Joshua presents an idealized version of how Israel emerged in the land of Canaan. The book divides neatly into several large sections: chaps. 1–5 (preparation for the conquest); chaps. 6–12 (the conquest and the individual battles); chaps. 13–22 (the apportioning of the land to the individual tribes, the Levites, etc.); and chaps. 23–24 (valedictory speeches by Joshua). The most famous section of the book is the second one, with its accounts of the conquest of Jericho (chap. 6), Ai (chaps. 7–8), and Gibeon (chaps. 9–10).[44] As we noted earlier, however, the notion of the conquest of the land of Canaan must be surrendered. There simply is no archaeological evidence for such, and in the specific case of Jericho the site seems to have been largely abandoned during the period under consideration here (c. 1400–c. 900).

Nevertheless, the battle accounts in Joshua 6–10 do not appear to have been invented out of whole cloth; instead, they are based on known military strategies from the ancient world.[45] One example is Joshua marching his troops *at night*, from his base camp at Gilgal to Gibeon (Joshua 10:9), implying an attack of the city at dawn from the east, during which the rising sun would have blinded the city defenders. This may explain the famous saying that "the sun stood still at Gibeon" (Joshua 10:11–12), an epic feature in the account, since Joshua and his troops needed the sun to stay in position just above the eastern horizon until the military operation was complete.

In light of such demonstrable military strategies embedded within the narratives of Joshua 6–10, should we consider the possibility that, notwithstanding the largely peaceful settlement by the Israelite tribes in the central hill country that this chapter has postulated, here and there an actual battle needed to be fought? One cannot discount this possibility, though in general such encounters would have been very occasional and on a very limited scale, especially as we recall the openness of the terrain to be settled by the Israelites.

There is one archaeological site that may support a conquest by the Israelites as reported in Joshua: Hazor in the Upper Galilee, excavated by Yigael Yadin during the years 1955–1958 and 1968, and more recently by Amnon Ben-Tor (since 1990). Both scholars concluded that the large Canaanite city at the site represented by Stratum XIII was destroyed by a major conflagration c. 1200 B.C.E., after which a much more modest city represented by Stratum XII developed.[46] The evidence conforms with the statement in Joshua 11:10–13 that the Israelites conquered Hazor and set the city ablaze. Indeed, in the conquest narratives, only here does one read that the Israelites set a conquered city on fire. As always, the picture is more complicated, because in the alternative account of Judges 4–5 the city of Hazor remains a Canaanite city; and even when Barak defeats Sisera in battle, there is no mention of the capture of Hazor, never mind the burning thereof.[47] This issue aside, the coherence of the archaeological evidence and the account in Joshua 11 is rather striking.[48]

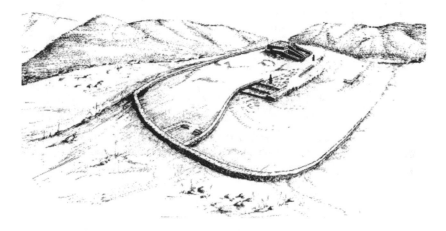

MT. EBAL altar site in artist's reconstruction.

The various battle accounts are interrupted in Joshua 8:30–35, which describes the building of the altar on Mt. Ebal and the gathering of the Israelites there, in fulfillment of the instructions commanded in Deuteronomy 27:1–8. Remarkably, the excavations by Adam Zertal on Mt. Ebal revealed an altar dated to the Iron Age I (12th–11th centuries) (see drawing above), along with faunal remains of sheep, goats, cattle, and deer.[49] One will assume, accordingly, an inherent historicity in the account in Joshua 8:30–35, for the archaeological site demonstrates that the Israelites of this time period performed ritual offerings at this altar.[50]

A second cultic site that deserves mention is in the northern reaches of the central hill country. In the 1980s, an Israeli kibbutznik accidentally discovered a bronze bull at a site near Mt. Gilboa, in the territory of Manasseh (see drawing on p. 86 and plate 6). Amihai Mazar then excavated the site, which he determined to be a cultic site, replete with altar dated to the 12th century B.C.E.[51] Most likely, the bull was intended to represent Yahweh (recall such passages as Exodus 32:4; 1 Kings 12:28; and Hosea 8:5–6), thereby giving us precious insight into the religion of early Israel, especially regarding a practice prohibited by the Torah and condemned by the prophets.

THE BRONZE BULL STATUETTE. Found at a hilltop cultic site near Mt. Gilboa, in northern Samaria. It measures about 4 inches high and dates to the 12th century B.C.E. This line-drawing shows three different views of the artifact; for the color photo, see plate 6.

One more cultic site in the central hill country was at Shiloh, where, according to the Book of Joshua 18:1, the Tabernacle was erected. The Tabernacle was the portable tent shrine that housed the Ark of the Covenant. According to the biblical tradition, the Tabernacle and its appurtenances were constructed in the Wilderness (Exodus 25–31 and 35–40) and then transported by the Israelites from place to place, until their entrance into the land of Canaan. Once the people settled in the central hill country, the Tabernacle found a permanent home in Shiloh. Note such expressions as "before Yʜwʜ in Shiloh" (Joshua 18:8), "in Shiloh before Yʜwʜ" (Joshua 18:10; 19:51), "the House of God in Shiloh" (Judges 18:31), "the feast of Yʜwʜ in Shiloh" (Judges 21:19), "the House of Yʜwʜ in Shiloh" (1 Samuel 1:24), and "the priest of Yʜwʜ in Shiloh" (1 Samuel 14:3), all indicative of the major role that Shiloh played in the religious life of Israel during this time period. And then references to the place stop.[52] In fact, when the Ark was captured by the Philistines in battle (1 Samuel 4) and then returned to the Israelites (1 Samuel 6), the people did not restore the Ark to Shiloh but rather deposited it in the house of a resident of Kiriath-jearim (1 Samuel 7:1).

What, then, happened to Shiloh? Archaeology provides a plausible answer. Israel Finkelstein, who excavated the site in 1981–1984, discovered there a typical Israelite central hill country village, replete with simple unpainted pottery, including collared-rim vessels (see image on p. 71), and with traces of some cultic activity—though, naturally, no evidence of the Tabernacle, which was made of perishable materials (wood, cloth, animal skins, etc.). The village was established in the 12th century B.C.E. and was destroyed in the 11th century B.C.E.[53] All of this coheres with the biblical passages cited above, which imply that Shiloh served as the cultic center of the Israelites in the central hill country for a century or so during Iron Age I. Its destruction presumably was wrought by the Philistines in connection with the battles described in 1 Samuel 4, even if the Bible does not state so explicitly. Centuries later, the prophet Jeremiah would evoke the destruction of Shiloh as a historical lesson for the people of Judah (Jeremiah 7:12, 14; 26:6, 9; see also Psalm 78:60).

Among the hundreds of toponyms mentioned in Joshua 13–22, listed within the tribal allotments, we call attention to one very interesting item: *ma'ayan mē neptōaḥ,* "the spring of Me-Neptoaḥ" (Joshua 15:9; 18:15). Because the Hebrew word *mē* means "waters of," readers of the Bible have interpreted this toponym as "the spring of the waters of Neptoaḥ," with only the last element as a pure proper noun. The term, however, is better understood as "the spring of Merneptaḥ," especially in light of the fact that final *r* was lost in Late Egyptian.[54] So while the pharaoh's name may have been written with the hieroglyphs *mr-n-ptḥ* (meaning "beloved of Ptaḥ"), the actual pronunciation of the first element would have been closer to what is preserved in Joshua 15:9 and 18:15, where it is further indicated that this particular spring is located on the boundary between Judah and Benjamin, identified as modern Lifta (with further apocopation of the original name), 5 km northwest of Jerusalem.

In his famous victory stela, Merneptah proclaims that he campaigned in Canaan, with specific mention of Ashkelon, Gezer, and Yano'am.[55] From the reference to "the spring of Merneptah" in the Book of Joshua, one should assume that this pharaoh's armies also reached the central highlands, perhaps Jerusalem itself. This point is only tangentially relevant to the history of ancient Israel, but it remains of great value and interest, nonetheless.

The Book of Joshua closes with the gathering of all Israel at Shechem for the renewal of the covenant. From such accounts we may conclude that Shechem served as the traditional "capital" of the tribal league before the establishment of the monarchy. Deuteronomy 27, notably, envisions the tribes gathering on Mt. Ebal and Mt. Gerizim, the two mountains that flank Shechem. Moreover, when Solomon died, and it was time to make Rehoboam king, the people again gathered at Shechem—and Rehoboam journeyed there (1 Kings 12), even though his seat of government was in Jerusalem. Once the northern tribes separated from the Davidic-Solomonic dynasty, it was only natural for Jeroboam I to establish Shechem as the first capital of the northern kingdom of Israel (1 Kings 12:25). This last passage is the final reference to Shechem in the historical books of the Bible, for the capital soon was moved to Tirzah and thence to Samaria. The author of Joshua 24, regardless of its historicity, thus situates the account against the backdrop of pre-monarchic Israel, when the city of Shechem still held prestige within Israelite society.

The Book of Judges

The Book of Judges contains an easily discernible redactional pattern: the prologue (chaps. 1–2), the cycles of stories concerning the individual judges (chaps. 3–16), and the epilogue focused especially on Dan and Benjamin (chaps. 17–21).[56] As noted earlier, Judges 1 provides an alternative account (to the Book of Joshua, that is) of the emergence of Israel in the land of Canaan, one more in keeping with the historical and archaeological evidence. Judges 2:10–13 refers to the Israelites' worshiping of Canaanite deities (see also Judges 3:7), which seems to imply that as long as Israel retained its desert and desert-fringe lifestyle in isolation from outside influences, the people remained loyal worshipers of the single god, Yahweh. But once they entered the land and settled in close proximity to their Canaanite neighbors, they began to worship other gods and goddesses.

A note is now due about the Hebrew word *šofṭim*, traditionally rendered "judges." Although the word can bear that meaning (e.g., Deuteronomy 16:18), in the Book of Judges we do not encounter any of the so-called judges adjudicating legal cases, except maybe Deborah (Judges 4:4–5). In this book the term *šofṭim* more typically means "leaders, chieftains," especially in a social or military context. Sometimes these individuals act alone (Ehud, Samson), at other times they muster troops (Barak, Gideon). So although time-honored tradition obliges one to retain the title "judges" when referring to these individuals, the reader should keep in mind the more accurate functional meaning of the term *šofṭim*.

As the Book of Judges segues from the prologue to the stories about the individual judges, it uses the above picture of apostasy as the backdrop for what transpires. The repeated pattern is as follows: Israel "does evil in the eyes of Yahweh"; the people are delivered into the hands of an enemy; they cry out to God; God raises up a savior; the "spirit of Yahweh" descends upon him; said leader defeats the enemy; and peace is restored—until the whole cycle starts all over again.[57] Well-developed accounts are provided for the six (or seven) major judges (Ehud, Deborah and Barak, Gideon, Abimelech, Jephthah, and Samson), whereas only brief notices are given for each of the seven minor judges (Othniel, Shamgar, Tola, Jair, Ibzan, Elon, and Abdon).

Also noteworthy is the internal chronology of the Book of Judges. First there are the periods of foreign rule: for example, 8 years under Cushan-Rishathaim (Judges 3:8), 18 years under Eglon (Judges 3:14), 20 years under Jabin (Judges 4:3), 40 years under the Philistines (Judges 13:1). Next, the narrative refers to long schematized periods of peace in the land: for example, the 40-year spans associated with Othniel, Deborah and Barak, and Gideon (Judges 3:11; 5:31; 8:28, respectively), along with the 80 years associated with Ehud (Judges 3:30).

When we add up all these numbers, we arrive at a total of 410 years for the events described in the Book of Judges, far too long a time span between the emergence of Israel in Canaan (mid-12th century B.C.E.) and the events described in the following Book of Samuel (the beginning of David's reign, e.g., may be dated c. 1000 B.C.E.).[58] The solution to this seeming conundrum is twofold. First, the years in the Book of Judges are not to be taken literally. Throughout the early books of the Bible, all manner of events span 40 years, including, most famously, the wandering in the desert (Exodus through Deuteronomy). Clearly this is but a schematic number used by the biblical authors writing in an epic style. Half that number is 20 (see Judges 4:3); twice that number is 80 (see Judges 3:30). No chronology can be adduced from these numbers, full stop.

Secondly, if there is any historical reality to any of these events, almost undoubtedly the individual episodes could have occurred simultaneously rather than sequentially. Note, for example, that the story of Ehud concerns the tribe of Benjamin only; the story of Samson focuses on a single Danite hero; the story of Gideon involves the tribe of Manasseh, along with some Galilean tribes, with the action occurring mainly in the Jezreel Valley; the story of Jephthah occurs in Gilead, with the battle against the neighboring Ammonites; and so on. Presumably all these stories arose as local traditions amongst the diverse tribes, until a later Israelite author combined them into the esthetically pleasing and theologically appealing narrative which is the final form of the Book of Judges.

Of all the various components of the Book of Judges, a special word needs to be said about Judges 5, known as the Song of Deborah, for it constitutes one of the oldest poems (and hence one of the oldest compositions) in the entire Bible. The poem details the battle between the Canaanites, led by Jabin and Sisera, and the Israelites, led by Deborah and Barak. Some scholars consider the poem to be composed contemporaneously (or nearly so) with the events described, that is, c. 1100 B.C.E. To be sure, from both a linguistic and a literary perspective, the poem is very old.[59] Moreover, the presence of both the prose account in Judges 4 and the poetic version in Judges 5 provides biblical scholars with a unique opportunity to see the transition from song to story.[60] In earliest Israel, stories were narrated in epic poetry, on a par with Ugaritic literature, for example. At some point, however, the ancient Israelite literati developed the characteristic narrative prose that permeates the Bible, especially in the grand chronicle that spans Creation (Genesis 1–2) and the reign of King David (through 1 Kings 2). Only a few poetic snippets, such as Judges 5, remained, but otherwise the shift to narrative prose was complete.[61]

Finally, it is important to note that—regardless of the engaging tales concerning the individual judges—the Book of Judges carries an important political message.[62] As is well known, a political crisis arose in Israel c. 1020, when certain forces sought to establish a monarchy, notwithstanding the strong opposition from the prophet Samuel (1 Samuel 8). The latter view held that a human king was an intolerable concession against the ideal tenet that only Yahweh could serve as king over Israel; while the former position held that the times had changed and that a human king was necessary to preserve Israel from destruction by the Philistines. In the end, the pro-monarchic stance won the day, as Israel moved to a monarchy, first under Saul, then under David. But the original tenet of Yahweh as king was never surrendered, for Israelite theologians continued to promote that image of Yahweh throughout the biblical period.[63]

One cannot know for sure when the Book of Judges took its final form, but given the presence of both pro- and anti-monarchic statements, quite possibly the compilation was achieved sometime in the tenth century, when the issue was still fresh in the minds of the Israelites. The most glaring anti-monarchic statement in the book is Judges 8:22–23: the people, impressed by Gideon's victory over the Midianites, offer him kingship,[64] to which the hero responds, "I will not rule over you, and my son will not rule over you; YHWH will rule over you."[65] The most glaring pro-monarchic statements are found first at Judges 17:6 and then in the final verse of the book, 21:25: "In those days there was no king in Israel, each-man would do whatever was right in his eyes,"[66] with reference to the dark chapters of Israel's history related in the epilogue to the Book of Judges (the story of the concubine at Gibeah, the war against Benjamin, etc.). Many scholars resolve the tension between the two positions by assuming that a later redactor combined a pro-monarchic source and an anti-monarchic source in creating the Book of Judges. Such need not be the case, though. To our mind, better to assume that the author/editor/redactor/compiler of the book simply wished to exhibit the ambivalence that all (or most) Israelites felt with the establishment of the monarchy—and thus he included both views.

4

The Early Monarchy
Saul, David, and Solomon

ANDRÉ LEMAIRE

THE EARLY MONARCHY WAS THE MOMENT of Israel's glory on the regional scene—a moment to be remembered and recalled for millennia. What led to the creation of the Israelite monarchy? In the words of William E. Evans, "The impetus ... [was] the Philistine threat."[1] As most historians recognize, this is certainly part of the truth. However, external pressure was not only from the Philistines: An Ammonite threat also played a role in bringing an end to the loose tribal confederacy—if indeed that is what it was—by which Israel had been led and protected. Moreover, internal (social, economic, and demographic) pressures must also be taken into account.[2] Charismatic tribal leaders who arose as needed were no longer enough to lead the emerging nation. The Early Kingdom of Israel lasted for about a century (c. 1030–931 B.C.E.). Three strong personalities occupied the throne: Saul, David, and Solomon. Then the United Kingdom split in two, with Israel in the north and Judah in the south.

Under Saul, the Israelite monarchy controlled a small, petty territory. Under David and then Solomon, Israel was transformed into a larger, unified kingdom eventually with vassal states subject to it. As the monarchy assumed a regional role, other powers in the ancient Near East (mainly Phoenicia and Egypt) had to take it into account.

The historian looks very fortunate in this period: The biblical record is copious because this period was later conceived as a kind of "golden age." The Bible probably devotes more space to this century than to any other in ancient Israel's history. Accounts of this period appear in both of the Bible's parallel histories—1 Samuel 8 to 1 Kings 11 and 1 Chronicles 3 to 2 Chronicles 9.

The principal difficulty in reconstructing the history of the period is that we are dependent almost exclusively on the Bible. The assurance that comes from a variety of sources is missing here, and the biblical account is often tendentious and includes traditions that are not reliable as history. It tends to idealize this period with legendary aspects. As underlined by J. Maxwell Miller: "The important question is not whether we should use the Hebrew Bible in our attempts to understand the origin and early history of Israel, but how we should use it. In my opinion, it should be approached critically, examined with the careful attention to its internal typology and stratigraphy that archaeologists give to their data, and then used very cautiously, alongside other kinds of evidence."[3] (For a summary of how scholars can date ancient Israel's kings, including David and Solomon, see "Why Do We Date David and Solomon to the Tenth Century?" [see Learn More box].)

To understand this period of Israel's history, we must therefore consider questions of literary criticism, as well as differences in the various traditions preserved in the Bible. Finally, we must consider the light archaeology sheds (or fails to shed) on the monarchy[4]—not an easy task, as exemplified by the contemporary controversy over the archaeology of the tenth century B.C.E.[5] Two divergent views of this century have emerged, one known as the so-called maximalist viewpoint, the other as the so-called minimalist. The former group contends that the biblical account of the United Monarchy has a historical core;[6] the latter practically tends to deny that the biblical traditions of this period have any basis whatsoever in history.[7] The main argument of the latter group is that there was no literary historiographical tradition before 800 B.C.E.[8] Such an a priori negation is contradicted by the inscriptions of Mesha and Deir 'Alla as well as by many smaller tenth–ninth century B.C.E. inscriptions, as stressed by most epigraphers.[9]

Why Do We Date David and Solomon to the Tenth Century?

In the ongoing scholarly debate over the historicity of David and Solomon, most attention has focused on the tenth century B.C.E. But why do scholars think these two kings should be placed in the tenth century in the first place? After all, the biblical writers only tell us how long both kings reigned, not specifically when they reigned. In a masterful *BAR* article ("How We Know When Solomon Ruled," September/October 2001), Egyptologist and biblical historian Kenneth Kitchen explains that datable records and events from ancient Assyria and Egypt help establish specific calendar dates for the reigns of almost all of Israel's kings, including David and Solomon. Not only did these foreign powers keep extensive lists of the reigns of their own kings, but they often mention surrounding states and kings that they conquered or subdued, including Israel and Judah. In this way, the reigns of Israel's kings are linked with the known dates of Assyrian and Egyptian rulers and their foreign campaigns.

Dating the excavated material remains that come from the time of David and Solomon, however, is a somewhat different matter. While there is increasing hope that advanced scientific techniques like carbon-14 dating will ultimately be able to date a particular archaeological level to within a decade or two of its use, archaeologists are still largely dependent on tried and true "relative" dating techniques—such as pottery analysis and stratigraphy—to understand the world that David and Solomon built (see Lily Singer-Avitz, Archaeological Views, "Carbon 14—The Solution to Dating David and Solomon?" *BAR*, May/June 2009). In the pages of *BAR* ("Pottery Talks: What Ceramics Tell Us About the Social World of Ancient Israel," March/April 2004), archaeologist Avraham Faust explored the social and political significance of a unique type of pottery that, according to the traditional chronology, was made and used primarily in the tenth century B.C.E., the time of the appearance of the first Israelite state, under David and Solomon. This so-called "red-slipped burnished ware," says Faust, is not only a key chronological indicator but also a material manifestation of Israel's emergence as a male-dominated state society under King David. –ED.

Actually many new small c. tenth-century inscriptions have been lately discovered.[10] However, that does not mean that all the historical tradition of the books of Samuel and Kings is early. The ensuing debates remind us that the results of literary criticism and the interpretation of archaeological discoveries are seldom clear-cut. One must therefore be very careful to distinguish what the biblical record says from the historical interpretation of it based on literary criticism and archaeology. Each reign presents different aspects of the problem.

THE ERA OF KING SAUL (C. 1030–1009 B.C.E.)

The Philistine Threat

The Bible depicts Saul as a study in contrasts. Although he was Israel's first king, he was ultimately rejected (1 Samuel 15:10). His dark, fitful personality suffers by contrast with the two legendary figures between whom he seems wedged—Samuel, the prophet-priest, and David, Saul's hero-successor.[11] The Bible describes Saul rising to the throne in the face of the Philistine military threat. The Philistines are known both from the Bible and from extrabiblical sources.[12] Egyptian inscriptions mention them as one of the so-called Sea Peoples. Apparently, they originally came from the Aegean area or from southern Anatolia.[13] Other Sea Peoples include the Tjekkar, the Sheklesh, the Danuna and the Weshesh. The Sea Peoples destroyed a number of cities of the Syro-Phoenician coast at the beginning of the 12th century B.C.E. and even tried to invade Egypt. However, they were stopped in a large-scale battle, fought both on land and on sea, in the eighth year of the reign of Pharaoh Ramesses III (c. 1177 B.C.E.). Reliefs and hieroglyphic accounts of this battle appear on Ramesses III's temple at Medinet Habu in Thebes.[14] The Sea Peoples settled in various parts of the Egyptian province of Canaan, probably with Egypt's agreement: the Philistines occupied the coastal plain between Gaza and Jaffa; the Tjekkar occupied the Sharon plain around the city of Dor; the Cherethites (Cretans?), perhaps another Sea People, settled the so-called Negev of the Cherethites (1 Samuel 30:14).

In the coastal plain, the Philistines organized themselves into a pentapolis, a confederation of five cities: Gaza, Ashdod, Ashkelon,

Gath, and Ekron. Each city was ruled by a *sèrèn*. (The only Philistine word that is known with certainty, *sèrèn* [Joshua 13:3; Judges 16:5, 8, 23, 27; 1 Samuel 5:8, 11] may be related to the Greek word *tyrannos*.)[15]

Eventually, the Philistine military expansion near Aphek brought the Philistines close to the territory occupied by the Israelite confederation.[16] The Philistines were apparently skilled warriors who used the most advanced military equipment of their time. Their weapons were made of both bronze, the predominant metal until about 1200 B.C.E., and iron, which was becoming increasingly available.[17]

PHILISTINE WARRIOR. The Philistines and other Sea Peoples inhabited several cities on the eastern Mediterranean coast in the early 12th century B.C.E. A large-scale sea battle between the Sea Peoples and Egyptian forces is depicted in wall reliefs from Ramesses III's mortuary temple at Medinet Habu, in Thebes. This detail of a warrior's face from one relief showcases the Philistines' characteristic battle headdress, which included a headband and upright strips that may be feathers, reeds, leather strips, horsehair or an unusual hairdo. The military threat posed by the warlike Philistines was one of the factors leading to the creation of the United Kingdom of Israel.

AMMONITE KING. This life-size limestone head, with plaited hair, curled beard, earrings and crown, is said to have been discovered near Amman, Jordan, a city whose name preserves its Ammonite origins. According to the Bible, the Ammonites, who lived east of the Jordan during the Israelite monarchy, were one of Israel's most important adversaries, second only to the Philistines.

According to the biblical record, the Israelites mustered in the hill country near Ebenezer overlooking Aphek.[18] A two-stage battle between the Israelites and the Philistines ensued. In the first phase of the battle, "Israel was defeated by the Philistines, who slew about four thousand men on the field of battle" (1 Samuel 4:2). In desperation, the

Israelites brought the Ark of the Covenant, which had been installed at Shiloh, to lead them in battle. In the second phase of the battle, the Israelites were again defeated, and the Ark was captured by the Philistines.[19] After the battle of Ebenezer (1 Samuel 4), the Philistines occupied at least part of the Ephraimite hill country. After their victory at Ebenezer, the Philistines installed garrisons (or governors) in the hill country of Ephraim and Benjamin, the most important of which was at Geba (1 Samuel 13:3–5).

Like the Habiru/Apiru of the Late Bronze Age, hundreds of years earlier, and the Jews of the Maccabean revolt, hundreds of years later, some Israelites took to the hill country and hid in natural caves (1 Samuel 14:11, 22).

The Choice of Saul

Facing these dire circumstances, the Israelite tribes determined that they must have a king. The story of the choice of Saul as king appears in three different traditions: In the first, Saul is looking for his father's lost she-asses; he meets Samuel who anoints him prince (*nasi*) over Israel (1 Samuel 9:3–10:16). In the second tradition, Saul is hiding among baggage at Mizpah when Samuel casts lots to choose the king (1 Samuel 10:17–27); in the third and most probably reliable tradition,[20] Saul, at the head of Israelite columns, has rescued Jabesh-Gilead from an Ammonite attack, and the people, with Samuel's agreement, proclaim their allegiance to Saul at Gilgal (1 Samuel 11–15). In each of these accounts, Saul is installed and anointed as king by Samuel, now an old man.[21]

Samuel was regarded as the last of the judges (1 Samuel 7:6, 15; 8:1–3), the charismatic leaders who emerged at times of crisis. Another tradition, probably a later one, regarded Samuel as a prophet (1 Samuel 3:20). He also officiated at the Tabernacle at Shiloh, where the Ark was kept, which means he was probably a priest. But Samuel's leadership was regarded as insufficient. The tribal elders apparently felt that the appointment of a king was a historical necessity: "Now appoint for us a king to govern us like all the nations," they told Samuel (1 Samuel 8:5). Saul, a Benjaminite, seems to have been chosen because he was tall and strong and well qualified to wage war against Israel's enemies.

Like earlier charismatic leaders, Saul's principal task was to conduct a war of liberation. Saul's successful expedition against the Ammonites at Jabesh-Gilead (1 Samuel 11:1–11) was no doubt an important consideration in his selection. Now he was called upon to lead the people against the Philistines, a people who were well organized, well equipped, and motivated by an expansionist ideology that included plans to bring the whole country west of the Jordan under its control.

The first battle—at Michmash—was a victory for Israel (1 Samuel 13:5–14:46). The decision to appoint a king seemed to have been a wise one. (Although, as Gary Rendsburg noted in the previous chapter, the establishment of a monarchy had been greeted with considerable ambivalence). Moreover, this was by no means the last battle of the war.

Saul the Warrior

"There was hard fighting against the Philistines all the days of Saul; and when Saul saw any strong man, or any valiant man, he attached him to himself" (1 Samuel 14:52).

The Philistine war thus became a guerrilla war, characterized by ambushes and surprise attacks against enemy posts. Generally, it did not involve great numbers of fighters. Saul had only "about six hundred men with him" near Gibeah (1 Samuel 14:2). Unfortunately, the Bible gives only brief intimations of the details of the continuing wars with the Philistines. Saul probably succeeded in driving the Philistines out of the central part of Israel. But the Philistines did not give up. They apparently attacked from the south, threatening Judah in a confrontation in which a young Judahite named David distinguished himself (1 Samuel 17).

Saul seems to have been generally successful as long as he fought in the hills, but his troops could not win a battle in the open plain. Witness what happened near Mt. Gilboa (1 Samuel 28–31). The Philistines attacked from the north through the Jezreel Valley. The Israelites should never have come down into the plain to fight.

> The Philistines fought against Israel; and the men of Israel fled before the Philistines, and fell slain on Mount Gilboa ... Thus Saul died, and his three sons, and his armor-bearer, and all his men, on the same day together. And when the men of Israel who were on the other side of the valley and those beyond the Jordan saw that the men of Israel had fled and

that Saul and his sons were dead, they forsook their cities and
fled; and the Philistines came and dwelt in them.
(1 SAMUEL 31:1, 6–7)

This sober presentation of an Israelite disaster has a ring of truth
even though, beginning in David's time, there were divergent traditions concerning the details of Saul's death (compare 1 Samuel 31:3–5
with 2 Samuel 1:6–10).

Other than the Philistine war, which seems to have been the prin-
cipal feature of Saul's reign, the biblical text mentions wars against the
Moabites, the Ammonites, the Edomites, the king of Zobah, and the
Amalekites (1 Samuel 14:47–48).

The main battle of the war with the Amalekites is described in
1 Samuel 15. The Amalekites were the Israelites' special enemies
because they were the first to confront Israel in the wilderness after
the Israelites left Egypt. Without provocation, the Amalekites are said
to have attacked Israel from the rear (Exodus 17:8–16).

Actually, Samuel is said to have instructed Saul and his men to kill
all the Amalekites and their animals, according to the tradition of
hérèm (compare Joshua 6:18; 7), which allotted the fruits of victory to
the Lord alone. However, Saul spared the Amalekite king Agag and
the best of the Amalekites' domestic animals. For this sin, Samuel
denounced Saul and declared that the Lord had irrevocably rejected
him. Samuel, the Bible tells us, "never saw Saul again ... And the Lord
was sorry that he had made Saul king over Israel" (1 Samuel 15:35).

Tentative Evaluation of Saul's Reign

We do not know how long Saul ruled. According to the traditional
Hebrew text (the Masoretic text), which unfortunately is badly
preserved at this point, Saul became king when he was one year old
(!) and his reign lasted only "two years" (1 Samuel 13:1).[22] Two years
seems improbable, and several commentators correct it to "twenty-
two years"; but this remains conjectural.

Although the length of Saul's reign is uncertain, two biblical
passages offer some information about the general economic and
political conditions under Saul:

Now there was no smith to be found throughout all the land
of Israel; for the Philistines said, "The Hebrews must not

make swords or spears for themselves"; so all the Israelites went down to the Philistines to sharpen their plowshares, mattocks, axes, or sickles; and the charge was a *pim* [= two-thirds of a shekel] for the plowshares and for the mattocks, and a third of a shekel for sharpening the axes and for setting the goads. So on the day of the battle, neither sword nor spear was to be found in the possession of any of the people with Saul and Jonathan; but Saul and Jonathan his son had them.

(1 SAMUEL 13:19-22)

This first passage reflects a nonspecialized society of peasants and shepherds in which even iron implements were rare.

The second passage describes Saul's family:

Now the sons of Saul were Jonathan, Ishvi, and Malchishua; and the names of his two daughters were these; the name of the firstborn was Merab and the name of the younger Michal; and the name of Saul's wife was Ahinoam daughter of Ahimaaz. And the name of the commander of his army was Abner the son of Ner, Saul's uncle.

(1 SAMUEL 14:49-50)

This passage demonstrates that Saul's kingship was essentially a family matter. The principal specialized responsibility, leadership of the army, was in the hands of Saul's cousin Abner.

It is difficult to give a balanced historical assessment of Saul's reign.[23] In the biblical tradition, he seems to be presented as the typical "bad" king,[24] in contrast to his adversary and successor David. This contrast is the central theme of the stories in 1 Samuel 16–27, the bulk of which could have been written by David's companion and priest Abiathar (see 1 Samuel 22:20) or someone close to him.[25] These chapters may contain some reliable information,[26] but it is presented in a one-sided and tendentious way. They describe, in sometimes divergent traditions, the stormy relationship between Saul and the young David. David had distinguished himself in the Philistine wars and had been given Saul's second daughter, Michal, in marriage. Saul became increasingly envious of David, accusing his son-in-law of conspiring against him. On several occasions, Saul tried to kill David. David fled to Judah, but Saul pursued him. Finally David took refuge in Philistine territory. Written from

David's viewpoint, the stories in 1 Samuel 16–27 tend to depict David as right in rebelling against Saul and seeking refuge in Philistine territory.[27] But they also reveal that people from Bethlehem in Judah joined Saul in battle when the Philistines tried to invade the central hill country from the southwest (1 Samuel 17:1). Saul obviously exerted some political influence south of Jerusalem in the northern mountains of Judah, preparing the way for the federation of Israel and Judah under David.[28]

The historicity of many of Saul's other wars, however, is doubtful. The wars against the Moabites, the Edomites, the king of Zobah and even the Amalekites (1 Samuel 14:47–48; 15) may simply be a transposition from David to Saul made by the later Judahite historian because he had so little information about Saul. Such wars far from Saul's home base seem improbable, especially when the Philistine threat was so strong and Saul's army was so poorly organized.

Unfortunately, we are left with little solid information about Saul or his reign. All that can be said with confidence is that Saul seems to have been named king so that he would lead the Israelites in their wars against the Philistines, which he did.

Saul's "kingdom" was not very large. It probably included Mt. Ephraim, Benjamin and Gilead.[29] He also exerted some influence in the northern mountains of Judah and beyond the Jezreel Valley. Instead of a capital or a palace, Saul maintained his tent "in the outskirts of Gibeah under the pomegranate tree which is at Migron" (1 Samuel 14:2) or in Gibeah, where he sat "under the tamarisk tree on the height with his spear in his hand, and all his servants [i.e., ministers] were standing about him" (1 Samuel 22:6).[30]

Saul's "kingship," as might be expected from the biblical record, left hardly a trace archaeologically speaking. Surveys and excavations in the hill country of Manasseh,[31] Ephraim,[32] and Benjamin,[33] and at sites like Izbet Sartah,[34] have revealed farms, small villages and open-air cult places on hilltops. To the south, in northern Judah, settlement was even sparser.[35] The fortified site of Khirbet ed-Dawwara, northeast of Jerusalem, had perhaps a hundred inhabitants, and this was large for Saul's kingdom. However, this site could well have been built as an Israelite center to receive refugees during the struggle with the Philistines.[36] Alternatively Khirbet ed-Dawwara could have been the place of the Philistine camp mentioned in 1 Samuel 13:5, 16.[37] The principal Israelite site of the previous period, Shiloh,[38] seems to have been destroyed in the mid-11th century B.C.E.[39] by an intense conflagration. This destruction is often attributed to the Philistines as a follow-up operation after their victory over the Israelites at Ebenezer (1 Samuel 4). Shiloh is mentioned only once in the stories of Saul and David (1 Samuel 14:3).

Archaeology seems to confirm that until the end of Iron Age I, that is, the beginning of the tenth century, Israelite society was essentially a society of farmers and stockbreeders without any truly centralized organization and administration.[40] Recent population estimates set "a figure of about 50,000 settled Israelites west of the Jordan at the end of the eleventh century."[41]

By contrast, Philistine urban civilization was flourishing in the 11th century, as revealed by recent excavations at Ashdod,[42] Tel Gerisa, Tel Miqne (biblical Ekron),[43] Ashkelon,[44] and mainly Tell es-Safi (Gath).[45]

Saul's reign apparently ended in total failure. After the rout on Mt. Gilboa and the lamented death of Saul as a hero (2 Samuel 1:19–27),[46] the Israelite revolt against Philistine domination seemed hopeless. Under the leadership of Saul's adversary, David, however, the fight for independence—the raison d'être of Saul's kingship—was taken up once again but with an opposite orientation: taking advantage of the Philistine presence in the Philistine plain and the western part of the Shephelah.

THE ERA OF KING DAVID (C. 1009/1001–969 B.C.E.)

With David's reign, we begin to see Israel emerge as a national entity. The loose confederation of tribes has been transformed into a strong chiefdom. Israel's political existence is confirmed by its king, its army, its royal cabinet, its extended territory, and its relations with neighboring countries. Even historians, such as Mario Liverani[47] and J. Alberto Soggin,[48] who hesitate to say anything about the early history of Israel, agree that from about 1000 B.C.E., "the History of Israel leaves the realm of pre-history, of cultic and popular traditions, and enters the arena of history proper."[49]

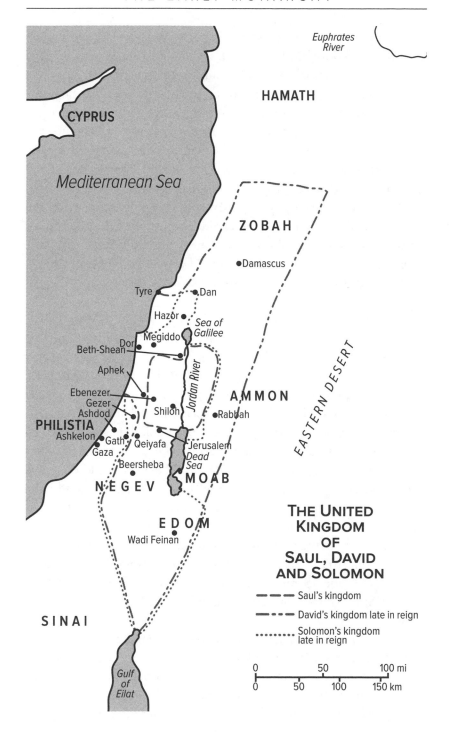

HAMATH

CYPRUS

Euphrates River

Mediterranean Sea

ZOBAH

•Damascus

Tyre•   •Dan

Hazor•
Megiddo•   *Sea of Galilee*
Dor•
Beth-Shean•

Aphek•

Ebenezer•   *Jordan River*
Gezer•
Ashdod•   Shiloh•   •Rabbah
PHILISTIA
Ashkelon•   •Gath   AMMON
Gaza•   •Qeiyafa   Jerusalem•
•Beersheba   *Dead Sea*

EASTERN DESERT

N E G E V   M O A B

E D O M
Wadi Feinan•

S I N A I

Gulf of Eilat

THE UNITED KINGDOM OF SAUL, DAVID AND SOLOMON

– – – Saul's kingdom

–·–·– David's kingdom late in reign

········· Solomon's kingdom late in reign

0		50		100 mi
0	50	100	150 km	

That does not mean, however, that everything is clear and that no historical questions remain. Indeed, a few scholars have recently gone so far as to deny that David really founded the kingdom of Jerusalem as a political power.[50] According to Ernst A. Knauf, "Archaeologically speaking there are no indications of statehood being achieved before the 9th century B.C.E. in Israel and the 8th century B.C.E. in Judah."[51] Although it may be true that Israel was more of a powerful chiefdom than a well-administered state or, still less, a centralized empire, there is no reason to deny the historicity of David's kingdom as *some* sort of political power. The methodological weakness of this extreme position is highlighted by two monumental ninth-century B.C.E. inscriptions written by enemies—Mesha of Moab[52] and Hazael of Damascus[53]—who designate the kingdom of Judah as *Be(y)t Dawid*, "the House of David," probably the official diplomatic name of this period.[54]

A Model King

The Bible tells the story of David's reign in detail (1 Samuel 16–1 Kings 2:11), reflecting its importance, as well as its length. David "reigned over Israel for forty years, seven in Hebron and thirty-three in Jerusalem" (c. 1009/1001–969 B.C.E.). His long reign was later regarded as Israel's "golden age"; David himself was seen as the model king.

David's later glorification may seem paradoxical in light of the fact that he was a Bethlehemite, from the tribe of Judah, and not from any of the original, northern tribes (Ephraim, Manasseh, and Benjamin). Furthermore, David was one of Saul's adversaries, who had been banned because he was considered the personal enemy of the first Israelite king. Moreover, at the time of Saul's death, David was serving as a mercenary in the army of the Philistines, Israel's bitter enemy.

According to 1 Samuel 16:1–13, David was the youngest son of Jesse. The prophet-priest Samuel "anointed him in the midst of his brothers; and the Spirit of the Lord came mightily upon David from that day forward."

The Bible offers two accounts of how David became part of Saul's household. In the first, Saul takes David into his service as his "armor-bearer" (1 Samuel 16:14–23). In the second version, David, having killed the Philistine champion Goliath in single combat (1 Samuel 17), is officially presented to Saul as a hero. The biblical account of David's rise to power may well represent an amalgamation of different traditions concerning the early relationship between David and Saul.

In any event, with the support of his friend Jonathan (Saul's son), David was "made ... a commander of a thousand [in the army]; and he went out and came in before the people. And David had success in all his undertakings; for the Lord was with him" (1 Samuel 18:13–14).

This happy situation did not last. David was soon accused of conspiring against Saul (1 Samuel 22:8). David decided it would be prudent to flee to the hill country:

> David departed from there and escaped to the cave of Adullam; and when his brothers and all his father's house heard it, they went down there to him. And every one who was in distress, and every one who was in debt, and every one who was discontented gathered to him; and he became captain over them. And there were with him about four hundred men.
> (1 SAMUEL 22:1–2)

Among them were Abiathar (the son of Ahimelech the son of Ahitub the priest of Nob, descendant of Eli the chief priest at Shiloh) and the prophet Gad (1 Samuel 22:5, 20). That these religious personalities joined David suggests the importance of Yahwism among David's partisans.

After some time hiding in various locations throughout Judah, including Keilah (1 Samuel 23:1–13),[55] as Saul pursued him, David sought refuge in Philistine territory:

> So David ... and the six hundred men who were with him [escaped to the land of the Philistines] to Achish son of Maoch, king of Gath. And David dwelt with Achish in Gath, he and his men, every man with his household and David with his two wives.
> (1 SAMUEL 27:2–3)

After a while "Achish gave him [David] Ziklag" (1 Samuel 27:6).[56]

During this period, David attempted to maintain good relations with the leaders of the territory of Judah by fighting Judah's enemy, the Amalekites (1 Samuel 17:8; 30:1–31). His efforts proved fruitful.

After Saul's death at the battle of Mt. Gilboa,

> David went [to Hebron in the territory of Judah] and his
> two wives also, Ahinoam of Jezreel, and Abigail the widow of
> Nabal of Carmel. And David brought up his men who were
> with him, every one with his household; and they dwelt in
> the towns of Hebron. And the men of Judah came, and there
> they anointed David king over the house of Judah.
> (2 SAMUEL 2:2–4)

This does not seem to have provoked any Philistine reaction, who,
at first, were apparently pleased that one of their vassals controlled the
territory of Judah. The same was not true, however, of Saul's descendants:

> Now Abner the son of Ner, commander of Saul's army, had
> taken Ishbosheth the son of Saul, and brought him over to
> Mahanaim;[57] and he made him king over Gilead and the
> Ashurites and Jezreel and Ephraim and Benjamin and all
> Israel. Ishbosheth, Saul's son, was forty years old when he
> began to reign over Israel; and he reigned two years.
> (2 SAMUEL 2:8–10)[58]

King David

A "long war" ensued between the house of Saul and the house of David
(2 Samuel 3:1). But in the meantime, a disagreement soon split Abner
and Ishbosheth (Eshbaal). Both of them were killed, apparently as a
result of personal vengeance (2 Samuel 3–4).[59] The way was open for
David to become the king of all Israel.

> All the elders of Israel came to the king at Hebron; and King
> David made a covenant with them at Hebron before the
> Lord, and they anointed David king over Israel.
> (2 SAMUEL 5:3)

The Philistines could no longer remain indifferent in face of the
unification of their longtime enemy Israel—joining forces with Judah.
They attacked twice in the central hill country, once near the Valley of
Rephaim and probably once near Gibeon. But David defeated them
both times (2 Samuel 5:17–25).[60] The Philistines then gave up their

efforts at military expansion.

After driving off the Philistines, David was free to attack the Jebusites[61] of Jerusalem and take the city, which until then had remained in Canaanite hands: "And David dwelt in the stronghold [of Jerusalem] and called it the City of David" (2 Samuel 5:9).

Jerusalem soon became not only the political capital of Judah and Israel, but also a religious center for all Israel. To accomplish this, David brought the Ark of the Covenant to the City of David (2 Samuel 6).[62] This was the Ark that, according to tradition, had accompanied Israel in the Sinai, that had rested in the Tabernacle of Shiloh before being captured by the Philistines, and that had remained in storage at Kiriath Yearim[63] after being returned by the Philistines. When David brought the Ark to Jerusalem, the religion of Yahweh became a unifying factor, strengthening the bond between Judah and Israel.

From the beginning of his career, David has shown himself to be a fervent Yahwist. His religious devotion is confirmed by the presence in his retinue of the priest Abiathar and the prophet Gad. David's devotion to Yahweh probably made it easier for the leaders of Israel to accept him as their king.

David cemented his relations with various political and national groups through marriage. His wives included Abigail of Carmel; Ahinoam of Jezreel; and Maacah, daughter of the Transjordanian king of Geshur (2 Samuel 3:2–5).[64]

Militarily, David had already developed a cadre of well-trained troops when he fled from Saul. These devoted soldiers were ready to follow him anywhere, and, in fact, had followed him from the wilderness of Judah to Gath, Ziklag, Hebron, and, finally, Jerusalem. These troops became his personal guard and the core of his regular army.[65] His nephew Joab served as chief of the army (2 Samuel 8:16).

After checking the Philistine advances on Israel's western border, David was free to expand his kingdom to the east. There he defeated the Moabites, who then became a vassal state, paying tribute to David (2 Samuel 8:2). As discussed below, David also fought with the Ammonites, although the precise sequence of these wars is unclear. According to the Masoretic Text, he also led a campaign to Edom, where he won a battle in the Valley of Salt. David then appointed "garrisons (or governors) in Edom; throughout all Edom he put garrisons, and all the Edomites became David's servants" (2 Samuel 8:14).

In the biblical tradition, after the Philistines, the Ammonites were Israel's most important adversary. The Ammonite war began as a result of a diplomatic incident. Nahash, the king of the Ammonites, had been David's friend. When Nahash died, David sent condolences to his son and successor, Hanun. But Hanun treated David's messengers with contempt: He cut away half of their beards and half of their garments, accusing them of being David's spies (2 Samuel 10:1–5). Hanun probably thought he could get away with this because of an alliance he had made with the Aramean kingdoms of northern Transjordan and southern Syria (1 Samuel 10:6).[66]

In retaliation, David's general, Joab, led an attack near the Ammonite capital. An Ammonite ally—Hadadezer the Rehobite, king of Zobah[67]—summoned other Arameans from "beyond the Great Bend of the Euphrates" to join forces against David (2 Samuel 10:16). David met and defeated this Aramean army at Helam (2 Samuel 10:17–18). He "took from him [Hadadezer] a thousand and seven hundred horsemen, and twenty thousand foot soldiers; and David hamstrung all the chariot horses, but left enough for a hundred chariots" (2 Samuel 8:4). (Apparently, chariots were not used much in David's army; otherwise, he would not have crippled so many horses.)

As a result of this enormous victory, David was able to conquer Rabbah, the Ammonite capital. David then "took the crown of their king (or of Milkom, their god) from his head ... and it was placed on David's head" (2 Samuel 12:30).

The Ammonites became David's subjects. In addition, the kingdom of Zobah, headed by Hadadezer, became David's vassal: "David put garrisons (or governors) in Aram of Damascus; the Syrians [Arameans] became servants to David and brought tribute" (2 Samuel 8:6). Finally, "All the kings who were servants of Hadadezer ... they made peace with Israel and became subject to them" (2 Samuel 10:19). Among them was Toi, the king of the important kingdom of Hamath (2 Samuel 8:9–10). David would have thereby extended his political influence from the Red Sea to the bend of the Euphrates.

By gaining control over international trade routes, the Israelite kingdom became an economic power. David became rich from the spoil and tribute brought to Jerusalem. Even the Phoenician king of

Tyre, Hiram, started trading with him, especially after David made Jerusalem his capital (2 Samuel 5:11–12).

The Inchoate Nature of the Early State

The expansion of David's kingdom altered the status of Jerusalem.[68] From a small declining Canaanite city-state with a territory of a few square miles, it became—probably with little physical change—the capital of the united Israelite and Judahite kingdoms. These kingdoms, after David's victories, extended far and wide. The borders of the United Kingdom stretched from Dan to Beersheba, but its vassal states extended far beyond. David's kingdom may have been a strong chiefdom, but it was not really an empire. His kingdom was still not yet well organized, nor did it have a strong central administration.

At least toward the end of David's reign, there was a kind of royal cabinet where David's general Joab played an important role[69]:

> Joab the son of Zeruiah was over the army; and Jehoshaphat the son of Ahilud was recorder, and Zadok the son of Ahitub and Ahimelech the son of Abiathar were priests; and Seraiah was secretary; and Benaiah the son of Jehoiada was over the Cherethite and the Pelethites; and David's sons were priests.
> (2 SAMUEL 8:15-18; compare 2 SAMUEL 20:23-26)[70]

The spoils of war, the levies from the administered territories, the tributes of vassal kings—all flowed into David's royal treasury. Justice was administered at the local level by the elders of the cities, but an appeal could now be taken directly to the king (2 Samuel 14:15).

David planned to build a new temple at Jerusalem (2 Samuel 7) and organized a census, probably as a basis for future administration, taxation, and circumscription (see 2 Samuel 24:1–9). Both the temple project and the census met internal opposition. Even the prophet Gad, one of David's oldest and most loyal companions, opposed the census; he did, however, support the construction of an altar on the threshing floor of Araunah the Jebusite, the site David purchased for the temple (2 Samuel 24:18).

Toward the end of David's reign, the guiding principles of the United Kingdom became organization and centralization. These were later applied more broadly by his son and successor Solomon.

The Problem of Succession

Internally, the problem of David's legitimacy as successor to Saul, and then of David's own successor, loomed large. It was doubtless exacerbated by the unstable union of the houses of Israel and Judah. This problem is treated at great length in the Bible. Indeed, this is the principal subject from 2 Samuel 6 through 1 Kings 2, often called the "History of the Succession."[71]

Initially, David tried to gain the goodwill of Saul's house.[72] He even married Michal, Saul's daughter. David also welcomed to his table on a regular basis Meribbaal (Mephibosheth), a cripple who was Saul's heir. True, this seeming act of kindness permitted David to control Meribbaal's activity (2 Samuel 9). And in the end David more or less abandoned Michal, who "had no child to the day of her death" (2 Samuel 6:23).[73] When David allowed the Gibeonites to take vengeance on seven of Saul's descendants, reconciliation between the two houses was no longer possible (2 Samuel 21:1–14).[74]

David's own house was also beset with rivalries and jealousies among his sons. His eldest son, Amnon, was killed by order of David's third son Absalom (2 Samuel 13). Absalom himself was killed by Joab, the general of David's army, after leading an almost-sucessful revolt against his father (2 Samuel 15–19). Absalom's revolt was connected with the rivalry between Israel and Judah and with Benjaminite opposition to David (compare the roles played by Shimei and by Sheba son of Bichri, both Benjaminites [2 Samuel 19:16–23; 20:1–22]).[75]

After Amnon and Absalom were killed, Adoniah became David's heir apparent. David's old retainers, including his general Joab and the priest Abiathar, were ready to support Adoniah (1 Kings 1:5–7). However, according to 1 Kings 1, the aged David apparently promised Bathsheba that their son Solomon would become king. With the help of the prophet Nathan, the priest Zadok, and the chief of the guards Benaiah, Solomon was recognized as king while David was still living. David himself died peacefully some time afterward (1 Kings 2:10–12).[76]

Assessing the Biblical Text

In the absence of any long text contemporary with the biblical tradition, a historical appreciation of David's reign is difficult.[77] A literary analysis of the biblical tradition seems to indicate, however, that a good deal of it could have been written either in David's or Solomon's time, close enough to the events to be reliable witnesses,[78] although there are doubtless later additions and glosses reflecting the influence of the so-called Deuteronomistic historians of later centuries.[79]

Of course, even early traditions are tendentious, and it does seem that most of the account of David's reign was written to glorify and justify David and his son Solomon. This is particularly true of the stories concerning David's accession, which reflect the most attractive side of his personality and justify his claim to the kingship.[80] One may note that David's marriages played an important role on his way to power and afterward.[81] The propaganda aspect is also obvious in the account of Solomon's accession, which explains how Solomon, although one of the younger sons of David, could be his legitimate heir; this justification would place it "with Solomon's reign."[82] The aged David's promise to Bathsheba to make her son king sounds more like literary artifice than history. Or perhaps Bathsheba, with the help of the prophet Nathan[83] and the priest Zadok, succeeded in convincing an old and weakened David to support their conspiracy to elevate Solomon and thus to legitimate what was in effect a coup d'état.[84]

The account of David's external policies also bears the marks of tendentiousness; the biblical text emphasizes David's military victories[85] more than his political control of the conquered territories. Even if David was victorious against the expansionist Philistines, he was apparently unable to control the Philistines' territory. The biblical statement that David "subdued" the Philistines (2 Samuel 8:1; 11–12) is ambiguous. Further, 2 Samuel 5:25 tells us that David defeated the Philistines only as far as Gezer, which lay on the eastern border of Philistine territory. Gezer itself did not become part of Israel until Solomon's reign. Actually, David seems to have kept good relations with the kingdom of Gath; he employed Gathites as his guard and they even fought on his side against Absalom. Finally "a kind of peaceful coexistence" with Philistines emerged.[86]

David's relations with Hiram king of Tyre must also be looked at critically. The Phoenicians were technologically superior to the Israelites, and David's relationship with them was essentially commercial; there was no vassal submission. Moreover, even this commercial relationship probably dated to the very end of David's reign or, even more likely, to the beginning of Solomon's reign.[87]

After the Ammonite war, if David indeed took for himself the Ammonite crown, he probably dismissed the ruling Ammonite king only to put in his place another son of Nahash: "Shobi the son of Nahash from Rabbah of the Ammonites," who supported David during Absalom's revolt (2 Samuel 17:27–29).

In the Aramean territories that David administered (Zobah and Damascus),[88] the governors were probably chosen from local leaders. In the vassal kingdoms (like Moab), their own kings continued to rule, although they paid tribute to David. Sometimes it is difficult to tell the difference between a vassal state and an allied kingdom, or even a good neighbor. For instance, Toi, king of Hamath, probably considered himself as a good neighbor rather than an allied king and certainly not a vassal (see 2 Samuel 8:9–10). Unfortunately, the identification of Toi king of Hamath with Taita (II?)[89] king of Walastina (or Palastina)[90] is disputed and remains somewhat uncertain.[91]

Even if David's sphere of influence did extend from the central Negev and Edom to the southern border of the kingdom of Hamath, we must realize that there are varying degrees of political control.[92] For example, David's influence over the outlying areas was often through good personal relations with the neighboring kings or local chiefs; his suzerainty was sometimes only nominal, mainly dependent on the military threat of his soldiers. As stated earlier, David's political sphere should probably be characterized as a strong chiefdom rather than an "early state" and not as an "empire."[93] Only at the very end of his reign did he begin seriously to organize and centralize his power. According to biblical tradition, David's reign was characterized by wars (see 2 Samuel 8; 10; 1 Kings 5; 17) and he was essentially a warrior; the few buildings attributed to him (2 Samuel 5; 9–11) are more likely to be connected with Solomon.

As would be expected, the archaeology of David's reign seems very sparse, aside from the possible destructions of Canaanite cities.[94] In the 1970s, Yohanan Aharoni argued that Dan and Beersheba were rebuilt by David and that the Iron Age gates of these cities could be dated to the beginning of the tenth century B.C.E.,[95] but few archaeologists today support his conclusions. More recently, Eilat Mazar has proposed identifying monumental archaeological fragments found north of the Ophel (City of David), in Jerusalem, with King David's palace.[96] However her general stratigraphic interpretation is far from clear[97] and a public building from Solomon's reign might eventually be a better candidate. Moreover, even though it could have been built or in use in the tenth century,[98] the date of the "Jebusite ramp," or Stepped-Stone Structure, built on the eastern slope of the City of David is still hotly debated.[99] It appears therefore—from the texts and from the archaeological excavations—that Jebusite Jerusalem did not change much during David's reign.[100]

KHIRBET QEIYAFA. This small but impressively fortified site, known today as Khirbet Qeiyafa, sat on the border between Judah and the Philistine kingdom of Gath during the late 11th–early tenth century B.C.E. While many have suggested Qeiyafa was a military outpost established by King David, it is also possible that it was a Philistine fort built to protect nearby Gath and its territories.

The best candidates for archaeological remains that may be dated during David's reign lie in Hebron and in the Judean Hills. Avi Ofer's excavations in Hebron and his survey of the hill country of Judah reveal a "breakthrough in the settlement history of the Judean Hills."[101] However, it is difficult to date any artifact or architecture to the *beginning* of the tenth century.[102] Most of the building activity in the tenth century probably occurred later, during King Solomon's reign. Yosef Garfinkel and Saar Ganor, however, have proposed that the ruins of Khirbet Qeiyafa,[103] south of Beth-Shemesh, are those of a Judahite town probably called Sha'araim (1 Samuel 17:52) that was fortified by David around 1000.[104] Nadav Na'aman,[105] on the other hand, interprets this site as connected with the Philistine kingdom of Gath and identifies it as "Gob," mentioned two or three times as a place where David and his men battled the Philistines (2 Samuel 21:16–19). In fact, this fortified town, being only 6.5 miles from Tell es-Safi/Gath, appears to be on the border between the kingdom of Jerusalem and the kingdom of Gath and could well also have been a fortress under the control of the "Canaanite" city of Beth-Shemesh. We may hesitate among the three political interpretations: Judahite, Philistine, or Canaanite.

Despite all these reservations, however, David's reign represents a glorious achievement. Seizing the opportunity occasioned by the weakness of Assyria and Egypt,[106] a strong and brilliant personality[107] joined the houses of Israel and Judah, made Jerusalem the capital of both and used this unification as the basis of his dominion. Within this favorable international situation, David created, for a short time, one of the most important powers in the southern Levant. He also laid the foundations of religious institutions that would support the worship of the Hebrew God Yahweh for centuries.[108] What is more, as is now known from the Tel Dan Stele and the Mesha Stele, the kingdom of Jerusalem was later designated by his name: "House of David."[109]

THE ERA OF KING SOLOMON (C. 970/969–931 B.C.E.)

David was occupied chiefly with fighting wars and with expanding his kingdom by both military and political means. Solomon was concerned mainly with consolidating the lands acquired by David and organizing the administration of the kingdom. But before he could turn to this, Solomon had to strengthen his position as king.

Threats to Solomon's Rule

During the early years of his reign, Solomon was confronted with an internal threat. As long as Adoniah, David's oldest surviving son, lived, this apparent Davidic heir was a danger; there was always the possibility that he would present himself as the legitimate successor to David. Solomon seized an early opportunity to rid himself of this threat: Adoniah was executed as soon as he was suspected of scheming against Solomon. David's powerful general Joab, one of Adoniah's supporters, was also executed, and Abiathar the priest, another of Adoniah's chief supporters, was exiled to his own estate in Anathoth (1 Kings 2:13–35). Solomon also put to death Shimei, a supporter of the house of Saul (1 Kings 2:36–46). In this way, the Bible tells us, "the kingdom was established in the hand of Solomon" (1 Kings 2:46).

Outside of Israel, the Egyptian pharaoh, probably Siamun, tried to take advantage of the change in rulers to intervene.[110] He organized a military expedition that seized and destroyed Gezer (1 Kings 9:16), a destruction that now seems confirmed by archaeological excavations.[111] Apparently Pharaoh did not go any farther; that is, he did not enter Solomon's territory. On the contrary, he gave one of his daughters to Solomon as a wife with the city of Gezer as her dowry (1 Kings 3:1; 7:8; 11:1).

Apparently no significant change in external policy occurred except, perhaps, a greater development in commercial relations with Hiram, king of Tyre (1 Kings 5:1–18), and, later on, the transfer of the land of Cabul (see below).

Like David, Solomon entered diplomatic marriages to ensure the fidelity of the neighboring Transjordanian kingdoms. He probably married "Naamah the Ammonitess" whose son later became King Rehoboam (1 Kings 14:21).[112] According to 1 Kings 4:21, like his father, "Solomon ruled over all the kingdoms from the River [the Euphrates] to Philistia, as far as the Egyptian frontier; they were bringing gifts (or tribute) and were subject to him all his life." However, this general and late (probably Persian period)[113] assertion needs to be qualified, especially for Philistia (see above) and for Damascus' kingdom (see below), as well as more generally for northern Syria and the Phoenician coast.

Solomon also reorganized the administration of his kingdom, a task to which he devoted considerable effort and for which biblical tradition accords him the title "wise" (*hakam*)—that is to say, he was both a clever politician and a good administrator. Various areas of administrative organization or reorganization can be distinguished.[114] First was the central government, in which a new royal cabinet was nominated:

And these were his high officials: Azariah the son of Zadok

was the priest; Elihoreph and Ahijah the sons of Shisha were secretaries; Jehoshaphat the son of Ahilud was recorder; Benaiah the son of Jehoiada was in command of the army; Zadok and Abiathar were priests;[115] Azariah the son of Nathan was over the officers; Zabud the son of Nathan was priest and king's friend; Ahishar was in charge of the palace; and Adoniram the son of Abda was in charge of the forced labor.

(1 KINGS 4:2–6)

In comparison with David's royal cabinet (2 Samuel 8:16), Solomon's appointments reflect a certain continuity, a son often inheriting his father's position. We can also detect Egyptian influence in the bureaucratic structure.[116] There are new officials, such as the man over the officers/governors, the man in charge of the administration of the palace, and the man in charge of the forced labor levy. In general, the bureaucracy becomes more complex and more pervasive.

Two sons of the prophet Nathan were made members of this cabinet, probably because of the prominent part their father played in the designation of Solomon as king (1 Kings 1:11–38).

Israelite territory now included a number of annexed Canaanite city-states, such as Dor, Megiddo, and Beth-Shean. As it expanded, Israel was divided into 12 administrative districts or provinces.[117] Each province had at its head a prefect or governor appointed by the king. Administration was thus centralized. In 1 Kings 4:8–19, we find a list of the governors with their territories and principal cities, which presents a good parallel to other ancient Near Eastern administrative lists.[118] At least two governors married daughters of Solomon (1 Kings 4:11, 15), another way of centralizing and controlling the government administration.

Each administrative district was required to provide for the king and his palace for one month a year (1 Kings 4:7, 27–28). This was a heavier economic responsibility than it might at first seem. It included the expenses of maintaining the royal harem, of providing for a number of functionaries, and of equipping the army with horses and chariots (1 Kings 4:28 = 1 Kings 5:8 [Hebrew Bible]). As in David's reign, the royal treasury also received income from royal properties. Although the royal treasury no longer received booty in Solomon's reign, the Jerusalem treasury was probably supplied with tribute from vassal lands in Transjordan.

Trade and Construction During Solomon's Reign

Solomon also developed an important new source of income from the international trade that became so important during his peaceful reign.[119] The government operated this trade, and the royal treasury profited from it in various ways: Trade with Phoenicia provided timber (cedar and pine) and technical aid (mainly for the construction of Solomon's official buildings). In exchange, Israel supplied agricultural products like wheat and olive oil (1 Kings 5:8–11 = 1 Kings 5:22–25 [Hebrew Bible]). In cooperation with the Tyrians, Solomon sent trading expeditions to Ophir[120] through the Red Sea.[121] These expeditions brought back gold, precious stones and tropical products (*almug* wood, ivory, apes, and baboons) (1 Kings 9:26–28; 10:11, 22). Caravans through the Arabian Desert began to arrive into Jerusalem (1 Kings 10:1–10).

Although Solomon's reign was comparatively peaceful (David had been almost continually at war), he nevertheless took care to modernize his army.[122] He equipped it with large numbers of chariots imported from Egypt, for which he imported horses from the kingdom of Que (Cilicia) (1 Kings 10:26–29).[123] Solomon also built special garrisons in various administrative districts for his chariots and their horses (1 Kings 4:26–28 = 1 Kings 5:6–8 [Hebrew Bible]; 9:19).

Solomon is also famous for his building activities. He constructed a wall around Jerusalem (probably around the new quarter: Ophel)[124] and built three fortified cities, Hazor, Megiddo, and Gezer (1 Kings 9:15). These building activities can be related to military defense (see 1 Kings 9:17–18).[125] Solomon's public works in Jerusalem were major accomplishments. It took him seven years to build the Temple (1 Kings 6:37–38) and 13 years to build his royal palace (1 Kings 7:1; 9:10). He also built a structure in Jerusalem known as the *millo*. No one today is certain what the *millo* was. The most likely suggestion is that it was some kind of terracing, since the word seems to be related to the Hebrew term for "fill."[126]

To plan and construct these official buildings, Solomon needed the technical aid of the Phoenicians, who provided assistance not only with the basic architecture and construction, but also with the decoration of the buildings and the acquisition of the raw materials (wood,[127] ivory, gold). These imports were expensive. Indeed, during the second part of his reign, "King Solomon gave to Hiram twenty cities in the land of

Galilee" (1 Kings 9:11–13), that is, "the land of Cabul"[128] (Asher with the rich plain of Acco), to balance the trade deficit between the two kings. To cast the many bronze objects decorating the Temple and the royal palace, Solomon used his metalworks in the Jordan Valley "between Succoth and Zarethan." The casting seems to have been supervised by a Phoenician who specialized in bronze craftsmanship (1 Kings 7:13–47). The origin of the metal is not specified (but see below).

The Bible's detailed description of Solomon's public buildings, especially of the Temple (1 Kings 5–6),[129] reflects the importance of these monuments to the king's glory. Actually, the description of the Temple in 1 Kings 5–6 probably takes into account further developments of this construction.[130] At first, the Temple seems to have been a kind of royal chapel attached to the royal palace that was used primarily by the king and his court. Its architecture may get some light by comparison to a temple discovered at 'Ain Dara (Syria)[131] and to a Judean temple at Tel Moza near Jerusalem.[132] Later, after the eighth-century reforms, these buildings served as a source of pride for the people. Moreover, such buildings helped legitimize the new political organization.[133] However, to build and maintain these symbols of power, Solomon needed a reservoir of cheap manpower. His solution was the *corvée*, forced labor required not only of non-Israelite peoples (1 Kings 9:20–21), but of Israelites as well. The statement in 1 Kings 9:22 that "of the people of Israel Solomon made no slaves" seems contradicted by several statements in Kings (1 Kings 5:13–18 = 1 Kings 6:27–32 [Hebrew Bible]; 11:28; 12:4). The *corvée* and the conscription of Israelites into Solomon's army (1 Kings 9:22) were probably the two principal sources of popular dissatisfaction with Solomon's reign.[134]

As often happens during long reigns, internal dissatisfaction grew in the latter half of Solomon's rule; at the same time, serious external threats surfaced. The biblical tradition gives us a few hints of the dissension inside Israel (1 Kings 11).[135]

The text speaks of two foreign adversaries (*satan*) of Solomon: The first one is "Hadad the Edomite [Aramean]." A member of the royal house of Edom (Aram),[136] Hadad sought refuge in Egypt and even married a sister of the queen (Tahpenes) before trying to go back to his country (1 Kings 11:14–22). The second adversary of Solomon was "Rezon the son of Eliyada," who fled from his master

Hadadezer, king of Zobah, and took to the hills as the chief of a small troop: "They went to Damascus, and dwelt there and made him king in Damascus" (1 Kings 11:23–24). (Actually, as we will discuss below, these two enemies might have been one and the same: "the Aramean Prince/*Rezon* Hadad son of Eliyada.")

In Israel itself, internal dissatisfaction led to a revolt spearheaded by Jeroboam, an Ephraimite who had the support of the prophet Ahijah from Shiloh: "Solomon sought therefore to kill Jeroboam; but Jeroboam arose and fled into Egypt, to Shishak king of Egypt and was in Egypt until the death of Solomon" (1 Kings 11:29–40).[137]

The dissatisfaction with Solomon's rule probably had many sources, but the biblical tradition insists principally on the people's objections, based on religious grounds, to Solomon's many foreign wives.

> For when Solomon was old his wives turned away his heart after other gods...He went after Ashtoret, the goddess of the Sidonians, and after Milcom, the abomination of the Ammonites...Then Solomon built a high place for Chemosh the abomination of Moab, and for Molech [Milcom][138] the abomination of the Ammonites, on the mountain[139] east of Jerusalem.
> (1 KINGS 11:4–7)

The biblical account of Solomon's reign closes by again mentioning the wisdom of Solomon (1 Kings 11:41; see 1 Kings 4:29–34 = 1 Kings 5:9–14 [Hebrew Bible]; 1 Kings 10:1–13) and by fixing the length of his reign at 40 years (1 Kings 11:42).

Biblical Text vs. History

As with David, it is difficult to assess as history the biblical traditions concerning Solomon's reign. In the absence of contemporary Hebrew texts or references to Solomon in ancient Near Eastern texts, we are dependent almost exclusively on the Bible and on archaeology. Yet the biblical materials have a long and complex history of their own, and the Solomon they present is largely a legendary figure.[140]

The principal parts of 1 Kings 1–11 contain an early literary tradition that appears to have been taken from a now-lost account of Solomon's reign, referred to in the Bible as the Acts of Solomon (1 Kings 11:41),

which was probably written not long after Solomon's death. The lost
account presented Solomon as a typically wise king since it could not
speak about his glory at war.[141] However, this early tradition is often
mixed with later Deuteronomistic additions and with emendations by
later editors.[142] For instance, two different literary traditions seem to
have been combined in 1 Kings 9:26–10:13, which concerns the journey
to Ophir and the visit of the queen of Sheba. Part of the early tradition preserved in the Book of Kings tries to justify and exalt Solomon.
This is even truer of later traditions.[143] For example, 2 Chronicles 8:3–4
refers to Solomon's expedition to northern Syria: "And Solomon went to
Hamath-Zobah and took it. He built Tadmor [Palmyra] in the wilderness and all the store-cities which he built in Hamath." However, the
Hebrew text of 1 Kings 9:15–18 does not mention Hamath-Zobah or
Tadmor, and these names are probably a conforming alteration of 1 Kings
9:15–18 by the author of Chronicles.[144] In the same way, the Hebrew text
of 1 Kings 9:19 mentions "Lebanon," in addition to Jerusalem, as a place
where Solomon conducted building activities; however, "Lebanon" is
missing in some manuscripts of the Greek translation known as the
Septuagint and probably has no historical basis.

Nonetheless, if we put aside overstatements and later additions
and discount for the flattering style of most of the texts, the principal
points of the early biblical tradition seem generally trustworthy. We
can rely most heavily on passages that are close in style to contemporaneous annals and administrative texts.[145]

Our extrabiblical knowledge of the history of the region during this
period provides information regarding several aspects of Solomon's
reign, especially in connection with his relations with Egypt,[146] but also
with Phoenicia and Sheba.[147] And archaeology helps us to understand
Solomon's reputation as a builder, as well as the social transformation
into an "early inchoate state"[148] that took place during his reign.

Relations with Egypt

Although Egypt is hardly mentioned as a political power in the biblical
accounts of David's reign, several pharaohs did play an important role
during Solomon's day. At the beginning of Solomon's reign, a pharaoh
attacked Gezer. This pharaoh, as earlier mentioned, was probably
Siamun, one of the last pharaohs of the 21st Dynasty.[149] Although

Egyptian texts thus far discovered do not confirm the matrimonial alliance between Solomon and Pharaoh's daughter, the event is factually presented in the Bible and is probably to be understood in the context of a strong Egyptian political and cultural influence on Solomon's kingdom; one may wonder whether the coup d'état of Solomon was possibly realized with Egyptian support.[150] Anyhow, by this marriage with Pharaoh's daughter, Solomon officially agreed to be in the sphere of Egyptian influence.[151]

As evidence of this Egyptian influence,[152] several studies have cited the design of the royal cabinet[153] and Solomon's organization of the country into 12 administrative districts.[154] Regarding the 12 administrative districts, however, some scholars contend that the influence went in the opposite direction,[155] although that does not seem very likely. It is also quite possible that the literary tradition of the 12 sons of Jacob and of the 12 tribes of Israel find its origin in this organization into 12 administrative districts, as Gösta W. Ahlström has suggested.[156] The notion of 12 tribes of Israel would be a retrojection from this period to the patriarchal age.

Another pharaoh mentioned in the biblical account of Solomon's reign (in connection with Jeroboam's revolt [1 Kings 11:26–42]) is called Shishak. This is Pharaoh Sheshonq, the founder of the 22nd Dynasty.[157] Shishak was a strong personality who wanted to restore Egyptian power, especially in the ancient Egyptian province of Canaan. His accession to the throne (c. 945 B.C.E.) probably marks a turning point in Solomon's reign. Instead of being a kind of benevolent godfather, Shishak was hostile to the Israelite king and supportive of all his opponents. Finally, in the fifth year of the reign of Solomon's successor and son, Rehoboam, Shishak organized a military expedition against the kingdom of Judah (1 Kings 14:25–28), which marched through Israel as well.[158]

It is therefore not surprising to find Shishak supporting Jeroboam's revolt. This political and military threat—and the independence of Damascus—probably increased the financial strains on Solomon. He received less tribute and had to spend more money on defense.

Relations with Phoenicia

A literary tradition sheds some light on the relationship between

Israel and Phoenicia at this time. Preserved in Phoenician annals, the tradition has been transmitted to us second- or third-hand through Menander of Ephesus, Alexander Dius Polyhistor, and Josephus.[159] Although we must read these works with some caution, because they evolved indirectly via two or three Greek intermediaries, they are part of a serious literary tradition; they reflect the use of actual Tyrian archives or annals telling about the principal military expeditions and building activities of the Phoenician kings.[160] Some kind of Solomonic annals probably existed as a contemporaneous parallel—and may well have been partly inspired by the Phoenician annals.[161] Thus Josephus quotes Dius Polyhistor, probably from his history of Phoenicia:

> On the death of Abibalus [Abibaal], his son Hirom came to the throne. He leveled up the eastern part of the city with embankments, enlarged the town, united it by a causeway to the temple of Olympian Zeus, which was isolated on an island, and adorned it with offerings of gold; he also went up to Libanus and had timber cut down for the construction of temples.[162]

Menander of Ephesus, as quoted by Josephus, writes of a similar tradition.[163] Even if these texts present historical problems of their own and differ in detail, they were probably based on the same annals of Tyre and thus shed some light on the cultural and commercial relations between Hiram and Solomon. Furthermore, other late traditions as well as some Phoenician inscriptions confirm the important part played by the Phoenicians, mainly by the Tyrians, in the maritime trade of the Red Sea during the first millennium B.C.E.[164]

As indicated above, the relations between Jerusalem and Tyre were essentially commercial and technical (for the constructions of the Temple and Palace). There was no dependence of Tyre vis-à-vis Jerusalem. At the opposite, in the second part of his reign, Solomon had to give to Hiram "the land of Cabul" including 20 towns (1 Kings 9:11–13). This is not to the glory of Solomon but very probably historical.[165]

Relations with the Kingdom of Sheba

Although in the Bible the story of the Ophir expedition through the Red Sea is now intertwined with the expedition of the queen of Sheba

(1 Kings 9:26–10:22), these two events should not be confused. The queen of Sheba did not come on Phoenician-Israelite ships plying the Red Sea but traveled instead on camels and brought with her primarily spices. These two features are characteristic of the Arabian Peninsula. Although the story of the queen of Sheba contains various literary and legendary themes and was clearly written to glorify Solomon, Assyrian texts of the eighth and seventh centuries do mention a kingdom of Sheba in Arabia and several queens of northern Arabian kingdoms.[166]

THE KHIRBET QEIYAFA OSTRACON. The text written in ink on this broken pottery sherd (called an ostracon) was found in the excavations of the tenth-century B.C.E. site of Khirbet Qeiyafa. It may be the earliest example of a Hebrew inscription, although it could equally be a rare example of an early Philistine or Canaanite writing. The scripts would be the same. Even if Hebrew, however, the text is too broken and poorly preserved to provide a continuous translation. Initial readings have isolated the words and phrases "Do not do," "serve," "judge," and "king," all of which seem to place the text in the realm of ethics and justice.

Other Assyrian texts, connected with Hindanu on the Middle Euphrates, show that the international South Arabian trade was already in place in about 890.[167] Furthermore, we now know that South Arabian script was used in the tenth century and probably before.[168] In light of these various inquiries, an official mission of Sheba (but probably not a queen)[169] could well have come from southern Arabia to Jerusalem in the second half of the tenth century B.C.E.[170]

Independence of Damascus

The confused story of Hadad the "Edomite" and "Rezon the son of Eliyada" (1 Kings 11:14–22) probably represents a distorted image of a historical tradition from an old source[171] concerning the first king of Damascus: the Aramean Prince (*Rezon*) Hadad son of Eliyada,[172] whose revolt Solomon apparently did not dare to crush by a military expedition (probably because Hadad was patronized by Pharaoh), which means that Solomon probably did not control any Aramean territory.

Writing

Epigraphic discoveries from the period of the United Monarchy are still very rare.[173] An exception is the famous Gezer calendar, a small limestone tablet containing a list of the 12 months with the agricultural work performed in each month.[174] However, this inscription may well be Philistine as well as Hebrew.[175] We meet the same problem of interpretation with the Tel Zayit abecedary and the Khirbet Qeiyafa ostracon.[176] The latter is often presented as a didactic Hebrew inscription from the beginning of the tenth century,[177] but an interpretation as an 11th-century list of Canaanite names cannot be excluded since Qeiyafa could have been a Philistine, Canaanite, or Judahite fort (see above). In any event, these inscriptions and a handful of shorter ones show, directly or indirectly, that alphabetic writing was known and used in Judah and Israel as well as in Philistia around the tenth century (see above).

Despite this paucity, the period of David and Solomon was probably an important period of literary creation, much of it composed to support ideological and political goals of the king. Although a matter of considerable scholarly dispute, Israelite historiography probably began at this time.[178] It may have begun with a history of David's accession written by Abiathar the priest or by someone close to him.[179] David and, even more so, Solomon probably promoted the writing of a history that brought together the early Israelite traditions originally connected with different sanctuaries (Shechem, Hebron, Beersheba, Shiloh, etc.).[180] The original unification of these early traditions may have been the work of the famous and much discussed Yahwist.[181] The Yahwist (also called J) is the earliest strand of tradition in the Pentateuch, according to the so-called documentary hypothesis, which divides the Pentateuch into four different strands, the others being E (for Elohist), P (Priestly code and history), and D (Deuteronomist). J could have established the tradition of the 12 sons of Jacob and was the first to present Abraham, Isaac, and Jacob as members of the same family.

THE STEPPED-STONE STRUCTURE. Located on the eastern ridge of the City of David, this massive stone structure originally stood nearly 90 feet tall and 130 feet wide at top. It is preserved to a height of 50 feet, making it one of the most imposing structures to have survived from ancient Israel. The Stepped-Stone Structure may have been built to support a large public building, quite possibly King David's palace, as recently proposed by archaeologist Eilat Mazar. Although scholars agree that the structure incorporates several centuries of building, the dating of the various elements is contested. The most recent excavations date its core to pre-Davidic times, suggesting it may have been part of the fortress that defended Jebusite Jerusalem when David successfully assaulted the city, in about 1000 B.C.E.

Solomon's state administration required officials who could read and write. The development of national historical and legal traditions, as well as a new royal ideology, also required literate scribes. We may therefore assume that there were scribes and probably schools in Jerusalem[182] and in the capitals of the administrative[183] as well as in some of the ancient Canaanite city-states. The tradition of Solomon "the wise ... who declared 3,000 proverbs and 1,005 songs" is clearly an exaggeration (1 Kings 4:32); nevertheless, the Solomonic period, probably in part under Egyptian influence (note the use of hieratic ciphers in later Hebrew epigraphy),[184] no doubt saw the birth of an important stream of Hebrew literature connected with royal ideology.

Solomon and Archaeology

Archaeology also sheds some light on the activities of Solomon as a builder and on the contemporaneous transformation of Israelite society. According to William G. Dever, the tenth-century B.C.E. architectural remains "are not only the earliest evidence we possess of monumental architecture in ancient Israel but [the buildings] are among the most impressive."[185]

The Solomonic Temple[186] was probably completely destroyed by the Babylonians in 587 B.C.E. After the Israelites returned from the Babylonian Exile, a second temple was built. This Temple was rebuilt by Herod the Great in the first century B.C.E. and subsequently burnt by the Romans in 70 C.E. According to Ernest-Marie Laperrousaz, however, part of the Solomonic retaining wall of the Temple Mount can still be seen on the eastern side of the Temple Mount as it exists today.[187] (This particular part of the wall begins north of the so-called straight joint that can be found on the eastern wall of the Temple Mount, 105.5 feet north of its southeast corner.) According to others, the Temple and the palace could well have been at the place of the Haram ash-Sharif.[188] Both interpretations remain hypothetical.

The excavations in the City of David (a spur south of the present Temple Mount), led by Yigal Shiloh, have uncovered the huge Stepped-Stone Structure probably built to support an enlarged platform on top of the northern part of the City of David. According to William G. Dever, "the most reasonable conclusion is that the stepped stone structure represents the "Jebusite" city of the Hebrew Bible."[189] The platform may have supported a public building—perhaps a royal palace as proposed by Eilat Mazar; or the Stepped-Stone Structure may also be the famous *millo* mentioned in 1 Kings 9:15. However, this last inter-pretation is conjectural and the dating of this structure is disputed (13th/12th or tenth century),[190] as is the date of the monumental archae-ological fragments (tenth or ninth century) found north of the Ophel, which could be connected with Solomon's palace.[191]

GEZER GATE. In 1 Kings 9:15, we read that Solomon fortified "Hazor, Megiddo and Gezer." In this view from inside Gezer, we see six chambers (three on each side) of a monumental gate dated to the tenth century B.C.E. Nearly identical gates have been discovered at Hazor and Megiddo, and for decades, archaeologists have believed that all three gates were evidence of Solomon's handiwork—mighty public works constructed by a powerful central authority. More recent excavators at Megiddo, however, using the so-called "Low Chronology," have redated the gate at their site to the ninth century B.C.E., nearly 100 years after Solomon. In renewed excavations at Hazor, the excavator confirms the tenth-century date of that gate.

As noted, in 1 Kings 9:15–17 we are told that Solomon rebuilt three Canaanite cities that became part of his kingdom—Hazor, Megiddo, and Gezer. Major excavations have been and are still conducted at each of these three cities, and Yigael Yadin, followed by many others, tried to demonstrate that these three cities were probably rebuilt in about the middle of the tenth century (the time of Solomon).[192] Yadin and other archaeologists have based their conclusions on the presence of almost identical fortification plans at all three sites.[193]

Each city is surrounded by a casemate wall[194] and has a gateway with three chambers on each side (i.e., with four pairs of piers) of nearly the same dimensions. Furthermore, the ashlar stones (hewn stones) of these three gateways are dressed the same way. All these similarities in design can best be explained as having been the work of the same architect or school of architects during Solomon's reign.[195] These dates and this interpretation have been corroborated by later excavations at Gezer by William Dever[196] and at Hazor by Amnon Ben-Tor.[197] The dating of the gate of Megiddo, however, is still a matter of dispute.[198]

The stratigraphy of Megiddo at the beginning of Iron Age II (beginning in c. 1000 or 980 B.C.E.) is not at all clear. So, for instance, the structures identified by early American excavators as Solomonic stables[199] were redated by Yadin to be ninth century.[200] Furthermore, their interpretation as "stables" is still a matter of dispute.[201] However, Graham I. Davies has shown that a similar, earlier building at Megiddo might well have been the Solomonic stables.[202] Most archaeologists date level VA-IVB at Megiddo to the tenth century, corresponding to the Solomonic period.[203] This dating has been questioned by David Ussishkin, who argues that, at least for the "Solomonic" gate, this level must be dated to the ninth century;[204] moreover, G.J. Wightman[205] and Israel Finkelstein[206] proposed a general shift in the dating, lowering what have been thought of as tenth-century remains to the ninth century. This proposal, however, is beset with major problems and has been rejected by many excavators at other sites.[207] Actually Amihai Mazar and Israel Finkelstein have now somewhat nuanced their chronological interpretation,[208] and Finkelstein lately admitted early Iron IIA could start about "mid-tenth" century[209]: with this dating, there would not be any problem to attribute the (re)building of Gezer, Megiddo, and Hazor to Solomon. One can only hope that the current excavations at Megiddo will clarify the dating of the relevant levels from that important site.

Another town mentioned in 1 Kings 9:18 is "Tamar in the wilderness," which has been identified with 'En Hazeva. Excavations led by Rudolph Cohen and Yigal Yisrael at this site have revealed a tenth-century level (Stratum VI), which seems to match with Solomonic building.[210]

More generally, many archaeological sites in ancient Israel seem to have been built or rebuilt about the middle of the tenth century.[211] These sites include new cities as well as fortresses. Indeed, a network of early Iron Age fortresses in the Negev may be connected with Solomon's reign.[212] Most of them were probably later destroyed by Pharaoh Shishak's military expedition to Palestine in about 925 B.C.E.[213]

Excavations at Khirbet en-Nahas in the Wadi Feinan area of Jordan, south of the Dead Sea, revealed "the largest Iron Age copper-smelting site in the southern Levant."[214] Even though the precise dates of this site had been debated,[215] thanks to C14 dating, it is clear that this important copper-smelting site was mainly in use in the tenth and ninth centuries.[216] Furthermore, farther south, there was also some tenth-century activity at Timna.[217] These 'Aravah mines could well be the source of the copper used to cast the many bronze objects decorating Solomon's Temple (1 Kings 7:13–47). Actually, one may compare the En Hazeva, Khirbet en Nahas, and Khirbet el-Kheleifeh tenth-century fortresses.[218] This possible Solomonic southward influence seems to fit in the fact that Solomon was under Egyptian influence.

From the point of view of archaeology, the general picture of ancient Israel in the mid-tenth century seems to be that of a transitional society. Israelite areas were inhabited not only by farmers and stockbreeders in villages but also, beginning in the tenth century, by some craftsmen, merchants, and functionaries who served in the army and in the government administration and lived in royal fortified cities (many of these having been built upon ancient Canaanite cities). Archaeology attests to the beginning of a process of reurbanization typical of an early state.[219] The beginning of this social change, from a tribal society to an early state under a central administration, probably accounts for the appearance of public buildings in the new fortified cities—governors' palaces, storehouses, and administrative buildings.[220] At about this time, we also begin to find many small precious objects. As Yohanan Aharoni notes, "The change in material culture during the tenth century is discernible not only in luxury items but also especially in ceramics" which are of a higher quality.[221] (See the Learn More sidebar, "Why Do We Date David and Solomon to the Tenth Century?" on p. 95.) The economic growth and development of new cities was probably connected with a population boom, natural in a period of peace and prosperity. In the area inhabited by Israel, the population could well have doubled in the century that extended from the beginning of Saul's reign to the end of Solomon's.[222] By this time, the sedentary population of the Judahite hills (not including the Shephelah and the Negev) made up probably only 3 percent of the total population of the country.[223]

Thus, though several legends developed later on, it is possible to draw the main points of historical Solomon: He was not at the head of an empire but only of Judah and Israel. He did not wage war, but he was a builder and initiated administration. His reign was apparently successful from the economical point of view because it was peaceful under the shadow of Egypt.

Social and Political Tensions

The beginning of the transformation of Israelite society into an early state and the burden of the new state's administrative structures[224] were resisted by many levels of Israelite society.[225] This was especially so among the "house of Israel" (the northern tribes), which wanted to retain its own religious and political traditions. Social tensions were also produced by the mixing of the populations in Solomon's military conscription and the forced levy (the *corvée*). All this certainly served to sharpen the antagonisms between Israel and Judah.[226] No doubt, members of the house of Israel resented the Judahites, who probably held the better positions in the civil government and in the military. Solomon's death and the political errors of his successor soon revealed the unstable base on which he and David had set their achievements and probably delayed the further evolution of Israelite and Judahite society into a well-organized national state. Moreover, that evolution would now occur in two separate states.

5

Israel and Judah
in Iron Age II

MELODY D. KNOWLES*

UPON THE DEATH OF SOLOMON (C. 930 B.C.E.), the nation that his
father, King David, established broke into two kingdoms. Over the
next several centuries, Israel and Judah gained in population and prosperity (although unevenly) as various world powers rose and declined
in the region. Ultimately, Israel fell to the Assyrians, in 701 B.C.E., and
Judah was conquered by the Babylonians, in 586 B.C.E.

SOURCES OF EVIDENCE FOR
RECONSTRUCTING THE PERIOD

Iron Age II in the Archaeological Record

Although the relative chronology of the Levant in the Iron Age is
well established, the absolute dates of the archaeologically obtained
datasets are debated. Even though there is general agreement as
to the sequence of the ceramic typology and the identification

* This chapter has been rewritten and updated from the version contributed by
Siegfried H. Horn and P. Kyle McCarter Jr. to the third edition (Washington,
DC: BAS, 2011).

and sequence of significant strata at major sites, such as Megiddo in the north and Lachish in the south, the exact dates assigned to the various strata and sequences are not universally accepted. This means that the proposed dates for the beginning and end of Iron IIA vary considerably. This is particularly significant for the period of the Divided Monarchy, because the proposed dates for Iron IIA concern the tenth–ninth centuries B.C.E.

According to conventional analysis, Iron IIA should be dated between 1000 and 925 B.C.E. (i.e., mostly during the time of the United Monarchy), but others have argued that it should be lowered to between 930/920 and the second half of the ninth century. This gap in dating is currently narrowing somewhat, thanks to evidence emerging not only from new analysis of stratigraphy and ceramic typology but also from radio-carbon dating. Amihai Mazar has argued recently that Iron IIA should be dated to 980–830, while Finkelstein and Piasetzky prefer a time frame between early second half of the tenth century and 800.[1]

The dates for the later periods are less contested, with Iron IIB ending between the fall of Samaria and the invasion of Sennacherib, that is, 720–701.

Within these time frames, the relevant archaeological evidence is similar to that used to reconstruct both earlier and later periods. Human-made artifacts and natural materials systematically recovered from controlled excavations shape our knowledge of the past. Domestic architecture, pottery assemblages relating to food storage and management, and burial remains give us a window into the structures and assumptions about family units as well as diet and economic patterns. Public buildings (for administration as well as worship), official texts, and destruction layers point to the function and role of the state on the local, national, and international level. Texts recovered from secure archaeological contexts also can provide invaluable insights in the period.

At any one archaeological site, all of this sometimes-complicated information must be read together for a full picture of life in any one period; it also must be analyzed in the context of other sites within the region to show larger regional patterns.[2]

The Divided Monarchy in the Biblical Texts

Like the archaeological record, the biblical evidence describing this period is not straightforward. The most extensive narratives come from 2 Kings and 1–2 Chronicles—both written centuries after the events they describe. Although it incorporates older materials and traditions, this literary corpus is also influenced by the current concerns of the authors and editors, as well as their artistic aim and skills.

The books of Kings' Deuteronomistic perspective, labeled as such by our modern scholarship, retells Israel's history based on religious ideas preserved in the Book of Deuteronomy: YHWH has chosen to enter into a covenant with Israel, and, in response, the people obey the divine law in order that they might flourish in the land. The theory is that the Deuteronomistic historian authored and edited the Deuteronomistic history, a text found in the biblical books of Deuteronomy, Joshua, Judges, 1–2 Samuel, 1–2 Kings, and parts of Jeremiah. The storyline stretches from the last days of Moses through the settlement of the land, the rise of the monarchical state, and the fall of both the northern Kingdom of Israel and the southern Kingdom of Judah. It may be that the work was put together during the reign of King Josiah of Judah (r. 640–606), but some argue that it is not earlier than Exilic, post-Exilic, or even Hellenistic.[3] In the account of the Deuteronomistic historian, the nation's success or failure is largely tied to the keeping of God's law, especially the centralization of worship in Jerusalem and the right treatment of society's weakest members.[4]

The other major biblical retelling of this period is found in the Book of 1–2 Chronicles. In comparison to the Deuteronomistic history, Chronicles is later and covers a longer swath of history: writing in the late Persian or Hellenistic periods, the author retells the story of the nation from Adam through the end of the Exile in Babylon. There is also a slightly different geographical focus: when Judah and Israel break up into two kingdoms, the author keeps the account much more focused on the story of the southern, Judean state and its kings. Yet the book also borrows large amounts of text from the Deuteronomistic history, and also retains some of its emphases, such as the importance of centralizing worship in Jerusalem.[5]

Like the archaeological data, the biblical texts only give partial information and can't be interpreted straightforwardly. And interpreting the two types of sources together is a nuanced project. The reader of the biblical texts must always keep in mind that the narratives are products of later periods with their own ideological programs, and that the retellings preserve accounts of past events even as they also alter them. Not only are the texts perspectival, they are also incomplete when it comes to reconstructing historical periods. Both Kings and Chronicles give the dates of the reigns of the various kings along with a judgment on their maintenance of a centralized cult, but we don't hear much about agricultural innovation, social organization, food-ways, or trade patterns. When trying to evaluate the literary texts and the archaeological record together, historians must be sensitive to the tendency to privilege the concerns of the Bible over archaeological data. Given this situation, the present chapter will attempt to carefully distinguish between the types of evidence being used to reconstruct this period, so that readers can better see the interpretive moves and come to their own conclusions.

THE EARLY YEARS

The Schism at the Death of Solomon

According to the biblical text, King Solomon was succeeded by his son Rehoboam (c. 930–913) as king over Judah (1 Kings 11:43; 2 Chronicles 9:31; 1 Kings 14:21; and 2 Chronicles 12:13, which also identifies his mother as Naamah from Ammon). The new monarch then traveled north to Shechem to lay claim to the throne of Israel as well. At least from Rehoboam's point of view, the visit was not a success, for it was at this point that he lost more than half of his father's and his grand-father's kingdom. When the gathered Israelites asked the new king whether he would lighten the workload that Solomon had demanded, Rehoboam replied that he would increase it. In response, the Israelites refused to proclaim him as their king. The Israelites then killed the head of Rehoboam's workforce, and the king of Judah retreated to his capital city, Jerusalem, to prepare for war (1 Kings 12:1–21; 2 Chronicles 10:1–11:1). It may be that the request for less work relates to the tax and/or labor burden required to support Solomon's building projects and palace maintenance described in 1 Kings 4:7–28. However, it is only the intensity of the workload and not its purpose that is named by the people in their reported wager to Rehoboam: "Your father made our load very hard for us. If you will lessen the demands your father made of us and lighten the heavy workload he demanded from us, then we will serve you" (1 Kings 12:4).

THE BUBASTITE PORTAL. In the fifth year of the reign of Rehoboam, "King Shishak of Egypt…took the fortified cities of Judah and came as far as Jerusalem" (2 Chronicles 12:2–4). Scenes depicting the military exploits of Pharaoh Sheshonq I (c. 945–924 B.C.E.)—biblical Shishak—decorate a doorway in the forecourt of the Great Temple of Amun at Karnak, in Thebes.

The inclusion of such details into the account of Rehoboam's loss of the north lend the narrative a particularly dramatic tone, and the literary foreshadowing also adds tension. Before Solomon died, the biblical account relates that Jeroboam, handpicked by Solomon to head a workforce, was confronted by the prophet Ahijah and given ten pieces of fabric as a sign that God would make him king over the ten tribes of Israel. When Solomon heard the news, Jeroboam fled to the court of Pharaoh Sheshonq in Egypt (1 Kings 11:26–40). Given this background, the mention that Jeroboam had returned and was part of the company of Israel meeting up with Rehoboam in Shechem sets a menacing tone, as does Rehoboam's request that he have three days to consider the people's appeal for a lessened workload. Additional direct quotations from the various parties add vividness to the account, as does the coarse euphemism used by the king's younger advisors when they coach Rehoboam's reply in reference to his virility: "my little finger [i.e., penis] is thicker than my father's waist!" (1 Kings 12:10). The final reply of the people of Israel as they defied Rehoboam's right to rule over their ten tribes is particularly striking:

> What share do we have in David?
> We have no inheritance in the son of Jesse.
> To your tents, O Israel!
> Look now to your own house, O David.
> (1 KINGS 12:16)

The break-up of David's kingdom is certainly a significant moment in the arc of national history, and this fact alone might account for the lengthy and detailed narrative. But the interpreter must consider whether the literary details themselves promoted the preservation of this particular account. That is, the drama of the storyteller's art made the narrative memorable, but whether the literary project is also accurate in all of the details is a different question.

In line with the interpretive stance of the larger text of Kings and Chronicles, the biblical narrative is clear that Rehoboam's loss of the north is due to the idolatry of his father. When Jeroboam is given the ten pieces of fabric to signal the coming schism, the prophet relates God's rationale: "This is because [Solomon] has forsaken me, and worshipped Astarte the goddess of the Sidonians, Chemosh the god of Moab, and Milcom the god of the Ammonites, and has not walked in my ways" (1 Kings 11:33; cf. 2 Chronicles 10:15). This same cause is given when Rehoboam attempted to reclaim the kingdom through military means. As he was assembling his troops in Jerusalem, the king received the following message from a man of God: "You shall not go up or fight against your kindred the people of Israel...for this thing is from me" (1 Kings 12:24; 2 Chronicles 11:4).

Sheshonq's Invasion

After the separation of Israel and Judah, Pharaoh Sheshonq I led a large Egyptian army across the Sinai Peninsula into Canaan. Sheshonq was a Libyan nobleman who founded the 22nd Egyptian dynasty and ruled in c. 945–924 B.C.E. Earlier, Pharaoh Siamun (r. 978–959) made common cause with Israel and Judah against the Philistines, but now (under the new ruler) Egypt turned its military might against its former allies in Canaan. Control over this region meant control over the trade routes along the coastal highway as well as the corridor running from Jezreel to Beth Shean. It also gave access to the Levantine copper industry at such sites as Khirbat en-Nahas in the Wadi Feinan area.[6]

In the biblical text, Sheshonq is known as Shishak, and it was in his court that Jeroboam found refuge when Solomon was seeking to kill him (1 Kings 11:40). It may be that Sheshonq's hospitality stemmed from his interests in thwarting the growing power of Solomon in Canaan. Once Solomon's kingdom was divided and Jeroboam returned to lead Israel, Sheshonq mobilized his armies and invaded in the fifth year of Jeroboam's rule.

A record of the invasion is inscribed on the Bubastite Portal, which is a large public gate leading to the Amun temple in Karnak in Thebes (modern Luxor), named after Sheshonq's hometown of Bubastis in the eastern Nile Delta. Inscribed onto the monumental structure, a 20-foot image of Sheshonq smites his enemies as the god Amun presents the king with rows and rows of bound prisoners. Below their necks are oval name-rings inscribed with names of the many places that Sheshonq conquered. The toponyms include sites north of Jerusalem, such as Gibeon, Rehov, Beth Shean, and Megiddo, as well as places in the southern Negev, such as Beersheba and Arad.[7]

Sheshonq's military campaign seems also to have left its mark in the archaeological record. There are possibly contemporaneous destruction layers throughout Judah and Israel, including at Tell el-Hammah, Tel Rehov, Beth Shean, Tel ʻAmal, and Taanach. A fragment of an inscription found at Megiddo has cartouches of Sheshonq and was presumably part of a victory stela set up to celebrate the pharaoh's conquest of the city and signaling the northern reach of his armies.[8]

A key question relates to the fate of Jerusalem during the Egyptian campaign. The biblical accounts give the impression that the incursion was solely directed at Jerusalem (1 Kings 14:25), or at Jerusalem and the fortified cities of Judah (2 Chronicles 12:4). No other city is named in either 1 Kings or 2 Chronicles, and the accounts read as if Sheshonq, who had given asylum to Jeroboam when he was a refugee, was now acting on his behalf in his ongoing conflict with Rehoboam of Judah (1 Kings 14:30; 2 Chronicles 12:15b). But in the biblical text Sheshonq didn't destroy the city. After setting out with a large army, the pharaoh only took treasures from the Jerusalem Temple and the palace and left (1 Kings 14:25–26).

Curiously, the Bubastite Portal doesn't name Jerusalem among the conquered sites. It may be that the city's name is listed in one of the areas of the inscription now obscured. Most likely, especially when considering other triumphal reliefs from Egypt, the text doesn't celebrate one particular military campaign, but rather depicts the pharaoh as victorious over the whole world. Given Egypt's interests in weakening the neighboring states, it seems likely that Egyptians did fight against Judah as well as its capital city.[9]

The Reigns of Rehoboam and Jeroboam

Having begun his reign in Shechem, Jeroboam soon moved his base of operations to Penuel, a town in Gilead that he is said to have fortified (1 Kings 12:25). Although some have speculated that Jeroboam withdrew to the Transjordan to seek refuge at the time of Sheshonq's incursion, the biblical narrative provides no reasons for the move. Nor is there any explanation why he eventually returned west and established a capital at Tirzah, as is implied by 1 Kings 14:17. In any case, Tirzah (now identified with the extensive tenth-century ruins at Tell el-Far'ah northeast of Shechem) was the capital of Israel during the reigns of Jeroboam's successors until the sixth year of Omri when Samaria was founded (1 Kings 16:23).

The paucity of information about Jeroboam's political headquarters in the biblical account contrasts sharply with the extended report on the national religious centers he established near the northern border at Dan and Bethel (1 Kings 12:26–33; see also 1 Kings 13:1–14:18), which emphasizes both the motivation and consequences of the building program.[10] According to the account, the king installed calves of gold at both sites, houses on the high places, different priests and a festival calendar (1 Kings 12:26–33). The purpose of this work was to construct national cult sites to replace Jerusalem. With Dan and Bethel set up, the people of Israel would not need to travel to Jerusalem in the rival realm of Rehoboam.[11]

But from the point of view of the Deuteronomist, Jeroboam's work was a fundamental breach of religious law and a flaunting of the divine will—it was Jerusalem, after all, that was foretold by Moses to be "the place that the Lord your God will choose" as the one acceptable place of sacrifice (Deuteronomy 12:13–14). The long-term consequences are foreshadowed in the fate of Jeroboam's son and heir apparent, who suffers an early death (1 Kings 14:17–18). Even though the king is eventually succeeded by another son, Nadab (1 Kings 14:20), "the sin of Jeroboam" (as the Deuteronomist calls it), was perpetuated by his successors and eventually causes the fall of the northern kingdom and the exile of its people (2 Kings 17:21–23).

Regardless of the ideological biases of the biblical account, Jeroboam's acts were not contrary to tradition. In terms of geography, Jerusalem held no special claim to religious authority, being a Canaanite enclave conquered by David and held by the kings of the southern kingdom. By contrast, Bethel was an ancient Yahwistic sanctuary, strongly associated with Israel's patriarchs (Genesis 12:8; 28:10–22), and Dan was also a premonarchic center of Yahwism (Judges 17–18). Although condemned in some biblical texts, there is also considerable evidence to suggest that bull iconography for God was employed in Israel from the earliest days. A small bronze bull figurine was found at a probable 12th-century B.C.E. cultic site in the heart of the region that was then being settled by Israelites in the hill country of Samaria.[12] The depiction of "Yahweh of Samaria" in bovine form on a pithos from Kuntillet 'Ajrud shows that bull iconography was still a viable form of religious expression at the beginning of the eighth century B.C.E.[13] Hosea's diatribes against "the calf of Samaria" and "the calf of Beth-aven" (Hosea 8:5–6; 10:5) show that it was still a part of the northern cult later in the eighth century B.C.E.

Rehoboam's own royal enclosure and cult area in Jerusalem is not accessible archaeologically, and not much can be clearly determined about the early emergence of Judah as a state. The defense system of fortified cities erected by Rehoboam throughout Judah mentioned

in 2 Chronicles 11:5–12 may reflect reality—Lachish Stratum IV has
a six-chambered gate and brick wall—or may reflect the later work
of Hezekiah.[14] Additionally, an inscription found at Tell Dan (c. 840
B.C.E.) refers to "the House of David," which indicates that the
continuing royal line was known in later periods.[15] It seems likely that
the southern kingdom under Rehoboam was small and relatively weak.

The Wars of the Early Divided Monarchy

The early years of the Divided Monarchy were characterized by almost
constant warfare between Israel and Judah. When Rehoboam died
after a reign of some 17 years (1 Kings 14:21), he was succeeded by his
short-lived son, Abijam (c. 913–911 B.C.E.; known as Abijah in the Book
of Chronicles), about whom little is said except that he was victorious
over Jeroboam in a major battle fought on the southern boundary of
Ephraim (2 Chronicles 13:3–20; cf. 1 Kings 15:7).

Jeroboam died a few years later, and his son Nadab (c. 908–907
B.C.E.), after only a couple of years' rule, was assassinated by Baasha
son of Ahijah, a member of the tribe of Issachar and one of Nadab's
senior officers (1 Kings 15:25–31). The coup took place during an
Israelite siege of the Philistine-controlled fortress of Gibbethon. This
may be taken as an indication of ongoing border disputes between
Israel and Philistia in this period, especially in view of the fact that
Gibbethon (usually identified with Tell el-Malat, just west of Gezer)
was under Israelite siege again a generation later when Baasha's son
was unseated in another military coup (1 Kings 16:8–10). Baasha, having
quickly secured his position by a massacre of the remaining members
of the family of Jeroboam (1 Kings 15:29), was able to stabilize the situation and establish himself in Tirzah as the new king of Israel. He
ruled for a substantial number of years (c. 907–884), though we are
told in 1 Kings 15:16 that his reign was troubled by constant warfare
with Judah, which was now ruled by the even more long-lived Asa (c.
911–870), Rehoboam's grandson.

At some point in the long reigns of these two kings (Baasha in
the north and Asa in the south)—the year is uncertain and disputed—
a series of events drew Damascus into the hostilities between Israel
and Judah (1 Kings 15:17–22; 2 Chronicles 16:1–6). Baasha's forces had
captured and fortified the border fortress of Ramah (modern er-Ram)

and imposed an embargo on Jerusalem, a few miles to the south. Asa sought the help of Ben-hadad, the king of Damascus.[16]

Appealing to a former or still-existing treaty between Jerusalem and Damascus, Asa asked Ben-hadad to invade Israel. He enticed the Aramean king with a large gift of silver and gold collected from the Jerusalem Temple and his own royal palace. Although Ben-hadad seems also to have had a treaty with Baasha (1 Kings 15:19), he accepted Asa's invitation and sent an Aramean army south to ravage Israelite cities in the region north of the Sea of Galilee. Thus, Asa's strategy was successful, and Baasha was forced to withdraw from Ramah and lift the embargo. The Israelite withdrawal gave Asa the opportunity to strengthen the northern border of Judah. According to 1 Kings 15:22, the Judahites took the building materials with which the Israelites had fortified Ramah, transported them to Geba and Mizpah,[17] and fortified those places, thus shoring up the Judahite frontier against Israel.

Although the silver and gold with which Asa bribed Ben-hadad might have been enough to entice him into action, it is also clear that the region he attacked had strategic importance to Damascus. The cities listed in 1 Kings 15:20 as having been conquered by Ben-hadad ("Ijon, Dan, Abel-beth-maacah") lie at the northern extreme of Israelite territory, on or beneath the western slope of Mt. Hermon in the direction of the watershed of the Litani River.

Control of this region provided Damascus with passage into the river valley and thus to the Phoenician port city of Tyre, situated only 6 miles south of the mouth of the Litani. Having access to Tyre without having to negotiate with Israelite intermediaries was a major advantage for the merchants of Damascus in the ongoing struggle for control of the important trade routes of northern Palestine.

Baasha's son and successor, Elah (r. c. 884–883 B.C.E.), succumbed to a coup early in his reign (1 Kings 16:8–20). He was assassinated in his palace at Tirzah while his army, commanded by Omri, was away from the capital besieging the Philistine city of Gibbethon. The assassin, a chariot officer named Zimri, quickly massacred the rest of Baasha's family—as Baasha himself had done to the family of Jeroboam. When word reached Gibbethon, however, the Israelite army proclaimed Omri king and set out for Tirzah. Zimri, after only a week's rule, took his own life. This was followed by a brief struggle for the crown, when

Omri's followers were challenged by supporters of a certain Tibni son of Ginath (1 Kings 16:21–22). Ultimately, Omri's supporters prevailed and he became king of Israel in Tirzah.

The pattern of royal assassinations in the early history of the northern kingdom creates an impression of political turmoil in Israel that contrasts with the stability that the Davidic dynasty gave Judah. Neither Jeroboam nor Baasha was able to establish a dynasty, since in each case the son and successor was removed in a coup early in his reign. Some have interpreted this as indicating that the northern kingdom had embraced a tradition of "charismatic" kingship, according to which leaders were expected to arise in times of crisis, receiving divine designation and popular acclamation (similar to the stories of the "judges," who ruled in the premonarchical period, or King Saul, who was subsequently rejected by the prophet Samuel, acting on behalf of Yahweh). Thus Jeroboam is designated and rejected as king by Ahijah the Shilonite (1 Kings 11:29–39; 14:6–16; see also 1 Kings 15:29), and Baasha is designated and rejected by Jehu son of Hanani (1 Kings 16:1–4, 12). Omri does succeed in establishing his dynasty, but its rule is prophetically condemned and, during the reign of Ahab, formally rejected by Elijah (1 Kings 21:20–24). It is unclear whether this pattern is a literary shaping years after the actual events took place or an indication of a distinctly northern ideal of kingship that differed from the dynastic principle, which became entrenched early in Judah.

THE DYNASTY OF OMRI

King Omri and the Restoration of Israel as a Trading Power

Although the biblical account of Omri's reign is cryptic (1 Kings 16:23–28), the king ushers in a season that is well attested in extrabiblical texts and in which Israel came to be known in the records of the neo-Assyrian Empire as *māt Bit-Ḫmri*, "the (land of) the House of Omri." Even though Omri ruled for only 12 years (c. 883–872), he accomplished a great deal: he founded a dynasty, built Israel into an important trading nation, and ushered in a period in which the nation would build its own internal infrastructure and extend and stabilize its boundaries. The biblical account, however, mentions only one of his accomplishments: the founding of Samaria.

Israel's Kings

The United Monarchy

Saul   c. 1030?–1009 B.C.E.
David   c. 1009/1001–969 B.C.E.
Solomon   c. 970/969–931 B.C.E.

The Divided Monarchy

Kingdom of Judah c. 930–587/6 B.C.E.		Kingdom of Israel c. 930–722 B.C.E.	
Rehoboam	c. 930–913	Jeroboam I	c. 930–908
Abijam (Abijah)	c. 913–911	Nadab	c. 908–907
Asa	c. 911–870	Baasha	c. 907–884
		Elah	c. 884–883
		Zimri	c. 883
		Omri	c. 883–872
Jehoshaphat	c. 870–846	Ahab	c. 872–851
		Ahaziah	c. 851–850
Jehoram	c. 846–841	Joram	c. 850–841
Ahaziah	c. 841	Jehu	c. 841–818
Athaliah	c. 841–835		
Jehoash	c. 835–801	Jehoahaz	c. 818–802
Amaziah	c. 801–783	Joash	c. 802–787
Azariah (Uzziah)	c. 783–732	Jeroboam II	c. 787–748
		Zechariah	748–747
		Shallum	747
Jotham	750–735	Menahem	747–738
		Pekahiah	738–737
Ahaz	735–727	Pekah	737–732
		Hoshea	732–724
Hezekiah	727–697		
Manasseh	697–642		
Amon	642–640		
Josiah	640–609		
Jehoahaz	609		
Jehoiakim	609–598		
Jehoiachin	598–597		
Zedekiah	597–586		

Omri's choice of Tirzah for the first years of his reign provided easy communication with the Jordan Valley via the Wadi Far'ah. (This may have been of paramount importance when Jeroboam moved the capital there from Transjordanian Penuel.) Otherwise, Tirzah was isolated, surrounded by hills that made access to the principal international trade routes difficult. After six years, Omri founded his royal residence at Samaria, northwest of Shechem, a choice that favored communication and trade.[18]

The site, a strategically located and easily defended summit in a fertile part of the Ephraimite highlands, overlooked one of the main roads into the hills from the coastal highway and the Mediterranean, about 25 miles to the west. Perhaps most importantly, the location permitted extensive contact with Phoenicia. In many respects, the most salient characteristic of the Omride dynasty was its close relationship with Tyre.[19]

Omri entered into amicable relations with King Ittobaal of Tyre (the biblical Ethbaal) and secured the alliance by marrying his son Ahab to Ittobaal's daughter Jezebel.[20] This couple was reviled by the biblical writers for being corrupt and promoting the worship of a foreign god. Nevertheless, their marriage cemented a diplomatic and commercial relationship with the prosperous mercantile cities of the Mediterranean coast that brought substantial wealth to the landlocked cities of Israel. Phoenicia gained a passage through the central hill country into the Transjordan, where caravans arrived from the south transporting luxury items (cf. Numbers 20:17; 21:22). The caravans were a source of immense wealth, and it was in the interest of Tyre and the other Phoenician ports to divert them west before they reached Damascus. The topography of the region determined the best route for this. It diverged from the King's Highway somewhere near Ramoth-gilead (possibly Tell er-Ramith, near the modern border of Jordan and Syria), descended through the Wadi Yabis into the Jordan Valley, continued on the other side through the Beth-Shean and Jezreel Valleys, and came out on the Plain of Akko with Tyre and the other Phoenician ports straight ahead.

Phoenician expansion eastward along this route in the tenth and ninth centuries B.C.E. can be seen in the archaeological record. A substantial amount of imported Phoenician pottery has been found at northern Israelite sites during this time. In addition, Israelite architecture shows the use of building materials imported from Phoenicia as well as Phoenician building techniques, such as ashlar masonry and ornamented Proto-Aeolic capitals.[21] Elegant ivories—Phoenician in style and probably in manufacture—have been found at a number of Israelite and Judahite sites of the tenth to eighth centuries.[22] Finally, near the Gihon spring in Jerusalem, fish bones were found that indicate trade from Phoenician harbors, such as Athlit or Dor, and a bulla depicting a Phoenician ship.[23]

This commercial arrangement with Phoenicia brought Israel into conflict with its immediate neighbor to the north, the Aramean state of Damascus. Though we have no biblical or extrabiblical report of Omri's foreign wars, there are indirect indications that he might have successfully pursued the struggle against Damascus begun in the reign of Baasha, when much of the northern Galilee fell to the depredations of Ben-hadad son of Tabrimmon. Excavations at such sites as Dan and Hazor, where archaeologists have found destruction levels that one could associate with Ben-hadad's raid, indicate that those cities were rebuilt quickly, often to a higher standard and with the Phoenician-influenced building techniques noted above.[24] This restoration might correspond to the rise of Omri, when the region was returned to Israelite control. Eventually, however, the conflict between Samaria and Damascus ended with the two states making common cause against the Assyrian threat, as explained below.

The Reign of Ahab

Ahab succeeded Omri as king and ruled 22 years in Samaria (872–851 B.C.E.). His reign continued the prosperous period for the northern kingdom begun by his father. By the middle of the ninth century B.C.E., Israel had an architecturally impressive capital city (Samaria), additional major cities (Dan, Hazor, Kinneret, Megiddo, Beth Shean, Tell Rehov, and Tell en-Nasbeh), as well as minor settlements in the Galilee and Samaria hills.[25]

Despite the biblical account of Ahab's reign being quite extensive (1 Kings 16:29–22:40), it is problematic for historical reconstruction due to its ideological shaping. The Deuteronomist is suspicious of kingship as an institution, because he saw the involvement of kings in foreign alliances lead to the worship of foreign gods and the royal administrative apparatus mistreat the poor. Thus, although Ahab's marriage to Jezebel of Tyre cemented a key political alliance, it is viewed negatively in stories like that of Naboth's vineyard (1 Kings 21) and the struggles with the prophet Elijah. In fact, there is little question that Yahweh was recognized in Samaria as the national God of Israel. Ahab's allegiance to Yahweh is demonstrated by the fact that the three of his children whose names we know all had Yahwistic names—two sons, Joram and Ahaziah, both of whom eventually became king, and one daughter, Athaliah, who became queen of Judah. But to show Yahweh's displeasure on Ahab's reign, the author also creatively adapts the historical narrative. There are only a few allusions to Ahab's substantial building projects and little reliable information about his foreign relations. For example, the accounts of Ahab's wars in 1 Kings 20 and 22:1–38 seem more likely to have come from a later era when Israel was weaker and were then placed in Ahab's reign so that Israel's king would be seen to suffer.[26] Most striking, there is no reference at all to Ahab's participation in the great anti-Assyrian coalition of 853 B.C.E. (see below), despite the major role he is known to have played, as shown by the Assyrian records.

Nevertheless, it is possible to give a general description of Ahab's reign based on a critical reading of the biblical text and drawing heavily on extrabiblical documents and the archaeological record of the period. As already noted, the first half of the ninth century is characterized archaeologically by extensive building projects throughout Israel. While these are likely to have begun during Omri's reign, it seems safe to assume that his son Ahab brought them to completion. This is true in particular of the Samaria acropolis, where excavations have shown the ninth-century royal palace to have been an architectural achievement of the highest order, with its finely dressed header-and-stretcher ashlar masonry, Proto-Aeolic capitals, and ivories.[27] This is the palace described in the summary of Ahab's reign in 1 Kings 22:39 as "the ivory house that he built." The same passage refers to "all the cities that he built" throughout Israel, and monumental structures have been found at sites like Dan,[28] Hazor,[29] Megiddo,[30] Jezreel (where the Omrides seem to have maintained a royal estate and/or a military base),[31] and many others.

Ahab also perpetuated the essentials of Omri's foreign policy. Since his queen was the Tyrian princess Jezebel, the alliance with Phoenicia remained strong, and Israel continued to benefit from the relationship. In the ongoing conflict with the Aramean kingdom of Damascus, including the contest for control of the east-west trade routes to the Mediterranean port cities, Israel probably maintained ascendancy during most of Ahab's reign. In his later years, however, he found it expedient to enter into a defensive alliance with King Hadadezer of Damascus to counter the threat posed by Assyria, a situation reviewed below.

During the dynasty of Omri, Israel seems generally to have held sway over Judah. Jehoshaphat (r. 870–846), who had succeeded his father, Asa, as king of Judah early in Ahab's reign, is said in 1 Kings 22:44 to have "made peace with the king of Israel." We learn in 2 Kings 8:26 that this peace was sealed by the marriage of Ahab's daughter Athaliah to Jehoshaphat's son Jehoram.

Omri and Ahab also exercised control east of the Jordan, at least in Gilead and as far south as the region north of the Arnon River, which was disputed with Moab. According to 2 Kings 3:4–5, King Mesha of Moab brought tribute during the reigns of Omri and Ahab, then rebelled when Ahab died.

A major inscription of Mesha, found at Dhiban (about 20 miles south of Amman)—ancient Dibon and Mesha's capital—indicates that "the land of Medeba" (the region surrounding modern Madaba, about 18 miles southwest of Amman) was under Israelite sway "during [Omri's] days and half the days of his son," which seems to indicate that the revolt began earlier than the time of Ahab's death.[32] A reasonable interpretation would be to assume that Ahab maintained firm control of central Transjordan until at least the latter part of his reign, when his participation with Damascus in the coalition against Assyria diverted his attention to the north. As explained below, a final, unsuccessful attempt to reimpose Israelite control over Moab was made by a later Omride, Joram (c. 850–841).

Assyrian King Shalmaneser III and the Rise of Imperial Assyria

After a long period of weakness at the beginning of the first millennium B.C.E., the upper Mesopotamian kingdom of Assyria, with its capitals on the east bank of the Tigris at Calah and Nineveh, arose to become a leading factor in the history of the Near East during the ninth to seventh centuries B.C.E.[33] The Assyrian kings were motivated first by a desire to control the trade routes through northern Syria into the mineral-rich mountain country of Anatolia, but eventually their ambition spread south into the middle Orontes region, southern Syria and even Palestine. By the time Ahab ascended the throne, in 872 B.C.E., it was already clear that the growing power of Assyria was a threat that would have to be reckoned with.

MESHA STELA. Erected by Mesha, king of Moab in the mid-ninth century B.C.E., this black basalt stela stands about 40 inches high and 24 inches wide. The inscription in Moabite, which is closely related to Hebrew, expresses Mesha's gratitude to his god Chemosh for delivering the Moabites from Israelite rule. Mesha claims he conquered Israelite territory east of the Jordan and humiliated the tribe of Gad. Among the towns mentioned is Dhiban (biblical Dibon), the site, about 20 miles south of Amman, where the stela was discovered. The Book of Kings also tells of a ninth-century Moabite rebellion; but the Bible and the stela may or may not refer to the same conflict. Each paints a different outcome from the other. André Lemaire and others have argued that the inscription, which is poorly preserved in places, contains one of the earliest extrabiblical references to "the House of David," that is, the dynasty of David (see the detail). Another reference to "the House of David" has been identified in the nearly contemporaneous Tel Dan Stela (see plate 7).

When Shalmaneser III (r. 859–824), who established a pattern of annual military campaigns into the neighboring territories, conquered the north Syrian state of Bit Adini, most of the states of northern Syria regularly paid tribute to Assyria. Quickly, however, a new anti-Assyrian coalition was formed by states farther to the south, who now felt threatened by Shalmaneser's relentless campaigns. The new alliance extended from Arvad, Byblos, and other Mediterranean coastal cities as far south as Ammon in Transjordan and even Arabia. The ringleader of the coalition—and the target of Shalmaneser's retaliation—was Irhulena of Hamath, ruler of a state situated in the rich agricultural lands of the middle Orontes region. Among the 12 kings allied with Irhulena, the most important were Hadadezer of Damascus and Ahab of Israel. So began Samaria's conflict with the empire that would eventually destroy it.

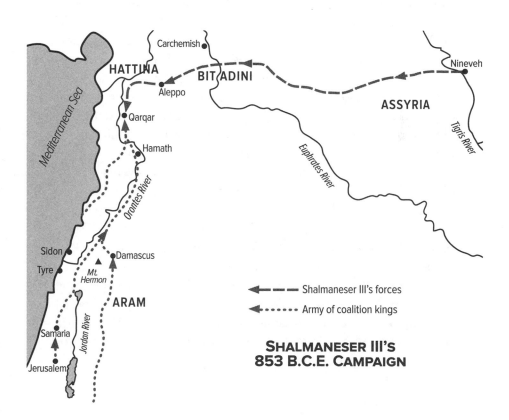

Shalmaneser III's forces
Army of coalition kings

**SHALMANESER III'S
853 B.C.E. CAMPAIGN**

The showdown began during Shalmaneser's sixth-year campaign (853), when the Assyrian army marched into central Syria for the first time, subduing three of Irhulena's towns and capturing the fortress of Qarqar (probably Tell Qarqur in the northern Gab or Orontes Valley, northwest of modern Hama). After the fall of Qarqar, the Assyrian army was confronted by the full forces of the coalition. According to Shalmaneser's own records in a text called the Kurkh Monolith, the main contributors to the opposition force were Irhulena of Hamath (700 chariots, 700 horsemen, and 10,000 foot soldiers), Hadadezer of Damascus (1,200 chariots, 1,200 horsemen, and 20,000 foot soldiers), and Ahab of Israel (2,000 chariots and 10,000 foot soldiers).[34]

After a brief respite from 852 to 850 B.C.E., when the Assyrian army was campaigning close to home, Shalmaneser resumed his assault on the coalition in his tenth year (849), marching west repeatedly in 848, 845, and 841. The persistence of Shalmaneser's attacks suggests that the alliance was effective, at least until Hadadezer of Damascus died during the 845 B.C.E. Shalmaneser's campaign or shortly afterward and the throne of Damascus was seized by Hazael.[35]

The Assyrian records designate Hazael as the sole target of Shalmaneser's 841 B.C.E. campaign, suggesting that the supporting coalition had dissolved with Hadadezer's death. After defeating Hazael and forcing him to retreat into Damascus,[36] Shalmaneser marched west to the Mediterranean coast, where he received tribute from Tyre, Sidon, and Israel. Israel's role in these events will be discussed below, but the point to be emphasized here is the isolation of Damascus—all of its former coalition members having chosen to capitulate rather than stand with Hazael against Assyria. Despite this isolation, however, and the devastation of his territory in 841, Hazael did not capitulate. Shalmaneser marched against Damascus once more, in 838, and then spent the rest of his reign campaigning in northern Syria to secure Assyrian control of that region. Hazael survived to become an increasingly powerful force in southern Syria and northern Palestine and to expand his territory at the expense of his neighbors, especially Israel.

ISRAEL AND JUDAH UNDER THE HEGEMONY OF DAMASCUS

Jehu's Revolt

During most of the time that Shalmaneser was pressing his cause against Damascus, Israel was ruled by Ahab's son Joram (c. 850–841). Ahab himself does not seem to have lived long after the battle of Qarqar (853), although Jezebel continued to exercise influence in her role as queen mother. Their older son, Ahaziah, succeeded Ahab as king, but after reigning for only a couple of years (c. 851–850), he died of injuries after falling through the railing of his balcony at Samaria (2 Kings 1:2–17). He was succeeded by his brother Joram.

Although the Assyrian records from Shalmaneser's campaigns in 848 and 845 do not mention Israel by name, they do indicate that Hadadezer of Damascus was still supported by a 12-king coalition, and we assume that Joram was among the 12, as his father had been before him. The biblical account of Joram's decade-long reign (2 Kings 3) is silent on this issue, alluding to international events only in connection with his unsuccessful campaign against Moab.

In Judah, Jehoshaphat was succeeded by his son Jehoram (r. 846–841).[37] His wife was Athaliah, daughter of Ahab and Jezebel. Jehoram's military endeavors were no more successful than those of his father. The account of his reign in 2 Kings 8:16–25 mentions revolts by Edom and Libnah (possibly Tell Bornah, north of Lachish), which the king tried but failed to suppress. When Jehoram died he was succeeded as king of Judah by his son Ahaziah.

Not long after Ahaziah's accession, and while Joram was still on the throne in Samaria, a high-ranking officer in the Israelite army named Jehu instigated a bloody purge that resulted in the deaths of the kings of both Israel and Judah. This was another in the series of military overthrows that had brought both Baasha and Omri to the throne of Israel earlier. In this case, however, we have a better understanding of the factors that led to the revolt. From the viewpoint of the biblical writers, the uprising was the inevitable consequence of outrage (both divine and human) over the religious policies and social abuses of the Omrides, especially Ahab. The story of Jehu anointed for his task by the hand of a prophet in 2 Kings 9:1–13 may reflect a contemporaneous dissatisfaction with the royal house of Omri. In addition, the successful revolts of Moab against Israel and of Edom against Judah greatly diminished the ability of both countries to benefit economically from the caravan trade. As the biblical account in 2 Kings 8–9 makes clear, however, the enemy on this occasion was not Moab or Assyria, but Israel's old anti-Assyrian ally, Damascus.

According to 2 Kings 8:28, the trouble began when Joram of Israel and Ahaziah of Judah marched into Transjordan "to wage war against King Hazael of Aram at Ramoth-gilead." We have already noted that after the death of Hadadezer in 845 B.C.E. and the seizure of the throne of Damascus by Hazael, the latter faced Shalmaneser alone. The confrontation at Ramoth-gilead suggests that Israel's Joram not only refused to support Hazael but became his open adversary.[38] In the perspective of the long-term relationship between Samaria and Damascus, this was a return to normalcy—another flare-up of the smoldering rivalry between the two states, like the one that occurred during the reigns of Baasha of Israel and Ben-hadad son of Tabrimmon of Damascus in the early ninth century B.C.E. This time, the principal cause of the hostilities between Samaria and Damascus likely was conflicting commercial interests involving the control of trade routes—a likelihood underscored by the location of the confrontation at the critical commercial junction of Ramoth-gilead.

The violent sequence of events that the prophet Hosea would later refer to as "the blood of Jezreel" (Hosea 1:4) is described in detail in 2 Kings 8:28–10:28. Joram was wounded in the battle and retreated to recuperate in the town of Jezreel, where he was soon joined by Ahaziah. Jehu was one of the ranking officers who remained at the front, and when Joram departed, the army turned to Jehu and proclaimed him king (2 Kings 9:13). According to the biblical account, Jehu then rode quickly to Jezreel, where he assassinated Joram, and then pursued and killed the fleeing Ahaziah. The coup was secured in the usual way—by tracking down and massacring the surviving members of the fallen Omrides. Ahab's descendants ("seventy sons") were executed by the intimidated city leaders of Samaria and their heads were sent in baskets to Jehu in Jezreel (2 Kings 10:1–11). The Israelite queen mother, Jezebel, was also killed in Jezreel.[39] The grim account of her death in

2 Kings 9:30–36 (hurled from the window of her palace, and her corpse consumed by dogs) reflects the strong animosity toward this foreign queen on the part of the prophetic tradition and the biblical writers, who interpreted her violent end as the fulfillment of Elijah's prediction in 1 Kings 21:23. The carnage extended to the Judahite kin of Ahaziah (2 Kings 10:12–14) and "the prophets of Baal, all his worshipers, and all his priests" (2 Kings 10:19).

Complicating this account, however, is an inscribed stela found at Tel Dan which claims that it was an Aramean ruler (Hazael?) who killed the kings of Israel and Judah: "[Jo]ram son of [Ahab], king of Israel," and "[Ahaz]iah son of [Jehoram, ki]ng of the House of David."[40] There are several ways to interpret this along with the rest of the evidence. Perhaps Jehu worked as an agent of Hazael, and the Aramean ruler then took credit for the deaths in his stela. The problem is that Jehu seems to have subsequently aligned with Assyria against Hazael (as described below). So Jehu either seized the throne after the deaths of Joram and Jehoram at the hand of Hazael and his armies, or Jehu and Hazael switched alliances when new circumstances presented themselves.[41]

Hazael's Ascendancy

In political and territorial terms, Jehu's revolt was disastrous for Israel. "In those days," we are told in the theological account in 2 Kings 10:32–33, "the Lord began to trim off parts of Israel." The passage goes on to describe Hazael's seizure of all of the Israelite territories east of the Jordan. As already noted, Shalmaneser III returned in 841 B.C.E. with Damascus as his principal target. After pursuing Hazael to Damascus and conducting a perfunctory siege of the city, Shalmaneser contented himself with marauding Aramean settlements in the Hauran, and then marched west to a headland on the Mediterranean coast called Ba'li-ra'si, probably Ras en-Naqura (Rosh ha-Niqra, about 12 mi north of the Akko spur), one of the peaks of the "Ladder of Tyre."[42] The so-called Black Obelisk of Shalmaneser III from Nimrud, which celebrates this campaign, includes a panel in relief depicting an Israelite king identified as "Yaw, son of Omri" prostrating himself in submission before the Assyrian monarch.[43] If the image was intended to depict Jehu, the gesture demonstrates that Jehu was now an enemy of Hazael and Damascus.

BLACK OBELISK. The reliefs on this 7-foot-tall, black stone monolith (left) depict the leaders of territories conquered by Shalmaneser III paying tribute to the Assyrian emperor. In the detail (above), a king of Israel (or perhaps his emissary) kneels before Shalmaneser, who appears to be admiring a vessel he has received. The annals of Shalmaneser III date the event to 841 B.C.E. The cuneiform inscription on the obelisk identifies the kneeling figure as "Yaw, son of Omri," leading scholars to identify the king as Omri's successor Jehu (c. 883–872).

The obelisk was discovered among the ruins of Nimrud, the royal seat of King Shalmaneser III of Assyria, on the eastern bank of the Tigris.

Following a final visit, in 838 B.C.E., also directed at Damascus, Shalmaneser departed and never returned. In fact, Assyria would not return in force to southern Syria and Palestine until the final years of the ninth century (805), as explained below. Having survived the onslaughts of Shalmaneser III, Hazael thus emerged as the dominant figure in the region, free to exact revenge for what he may have regarded as Jehu's treachery and to realize his ambition in expanding the hegemony of Damascus at the expense of Israel, Judah, and other neighbors.

When Ahaziah of Judah was assassinated, his mother, Athaliah (daughter of Ahab and Jezebel and widow of Jehoram of Judah), seized power (2 Kings 11:1–3). To consolidate her position, she attempted to eradicate the royal family of Judah. This part of her plan was foiled, however, by Ahaziah's sister Jehosheba, who hid her infant nephew, Jehoash son of Ahaziah, from Athaliah's executioners.[44] She then took the young Davidide secretly to the Temple and entrusted him to the protection of the high priest Jehoiada.[45] Jehoash remained in hiding in the Temple during the seven years that Athaliah ruled in Jerusalem (841–835 B.C.E.).

The reference in 2 Kings 11:18 to the dismantling of a "house of Baal" after Athaliah's death suggests that she attempted to introduce the Tyrian religion of her mother into Jerusalem (cf. 2 Chronicles 24:7), but otherwise the biblical record provides no information about her reign. It represented an interruption in the continuity of Davidic rule in Judah, and the biblical writers' silence on the subject is probably a reflection of their contempt for Athaliah, which they make clear in describing her ruthless acquisition of power and the degrading manner of her removal from office.

When Jehoash was seven years old, Jehoiada, operating under heavy guard, publicly presented him in the Temple and proclaimed him rightful king of Judah. When Athaliah arrived with a cry of treason, she was led outside of the Temple precincts and summarily executed (2 Kings 11:4–20).

The biblical account of Jehoash's reign deals primarily with the relationship between the royal palace and the Temple (2 Kings 11–12). A proclamation is said to have been issued in the king's name requiring that all contributions of silver brought to the Temple be turned over to the priests (later the repairmen), who were then to use the funds to repair the Temple. An inscribed potsherd may relate to this project;[46] it refers to an order in the name of Jehoash (called Ashyahu here) for a small amount of silver to be contributed to the Temple: "As Ashyahu the king commanded you to give into the hand of [Ze]chariah silver of Tarshish for the House of Yahweh: three shekels."[47] Since Zechariah is the name of a prominent priest of the period—the son of the high priest Jehoiada—the expression "into the hand of Zechariah" suggests that the ostracon reflects the situation early in Jehoash's reign when contributions of silver were made to the Temple through a priestly intermediary. According to the account in Chronicles, the Temple restoration proceeded well until Jehoiada's death, after which Jehoash fell under the influence of "the officials of Judah" (2 Chronicles 24:17), who persuaded him to abandon the project. When Jehoiada's own son, Zechariah, publicly objected, he was stoned to death.

THREE SHEKELS OSTRACON. This Hebrew inscription appears to be a receipt for a donation of three silver shekels to "the House of Yahweh," that is, the Jerusalem Temple. The inscription states that King Ashyahu has commanded that the money be given to one Zechariah. Although the Bible mentions no king of Judah named Ashyahu, this name may be a form of Joash or Jehoash. The inscription probably dates to the early years of King Jehoash of Judah (835–801 B.C.E.), who, according to 2 Kings 12:4, proclaimed that all contributions to the Temple should be turned over to the priests for repairs. Zechariah was a prominent priest at the time (2 Chronicles 24:20). Some scholars have voiced concerns about the ostracon's authenticity.

Though the Chronicler blames "the officials of Judah" for Jehoash's abandonment of the Temple project, the decision may have been forced on him by external circumstances—specifically, by the threat to Judah posed by Hazael of Damascus, who was left with a free hand to satisfy his territorial ambitions. According to 2 Kings 12:17–18, Hazael, after conquering the Philistine city of Gath, turned east to threaten Jerusalem.[48] Jehoash was able to save the city only by paying the Aramean king a heavy tribute amassed by emptying the treasuries of both the Temple and the royal palace.[49] However rich this extorted treasure may have been, it was not the primary economic benefit of Hazael's coastal campaign. His conquests in Philistia and Judah gave him jurisdiction over the primary coastal highway, and since he already controlled the principal trade route east of the Jordan, Hazael now had a virtual monopoly on commercial traffic passing through Palestine and direct access to both the Egyptian and the Arabian markets.[50]

EIGHTH-CENTURY PROSPERITY

The Resurgence of Israel and Judah

The ascendancy of Damascus over Israel and Judah extended from the 830s B.C.E. until the early eighth century B.C.E. Hazael died sometime before 805, when his son Ben-hadad II (Aramaic Bir-hadad, also known as Mari') first appears in Assyrian records.[51]

During Jehoahaz's reign over Israel (818–802), Ben-hadad II was able to maintain the domination of Israel that Hazael had established (cf. 2 Kings 13:3). He had the misfortune, however, to come to the throne at about the time that Assyria began to reassert itself in Syria-Palestine. The revival of Assyrian power was the achievement of Adad-nirari III (r. 811–783), who turned his attention to the West. By the time Adad-nirari's second western campaign was over, in 796, Ben-hadad II had been subdued. According to an inscription from the same year, Adad-nirari received tribute from "Mari' of Damascus ... Joash of Samaria, the Tyrians, and the Sidonians."[52]

The return of Assyria brought an end to the aggressive policies of Damascus, and Ben-hadad II and his successors were now obliged to submit to Assyria and pay tribute on a regular basis. For the kings of Israel, Judah, and the other regional states that had suffered at the hand

of Damascus, the arrival of Adad-nirari III was a welcome development. It has even been suggested that Adad-nirari is the unidentified
"savior" of Israel who helped the people escape from the land of the
Syrians (2 Kings 13:5). In any case, Joash of Samaria was subsequently
able to defeat Ben-hadad II three times and recover Israelite towns
lost to Hazael (2 Kings 13:25).

The Edomite campaign of Amaziah of Judah (c. 801–783)—reported
briefly in 2 Kings 14:7, with an expanded account in 2 Chronicles
25:5–16—may also have been inspired by the weakening position of
Damascus and the consequent hope on Amaziah's part that he could
recover the territory and trade access that had been lost to Edom in
the days of his great-grandfather, Jehoram (cf. 2 Kings 8:20–22). In the
flush of a victory at the Edomite stronghold of Sela (possibly el-Sela,
southwest of Tafila, Jordan), however, Amaziah overreached himself
and sent a defiant message to Joash (2 Kings 14:8–14; 2 Chronicles
25:17–24), apparently believing that the Israelite army was either too
weak or too preoccupied with Damascus to respond. This proved to
be a catastrophic miscalculation. Joash marched to Beth-Shemesh in
the Shephelah and routed the Judahite army, taking Amaziah prisoner.
He then proceeded to Jerusalem, where he broke down the northern
wall, looted the treasuries of the Temple and the royal palace, and
returned to Samaria with hostages. As a result, when Amaziah's son
Azariah became king in 783, Judah was dominated by Israel, a situation reminiscent of the heyday of the Omride dynasty.[53]

The Reigns of Jeroboam II and Azariah

Joash's policies—and his success in the ongoing conflict with
Damascus—were continued by his successor, Jeroboam II. The
long reigns of Jeroboam II in Israel (787–748 B.C.E.) and Azariah in
Judah (783–732 B.C.E.) correspond to a period of prosperity in both
kingdoms. This was possible not only because of the weakness of
Damascus but also because of the absence of Assyria, which would not
again pose a serious threat to Israel until the first western campaign
of Tiglath-pileser III, in 743–738. After Adad-nirari's 796 incursion
into Syria, the Assyrian armies were generally engaged near home.
For many of these years, the Assyrian Eponym Chronicle indicates
that there was no foreign campaign, and, when there was, it was often

directed "against Urartu." Urartu, the biblical Ararat, was the region around Lake Van, north of Assyria. The Urartians had been gradually expanding westward since the end of the reign of Shalmaneser III, who had held them in check, and by the beginning of the eighth century they had taken control of much of Anatolia and Syria north of Aleppo. Because of the distractions caused by domestic unrest and the conflict with Urartu, the Assyrian kings of this period seem to have paid little attention to southern Syria. Only five Syrian expeditions are listed in the Eponym Chronicle, and only one of these—a campaign in 773—is designated as "against Damascus."[54] Nevertheless, the fortunes of Damascus remained in decline. The devastation inflicted by Adad-nirari III seems to have left the once-powerful state broken and vulnerable.

This turn of events worked to the advantage of Israel, whose resurgence, begun under Joash, grew during the reign of his son Jeroboam II. According to 2 Kings 14:25, Jeroboam restored the border of Israel from the town of Lebo (modern Lebweh), at the southern boundary of the state of Hamath on the Orontes, to the Dead Sea. This claim seems overblown and influenced by the editor's vision of the ideal borders of the Davidic-Solomonic empire.[55]

According to the archaeological record, Israel at its largest did not stretch beyond Dan in the north. Yet even though the territory under Jeroboam II was smaller than biblical account asserts, Israel experienced material prosperity during his reign. The critical oracles of the eighth-century prophet Amos confirm the prosperity of the period while condemning the associated social and religious corruption.[56] In Amos's view, an exploitative ruling class was oppressing the poor and governing corruptly, "trample[ing] on the needy and bring[ing] ruin to the poor of the land ..." (Amos 8:4).

Excavations conducted at Israelite sites also show that the first half of the eighth century B.C.E. was a period of extensive construction, characterized by the renovation, refurbishment, and expansion of existing cities. Examples include the high place at Dan, fortifications and other structures at Megiddo, as well as the massive citadel and fortification system of Hazor.[57] Nationwide, there was a substantial population increase. The fortress at Kuntillet 'Ajrud indicates that probably in the first half of the eighth century, Israel controlled the desert trade routes in this southern territory.[58]

The trade advantage that Jeroboam achieved resulted in an accumulation of wealth, indicated by the discovery of luxury items in eighth-century archaeological strata. Most striking of these are the elaborately carved ivory inlays found at various sites in the northern kingdom, especially at Samaria.[59] Carved ivory was an art form of Phoenician and north Syrian inspiration, so that its presence in the archaeological record points to a renewal of Israelite contact and cooperation with Phoenicia, which was essential to a robust trade economy. An immense hoard known as the Samaria ivories was found in the ruins of the royal palace at Samaria, and testify to the wealth of the aristocracy and social stratification.[60] It is not surprising, therefore, that references to ivory play a part in Amos's invective against the excesses of the rich (Amos 3:15; 6:4).

The epigraphic record also sheds light on life in Samaria during the reign of Jeroboam II. The most impressive Hebrew seal from the early to mid-eighth century B.C.E. is surely the seal of "Shema', the servant of Jeroboam," a high official of the Samarian government stationed at Megiddo, where the seal was found.[61] The largest corpus of Hebrew inscriptions from any period of history in the northern kingdom comes from this period: the so-called Samaria ostraca were found in the ruins of an administrative structure on the acropolis immediately to the west of the royal palace.[62] Dating formulae indicate that the ostraca come from the 9th–17th years of an unnamed king, almost certainly Jeroboam II, so that they fall between the years 779 and 771. They record regional shipments of agricultural goods, thus shedding light on the support given by large estates to the activities of the court in Samaria. An especially interesting feature of the Samaria ostraca is the number of personal names in them that contain the theophoric for Yahweh (in the form *Yaw*, 11 in total), El (5 in total), and Baal (7).[63] It is difficult to assess the significance of this observation for the religion of Israel in the period. The Baal names might belong to foreigners (perhaps Phoenicians) who owned property in the vicinity of Samaria, or to Israelites who either worshiped a foreign god or used his name as an epithet in its general meaning "Lord"—a practice acceptable for Yahweh in this period (cf. Hosea 2:16). The significance of the ostraca is clearer in terms of what they say about social structure: Israelite landowners were sending produce to their monarch for the use of the court and guests of the king, and a scribal class existed to oversee and record the process.[64]

Judah, too, was prosperous in this period under the rule of Azariah (also known as Uzziah; 783–732). Although Azariah reigned over Judah even longer than Jeroboam over Israel, the account of his reign in 2 Kings 15:1–7 is very brief, and there is no mention of victories in foreign wars or other international achievements. The account in 2 Chronicles 26:1–23 is somewhat longer and presents Azariah as an effective military leader who reorganized the Judahite army and greatly increased its size and readiness. It also describes successful military campaigns that he conducted. Keeping in mind that Judah, since Joash's defeat of Amaziah early in the century, had been in the service of Israel as a junior ally, it may be that Azariah's build-up of the Judahite army and his various military enterprises were encouraged and abetted by Israel as part of Jeroboam's overall plan to reclaim control of the major trade routes of the region.[65] It is in this light that we should probably interpret Azariah's goals in the wars he is said to have conducted against the Philistines and two Arabian groups, the Arabs of Gurbaal (otherwise unknown) and the Meunites (2 Chronicles 26:6–7).[66]

After his Philistine campaign, during which he breached the walls of Gath, Jabneh, and Ashdod, Azariah is said to have built "cities" in Philistine territory. These are most likely to have been fortified garrisons positioned to guard trade routes that ran through disputed territory and connected with roads farther south, which he seems also to have secured with protective fortresses—note the reference in 2 Chronicles 26:10 to Azariah's erection of "the towers in the wilderness." These activities brought him in conflict with the Meunites, a northwestern Arabian tribe who seem at this time to have controlled access from the Philistine ports through the Beersheba depression and the Wadi Zered (the modern Wadi el-Hasa) to the southern end of the King's Highway and the Hejaz route. After defeating the Meunites, Azariah evidently left the fortresses in place as guardians of this highly lucrative thoroughfare, but diverted its wealth to Judah by imposing tribute on them (2 Chronicles 26:8).[67] It was probably after gaining control of the southern trade corridor that Azariah recovered the seaport of Elath[68] on the Gulf of Aqaba from Edom and rebuilt it (2 Chronicles 26:2; cf. 2 Kings 14:22).[69]

Although Azariah's domestic accomplishments may have been considerable—the Chronicler's account credits him with assembling large herds of cattle and employing farmers and viticulturists in the fertile parts of Judah (2 Chronicles 26:10)—he is remembered principally for having been a "leper."[70] After his diagnosis he had to live in quarantine, and his son Jotham ruled Judah as his coregent (2 Kings 15:5).[71] Since "leprosy" was determined by an examination by priests, who prescribed whether quarantine was required and how long it would last (Leviticus 13–14), Azariah's exclusion from power may have been the result of a continuation of the struggle in Judah between the king and the priesthood that had created turmoil during the reign of Jehoash in the late ninth century.[72] In any case, as a "leper," Azariah was apparently assigned a special burial place in the vicinity of—but apart from—the royal tombs (2 Chronicles 26:23; contrast 2 Kings 15:7). A plaque inscribed with his name found in Jerusalem suggests that he was reburied in the late Herodian period.[73]

Everyday Life During the Divided Monarchy

The rise of the Israelite and Judahite states in the early centuries of the first millennium B.C.E., the emergence of strongly centralized governments based in the capital cities of Samaria and Jerusalem, and the growth of large regional centers, such as Hazor, Megiddo, and Dan in the north and Lachish and Beersheba in the south, led to a highly stratified society in both kingdoms. The upper stratum consisted of the king, his family, and a group that maintained the royal estates and ruled the regional centers as governors. Of somewhat lesser stature were artisans and scribes and skilled laborers of various kinds. Most of the rest of the population—indeed, the vast majority—were agriculturalists. The lucrative international trade that flourished when Israel enjoyed good relations with Phoenicia and Judah with Philistia, and when the competition with Damascus was successful, was a source of substantial wealth for the king and the upper class.

The everyday livelihood of most of the ordinary citizens of Israel and Judah throughout the history of the monarchy, however, consisted of family-based farming and horticulture, usually supplemented by the maintenance of small flocks of sheep and goats. In the lowland areas the staple crops were grain (wheat, barley, and millet), while in the higher elevations and the western slopes of the hill country cereal farming was mixed with viticulture and arboriculture: the cultivation of figs, pomegranates, dates, sycamores, and especially olives.[74] In some areas, olive oil or wine could be produced in sufficient quantities to accumulate surpluses that provided a valuable export commodity.

Archaeological evidence indicates that the basis of this production throughout the Iron Age was the extended family or, to use the biblical term, the "father's house" (*bêt ʾāb*). This is shown by the widespread persistence throughout the period of the "four-room," or "pillared" house, which consisted of a central courtyard enclosed by rooms designed to house not only an extended family unit but also livestock and to provide agricultural storage. Several such households constituted a clan, which lived together in the same village or at least in relatively close proximity to each other. A group of clans formed a tribe.[75]

The stockpiling of crop surpluses in individual households rather than communal storage facilities indicates that agriculture was largely family-based. However, there is also evidence from domestic structures for specialization. Several "pillared" houses from the eighth century were found in the southern town of Tell Halif. One of these, A8 House, had a room in which were found items related to food preparation and textile fabrication for a single family: an oven, cooking pot, oil lamp, and loom weights. But another room suggests the production of commodities on a larger scale: a grain grinding installation and storage vessels large and numerous enough to suggest an enterprise larger than what would be needed to support a single family. Other remains from the same town suggests that at least some bread making was also done on a large scale.[76] So although agriculture and food production was largely pursued in small family units, there are examples of larger-scale specialization during this period.

Given the central position of the family in the economy and social organization of the two states, women's influence in society is assumed to have been pervasive despite their relative invisibility in the surviving texts. The critical tasks of childbearing, child-rearing, spinning, weaving, and sewing were all done by women, and women also took part in farming and caring for livestock.[77] A number of personal seals and seal impressions bearing the names of female Judahites from the seventh and early sixth centuries indicate the involvement of women in more formal, legal and economic transactions.[78] "Meshullemeth daughter of Elichen" appears in a list of the recipients of specified commodities on an ostracon from the early sixth century, indicating her business transactions during the final days of the Kingdom of Judah.[79] At the highest social level, the principal wife of the kings could exercise authority as queen and, after her husband's death, queen mother. The narratives about Queen Jezebel in 1 Kings 16–21, although largely negative, assume a great deal of power for the wife of the reigning king, and the text has a queen mother, Athaliah, ruling Judah as its principal sovereign for several years (c. 841–835).

Religion in Israel and Judah

Archaeology has dramatically altered our view of the practice of religion in Judah and Israel during the Iron Age. Although the biblical writers of Jerusalem stressed devotion to the single God Yahweh, many worshippers of Yahweh worshiped their deity according to different traditions, some already hundreds and even thousands of years old. Significantly, the archaeological evidence provides many examples of deviations from the major tenet of the biblical texts: the exclusive worship of Yahweh in the single temple in Jerusalem. In addition to widespread and ongoing worship within a domestic context, the archaeological finds also indicate that there was a shift to the centralization of the public cult both in the north and the south in the eighth century.[80]

In the 1970s two ruined buildings dating to the early eighth century B.C.E. were excavated at Kuntillet 'Ajrud, a remote site on the Sinai Peninsula. These buildings give us a picture of religious practice during this time.[81] The better preserved of the two buildings yielded an unusually large amount of written material, including Hebrew inscriptions written in ink on *pithoi* (large storage jars) and on plastered walls, as well as incised onto large stone bowls.

Although its nature and function are still not fully understood, the site is located at the junction of three of the principal roads crossing the northeastern Sinai, and it is tempting to associate it in some way with Amaziah's interest in controlling the trade routes south and east of Judah, as shown by his Edomite campaign.

KUNTILLET 'AJRUD. Travelers may have stopped for rest and refreshment at this desert way-station halfway between Beersheba and Elath. The ruins of two late-ninth- to early eighth-century B.C.E. buildings are visible on the isolated hilltop, which overlooks three major routes across northeastern Sinai. Archaeologists have discovered abundant evidence here of early Israelite worship, predating the great religious reforms of Hezekiah and Josiah.

The corpus includes inscriptions written in both the northern (Israelite) and southern (Judahite) dialects of Hebrew, which may put the site in the context of Judah's subjugation by Joash, whose name actually appears on one of the *pithoi* where it belongs to one who bestowed a blessing.[82]

The content of the Kuntillet 'Ajrud inscriptions is substantially religious, shedding invaluable light on the nature of Israelite religion at the dawn of the eighth century B.C.E. In view of the later movement towards cult centralization in Judah, for example, it is important to note that at 'Ajrud the name of the God of Israel is always qualified by a geographical designation, so that it appears not simply as "Yahweh" but as "Yahweh of Samaria" or "Yahweh of Teman." The first designation was the local form or manifestation of the God of Israel as worshiped in the capital of the northern kingdom. "Yahweh of Teman" was probably the local Yahweh of the region around 'Ajrud itself: biblical Teman, which means "Southland," was a region, and in modern times Kuntillet 'Ajrud has been given the Hebrew name Horvat Teman, "the Ruin of Teman."

YAHWEH AND HIS ASHERAH. "I have blessed you by Yahweh of Samaria and his asherah," declares the Hebrew inscription on this pithos, or storage jar, from Kuntillet 'Ajrud. The accompanying painting depicts two grotesque figures standing side-by-side with arms akimbo. The larger figure, at left, has a man's torso and posture, but a bovine face, horns and a tail. The smaller figure has a human body with breasts and a bovine face and tail. A seated musician appears at far right. Some scholars identify the two standing figures as Yahweh and Asherah (although others have suggested that both depictions represent the Egyptian deity Bes). A goddess by the name of Asherah is mentioned with contempt in the Bible; this inscription suggests that in the late ninth or eighth century B.C.E., she was conceived of as Yahweh's consort.

FERTILITY FIGURINE. Excavated in the Jewish Quarter of Jerusalem's Old City, this clay figurine may be a household fertility amulet representing the Canaanite goddess Asherah. The pillar-shaped body may represent a tree, a motif connected with Asherah.

For the ancient advocates of cult centralization, these local cults posed a threat to the authority of the central sanctuary. For the opposing advocates of incipient monotheism in the biblical form (i.e., those who stressed the oneness of Yahweh and insisted on the exclusive worship of this one god), the local cults posed another kind of threat because local manifestations of a deity tended to attain quasi-independent status.

In addition to the information that the site reveals about worship of Yahweh outside of a single site, we also see the connection of Yahweh with a female consort: "his Asherah." For example, the aforementioned blessing of Joash is invoked "by Yahweh of Samaria and his Asherah."

Goddesses known as "Asherah" are known from several ancient Near Eastern societies, and a goddess by that name is mentioned several times in the Bible with contempt (1 Kings 18:19, etc.). The biblical text also employs the term for an object used in worship: an *asherah* (plural *asherim*). This was a wooden object of some kind, perhaps a simple pole but also possibly a carved female image (cf. 2 Kings 21:7) or sacred tree, and part of the conventional paraphernalia of a local shrine, or "high place." Since the Hebrew term may originally have meant something like "track" or "trace," "the asherah of Yahweh" may have signified the presence of Yahweh, with the cult object serving as a concrete representation of the divine presence. However, one of the *pithoi* found at Kuntillet 'Ajrud has a blessing invoking "Yahweh of Samaria and his asherah," inscribed immediately above a drawing of two figures standing side-by-side. Both figures combine human and bovine features—human torsos and posture with bovine faces, horns, tails, and hoofed feet. One of the figures has breasts, as does an additional figure seated nearby and playing a harp. Taken together, all this suggests that worshipers at Kuntillet 'Ajrud understood that Yahweh had a female consort.[83]

ARAD TEMPLE. Limestone incense altars flank the steps leading into the Holy of Holies, or innermost chamber, of the temple to Yahweh at Arad, in the Negev; at the rear of the niche are two sacred standing stones. Built in the tenth century B.C.E., the Arad temple remained in use until it was destroyed during the religious reforms of either Hezekiah in the late eighth century B.C.E. or Josiah in the late seventh century. When the temple was abolished, the altars were reverently laid on their sides and covered with earth.

The finds at Kuntillet 'Ajrud suggest that the negative perspective on Asherah in the biblical texts actually betrays the fact of her widespread worship in popular religion throughout Israel and Judah. Depictions of the goddess Ištar as well as Asherah imagery in numerous small house shrines in Israel, and the prevalence of female figurines throughout Judah and Israel also point to this conclusion.[84]

BEERSHEBA HORNED ALTAR. Dating to the eighth century B.C.E., this is the first example discovered of an Israelite horned altar for animal sacrifice. Contrary to biblical law (Exodus 20:25), the 63-inch-tall altar was built of hewn stones. It also has a serpent motif incised on one of its blocks. Sacrifices had apparently been burnt on the altar, for the top stones were blackened. The Beersheba altar provides rare evidence of religious rituals carried out in a Judahite city other than Jerusalem.

Although the altar had been disassembled and its blocks reused in a wall, archaeologists had no trouble distinguishing the calcareous sandstone of the altar blocks from the common limestone of the rest of the wall.

The existence of a public worship site at Kuntillet ʿAjrud from the early eighth century should be linked to other sites in Judah during this time. There was a temple in Arad which was probably in service in the eighth century (Stratum X), and it existed for approximately 50 years (Strata X–IX), before it was carefully put out of service during the time of Hezekiah.[85] Large standing stones (*masseboth*, in Hebrew) were found in the Arad temple, and hundreds more of unhewn stone pillars have been found in surveys of the Negev and Sinai deserts, often deliberately arranged in pairs or triads and dating back as far as the tenth millennium B.C.E. It is likely that such objects were thought to represent the physical presence or abode of the deity.[86] A large altar from the eighth century has been reconstructed at Beersheba. At 63 inches tall, the altar is large enough for animal sacrifice, and the remains of burn marks indicate that it was used for such. When considered together, such evidence indicates a vibrant religious life in the south during this period outside of Jerusalem.

Worship sites in the north point to a general reorganization upon the rise of the Omride kingdom. Abel Beth Maacah was occupied for most of the Iron Age, and after a public complex devoted to ritual activity in the 11th–10th centuries was destroyed by fire, a new structure was rebuilt in its place. In addition to demonstrating at least a geographical continuity with earlier practice, the rebuilt Israelite worship space also provides intriguing evidence for religious life. Associated with the building is a stone-paved courtyard and a round raised platform of stone and brick. On this platform was found a jar full of 425 astragali—small ankle-bones of sheep, goats, and deer that may have been used for divination or other ritual activity.[87] Evidence from the ninth century B.C.E. indicates that domestic shrines were used at Megiddo and that other small places of worship were in use at Tel Amal and Taanach. Yet none of these continued into the eighth century, and there is no architectural evidence for large-scale public worship during this period outside of Samaria, Bethel, Dan, and Penuel.[88]

Popular Religion in Ancient Israel

Archaeology has dramatically altered our view of ancient Israelite religion. While the biblical writers and the priestly circles of Jerusalem stressed Israel's exclusive devotion to the single, all-powerful and unseen God Yahweh, some everyday Israelites often worshiped their national God according to religious traditions that were already hundreds and even thousands of years old.

Among the relics of this more traditional Israelite religion are small ceramic altars and house shrines that were used for private rituals in domestic and small-scale industrial contexts. While the deity (or deities) to whom these altars and shrines were dedicated remains uncertain, archaeologists Amihai Mazar and Nava Panitz-Cohen reported in *BAR* ("To What God?" July/August 2008) that several of these objects found at the Israelite site of Tel Rehov in the Jordan Valley reflect much earlier, Canaanite cultic traditions and religious ideas. In a separate *BAR* article ("A Temple Built for Two," March/April 2008), the esteemed American archaeologist William G. Dever proposes that many of the house shrines found at Iron Age sites in Israel were meant to be private "temples" for the Canaanite mother-goddess Asherah, who was often recognized as the consort of Yahweh. He argues that while there was indeed a general reluctance among even everyday Israelites to depict the God Yahweh in physical form, many of the shrines are replete with explicit or symbolic depictions of his consort, Asherah.

Archaeologist Uzi Avner discusses with *BAR* readers ("Sacred Stones in the Desert," May/June 2001) an even older—but no less enigmatic—religious tradition adopted by the Israelites: standing stones, or *masseboth*. Avner's surveys of the Negev and Sinai deserts found hundreds of unhewn stone pillars, often deliberately arranged in pairs or triads, that date as far back as the tenth millennium B.C.E. Based on numerous biblical passages that mention such *masseboth*, as well as other historical and ethnographic evidence, Avner argues that these stones were thought to represent the physical presence or abode of the deity. Indeed, two such stones were found in the inner sanctum of the temple to Yahweh at the Israelite fortress at Arad in the Negev, perhaps representing the Israelite God and his Asherah. –ED.

ISRAEL AND JUDAH UNDER THE ASSYRIAN EMPIRE

Tiglath-pileser III

Following Adad-nirari III's 796 B.C.E. campaign to Syria, a long period of Assyrian weakness began. The Assyrian kings were unable to gain the upper hand in their competition with Urartu for control of Anatolia and northern Syria. With the accession of Tiglath-pileser III (r. 745–727), however, the situation changed rapidly.[89] After moving quickly to reorganize the kingdom administratively, the king embarked on his first western campaign in 743. He broke the power of Urartu almost immediately and in 740 conquered Arpad, which was the key to the control of northern Syria. This led to a surrender of most of the other states of northern and central Syria, including Hamath. Not content with this victory, Tiglath-pileser continued his march westward and extended the Assyrian Empire to the Mediterranean coast. In 738, at the end of this first western campaign, he received tribute from Rezin of Damascus and Queen Zabibe of Arabia (see below), as well as Menahem of Israel.[90]

Although computing the reigns of the kings of Israel and Judah in 2 Kings 15 is not always straightforward,[91] it is clear that Menahem had ascended to the throne of Israel after a series of royal assassinations that brought the dynasty of Jehu to an end (2 Kings 15:8–22). Jeroboam II had died in about 748. His son Zechariah (r. c. 748–747) succeeded him but was publicly assassinated by a certain Shallum son of Jabesh (c. 747) after a reign of only six months. One month later Shallum himself was assassinated by Menahem son of Gadi, who had marched against Samaria from the old Israelite capital city of Tirzah. Menahem then ruled for a decade (c. 747–738). Witnessing the arrival of Tiglath-pileser in the West, he kept his throne by paying tribute to Assyria. Two years after his death, however, his son and successor, Pekahiah (r. c. 738–737), was unseated in an anti-Assyrian coup led by Pekah son of Remaliah and an army of Gileadites.[92] Menahem and Pekahiah had ruled Israel for 12 relatively stable years in very dangerous times. Yet the price they paid for peace with Assyria was very high. According to 2 Kings 15:20, the wealthy in the land had to give 50 shekels each to the Assyrian king, and we can assume that anti-Assyrian sentiment in the kingdom was strong. It is likely that the revolt was also stimulated and supported by Rezin of Damascus, following in the footsteps of his ninth-century predecessors, Hadadezer and Hazael.[93]

BULLA OF KING AHAZ. "Belonging to Ahaz (son of) Jotham, King of Judah," reads the Hebrew inscription impressed onto this lump of clay, which was originally used to secure a papyrus scroll. Ancient bullae and seals are not uncommon, but this is one of the first that can be attributed to a Hebrew king: Ahaz, who ruled over Judah from 735 to 727 B.C.E.

For most of his reign, Menahem's contemporary in Judah was Jotham (c. 750–735), who was still ruling as coregent for his leprous father, Azariah.[94] The account of Jotham's reign in the Book of Kings provides little information about his achievements, except that "he built the upper gate of the house of the Lord" (2 Kings 15:32–38). The Chronicler gives him credit for additional construction projects in Jerusalem, especially on the city's fortifications, including the wall of the Ophel, defensive towers, and anti-siege devices on the walls (2 Chronicles 27:9, 15). Such building projects were probably motivated by a concern over the possibility of an invasion—not by Assyria, which did not yet pose a direct threat to Judah, but by Israel and Damascus. Such a concern was not ill-founded or premature. At some point, probably late in Jotham's reign, Pekah and Rezin began making incursions into Judah (2 Kings 15:37), anticipating their full-scale assault on Jerusalem in the time of Ahaz (see below). Although the initial motivation for the alliance of Samaria and Damascus may have been territorial expansion in support of their trade ambitions, their later attack on Ahaz might have been an attempt to force him to join the anti-Assyrian coalition that had formed in southern Syria and Palestine. Despite the pressure his northern neighbors brought to bear, however, Jotham did not yield, and his determination to remain unaligned, if not pro-Assyrian, is understandable. To Judah, which had not been among the nations that paid tribute to Tiglath-pileser III in 738, the Assyrian threat must have still seemed remote, and no doubt Jotham thought it wise not to antagonize Tiglath-pileser.

After a few years in which the Assyrian army was occupied north and east of Syria campaigning against the Urartians and Medes,[95] Tiglath-pileser set out on his second western campaign (734–732), which ended triumphantly with the fall of Damascus. The biblical account of this campaign (2 Kings 16:5–9) claims that it was launched in response to a petition to Tiglath-pileser from Ahaz (735–727 B.C.E.), who was now king of Judah.[96] Rezin and Pekah had joined forces again and laid siege to Jerusalem. Earlier scholars argued that Damascus and Israel launched the "Syro-Ephraimite war" to intimidate Ahaz, so that he would renounce his policy of neutrality and join the anti-Assyrian cause,[97] but it seems likely that the initial motivation of Rezin and Pekah was probably more commercial than conspiratorial. That is, the Aramean-Israelite coalition was formed in the first place out of a mutual interest in territorial expansion, especially into Transjordan, and the driving incentive for this expansion was commercial ambition, not hostility to Assyria, which may not yet have been perceived as an immediate threat.[98] Phoenician and Philistine participation in the alliance was probably also motivated by a primary interest in the control of trade routes, and the same was true of the involvement of Arabian tribes under the rule of Queen Samsi. Nevertheless, Tiglath-pileser regarded the new trade alliances as anti-Assyrian, and it was suspicions of this kind that led to Assyrian military intervention. In any case, if it was the intention of Rezin and Pekah to pressure Ahaz to resist Tiglath-pileser, the plan backfired. According to the biblical sources, Ahaz was indeed intimidated,[99] but instead of joining the resistance to Assyria, he voluntarily entered into Assyrian vassalage. He sent a message of subservience to Tiglath-pileser together with a gift of silver and gold from the Temple and palace treasuries. The biblical account concludes by indicating that the Assyrian king responded favorably and led his forces into Syria, where he captured Damascus, exiled its population, and executed Rezin.

TIGLATH-PILESER'S 734–732 B.C.E. CAMPAIGNS

Despite the limited perspective of the biblical account of these events, which naturally centers on the involvement of Judah, we know from Assyrian sources that Rezin and Pekah were involved in a larger anti-Assyrian movement in the West, which included Hiram of Tyre as well as the kings of two Philistine cities: Mitinti of Ashkelon and Hanun (or Hanno) of Gaza. Although the Damascene Rezin, as the ringleader of the coalition, was clearly the primary target of the larger Assyrian campaign, Tiglath-pileser's strategy seems to have been to subdue the other coalition members first in order to isolate Damascus. Thus in 734 B.C.E., which is designated "to Philistia" in the Assyrian Eponym Chronicle, he moved to subdue the western allies of Damascus and the northern kingdom of Israel.[100] Although the annalistic fragments are too incomplete to permit more than an approximation of his itinerary, he seems to have begun by marching down the Phoenician coast, capturing Byblos and other cities until he came face-to-face with Hiram of Tyre (the namesake of the Hiram of Tyre who helped Solomon build the Temple), who capitulated and paid tribute. Tiglath-pileser then proceeded south to Ashkelon, where he accepted the Philistine Mitinti's surrender and an oath of loyalty. When the Assyrian army reached Gaza, Hanun fled to Egypt, from which he would later return to accept vassalage and to rule over the port of Gaza as an Assyrian imperial entrepôt. The southernmost point reached on the 734 B.C.E. march was the "the Wadi of Egypt" (the Wadi el-'Arish, the traditional southern boundary of Palestine), where Tiglath-pileser fought the Meunites, a group that Azariah had subdued decades earlier, after his own Philistine campaign.

Having now subdued the entire coastal plain south of Phoenicia, Tiglath-pileser formally annexed the region from Dor and the Plain of Sharon south to Philistia as an Assyrian province called Du'ru (Dor). He also incorporated the Philistine states as vassaldoms and marked the southern boundary of the Assyrian Empire with a stela erected at the Wadi of Egypt. At that time he accepted tribute not only from the kings defeated on the march (Tyre, Ashkelon, Gaza) but also from Kaushmalaku of Edom, Salamanu of Moab, Sanipu of Bit-Ammon, as well as Ahaz (*Ia-u-ḫa-zi*) of Judah.[101] The three Transjordanian states, including Judah, seem to have bought their safety by offering tribute and by avoiding alliances with Rezin's coalition. They remained semi-independent as vassal states.

Over the next two years (733–732 B.C.E.), both of which are designated "to Damascus" in the Eponym Chronicles,[102] Tiglath-pileser turned his attention to Damascus and Israel. The fragmentary nature of the annals permits only an approximation of the sequence of events, but it seems clear that Damascus was placed under siege at the beginning of the campaign.

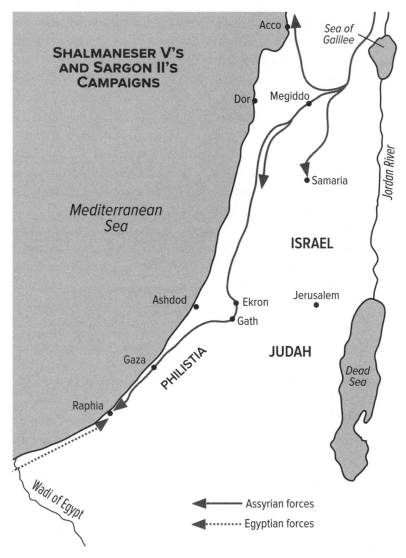

SHALMANESER V'S
AND SARGON II'S
CAMPAIGNS

Acco

Sea of Galilee

Dor   Megiddo

Samaria

Mediterranean
Sea

ISRAEL

Jordan River

Ashdod   Ekron   Jerusalem

Gath

Gaza   JUDAH

PHILISTIA

Raphia   Dead
Sea

Wadi of Egypt

⟵——— Assyrian forces
⟵········· Egyptian forces

Then, leaving part of his army to carry out the siege, Tiglath-pileser marched through northern Israel, capturing all of Naphtali and the Upper Galilee, as well as northern Transjordan (2 Kings 15:29).[103] Under the Assyrian policy of deportations, Israelites for the first time went into exile, as the captives—a total of 13,520, according to a fragmentary text[104]—were led off to Assyria. The rest of Israel was spared when Hoshea son of Elah assassinated Pekah and took his place as king in 732 B.C.E. (2 Kings 15:30). He quickly sent a message of fealty to

Tiglath-pileser, ensuring that most of Israel at least would be spared.[105] Large tracts of former Israelite territory did not survive, however, and they were incorporated into three Assyrian provinces: Du'ru (Dor, already annexed after the 734 campaign), Magidu (Megiddo, consisting of the entire Galilee as far south as Megiddo and the Jezreel Valley), and Gal'aza (Gilead, consisting of Israelite Transjordan as far north as Ramoth-gilead).[106] Also in 732, the city of Damascus fell to Tiglath-pileser's troops and was incorporated into the empire. Little information about the fall of Damascus is preserved in Assyrian records, except that Rezin was executed and his hometown of Hadara was destroyed in reprisal (cf. 2 Kings 16:9).[107]

It is important not to overlook the economic motivations and consequences of Tiglath-pileser's conquests in the West. By incorporating into the empire Syria, Phoenicia, and the entire Mediterranean coast as far south as the Wadi el-'Arish, Assyria attained direct control of the major Syrian trade routes and the great coastal highway, the Via Maris, which was the land route to Egypt. Since the Transjordanian states remained semi-independent tributaries (i.e., states that paid tribute), Assyria did not directly control the King's Highway with its connection to the lucrative caravan route from the northern Hejaz and farther south. But this hardly mattered, since Assyria's sovereignty over Damascus as well as the Phoenician and Philistine port cities gave it control of all the regional outlets for this highly profitable traffic. It is thus no surprise that we find an Arabian queen listed as paying tribute following both of Tiglath-pileser's western campaigns: The last name in the 738 B.C.E. tribute list is "Zabibe, queen of the land of Arabia."[108] When Damascus, Israel, and Tyre submitted to Tiglath-pileser of Assyria in 738, the trade from South Arabia to Damascus and from there to Mediterranean ports was in threat. Hence Zabibe's payment of tribute was probably an attempt to protect her interests and keep the routes open. The 738 tribute list contains an abundance of luxury goods that were bartered in the South Arabian trade, including precious metals and ivory, exotic woods, and the hides of elephants.

Near its southern end, the principal western bifurcation of the King's Highway ran south of the Dead Sea through the Wadi Hesa-Beersheba depression, then passed through Judahite territory and emerged at Ashkelon or another of the Philistine ports. A South Arabian

inscription dating to the late seventh century B.C.E. records the movements of a South Arabian trading caravan through the southern territories of both Gaza and "the towns of Judah."[109] This route was still free
from Assyrian interference after 738 B.C.E., but Tiglath-pileser's 734
incursion into Philistia brought it under Assyrian control. The name
of Samsi, who succeeded Zabibe as "queen of Arabia" at this time, has
not survived in the damaged tribute list of 734,[110] but it must have been
there, given her appearance in other texts.[111]

Mitinti of Ashkelon, who submitted to Tiglath-pileser in 734, later
rebelled, and the annals seem to associate this rebellion with that of
Samsi's. Whether these two acts of defiance were jointly planned or
simply happened simultaneously, they should probably be interpreted
as desperate attempts to restore the independence of the spice and
incense trade. Both rebellions were quickly suppressed—Mitinti's when
he died and his son and successor submitted to Tiglath-pileser, and
Samsi's when she surrendered, paid tribute and accepted an Assyrian-
appointed overseer—but they serve as good illustrations of what was
at stake economically in Tiglath-pileser's Philistine excursion.[112]

The Fall of Samaria

Israel enjoyed a brief period of stability after 732, while Hoshea (732–
724) was a loyal vassal of Tiglath-pileser.[113] But in 727, when Tiglath-
pileser died and was succeeded by Shalmaneser V (727–722), Hoshea
became embroiled in a revolt that broke out in the western part of the
empire. We have no Assyrian historical records from Shalmaneser V's
reign, but the general sequence of events can be reconstructed from
the Eponym Chronicle, itself poorly preserved at this point, in
combination with information that survives third-hand, from the
annals of Tyre.[114] Evidently Shalmaneser campaigned in Phoenicia
in his first regnal year (727), accepting tribute and then withdrawing.
Subsequently, a group of Tyrian vassal cities revolted against Tyre and
appealed to Assyria for help. In response, Shalmaneser marched west
again (in 725?) and began a siege of Tyre that was lifted without success
after five years—after Shalmaneser's reign had ended.

With this framework in mind, we can better understand the brief
biblical account of Hoshea's reign and the fall of Samaria in 2 Kings
17:1–6. The statement in 2 Kings 17:3 (that Shalmaneser marched against

Hoshea and accepted his tribute and fealty) suggests that Shalmaneser visited Israel on his way to or from Phoenicia or even that Samaria was one of the "Phoenician" cities recorded in the Tyrian annals as paying tribute to the Assyrian king in that year. According to 2 Kings 17:4, however, Hoshea subsequently antagonized Shalmaneser by conspiring against him and communicating with Egypt—presumably in search of support against Assyria—and by withholding the annual tribute he had been paying. Shalmaneser responded by arresting Hoshea. Then, with Hoshea in Assyrian custody, Shalmaneser marched to Samaria and laid siege to the city (2 Kings 17:5). It is tempting to associate these developments with the events of 725 and Shalmaneser's attack on Tyre.

A RECORD OF SHEBA'S TRADE WITH JUDAH. This fragmented but well-preserved South Arabian inscription mentions, among other things, a trading expedition from the kingdom of Sabaea (biblical Sheba) to "the towns of Judah." Believed to date to around 600 B.C.E., this inscription confirms Judah's role in the lucrative Arabian trade that was one of the primary economic drivers of Iron Age geopolitics from at least the time of King Solomon.

If this reconstruction is correct, it suggests that Samaria and Tyre had probably formed an alliance against Shalmaneser, reminiscent of the anti-Assyrian coalitions of the past, and that Egypt was encouraging (if not actively supporting) the alliance. It further suggests that the sieges of Tyre and Samaria probably began at about the same time, in 725 or 724.

At that time, Hoshea's appeal to Egypt having evidently gone unheeded, Shalmaneser "invaded all the land"—that is, overran and devastated Israel as a whole—and put the capital, Samaria, under siege (2 Kings 17:5–6; 18:9–10). The siege lasted three years, concluding in 722 with the fall of Samaria, and thousands of Israelites were led into exile. The biblical account of these events is telescoped, giving the impression that the same king of Assyria was responsible for the fall of Samaria and the deportation of the Israelites, but this was not the case. Shalmaneser V died only a couple of months after the conclusion of the siege, in the winter of 722. The Babylonian Chronicle records that Shalmeneser V "destroyed Samaria,"[115] yet the final disposition of Samaria and the exile of the Israelites was left to his successor, the usurper Sargon II (722–705). In his annals and other inscriptions, Sargon boasts of having "besieged and conquered Samaria," likely an overstatement aimed to enhance his accomplishments in the first year of his reign.[116]

Sargon II was prevented from giving his immediate attention to Samaria by two major revolts in the empire that erupted when he seized the throne. One of these took place in Babylon and was an outburst of nationalistic fervor under the leadership of the Chaldean prince Marduk-apla-iddina II—the biblical Merodachbaladan (2 Kings 20:12 = Isaiah 39:1)—who proclaimed himself king of Babylon.[117] Sargon needed 12 years to dislodge him from the throne. The other revolt, which took place in the western provinces, was initiated by Ilu-bi'di of Hamath and Hanun of Gaza, who had also rebelled against Tiglath-pileser, in 734. The revolt of Ilu-bi'di and Hanun quickly spread to several other cities, including Damascus and Samaria.[118] It was this revolt that brought Sargon west in 720 and gave him the opportunity to complete the incorporation of Samaria into the empire and to initiate the deportation of its citizens. Sargon trapped and destroyed the forces of Hamath in the fortress of Qarqar, where Shalmaneser III had fought Hamath and its allies 133 years earlier. When the region had been pacified and Ilu-bi'di executed, the Assyrian army marched down the coast toward Gaza to deal with Hanun. Like Hoshea a few years earlier, Hanun had appealed to Egypt for help, and in his case the pharaoh responded and sent his viceroy (*turtānu*) with a contingent of troops. Sargon met the combined forces of Gaza and Egypt at "the city of the Wadi of Egypt," that is, Raphia (about 15 miles southwest of Gaza), where he won a decisive battle, capturing Hanun and driving away the Egyptian army. With the Assyrian victory, Egypt, for the first time, agreed to pay tribute to Assyria, as did South Arabian leaders[119] who, confronted with another show of Assyrian power in southern Palestine, were anxious to maintain good relations with Sargon to protect their trade interests in the region.

It was probably during the first, northern phase of the 720 campaign that Sargon began the deportation of Israelites—one summary inscription indicates that 27,290 people were affected.[120] Although the Assyrian practice of deporting captive peoples had already begun in the ninth century B.C.E., it was Sargon II and his predecessor, Tiglath-pileser, who gave it its greatest notoriety, not only by employing it on a much vaster scale than their predecessors but also, in Sargon's case, by introducing the policy of two-way relocations. Conquered peoples from the western portions of the empire were resettled in Assyria and in the eastern provinces, while captives from the eastern and southern regions were resettled in the West. In clay prisms found at Nimrud, Sargon refers to his deportation of people both from and to Samaria.[121] He does not indicate the places of origin of the peoples transported to Samaria, except that they came from countries he conquered. The biblical account gives more detail: We are told in 2 Kings 17:6 that Sargon transported captive Israelites to Assyria, and in 2 Kings 17:24 we read that he repopulated the cities of Samaria with peoples from Babylonia and Elam (southwestern Iran).[122] More specifically, the Israelites were resettled in Halah (northeast of Nineveh), on the Habor (the Khabur River, a tributary that flows south into the Euphrates from the highlands of southeastern Turkey and northeastern Syria), and in the highlands[123] of the Medes (northwestern Iran).[124]

Hoshea's former kingdom was reorganized as the Assyrian province of Samerina (Samaria). The city of Samaria continued under Assyrian supervision to serve as the provincial capital,[125] and the Assyrians

BULLAE OF KING HEZEKIAH. When this damaged seal impression (bottom left) was originally published, it was too fragmentary to allow scholars to reconstruct the inscription and thus to realize to whom the seal had originally belonged. Fortunately, a more complete impression (top) of the same seal later surfaced in a private London collection. The better-preserved inscription clearly reads: "Belonging to Hezekiah (son) of Ahaz, king of Judah." Above the inscription appears a winged scarab—a symbol found in hundreds of inscriptions dating to the reign of Hezekiah (727–697 B.C.E.).

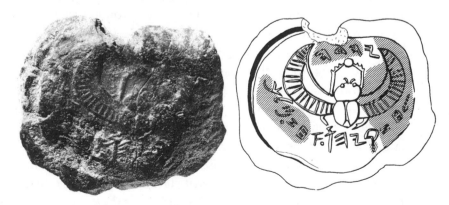

profited from the agricultural surplus of the countryside and the trade along the Via Maris.[126] The once independent state of Israel, the northern kingdom, which had enjoyed periods of considerable regional power under the Omrides and the last kings of the Jehu dynasty, was no more. In its place were the four Assyrian provinces of Dor, Megiddo, Gilead, and Samaria.

Sennacherib's Invasion of Judah

King Ahaz of Judah died in about 727 B.C.E. He was succeeded by his son Hezekiah (727–697), who presided over a critical period in the history of Judah, introducing cultic reforms that charted the course for the subsequent development of Israelite religion. He also adopted a bold policy toward Assyria, based first on defiance and then on concilation, that defined Judah's position in the international affairs of the seventh century.

As it happens, Hezekiah's pivotal reign is one of the best documented of any king of Israel or Judah, both in biblical and extrabiblical texts. It is extensively reported in the books of Kings and Chronicles, and it is the setting of a substantial number of the oracles and narratives collected in Isaiah 1–33. The Assyrian annals also provide a full account of Hezekiah's rebellion against Assyria and subsequent capitulation. A number of larger and smaller Hebrew inscriptions have survived from Hezekiah's reign, ranging from the Siloam tunnel inscription to the extensive corpus of *lmlk* jar handles to numerous personal seals and seal impressions belonging to the leading citizens of the day, including some of King Hezekiah himself.[127] In the Deuteronomistic historian's summary of his reign (2 Kings 18:1–8, esp. v. 4) we are told that Hezekiah "removed the high places" (local shrines), "broke down the pillars" (standing stones that marked the sacredness of the shrines), "cut down the sacred pole" (the *asherah*), and smashed Nehushtan, "the bronze serpent that Moses had made" (an otherwise unknown but obviously long-venerated cult object).[128] All of these, except the last one, are often-mentioned Israelite cult objects that earlier kings were condemned for failing to abolish, and none of them is Assyrian. It would be a mistake, therefore, to associate Hezekiah's religious reforms with his revolt against Assyria in the closing years of the eighth century. On the contrary, he is more likely to have initiated these reforms early in his reign, before Sennacherib threatened the country and before the elimination of local places of worship might have demoralized the citizenry outside of Jerusalem.[129] The Chronicler states that Hezekiah began to purify the Temple immediately, in the first month of the first year of his reign (2 Chronicles 29:3). However this claim was intended to emphasize the piety of an ancient and revered king, it may be only slightly exaggerated.[130] The grim example of Samaria gave credence to the voices of prophets like Hosea, who had warned that the gross religious improprieties in the northern kingdom would lead to disaster and exile, and Hezekiah may have hoped that religious reform would help Judah avoid the fate of Israel. Indeed, there is evidence that the temple at Arad, built in the eighth century (Stratum X), continued in use for approximately 50 years before it was carefully put out of service during the time of Hezekiah.[131]

For the first two decades of his reign, Hezekiah seems to have remained a loyal vassal of Assyria. There is no Assyrian record of an attack on Judah by Shalmaneser V or Sargon II during this period.[132] When Ashdod rebelled against Assyria, in 714, Hezekiah evidently refused to become involved, despite the seditious messages Ashdod is said in one of Sargon's inscriptions to have sent to Judah.[133] Ashdod had active support from Shabaka (716–706), the Cushite ruler of Egypt, who had moved to assert the rule of the strong 25th Dynasty over the entire Nile Valley after the death of the dynastic founder, his brother Piankhy. The "Oracle concerning Ethiopia [i.e., Cush]," in Isaiah 19, with its reference to "sending ambassadors by the Nile," is often taken as an indication that Shabaka contacted Hezekiah, urging him to join the revolt. If so, Hezekiah evidently refused, perhaps swayed by Isaiah's counsel (cf. Isaiah 20:6), and the decision proved to be the safe one, since by 712 Sargon had smashed the revolt in Ashdod[134] and had at least intimidated its Egyptian supporters—this is the background of the threats against Egypt and Ethiopia (Cush) in Isaiah 20.[135]

Hezekiah's policy of compliance with Assyria ended dramatically with the death of Sargon II and the accession of his son Sennacherib (705–681). Viewed in broad perspective, the reign of Sennacherib was a period of relative tranquility in the western provinces of the empire. This was partly because the Assyrian army was heavily committed to a long and difficult struggle with Babylon, but it was also because the conquest of the West was now complete. Although Sennacherib's successors would attempt to extend its boundaries to the Nile, the empire had reached its natural limits. Moreover, the imperial administration, to which Sennacherib made a number of improvements, was in place and working, and this brought an unaccustomed stability to Syria-Palestine—the so-called *Pax Assyriaca*. It is somewhat ironic, then, that just as this Assyrian Peace was taking hold in the West, Sennacherib sent an army across the Euphrates—his only western campaign—with Jerusalem as its principal target and destination.

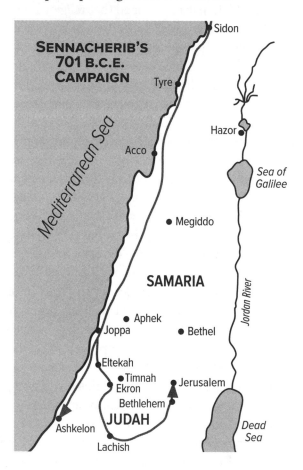

Sargon II had been killed in battle in Asia Minor, and news of his death sparked hope throughout the empire that Assyrian power would diminish. Almost immediately a rebellion broke out in Babylon, led again by Merodachbaladan, who had also opposed Sargon at his accession (722 B.C.E.). He was supported by a coalition of Babylonian ethnic groups, including his fellow Chaldeans, as well as Arameans and Elamites. Merodachbaladan may also have tried to foment unrest in the West,[136] where, in any case, a major revolt was brewing. The ringleaders were King Luli of Sidon in the north and Sidqia (*Sid-qa-a-a*) of Ashkelon and Hezekiah of Judah in the south. The people of Ekron also joined in, deposing their pro-Assyrian king Padi and consigning him to the custody of Hezekiah, who had "attacked the Philistines as far as Gaza and its territory, from watchtower to fortified city" (2 Kings 18:8), evidently attempting to force other Philistine states into the fold. Egypt supported the revolt hoping to reassert control over the territories and trade routes lost to Tiglath-pileser and Sargon.

Earlier, after Sargon's suppression of the 714–712 B.C.E. revolt in Ashdod, Pharaoh Shebitku (706–790), the successor of Shabaka, had made friendly overtures to Assyria in order to stabilize the position of the 25th Dynasty in Egypt by reducing the threat from Assyria. Now, however, Shebitku was ready to support rebellion against Assyria.

In 701, having ousted Merodachbaladan and brought things somewhat under control in Babylonia, Sennacherib marched against the western rebel states, beginning with Sidon.[137] When the Assyrian army arrived, the Phoenician cities surrendered without a fight. Luli fled to Cyprus (cf. Isaiah 23:12), where he later died, while Sennacherib installed Ittobaal (*Tuba'lu*) on the Sidonian throne. The Assyrian annals boast of the submission at this time of a number of western states ("all the kings of Amurru"). Some or all of these—including the Transjordanian states of Ammon, Moab, and Edom—may originally have supported the coalition, so that their surrender left Ashkelon, Ekron, and Judah isolated. Sennacherib stormed down the coast and accepted the surrender of Ashkelon, deporting Sidqia to Assyria and replacing him with Sharruludari, who, despite his Assyrian name, is said to have been the son of a former king of Ashkelon who had been loyal to Assyria. At this point Sennacherib spent some time destroying and looting towns and cities, such as Joppa, that had been dependent on Ashkelon. Before he was ready to march on Ekron, he was intercepted at Eltekeh (Tell esh-Shallaf, north of Jabneh) by a very large Egyptian expeditionary force that had responded to a request from

Ekron for help.[138] Though the annals claim that Sennacherib defeated the Egyptians, he may have merely escaped them—or at best repulsed them—and their continuing presence in the region was probably a factor in his decision to withdraw permanently from Palestine before consummating his siege of Jerusalem. In any case, he moved from Eltekeh on to Ekron and captured the city, punishing the rebels but sparing those who had remained loyal to Assyria; he would eventually bring Padi back from Jerusalem and restore him to his throne.[139]

WALL RELIEF FROM SENNACHERIB'S PALACE AT NINEVEH. A family from the conquered Judahite city of Lachish walks barefoot into exile. According to the Assyrian annals, Sennacherib (705–681 B.C.E.) besieged and captured 46 of Hezekiah's fortified cities. Sennacherib's greatest success was against Lachish— then the second most important city in Judah—which guarded the southwestern entrance into the passes to Jerusalem. The Assyrian war camp at Lachish, which is depicted in the Nineveh reliefs, became the headquarters for the entire Judahite campaign.

Sennacherib decorated the central ceremonial room of his Nineveh palace with reliefs like this depicting the conquest of Lachish. Other panels from the series show the Assyrians storming the city, executing the Judahites and carrying off booty.

After the capture of Ekron, the Assyrian army marched into Judah. For this stage of Sennacherib's campaign, we have fairly extensive accounts not only in the Assyrian annals, on which we rely for almost all we know about the earlier stages, but also in the Bible. The biblical account in 2 Kings 18:13–19:37 (= Isaiah 36–37) consists of two distinct sections that most likely derive from different sources. The opening section (2 Kings 18:13–16) is a straightforward summary of the events, describing the devastation of the Judahite countryside inflicted by the Assyrian army and Hezekiah's payment of tribute to Sennacherib. The businesslike tone of this passage and the absence of ideological or even interpretive expansion suggest that it is a quotation from an early annalistic source. Although much more compact than the Assyrian account, it corresponds closely—sometimes remarkably so[140]—to the picture given there, so that these two annalistic sources (Judahite and Assyrian) tend to corroborate each other.

The other section (2 Kings 18:17–19:34) is a long discursive narrative detailing demands for the surrender of Jerusalem made by Sennacherib's officers and placing special emphasis on the role of the prophet Isaiah in convincing Hezekiah not to surrender.[141] This material probably originated in prophetic circles associated with Isaiah, and its language and ideology indicate it was transmitted in the Deuteronomistic tradition. For these reasons the historical value of this second section of the biblical account of the invasion is now often discounted.[142]

According to the Assyrian annals, Sennacherib besieged and captured 46 of Hezekiah's fortified cities (cf. 2 Kings 18:13), turning many of them over to the Philistine states that had been loyal to Assyria. Most of these captured cities, we assume, were on Judah's western frontier, which, with Hezekiah's Philistine allies reduced to vassalage or worse, was vulnerable and unable to resist the Assyrian onslaught.[143]

Sennacherib's principal success in this part of the campaign was against the fortress city of Lachish in the Judahite Shephelah that guarded the southwestern entrance into the passes to Jerusalem. Lachish is not specifically mentioned in Sennacherib's annals—it was presumably one of the 46 captured cities—and the siege is not reported in the Bible (though the presence of the Assyrian army at Lachish is mentioned several times in 2 Kings 18–19). Nevertheless, the siege is very well documented, both by the reliefs found in the ruins of Sennacherib's palace at Nineveh that depict the siege and by the excavation of Lachish.[144] The old annalistic summary at the beginning of the biblical account states that Hezekiah sent a message of contrition to Sennacherib while he was at Lachish, asking the Assyrian king to withdraw and promising, "whatever you impose on me I will bear" (2 Kings 18:14). This suggests that the Assyrian war camp at Lachish, which is depicted in the Nineveh reliefs, was the headquarters for the entire Judahite campaign including the siege of Jerusalem, which must have already been well advanced before Hezekiah dispatched his submissive message.

SILOAM INSCRIPTION. Discovered in 1880, this inscription celebrates the completion of Hezekiah's tunnel. Carved into the wall of the tunnel about 20 feet from its end at the Siloam Pool, the text describes how the workmen tunneled toward each other to build the channel: "While the stonecutters were still wielding the axe, each man towards his fellow, and while there were still three cubits to be cut through, they heard the sound of each man calling to his fellow, for there was a *zdh* [fissure?] in the rock to the right and the left. And on the day of the breakthrough the stonecutters struck each man towards his fellows, axe against axe, and the waters flowed from the source to the pool, for 1,200 cubits."

Neither the Assyrian nor the biblical account indicates how long Jerusalem was under siege before Hezekiah submitted, but it was long enough for the Assyrian army to erect earthworks against the city gates and ravage the surrounding countryside while keeping Hezekiah confined, as Sennacherib boasted, "like a bird in a cage."[145] It may seem surprising that the city wall was never breached,[146] but Jerusalem was not as vulnerable as the cities on Judah's western frontier. The four years it had taken Sennacherib to subdue Merodachbaladan had given Hezekiah time to make elaborate preparations, especially in the capital city itself. According to 2 Chronicles 32:5, he had rebuilt and strengthened the city wall of Jerusalem and the *millo*.[147] He also added "another wall" that was "outside" the first.[148] Hezekiah's most remarkable achievement in this regard, though, was the construction of a tunnel to protect the city's water supply. The Gihon Spring, Jerusalem's principal source of water, was situated at a vulnerable location in the Kidron Valley outside the city wall.

HEZEKIAH'S TUNNEL. Anticipating an attack by Sennacherib of Assyria, the Judahite king Hezekiah (727–697 B.C.E.) built a 1,749-foot-long tunnel to bring the water of the Gihon Spring within the city walls of Jerusalem. This successful building project (with its fresh supply of water, Jerusalem managed to withstand the Assyrian siege) is referred to in 2 Kings 20:20 and 2 Chronicles 32:4.

Hezekiah's workers sealed access to the Gihon and the other water sources outside the city (2 Chronicles 32:3–4) and excavated a tunnel, still extant, that diverted the water under the hill to a collecting pool in the western part of the city, within the walls (cf. 2 Kings 20:20; 2 Chronicles 32:30). This remarkable engineering feat—the excavation of a tunnel 1,749 feet long and in places 100 feet beneath the streets of the city—was described and commemorated in an inscription found in 1880 and dubbed the Siloam Inscription.[149] It is also possible that a fragment of a monumental inscription from the City of David mentions Hezekiah and the pool he may have had built to collect the diverted waters.[150] Preceding his reference to Hezekiah's tunnel, the Chronicler indicates that Hezekiah maintained numerous storehouses for agricultural goods and cities for quartering livestock (2 Chronicles 32:28–29). These also should probably be seen as part of his preparations for the invasion. The possibility that Hezekiah reorganized the kingdom fiscally, dividing it into four administrative districts for the distribution of supplies, arises from the study of a large group of stamps found on jar handles and whole vessels—more than 1,200 of them from numerous sites— each of which bears the depiction of a winged scarab and the phrase *lmlk*, "Belonging to the king," followed by the name of one of four towns, which may have been central distribution depots.[151] Given the narrow time frame in which the marked jar handles were produced and the use of the jars for the storage of liquids (especially wine), it is likely that they, too, indicate that Hezekiah was stockpiling resources so as to withstand a siege.[152]

In the end, the siege of Jerusalem was lifted, and the Assyrian army departed. Although there may have been other factors,[153] Hezekiah's preparations probably made the completion of the siege seem more difficult than it was worth to Sennacherib, especially since he had already achieved his major goals. The revolt in the West had been completely quelled, and all the leading rebel states (Sidon, Ashkelon, and Judah) had submitted and accepted vassalage status— the former two with new kings of Sennacherib's choosing. Hezekiah was still on the throne of Jerusalem, but many of the towns and cities of Judah had been destroyed,[154] Padi had been freed from his custody and returned to Ekron, and Hezekiah himself had accepted vassalage and paid an extremely high price to keep his throne.[155] To supply the precious metals required by Sennacherib, Hezekiah emptied both the palace and Temple treasuries and stripped the gold ornamentation from the entryway of the Temple (2 Kings 18:15–16). With the Egyptian army probably still operating somewhere in the region, Sennacherib must have been content to go home and leave the Egypt problem for his successors.[156]

The Reign of Manasseh and the Assyrian Conquest of Egypt

Hezekiah died in 697 and was succeeded by his son Manasseh (697– 642). Judah was now a very small state, fully under the control of Assyria. Manasseh was a loyal vassal throughout most of his long reign. He is named several times in Assyrian records as one of the western kings required to transport materials to Nineveh or elsewhere for imperial building projects or to supply troops for the Assyrian assault on Egypt.[157] By complying with the demands of the Assyrian administration, he managed to reign mostly in peace for 55 years (2 Kings 21:1 = 2 Chronicles 33:1). To that extent, Judah can be said to have been a beneficiary of the *Pax Assyriaca* in Syria-Palestine. Nevertheless, Manasseh is judged extremely negatively in the Bible, especially in the account of his reign (2 Kings 21:1–18) where he is condemned not for his loyalty to Assyria but for his religious policies. The principal author of the account in Kings was an Exilic historian of the Deuteronomistic school, thus an advocate of the religious reforms of Hezekiah (Manasseh's father) and Josiah (Manasseh's grandson). The writer was trying to explain why Jerusalem fell despite these reforms, and he likely fixed on Manasseh because Manasseh was a counterreformer. In 2 Kings 21:10–15, the historian recites an oracle of Yahweh, attributed to unnamed prophets, that lays explicit blame on Manasseh for the fall of Jerusalem and the Exile of its people.

It was once assumed that Manasseh's religious policies were the inevitable result of his Assyrian allegiance, but this was not the case. As already noted in connection with Hezekiah's reforms, Assyria imposed no cultic restrictions on vassal states, permitting them to continue their indigenous religious customs. The list of cultic practices for which Manasseh is condemned in 2 Kings 21:3–7 includes no reference to the worship of Assyrian gods. The cultic changes made by Manasseh were, instead, revivals of old Israelite and Judahite practices that had been accepted in the time of his grandfather, Ahaz, and earlier, but set aside by the reforms of his father, Hezekiah. In particular, "he rebuilt the high places that his father, Hezekiah, had destroyed" (2 Kings 21:3), thus reversing the movement toward cultic centralization that lay at the core of Hezekiah's reform program. Manasseh's reversion to this and other abandoned practices was harshly condemned by reformers and biblical writers living in the time of Josiah and later.[158] But from another point of view, Manasseh's actions may be understood as a kind of reform in themselves—that is, as a counterreformation, involving a wholesale rejection of the innovative religious policies of Hezekiah, which, as Manasseh probably saw it, had not succeeded in protecting Judah from Assyria.

Manasseh was a vassal of three Assyrian kings. When Sennacherib was assassinated, in 681, by his sons (cf. 2 Kings 19:37), it led to a power struggle that resulted in the accession of his youngest son, Esarhaddon (681–669), who had been Sennacherib's designated heir and not one of his assassins. Much of Esarhaddon's reign was spent to conquer Egypt, an enterprise that was completed by his son Assurbanipal (668–627).

Throughout most of this period, Egypt was ruled by Taharqa (690–664), the biblical Tirhakah, whose reign was remarkable for both its achievements and disasters. It was the high point of the Cushite period (25th Dynasty), marked by prosperity and building activities especially in the dynasty's homeland of Nubia. But the 25th Dynasty also suffered the first successful invasion of Egypt in a thousand years (since the Hyksos period).

At the time of Esarhaddon's accession, in 681, the Assyrian Empire extended to the border of Egypt. Esarhaddon thus inherited full control of the coastal trunk road, the King's Highway east of the Jordan, and all the northern outlets available to the South Arabian trade. With the consolidation of Egypt under Pharaoh Taharqa, however, Assyria had a serious rival for control of commerce (by land and sea) in the eastern Mediterranean. A clash was inevitable. The pattern developed that Assyria became increasingly aggressive toward Egypt while Taharqa acted covertly or openly to support anti-Assyrian uprisings in the western provinces of the empire.

Before he could turn his attention to the conquest of Egypt, however, Esarhaddon was obliged to spend a few years defending his northern borders against the Medes[159] and the incursions of Eurasian horse nomads, including Cimmerians[160] and Scythians.[161] He then had to deal with a series of revolts in the West, which can be seen as the opening rounds in his fight with Egypt. Tyre and Sidon, which had been united when Luli had rebelled against Sennacherib, were now rivals. King Baal of Tyre was, like Manasseh, one of Assyria's most submissive vassals, and as a reward Esarhaddon made a treaty with him giving him certain trade privileges, such as free entry into all Mediterranean ports. Abdimilkutti of Sidon, provoked by what must have seemed to him unfair advantages for his rival, eventually decided to rebel, most probably with the encouragement and assurances of Pharaoh Taharqa.[162] In response, Esarhaddon marched west in

678 and besieged Sidon; within a year he had captured and beheaded Abdimilkutti and cast the city into the sea, reassigning portions of Sidonian territory to Tyre.

According to the Babylonian Chronicle, the first major battle between the Assyrian and Egyptian armies in Esarhaddon's reign occurred in his seventh year (674), when "the army of Assyria was defeated in a bloody battle in Egypt."[163] Nothing more is known of this conflict, but it seems to have been a serious setback for Assyria, since Esarhaddon did not return west until his tenth year (671). At that time, having accused his old ally Baal of Tyre of conspiring with Taharqa, Esarhaddon marched past Phoenicia, leaving troops to enforce an embargo on food and water against Tyre, and proceeded south past the then-Egyptian fortress of Ashkelon to the Wadi of Egypt. From there the invasion of Egypt was launched in earnest. The Assyrian army crossed the Sinai using camels and waterskins provided by "all the kings of Arabia."[164] Esarhaddon reached the Egyptian capital city of Memphis after fighting three battles in 15 days. The city capitulated, and the queen and crown prince were captured, but Taharqa fled south into Upper Egypt, where he still had control, and began to reorganize his forces.[165]

Esarhaddon, probably representing himself as the liberator of Egypt from Cushite rule,[166] accepted the surrender of local rulers of Lower Egypt and departed, leaving the Nile Delta in their hands. As soon as the Assyrian army had withdrawn, however, Taharqa returned north and seized power again. This provoked Esarhaddon to launch another campaign against Egypt, in 669, but the Assyrian king died at Haran shortly after setting out,[167] and it remained for his son Assurbanipal (669–627) to finish the war with Taharqa. In 667, Assurbanipal sent an army to Egypt led by his viceroy (*turtānu*).[168] This expeditionary force was supported by ground troops supplied by the Assyrian vassal kings, including Manasseh of Judah,[169] and it was reinforced by naval fleets launched from coastal vassal states. Taharqa was once again defeated at Memphis and fled south. This time, however, the Assyrian army pursued his troops up the Nile, establishing control as far south as Aswan. Taharqa himself escaped to Nubia.

As the Assyrian army withdrew, it again entrusted Egypt to local rulers who had pledged loyalty, and again the local rulers betrayed the

Assyrians and conspired with Taharqa, who in 666 again returned to power. In reprisal, Assurbanipal sent soldiers to seize the disloyal rulers, executing many but bringing two (Necho of Sais and his son Psammetichus) to Nineveh. In 665, Assurbanipal established the former as Necho I (r. 665–664) the first king of the 26th (Saite) Dynasty. Taharqa died the following year, having first named his son Tantamani or Tanwetamani (r. 664–656) as his successor. When Tantamani attacked the Assyrian troops at Memphis and seized the city, Assurbanipal again sent the Assyrian army into Egypt, where it took back control of Memphis and marched on Thebes in the south. Thebes was captured and sacked in 664/663 (cf. Nahum 3:8–11). Though Tantamani remained (at least nominally) in power as the Egyptian ruler controlling Upper Egypt from Nubia until his death in 656, Lower Egypt was now governed from Sais by Necho's son, Psammetichus I (r. 664–610).

The Assyrian Empire was now badly overextended, and Egypt soon became independent again. After the rebellion of 666–665, Assyria recognized Necho and then Psammetichus as sole king of Egypt on condition that neither would foment rebellion against Assyria. In 656, with the death of Tantamani and the end of the 25th Dynasty, Psammetichus was able to extend the rule of the 26th Dynasty south to Thebes.[170] Meanwhile the Cimmerians, now well established in Asia Minor, continued to threaten Assyria's Syrian holdings. These factors destabilized the empire, but the first critical blow came from Babylon, where a major revolt erupted in 652 at the instigation of Assurbanipal's own brother Shamash-shum-ukin, whom their father, Esarhaddon, had appointed as vice-regent in Babylon. This revolt soon spread.[171] In the East it was supported by Chaldean nationalists as well as Arameans and Elamites, the same groups who had backed Merodachbaladan earlier. In the West the primary supporters of the revolt seem to have been Arabs,[172] who probably perceived the vulnerability of Assyria as an opportunity to liberate the trade routes of the southern Levant. Although the Assyrian forces were able to contain the various Arab incursions associated with Shamash-shum-ukin's revolt, the victory was only temporary, since at this time much of Transjordan began to be overrun by Kedarites and other Arabian tribes who did not recognize Assyrian sovereignty. By 648, Assurbanipal had quelled the revolt in Babylon, but it was a foreboding of the fate of the empire.

We have no direct evidence of the way the news of the revolt in Babylon, and of Assyria's other troubles in the mid-seventh century, was received in Judah. Apart from its polemic against Manasseh's religious policies, the Kings account of Manasseh's reign (2 Kings 21:1–18), with its Deuteronomistic orientation, provides little information about Manasseh's activities.[173] The Chronicler's account supplies additional details, suggesting that in the last decade of his reign, with Assyria substantially weakened, Manasseh may have begun to move Judah toward independence (2 Chronicles 33:1–20). In particular, the Chronicler credits Manasseh with building "an outer wall for the City of David, west of the Gihon, in the wadi" and assigning military officers to "all the fortified cities of Judah" (2 Chronicles 31:14). The Chronicler does not indicate when in Manasseh's reign these things were done, but it seems probable that they began at the time of the revolt in Babylon (652–648). The activities described are reminiscent, on a smaller scale, of Hezekiah's preparations for his revolt against Sennacherib, and they sound very much as if they were designed to strengthen Judah in preparation for a declaration of independence against Assyria. Manasseh's "outer wall" in Jerusalem may have been identified archaeologically,[174] and excavations throughout Judah have found substantial evidence of refortification in the latter part of the seventh century. Most of this building should probably be associated with Josiah, but it may have begun during the last days of Manasseh.

THE FINAL YEARS OF THE KINGDOM OF JUDAH

The Reign of Josiah and the End of the Assyrian Empire

According to 2 Kings 21:23-24 (= 2 Chronicles 33: 24-25), Manasseh's son and successor, Amon (r. 642–640 B.C.E.), was assassinated by his own courtiers ("the servants of Amon"). The assassins in turn were then executed by "the people of the land," who proceeded to set Amon's eight-year-old son Josiah on the throne.[175] Since Josiah came to the throne as a minor, Judah was probably ruled at first by a regent or group of regents—perhaps Josiah's mother or one of "the people of the land" who set him on the throne—but we are not told. In fact, the biblical writers, who are interested almost exclusively in Josiah's religious reform, report nothing about his reign before his 18th year (622), when the reform began.

By this time, Assurbanipal had died (627). After a period of chaos, his son Sin-shar-ishkun (r. 623–612) succeeded him, but not before Assyria had descended into civil war and permanently lost control of Babylon, which was now ruled by the Chaldean Nabopolassar (r. 625–605).[176] In short, the Assyrian Empire was in its death throes. This meant that Judah was, in effect, an independent state again, and Josiah was free to institute administrative reforms and continue to strengthen his territory and the capital city of Jerusalem.[177]

The overriding interest of the biblical writers, however, was Josiah's religious reform, which is reported in detail in 2 Kings 22:1–23:30. The chief characteristics of this reform were cult purification and centralization to the Jerusalem Temple. This included the attempt to eliminate the "high places" (bāmôt, the local places of sacrifice and worship throughout the kingdom), and the exclusion of the regional priests from priestly service in Jerusalem (2 Kings 23:8). Other measures included the destruction of religious objects such as vessels made for Baal and Asherah, as well as images of horses dedicated to the sun (2 Kings 23:4–7; 10–14).

According to 2 Kings 22:8, the reform was set in motion by the discovery of "the book of the law in the house of the Lord" by Hilkiah, the high priest. When this scroll was shown to Josiah, he summoned the people of Judah to the Temple in Jerusalem, where he read them everything that was in the document. He then vowed to instigate religious reforms in conformity with the rules that were written there. It is not clear from the Kings and Chronicles accounts of these events whether the reform was initiated by the accidental "discovery" of a scroll (as the books of Kings suggest) or whether an already ongoing reform program received its crucial impetus when a scroll was brought forward by the priests. Although 2 Kings 22:3 dates the discovery to Josiah's eighteenth year, 2 Chronicles 34:3 states that the king had begun to "seek the God of his ancestor David" in his eighth year, "while he was still a boy," and had begun instituting reforms by his twelfth.

PLATE 1 · THE SINAI PENINSULA. This view of the "great and terrible wilderness" (Deuteronomy 8:15) traversed by the Israelites on their Exodus wanderings was taken by a NASA satellite, miles out in space; it also includes the Nile Delta (top left), most of the Egyptian Eastern Desert (between the Nile and the Red Sea), and the land of Canaan (top right). (See chap. 2.)

PLATE 2 · TOMB PAINTING FROM BENI HASAN, EGYPT. Leaning over his ibex, a figure named Abisha and identified by the title Hyksos leads brightly garbed Semitic clansmen into Egypt to conduct trade. Dating to about 1890 B.C.E., the painting is preserved on the wall of a tomb carved into cliffs overlooking the Nile at Beni Hasan, about halfway between Cairo and Luxor.

Foreign groups often sojourned in Egypt, especially in pursuit of trade. In the early second millennium B.C.E., numerous Asiatics infiltrated Egypt, some of whom eventually gained control over Lower Egypt for about a century and a half. The governing class of these people became known as the Hyksos, which means "Rulers of Foreign Lands." Knowledge of this period of Asiatic rule in Egypt may have affected the biblical account of Joseph's rise to power. (See chap. 2.)

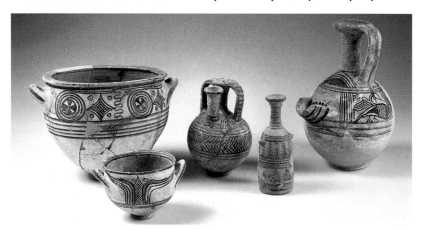

PLATE 3 · PHILISTINE POTTERY. The fine craftsmanship of these pitchers and bowls challenges the traditional characterization of the Philistines as a boorish, warlike people devoid of an aesthetic sensibility. Known as bichrome ware because it was decorated with two colors—black and red—this pottery displays typical Philistine designs, including birds (visible on the wine decanter, at right), checkerboards, spirals and other geometric patterns. (See chap. 4.)

PLATE 4 · CANAANITE CULT STAND FROM TAANACH. Four tiers of cryptic scenes ornament this tenth-century B.C.E. pottery stand from Taanach (about 5 miles southeast of Megiddo). A shallow basin—presumably for offerings or libations—crowns the 21-inch-high stand. The bottom register depicts, in high relief, a nude female figure, perhaps the mother-goddess Asherah, holding the ears of two lions. Winged sphinxes flank the opening in the second register. Lions appear again on the third register; between them, two goats nibble on a stylized tree—perhaps a "tree of life"—a motif associated with Asherah. Two columns frame the top scene, which depicts a horse or calf with a winged sun-disk above its back.

Although the images are often identified as the Canaanite deities Baal (represented as a bull) and Asherah, it has recently been suggested that they actually represent the Israelite deity Yahweh (represented by the horse and by the empty space in the second register) with Asherah as his consort. (See chaps. 3 and 4.)

PLATE 5 · IVORY CHERUB. Modeled in ivory, this 5-inch-tall ivory plaque, dating to the ninth or eighth century B.C.E., depicts a winged creature with an exquisite human face, the forequarters of a lion and what may be the hindquarters of a bull. Such composite creatures, like the Egyptian sphinx, were common in the ancient Near East, where they were often associated with divinity. This ivory, probably from Arslan Tash in northern Syria, recalls the cherub described by the prophet Ezekiel as combining characteristics of humans, lions, bulls and eagles (Ezekiel 1:10). Mentioned more than 90 times in the Hebrew Bible, cherubim guarded the gates of the Garden of Eden and stood over the Ark in the Holy of Holies in the Temple.

Solomon's "great throne of ivory," described in 1 Kings 10:18, may have been decorated with such ivory plaques. Ornamenting thrones and beds with ivory was a well-known specialty of the Phoenicians, Solomon's trading partners. (See chap. 4.)

PLATE 6 · ISRAELITE BULL FIGURINE. Dating to about 1200 B.C.E., this 4-inch-tall bronze statue was discovered at a cultic site near biblical Dothan, in the heart of the hill country that was then being settled by the Israelites.

Although the biblical writers consistently condemn the iconography of young bulls, archaeological finds such as this indicate that the bull was an early Israelite symbol of divinity. This figurine may resemble the bull statues erected by Jeroboam (c. 930–908 B.C.E.) at Bethel and Dan (1 Kings 12:26–33). (See chap. 3.)

PLATE 7 · TEL DAN STELA. An Aramean king—probably Hazael of Damascus—boasts of his victories over "[Jo]ram son of [Ahab], king of Israel," and "[Ahaz]iah son of [Jehoram, ki]ng of the House of David," in this Old Aramaic inscription from Dan. The dates of the reigns of the biblical kings Joram of Israel (c. 850–841 B.C.E.) and Ahaziah of Judah (c. 841 B.C.E.) provide a mid-ninth-century B.C.E. date for the inscription. The reference to "the House [or dynasty] of David" suggests that Judahite kings traced their descent back to an actual David who lived a century earlier. It is the earliest appearance of the name of David outside the Bible. (See chap. 5.)

PLATE 8 · IVORY POMEGRANATE FROM SOLOMON'S TEMPLE. This exquisite carving was long thought to be the only surviving artifact from Solomon's Temple in Jerusalem. A small hole bored into the bottom of the ivory indicates that it probably served as the decorative head of a ceremonial scepter carried by Temple priests. Several such pomegranate scepters have survived, one of which is pictured here. The inscribed pomegranate reads around the neck "Holy to the priests, belonging to the H[ouse of Yahwe]h." Although most paleographers, including André Lemaire and the late Nahman Avigad, regard the inscription as unquestionably authentic, dating to the late eighth century B.C.E., some Israeli officials and archaeologists contend the inscription is the work of a modern forger. (See chap. 5.)

PLATE 9 · HERODIUM. To protect himself in case of insurrection, Herod the Great
(37–4 B.C.E.) built a string of palace-fortresses—including this volcano-like
structure that he named after himself—in the Judean wilderness. At Herodium,
Herod started with a natural hill and then created an artificial mountain over it.
Inside he fashioned a palace that included living rooms, a reception and dining
hall, a colonnaded courtyard, cisterns and a bathhouse. Four massive towers
and a double wall protected the intimate palace. At the foot of the mountain, a
135-foot by 21-foot basin (visible in the left foreground) served as a reservoir,
a pool and a lake for small sailboats; picnickers may have enjoyed the circular
pavilion at the center of this desert oasis. Herod was buried at Herodium,
according to Josephus, and Israeli archaeologist Ehud Netzer has identified the
tomb at the foot of the mound. (See chap. 8.)

PLATE 10 · MASADA. This imposing citadel—built by Herod the Great (37–4 B.C.E.) on an isolated plateau at the edge of the Judean wilderness—is associated with a legendary act of defiance. According to the first-century C.E. Jewish historian Josephus, a band of Jewish fighters, unwilling to concede defeat during the First Jewish Revolt against Rome, held out at Masada for more than three years against a large imperial army after the fall of Jerusalem (70 C.E.). Masada fell in 73 or 74 C.E., when the Romans built a ramp on a spur on the western side of the plateau. (See chap. 8.)

It is also true that, even in the account in Kings, Temple repairs were already underway before the finding of the scroll (2 Kings 21:3–7). A final possibility is that an account about finding a scroll that correlated with anticipated reforms was composed only later—to give the reforms divine sanction.[178]

Based on the parallels between Josiah's reform measures as set out in 2 Kings 23 and the laws for worship recorded in Deuteronomy, some have argued that Josiah's "book of the law" was part of the biblical Book of Deuteronomy in an early form. For example, Josiah's instructions to abolish various cultic practices conform to prohibitions in Deuteronomy. These include the cult of Asherah and the "asherim," or sacred poles (2 Kings 23:4; 6; 7; 14; Deuteronomy 7:5; 12:3; 16:21; 17:3); the "pillars" (2 Kings 23:14; Deuteronomy 7:5; 12:3); the "high places" (2 Kings 23:13; Deuteronomy 7:5; 12:2–3), and many others. Compare also Josiah's observance of the Passover in Jerusalem "as prescribed in this book of the covenant" (2 Kings 23:21–23) with the commandment to observe Passover "at the place that the Lord your God will choose" in Deuteronomy 16:1–8.

Any religious reforms that Josiah carried out as king would also involve political dimensions. In terms of national ideals, the assertion of the centrality of Jerusalem would unify the country and strengthen the central government. The changes would also have vindicated those who still supported the principles of Hezekiah's reform and, by the same token, repudiated those who had defended Manasseh's policies. And although the nation was largely hemmed in by the waning power of Assyria on the East,[179] and the encroaching strength of Egypt along the Mediterranean coast, Josiah may have been looking to the north to expand his territory.[180] The biblical account gives special attention to the cancellation of the cult established by Jeroboam I at Bethel (2 Kings 23:15–20), and this would not have been possible if Josiah had not been able to expand his influence north into the territory of the former Assyrian province of Samerina (Samaria).

Things were changing quickly in international power structures. After the accession of Sin-shar-ishkun, the failing Assyrian Empire lasted little more than a decade before the critical blow was struck by the Babylonians and the Medes. The Babylonian Nabopolassar organized the anti-Assyrian forces—Chaldeans, Arameans, and Elamites—who had supported the Shamash-shum-ukin rebellion (652–648) and the rebellions of Merodachbaladan still earlier. By 616 B.C.E., Nabopolassar was ready to begin his advance north and west against Assyria. At about the same time, however, the Medes under Cyaxares began their own assault on Assyria from the north. In 614, the Medes captured the ancient Assyrian capital of Ashu and entered into an alliance with Nabopolassar. Then, in 612, Nineveh, which had been the imperial Assyrian capital since the time of Sennacherib, fell to the combined forces of the Babylonians and Medes. Sin-shar-ishkun seems to have died when the city fell, and Ashur-uballit II (r. 612–609) became the last Assyrian king, setting up a rump government in Haran, about 100 miles west of Nineveh. Though the Babylonians were not yet secure enough in central and northern Mesopotamia to attack Haran and finish the job, the fall of Nineveh signaled the end of Assyria. It was a major turning-point in the history of the ancient Near East and sent shock waves reverberating throughout the region. The biblical monument to this event is the Book of Nahum, which is entirely devoted to the prophet's "oracle concerning Nineveh" (Nahum 1:1).

Egypt played a prominent and somewhat surprising role in these events. As explained earlier, Egypt had been united since 656 B.C.E. under the 26th, or Saite, Dynasty. Psammetichus I (r. 664–610) had come to the throne as a protégé of Assyria. With the eclipse of Assyria, he became an independent and powerful ruler, not only presiding over the so-called Saite Renaissance at home, but also expanding north to take control of most of Philistia and coastal Palestine as far north as Phoenicia.[181] According to the testimony of Herodotus, Psammetichus took Ashdod by siege[182] and, on another occasion, negotiated the end of an incursion of Scythians into southern Palestine after they had plundered "the Temple of Aphrodite" in Ashkelon.[183] These reports lack direct substantiation in Near Eastern records, but they are plausible and seem to indicate Egyptian domination of Philistia in the latter part of the seventh century B.C.E.

Despite his departure from his old vows to Assurbanipal, however, the aging Psammetichus decided to come to the aid of Assyria in its hour of need. Egyptian troops fought alongside the Assyrians against Nabopolassar and his allies in 616, and under Psammetichus's successor, Necho II (r. 610–595), their support continued until 609.

It is not clear what motivated the Egyptian kings to adopt this policy of attempting to help Assyria survive. Perhaps they envisioned joint Assyrian-Egyptian control of Syria-Palestine. Perhaps they were attempting to position themselves so that when Assyria fell, Egypt would be heir to its empire in the West. It seems likely, in any case, that they wanted to preserve the status quo, as Egypt was beginning to thrive again, and were apprehensive about any future victories for the Chaldeans and the Medes.

In 610 B.C.E., the army of the Medes entered Assyria and joined forces with the Babylonians, who already had Scythian support, and in October the Babylonian and Scythian armies advanced on Haran, the last capital of Assyria. Ashur-uballit abandoned the city and fled west to await the arrival of his Egyptian allies. In 609, Necho II set out and marched north. When the Egyptian army was crossing through the Megiddo pass, Josiah confronted it, and Necho captured and killed him.

The circumstances under which Josiah was killed are not clear. The biblical account is cryptic: "King Josiah went to meet him; but when Pharaoh Necho met him at Megiddo, he killed him" (2 Kings 23:29). It is usually assumed, on the basis of 2 Chronicles 35:20–24, that Josiah was trying to intercept the Egyptian army. But the king may not have gone to Megiddo with a hostile encounter in mind. He may have been seeking an audience with the new pharaoh or attempting to enter into some kind of negotiation. At any rate, the encounter became antagonistic and Judah's king was killed.

After this, the Egyptian army proceeded north and, according to the Babylonian Chronicle, crossed the Euphrates in July of 609; then, joining forces with the Assyrians, they marched against Haran.[184] The results of a four-month siege seem to have been inconclusive—Ashur-uballit may never have reentered the city—but the time was sufficient for the Egyptian army to take control of Syria as far north as Carchemish (cf. 2 Chronicles 35:20), establishing its field headquarters at Riblah in the northern Beqa' (Tell Zerr'a on the Orontes, 21 mi south of Homs).[185] Necho summoned a group of Syro-Palestinian rulers to Riblah to require them to swear oaths of loyalty to Egypt. Among them was King Jehoahaz of Judah (2 Kings 23:33), Josiah's youngest son,[186] whom "the people of the land" had made king when his father was killed (2 Kings 23:30). Necho deposed Jehoahaz and replaced him with his brother Eliakim, changing his name to Jehoiakim (2 Kings 23:31–35), and imposed a heavy tribute on Judah. Judah's brief period of independence—between the direct control of either Assyria or Egypt control—was now over.

NEBUCHADNEZZAR'S CAMPAIGNS

Egypt dominated Syria-Palestine for a few years, holding the Babylonians at bay until 605, when the Babylonian crown prince Nabu-kudurri-usdur (the biblical Nebuchadnezzar or Nebuchadrezzar) was given charge of field operations in the West. The Babylonian Chronicle reports that under his leadership the Egyptian army was routed in a decisive battle fought at Carchemish.[187] Necho fled south, but Nebuchadnezzar overtook him at Hamath and defeated him again.

The Egyptian king then returned to the banks of the Nile, leaving Syria in Babylonian hands. By that time the Assyrian Empire was a thing of the past, and its former territories divided between the Medes and the Babylonians. The Medes took the Assyrian heartland and northern territories, while the Babylonians took the rest of Mesopotamia and the western territories, which included rights to not only Syria but also Palestine, so that a further showdown between Babylonia and Egypt was inevitable.

The Fall of Jerusalem

The predicament of Judah in the final years before the destruction of Jerusalem was similar to that of Israel before the fall of Samaria. Both were small states swallowed up by great imperial powers, and both had attempted to avoid this fate and maintain some measure of independence by oscillating between policies of appeasement and defiance. As we have seen, Hezekiah's revolt after the death of Sargon II (in 705) followed the Israelite pattern of defiance in the form of resistance to Assyria that was secured by an alliance with the neighboring states of Sidon and Ashkelon. But when Sennacherib invaded Judah, in 701, and placed Jerusalem under siege, Hezekiah was forced to shift to a policy of appeasement, paying a heavy tribute to ensure the survival of his kingdom. This policy continued through most of the long reign of Manasseh (697–642), whose loyalty to Sennacherib and his successors kept Judah secure.

When the Assyrian Empire collapsed in the last decades of the seventh century B.C.E., Judah's position became more precarious. The vacuum left by Assyria's demise was now filled by not one but two great powers. The kings of the 26th Egyptian Dynasty, who had been allied with Assyria, asserted their power along the coast of Palestine. At the same time, Babylon rose to preeminence under Nabopolassar and Nebuchadnezzar and began to take an interest of its own in the affairs of Palestine. These developments left Judah in the treacherous position of having to conduct its policies of resistance and appeasement in relation to two competing superpowers.

Nebuchadnezzar probably intended to follow up his victories at Carchemish and Hamath by continuing to march south into Palestine, but he was prevented from doing so by the death of his father,

Nabopolassar, which required him to return to Babylon in August 605, and accept the crown as Nebuchadnezzar II (r. 605–562), the second king of the neo-Babylonian Empire.

LACHISH LETTER. In 1935, while excavating a burned guardroom beneath a gate tower that had been destroyed by Nebuchadnezzar's army, archaeologists at Lachish found a small archive of wartime correspondence addressed to a certain Ya'ush, evidently the governor or commanding officer of Lachish, from a subordinate named Hawshi'yahu (both names contain forms of the name Yahweh). Written on inscribed potsherds called ostraca, the letters paint an intriguing picture of maneuvers taking place on the southwestern frontier of Judah. Most scholars believe that the ostraca were written on the eve of the destruction of Jerusalem in 586 B.C.E.

The last four lines of this letter read, "And let [my lord]know that we are watching for the signals of Lachish, according to all the signs which my lord has given, for we do not see Azekah." This recalls Jeremiah's prophecies about a time when "the army of the king of Babylon was fighting against Jerusalem and the cities of Judah—against Lachish and Azekah, for these were the only fortified cities that remained of all the cities of Judah" (Jeremiah 34:7).

Within a year, however, Nebuchadnezzar was back in the field, marching through Syria-Palestine and encountering minimal resistance, since Necho II was now back in Egypt licking his wounds and rebuilding his forces (see also 2 Kings 24:7). In this western campaign of 604, Nebuchadnezzar concentrated on Philistia, especially Ashkelon, which he sacked in December 604, capturing its king, Aga.[188] Judah was understandably intimidated by having the Babylonian army relatively nearby. A fast was proclaimed in Jerusalem (Jeremiah 36:9), and Jehoiakim, despite his pro-Egyptian leanings, submitted to Nebuchadnezzar and, according to 2 Kings 24:1, became his vassal for three years (604–602).

Nebuchadnezzar suffered one of his few setbacks in the winter of 601/600, when he attempted to invade Egypt and was repulsed, probably at the fortress of Migdol.[189] Nebuchadnezzar was forced to withdraw to Babylon, where he remained for a full year and rebuilt his army. This gave Necho the opportunity to campaign along the southern coast of Palestine, capturing Gaza (cf. Jeremiah 47). Jehoiakim, sensing that the balance of power had shifted again, ceased to pay tribute to Babylon and tried to restore himself in the favor of Necho, who was building a coalition against Babylon.

This proved to be a fatal error of judgment. Nebuchadnezzar returned to Palestine in 599 without much show of force, sending out only raiding parties to attack and plunder the camps of the Kedarites and other Arab tribes.[190] On his next visit, however, he returned with his forces fully restored. Intent on reprisal against Jehoiakim for having withheld tribute, he marched on Jerusalem in the winter of 598/597 and put the city under siege in January. Not long before this, in 598, Jehoiakim had died and was replaced by his 18-year-old son Jehoiachin. Jerusalem capitulated with no great resistance on the second day of the Babylonian month of Adar in the seventh year of Nebuchadnezzar—that is, March 16, 597 B.C.E.

Nebuchadnezzar, apparently content with the removal of Jehoiakim, followed a policy of relative leniency and ordered no general destruction of the city. He did, however, take Jehoiachin into exile, along with much of the royal family, many members of the court, and other leading citizens and artisans. According to 2 Kings 24:14, this first deportation from Jerusalem involved 10,000 people; according to 2 Kings 24:16, the number was 8,000 (7,000 prominent people and 1,000 skilled craftsmen); and according to Jeremiah 52:28, it was 3,023, a number that may include only the male heads of households. Nebuchadnezzar made vassalage treaty with a third son of Josiah, Jehoiachin's uncle Mattaniah, whom he placed on the throne, changing his name to Zedekiah.

BULLA OF JEREMIAH'S SCRIBE. "Belonging to Berekhyahu, son of Neriyahu, the scribe," reads the inscription on this clay bulla, which appears to have been impressed with the seal belonging to the prophet Jeremiah's scribe and faithful companion Baruch. The Bible recounts that "Baruch son of Neriah ... wrote on a scroll at Jeremiah's dictation all the words of the Lord that he had spoken to him" (Jeremiah 36:4). The biblical names appear on the bulla with the suffix *yahu*, a form of Yahweh.

An even more arresting impression appears on the upper left edge of the late-seventh to early-sixth-century B.C.E. bulla: the whorls of a fingerprint, presumably left by the biblical scribe himself.

During his reign, Zedekiah faced the same predicament that had doomed Jehoiakim, and he made the same mistake. Soon after he was crowned, Nebuchadnezzar conducted repeated campaigns in Syria-Palestine, but with the memory of the Babylonian defeat of 601/600 still fresh, Judah and the other Palestinian states do not seem to have been entirely intimidated. Egypt remained ambitious and formidable under the successors of Necho II—Psammetichus II (r. 595–589) and Apries, the biblical Hophra (r. 589–570). In these circumstances, anti-Babylonian plotting began almost immediately, and in 594 Zedekiah seems to have convened an international group of conspirators in Jerusalem to plan a revolt, with representatives from Edom, Moab, Ammon, Tyre, and Sidon (cf. Jeremiah 27:3). This conspiracy collapsed quickly when Nebuchadnezzar marched into Palestine in his 11th year (594/593). Jehoiachin sent word to him assuring him of Judah's loyalty, but the events foreshadowed what was to come.

The walls were breached in July of 586. Zedekiah was captured while trying to escape under the cover of night and was led before Nebuchadnezzar, who put the Judahite king's sons to death before his eyes, then blinded the king and sent him into exile. The Babylonian leader commanded that the city and its Temple be razed, and the order was carried out in August. According to Jeremiah 52:29, there was an additional deportation of 832 people, a number that may include only male heads of households.

There was no immediate plan to rebuild the city or repopulate it with foreign captives (which was not, in any case, Babylonian policy), and there was no plan for Jerusalem to become a provincial capital, probably because of its long history as a center of rebellion.[191] Nebuchadnezzar installed a cadre of pro-Babylonian Jews, led by a Judahite aristocrat named Gedaliah son of Ahikam, in a governance role at the town of Mizpah, 8 miles northwest of Jerusalem (2 Kings 25:23).[192] Soon after his appointment as governor, Gedaliah was assassinated by a Davidide named Ishmael (2 Kings 25:25). Members of Gedaliah's regime, fearing Babylonian reprisals, fled to Egypt (2 Kings 25:26), taking Jeremiah with them, while Ishmael and his followers fled to Ammon to escape the vengeance of Gedaliah's remaining supporters (Jeremiah 41:15).

In this way the Kingdom of Judah suffered the same fate as the Kingdom of Israel. Like Hoshea before them, Jehoiakim and Zedekiah were unable to find the right combination of resistance and appeasement that would permit their small kingdom to survive in an international arena dominated by two larger and more aggressive superpowers.

6

Exile and Return
From the Babylonian Destruction to the Beginnings of Hellenism

ERIC M. MEYERS

THE INDEPENDENT KINGDOM OF JUDAH finally came to an end
when the neo-Babylonian ruler Nebuchadnezzar crushed Zedekiah's
rebellion and destroyed Jerusalem in 586 B.C.E. The Book of Kings
and Jeremiah arrestingly recount the series of humiliations Judah faced.
The neo-Babylonians (as distinguished from the earlier Babylonian
Empire of the third millennium B.C.E.) executed Zedekiah's sons
before his eyes, then blinded and imprisoned him; they burned the
Temple and slaughtered the Temple officials, military commanders,
and noblemen; and they deported many of the survivors to Babylonia
(2 Kings 25:7–21; Jeremiah 39:1–10; 52:1–16). The rebellious Zedekiah
was deposed, and the grandson of Shaphan, Gedaliah, was appointed
as governor[1] in his place. Thus ended Judah's Davidic monarchy (see
2 Kings 25; Jeremiah 39; 52). Zedekiah, blinded and humbled, was
deported to Babylonia along with many of Judah's elites. A new chapter
in Israel's history had begun.

THE NEO-BABYLONIAN PERIOD

This period has traditionally been referred to as the Exile. The word "exile" and associated terms such as "exilic" and "postexilic," however, are not without problems. They give priority to the perspective of those who saw themselves as descendants of the "remnant" who survived in Babylonia and then returned to Israel. As such, "Exile" excludes, or at least marginalizes, several important developments in the history of Judah and the Judeans in the sixth–fourth centuries B.C.E. For example, what about the reduced but still notable population that remained in the land of Israel? What about the immigrants to areas other than Babylonia, such as Egypt and Transjordan? What about those deportees who chose to remain in Babylonia and elsewhere even after the Exile "ended"?[2]

The biblical accounts of life after the fall of Jerusalem are unfortunately fragmentary. The biblical writers and editors seem to have regarded the events of the neo-Babylonian period as less interesting than what those events meant or what they produced. The Exile was interpreted as deserving divine punishment for breaking Israel's covenant obligations (see Jeremiah and the Deuteronomistic History) or for allowing impurities to defile the land (see Leviticus 18; Ezekiel; Chronicles). Once Jerusalem had fallen, the biblical writers turned their gaze toward Babylonia and searched for new understandings of the meaning of history.

Life in the Land After the Fall of Jerusalem

Accordingly, the one-sided focus in biblical texts on the desolation of Jerusalem and Judah is somewhat distorted. Jeremiah 40:7 says that only "the poorest of the land" remained, a statement undermined, for example, by the presence of Judean administrative functionaries in Mizpah, north of Jerusalem. Even more extreme, 2 Chronicles 36:21 asserts that the Exile meant an effective emptying of the land, that it took place "to fulfill the word of the Lord by the mouth of Jeremiah, until the land had made up for its sabbaths. All the days that it lay desolate it kept sabbath, to fulfill seventy years."[3] These kinds of claims about the extent of the destruction have been vastly overstated to fit neat theological categories. On the contrary, for many, life in fact continued in Judea much as before.[4]

True, recent analysis of settlement patterns and population size in the seventh–fifth centuries B.C.E. has shown that the destruction of Jerusalem and surrounding areas, particularly the western border of Judah, was indeed very real. In the sixth century B.C.E., urban life in Judah declined precipitously. From 150,000 persons in the seventh century, Jerusalem was reduced to between 1,500 and 2,750, though a few scholars would place that number as low as several hundred souls.[5] From Iron Age II (the biblical period) to the Persian period (after the neo-Babylonian period), the settled area in the environs of Jerusalem, as well as in the Shephelah, was decimated.[6] Life carried on, but Jerusalem was but a shadow of its former self. Deep poverty likely characterized life in the Holy City. The dire, visceral imagery of Lamentations (e.g., Lamentation 1:4: "The roads to Zion mourn, for no one comes to the festivals; all her gates are desolate, her priests groan; her young girls grieve, and her lot is bitter"), though undoubtedly shaped by literary conventions, likely captures the flavor of life, such as it was in Jerusalem, as does Haggai 1:6.[7]

The destruction in Jerusalem occasioned a region-wide economic depression, even collapse, particularly in the southern and the eastern parts of Judah.[8] Judah may even have ceded territory to neighboring peoples; a few prophetic texts hint of significant losses at this time—to the Edomites (Obadiah 19; Ezekiel 36:5), Ammonites (Jeremiah 49:1; Ezekiel 25:10), as well as to the Philistines and Phoenicians (Obadiah 19; Ezekiel 25:15, 26).[9]

On the other hand, the entire land was by no means empty in the sixth century.[10] The Babylonian destruction of Judah was thorough and severe, but it was not wanton. The siege of Jerusalem was a part of a Babylonian strategy of escalating punishments for Judah's successive treaty violations. After wresting supremacy from the Egyptians—a feat solidified with their victory at Carchemish—the neo-Babylonians responded to Jehoiakim's rebellious alliance in 597 B.C.E. The neo-Babylonians invaded Judah and deported Jehoiakim's successor, Jehoiachin, along with others among Judah's elite, but allowed another member of Judah's Davidic dynasty, Jehoiachin's uncle Zedekiah (Mattaniah) to remain on the throne. From the Babylonian standpoint, Zedekiah's subsequent attempt to resist Babylonian authority was the final straw. Factions in Judah had repeatedly sought to assert its independence. Recognizing this, in 587 B.C.E. Nebuchadnezzar's general[11] Nebuzadaran decided to end Jerusalem's political, as well as cultural, autonomy. The Babylonian campaign was carefully designed to eliminate key Israelite holdings such as Jerusalem. Israeli archaeologist Oded Lipschits contends that the Babylonians barred the people from living in Jerusalem and set up an alternative administrative center in Mizpah. They appointed Gedaliah, a non-Davidide, as governor, perhaps even before they destroyed the Holy City.

The material culture unearthed by archaeology in Benjamin and the northern hills of Judah indicates that, in the interest of maintaining an administrative outpost in the area, the Babylonians left Benjamin untouched. To a far greater extent than in Jerusalem and its environs, archaeologists find evidence of continuous occupation in Mizpah (Tell en-Nasbeh[12]), Gibeah, Tell el-Ful, and elsewhere. In Benjaminite territory, from Sobah and Jericho to the west and east as well as in Mizpah and Ramat Raḥel to the north and south, archaeologists have found more than 40 seal impressions likely dating to the sixth century B.C.E. (found on site but not in stratigraphically secure locations) reading the still undeciphered *MṢH/MWṢH*.[13] Though the word the impressions contain has not yet been understood, they come from six stamp designs suggesting a standardized production of some commodity. Of the 43 examples of these seal impressions, 30 originate in Mizpah. This solidifies the identification of Mizpah as an active administrative city during the neo-Babylonian period.

If Mizpah served as the de facto capital of Judea after the destruction, it likely did so as an arm of the Babylonian bureaucratic structure. The extent of Babylon's administrative presence in the provinces is a matter of some controversy. Some scholars have assumed that the neo-Babylonians succeeded to the administrative network already put in place by the neo-Assyrians. Upon closer examination, this suggestion does not seem to hold up, however. The neo-Assyrians replaced smaller, long-standing kingdoms and their political and religious institutions and assimilated their populations. The neo-Babylonians, on the other hand, took over already-conquered areas with established administrative networks.[14] During the first decades of their empire, the neo-Babylonians either chose not to mobilize these bureaucratic resources or did not have the time or wherewithal to do so. The neo-Babylonian administration in the early years was mostly ad hoc. They made little attempt to build up trade networks or maintain fortresses. They simply filled their coffers by means of periodic campaigns through their empire.[15] It is unlikely that Babylon took over Assyria's institutions wholesale, though the evidence of the *MṢH/MWṢH* seal impressions suggests that a measure of administrative control was instituted sometime in the early sixth century B.C.E.

EXILIC SEAL IMPRESSION. Made by a sixth-century B.C.E. seal only three-fourths of an inch long, this impression reads "Belonging to Yehoyishma, daughter of Sawas-sar-usur." Yehoyishma, which includes the divine element *yeho*, a form of Yahweh, is a type of name that originated in Babylonia during the Exile. Sawas-sar-usur is a well-known neo-Babylonian name that means "Shamash [the Babylonian sun-god] protect the king!" Thus, the Jewish woman who owned this seal had a Yahwistic name, but her father had a neo-Babylonian pagan name.

Israeli archaeologist Nahman Avigad suggested that one of the first exiles in Babylonia gave his son the local name Sawas-sar-usur. By the time this man had a daughter, there was a resurgence of national and religious feeling among the Jews in Exile. Perhaps seeking divine help to return to Jerusalem, Sawas-sar-usur gave his daughter a Jewish name that means "Yahweh will hear."

Given Mizpah's prominence and Jerusalem's destruction and decimated population, the question arises as to whether the ancient Israelite cult site at Bethel, a few miles north of Mizpah, was revived as the principal place of sacrifice and worship. The evidence is scant, limited to a few hints in biblical passages such as Jeremiah 41:4–8, which speaks of meal offerings and frankincense to present at the House of the Lord.[16]

Mizpah and sites in Benjamin remained the population centers of Judah at least until the mid-fifth century B.C.E. The history of the area after the early sixth century, however, is little known. Judahite royalists, chief among them Ishmael son of Nethaniah, viewed the Babylonian-appointed Gedaliah as a collaborator and for this reason assassinated him shortly after he took power. Other pro-Davidic sympathizers fled to Egypt, among them the prophet Jeremiah (Jeremiah 43:7). Whether or not as a punishment for Gedaliah's murder, the neo-Babylonians also took a third wave of deportees back to Babylon in 582 B.C.E.[17]

Settlement patterns in Benjamin and the northern hill country indicate that Mizpah remained the de facto capital of Judea until well into the Persian period.

Life in Babylonia

Texts regarding living conditions in Exile during the neo-Babylonian period (Daniel 1–6; 1 Esdras 4; Tobit; Esther) depict Israelites developing strategies for coping with and occasionally even thriving in the Diaspora.[18] However, these stories owe more to literary conventions than to historical events. How to live faithful Jewish lives in Exile is of great interest, but hard information is scant.

According to Ezekiel (1:1–3, 3:15, 23), Judeans lived in the vicinity of Nippur, at Tel Abib near "the river Chebar." A recently published set of trilingual texts comes from the Babylon-Borsippa region at a place named "al-Yahudu" (meaning something like "Judah-ville").[19] In some of these texts, "al-Yahudu" lacks the gentilic ending, suggesting that it was less an ethnic enclave than a place whose name recalls its original inhabitants.[20] The texts also include a number of Judean (Yahwistic) names of people active in commodity and property transactions as both creditors and debtors. The earliest of these texts dates to 572 B.C.E. (not long after the Babylonian destruction in 586 B.C.E.). In general, they reflect the extent to which Judeans quickly integrated themselves into the Babylonian economy.

Other place names with Judean exiles are mentioned in

Ezra—Tel-melah, Tel-harsha, Cherub, Addan, Immer (Ezra 2:59; Nehemiah 7:61) and Casipha (Ezra 8:17), but nothing about them is known.

Many deportees no doubt felt the loss of their homeland deeply. The classic statement is Psalm 137: "For there our captors asked us for song, and our tormentors asked for mirth, saying 'Sing us one of the songs of Zion!' ... If I forget you, O Jerusalem, let my right hand wither!"

The predictions of the prophet Hananiah (Jeremiah 28:2–4) hint at the hope for a quick return. Perhaps this was incited by a period of unrest that threatened Babylon's power in 595 B.C.E.

> Thus says the Lord of hosts, the God of Israel: I have broken the yoke of the king of Babylon. Within two years I will bring back to this place all the vessels of the Lord's house, which King Nebuchadnezzar of Babylon took away from this place and carried to Babylon. I will also bring back to this place King Jeconiah [Jehoiachin] son of Jehoiakim of Judah, and all the exiles from Judah who went to Babylon, says the Lord, for I will break the yoke of the king of Babylon.
> (JEREMIAH 28:2-4)

Hananiah's prophecy failed to come to pass, however, and the exiles were left with little alternative but to adapt to their new home. Jeremiah's advice was to do so. In a letter to the Judeans, he rejected oracles of hope (Jeremiah 29:8–9) and asked the exiles to "build houses and live in them; plant gardens and eat what they produce" (Jeremiah 29:5).

The exiles appear to have followed Jeremiah's advice. A set of Babylonian inscriptions known as the Weidner documents record the distribution of daily rations to Judah's former king Jehoiachin and his family.[21] These rations, which were 20 times the standard individual allotment,[22] indicate that Jehoiachin, referred to by the title "king of Judah" in these documents, was treated with some measure of respect. Judeans, on the other hand, may have interpreted the situation differently: 2 Kings 25:27 notes that Jehoiachin was released from his "prison" by Nebuchadnezzar's successor Awel-Marduk (biblical Evil-Merodach).

Discovering a Universal God

The imperial conquests of Assyria and Babylon brought an end to the independent kingdoms of Israel and Judah. The leading residents of both states—the royalty, military, priesthood, and artisans—were exiled and resettled to various corners of Mesopotamia.

Archaeological evidence suggests that many of these deportees managed to survive and even prosper in their new settings. As explained by K. Lawson Younger Jr. in his *BAR* article "Israelites in Exile" (November/December 2003), both the Bible and various Assyrian documents show that while many Israelites and Judeans experienced hardship, at least some managed to achieve positions of relative importance within Assyrian society—as soldiers, bureaucrats, or even priests.

As André Lemaire described in *BAR* ("The Universal God: How the God of Israel Became a God of All," November/December 2005),* the experience of exile also prompted a historic theological development. Before the Babylonian conquest, YHWH the God of Israel had always been attached to the land occupied by Israel and Judah. Moreover, following the reforms of Hezekiah and Josiah (see chap. 5, pp. 188, 202), YHWH could be worshiped only at the Jerusalem Temple, which now lay in ruins. What were the exiles to do in a foreign land, with no house for their God?

Answers to this dilemma are found in prophetic texts from the period of Exile—Ezekiel and Deutero-Isaiah. These prophets explained that the catastrophe of the Babylonian conquest was not the result of YHWH's impotence, but rather was due to the people's repeated disregard for YHWH's commandments. Moreover, YHWH was fundamentally different from the local Babylonian gods, who were merely powerless objects of wood and stone, forged by human hands. Meanwhile, the exiles learned that YHWH could be reached wherever their prayers would find him.

The impotence of Babylonian gods was dramatically confirmed when Babylon was conquered in turn by the Persian king Cyrus the Great (539–530 B.C.E.). It was then that the prophet confirmed the truth of YHWH's nature—as creator of all things, the one, true, universal God (Isaiah 45:21–22). The author of Deutero-Isaiah sees Cyrus as God's instrument, who inspired this profound insight. However it came about, this new understanding would forever change the Israelites' conception of their God. -ED.

---

*Later expanded in Lemaire's book *The Birth of Monotheism* (Washington, DC: BAS, 2007).

The Murashu archive tablets provide further evidence that the Judeans integrated into Babylonian society and economy. Consisting of more than 700 cuneiform tablets of administrative and economic content from Nippur, they document many West Semitic and Yahwistic names. Although less applicable to the neo-Babylonian period than the al-Yahuda tablets because they were composed in the mid-fifth century, the Murashu archive documents Judean participation in a variety of economic transactions. Moreover, there is little indication that the Judeans were slaves; rather they appear to have been agricultural producers living as semi-free tenants on royal lands.[23]

Thus, although the Babylonians forcibly removed peoples from their homelands, they did not greatly interfere with their cultural autonomy. Many Judeans, to be sure, felt their displacement as a devastating loss.[24] One can draw parallels to other displaced populations throughout history to understand the exiles' experience.[25] Perhaps because so much that the Israelites thought secure was lost—not just the city and its Temple, but also the foundational theological concept that God would reside in and protect Zion—the neo-Babylonian period became a crucible of creative reinterpretations of history both recent and distant. In other words, the exiles turned the tragedy of the Exile into a triumph of the spirit. More particularly, the Exile was interpreted not as a punishment (or not as a punishment alone) but as a new beginning (see the box "Discovering a Universal God" on p. 220). Jeremiah, consistent with his pro-Babylonian (or anti-rebellion) position during the last days of Judah, interpreted the Exile as divinely willed. The prophet regards the exiles as the recipients of God's favor and those who were not forcibly relocated as rejected afterthoughts:

> The Lord showed me two baskets of figs placed before the Temple of the Lord ... One basket had very good figs, like first-ripe figs, but the other basket had very bad figs, so bad that they could not be eaten ... Then the word of the Lord came to me: Thus says the Lord, the God of Israel: Like these good figs, so I will regard as good the exiles from Judah, whom I have sent away from this place to the land of the Chaldeans. I will set my eyes upon them for good, and I will bring them back to this land. I will build them up, and not tear them down; I will plant them, and not pluck them up. I will give

them a heart to know that I am the Lord; and they shall be
my people and I will be their God, for they shall return to me
with their whole heart. But thus says the Lord: Like the bad
figs that are so bad they cannot be eaten, so will I treat King
Zedekiah of Judah, his officials, the remnant of Jerusalem who
remain in this land, and those who live in the land of Egypt. I
will make them a horror, an evil thing, to all the kingdoms of
the earth—a disgrace, a byword, a taunt and a curse in all the
places where I shall drive them.

(JEREMIAH 24:1-2, 4-9)

This theology foreshadows coming conflicts in the subsequent
Persian period. Similar ideas also appear in Ezekiel (11:14–20), where
the land left behind becomes a place of abomination that those
renewed by God in exile must eradicate so that God may once again
dwell in the land. In the eyes of these prophetic theologians, God
had great things in store for Israel when its faithful remnant returns
from its sojourn.

Other theological and religious developments can also be traced
to this fertile time. The radical otherness of Ezekiel's deity, not to
mention the idealized, fabulous Temple in Ezekiel 40–47 (sixth c.),
coupled with the soaring polemics of Deutero-Isaiah (Isaiah 40–55,
sixth c.), suggest that exclusive monotheism (as opposed to a local,
national deity tied to the land) comes to full flower in the neo-Babylonian and Persian periods.[26] Precursors to apocalyptic literature, particularly Ezekiel 38–39, Deutero-Zechariah (Zechariah 9–14; fifth c.), and
Joel, also emerge after the destruction of Jerusalem, perhaps reflecting
the influence of Persian dualistic thought.[27]

Though evidence for actual ancient synagogues does not appear
until the last centuries of the Second Temple period, Ezra's reading
of "the Book of the Torah of Moses" at the Water Gate (Nehemiah
8) may be a first step in that direction. It may be seen as an extension of the Iron Age practice of using city gates for public and cultural
purposes that now included the public reading of Scripture.[28] Ezekiel's
idea of a "diminished sanctuary" (miqdash me'at) in 11:16 may perhaps
refer to the origin of the synagogue, with the displaced population
learning to create in exile an alternative form of religious worship
without the Temple. Learning to pray without benefit of the Temple

in Jerusalem was surely one of the most important positive and creative responses to the tragedy of the Exile. This notion, secured with the establishment of the later synagogue, was one of the major building blocks of the diaspora communities.

THE PERSIAN PERIOD

The neo-Babylonians had only a short time to enjoy their newly won hegemony. By the early 540s, Persia to the east had defeated and subsumed its neighbor Media. Babylonia itself was already embroiled in internal controversy. The Babylonian ruler Nabonidus was developing a royal ideology, portraying himself as a historically minded archivist and builder who restored the traditions of the past. The Marduk priesthood, however, regarded Nabonidus as a dangerous innovator who angered Marduk with his devotion to the cult of the moon god Sin.[29]

The resulting political instability weakened the Babylonian state, and in 539 B.C.E. the Persian king Cyrus captured Babylon. Some contemporary sources, including the Nabonidus Chronicle and the Persian Cyrus Cylinder, suggest that Nabonidus was so unpopular that the Babylonians welcomed Cyrus and enabled him to obtain power in a virtually bloodless coup. Although this version of events may owe more to the propagandistic aims of the texts than to historical reality,[30] Cyrus no doubt did find some support in Babylonia for his campaign. Cyrus returned the favor by depicting himself as a supporter of Marduk: "Marduk, the great lord, caused the magnanimous people of Babylon [to ...] me, (and) I daily attended to his worship ... I sought the welfare of the city of Babylon and all its sacred centers."[31] The famous Cyrus Cylinder, dated c. 539/538 B.C.E., now in the British Museum, depicts Cyrus as a patron of Babylon. However, his policies should be considered as Persia's response to Babylonian politics, not as an empire-wide policy of religious tolerance.[32] Nevertheless, the generosity of spirit reflected in the cuneiform Cyrus Cylinder, which reflects the diversity of the many constituent peoples and languages that fell under Persian hegemony, is also found in the Bible's description (Ezra 1:2–4; 2 Chronicles 36:23).

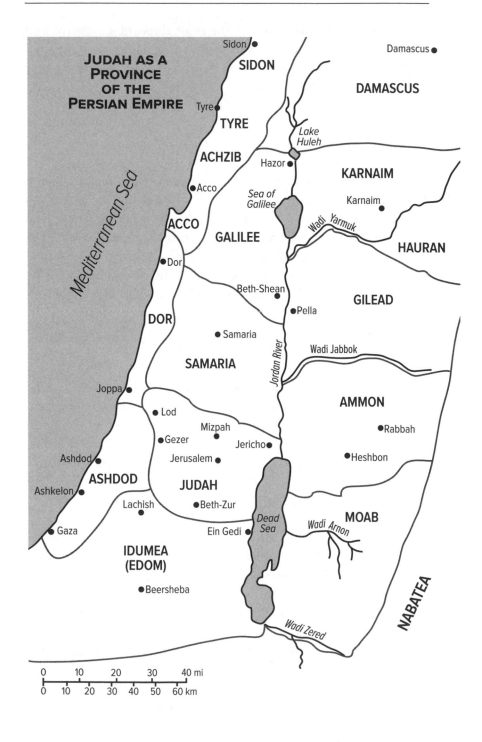

CYRUS CYLINDER. The inscription written in cuneiform on this 10-inch-long clay barrel tells how the great god Marduk chose Cyrus (559–529 B.C.E.) to supplant the impious tyrant who was then king of Persia, and of how Cyrus went on to conquer the equally odious king of Babylon, Nabonidus. It then proclaims, "I am Cyrus, king of the world, great king," and describes his new religious policy of toleration, which allowed subject peoples to return to their homelands and repair their ruined sanctuaries.

The Bible records a similar decree of Cyrus that permitted the Jews to resettle Jerusalem and rebuild their Temple in about 539 B.C.E. (2 Chronicles 36:23 and Ezra 1:2–3).

In the biblical version, Cyrus fulfills the quasi-messianic hopes of Deutero-Isaiah (see Isaiah 44:28; 45:1) and heralds the end of the Exile. Coming on the heels of Cyrus's decree allowing exiles to return, the words of Ezra indicate widespread support for the reconstruction of the Jerusalem Temple:

The heads of the families of Judah and Benjamin, and the priests and the Levites—everyone whose spirit God had stirred—got ready to go up and rebuild the house of the Lord in Jerusalem. All their neighbors aided them with silver vessels, with gold, with goods, with animals and with valuable gifts, besides all that was freely offered. King Cyrus himself brought out the vessels of the house of the Lord that

Nebuchadnezzar had carried away from Jerusalem and placed in the house of his gods. King Cyrus of Persia had them released into the charge of Mithredath the treasurer, who counted them out to Sheshbazzar the prince of Judah. And this was the inventory: gold basins, thirty; silver basins, one thousand; knives, twenty-nine; gold bowls, thirty; other silver bowls, four hundred and ten; other vessels, one thousand; the total of the gold and silver vessels was five thousand four hundred. All these Sheshbazzar brought up, when the exiles were brought up from Babylonia to Jerusalem.
(EZRA 1:5–11)

With this magnanimous offer, gladly accepted by the exiles, a new chapter in Israel's history began. But it is by no means clear how many exiles returned with Sheshbazzar considering the words of Haggai about two decades later who complains about the lack of work on the Temple and how it still lay in ruins (Haggai 1:4). The response seems to have been underwhelming.

Demography and the Delayed Restoration

If Cyrus's defeat of the hated Babylonians raised hopes and expectations of a speedy restoration, the early Persian period failed to live up to that promise. Sheshbazzar, denominated as "the prince of Judah,"[33] is credited with having laid the Temple's foundations (Ezra 5:6–17), but this is contradicted by Ezra 3.[34] Precisely who Sheshbazzar was and what he did, unfortunately, is lost to history, even to the tradents who composed Ezra-Nehemiah. The list of returnees in Ezra 2, because it comes on the heels of the description of the return of the vessels under Sheshbazzar, might be thought to imply a sizable return, but the list of names includes returnees like Zerubbabel from a second, later return (Ezra 2:1). The notion of a clean end to the Exile accompanied by a mass return in 539/538 B.C.E., as suggested by Ezra 1–3,[35] and assumed by many scholars, does not hold up under scrutiny. By the second half of the sixth century B.C.E., many of the exiles had successfully accommodated themselves to life in Babylonia. The same demographic situation that characterized the neo-Babylonian period in ancient Judah is also true for the early Persian period. Any return that may have taken place at the dawn of the Persian Empire left no traces in the settlement patterns in Yehud, as it is called as a Persian province.[36] The residents of Yehud lived in deep poverty and had few complex social institutions.

The late-sixth-century prophets Haggai and Zechariah attest to Yehud's battered economy. Writing in about 520 B.C.E., a generation after Cyrus's conquest of Babylon, Haggai addresses the inhabitants of Yehud in vivid terms (Haggai 1:5–6):

> Thus says the Lord of hosts: Consider how you have fared. You have sown much, and harvested little; you eat, but you never have enough; you drink, but you never have your fill; you clothe yourselves, but no one is warm; and you that earn wages earn wages to put them into a bag with holes.

As a remedy for the people's economic ills, Haggai encouraged his fellow Judeans to regain the Lord's favor by rebuilding the Temple, to finish the task that was to have begun in the time of Cyrus. Indeed, the fact that Jerusalem lacked a temple years after Judah was no longer barred from rebuilding it created a problem even for the historian who wrote Ezra 1–6; he attributed the delay to outside interference, namely the machinations of non-Judean enemies. This strategy is also mirrored in Nehemiah's first-person tale of the same events. However, to explain the delay in rebuilding the Temple required the historian to resort to creative chronology, jumbling events that took place over several time periods to create the illusion of unified opposition to the rebuilding of the Temple. The most jarring example of this technique can be found in Ezra 4:23–24:

> Then when the copy of King Artaxerxes' [465–424 B.C.E] letter was read before Rehum and the scribe Shimshai and their associates, they hurried to the Jews in Jerusalem and by force and power made them cease. At that time the work on the house of God in Jerusalem stopped and was discontinued until the second year of the reign of King Darius of Persia [520 B.C.E.].

Aside from the chronological disjunction—Artaxerxes I ruled nearly a century *after* Darius—the letter from Artaxerxes[37] cannot refer to the Temple project that was finished in 515 B.C.E. Rather, it would seem to relate to the construction of Jerusalem's wall in the mid-fifth century B.C.E., though, curiously, this letter makes no appearance in the primary narrative account of the wall project in Nehemiah 1–7; 13.

The people of Yehud did complete the Temple, however, during the reign of Darius I, most likely in 515 B.C.E. This date remains the scholarly consensus, notwithstanding Diana Edelman's attempt to attribute the Temple's construction to the mid-fifth century.[38]

YEHUD STAMPS AND COIN. From Tell en-Nasbeh (biblical Mizpah) in the north to Beth Zur in the south, from Gezer in the west to Jericho in the east, archaeologists have discovered jar handles and coins stamped Yehud, the name for Judah in the Persian period (539–332 B.C.E.). The distribution of these stamps helps modern scholars to establish the borders of Judah at this time.

A falcon with spread wings shares space with the Yehud stamp on the obverse of a small fourth-century B.C.E. silver coin discovered near Jericho. A lily appears on the reverse. The two pottery handles, found at Ramat Rahel and also dating to the fourth century B.C.E., probably came from wine jars. The Yehud impression was literally an official stamp of approval.

The debate on the chronology of the Temple's rebuilding nevertheless points up a central problem with the Persian-era Second Temple: We have no concrete contemporary descriptions of the edifice nor an account of its construction, biblical or otherwise, in striking contrast to the meticulously rendered descriptions of the Tabernacle (Exodus 25–31; 35–40), Solomon's Temple (1 Kings 6–7), and Ezekiel's re-imagined temple (Ezekiel 40–44).[39] As Carol Meyers has observed, "It is perhaps ironic that the temple building that survived the longest—almost exactly five centuries—evoked the least descriptive material in the literary record."[40] Extrabiblical literary and iconographic descriptions of the Second Temple largely refer to Herod's rebuilding of the Second Temple, rather than the smaller earlier Temple.

The absence of any detailed description of this earlier Temple does not mean, however, that the biblical writers found it to be insignificant. The Temple is the centerpiece of the restoration theologies in the Books of Haggai and Zechariah (particularly Zechariah 1–8) and Ezra-Nehemiah. In each of these biblical books, the religious significance of the Temple is inextricable from its political and social functions.

The rebuilding project was led by a Davidic heir, Zerubbabel son of Shealtiel, newly appointed governor of Yehud. Zerubbabel receives no title in Ezra, but Haggai and Zechariah invest great hopes in him. Haggai refers to Zerubbabel as "governor" and describes him in near-messianic terms, referring to him as the Lord's "signet ring" (Haggai 2:23). Though Haggai and Zechariah stop short of calling Zerubbabel a king, both prophets describe him with language that resonates with ancient Near Eastern kingship ideology. The imagery of divine sponsorship of public buildings, especially in Zechariah 4:6–10, is especially noteworthy.[41] Zechariah 1–8 envisions a diarchic government, with Zerubbabel paired with Joshua son of Jehozadak as high priest. This early Persian-period configuration may represent the first indications of the increasing power of the high priesthood that was so dominant in the Hellenistic period.[42] In any event, on the heels of the lofty praise by Haggai and Zechariah, Zerubbabel suddenly disappears from our sources and his fate is unclear.

Zerubbabel's brief governorship perhaps suggests that, in allowing an heir to the Davidic dynasty to govern, Persia did maintain a policy of allowing some measure of political and religious autonomy in their colonies. Persia's attitude toward their territorial possessions, however, should not be reckoned as one of systematized religious "tolerance." The Persian crown supported some local cults, but their policy was strategic and ad hoc; they provided support for temples when it served their purposes, whether for defense or for increasing revenue to the central government. In this regard, the Cyrus Cylinder's allusions to particularly Babylonian concerns reveal Persia's pragmatic, not programmatic, aims. Although Persia projected itself as the source of peaceful order throughout the empire,[43] it could respond to perceived sources of rebellion swiftly and decisively, as shown in the accounts of the campaigns of Darius I recorded in the Behistun inscription. Darius's skillfully executed and propagandized ascent to the Persian throne in 522 B.C.E. was followed by a thoroughgoing reorganization of the empire's administrative networks including the establishment of satrapies, roads, and major building projects. Zerubbabel's appointment and/or the funding for the rebuilding of the Temple may have come as a small aspect of this reorganization. In fact, the inability of the people of Yehud to rebuild the Temple earlier under Sheshbazzar may have been due to a cause as prosaic as the lack of an economic or demographic base strong enough to support the project.

Thus Persia was not a tolerant, hands-off ruler. On the other hand, Yehud was not the focal point of its concerns in the West, where Greece occupied Persian military concerns. Persia was surely focused on maximizing tribute and "gift" revenues. It ran a meticulous bureaucracy[44] facilitated by a well-maintained road system; Yehud and Samaria played a significant part in this network. But the importance of Yehud to Persia's overall strategic goals has often been exaggerated. To quote Pierre Briant in this regard, "[T]he importance of Judah is only an 'optical illusion' created by the uneven distribution of evidence."[45] Perhaps it is best to think of Persia's policy toward its outlying provinces as attentive but somewhat aloof, even if punctuated with occasional targeted interventions, as in the case of Sheshbazzar, Zerubbabel, Nehemiah-Ezra, and a possible administrative consolidation in the fourth century B.C.E.

Nehemiah and Ezra

In the sixth and early fifth centuries B.C.E., life in Yehud continued much as it did in the neo-Babylonian period, with the territory of

Benjamin and the city of Mizpah maintaining their relative prominence and with Jerusalem (and the rest of Judah) remaining largely
depopulated.

The Book of Ezra presents the early return of the exiles as the
fulfillment of Jeremiah's prophecies (e.g., Jeremiah 25:12). As already
noted, this time period is not described in any detail in the biblical
texts, as if the ancient writers were themselves aware of the lack-
luster response to the end of the neo-Babylonian Empire. Beginning
in the mid-fifth century, in contrast, political events are detailed in the
Bible and begin to manifest themselves in extrabiblical evidence as
well. Archaeological surveys show that at this time, what we might call
Persian II, Benjamin was becoming depopulated and at the same time,
the population of the Shephelah (the low hills southwest of Jerusalem)
and Jerusalem increased.

Additionally, a series of stamp seals from this period inscribed
YHD (Yehud) evidence a new bureaucratic system. The distributions
of these *YHD* seals may be compared with the *MWṢH* seals of the
neo-Babylonian period, now suggesting that the administrative center
of government had shifted from Mizpah back to Jerusalem.[46]

Until this time, Persianized motifs on seals were mostly absent.
Beginning in the late fifth century B.C.E., however, we begin to see
much greater Persian influence in the local iconography.[47] In Anatolia
and Egypt, Persian artistic influence can be seen much earlier,
suggesting that Yehud was late to feel Persia's ruling hand.

Turning to the wider global context of the mid-fifth century, we
see Persia struggling to fend off rebellions in the West and in Egypt,
while at the same time challenging Greece militarily. All this may have
encouraged Persia to shore up its frontier areas, including Yehud, by
building networks of military fortresses and garrisons.[48] Although
some scholars have questioned the date and the importance of these
fortresses, the cumulative evidence indicates that the mid-fifth century
marked a time of increased Persian interest in Yehud. The Books of
Ezra and Nehemiah, whose stories drop off after the completion of the
Temple, pick up the thread in the mid-fifth century with the missions
of Ezra and Nehemiah. Second Zechariah (chaps. 9–14) reflects the
uncertainly of this period especially in its focus on the future restoration of the kingdom of David.

Nehemiah's journey from Susa, one of the Persian capitals, to Jerusalem reflects a significant sign of Persian intervention into an area that had otherwise seen little attention from Yehud's imperial masters. The poverty and underdeveloped infrastructure in Jerusalem through the sixth and early-fifth centuries seems surprising nearly a century and a half after the fall of Jerusalem and 75 years after the completion of the Temple.[49] However, despite Nehemiah's characteristically exaggerated language, his description of Jerusalem, even with a rebuilt Temple, as poor and depopulated is eminently plausible.

Artaxerxes commissioned Nehemiah as the Yehud governor[50] and provided him with a military escort, official travel permissions, and access to timber supplies (Nehemiah 2:7–9). This suggests an effort to reconfigure the Persian administration of Yehud and centralize it in Jerusalem. Nehemiah took full advantage of the Persian king's blessing, leading the effort to rebuild the wall around Jerusalem.[51] He likely also built a governor's residence and fortress near the city. Recent excavations in the City of David led by Israeli archaeologist Eilat Mazar have found a small segment of wall, resting *atop* a sixth–fifth century (and therefore later) pottery assemblage, which may be a remnant of this construction project reported in the Book of Nehemiah,[52] although the identification of the segment as part of "Nehemiah's Wall" has been contested.[53]

Nehemiah describes the wall as an attempt to unify the people of Yehud. But the wall also created fierce opposition from neighboring peoples, such as Sanballat of Samaria, Tobiah of Transjordan, and Geshem of Arabia. Nevertheless, Nehemiah's enemies maintained significant ties with Yehud's elite, as may be inferred from Tobiah's connection with the high priest Eliashib (Nehemiah 13:4–9). Similarly, Sanballat and Tobiah were both likely worshipers of Yahweh and considered themselves part of the same people as those of Yehud— and were so considered by the people of Yehud.

That there were significant internal divisions in Nehemiah's Yehud becomes clear in the context of Nehemiah's other reforms, both religious and economic. Nehemiah relieved the debt of struggling small farmers (Nehemiah 5), regularized the distribution of Temple tithes to the Levites (Nehemiah 13:10–14, 31), restricted mercantile activity on the Sabbath (Nehemiah 13:15–22), and condemned exogamous marriages (Nehemiah 13:23–29). These reforms can be understood as part of his effort to restore glory to the city, but they also reveal Nehemiah's sensitivity to Persian administrative goals. These reforms suggest that Nehemiah was commissioned by Persia for the purpose of maximizing tax and tribute revenues[54] and minimizing the potential threat of homegrown sources of power. Because the Temple maintained an economic function as well as a religious function,[55] the prohibition against non-Temple-related economic activity on the Sabbath day would have funneled worshipers' resources more efficiently through the religio-administrative system. The reorganization of Levitical portions worked in the same direction. One small example: Nehemiah forcibly removed Tobiah from a chamber in the Temple "where they had previously put the grain offering, the frankincense, the vessels, and the tithes of grain, wine, and oil, which were given by commandment to the Levites, singers, and gatekeepers, and the contributions for the priests" (Nehemiah 13:5). Tobiah's offense was not solely his physical presence, though Nehemiah reports having the Temple cleansed as if contaminated by a foreign object, but Nehemiah also objected to Tobiah's influence over the flow of goods through the Temple.

Nehemiah's protracted complaints against Tobiah, as well as against Sanballat and Geshem, point to another area in which the newly appointed governor of Yehud was acting in Persia's and, consequently, his own interests. Sanballat was part of a well-established family in Samaria, a family that had held control over the governorship for generations.[56] Geshem's history is more shrouded, but it is likely he was a ruler of Kedar. Tobiah could very well have been governor of Ammon,[57] but as the story of his presence in the Temple suggests, he was also a wealthy person, likely an early exemplar of the influential Tobiad family mentioned in Zechariah 6:14 whose descendants later held a most impressive archaeologically preserved compound at 'Iraq el-Amir in Transjordan.[58] The cooperation of large landholders with the highest levels of the priesthood represented a potential threat to the control maintained by Persia through official channels. Perhaps to reverse this, Nehemiah reestablished the practice of allowing the Temple's goods to flow through lower-level Temple functionaries, such as the Levites. This was inevitably at the expense of people like Tobiah and Eliashib. The relief of debt granted to small landholders and tenant farmers (Nehemiah 5) would also have reduced the control of wealthy creditors.[59] None of this means that Nehemiah was following a laundry list of specific Persian directives.[60] Given Persia's inclination toward local autonomy, however (of course within established parameters), along with Yehud's small, though not insignificant, strategic importance, Nehemiah likely exercised considerable discretionary power to pursue his own interests. In many ways, Nehemiah's situation was similar to Zerubbabel's, when an effective governor served the interests of both the empire and the newly established province of Yehud.

Ezra's part in the reconstruction of late-Persian-period Yehud is uncertain. The narrative of Ezra-Nehemiah places Ezra's mission—like Nehemiah's—as an official commission from the Persian king. But it is presented as prior to Nehemiah's. Compelling arguments have been made for Nehemiah's chronological priority, however.[61] The problem is far from solved.

Ezra's story is apparently patterned upon Nehemiah's—yet it is different. Ezra rejects the Persian military escort that Nehemiah accepts (Ezra 8:22; Nehemiah 2:9). Ezra arrives with an open letter from Artaxerxes and waits three days before declaring a public fast (Ezra 8:15–23); Nehemiah arrives with directives known only to himself and conducts a secret, nighttime inspection at the end of three days (Nehemiah 2:11–16). Ezra hears of exogamous marriages and tears his hair and clothes in ritual mourning (Ezra 9:3–4); Nehemiah reacts violently and tears the hair and clothes of the offending husbands (Nehemiah 13:23–27). In each case, the comparison portrays Ezra more positively than Nehemiah. Ezra also proclaims the Torah as the law of the land. Some scholars argue that this was the "Persian authorization of the Torah."[62] Proponents of this theory suggest that Ezra's public reading and oral translation of the "Book of the Law of Moses" (Nehemiah 8) was related to an empire-wide policy of ratifying local legal customs and giving them the official backing of the crown (see Ezra 7:26: "All who will not obey the law of your God and the law of the king, let judgment be strictly executed on them"). The actual content of the Pentateuch, however, does not quite fit the description of a law code.[63] Ezra's glorious commission from Artaxerxes in Ezra 7 could still plausibly relate to the Judean exiles alone, although Persian imperial "policy" was generally respectful of local legal traditions.[64]

The authenticity of the commission to Ezra in Ezra 7 (along with the other Aramaic documents in Ezra 1–6) is uncertain. It is not clear why Artaxerxes would send a nongovernmental official to establish the Persian law (Ezra 7:25–26) before, or at least independently of, sending a governor to establish a new administrative center in Jerusalem.

Although the biblical text portrays Ezra as a formative figure in which the "reader" and "scribe" of the Torah is magnified into a full-blown "Second Moses,"[65] for the historian, this version of Ezra's story unfortunately raises more questions than it answers. There can be little doubt, however, that by the mid-fifth century, when Ezra is portrayed as having brought the Law to Judea, a distinctive accomplishment of the Babylonian diaspora was the editing and promulgation of a large portion of what was to become the Hebrew Bible. Such a task could have been accomplished by a relatively small and talented group, and the elites who survived deportation would have included individuals with the necessary skills. Moreover, the distress of exile—the loss of homeland and Temple—would have brought urgency to this undertaking. As part of the endeavor, certain editorial changes would have been required. For example, the Deuteronomistic History would need to be amended to account for the new circumstances of the post-Exilic era. Similarly, prophetic works would need to reflect theological developments. The renewed texts would then become the centerpiece of worship both at the rebuilt Jerusalem Temple and in the network of synagogues that would evolve first in the diaspora and later in the homeland.

Temples at Elephantine and Gerizim

Contemporaneous with Nehemiah and Ezra, and shortly thereafter, the activities of a Jewish community on the Egyptian island of Elephantine appear on the historian's radar screen.

Judeans in Egypt are alluded to in several sources. The *Letter of Aristeas* records a legend that Judeans served as auxiliaries during a military campaign of Pharaoh Psammetichus II[66] in 591 B.C.E. Jeremiah alludes to Judean settlements in Migdol, Tahpanhes, Memphis, and Pathros (Jeremiah 44:1–14). An oracle in Deutero-Isaiah anticipates the return of Judeans from far-flung places, including "from the land of Syene" (Isaiah 49:12). Those Jews who designated themselves

"Syenians"[67] (probably the residents of Elephantine) arrived in Egypt even before the Persian period.

The discovery of a Judean settlement with a cache of Aramaic documents on the Nile island of Elephantine (or "Yeb") revealed a treasure trove of information about the life and religious practices of a Diaspora community otherwise unknown. The island was the site of a former military colony. The Elephantine papyri, as they are known, include several collections of letters and administrative documents.[68] The most intriguing of these is the "Jedaniah archive," which contains 11 letters and other documents written for, addressed to, or concerned with the late-fifth-century leader of the Jewish community. Included is the famous "Passover letter" from an otherwise unidentified leader named Hananiah that purports to instruct Jedaniah "and his colleagues of the Jewish Troop" in the proper observance of Passover.[69]

ELEPHANTINE PAPYRUS. Following the destruction of Jerusalem in 586 B.C.E., a Jewish community thrived on Elephantine Island, in the Upper Nile River. This well-preserved papyrus—folded several times, bound with a string, sealed with a bulla and endorsed—was discovered among a hoard of letters, deeds and other documents belonging to the community. According to the papyri, a Jewish temple, oriented toward Jerusalem, stood on Elephantine Island in the sixth and fifth centuries B.C.E.

The military colony at Elephantine included Babylonians, Bactrians, Medes, Persians, Arameans, and others who lived alongside the Judeans.[70] One group of texts in the Jedaniah archive gives us a snapshot of what appears to be friction between the Judeans and some of their neighbors. Two drafts of a letter by "Jedaniah and his colleagues the priests" addressed to the governor of Yehud, Bagavahya,[71] pleads for assistance in rebuilding their temple to the god "Yahu" (YHW, an alternate form of YHWH, the Israelite God). The Judeans complain that priests of the Egyptian goat deity Khnum, whose temple stood near Yahu's, had destroyed the Judean temple, with the permission of the loathed local authority Vidranga. This letter is dated to 410 B.C.E. The destruction may have been due to the Khnum priests' dislike of sheep and goat sacrifices at Yahu's temple; after all, the Khnum priests served a goat deity. Jedaniah and the priests mention that their temple, otherwise unknown to the modern world until the discovery of these papyri, had stood since before the Persian king Cambyses entered Egypt in 525 B.C.E. The letter notes that the Judeans responded to the destruction of their temple with a series of penitential practices characteristic of Persian period texts: wearing of sackcloth, fasting, and prayer (see Jonah 3:5–9; Nehemiah 9:1–2). Whether the Elephantine community's appeal for help to the Jewish homeland was successful remains unknown, though one further document does describe a proposal on the part of the community to offer financial support and cease its animal offerings (perhaps in response to pressure from the Khnum priests) and may represent a compromise.

Another Elephantine archive—of Mibtahiah, the aunt of Jedaniah—deals with her life and estate. These documents provide valuable insights into the lives of Judean women—or at least one wealthy Judean woman. She appears to have been married twice, first to a Jezaniah and then to an Egyptian-named man, Eshor. Her marriage contracts indicate she had significant legal control over her marriage and property. She retained the right to initiate divorce proceedings, in marked contrast with later Jewish practice. She would also retain her own property in the event of the marriage's dissolution. Upon her first marriage, her father drew up a contract that granted his future son-in-law building rights on his daughter's land. Mibtahiah required her second husband, Eshor, to swear that he had no other heirs outside of any future children with her; further, he would bequeath all his property to her in the event of his death before any heirs were born. Mibtahiah was also a party to litigation, in which she agreed to a settlement with one Peu son of Pahe regarding goods that she had entrusted to Peu.

In the lawsuit against Peu, Mibtahiah swore by the Egyptian goddess Seti, while another document notes that she swore by YWH. Other deities also appear in these documents. All this suggests that the Elephantine Jewish community practiced a syncretistic form of

Yahwistic religion. On the other hand, no deity but Ywн is mentioned in the context of the temple.

The prophet Jeremiah, a rigorous Yahwist, took a dim view of Judean settlements in Egypt, charging that they made offerings to the "Queen of Heaven" (Jeremiah 44:15). However, Jeremiah does not specifically speak of Elephantine.[72]

Elephantine contacts with officials of Yehud and Samaria suggest that the Jewish inhabitants of Elephantine understood themselves to be somehow connected to their homeland. Yet, because they migrated to Egypt on their own accord, they may not have understood their religion to be in crisis as many in Babylon surely did and thus felt no pressure to emphasize religious boundaries between Judeans and non-Judeans. Multiple deities and their iconographic traditions were always a part of life for some Israelites.[73] "Syncretistic" elements in the lives of the Jews of Elephantine are best understood as a continuation of this aspect of earlier Israelite religious culture, fostered by life in a multiethnic society.

Whether the temple to ywн on Elephantine was constructed as a rival to the Jerusalem Temple is unclear. Another temple, however, the Judean temple at Gerizim, may well have been such a competitor. Ultimately it became the temple of the Samaritans. Our understanding of the origins of this sanctuary, however, is spotty. Josephus's claim that it was constructed in the Hellenistic period (*Ant.* 11.302–312) has been undermined by the recent excavations on Mt. Gerizim showing that the sanctuary at Gerizim dates back to the fifth century B.C.E.[74] These excavations have also uncovered hundreds of short votive inscriptions, many of which probably date to the Persian period.[75] The inscriptions are reminiscent of the refrain "remember me, O God, for good" in Nehemiah's valedictory (Nehemiah 13:31, and variations at 5:19; 6:14; 13:14, 22, 29) and reflect the existence of a thriving cult site. (One man made an offering for himself, his wife, and his sons "for good remembrance before God in this place.") These inscriptions resonate with Nehemiah's strident assertion that Sanballat, Tobiah (compare Zechariah 6:14), and Geshem shall have no "historic right" (Nehemiah 2:20 NRSV; Hebrew Bible has *zikkaron*, or "remembrance") in Jerusalem. Does this dispute hint at the beginning of the "Samaritan schism" or the break between Jews who worship at Jerusalem and those who worship at Gerizim? The Persian-period establishment of a temple at Gerizim suggests that the later tensions between Samaritans and Jews go back at least to the time of Nehemiah.[76] At this early stage, however, no clear religious differences between the two Yahwistic sanctuaries can be identified.

Literary Activity in the Neo-Babylonian and Persian Periods

Religious diversity within Yahwism of the Persian period fits uneasily with the biblical description. The Bible's strict focus on the restored cult in Jerusalem is driven by an Exilic and, to a lesser extent, Jerusalem-based perspective. The Babylonian exiles responded to the destruction of Jerusalem with great creativity, refining and defining matters of identity formation that were latent prior to the Exile, but became explicit only later. Much of the consolidation and editing—or even composition—of biblical narratives date to the neo-Babylonian and Persian periods.

Some scholars point to the absence of any significant urban culture in impoverished Yehud as militating against the supposition of a sophisticated literary culture.[77] The loss of the complex social institutions required to support scribal activity may account at least in part for the dearth of Hebrew inscriptions. Instead, Aramaic seems to be the preferred language, perhaps due to Persia's use of Aramaic, the lingua franca in international dealings.[78]

If the inclination and wherewithal to produce Hebrew inscriptions was not present in Yehud, how then can we account for the robust literary activity mostly preserved in Hebrew? We have numerous biblical texts that are assumed to be written in the Persian period: Haggai, Zechariah, Malachi, Ezra-Nehemiah, Chronicles, some psalms, Isaiah 55–65 (Trito-Isaiah), Jonah, and Joel.[79] Haggai and Zechariah especially describe the impoverishment of Yehud and their disappointment at the incomplete restoration of the Temple. They seem to provide a maximalist view of the Return in a minimalist social context. Although small, the population of Yehud was nevertheless called upon to support a full Temple bureaucracy, which may have included Aaronide, Zadokite, and Levitical priests (Ezra 8:15–36; Nehemiah 7:1, 39, 43); singers and gatekeepers (Nehemiah 7:1, 23, 45), Temple servants (Nehemiah 3:26, 31; 7:46; 11:19) and a scribal class (Ezra 8:1, 9), not to mention military officials, artisans, and attendants of the governor. According to the latest social-scientific scholarship, however, it takes only between 5 and 10 percent of elites or specialists in a society to produce a scribal oeuvre in preindustrial societies.[80] By way of analogy, consider that the small community at Qumran was responsible for great literary productions (the Dead Sea Scrolls), some of which were written in what was then archaic Hebrew. In all likelihood, as already indicated, the literary production of the Babylonian Exile and of Persian Yehud included the promulgation and consolidation of the Pentateuch and the Former Prophets (Joshua, Judges, Samuel, and Kings), known collectively as the Primary History, and the beginning of the process that led to the collection of the three major prophets (Isaiah, Jeremiah, and Ezekiel) and of the Book of the Twelve Minor Prophets. Collectively this represents a creative response to the crisis of the Exile, a flowering of imagination and hope in the midst of a land that had not yet pulled itself out of its economic, political, and social difficulties. It is nothing less than an astonishing literary achievement.

The Fourth Century and the End of the Persian Period

For the years following the time of Ezra and Nehemiah, narrative accounts of events are few and far between. Josephus (*Ant.* 11.297–301) tells a story of the high priest Johanan (410–371 B.C.E.) who murdered his brother Jeshua in a dispute concerning control of the high priesthood.[81] Jeshua had been supported by the Persian functionary Bagoses. This story hints at Persian intervention in the affairs of the high priesthood (see Nehemiah's dispute with Eliashib [Nehemiah 13:4–9, 28–29]) and foreshadows tales of bitter disagreements over and politicization of the high priesthood during the subsequent Seleucid and Hasmonean periods.

The first-century B.C.E. Greek historian Diodorus Siculus mentions conflicts in the fourth century B.C.E. along the Persian western frontier (the "Revolt of the Satraps" and the "Tennes Rebellion" in Phoenicia) that supposedly rocked the entire region. These events were likely localized, however. There are no reports of Judea or Samaria being involved in them, although they may reflect tensions elsewhere in the empire.[82]

The archaeological evidence for the end of the Persian period is much richer than the narrative material and helps fill out the larger context of what was going on in Yehud. Israeli archaeologist Ephraim

Stern has claimed that the Persian period witnessed an unprecedented reduction in the number of cultic figurines (so-called Judahite pillar figurines of the pre-Exilic period) and sanctuaries found in excavations in Samaria and Yehud.[83] Stern interprets this as evidence for the increased centrality of the Jerusalem and Gerizim temples in the religious life of the Judeans and Samarians, though the report of Nehemiah's religious reform may suggest otherwise; at any rate, no sources directly polemicize against the Iron Age Judahite pillar figurines or otherwise indicate that they were rejected by the temple establishment.

On the political front, in addition to the western rebellions, Persia lost and then reconquered Egypt. Instability in the empire appears to have induced Persia to solidify its administrative institutions in the Levant.

Oded Lipschits and David Vanderhooft point to a break in the paleography and orthography of the *YHD* stamp impressions from the sixth–fifth centuries and those of the fourth–third centuries, which display no governors' names, more use of paleo-Hebrew script, and a change in the spelling of the name Yehud (from YHWD to YHD or the abbreviated YH).[84] This shift has two implications: First, it suggests the possibility that Persia, upon losing control over Egypt, tightened its control over Yehud and other territory along the border of Persia's newly reduced holdings in the Levant. Additionally, the fact that the typological break among the *YHD* stamp impressions lies between the sixth–fifth and fourth–third centuries means that the end of Persian rule appears not to have significantly disrupted the economic and political institutions in Yehud.

Similarly, a large number of unprovenanced Idumean Aramaic ostraca from the fourth century B.C.E. offer insight into the economic administration of this region and suggest that the tax system after the arrival of Alexander the Great did not differ significantly from the policies under the Persians.[85]

In short, the end of the Persian period did not mark a radical or immediate break. When the armies of Darius III were finally defeated by Alexander, the Achaemenid Persian Empire fell. The empire did not self-destruct due to a lack of strong administrative oversight or economic or military weakness.[86] The success of Persia's royal ideology of peace and order, granting limited home rule and respecting local and

ethnic religious practices, and indeed the success of its satrapal administrative system, meant that Alexander found much to emulate in
Persian institutions.[87] Then again, Alexander's conquest was followed
almost immediately by severe political instability, which eventually
opened the door for local Hasmonean independence.

Not only did aspects of the Persian period carry over into the
Hellenistic period, but elements of Hellenism began to seep into
Samaria and, to a lesser extent, Yehud, well before Alexander's conquest.
The Wadi Daliyeh papyri and seal impressions provide a glimpse of
the international, Greek- and Phoenician-influenced culture of the late
fourth century B.C.E. These were discovered in 1962 by the Ta'amireh
Bedouin who had discovered the Dead Sea Scrolls only 15 years earlier.
In the central hill country halfway between Jericho and Samaria in a
series of caves located at the heart of the Wadi Daliyeh, they uncov-
ered a trove of papyri, many of which bore seal impressions depicting
Persian and Greek figures. Months later the Bedouin sold the cache
to the American Schools of Oriental Research in Jerusalem; director
Paul Lapp then undertook systematic excavations of the caves the
Bedouin had identified. The first papyrus unrolled revealed a date
of 336/335 B.C.E., ultimately leading to Frank Moore Cross's theory
that the papyri were taken to the caves by Samaritans fleeing from
Alexander the Great's forces. The papyri and many small finds and
coins of Wadi Daliyeh thus provide a rare glimpse of Palestine in the
last days of Persian control.

Although the papyri are economic documents and offer no narrative context, they enable scholars to reconstruct the names of the
governors of Samaria and document legal customs of the time. The
appearance in the papyri of the name of one Sanballat, active and flourishing in Samaria in the first half of the fourth century, has led scholars
to suggest that an eponymous great-grandson of Nehemiah's enemy
Sanballat was governor of Samaria in 335 B.C.E. The seal impressions include numerous Greek images—Heracles, Hermes, Pericles,
and Dionysian satyr images. But they also include Near Eastern
iconography such as sphinxes and what Mary Joan Winn Leith calls
the "Persian-hero" motif, a variant on the Near Eastern "Master of
Animals" motif showing the king holding animals aloft.[88] The iconography of these seals nevertheless strongly underscores the presence

of Greek-influenced culture prior to Alexander. The Greek motifs may have been mediated through Phoenician styles. And the variety of styles suggests an already-internationalized culture and economy.

Numismatic evidence too indicates Greek influence in the late Persian period. Although Persian coins appear with some regularity in the fourth century, only one Persian coin has been found in Israel from this later period, while dozens of Greek-Phoenician examples have surfaced displaying what appears to be standardized imagery, such as the Athenian owl.[89] Additionally, Attic black-ware pottery from Greece turns up in fifth- and fourth-century B.C.E. excavations in Palestine with great regularity, signaling closer ties with the Greek mainland, ironically in the Persian period. This black glazed pottery was a highly prized luxury item even in areas controlled by the Persians and is most frequently found at coastal sites.

Any full evaluation of the extent and nature of the penetration of Greek culture into Samaria and Yehud would require an investigation into the next phase of Jewish history (see next chap.). The evidence of the late-Persian-period material, in general, suggests that later cultural Hellenism may have been preceded by a kind of economic Hellenism; that is, an internationalized mercantile economy based on money. The widespread appeal of Attic black-ware pottery throughout the Persian period, along with the other evidence from the fourth century, indicates that, notwithstanding the ongoing conflicts between Persia and Greece, Greek art and culture was very much part of the realia of Achaemenid Palestine long before Alexander. A new world was opening up and the small Jewish community in Yehud was more than ready and able to meet the new challenges introduced by Alexander and his followers.

7

Judea in the Hellenistic Period
From Alexander the Great to Pompey (334–63 B.C.E.)

JOHN MERRILL*

A New Geopolitical Reality

IN 334 B.C.E., THE NEWLY CROWNED KING OF MACEDONIA, the 22-year-old Alexander, led his army across the Strait of Hellespont (modern-day Dardanelles) with the goal of conquering the Persian Empire. Within a year, the Macedonians defeated the Persian forces of Darius III in two decisive battles. Alexander then turned south, proceeding along the Mediterranean coast toward Egypt.

Along with other rulers in Alexander's path, the Judean high priest Jaddua faced an existential choice—to stay loyal to his Persian overlord or to support the Macedonian newcomer. The island city of Tyre and some other city states rejected Alexander's overtures and were severely punished. According to the Jewish historian Flavius Josephus, Jaddua at first demurred but then became reconciled with Alexander, thereby sparing Jerusalem from Tyre's fate. Jaddua's decision was a prudent one because, after taking control of Egypt, Alexander returned up the coast

---

* This chapter has been rewritten and updated from the version contributed by Lee I. Levine to the third edition (Washington, DC: BAS, 2011).

and then marched east for a final confrontation with Darius. His fierce Macedonians overwhelmed the numerically superior Persians at the Battle of Guagamela, and Alexander stood astride the entire former Persian Empire, in addition to all of Greece.

When Alexander died, in 323 B.C.E., his surviving generals fought among themselves for control of the empire. It was a tumultuous time. Armies marched back and forth across the land; treaties were made and broken. Local regimes such as Judea experienced the destabilizing effects of conflict after some two centuries of comparative tranquility under Persian rule. Jerusalem itself was occupied and reoccupied on multiple occasions by contending armies. As part of an eventual peace settlement between the exhausted Macedonians, Ptolemy son of Lagos[1] was recognized as king of Egypt in 301, establishing a long-lived dynasty based in the newly created city of Alexandria. Seleucus commenced a parallel dynasty in Syria and Mesopotamia, head-quartered at Antioch. Coele Syria, a collection of provinces that lay between these two regimes and that included Judea,[2] was grudgingly ceded to Ptolemy, who had seized it when Seleucus was preoccupied. Greek became the official language of the region, although indige-nous peoples, including Judeans, continued to speak Aramaic. Greek culture—including institutions, behavioral norms, religion, and philos-ophy—became dominant. Accordingly, the approximately 260 years of Macedonian rule have been termed "the Hellenistic period."*

Finding themselves caught, as it were, between two powerful and warlike kingdoms—the Ptolemies and the Seleucids—would be a new experience for Judeans of the third century B.C.E. During the preceding period of Persian hegemony, all the major wars occurred well beyond Judean borders; Judeans were permitted a large measure of self-government and were free to pursue their own cultural, religious, and economic interests, for the most part unmolested. Now, however, in addition to their strategic location in the event of a fresh outbreak of hostilities, they would be an increasingly tempting source of tribute for the Ptolemaic and Seleucid rivals. This new fact of geography was to become, over time, the single most important dynamic to affect Judean history during the Hellenistic era.

* "Hellas" was the ancient name for Greece, and Greek-speaking people called themselves "Hellenes."

Contrasting Governing Styles

The Persian approach to governing subject territories seems to have afforded substantial autonomy to trusted local satraps, provided that they kept the peace and met their tribute obligations. The Macedonians, who displaced the Persians, followed a policy of "spear-won land." That meant that all conquered territory belonged to the victorious king, who could dispose of it as he chose. Some subject dynasties, including the Tobiads based in Ammon in the Transjordan, seem to have managed deftly the transition from Persian to Ptolemaic control.

Recent scholarship, however, provides vivid evidence of the fate of a local satrapy that failed the loyalty test. An article by Andrea Berlin in the November/December 2019 issue of *BAR* ("Zenon's Flour: Grains of Truth from Tel Kedesh") describes the results of extensive excavations at Tel Kedesh in northeast Galilee and suggests that the site during the period of Persian hegemony was a thriving and affluent outpost of the coastal city of Tyre. Tyrian kings had been loyal supporters of their Persian overlords. Indeed, Tyrian vessels led by King Matten played an important role in the Battle of Salamis against the Greeks in 480 B.C.E. However, the Tyrians made a fatal misjudgment in opposing Alexander, and their island city was destroyed.* The excavations at Tel Kedesh provide vivid evidence of the consequences. The facility was converted to a comparatively drab utilitarian outpost, apparently administering the surrounding region that had been removed from Tyrian control and added to the Ptolemies' royal estates.

Jerusalem, for its part, seems to have avoided the fate of Tyre. Jaddua, the last high priest of the Persian era, managed to accommodate to the Macedonians and maintain a degree of political independence.** —ED.

* John Grainger (*Hellenistic Phoenicia* [Oxford: Oxford Univ. Press, 1991], 35–36) has suggested that the Tyrians acted as they did because the Persian king ordered them to mount a stiff challenge. The vehemence of Alexander's response—and the enmity his Ptolemaic successors felt for Tyre—was undoubtedly prompted by the fact that the Tyrians had thrown the mutilated bodies of Alexander's emissaries over the city walls (Curtius 4.2.15).

** Tcherikover, *Hellenistic Civilization* (see n. 21), 59.

To those Judeans mindful of their past, their new situation might well have been a source of consternation. After all, three centuries earlier the then kingdom of Judah had been caught between the superpowers of that era—Babylon to the north and east and Egypt to the south. The results had been disastrous, as we learned in chap. 5.

In the early days of Ptolemaic rule, such intimations of impending crisis would have been unrecognized by most Judeans because once the Ptolemies and Seleucids (however grudgingly) agreed to a settlement, life in Judea went on more or less as it had before, under Persian auspices. Judea was an agricultural economy, and most of the population worked from dawn to dusk simply to pay taxes and tithes and to support themselves. Whether their taxes were being paid over to the new hegemon in Alexandria rather than the former one at Susa would have seemed, at least in the beginning, a distinction without a difference to most Judeans.

Assessing the Extent of Hellenization in Judea

Over time, however, it was impossible for Judeans to remain completely insulated from the Hellenistic world around them. New cities were being founded throughout Coele Syria, based on the Greek constitutional model of the *polis*, and were populated by retired, Greek-speaking soldiers. These *poleis* served as centers of Greek life, worshiping Greek deities and supporting one another through joint commercial, cultural, and athletic activities. Ptolemaic bureaucrats roamed Coele Syria, including Judea, looking after the king's interests; Greek-speaking merchants offered luxurious trade goods and potentially lucrative commercial opportunities. These developments, while increasingly pervasive, would not have come as a shock to many Judeans because, as Eric Meyers pointed out in chap. 6, archaeology reveals significant penetration of Greek culture even before the end of the Persian period.

As Lee Levine has described, scholars have staked out maximalist (Bickerman, Hengel) and minimalist (Tcherikover, Sandmel, Millar) positions on the extent to which such cultural interactions—termed "Hellenization"—affected Jewish society.[3] Much depends on which part of that social order one is talking about (e.g., the urban aristocrat vs. the rural farmer), as well as the time period in question. On the latter point, it is useful to divide the entire Hellenistic era into three distinct time periods—the century of Ptolemaic rule, from c. 301 to the transfer of authority to the Seleucid regime, in 200; the period of growing instability and unrest under the Seleucids, leading to the Maccabean Revolt (167–142); and the era of Judean expansion and independence during the

Hasmonean dynasty, ending with the Roman conquest of Judea in 63. Each of these historical periods exhibited a distinct set of interactions with the Hellenistic world, and we will deal with them separately below.

Hellenization Under the Ptolemies (301–200 B.C.E.)

While the growing pervasiveness of Greek culture may have been unsettling to some Judeans, the Ptolemaic regime offered undeniable opportunities to others. Josephus[4], citing the Greek historian Hecataeus of Abdera, makes reference to a certain Hezekiah, a senior priest no less, who migrated to Alexandria and became a valuable minister in the court of Ptolemy I (r. 305–283) (*Ag. Ap.* 1.187–89). If this reference is historically authentic, Hezekiah would be the first in a lengthy list of Jews who prospered under Ptolemaic auspices, during and even well beyond the century in which the Ptolemies controlled Judea. Many of these became Alexandrian expatriates, but nevertheless played important roles in Judea's history.

According to the *Letter of Aristeas*, a translation of the Torah into Greek was commissioned by Ptolemy II Philadelphus (r. 283–246). Supposedly, the translation was carried out by 72 sages, who were both experts in the Torah and well versed in Greek—hence the designation Septuagint (Latin for "70") for the Greek version of the Hebrew Bible. As Lee Levine observed, the historical authenticity of this account may be questioned, but the creation of the Septuagint testifies to the penetration of Greek language into Jewish scholarly circles, if not during the third century then by the second century at the latest, when the *Letter of Aristeas* was composed.[5]

During the reign of Ptolemy II, we also have graphic evidence of the presence of Ptolemaic functionaries in Coele Syria, in the form of some 2,000 papyri consisting of the administrative files of a certain Zenon, a bureaucrat in the service of Ptolemy's finance minister Apollonius. In February 259 B.C.E., Zenon traveled by sea to the port of Strato's Tower on the Mediterranean coast. From there, he went to Jerusalem and then onward to nine more locations. The exact nature of his mission is unclear, but he seems to have been conducting an auditing function of some kind, ensuring that income-producing properties were performing adequately for the Ptolemaic regime.

The term of the next Ptolemy in line, Ptolemy III Euergetes

(r. 246–222) provided the most striking example of opportunism by a Judean aristocrat. According to Josephus, a certain Joseph son of Tobiah and nephew[6] to the high priest Onias II, was able to secure from Ptolemy III the tax collection franchise for all of Coele Syria. Joseph out-bid all the competitors, managed to hold the concession for a reported 22 years, and thereby became Coele Syria's wealthiest man. Josephus uses the term "tax farming" to describe the process of allocating tax collection privileges based on competitive bids. It is not known whether this was an innovation of the Hellenistic era, although Josephus's use of the term "tax farming" is the first appearance of that notion in historical literature. In any event, Joseph's spectacular success must have come in no small measure at the expense of the taxpayers at the bottom of the economic pyramid. The practice of tax farming was to become an important source of social unrest in subsequent years.

The Ptolemaic court continued to provide opportunities to Judeans even after control of Coele Syria passed to the Seleucids, in 200. For example, 2 Maccabees 1:10 provides the text of a letter dated around 162[7] that Judas Maccabeus addressed to a certain Aristobulus, a member of the Judean priesthood who was apparently both a leader of the Jewish community in Alexandria and a counselor to Ptolemy VI. In approximately the same year, Onias IV, the son of the deposed high priest Onias III, fled to Egypt, where he was welcomed by Ptolemy VI and allowed to build a new temple in Heliopolis. A generation later, his descendants Chelcias and Ananias became generals in the Egyptian army (*Ant.* 13.285).[8]

In addition to the foregoing examples of active connections between Jerusalem aristocrats (especially senior members of the priesthood) and the Ptolemaic regime, the archaeological record, although less decisive, is also suggestive of Hellenistic cultural influence in Judea. For example, coins minted in Jerusalem bear the likeness of Ptolemy I and his wife, Berenike, together with the image of an eagle signifying Ptolemaic hegemony. While these small-denomination coins could possibly be interpreted as welcoming Ptolemaic authority by the Jerusalem establishment, in reality Ptolemaic approval was required to mint coins in the locations under their control, and the format of the Jerusalem coins followed the central model. At a minimum, the coins were likely a constant reminder to Judeans that they were subject to Ptolemaic rule.

Perhaps more telling, with respect to the infiltration of Hellenistic culture in Judea, is the discovery of some 1,000 jar handles indicating that the jars contained wine produced in Rhodes during the Hellenistic era. This seems to indicate that at least some elements of the Judean population—those who could afford it—had acquired a taste for high-end Greek beverages. Of interest as well, the archaeological record shows that some Jerusalemites set their tables with imported dishes, which included black slipped and painted plates, as well as bowls and drinking cups from Athens, Antioch, and Alexandria. While the remains of such items datable to the Ptolemaic period are insufficient to gauge the intensity of their use, the simple fact of their appearance in Jerusalem demonstrates that foreign goods could and did make their way into the city.[9]

Without a doubt, the most striking example of the impact of Hellenistic tastes on Jewish material culture may be seen in the archaeological remains of the mausoleum[10] built by Hyrcanus,[11] son of the aforementioned Joseph the tax collector, at the Tobiad family's 150-acre estate east of the Jordan River, between Jericho and Amman, in modern Jordan. The structure's classical dimensions exceed even those of the fabled tomb of Mausolus, the seventh wonder of the ancient world. Measuring 217 by 148 feet, its base is built with massive limestone monoliths, some weighing as much as 30 tons, creating an island in the middle of an artificial lake. Four elaborately carved lions adorn each cornerstone, while marble eagles perch at each corner of the rooftop. The lakebed is now dry, but in ancient times, the reflection on the water's surface of the alabaster walls would have been a grand and graceful sight. The impressive structure testifies to the cosmopolitan proclivities of at least one family of Jewish aristocrats during this time period.

In addition to material evidence, scholars have noted an awareness of ideas from the outside world contained in the Jewish literature produced during this period. One example is the biblical Book of Ecclesiastes (Qoheleth), which, as Lee Levine observed, "reflects a situation wherein faith and certainty had been lost, and in their stead, doubt, hesitancy, and skepticism had surfaced."[12] The author of Ecclesiastes also dismisses as vanity—i.e., "air" or "nothingness"—certain ideals held dear in the Hellenistic world such as athletic prowess, warcraft, and even learning: "Again I saw that under the sun the race is not to the swift, nor the battle to the strong, nor bread to the wise, nor riches to the intelligent, nor favor to the skillful; but time and chance happen to them all" (Ecclesiastes 9:11).[13]

During the disruptive period in which authority for Palestine had been transferred from the Ptolemies to the Seleucids, Ben Sira composed a work that rejects the deep skepticism of Ecclesiastes, offering instead a reaffirmation of traditional Jewish values: fear of the Lord, obedience to his commandments, and respect for iconic figures of Jewish history.[14] Ben Sira also introduces a number of themes relevant to the historical period: growing tension between rich and poor (4:1–10); respect for the priesthood and sanctity of the Temple (7:29–31); and resistance to foreign interference (36:1–12).

The Seleucid Conquest and Its Aftermath

Regardless of how one assesses the influence of Greek culture on Judeans, it occurred under conditions of comparative tranquility during the period of Ptolemaic hegemony. Toward the end of the third century B.C.E., however, that would change with far-reaching consequences. The geopolitical tectonic plates began to shift with the ascension of Antiochus III to the Seleucid throne in 223. Assuming the title "the Great," Antiochus aspired to reconsolidate the empire of the other "Great"—Alexander—the centennial of whose death coincided with the beginning of his rule. Coele Syria, then Egypt itself, were marked for conquest. In 219, Antiochus launched a major expedition against Ptolemy IV,[15] only to see his forces suffer a humiliating defeat two years later at Raphia, just north of the Egyptian border. For the time being, Coele Syria, including Judea, remained in Ptolemaic hands.

Ptolemy IV's grip on power, however, would have been tenuous at best. Corruption, dynastic rivalry, currency debasement, and incipient insurrection all threatened to undermine his regime.[16] Meanwhile, Antiochus's goal of conquest was undiminished, despite his recent setback. These developments would not have gone unnoticed by the Jerusalem establishment, especially those like Joseph the tax farmer, who had a significant stake in the outcome of the Ptolemaic-Seleucid rivalry. Meanwhile, a parallel rivalry was playing out within Joseph's own family. Joseph had seven sons by a first wife, and an eighth, named

Hyrcanus, by his brother's niece.[17] The stage was set for internecine conflict, especially as Joseph himself was approaching old age, and his financial empire was soon to be up for grabs.

In 210, a son—the future King Ptolemy V—was born to Ptolemy IV. Dignitaries from throughout the realm were summoned to celebrate the event. Curiously, according to Josephus, Joseph and his seven elder sons demurred, leaving young Hyrcanus to represent the family. A reasonable interpretation is that the Tobiads considered Ptolemy the likely loser in the coming renewal of hostilities. Be that as it may, Hyrcanus made a great success in Alexandria, albeit at considerable cost to the family treasury. His performance so enraged his elder brothers that they plotted to kill him on his return. Hyrcanus, however, was forewarned, and during the attempted ambush two of the brothers were killed instead. Now out of favor in Jerusalem, Hyrcanus withdrew to the family compound across the Jordan, where the fabulous architectural monument described above still stands (see p. 251). There, he apparently took on the role of governor on behalf of the Ptolemaic regime (*Ant.* 12.196–222).

In 204, Ptolemy IV died, leaving the six-year-old Ptolemy V to rule his kingdom and triggering a power struggle between his widow (and sister), Arsinoe III, and two of his former ministers. Antiochus seized the opportunity and struck again. In 200, he routed the Egyptian army at the Battle of Panium, near the headwaters of the Jordan River. The century of Ptolemaic hegemony was ended, and Coele Syria now was in Seleucid hands. Josephus, citing Polybius, reports that as the contending armies marched back and forth through Coele Syria, the local populations were "shaken like a storm-tossed ship" (*Ant.* 12.130). Judea, in the end, supported Antiochus, welcomed him into Jerusalem, and provided him amply with supplies. Undoubtedly, this gesture toward the Seleucid side was led by the Tobiad family (excluding Hyrcanus), who were among the city's leading citizens. In response, the grateful monarch recognized the authority of the Jerusalem establishment—that is, the high priest and his ruling council (*gerousia*)—and decreed that the Jews could live "according to the laws of their own country" (*Ant.* 12.142).

Following his victory at Panium, Antiochus would have proceeded to complete his goal of conquering Egypt but was dissuaded from doing so by the new rising power in the Mediterranean world: Rome. Pressured into making peace, Antiochus in 195 concluded a treaty with Ptolemy V, in which he gave his daughter Cleopatra in marriage, along with the revenues from Coele Syria as a dowry. That, at least, was the Egyptian understanding of the terms. Antiochus and his descendants would subsequently deny the claim, while Cleopatra and her descendants would persist in asserting it. This dispute set the stage for further conflict.

Throughout the rivalry between the Seleucids and Ptolemies, it seems inevitable that Judeans would be drawn to one side or the other. There was a long tradition of Judeans migrating to and prospering in Alexandria; these undoubtedly had friends and relatives still living in Judea. On the other hand, especially starting with Antiochus, many like the Tobiads saw their interest served by backing the stronger hand. The tension between pro-Ptolemaic and pro-Seleucid factions in Judea was to become a major factor in the turbulent history of this period.

Eventually, Antiochus III's ambitions got the better of him. His army was crushed by the Romans at the Battle of Magnesia, in 190, and he was forced to pay a staggering indemnity of 15,000 talents. This financial obligation was inherited by his successors and became an enormous burden on all taxpayers in the realm. Antiochus was murdered in 187 while in the process of looting a temple in the eastern part of his realm and was succeeded by Seleucus IV. At about this time,[18] Josephus reports, the Tobiad patriarch Joseph died, and his uncle Onias II was succeeded as high priest by his son Simon II. In the wake of these changes to the power structure, Josephus relates that a "war" broke out between Hyrcanus and his surviving elder brothers (*Ant.* 12.229). The term "war" may seem something of an exaggeration; however, the population of Jerusalem may have been as small as 5,000,[19] and the contending households each commanded security forces numbering in the hundreds. So the accompanying street fighting, ambushes, and assassinations could have well felt like "war." According to Josephus, the high priest Simon sided with the elder Tobiads because "he was of kin to them" (*Ant.* 12.229). This renewal of hostilities could reasonably be characterized as a continuation of animosity between pro-Ptolemaic and pro-Seleucid factions within Jerusalem. Hyrcanus once again found himself outnumbered and he withdrew to his fortified compound across the Jordan, where he completed work on the fabulous monument described above.

The Hellenist Reform Movement

In approximately 182 B.C.E., Simon II died and was succeeded by his son Onias III. The latter's term as high priest seems to have started smoothly enough, according to Jason of Cyrene's account in 2 Maccabees 3:1: "While the holy city was inhabited in unbroken peace and the laws were strictly observed because of the High Priest Onias and his hatred of wickedness."

This tranquil status quo was about to be upset in dramatic fashion, but before proceeding to those events, it is useful to consider exactly what that status quo consisted of. From the beginning of the Hellenistic era,[20] the Judean high priest had served as both the religious and political leader (*prostates*) of the Jewish people.[21] The position of high priest was hereditary, passing from father to eldest son, and was understood to have continued in dynastic succession from David and Solomon's high priest Zadok, and thence back to Moses's brother Aaron. As such, high priests were held in great reverence by the Jewish people. The high priest presided over a Temple hierarchy whose senior officials, such as the Temple Captain (second in command) and Temple Treasurer, were typically close family members, as well as a ruling council (*gerousia*), whose members included senior priests, military commanders, and wealthy landowners, often the same individuals.[22]

The senior priests, even if not in the direct line of descent for the high priesthood, considered themselves Zadokites,[23] by virtue of extended genealogical connections, and comprised the sect of the Sadducees, identified by Josephus[24] as important players in the coming period of Judean history. In addition to these senior priests, the Temple was staffed by large numbers of both junior priests and Levites who served on a rotational basis[25] because they were far too numerous to serve all at once. The total population of junior priests and Levites likely totaled some 8,000–10,000 individuals, of whom not more than 20 percent lived in Jerusalem, with the rest widely distributed in the villages and towns of the countryside, where they engaged in agriculture, animal husbandry, and various crafts, to support themselves and their families when not on duty at the Temple. Nevertheless, their privilege of Temple service was jealously guarded, and their loyalty to the Temple cult and senior priesthood was strongly held. Those loyalties would in due course be severely tested.

The trouble that would upset this status quo began when a dispute over the administration of the city market arose between Onias III and a certain Simon "who had been made Captain of the Temple" (2 Maccabees 3:4). A number of distinguished students of this era[26] have opined that Simon and his two brothers, who will appear shortly, are three of the elder pro-Seleucid Tobiad brothers who were joined by Onias's father Simon II in the conflict with Hyrcanus. While the evidence may not be decisive,[27] the three brothers were so closely allied with the Tobiads' interests, that whether they themselves are Tobiads is immaterial to understanding the political alignments in Jerusalem. In any event, Onias III prevailed and Simon was exiled from Jerusalem (2 Maccabees 3:5).

Simon appealed to the Seleucid governor of Coele Syria and Phoenicia, Apollonius of Tarsus, to whom he revealed that the Jerusalem Temple contained substantial wealth that could be appropriated by King Seleucus IV. The ever-cash-strapped king responded eagerly and dispatched a senior official, one Heliodorus, to confiscate[28] the Temple funds.[29] Upon Heliodorus's arrival in Jerusalem, Onias III confirmed that, indeed, there were considerable sums in the Temple vaults and, moreover, that a goodly portion belonged to none other than Hyrcanus, son of Tobias (2 Maccabees 3.11). Onias asserted, however, that to confiscate these funds was utterly impossible as that would violate the holiness and sanctity of the Temple that was trusted throughout the world (2 Maccabees 3.12). Heliodorus nevertheless persisted, and as word spread of his intention to violate the sanctity of the holy sanctuary, 2 Maccabees reports that the whole population of Jerusalem reacted with anguish. Of interest is the role of the city's women in the outpouring of emotion:

Women girded with sackcloth [...] thronged the streets. Some of the young women who were kept indoors ran together to the gates, and some to the walls, while others peered out of the windows. And holding up their hands to heaven, all made supplication (2 Maccabees 3:19–20).[30]

THE HELIODORUS STELA. This fragmented Greek inscription, dating to 178 B.C.E., gives King Seleucus IV a free hand to interfere in the affairs and treasuries of the sanctuaries of Syria and Palestine.

While the upper portion of the inscription surfaced on the antiquities market, several pieces from its bottom were recently excavated by a volunteer at the site of Maresha in southwestern Israel, where the stela was presumably installed for public viewing.

When Heliodorus arrived at the entrance to the Temple treasury, according to 2 Maccabees, he was confronted by two angelic warriors, who beat him nearly to death. Of course, this part of the story is metaphorical, but the implication is that attempts by secular authorities to violate the sanctity of the Temple would be met by divinely inspired resistance. Moreover, the agents of that resistance would have been the Temple security forces, a paramilitary Levitical order, who are called "Gatekeepers" in 1 Chronicles 9 and 26, and who will be important players as the drama unfolds.

The report of Heliodorus's failed mission would not have pleased Seleucus IV, and the discovery of some bond of trust between Onias III and the pro-Ptolemaic Hyrcanus would have unsettled the king even more. Meanwhile, Simon continued to agitate against Onias with the Syrian governor while dispatching agents to assassinate his political enemies in Jerusalem. Onias "appealed to the king,"[31] but before the matter could be resolved, Seleucus was killed[32] and succeeded, in 175, by his brother Antiochus IV.[33] At this point, 2 Maccabees introduces Jason, the brother of Onias, and relates that Jason bribed Antiochus to appoint him high priest instead. Importantly, Jason agreed to pay Antiochus 150 talents for the privilege of establishing a gymnasium in Jerusalem and enrolling the Jerusalemites as "citizens of Antioch" (2 Maccabees 4:9).

Scholars agree that Jason's "reform" involved converting Jerusalem into a Greek *polis*,[34] establishing Greek institutional forms such as a gymnasium for athletic training and an *ephebium* for the education of youth. Those enrolled as "citizens" were presumably the city's affluent residents, as only they could afford the expenses associated with these new institutions.[35] Importantly as well, civic authority was transferred away from the high priest and to officials selected by the comparatively exclusive group of citizens.[36] Jerusalemites were now able to participate in cultural and athletic events on an equal footing with other Greek cities, and were able to avail themselves of the associated commercial opportunities. Scholars note that these changes, although seemingly a dramatic departure from past practice, were political and economic in nature and did not, at this stage, alter the religious life of the city.[37] These reforms are collected in scholarly commentary under the blanket heading "Hellenization," and those advocating them are called "Hellenizers."

Heliodorus Stela

An article in the November/December 2008 issue of *BAR* ("Inscription Reveals Roots of Maccabean Revolt") featured a newly discovered but fragmentary limestone stela from the reign of the Seleucid king Seleucus IV that provided fresh insight into the tumultuous events leading up to the Maccabean revolt of 167 B.C.E. The stela's Greek inscription, written as a series of correspondences between Seleucus, his chief advisor Heliodorus and two lower royal officials, publicly proclaimed the Seleucid king's right to interfere in the affairs and treasuries of religious sanctuaries throughout Syria-Palestine, including the Jerusalem Temple. Before breaking off, the last line of the preserved text mentioned one Olympiodorus whom the king had appointed to administer temple affairs in the region.

Seleucus's brother and successor, Antiochus IV, took these exploitive policies even further. He continued to meddle in Judean affairs for financial gain but also set up an altar to Zeus in the Jerusalem Temple and imposed a series of harsh bans on traditional Jewish observance. By 167 B.C.E. the Jews had suffered enough at the hands of the Seleucids and, led by Mattathias and his son Judah Maccabee, arose in open revolt. The retaking of the Temple by Jewish forces and the miraculous relighting of the menorah for eight days with oil enough for only one are the basis for the Hanukkah festival (2 Maccabees 6–10).

Remarkably, three additional fragments from the lower portion of the same stela were recently excavated by a young volunteer at the site of Maresha in southwestern Israel (Dorothy D. Resig, "Volunteers Find Missing Pieces to Looted Inscription," *BAR*, May/June 2010). The new pieces not only secure the stela's authenticity and original provenance, but also list Olympiodorus's qualifications for administering the temple treasuries. –ED.

How was this so-called Hellenistic "reform" greeted by the population of Jerusalem? On the one hand, when Jerusalem was visited by Antiochus IV, he was "welcomed magnificently by Jason and the city and was ushered in with blaze of torches and with shouts" (2 Maccabees 4:22). On the other hand, we learn from modern political activity that a relatively small group of sign-waving advocates can appear, if properly positioned for TV cameras, as a mighty throng.

Similarly, even the few hundred "citizens" of the new *polis*, along with their associated security forces and householders, could have convincingly provided the welcome reported in 2 Maccabees while the rest of the populace remained skeptical or even opposed.

The author of 2 Maccabees excoriates Jason for his supposed perfidy in ousting his own brother from the high priesthood, but it is possible to apply a more charitable interpretation to the story. Onias III's position was tenuous at best. The powerful Tobiads were attacking him in Jerusalem and using their influence with the Seleucid regime against him. The revelation of his apparently pro-Ptolemaic connection was inflammatory, and the new king, Antiochus IV, was a man of volatile disposition. Jason's gambit may simply have been a compromise to appease the Tobiads by giving them control of civic affairs while keeping the priesthood in the family. Jason's compromise, if that is what it was, apparently included reinstating the brother of Simon named Menelaus[38] as Temple treasurer. In 172, Menelaus traveled to Antioch to deliver the scheduled payment to the king and took advantage of the opportunity to offer an even larger sum—300 talents more—to have himself appointed high priest. Jason was forced to retire across the Jordan to Ammon, where he presumably found protection from Hyrcanus.

Given the huge sums due, it is not surprising that Menelaus soon fell behind on his required payments. Summoned to give account, he looted some gold vessels from the Temple. Word of this sacrilege reached Onias III, and when the latter raised a protest, Menelaus arranged to have him assassinated. The people of Jerusalem reacted to these events with mixed outrage and horror. The sacred office of the high priest was being auctioned like a commercial franchise; the holy sanctuary was being looted; and the legitimate high priest, a man esteemed for holiness, had been murdered. A large crowd converged upon the Temple, where a third brother, Lysimachus, had been left in charge. Before the melee ended, Lysimachus lay dead and bleeding at the entrance to the Temple treasury (2 Maccabees 4:42).

Matters seem to have settled down, at least temporarily. But in 168, Antiochus IV led an army to invade Egypt,[39] only to be thwarted by the Roman Senate. During this humiliation, rumors reached Jerusalem that the king had been killed. This prompted Jason to return at the head of a force of "no fewer than a thousand men," (2 Maccabees 5.5) presumably furnished at least in part by Hyrcanus. The city was plunged into civil war, with a significant part of the population supporting Jason (according to *Ant.* 12.240), but the latter was forced to withdraw back to Ammon at the approach of Antiochus and his army. The king apparently construed the civil conflict as a Ptolemaic-inspired rebellion[40] against his own regime, and proceeded to attack the city, massacre the inhabitants, and loot the Temple. Antiochus left a certain "governor" to oversee Jerusalem affairs, and later[41] sent Apollonius with an armed force, who killed more victims, took slaves, and built a citadel called the Akra for housing a permanent garrison. The likely remains of that massive structure appear to have been identified on the northwest side of the City of David.[42]

Not long thereafter, in December 167, Antiochus launched an entirely unprecedented religious persecution considered by many to be "the most decisive episode [...] of the entire Second Temple period."[43] According to the sources, customary practices such as Sabbath adherence and circumcision were brutally punished; citizens were forcibly required to sacrifice to pagan idols and to eat defiled foods. The Temple was stripped of its traditional artifacts, and a statue of Zeus was set up in the sacred sanctuary. This final act of desecration would be called by the prophet Daniel "the Abomination of Desolation" (Daniel 9:7).

Historians of this era have puzzled over the ferocity of the ban of the Judeans' religion, which was unprecedented. Alexander the Great, after all, had been quite respectful of local deities, and the Hellenistic world followed this model. As often happens when strong explanatory evidence is lacking, theories abound.[44] Perhaps the one that comes closest to the mark was postulated by Tcherikover, who opined that the persecution was in response to what Antiochus came to believe was a religiously inspired revolt.[45] The evidence of a full-scale revolt falls short, but religiously inspired resistance may well have been the case. When Antiochus looted the Temple, the first line of defense would have been the Levite security forces—the so-called Gatekeepers. These would have been among the victims of the massacres reported by both books of Maccabees.[46] However, the Gatekeepers on duty at the time (1 Chronicles 9:22 puts their number at 212) would have been only a small fraction of the total membership of this paramilitary Levitical order, because they served on a rotating basis.[47] Thus, there would have been large numbers of off-duty Gatekeepers in both Jerusalem and the surrounding countryside, thirsting to revenge the massacre of their comrades, not to mention the looting of the Temple, whose treasures they had a sacred duty to protect. This cadre would have provided leadership for a significant resistance, if not open revolt, by a population large numbers of whom not only had not benefited from the Hellenistic reforms, but saw them as sacrilegious. Moreover, when the full-scale rebellion did break out, we find "Hasideans" described as "mighty warriors"—the same language that 1 Chronicles 26 uses to describe Gatekeepers—in the vanguard of the fighting (see below, p. 263).

The Maccabean Revolt

It did not take long for Antiochus's heavy-handed policy to provoke open revolt. Many devout Judeans had fled Jerusalem to avoid persecution. Among these was Matthias son of Hasmoneus,[48] a priest who with his five sons retired to their ancestral village of Modi'in, some 20 miles northwest of Jerusalem. As 1 Maccabees tells the story, a group of the king's soldiers pursued the family to Modi'in, where their officer ordered the villagers to partake of a prohibited sacrifice. Matthias refused, asserting that he and his sons would not deviate from their religion either "to the right hand or to the left."[49] When one of the villagers meekly complied, Matthias drew his sword and struck him down, then turned and killed the officer. The revolt had officially begun.

Of course, 1 Maccabees is a work designed to glorify the Hasmoneans, and it is useful to understand, from that point of view, how the revolt was characterized. For one thing, the first blow in the uprising was struck not against the Syrian soldiers but against the apostate Jew. Next, in praising Matthias's act, 1 Maccabees repeatedly invokes the zeal of Phinehas, the iconic figure who earned for his descendants the perpetual right to serve as high priest—with the attendant social and economic benefits—by slaying another apostate Jew (cf. Numbers 25:6–15). Third, the Hasmoneans were soon joined by others who "offered themselves willingly for the law," showing again that there was a religious basis for the revolt. Fourth, these early joiners are called "Hasideans," a Greek rendering of the Hebrew *Hasidim*, meaning holy or pious. Fifth, the Hasideans are described as "mighty warriors of Israel" (1 Maccabees 2:42) which is the same terminology that 1 Chronicles 26 uses to describe Levitical Gatekeepers,[50] supporting the notion above that this paramilitary order was in the vanguard of the resistance. And finally, the rebels proceed to attack not their military opponents but rather "sinners" and "renegades" or "outlaws" (*paranomoi*). For all the foregoing reasons, whether or not the earlier resistance to Antiochus was religiously motivated, the resulting rebellion unquestionably was (at least in the minds of the authors of 1 and 2 Maccabees).

Hasmonean Rulers of Judea, 142–37 B.C.E.

Simon	142–134
John Hyrcanus	134–104
Aristobulus	104–103
Alexander Jannaeus	103–76
Salome Alexandra	76–67
Aristobulus II	67–63
John Hyrcanus II	63–40
Mattathias Antigonus	40–37

Thus, while the revolt ultimately led to an independent Jewish state, its genesis was not as a war of independence but rather a civil conflict between Jews willing to live according to Hellenistic cultural norms and those committed to retaining their traditional way of life. Leadership of the movement was passed from the elderly priest Matthias to his oldest son Judas, named Maccabeus,[51] from whom the Maccabean Revolt takes its name.

Judas and his determined Hasidean[52] followers managed to retake control of Jerusalem, whereupon they cleansed and rededicated the Temple, in December 164 B.C.E.—an event celebrated ever since as Hanukkah. Judas was killed in combat in 160, and the mantle of leadership passed to his brother Jonathan, who withdrew into the wilderness. From this low ebb in their fortunes, the Hasmoneans gradually gained ground, until their guerilla tactics had taken control of much of the countryside, leaving the "renegades" and their Syrian supporters holding out in fortified sites. Then in 152, dissension within the Seleucid family led the disputing parties to sue for peace and to offer Jonathan the high priesthood.

This was the beginning of a dynasty in which Hasmoneans would hold this office for more than a century. Jonathan lived another ten years, but in 143 he was captured by the Seleucid general Tryphon and executed, to be succeeded by his older brother Simon. A year later, Simon besieged the Syrian garrison at Jerusalem and evicted its occupants. The year 142, therefore, marks the end of the civil war after 25 years of conflict. Simon then made an alliance with the latest Seleucid ruler, Antiochus VII (r. 138–129), only to be assassinated by his own son-in-law, an otherwise unknown Ptolemy son of Abubus.[53] The traitor dispatched agents to do away with Simon's eldest son, John Hyrcanus, but the intrepid Hyrcanus, himself a proven military commander, got wind of the plot, killed his would-be assassins, and in 134 was declared high priest in Jerusalem by acclamation.

Hyrcanus offered his first sacrifice as high priest, then hastened to exact revenge upon his father's assassin. Ptolemy was sequestered in a fortress near Jericho where he still held Hyrcanus's mother and brothers captive. Josephus provides a gripping scene, in which Ptolemy brings Hyrcanus's mother to the wall in view of the opposing forces and threatens to kill her unless they give up the siege. She, however, urges her son to persist, even if it means her death (*Ant.* 13.230–32). Her courage in the face of extreme torment is echoed in the parallel tale of the martyrdom of a mother and her sons in 2 Maccabees 7:1–42. The lesson of both accounts seems to be that if a woman—particularly a mother—displays such courage, how can a man (or a son) do any less?

Hyrcanus did not have long to enjoy his new position. Antiochus VII attacked Jerusalem in force, surrounded the city, and began a debilitating siege. Traces of that intense military action have been discovered by archaeologists in the form of ballista balls and arrowheads in excavations at the Jaffa gate.[54] According to Josephus, Antiochus agreed to a suspension of hostilities so the Jerusalem residents could observe the holy week of Tabernacles. Then Antiochus offered to lift the siege if the Judeans would pay a reparation fee of 500 talents and accept the re-establishment of a Syrian garrison as security for payment. The Judeans' objection indicated the insular nature of the new regime: "They could not," they asserted, "associate with other people or converse with them" (*Ant.* 13.247). Antiochus agreed to take hostages instead but tore down the city's defensive wall as a precaution against further insurrection. In 129, Antiochus was killed in fighting against the Parthians, and this marked the beginning of an independent Hasmonean state.

Sectarian Participation in the Revolt?

At the point in his narrative in *Antiquities* that can be dated to c. 144–43 B.C.E.,[55] Josephus interrupts the flow of events to record the following: "Now at this time there were three schools of thought among the Jews ... the first being that of the Pharisees, the second that of the Sadducees, and the third that of the Essenes" (*Ant.* 13.171).

A reasonable inference is that Josephus understood the groups he calls "schools," but which scholars typically speak of as sects, to have been relevant to the historical situation as of the time (i.e., "*at this time*") he injects them into his narrative; otherwise the passage would be a complete non-sequitur. As Lee Levine has observed, the notion that the sects coalesced around this time is supported by various literary sources.[56] In addition, the Pharisees and Sadducees are portrayed by Josephus as up-and-running sects, indeed prominent members of John Hyrcanus's court[57] only a few years after the date of this introduction.

If, as Josephus seems to be telling us, the three sects were in existence c. 144–143, they did not materialize out of thin air, and it seems reasonable to inquire what roles they might have played in the immediately preceding history—that is, the Maccabean Revolt itself. Looking first at the Sadducees, the insurgency needed capable military leadership, and senior priests (i.e., Sadducees) were traditionally military commanders, a role that they would retain throughout the Hasmonean regime.[58] Turning to the Pharisees, fighting forces are more effective if animated by a moral imperative, and this is where scribes, who could provide such guidance, would have been important. Josephus repeatedly tells his readers that Pharisees were acknowledged expert interpreters of the law upon whom much of the Judean population relied. While the term "Pharisee" may not have been coined at the beginning of the revolt, there were certainly Pharisee-like figures in Judea, such as "Eleazar, one of the scribes in high position" (2 Maccabees 6:18), who taught an indelible lesson about adhering to the Law.[59]

The case for the involvement of the Essenes, or perhaps more properly proto-Essenes, is less obvious but intriguing. To begin with, the terms 'Essene' and 'Hasidean' likely have a common root in the Hebrew *Hasidim*. This is because Josephus's Greek *Essenoi* that first appears in *J.W.* 2.119 is a transliteration (i.e., phonetic rendering) of an Aramaic term,[60] and the most plausible candidate is *hysn*,[61] which is the Aramaic equivalent of the Hebrew *hasidim*. Philo seems to be confirming this etymology when he says in three separate statements[62] that the name of the Essenes is derived from their holiness.

For its part, the Greek *Assidaioi* of both 1 and 2 Maccabees is generally accepted to be a transliteration of the Hebrew *Hasidim*. The apparent linguistic connection between *Assidaioi* and *Essenoi* gives rise to the hypothesis that the Essenes evolved from the same "holy" or "pious" group that comprised the Hasideans of the revolt. Said another way, the Hasideans could reasonably be imagined to be precursors of the Essenes. Moreover, that understanding of Essene origins can be extended further because, as described earlier, the Hasideans are called "mighty warriors" (Greek: *ischyroi dynamei;* Hebrew: *gibbore hayil*), which is the same term that the Chronicler uses to describe Levite Gatekeepers.[63]

The Gatekeepers were a paramilitary force numbering in the thousands and distributed throughout the villages and towns of Judea. Accordingly, when 2 Maccabees 8:1 reports that "Judas ... and his companions secretly entered the villages and summoned their kindred and enlisted those who had continued in the Jewish faith, and so they gathered about six thousand," one can see that a fighting force could be quickly assembled because *it was already in existence.* Thus, we can discover, if not the Essenes, at least their forerunners, as providing a third ingredient of a successful revolt—a cadre of skilled and determined fighters.

The foregoing identification of the precursors of the Essenes as mighty warriors will undoubtedly raise many eyebrows because the Essenes in later history are portrayed as a rather passive group. Philo even says they decline to use their artisan skills to fabricate weapons.[64] However, at the end of this chapter, we will suggest a theory about how descendants of the Maccabean-era Levites could have become core members of what would be known to Josephus as the Essene sect. In the meanwhile, it is worth keeping in mind that, notwithstanding Philo, the sectarian literature itself is filled with echoes of an earlier militaristic orientation.[65] It is also useful to consider that there were unquestionably Levites among the Essenes (cf. CD 3.21; 4.2; 14.3), and as gatekeeping was one of the principal Levitical functions, it seems reasonable to suppose that at least some Levites in the sect were descendants of the Maccabean-era Gatekeepers, especially in view of the militaristic language noted above.

The Hasmonean cause certainly benefited from the ever-increasing dysfunction of the Seleucid regime. Notwithstanding that benefit, the Maccabees at various critical moments still faced seemingly insurmountable odds. In reflecting on their final success, one could detect certain elements in common with other successful revolts in history—to wit, charismatic and able leadership, a strong moral imperative, and an aroused population willing to fight. One can also associate each of these elements, respectively, with the Sadducees, Pharisees, and Essenes, or at least with precursors of those groups. During the revolt, the sectarians (or precursors) worked together toward a common goal. As so often happens in history, however, alliances formed in the heat of revolution do not always survive after the ultimate victory, and sectarian rivalry would eventually be the undoing of the fledgling Jewish state.

Territorial Expansion

Not unlike in other successful revolutionary movements,[66] Hyrcanus and his successors in the flush of victory embarked on an aggressive program of territorial expansion, whose goal was in part to spread the ideology that underlay the revolt—in this case, a religious ideology—in part for security reasons, and in part for economic advantage. From the comparatively small and isolated sub-province at the beginning of the Hellenistic period, Judea under the Hasmoneans would become a significant political entity that encompassed an area roughly the size of David and Solomon's kingdom. And indeed, as Lee Levine has observed, the language of 1 Maccabees reflects a conscious attempt by the authors to compare their Hasmonean patrons to the Jewish heroes in the Book of Judges and the glorious achievements of David and Solomon.[67]

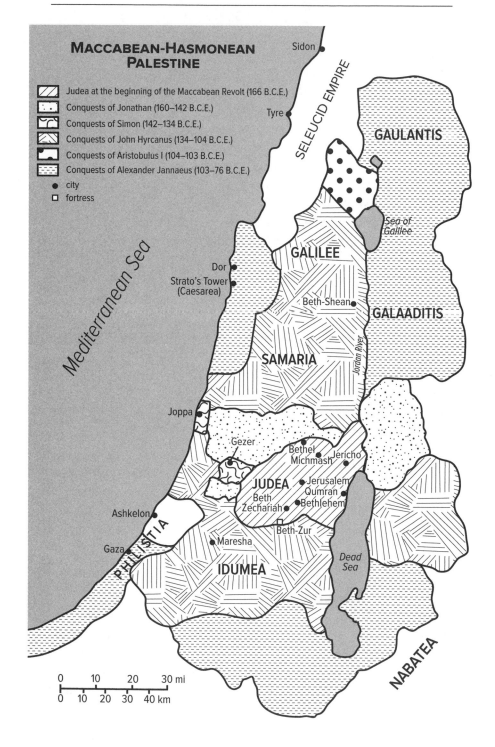

MACCABEAN-HASMONEAN PALESTINE

Judea at the beginning of the Maccabean Revolt (166 B.C.E.)
Conquests of Jonathan (160–142 B.C.E.)
Conquests of Simon (142–134 B.C.E.)
Conquests of John Hyrcanus (134–104 B.C.E.)
Conquests of Aristobulus I (104–103 B.C.E.)
Conquests of Alexander Jannaeus (103–76 B.C.E.)
• city
□ fortress

Sidon

SELEUCID EMPIRE

Tyre

GAULANTIS

Sea of Galilee

GALILEE

Dor
Strato's Tower (Caesarea)

Beth-Shean

GALAADITIS

Mediterranean Sea

Jordan River

SAMARIA

Joppa

Gezer

Bethel
Michmash
Jericho

JUDEA
Jerusalem
Qumran
Bethlehem
Beth Zechariah
Beth-Zur

Ashkelon

PHILISTIA

Gaza

Maresha

IDUMEA

Dead Sea

NABATEA

0   10   20   30 mi
0 10 20 30 40 km

Consistent with that vision, Jerusalem would grow from a 30-acre site with some 5,000 inhabitants clustered around the City of David and the Temple Mount to a full-fledged 130-acre city accommodating an estimated population of 30,000.[68] The Jerusalem Temple, of course, would continue to command center stage, and both its daily rituals and special festival events would be a source of both intense devotion and, later, divisiveness.[69] The Hasmoneans accrued significant wealth and power, as they and their political supporters came to control the newly conquered seaports, trade routes, and agricultural lands, the revenue from which was free of tribute obligations to external hegemons.[70]

HASMONEAN COIN. Hellenistic and Jewish iconography are blended in this bronze prutah minted by John Hyrcanus I (r. 134–104 B.C.E.). The obverse depicts a double cornucopia, a pagan symbol, but one that was inoffensive to Jews.

The reverse side of the coin, by contrast, demonstrates Jewish nationalism. The language of the inscription, including the name and title of the ruler, is Hebrew, not Greek: "Jehohanan the High Priest and the council of the Jews." Moreover, the coin is inscribed in an ancient Hebrew script used nearly a millennium earlier, at the time of the Davidic and Solomonic monarchies, as an expression of the Hasmoneans' identification with a glorious past, when Israel was first an independent nation.

Simon had already conquered Gezer and, according to 1 Maccabees 13:43–48, expelled that city's gentile inhabitants and replaced them with observant Jews. Simon also captured the major port city of Joppa. Hyrcanus aggressively continued this territorial expansion, subduing various ethnic groups that in the past had threatened Judea's territorial integrity—Idumea in the south and the Samaritans in the north (*Ant.* 13.254–83). Hyrcanus's son Aristobulus I added Iturean territory and, possibly, northern Galilee (*Ant.* 13.318–19). After Aristobulus's premature death (see below, p. 277), his brother Alexander Jannaeus, perhaps the most expansionist Hasmonean of them all, proceeded to annex territories in almost every direction: Strato's Tower (later Caesarea Maritima) and Dor in the northwest, Gaza in the southwest, and much of Golan and Gilead in the northeast (*Ant.* 13.320–97).

Religious Intensity

As noted, the Hasmoneans' territorial gains were accompanied by forceful religious zeal, including policies mandated by Deuteronomy, such as the deportation of non-Jewish populations, the destruction of their idols and shrines, and the introduction of observant Jewish populations. In some cases, whole populations (Idumeans and Itureans) were converted to Judaism.[71]

Recent archaeological work[72] provides a further insight into the extent of religious intransigence during this period. Finkelstein offers intriguing evidence that many of the geographical sites mentioned in the books of Ezra, Nehemiah, and Chronicles were uninhabited prior to the Hasmonean era. This means that at least some portion of those biblical books could not have been composed before that period because the sites referenced in them did not exist. We have already noted (see p. 267) that the organization and numbers of Levitical Gatekeepers in 1 Chronicles 9 and 26—although purportedly describing David's kingdom—likely reflect conditions during or not long before the Hasmonean period. The Book of Ezra, for its part, contains strong Deuteronomic formulations and even extends the ban on intermarriage with the seven indigenous nations to a rather harsh (at least to modern sensibilities) blanket proscription against intermarriage with all non-Jews.[73] Based on the date of composition (per Finkelstein), it would appear not that the Hasmoneans were following Ezra, but rather that the author of Ezra was endorsing existing Hasmonean policy.[74]

Archaeology adds to the picture of the religious intensity of the Hasmonean regime provided by literary sources. For example, the reaffirmation of a distinctly Jewish culture is reflected in daily household objects from Judea and Galilee, which in the Hasmonean era exhibit a consistent and apparently deliberate return to simplicity. Cooking pots, storage jars, and small dishes recovered from sites both north and south, while manufactured locally, look exactly alike. Gone as well are the imported or luxury items found in pre-Hasmonean locations (see p. 251) and, conspicuously, in contemporary but non-Jewish towns, such as Marissa and Dor. In their everyday lives, Judeans and Galileans consciously distanced themselves culturally, both from their neighbors and their own, more culturally syncretic past.[75]

During the same period, stepped pools (*mikva'ot*) begin to appear at a number of settlements in Judea, and one more is added at Gamla in the Golan. These installations seem to indicate a growing concern for ritual purity and to advertise a distinct ethnic identity.[76]

Cultural Synthesis

Other archaeological evidence, however, may provide a more mixed picture. Lee Levine has offered three examples that are thought to support the notion, advanced by Elias Bickerman, of a cultural synthesis of Jewish and Hellenistic elements.[77] The earliest candidate is the Maccabean funerary monument described in 1 Maccabees 13:27–29 for which not a single stone remains. However, Andrea Berlin has pointed out that the structures described in 1 Maccabees—pyramids surrounded by massive columns displaying full suits of armor—seem to imitate Hellenistic funerary monuments found elsewhere in Asia Minor.[78] Another example is the magnificent Hasmonean palace excavated by the late Ehud Netzer near Jericho that displays the sort of fine amenities—a swimming pool, baths, a grand pavilion, frescoed walls, and so forth—seen elsewhere in the Hellenistic world. The Hasmonean royal family was apparently not alone in adopting Hellenistic architectural forms. The tombs of wealthy Jerusalem aristocrats follow well-known Hellenistic styles, including pyramidal form, columned facades, friezes, and so forth. Notwithstanding these outward displays of wealth, virtually all of the foregoing Hellenistic forms retain a distinctly Jewish character. For example, between the Hasmonean palace and its pool were several ritual baths (*mikva'ot*), and virtually none of the funerary monuments include the sorts of figural representations common in non-Jewish tombs throughout the Hellenistic world, including Palestine. It is not clear that the adoption of these internationally recognized status symbols necessarily implies a parallel adoption of cultural mores. Whatever one might conclude about the extent of cultural syncretism these examples convey, there seem to have been well-defined limits.

Lee Levine has provided further evidence of cultural synthesis, including the *Additions* to the Book of Esther, written in Hasmonean Jerusalem by a priest named Lysimachus in a refined Greek literary style, and brought to Alexandria by a Levite named Ptolemy. The *Additions* have the effect of modifying the themes of Esther toward a more Jewish outlook, and represent a striking contrast between the obviously Hellenistic education of the author and his strong Jewish loyalties.[79] Further elements of cultural synthesis may be found in forms of marriage contracts first attested in Egypt, and the Pharisaic system of higher education (*beth midrash*) that appears to be modeled on Greek philosophic schools.

How are we to reconcile the intense and seemingly insular religious orientation of Jews in the Hasmonean era with the apparent acceptance of elements of Hellenistic culture? The answer that suggests itself is that the Maccabean revolt was not an uprising against Hellenistic culture *per se* but rather a reaction to the forceful imposition of unfamiliar and to many Judeans uncomfortable behavioral norms and, subsequently, a brutal and unprecedented suppression of the Jewish religion itself. Just as scholars have termed the first set of changes a "Hellenistic reform" movement, the revolt and subsequent regime could reasonably be termed a counter-reformation that sought to obliterate any re-emergence of the original reform. Moreover, in addition to being sponsored by a relatively small group of Jerusalemites, the reform was enforced by a Seleucid king (Antiochus IV). The Seleucids and the Hellenizing "renegades" therefore bore the brunt of Jewish animosity,[80] while many Judeans remained pro-Ptolemaic and maintained extensive familial and cultural connections to fellow Jews in Alexandria. These connections not only survived but apparently continued to flourish during the Hasmonean era, as evidenced by such Jewish figures as the Aristobulus to whom Judas Maccabeus's letter was addressed; the grandson of Ben Sira who migrated to Alexandria in the early years of the Hasmonean dynasty; the Jewish general in Cleopatra's army who spoke in support of Alexander Jannaeus;[81] or the priest Lysimachus, who composed the *Additions* in Greek. It is not accidental, in this context, that the Hasmonean royal family employed both Greek and

Hebrew names, or that one of them, Aristobulus I (the first to take the title king), was termed by Josephus "a lover of the Grecians" (*Ant.* 12.318). Thus, despite the stern religious orientation of the Hasmonean regime, there was a robust set of relationships with Alexandrian Jews, through which certain cultural adaptations could flow.

Religious Sects

As noted earlier, Josephus introduces the three principal Judean sects—the Pharisees, Sadducees, and Essenes—in the portion of his narrative that occurs during the mid-second century B.C.E.,[82] that is, near the end of the Maccabean revolt and the beginning of the Hasmonean regime. We suppose that Josephus inserted his brief commentary on the sects at this point because each of them, or at least their forerunners, had played meaningful roles in the successful revolt. Importantly as well, Josephus knew that the sects (at least two of them)[83] would also be central to the history that followed the revolt, including eventual fall of the Hasmonean regime.

Lee Levine has opined that religious sectarianism was an unusual phenomenon in ancient Judaism, and that the upheavals in the second century B.C.E. seem to have been a catalyst for the emergence of such groups.[84] The reasons for that emergence are, of course, complex, but at the risk of over-simplification, we can observe in our own era that when a people binds itself to the rule of law, disputes inevitably arise as to the interpretation of that law. All Jews subscribed to certain common beliefs: that there was one all-powerful God, to be worshiped in one Temple in one particular city (Jerusalem); God had chosen his people (Israel) and made a covenant with them, the essence of which was that if they would scrupulously obey his commandments, he would reward them with a glowing future.[85] However, the devil, so to speak, was in the details, and differences would inevitably arise as to when and how the rules were to be obeyed. Such differences in turn were clearly the source of Jewish sectarianism, and the intensity of sectarian dissension that emerged would seem to be in direct proportion to the degree of commitment to the law that the failed Hellenistic "reform" effort had inspired. As we have seen, the Maccabean revolt in its most elemental form was about Mosaic Law—whether to follow it strictly, deviating neither "to the right hand nor to the left,"[86] or to accept the imposition of a new polity that diverged significantly from tradition. All participants in the victorious outcome understood that adherence to the law provided the moral justification for the insurrection, as well as securing divine support for the eventual victory.

In this context, it should not be surprising to discover the Pharisees, as expert exponents of the law, in prominent positions in the new regime. Josephus reports that "Hyrcanus was a disciple of theirs," and further that "these (the Pharisees) have so great a power over the multitude, that when they say anything against the king, or against the high priest, they are presently believed." (*Ant.* 13.288–89).[87] In addition, the Pharisees claimed to be the exclusive custodians of oral traditions (*Ant.* 13.297) that (according to rabbinic tradition [*M. Avot* 1.1]) had been given by God to Moses in addition to the written laws. Accordingly, the Pharisees presented themselves as the sole legitimate bearers of Mosaic tradition,[88] a position that in due course would be vigorously opposed by the other two sects. In the beginning of his term, though, Hyrcanus considered them valued members of his ruling council,[89] alongside the aristocratic Sadducees.

The Sadducees, as described earlier, were members of the senior priesthood who likely took their name from the Hebrew *Zadikim*, signifying the extended family who claimed ancestral connections to David and Solomon's high priest Zadok. This relatively small group of Judean aristocrats held high positions in the Temple, government bureaucracy (especially in diplomatic roles), and the military.[90] Some scholars have suggested that these supposed descendants of Zadok would have strenuously objected to the Hasmoneans' qualifications for the office of high priest. This theory, though, seems debatable. First, the last priest in the direct line of succession was Onias IV, son of the deposed Onias III. Following the latter's assassination, Onias IV had fled to Egypt, where he was welcomed by Ptolemy VI. This left a vacuum for which the Hasmoneans would seem as qualified as any other candidate to fill. Further, a certain Ananias, a descendant of Onias IV who had become a general in Cleopatra's army, overruled the queen's advisors when they urged her to attack and depose Alexander Jannaeus, saying that Jannaeus was a kinsman,[91] whom it would be unjust to deprive of the authority that "belonged to him" (*Ant.* 13.354). It is difficult to imagine a stronger endorsement of Hasmonean qualifications than this statement of support by a direct descendant of the last authentic Zadokite.[92] In any event, the Sadducees consistently supported the Hasmoneans and enjoyed senior positions in the religious, bureaucratic, and military hierarchy.[93]

The third sect identified by Josephus as being active in the mid-second century B.C.E.—the Essenes—plays no visible role in the history of the Hasmonean regime. If, as we supposed,[94] Levitical Gatekeepers were forerunners of the Essene sect, they would have settled back into their villages and towns in comparative anonymity at the end of the revolt. There, when not on duty at the Temple, they would have needed to find employment in agriculture, animal husbandry, or crafts to support themselves and their families.[95] What became known to Josephus as the sect of the Essenes seems to have originated when certain Levites and priests became alienated from the Hasmonean regime and withdrew from mainstream Judean society to form a separate community, which they described as the *Yahad.* Exactly what circumstances led to this withdrawal is much debated and will be discussed in more detail at the end of this chapter. Over time, however, the core group of sectarians were joined by other disaffected Jews, such that by the first century C.E., the sect reportedly comprised some 4,000 members[96] living in self-sufficient enclaves in many villages and towns.[97]

Sectarian Rivalry Under John Hyrcanus (134–104 B.C.E.)

The symbiotic relationship between John Hyrcanus and the Pharisees was not to last. Josephus reports that Hyrcanus's success moved many to envy him, and that the foremost of these were the Pharisees (*Ant.* 13.288). Secret meetings were held to air complaints (*J.W.* 1.37), and in due course opposition broke out into the open. Matters came to a head, according to Josephus, at a dinner held by Hyrcanus to honor the Pharisees (recalling that in the aftermath of the revolt, he had become "a disciple of theirs"). During that event he inquired of his guests as to whether they found any aspect of his behavior lacking. "Yes," said one of the guests, and stated that if Hyrcanus truly desired perfect righteousness, he must give up the high priesthood and confine himself to civil matters. When Hyrcanus demanded to know on what possible grounds he should give up his position, his interlocutor (named Eleazar) replied, "... because it is understood by many ... that your mother had been a captive in the days of Antiochus Epiphanes" (*Ant.* 13.292).[98] Apparently convinced that Eleazar would not have been bold enough to make such a scurrilous charge without being confident of a supporting consensus among his Pharisaic guests, Hyrcanus's response was swift and comprehensive. He put a stop to the many decrees the Pharisees had been issuing (presumably on points of law), and imposed punishments on those who persisted in following the Pharisees' directives (*Ant.* 13.296). Presumably, he also dismissed them from his ruling council. At this point in his narrative, Josephus reveals that the dinner episode was a sort of tip of the iceberg in a larger dispute over legal (halakhic) matters between the Pharisees and the Sadducees, with the former claiming the force of Oral Law and the latter insisting on written.[99] The Pharisees had a significant popular following,[100] and Hyrcanus's prohibition of their rulings caused a rebellion, which in his earlier history, Josephus calls "open war" (*J.W.* 1.67). Hyrcanus, however, controlled the military and the Temple priesthood, whose Sadducean members stood firmly at his side, and the rebellion was put down. Hyrcanus, Josephus says, went on to live out the rest of his term in peace; however, the dispute between the Pharisees and the Sadducees was far from over.

From his report on the Pharisee-led rebellion, Josephus leaves out (or perhaps was unaware of) a material bit of information: Hyrcanus's oldest son and heir apparent, Aristobulus I, was married to a certain Salome Alexandra,[101] whom rabbinic sources reveal to be the sister of a leader of the Pharisees, one Simeon ben Shetah (*b. Sotah* 47a; *b. Ber.* 48a). A plausible inference is that this was a diplomatic marriage, a fence-mending exercise in the wake of the revolt. If that was indeed the intent, however, it failed, because Salome Alexandra eventually went on to become the instrument of the Pharisees' return to power.

The Short, Unhappy Reign of Aristobulus I (104–102/3 B.C.E.)

John Hyrcanus died in 104 B.C.E. His eldest son, Aristobulus I, succeeded to the high priesthood and ignored his father's final testament that left civil authority in the hands of Hyrcanus's widow. Instead, Aristobulus imprisoned his mother and allowed her to starve to death while also declaring himself king and confining his three youngest brothers. Aristobulus's next eldest brother, Antigonus, however, was much loved by the new king and a trusted military commander. In a complicated tale of court intrigue, Josephus relates that the new king's wife—who the text labels Salina, but who is better understood to be Salome Alexandra (see n. 101)—contrived to have Antigonus murdered.[102] Shortly thereafter, in 103, the bereaved Aristobulus died of symptoms that have caused speculation that he was poisoned,[103] leaving his widow Alexandra in charge. The queen, as we will discover, proved to be one of the most striking female personalities of the Second Temple period. She proceeded to release the remaining three brothers from confinement and to marry the eldest survivor, Alexander Jannaeus, who was apparently 15 years her junior.[104] It is worth noting that Jannaeus likely adopted one or both of Alexandra's sons by Aristobulus I—Hyrcanus II and Aristobulus II—as part of the marriage arrangement.[105]

Josephus says that the newly widowed queen chose Jannaeus, because in addition to being the eldest, he was "of more even disposition" (*Ant.* 13.320), implying that he could be easily manipulated by an experienced and (apparently) ruthless courtier like Alexandra. One can only guess how Alexander's evenness of temper fits in to the plot, but Josephus rarely drops such tidbits into his narrative without suggesting something relevant. In this case, a reasonable conjecture is that she hoped to persuade Alexander to relinquish the high priesthood and content himself with the royal crown. This, after all, had been the Pharisees' objective all along. If that was her plan, she had miscalculated. Jannaeus became both king and high priest, and Alexandra would need to wait 27 more years to accomplish her goal.

Alexander Jannaeus: The Lion of Wrath (103–76 B.C.E.)

In the tradition of his Hasmonean forebears, Jannaeus wasted little time before launching an aggressive program of military expansion. Proceeding first against the coastal cities of Gaza, Ptolemais, Strato's Tower (later Caesarea Maritima), and Dor, he became enmeshed in a diplomatic imbroglio involving Cleopatra, queen of Egypt, and the latter's son Ptolemy, whom she had evicted from her realm. Jannaeus suffered a devastating defeat by Ptolemy's army but was spared an even worse disaster (the loss of his crown) by the intervention of Cleopatra, whose army fortuitously was commanded by the Jewish generals Chelcias and Ananias, descendants of Onias IV. Their support of Jannaeus, against the advice of Cleopatra's ministers, marks a strong endorsement of Jannaeus's Hasmonean credentials. Here, after all, were the direct descendants of the last legitimate Zadokite priest, with a perfect opportunity to extinguish the Hasmonean line. Not only did they decline to do so, they argued to keep Jannaeus in power against the advice of other senior officials (see above, p. 277). In due course, both Cleopatra and Ptolemy withdrew to their respective home bases, and Jannaeus completed his conquest of the coastal cities.

Upon his return to Jerusalem, Jannaeus discovered his own people in a rebellious mood. The source of the Judeans' discontent has been much debated, but Josephus's account provides a rather compelling clue. At a Feast of Tabernacles in around 96,[106] Jannaeus—presiding as high priest—was preparing to make the traditional offering when the assembled onlookers began shouting insults and pelting him with citrons.[107] The crowd, Josephus pointedly reports, "reviled him as descended from a captive and therefore unworthy of the dignity of his office" (*Ant.* 13.372). Attentive readers will recall that this is precisely the accusation the Pharisees had levelled against his father Hyrcanus a generation earlier. It is difficult in this context to escape a conclusion that the Pharisees had retained considerable influence with Jerusalem's population and were the instigators of the disturbance and, moreover, that this episode represented a renewal of the sectarian dispute between the Pharisees and their Sadducean rivals.

Jannaeus called out his mercenary guards to disburse the crowd, albeit with significant casualties.[108] Thereafter, a six-year civil war ensued—a back-and-forth affair with Jannaeus, at times engaged with foreign enemies and at others fending off domestic foes. Moreover, there appeared to be no middle ground for resolving the sectarian dispute. When Alexander inquired of his domestic enemies what he might do to restore peace, they replied that only his death would satisfy them (*Ant.* 13.376).

In due course, the leaders of the rebellion, whom Josephus does not identify but who are necessarily Pharisees, invited the latest Seleucid contender, Demetrius III Eucerus, to join their cause. Demetrius arrived with a great army, and a series of fierce battles followed with great casualties on both sides. When Demetrius retired back to Syria, Jannaeus was able to capture the leaders of the rebellion. Josephus's report of what happened next stands as a gruesome reminder of the intensity of sectarian rivalry: "He (Jannaeus) brought them to Jerusalem and did one of the most barbarous actions in the world to them, for as he was feasting with his concubines, in sight of all the city, he ordered about 800 of them to be crucified; and while they were living, he ordered the throats of their wives and children to be cut before their eyes" (*Ant.* 13.380).

While many of Josephus's accounts bear the marks of poetic amplification, there is confirming evidence that Jannaeus crucified the leaders of the insurrection (although the number 800 may be exaggerated) and that the victims of his wrath were Pharisees. Among the Dead Sea Scrolls is a so-called pesher, or interpretation of a biblical passage, in this case a prophecy of Nahum. The prophet's words, the authors say, refer to Demetrius's invasion at the urging of the Pharisees[109] and the "Lion of Wrath" (i.e., Jannaeus), who wrought vengeance on the Pharisees by crucifying them (4Q169 1.8).

Queen Salome Alexandra and the Pharisees (76–67 B.C.E.)

When Alexander Jannaeus died, in 76, he had on his deathbed supposedly counseled Queen Alexandra to turn control of the government over to the Pharisees.[110] The queen proceeded to do exactly that—she "spoke to the Pharisees and put all things into their power" (*Ant.* 13.405). Presumably, this change of control entailed replacing the Sadducean incumbents, who held key ministerial and Temple positions and were members of the ruling council, with Pharisees. Queen Alexandra also appointed the eldest of her two sons, Hyrcanus II, as high priest. Josephus explains that Hyrcanus "delighted in a quiet life" and was "unable to manage public affairs" (*Ant.* 13.407), and that "he permitted the Pharisees to do everything" (*Ant.* 13.408). In commenting on this historical era, later rabbis (who viewed the Pharisees as their forebears) portrayed it as a halcyon age, a time of peace and prosperity. But to the displaced Sadducees, it would soon become what some scholars have called a "reign of terror."[111]

Not surprisingly, the newly empowered Pharisees wasted little time in seeking retribution from their former adversaries, especially those deemed complicit in the crucifixions. The first to feel the executioner's blade was a certain Diogenes, but others followed in quick succession (*Ant.* 13.410). The alarmed Sadducean survivors appealed to Aristobulus II, the queen's younger son, and the latter helped persuade his mother to allow these former senior military leaders,[112] ministers, and priests to evacuate Jerusalem and settle into the fortresses in the periphery of the country[113] if they promised to "live in private station (t)here" (*Ant.* 13.415). This temporary solution would be short-lived, however. In due course the queen fell ill, and Aristobulus could see that with his weak-willed elder brother nominally in charge,[114] the nation and his own family would in effect be subject to the Pharisees (*Ant.* 13.423). Accordingly, Aristobulus fled Jerusalem and within two weeks was joined by his father's former officials, who had established themselves in the peripheral fortresses. Alexandra died before she could respond, but the stage was set for a renewal of a civil war that is frequently characterized as a dispute between the two brothers. However, careful readers should understand that it was a conflict born of bitter sectarian rivalry, with the brothers being the figureheads to which the sects attached themselves.

Josephus's epitaph on Salome Alexandra is unflattering and particularly discordant to the modern ear. He faults Alexandra with the ultimate demise of the Hasmonean family, brought about by "a desire (for power) that does not belong to a woman" (*Ant.* 13.431). In this regard, Josephus is betraying a rather transparent bias: Contrary to what is often supposed of him, Josephus was never a member of the Pharisaic sect;[115] instead, in his own career, Josephus ran afoul of several prominent Pharisees.[116] In his autobiography, Josephus proudly claims descent from the Hasmonean family, who were for much of their dynastic existence mortal enemies of the Pharisees. Salome was a woman whom fate had cast in a leadership role customarily played by men; she was a Pharisaic sympathizer in a court dominated by their rivals. And as a woman she could not take the title of high priest on the two occasions when the deaths of her incumbent high priest husbands might otherwise have permitted such a succession. In the final analysis, subject to those limitations, she played a difficult hand as well as it might have been expected.

Aristobulus II (67–63 B.C.E.) and Pompey's Conquest of Jerusalem

Upon Aristobulus's retreat to the country, Josephus relates that "a mighty influx of people came to Aristobulus from all parts"

(*Ant.* 13.427). This statement would seem to contradict Josephus's earlier assessments about the extent of the Pharisees' popular support, as well as his view that the Sadducees persuaded only the rich. Aristobulus advanced on Jerusalem with a substantial force, and, for the sake of peace, Hyrcanus relinquished both the high priesthood and the royal crown (having held the latter for barely three months). However, this settlement among the brothers failed to produce a lasting peace. The governor of Idumea, named Antipater, whom history would come to know as the father of Herod the Great, persuaded Hyrcanus to flee to the neighboring kingdom of Nabatea.[117] With promises of territorial concessions, King Aretas of Nabatea besieged Jerusalem with a large army, leaving Aristobulus, Josephus claims, with no one on his side but the priests (*Ant.* 14.20). But Josephus seemingly contradicts himself (again) when only a few paragraphs later he says that Aristobulus attacked Aretas and Hyrcanus "with a great army and beat them in the battle" (*Ant.* 14.33).[118] The contradiction may be explained by the fact that Aristobulus, while in Jerusalem, had only the support of the priests (and Levites) on duty at that time. Since most priests and Levites served on a rotating basis, however, the number of those actually in Jerusalem during Aretas's siege would have been only a fraction of the total. If those outside Jerusalem quickly mobilized to Aristobulus's defense, it would explain why he suddenly appears with "a great army."[119] The distribution of priests and Levites throughout Judea would also explain why, as we will see in the next chapter, the Hasmoneans in their various attempts to recover the kingdom after Pompey's conquest never failed to attract widespread support and to quickly gain control of the territory outside Jerusalem.

During the stand-off that followed, an event transpired that provides grim evidence that the sectarian hostility now imperiled noncombatants wishing to stay neutral. A certain Onias, a "righteous man, beloved of God" and someone who could successfully pray for rain,[120] had gone into hiding at the outbreak of hostilities, but the supporters of Hyrcanus—read, Pharisees—found him out and brought him in custody to their besieging camp. His captors insisted that he use his powers against their enemies—read, Sadducees. Onias prayed instead that God would favor neither side. No sooner had he made this prayer than the outraged followers of Hyrcanus stoned him to death (*Ant.* 14.22–24).

In due course, both factions appealed to Pompey, the Roman general who had conquered Syria and was now encamped in Damascus and on the lookout for further prizes. A complicated series of pleadings followed, but the upshot was that Aristobulus found himself outmaneuvered and in custody. His supporters barricaded themselves in the Temple compound while a full Roman legion supported by Hyrcanus's faction began a siege. It is a measure of the fierce tenacity of the Sadducean partisans (as well as the strong defensive character of the Temple) that they held out for three full months. Eventually, Roman siege engines battered down the defensive walls, soldiers and their Judean allies stormed the gap, and a slaughter of defenders followed. Priests within the Temple carried on their regular prayers and sacrifices, seemingly indifferent to their imminent demise, until they, too, were cut to pieces. The striking feature of this carnage is the extent to which it was carried out by Jewish partisans: In *Antiquities* the reader learns that "some (Jews) were killed by Romans and some by one another" (*Ant.* 14.70). But in this later work, Josephus seems to have watered down the truth, because in *Jewish War* he stated plainly, "the greatest part of them were killed by their own countrymen" (*J.W.* 1.150).

Pompey rounded up and executed any members of the opposition left alive. He reinstated Hyrcanus as high priest (but, conspicuously, not as king), and shipped Aristobulus and his family off to Rome in custody. The era of Judean independence was ended, and the era of Roman domination begun.[121]

WE NOW TURN TO THE THIRD of Josephus's principal sects, the Essenes, who have been conspicuously absent from the historical narrative to this point, except to the extent that the "Hasideans" (*Hasidim*), who were the plausible forerunners of the sect, appeared in the vanguard of the Maccabean forces. However, the subsequent Hasmonean narrative outlined above is an essential prerequisite to evaluating who the Essenes were and how their sect evolved, and so we place that discussion below, following our outline of the relevant history.

We begin by fast forwarding two millennia. The year is 1896 C.E., and a Jewish scholar named Solomon Schechter had secured permission to examine an enormous collection of ancient manuscripts that had lain untouched for centuries in the *genizah*[122] of the Ben Ezra Synagogue in Cairo, Egypt. Among the many thousands of documents that Schechter reviewed was a text that has since become known as the Damascus Document. Schechter surmised— correctly, as it would turn out—that the document was a medieval copy of an even more ancient writing, most likely from the first century B.C.E.

In substance, the text seemed to be a constitution of sorts, the foundational beliefs of a Jewish group who had separated themselves intellectually—and perhaps physically—from mainstream Judaism in order to lead lives (in their view) of more perfect holiness. When the text was published (c. 1910), it created a flurry of interest because some of the figures described—such as a "Teacher of Righteousness"— seemed to resemble personages of early Christianity. That notion was quickly rejected by scholars, however; interest died down, and the Damascus Document became a curiosity relegated to the pages of academic journals. Then in the 1940s, the Damascus Document resurfaced as part of an extraordinary archaeological discovery.

The Dead Sea Scrolls

In 1947, two Bedouin tribesmen arrived in Bethlehem (their market town) with some curious artifacts to sell. The objects were seven ancient scrolls, carefully wrapped in linen and safely stored in cylindrical clay jars. From Bethlehem, the scrolls worked their way through the labyrinthine pathways of the antiquities market, and by 1954 all seven had been acquired by the Israeli government.[123] Meanwhile, an intensive search was launched for more scrolls. The site of the original Bedouin discovery was located in the wilderness region near northwest corner of the Dead Sea and identified as Cave 1. More finds were made in Caves 2 and 3. Thinking they had exhausted the possibilities, archaeologists then began to excavate the ruins of the nearby ancient site—Khirbet Qumran—that they guessed might have some relation to the scrolls. When the excavators retired for the evening, the Bedouin kept on searching, and in the limestone marl terrace adjacent to the site, discovered what would be the mother lode of scrolls in Cave 4.

THE DAMASCUS DOCUMENT (4Q271, fragment 3) tells the story of the Essene origins. It also mentions the "Teacher of Righteousness," who had led or perhaps even founded a community—possibly at Qumran.

The scrolls excavated by the Bedouin were in deplorable condition. Although a total of more than 500 separate manuscripts were eventually identified, they had to be pieced together from more than 25,000 fragments. In the process of that Herculean effort, it became clear that two of the texts were partial remains of none other than the Damascus Document. And now, the complete copy identified by Solomon Schechter could tell the world what the remains of Cave 4 were too fragmentary to reveal: that sometime in the second or first century B.C.E. a figure known as the Teacher of Righteousness had led, or perhaps even founded, a community of like-minded devotees whose beliefs and practices are still a source of scholarly fascination and discussion.

The Essenes

Not surprisingly, the identity of the cryptic "Teacher" and his group of followers—who referred to themselves by the Hebrew term *Yahad*, or "community"—was much debated, but a consensus was reached and still holds today that they were Essenes. Both Josephus and Philo of Alexandria left extensive descriptions of the Essenes that mirror very closely what the scroll authors say about themselves. In all, some 20 close parallels have been identified, and the relatively few discrepancies are easily explained by the fact that Josephus and Philo lacked direct experience[124] and/or chose to emphasize some characteristics (such as celibacy) they thought would be intriguing to their readers.

The portrait that emerges from the scrolls—especially the so-called Community Rule (labeled 1QS)[125]—is one of a tight-knit organization that held property in common, shared common meals, engaged in common prayer, and, above all, subscribed to a rigorous set of beliefs and practices with stern penalties for deviation. Most of the sectarians reportedly practiced celibacy,[126] but the community managed to preserve itself over many generations by attracting new initiates. Their ability to maintain a continuing stream of new members was in large part due to one of their more idiosyncratic views—that the world was imminently coming to an end and that only individuals who repented of their sins, reformed their behavior, and joined the community would be saved. The strong appeal of this message is supported by the fact that proselytes were willing to undergo a very rigorous multiyear period of indoctrination before becoming full members, an event that was marked by a ritual immersion, or baptism. Curiously, the sectarians also held that some had been predestined by God for salvation, while others were doomed. The contradiction between their notion of predestination and their call for repentance—seemingly an act of free will—is one that their writings fail to resolve and that has confounded many students of their beliefs.

Another distinctive feature of the community was their reliance on a solar calendar, in contrast to the rest of Jewish society, which employed a lunar calendar. This necessarily caused their festival dates to fall on different days than those of other Jews, and that according to some scholars is the reason[127] why they withdrew from the rest of society—that is, to ensure that celebrations were occurring at their "appointed time" as prescribed in the Bible.

A further important fact that comes through clearly in the sectarian writings is that the leaders of the sect were "sons of Zadok." This is interpreted literally by some scholars to mean that the leaders of the sect were Sadducean priests while others suggest that "Sons of Zadok" could be an honorific term referring simply to righteous persons.[128] Their texts are replete with military nomenclature,[129] suggesting a military orientation not only of the leadership but also of the core membership. The sectarians also exhibit a distinct animosity toward the Pharisees, whom they describe as "seekers after smooth things."

Scholars have also noted some striking parallels between the scroll sectarians and early Christians[130] that at least one expert has termed "extraordinary."[131] Since the Christian doctrines did not emerge in any discernible way until roughly a century later, discussion of these parallels is the purview of the next chapter.

QUMRAN. The settlement at Khirbet Qumran and the surrounding caves are traditionally associated with the Essenes.

Qumran

As noted earlier, archaeologists began to excavate the ancient ruins of Qumran because it was located not far from where the scrolls were found, and it was thought that the site might have some relationship to the scrolls. Those excavations were led by the late Father Roland de Vaux, head of École biblique et archéologique française de Jérusalem, and seemed to produce confirming evidence of a possible connection between the site and the scrolls. For example, pottery fragments from the site closely match those found in the caves; coin findings suggest a dating contemporaneous with the paleography of the scrolls; and several inkwells imply a scribal activity. Moreover, there are a number of conspicuous ritual baths, or *mikva'ot*, that seem to confirm the religious nature of the occupants.

Once the texts were firmly identified as Essene documents, scholars noted that Pliny the Elder had described an Essene settlement located between Jericho and Ein Gedi—that is, almost precisely where the Qumran site stood.[132] One could think that this would be the decisive identification of Qumran as an Essene site, but in the scholarly world things are rarely that uncomplicated. Many other possible identifications have been proposed, often with well-argued rationales and convincing evidence: Qumran was a fortress, a country agricultural estate, a pottery factory, and so forth. None of these identifications, however, necessarily precludes an Essene occupation of the site. Moreover, no alternative site has been identified that plausibly satisfies Pliny's description.

As early as the 19th century, explorers of the region consistently identified Qumran as a military site.[133] Their reasoning remains valid today: the location on an elevated plateau, providing both defensibility and a clear view of the approaches from both ends of the Dead Sea; the fortified tower; and the strategic location in relation to the main fortress of Hyrcania, built by John Hyrcanus to guard the approaches to Jerusalem.[134] The nonmilitary aspects of the site's archaeology, such as its pottery manufacturing facility and agricultural structures, are all consistent with a community desiring to live in self-sufficient isolation, just as Josephus and Philo describe the Essenes and how their own literature describes them. How Qumran made the transition from a military outpost to an Essene settlement is explained by the following remarks on historical context.

The Essene Community at Qumran in Its Historical Context

The Damascus Document contains a preamble that is generally construed to be a self-account of the sect's origins. They consider themselves "a root of planting" from Aaron and Israel, beginning "three hundred and ninety years from the time He (the Lord) handed them (the faithless) over to the power of Nebuchadnezzar..." (CD 1.5). Taking this statement at face value and dating it by modern reckoning of Nebuchadnezzar's conquest of Jerusalem (586 B.C.E.) yields a date of 196 B.C.E. From that time, members of the sect had been "like blind men, groping for the way twenty years," at which point God "raised up for them a Teacher of Righteousness to guide them in the way..." (CD 1.8–11). The arrival of the Teacher, then, would be dated to 176 B.C.E, which coincidentally was approximately when trouble started in Judea with the ascension of Antiochus IV Epiphanes to the Seleucid throne. If we were then to assume a duration for the Teacher's ministry of some 30 years, we could calculate that the events alluded to in the various scroll texts occurred sometime around 146 B.C.E. This was the time when, as we have seen, the disputing Seleucids had allowed Jonathan Maccabeus to assume the high priesthood. Since the Teacher of Righteousness is portrayed as having a conflict with someone called The Wicked Priest near the end of the Teacher's life, the Wicked Priest was identified as Jonathan, or possibly his brother and successor, Simon. The conflict between the Teacher and the Priest was therefore assumed to have something to do with the notion that the Hasmoneans had improperly usurped the high priesthood. In protest, the sectarians were thought to have withdrawn from Jerusalem and settled in the wilderness—at Qumran. In the foregoing simplified form, that understanding of the sect's origins prevailed for many years.[135]

More recent scholarship, however, has questioned this version of the sect's origins. For one thing, the numismatic evidence at Qumran suggests an occupation no earlier than the reign of Alexander Jannaeus (r. 103–76).[136] For another, close examination of the texts reveals a strong antipathy to the Pharisees and, indeed, in the Nahum pesher (4Q169), the sect's apparent approval of Jannaeus's crucifixion of his Pharisaic opponents. The Nahum pesher as well as the Habakkuk pesher refer to the arrival of the *kittim*—that is, the Romans—and, as we have seen, Pompey's Romans did not arrive on the scene until 63 B.C.E. In view of this evidence, some scholars have revisited the chronology implied by the Damascus Document and concluded that it is misleading to take it literally.[137] That is, we cannot be sure exactly how the ancients dated Nebuchadnezzar's conquest. Various passages in Josephus and certain biblical texts imply quite divergent estimates of when such earlier events occurred. Moreover, the figure of 390 years may well be a symbolic expression, like Daniel's 70 weeks of years (Daniel 9:24), not meant to be used with precision.

For all the above reasons, many scholars today would prefer a different historical context for the establishment of the community that produced the scrolls. The issue is far from settled, but one such context that stands out is the sectarian rivalry between the Pharisees on the one side and the Hasmoneans with their Sadducean supporters on the other.[138] Some scholars are now focusing, in particular, on the period when Salome Alexandra turned power over to the Pharisees and the latter conducted a purge of their Sadducean opponents. In these new perspectives, Hyrcanus II would become the Wicked Priest and Simeon ben Shetah (leader of the Pharisees), the Man of the Lie.[139] The Teacher of Righteousness would be seen as a Sadducean priest whose halakhic views conflicted with those of the Pharisees, causing him to be persecuted, exiled, and (possibly) killed by them. Scholars advancing this version of events call attention to certain thanksgiving hymns, which they see as compositions either by the Teacher himself or by one or more disciples who were close to the Teacher's thinking.[140] The hymns describe an individual favored by God and having an understanding of God's regulations, who is made to suffer at the hands of his persecutors—called "seekers after smooth things," meaning Pharisees—because of these beliefs. The debate on these matters is ongoing, but there do seem to be reasonable grounds for revisiting the original notion that the scroll sect withdrew from Judean society as a rejection of the Hasmonean regime.

The new theories may also provide a useful framework for examining how the descendants of the "mighty warriors" of the Maccabean era might have become initial members of the *Yahad* nearly a century after the beginning of the revolt. The conflict between the Sadducees and the Pharisees, especially as it became bloodier, would have been an emotionally wrenching time for that generation of Levitical

Gatekeepers. Mindful of their traditions, they would have held the Pharisees in high esteem out of reverence for the law while being simultaneously compelled to loyalty to the Temple and its senior priests. The choice would have been excruciatingly difficult, because—as the story of Honi the Circle Drawer illustrates—it was not possible to stay neutral. It is tempting to imagine that this conflicted period is echoed in the Damascus Document's lines about "... men ... like the blind and like those groping for the way" (CD 1.9).

Matters would have come to a head when one of their respected leaders—the so-called Teacher of Righteousness and possibly a Sadducean priest or simply an intellectual leader revered for righteousness—was reviled by the newly empowered Pharisees and expelled[141] from Jerusalem. If this occurred during the period when Salome Alexandra gave power to the Pharisees, the time frame would be c. 76–67. The Teacher's place of exile is referred to as Damascus, and the Damascus Document repeatedly mentions a covenant between the Teacher and those who followed him there. Since members of this new covenant conspicuously included Levites,[142] and since gatekeeping was one of the principal Levitical functions, it seems safe to imagine that some of the Teacher's original followers were Gatekeepers. If so, they would have been the fourth- or fifth-generation descendants of the "Hasideans" of the Maccabean era. Not all of these early followers apparently held fast to the covenant. CD 19.14 refers to "warriors who went back to the Man of the Lie." The latter figure is presumed to be a Pharisaic leader, and the fact that some of the Teacher's original followers returned to the Teacher's opponent speaks strongly of the conflicted loyalties these individuals must have felt. Moreover, they are called "warriors," a militaristic characterization consistent with their status as Gatekeepers.

The Essene settlement at Qumran would also seem to comport well with these new theories. Whether or not Qumran was the Teacher's original place of exile,[143] the site almost certainly would have been among the "twenty-two strong places" (*Ant.* 13.427), to which the victims of Pharisaic persecution fled. As such, it would have been a natural location for the headquarters of the newly established *Yahad.* Indeed, the Gatekeepers, who were early members of the sect, may well have been among Qumran's original military garrison. Given the purity concerns of the Hasmonean regime, this would account for the presence of *mikva'ot* at the site. Aristobulus II's assumption of the high priesthood might have given the covenanters hope of returning to their former lives. But with the bloodbath that accompanied Pompey's conquest, members of the *Yahad* would have had little choice but to wait patiently for the hoped-for Lord's day of reckoning.

Retrospective

Arguably the single most important sociopolitical dynamic in Judea during the Hellenistic period was not the extent of cultural synthesis (or lack thereof) but rather the degree of factional rivalry within Judea itself. This began with the tension between pro-Ptolemaic and pro-Seleucid parties and it culminated in the rivalry between religious sects. It is difficult to read the histories of Josephus and not be struck by the intensity of the sectarian tensions—triggering at least three seemingly bitter civil conflicts and the slaughtering of opponents and culminating in Roman domination.

Some have suggested that Judea would have fallen to Rome with or without these internal disputes.[144] That sort of alternative history is, of course, unknowable. But if the Jews had presented a united front, they might have retained a larger measure of independence, even while paying the necessary tribute to Rome. Antipater and his son Herod would go on to exploit the lack of Jewish cohesiveness, as readers will discover in the next chapter. Elsewhere in the empire, Rome was content to govern vassal states with native dynasties, but because the Jews could not unite behind one of their own,[145] they ended up with Herod (at best a half-Jew)[146] as king and with high priests appointed rather than succeeding in dynastic fashion as God had prescribed.[147]

8

The Era of Roman Domination

MUCH OF WHAT WE KNOW ABOUT JUDEA in the era of Roman domination comes from the writings of the Jewish historian Flavius Josephus.
Josephus was born of a priestly Jerusalem family in 37 C.E. In his autobiography, he proudly traces his descent to the Hasmoneans, who, as
we saw in the previous chapter, ruled Judea as an independent state for
about 70 years. After war broke out between Judea and the Romans
in 66 (the so-called First Jewish Revolt), Josephus was appointed by
the ruling council in Jerusalem to lead the war effort in Galilee, which
happened to be in the direct path of the Romans' advance.

Preamble: Josephus as a Historical Source

Josephus participated heroically (in his telling) in the defense of
Jotapata, one of Galilee's best-fortified towns, but then surrendered
(or was captured) and went on to become a useful advisor to the
Roman commander and later emperor, Flavius Vespasian, and then
to Vespasian's successor, Titus.

After the war, Josephus followed Titus to Rome and took up residence in the Flavian household (hence his *gentilicium* Flavius). There,

---

* This chapter has been rewritten and updated from the version contributed by
Shaye J.D. Cohen to the third edition (Washington, DC: BAS, 2011).

he proceeded to write a detailed history of the conflict titled *The Jewish War* (henceforth, *J.W.*). Its stated purpose was to discourage other Roman vassal states from similar insurrection. *Jewish War* was composed initially in Josephus's native Aramaic and then translated to Greek. The Aramaic version, however, has been lost, and what remains is the Greek translation compiled with Roman readership in mind, with the help of translators who apparently were skilled in classical Greek. Sometime after publishing *J.W.* (around 73), Josephus began work on a second, more ambitious project—a complete history of the Jewish people, from Creation to the onset of the war. Titled *Jewish Antiquities* (henceforth, *Ant.*), that work was published around 93 and was intended to present the Jewish people to Roman readers in a favorable light. Because *J.W.* begins its narrative in approximately 175 B.C.E., the two histories overlap for a period of about 250 years.

Few historians of Josephus's era took great pains to temper their own biases, and Josephus was no exception. Sometimes his agenda is transparent, and sometimes it can only be inferred. One of the main challenges in using Josephus to reconstruct Judean history is to ferret out those biases. This task is further complicated by language issues; specifically: how well did Josephus's "helpers" understand what his Aramaic was trying to convey in *The Jewish War*, and how fluent had Josephus become in Greek when he later composed *Jewish Antiquities* in that language?

Josephus relied on secondary sources, especially for events prior to his own time. Most of these originals have been lost, so there is no way of knowing how well Josephus captured their content or even how accurate that content was in the first place. Indeed, when he treats the same event separately in his respective histories, there are often inconsistencies. Josephus's coverage of Herod the Great and his father, Antipater, for instance, are based largely on a history (now lost) compiled by Herod's trusted advisor Nicholas of Damascus. There is, therefore, a necessarily pro-Herodian slant to these accounts, even though Josephus himself considered Herod a "common man," that is, lacking royal ancestry.

Josephus also exercises considerable literary license, inflating numbers and attributing elaborate speeches to some of his protagonists that are transparently rhetorical flourishes of his own invention.

Further, because two brief passages seem to support the historicity of Jesus Christ, Josephus's writings were painstakingly preserved by generations of Christian monks, laboriously copying manuscripts that apparently at least some of the copyists could not themselves read. That is, the material that has survived is corrupt in many places: lines are missing, words misspelled, and proper names often garbled beyond recognition.

For all the foregoing reasons, students of Josephus have often found his writings to be elusive, ambivalent, and sometimes contradictory, such that decoding Josephus is a major challenge.

JUDEA AS A ROMAN TRIBUTARY (63–37 B.C.E.)

Judea in the Aftermath of Pompey's Conquest

From Josephus's description of the battle for Jerusalem in 63 B.C.E., it would appear that all the partisans of the Hasmonean king Aristobulus were either killed outright, rounded up and executed in the aftermath of fighting, or shipped to Rome as slaves. These casualties would have included the Sadducean priests holding permanent positions at the Temple,[1] rural priests and Levites in Jerusalem for their two-week course of service, and any other Sadducean aristocrat unfortunate to find himself in Jerusalem at the time.[2] The elimination of the Sadducean faction would have been extremely thorough, because their Jewish opponents knew better than the Romans exactly who they were and had participated energetically in their slaughter.[3]

What, then, was the remaining power structure in Jerusalem, once the Sadducees had been purged? Before his departure, Pompey had confirmed Hyrcanus as high priest, transferred many of the territories previously conquered by the Hasmoneans to the new Syrian province under Roman jurisdiction,[4] and declared Jerusalem a Roman tributary.[5] Hyrcanus, therefore, would have been free to manage affairs as before, albeit with a much reduced territory, provided the peace was kept and tribute paid. However, Hyrcanus is repeatedly characterized by Josephus as wholly lacking in energy and determination.

His Council of Elders (later *Sanhedrin*), therefore, would have become the de facto authority in Jerusalem. And that body—by the process of elimination that had just occurred—would necessarily have been comprised predominantly of Pharisees.[6] As we will see, however, the span of control enjoyed by Hyrcanus and his Council of Elders did not extend much beyond Jerusalem, in all likelihood because pro-Hasmonean sentiment remained strong among the rural priests and Levites. Moreover, Antipater (and later Herod) increasingly ingratiated themselves with their Roman overlords reducing thus Hyrcanus's status to that of a figurehead.[7]

Hasmoneans Attempt to Regain Power (63–50 B.C.E.)

Approximately five years after the fall of Jerusalem, Alexander, the eldest son of Aristobulus, eluded Roman custody and returned to Judea. Josephus reports that Alexander received considerable support from the Judean population, such that he effectively controlled the countryside, and Hyrcanus was "not able to oppose him" (*Ant.* 14.82). Alexander occupied and strengthened a number of peripheral fortresses before proceeding toward Jerusalem. He was intercepted, however, by Roman forces led by Marcus Antonius, who is known to English speakers as Mark Antony or simply Antony. Alexander's forces put up a determined fight, but on the arrival of Rome's next governor, Gabinius, the Judeans were forced to agree to terms and cease hostilities.

Soon thereafter, Aristobulus himself arrived on the scene, along with his younger son Antigonus. Once again, many Judeans rallied to his support, but once again the rebel forces were defeated by Roman soldiers led by Antony. From these two episodes, it would appear that Hyrcanus and his ruling council had little support outside Jerusalem and required Roman military intervention to survive.

The next year (c. 56 B.C.E.) found Gabinius and Antony in Egypt, saving the regime of Ptolemy XII in exchange (so the story went) for the astronomical sum of 10,000 talents.[8] Seizing the opportunity provided by the Romans' absence, Alexander raised yet another army and regained control over the countryside. Gabinius dispatched Antipater to negotiate, but the majority of Alexander's followers chose to fight. A furious battle ensued at the foot of Mt. Tabor in eastern Galilee. The result was a great slaughter, with the Romans characteristically on the winning side. Alexander was marched off to Antioch in custody. He would not escape again.

The Hasmoneans had led three separate uprisings against the Romans in the space of so many years. In each case, they apparently secured significant popular support, rapidly taking control of the countryside and leaving Hyrcanus II and his ruling council (predominantly Pharisees) stranded in Jerusalem. Logic suggests that the source of that support was the rural priests and Levites who had both the military skills and the allegiance to Hasmonean traditions. Moreover, if recent scholarly thinking about the origins of the Qumran sectarians is applied, members of the *Yahad* would have been sympathetic to, if not participants in, the Hasmonean uprisings. However, by 50 B.C.E., all of those efforts had been crushed by the Roman military, with significant casualties. The sectarians appear to have come to believe that human action against the forces of evil was futile. Notwithstanding these many setbacks, however, their writings evidence a strong conviction that God would favor them with victory in the end. But it would be at a time of God's choosing, known only to him. In the meanwhile, they committed themselves to living in perfect righteousness, in anticipation of that day.

In the spring of 54 B.C.E., Gabinius returned to Rome and was replaced by Marcus Licinius Crassus. Crassus was said to be Rome's wealthiest man and had been part of a triumvirate that also included Pompey and the rising star of the Roman Republic, Gaius Julius Caesar. Crassus was determined to match the military exploits of his fellow triumvirs—Pompey, already a renowned general, and Caesar, who had been commissioned by the Senate to quell a Gallic uprising and was earning fame and fortune in the process. To equal or exceed his fellows, Crassus aimed to conquer Parthia, the vast territory in modern-day Iran. For that purpose, he needed seven legions, and so determined to augment his already considerable resources by appropriating the wealth of the Jerusalem Temple. According to Josephus (*Ant.* 14.106), Crassus was opposed by only a single priest, and carried away 8,000 talents. The Temple's defensive forces seem to have deteriorated badly from the days when Heliodorus was scourged by angels,[9] and determined priests held off against Pompey's legion for three full months. Be that as it may, Crassus did not escape unpunished. His generalship fell short of his ambition, and he and his son perished (along with 25,000 soldiers) in one of the worst military defeats in Roman history.

Under the leadership of Gaius Cassius Longinus, the remnant of Crassus's army limped back to Syria in time to confront yet another uprising—the fourth in so many years—of former Sadducean partisans. This one was led by a certain Pitholaus, identified as a follower of Aristobulus (*Ant.* 14.129). Cassius was alerted by Antipater and the rebels were defeated and Pitholaus killed. Hyrcanus and his ruling council had once again been spared, but Antipater was inexorably becoming the Romans' man in Judea.

Judea During the Dictatorship of Julius Caesar

Meanwhile, political dysfunction had gripped the Roman senate. Many were calling for Caesar's return in the hope of restoring order. Others rejected that idea, fearing—correctly as it would turn out—that Caesar would become a dictator. In 50 B.C.E., Antony returned to Rome and sponsored legislation mandating Caesar's return, and when that motion failed, he traveled north to where Caesar was stationed with his army. In January 49, Caesar led his forces south across the Rubicon, the northern border of Italy proper, in defiance of the Roman constitution. Pompey was commissioned to form a new army to oppose Caesar. For that purpose, he traveled to the East, where he still had many supporters. In due course, the opposing forces met at Pharsalus near Thessalonica in eastern Greece. Caesar and Antony routed Pompey's makeshift army, and the defeated general fled to Egypt.

Caesar set off in hot pursuit and arrived in Alexandria—only to discover that Pompey had been murdered and a civil war was raging between Cleopatra VII and her brother. Caesar sided with Cleopatra but soon found himself surrounded and outnumbered. He was rescued from this difficulty by none other than Antipater, whose timely arrival with reinforcements once again displayed his uncanny ability to ingratiate himself with leading Romans.[10] When Caesar eventually returned to Roman headquarters at Antioch, he reconfirmed Hyrcanus II as high priest, then (according to Josephus) inquired of Antipater as to what position would be suitable for himself. Josephus has already explained twice in this episode that it was "Antipater, who managed Jewish affairs" (*Ant. 14.* 127, 139), so Caesar simply confirmed what was already de facto. He named Antipater Procurator of Judea and made him a Roman citizen as well. After seeing Caesar off, Antipater hastened back to Jerusalem and proceeded to appoint his two sons as deputies—Phasael as governor of Jerusalem, and the 25-year-old Herod as governor of Galilee.[11]

One can only imagine the consternation felt by the members of Hyrcanus's ruling council, to discover that the man who had been instrumental in preserving them in power by defeating their Sadducean rivals, had now become their overlord. The rash young Herod wasted little time in providing an opportunity to undermine the new procurator. He hunted down and executed a certain Hezekiah, described by Josephus as a "bandit leader" who had been conducting raids across the Galilean border into Syria. A number of scholars have identified this Hezekiah as one of Aristobulus's partisans,[12] and indeed, his son Judas would lead an insurrection following Herod's death, in 4 B.C.E. (*Ant.* 17.271). The wives of the slain raised an outcry in Jerusalem,[13] and the members of the ruling council lobbied with Hyrcanus to bring Herod to trial.[14] Herod, though, arrived with his bodyguard and cowed his accusers into silence. Significantly, a certain Sameas, a Pharisee and prominent member of the Sanhedrin, spoke favorably of Herod and was later rewarded when Herod became king.

Roman Civil War Prompts Antigonus to Return

On the 15th of March 44 B.C.E., the foundations of the Roman world were rocked again. Julius Caesar was assassinated, and a new civil war begun. The antagonists were Caesar's assassins, Cassius Longinus and Marcus Brutus, on one side, and Caesar's right-hand man Antony together with Caesar's nephew and adopted son, Octavian, on the other.

Not surprisingly, Caesar's demise shifted the political ground in Judea. Now Antipater's position was at best ambivalent. Plots and counterplots unfolded, but in the end, Antipater had been poisoned and the perpetrators[15] struck down by Herod's men. Upon news of Antipater's death, Aristobulus's son Antigonus appeared with yet another army, but Herod's own forces drove him back across the border. The re-emergence of Antigonus—the fifth Hasmonean-inspired insurrection—had apparently convinced Hyrcanus that he had to choose between being overthrown by Antigonus or sheltering under the protection of Herod. The latter option was clearly less unattractive, and an alliance between Hyrcanus and Herod was sealed by the betrothal of Hyrcanus's granddaughter Mariamme.[16]

In October 42 B.C.E., the allied forces of Antony and Octavian defeated Cassius and Brutus at the Battle of Philippi, in eastern Greece. The victors divided their responsibilities, with Octavian returning to Italy and Antony presiding in the East. The Jerusalem aristocrats made repeated efforts to turn Antony against Herod, but the strength of Herod's family connection to Antony, supplemented by lavish bribes, left his standing unscathed. Antony then traveled to Alexandria, to take up with Cleopatra where Caesar had left off.

Antony's absence from Asia tempted the Parthians to invade. As they gobbled up territory, Antigonus seized the opportunity to ally himself with them, offering a lavish bribe if the Parthian prince Pacorus would restore him to the Judean throne. As witnessed many times before, the population of the countryside soon flocked to the Hasmonean Antigonus's cause. In 40 B.C.E., Jerusalem was conquered, Hyrcanus taken into custody, Phasael committed suicide, and Herod was forced to flee. As a measure of the partisan animosity that still prevailed, Josephus says that Antigonus bit off Hyrcanus's ears, creating a disfigurement that would forever bar the latter from serving as high priest (*J.W.* 1.270).[17] Antigonus was proclaimed as king and high priest, but his tenure would be short lived. To win his position, he had allied himself with Rome's mortal enemy, and that would be his ultimate undoing.

Herod Reconquers Jerusalem

Herod fled south to the comparative safety of Idumea, leaving his family at the hilltop fortress at Masada. He then proceeded on to Egypt, where he hoped to enlist the support of his long-term family friend Antony. The latter, however, had departed for Rome to deal with a feud that had begun between his relatives and Octavian. Despite dangerous winter conditions, Herod sailed off in pursuit. After being shipwrecked near Rhodes, he eventually found his way to Italy. Fortunately for Herod, Antony and Octavian had reconciled their differences and were now focused on the Parthian threat in the East. After some discussion (and the customary bribe to Antony), it was agreed that Herod would be designated not merely procurator, but king of Judea instead.[18] Judea was of strategic importance to the Romans because it controlled the gateway from the East into Egypt, which had now become an essential source of Roman grain. The Romans needed a leader in Judea they could count on, and by allying himself with the Romans' archenemy, Parthia, Antigonus had paved the way to be replaced by Herod. Herod was now Rome's client and loyal friend, and the Roman senate rubber-stamped a resolution to win the kingdom back.

Herod returned to Palestine in the spring of 39 B.C.E. However, the promised Roman aid was delayed nearly two years, as the body of Roman forces were preoccupied with the Parthians. While waiting for the Romans, Herod removed his family to the comparative safety of Samaria, where he married Mariamme and thereby grafted himself to the Hasmonean royal line. In due course, the Roman military arrived under the command of Gaius Sosius, and in the spring of 37 B.C.E., Herod's and Sosius's joint armies began the siege of Jerusalem.[19]

The attack on Jerusalem followed a familiar pattern. The Romans erected earthen ramps from which to deploy siege engines against the city's defensive walls. The defenders fought back vigorously, but soon enough the walls were shattered and legionnaires poured into the city, slaughtering indiscriminately like "a company of madmen" (*Ant.* 14.480). Antigonus was captured and removed to Antioch, where, at Herod's urging, he was executed.[20]

THE HERODIAN ERA (37 B.C.E.—6 C.E.)

Herod Establishes His Kingdom

Although Antigonus and his partisans had been eliminated,[21] Herod's new crown was not destined to sit securely on his head. Many or even most of his Jewish subjects considered him at best a half-Jew,[22] a *prima facie* disqualification to be king under their sacred law (e.g., Deuteronomy 17:15, "you are not to put a foreigner over you"). Of course, Herod had his apologists, then as now,[23] but Josephus made it clear that, in addition to his father being an Idumean—a race of ethnic Arabs who had been converted to Judaism under duress—his mother,

Cypros, was an Arabian noblewoman (*J.W.* 1.181).[24] While scholars may argue Herod's Jewishness or lack thereof, insurrection against Herod always seemed to be simmering, and his unavoidable family tree was likely a contributing factor.

Herod understood that he had to restore the form, if not the fact, of normalcy as soon as possible. For that purpose, he needed a new high priest, a position for which he himself was even less qualified than for that of king. With Hyrcanus II, who might have been compliant, still in Parthian custody and unable to serve in any event because of his disfigurement, Herod's solution was characteristically Machiavellian. He appointed a priest from the Babylonian diaspora named Ananel, an individual with obscure genealogical credentials,[25] but one whose primary qualification would be personal loyalty to Herod. Herod needed to surround his new high priest with an equally compliant Sanhedrin. For that purpose, two notable Pharisees were close at hand—Pollio and Sameas—who during the recent siege of Jerusalem had urged the citizens to accept Herod as their ruler (*Ant.* 15.3).[26] Pollio and Sameas, then, would become leaders of a reconstituted Sanhedrin, whose roster would presumably be filled out with further like-minded members.

Herod's underlying insecurity undoubtedly contributed to the volatility of his disposition, which oscillated between exhilarated highs and suicidal lows. As we have seen, Herod had adroitly grafted himself into the Hasmonean bloodline by marrying Mariamme, the one woman in whom the rival family factions were united.[27] He also lured Hyrcanus II back to Jerusalem, where he could keep a close eye on him. However, these stratagems would ultimately prove self-defeating, as they would bring into Herod's household the most plausible rivals to his own position. Early in his kingship, for example, he appointed Aristobulus III, Mariamme's younger brother, to be high priest. In 35 B.C.E., the young man presided in public for the first time at the Feast of Tabernacles, a pilgrimage event that drew large numbers of celebrants from the countryside. Josephus sums up the reaction of the crowd as follows: "A warm impulse of affection towards him [Aristobulus III] appeared among the people, and the memory of the actions of his grandfather [Aristobulus II] was fresh in their minds" (*Ant.*15.52).

Remarkably, young Aristobulus III evoked memories of Aristobulus II, who had led successive revolts against the Roman-backed regime[28] and had been dead for 15 years, and not of his other grandfather—Hyrcanus II, the long-term Roman client, who must have been physically present at the event. This report suggests that anti-Roman and pro-Hasmonean sentiments continued unabated in the rural population. Herod was understandably alarmed, and a short time later arranged for the murder of his young brother-in-law in a transparently staged drowning accident.

After the tragic death of Aristobulus III, Herod returned Ananel to the high priesthood and thereafter continued to appoint and depose high priests at will. These new priests and their families formed what has aptly been called "a new aristocracy,"[29] who derived their status and prestige, not to mention considerable wealth, from their usefulness and personal loyalty to Herod. The practice of appointing high priests, as opposed to strict genealogical succession as mandated by Mosaic Law,[30] would be continued by later Roman governors and would be a significant source of dissension among the subject Jewish population.

Four years later, the unstable co-emperorship of Antony and Octavian unraveled. Challenges were issued, armies and navies assembled, and on 2 September 31 B.C.E., the opposing forces met at Actium on the western coast of Greece. Octavian was the victor, and this outcome was a potential disaster for Herod, who had backed his long-time patron Antony. The impending crisis elevated Herod's innate insecurity to a boiling point, and he contrived to have the elderly[31] Hyrcanus II executed on trumped-up charges of treason. In reality, Herod foresaw that Hyrcanus II would be his logical replacement, should the new sole emperor Octavian choose that option.

Herod, however, managed to make his peace with Octavian. The latter was a practical man, and a reliable source of tribute—together with political stability—outweighed whatever personal considerations he may have felt. Once again, Herod's ability to ingratiate himself with leading Romans proved to be the saving skill set. Upon returning to Judea, however, Herod suspected[32] Mariamme of infidelity, and she too was executed. According to Josephus, the death of Mariamme propelled Herod into a downward spiral of paranoid dejection that led to the execution of Mariamme's mother, Alexandra, as well as half a dozen or more formerly loyal retainers and his own brother-in-law Costobarus.[33]

Perhaps to lift his downcast spirits, Herod embarked on a number of cultural innovations, including athletic events, where lavish prizes attracted the most acclaimed contestants, and gladiatorial displays in which both men and animals fought to the death. To his conservative Jewish subjects, such goings-on represented "barefaced impiety," according to Josephus (*Ant.* 15.275). Herod called together "the most eminent men among them" for consultation and pointed out that the "trophies" with which Herod had adorned the stadium, and that had been construed as prohibited images, were nothing but blocks of wood.

The "eminent men," who no doubt included Herod's compliant priesthood and (likely) the Pharisaic Sanhedrin members, reportedly put aside their larger reservations about the impiety of the events and were satisfied with this rationalization. Not all Judeans, however, were willing to compromise their principles. Ten such pietists entered into a pact to assassinate the king with daggers. One of Herod's many spies got wind of the plot, and the conspirators were arrested and put to death "after patiently enduring every torment" and having declared that their motives were noble and pious (*Ant.* 15.289). This would be one of several episodes in Josephus's account of Herod's career that demonstrates an intense religiously based animosity to his regime, albeit one that simmered beneath the level of the aristocracy.

Herod the Visionary Builder

Forewarned, Herod set out to strengthen his security precautions. He beefed up his private peacekeeping force, placed garrisons around Judea, and expanded his network of spies. His rule became one of increasing terror and brutality,[34] reminiscent of a modern police state. Then, having tightened his grip on power, Herod set out to deploy the vast resources at his disposal in a series of monumental building projects that would forever leave his mark on history.

The first of these was at a site that Herod found particularly appealing, as it involved a hill that rose precipitously some 300 feet from the hardscrabble ground, about 8 miles south of Jerusalem. It was here that Herod had fended off Antigonus's pursuing partisans when, in 40 B.C.E., he had been forced by the Parthian invasion to flee Jerusalem. To commemorate that dramatic moment, Herod ordered his engineers to hollow out the interior of the hilltop and enclose therein four stately towers. Three of these were constructed as luxurious residential spaces, while the fourth was built of solid stone, and its purpose remains obscure even today. The hilltop compound was accessed only by a single narrow path, and easily defensible. At the base of the hill was a circus for racing events and a pillared pavilion. Herod named the place Herodium, and Josephus reports that his will provided that he be buried there.[35]

Herod also refitted the old Hasmonean hilltop fortress at Masada, near the southwest corner of the Dead Sea. He intended it as a secure refuge for himself and his family in the event of insurrection. It featured luxury residential quarters, including an open-air private bath with an expansive view of the Dead Sea. More practical considerations included enormous cisterns capable of supplying many years' worth of water, and extensive granaries.

Other projects included Herod's luxurious winter palace at Jericho, and a fortified compound he called Sebaste, in Samaria. But as if challenged to outdo himself, in approximately 22 B.C.E., he began construction of an entire city at the old coastal site called Strato's Tower, eventually renamed Caesarea—after his patron Octavian. When in about 12 years the project was complete, the city's harbor had been enlarged—a remarkable engineering feat—to rival the size of Piraeus, the famous Athenian port, and it was accessed by wide stone-paved avenues that passed a theater and a hippodrome.

In the midst of this seemingly manic succession of building projects, Herod paused briefly, in about 22 B.C.E., to marry a new wife, Mariamme, who was referred to as Mariamme II to distinguish her from Mariamme I, Herod's earlier, Hasmonean wife. As part of that arrangement, Herod appointed her father, Simon Boethus, to be high priest. Josephus explains that Herod made this appointment so that Simon would have sufficient standing to qualify as his father-in-law. However, there was surely more to the decision.

The Boethusians were a prominent Alexandrian family that likely understood how to manage the wealth of the Temple while keeping mindful of where Herod's personal interests lay. Indeed, Boethusians continued to occupy the office well past Herod's divorce from Mariamme II, some 15 years later. Whatever Herod's exact motivation, he continued to appoint high priests at will, in violation of both tradition and Mosaic Law (e.g., Exodus 29:29).

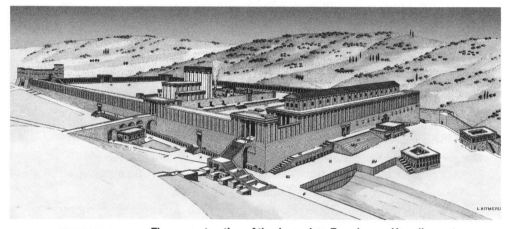

HEROD'S TEMPLE. The reconstruction of the Jerusalem Temple was Herod's most ambitious project. Pictured here is an artistic rendering of how the fabulous structure would have appeared before it was destroyed by Romans in 70 C.E.

In 19 B.C.E., Herod began what would be his most ambitious architectural undertaking, the reconstruction of the Jerusalem Temple. As a first step, his engineers enlarged the elevated platform that formed the base of the Temple compound, using massive ashlar blocks with supporting arches to nearly double the structure's size—to some 36 acres. The junction between the original foundation that supported Solomon's Temple and the Herodian addition is clearly visible to this day.[36] The southern projection of the Temple Mount now soared to a dizzying height above the Kidron Valley, and was encompassed by a dramatic three-tiered stoa supported by 162 pillars 30 feet high. The Temple was surrounded by a low balustrade, or *soreg*, with warning signs declaring that gentiles must not enter upon pain of death.[37] Within that barrier there were three progressively exclusive courtyards, the outermost for women, the next for men, and the innermost, containing the altar, for priests only. The area of the altar was enclosed by towering marble walls rising to great height and adorned in gold laminate. By the time the project was completed, around 10 B.C.E., it would have easily qualified as the eighth wonder of the ancient world.

Herod's Legacy

Unfortunately for Herod, he was not destined to enjoy his many architectural accomplishments in peace. In the final years of his life, he became convinced that his own family members were plotting his overthrow. It is difficult to determine whether those suspicions were justified, because Herod ordered that possible informants be tortured. Victims subjected to sufficient anguish are more likely to confirm than deny what their tormentors want to hear. As his health and mental state deteriorated, he executed his most likely heirs—his two sons by Mariamme I, Alexander and Aristobulus, and his eldest son, Antipater. He tortured and put to death dozens of real or imagined conspirators, including an astonishing reported total of 300 military officers.

By the winter of 5/4 B.C.E., rumors of Herod's declining health had begun to percolate through the Judean population, prompting those with grievances to become more outspoken. Josephus describes a particularly dramatic episode in which two "men of learning" exhorted their disciples to destroy a massive golden eagle—the symbol of Roman hegemony—that Herod had ordered installed over the "great gate" of the Temple.[38] The young men dutifully complied, hacked the hated icon to pieces, and were promptly arrested with their teachers and brought to trial. The accused freely confessed their responsibility for destroying the sacrilegious icon and declared that they did not fear death because they were certain of a happy after-life. Although the accused had acted properly according to Jewish law, the magistrates who heard the case had no choice but to render a guilty verdict to avoid Herod's wrath. Herod enforced the verdict by ordering the condemned to be burned alive.

In the spring of 4 B.C.E., Herod could see that his death was imminent, as he was in pain that "so greatly afflicted him in all parts of his body" (*Ant.* 17. 175). However, according to Josephus, Herod anticipated that his ungrateful Jewish subjects would celebrate rather than lament his death. To ensure that his death would bring about a national wave of mourning, he therefore ordered that "notable Jews from all parts of the nation" be summoned to Jericho and sequestered in the hippodrome, and that upon his death, they be executed *en masse*. This plan—if at all authentic—was never carried out.

The Herodians

The Wives and Descendants of Herod the Great, Governor of Galilee (r. 47–37 B.C.E.), King of the Jews (r. 37–4 B.C.E.)

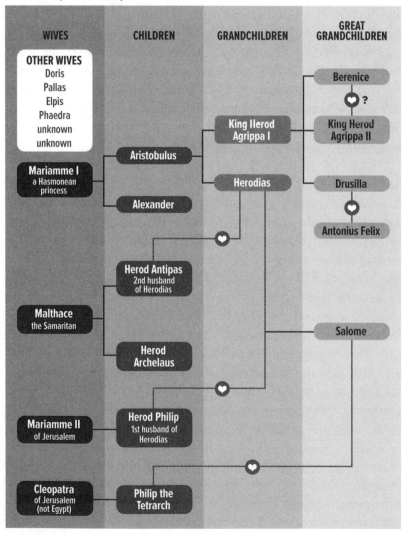

Although some scholars have questioned whether it was real, that kind of extreme enmity on the part of the Judean population should not be especially surprising. Herod taxed his subjects heavily to support his extravagant building projects as well as to keep his Roman patrons happy. On a number of occasions, he also severely offended his people's religious sensibilities, to the point that some were willing to die in protest. The very fact of Herod's kingship would have been deemed sacrilegious to at least some strict observers of Mosaic Law, and his arbitrary selection and removal of high priests was a *per se* violation. Finally, but by no means least: if Josephus's reporting is even moderately accurate,[39] Herod arrested, tortured, and put citizens to death, seemingly indiscriminately.

The people's expression of animosity toward these and other aspects of Herod's rule were soon expressed out loud during the first public appearance of Herod's nominated successor, Archelaus. "Reduce our taxes!" the assembled crowd implored. "Release the prisoners! Relax the tariffs in the marketplace!" And then, perhaps the most telling demand of all: Remove the high priest appointed by Herod and choose another, who would serve in accordance with the law and ritual purity (*Ant.* 17.208).

Josephus had previously offered this explanation of the suffering caused by Herod's grievous illness: "God was inflicting just punishment upon him for his lawless deeds" (*Ant.* 17.167). Then, as if to close the case, Josephus provides this epitaph: He was a man who was cruel to all alike and one who easily gave in to anger and was contemptuous of justice" (*Ant.* 17.191).

Herod changed his will repeatedly in the weeks before his death (in the spring of 4 B.C.E.) and eventually settled on Archelaus, the 19-year-old, eldest of two sons by an otherwise obscure Samaritan wife Malthace. The designated heir was a feckless stripling, more interested in feasting with his friends than governing a restive nation.[40] The will was soon disputed, and a multitude of petitioners traveled to Rome to make their case with Augustus, who, arguably, was being forced to choose from among a number of unattractive options.[41] Herod had, after all, already executed the heirs most likely to be successful. In the end, the weary emperor named Archelaus ethnarch of Judea, withholding both the title of king[42] and the territories of Galilee and Perea, which he assigned to Archelaus's younger brother Antipas.[43] Whether intentional or not, Herod's choice of a successor became his final act of vengeance against his Jewish subjects, as Archelaus's incompetence ultimately subjected the nation to an even more disastrous outcome.

Meanwhile, back in Judea, Herod's death had been like lifting the lid from a boiling cauldron, and a full-scale revolt was underway. A group of rebels assaulted and burned the palace at Jericho; another band attacked a column of Roman soldiers at Emmaus; a certain Judas, son of that Hezekiah whom Herod had executed in 47 B.C.E.,[44] broke into the armory at Sepphoris. But most unsettling of all, a great gathering of Pentecostal celebrants from the countryside had surrounded and trapped an entire Roman legion in Jerusalem. The siege was lifted only when the Syrian governor Quintillius Varus arrived with two other legions. The uprising was suppressed, but a reported 2,000 victims were crucified as a warning against further insurrection.

Ten years later, a delegation of "leading men among the Jews" arrived in Rome to bring complaints to Caesar about Archelaus's failures of governance. By then the emperor's patience had apparently run thin, and the ethnarch was summoned to Rome and then banished. Judea was henceforth governed as a Roman province, under the general oversight of the Roman governor at Antioch, but with a Roman prefect looking after local matters. The Herodian era was at an end.

JUDEA AS A ROMAN PROVINCE (6–73 C.E.)

Observations About Roman Administration

The Romans generally preferred to govern their vassal states in the East through native dynasties.[45] Local rulers were more or less free to govern as they pleased, as long as they kept the peace, looked after Roman interests, and made timely tribute payments. The removal of Archelaus was a departure from that practice and deserves some examination. According to Josephus, Augustus's decision was prompted by a "delegation of the principal men of the Jews (who) accused (Archelaus) of cruelty and intolerable tyranny" (*Ant.* 17.342). However, it is difficult to imagine that the supposed predations of Archelaus could have come close to rivalling those of Herod, and the latter's administration had been apparently acceptable to Rome.[46] It is somewhat conjectural, but one suspects that Archelaus had been lax in revenue gathering, peace-keeping, or both. In this context, the "delegation of principal men" would have been Sanhedrin members who convinced Augustus that they could govern more efficiently than the young ethnarch. The fore-going reasoning is supported by two facts. First, the newly appointed prefect, Coponius, immediately named Joazar son of Boethus to be high priest. This Joazar had been deposed ten years earlier by Archelaus, likely because he had led a similar delegation to plead for autonomy rather than a continuation of Herodian rule.[47] Second, Joazar proceeded soon after his appointment to publicly support the so-called Census of Quirinius, intended to improve the effectiveness of tax collection.

However it came about, the effect of this change in Roman policy had far-reaching implications for Judea. Roman prefects would continue the practice of appointing and deposing high priests at will, and since high priests in turn controlled or at least significantly influenced the composition of the Sanhedrin, the entire structure of government would depend to a great extent on the competence, temperament, and integrity of the prefect (later procurator). Prefects, in turn, were appointed by the Roman emperor, and the quality of prefects would therefore depend on the emperor's perspicacity. Augustus was a prudent, careful, albeit ruthless ruler (when neces-sary); but the emperors who followed him were increasingly erratic. For example, after succeeding Augustus in 14 C.E., Tiberius grew indif-ferent to ruling at all, eventually sequestering himself on his island resort at Capri and turning day-to-day affairs over to the commander of the Praetorian Guard, Lucius Aelius Sejanus. In part because of his unconcern over matters of state, Tiberius in 37 designated his great-nephew, the 25-year-old Caligula, to succeed him. The latter's mega-lomaniac instability led to his assassination by his own guards in 41 and the selection of the diffident but marginally competent Claudius. When Claudius died, in 54, the quality of emperors descended into a 14 year downward spiral with Nero.

All prefects and later procurators were understood to be avaricious;

the ability to enrich oneself, apparently, was one of the perquisites of the office. Responding to complaints that he used to leave local governors too long in office, Tiberius joked that he did so to spare their subject populations from excessive predation. That is, once the incumbent had initially sated his greed, he was expected to relax his predatory tendencies, whereas a fresh appointee would begin anew to wring wealth from his assigned territory (*Ant.* 18.170–77). Moreover, in addition to being money-hungry, prefects could also be temperamental, capricious, and even cruel. Thus, although we know comparatively little about many of these local officials as individuals, we nevertheless can infer a great deal about the general type. The deposition of Archelaus had cast Judea into the death-grip of Roman bureaucracy.

One particular family of priests, moreover, managed to ingratiate themselves with Roman authorities. Soon after the aforementioned Joazar endorsed the new census, he was replaced by a certain Ananus son of Seth. Curiously, neither Josephus nor any other written records offer information about this figure other than the fact of his high priesthood—the office he was to occupy for 9 years (6–15 C.E.) and then see five sons[48] and one son-in-law follow him. In all, they served for at least 37 years, or more than half the entire 64-year period of Roman administration. This demonstrates the tight (and mutually profitable) relationship between the priestly aristocracy and the local Roman governors that cannot have been lost on the Jerusalem population.[49]

Judaism in the First Century C.E.

The basic outlines of Jewish beliefs and practices do not appear to have changed a great deal, if at all, from the earlier Hellenistic era.[50] The central tenet of Judaism was the belief in one all-powerful God, who had created the world and chosen the Jews to be his special people, who would be rewarded or punished in accordance with their obedience to his commandments that had been communicated via Moses.[51] The main elements of those rules were circumcision, Sabbath adherence, and avoidance of prohibited foods. While some of the specifics, inevitably, would be vigorously debated, there was general agreement on the foregoing broad outline.

Over time, the access to God through Temple rituals had come to be supplemented by individual prayer and study of scripture. The institutional setting for this form of individual piety was the *synagogue* ("assembly," or "gathering") or *proseuche* ("prayer house"). The earliest synagogue identified by archaeologists was built in the third century B.C.E. in Egypt, and by the first century C.E., there were synagogues in many towns and villages throughout Judea as well as the diaspora.[52] The corollary to individual prayer was individual responsibility for observing the commandments.

A new form of religious literary genre had also begun to emerge, referred to by modern scholars as *apocalyptic*—that is, revelatory. The essence of apocalyptic thinking was the sense that the current age was coming to an end (the so-called *eschaton*, or end of time), in which the old order would be overturned by God. In its place, God would inaugurate a new regime wherein the virtuous would prosper and the wicked would be eternally punished. While it is unclear how widely these views were held, the notion that rewards and punishments would occur after death, or at the end of time, or both, represented a significant departure from the former view that God rewarded and punished humans in this life. At least one form of the apocalyptic worldview foresaw that all of Israel would be redeemed, and gentiles would recognize the Lord and accept the hegemony of the Jews. Another variation, however, held that individuals would receive their just deserts, and no one would be saved from punishment merely by virtue of being a Jew.

Related to apocalyptic thinking was a growing belief in individual resurrection. While the concept of bodies being re-constituted by God after death had received only sporadic references in biblical texts (e.g., 2 Maccabees 7:14; Isaiah 26:19; Ezekiel 37:1–6; Daniel 12:2–3), there was a certain logical connection between the belief in reward and punishment at the end of time, on the one hand, and in resurrection on the other. How else could one rationalize the fact that some who eagerly awaited the end of time have died before the event occurred?[53] The use of ossuaries (boxes for storing the bones of the deceased) is thought by some scholars to indicate a rather widespread belief in resurrection in the first century C.E.[54]

Religious Sects in the First Century C.E.

Scholars often assume (implicitly, at least) that the major Jewish sects or schools that Josephus introduced in c. 144–143 B.C.E. (*Ant.* 13.171) continued more or less intact into the first century C.E.[55] This assumption deserves close examination.

Take the Sadducees as a case in point. As we saw in chap. 7, the Sadducees during the Hasmonean era comprised a priestly aristocracy that held senior religious, ministerial, and military positions in the Hasmonean regime. The term "Sadducee" appears to have been derived from a supposed ancestral connection to David and Solomon's high priest Zadok. The last high priest in the direct line of Zadokite descent, Onias IV, had fled to Egypt, leaving a succession vacuum that the Hasmoneans filled. Whether the Hasmoneans themselves had Zadokite credentials is an open question, but the evidence is clear that after the rift between John Hyrcanus and the Pharisees, the Sadducees and Hasmoneans were closely allied.[56] That changed dramatically when Salome Alexandra removed the Sadducees from positions of authority and replaced them with the Pharisees. In response to that change of control and the installation of Pharisaic religious protocols, some Sadducees appear to have withdrawn from Judean society and became leaders of Essene communities.[57] Others, however, rallied behind Aristobulus and his sons in an effort to win the kingdom and their positions of authority back. The disenfranchisement of the Sadducees was completed by Pompey's invasion, and five separate efforts by the Sadducees to regain power were thwarted by the Roman military. The final blow to any Sadducean hopes was struck when Herod and Sosius reconquered Jerusalem in 37 B.C.E. To the extent that there were any descendants remaining from the Sadducees of the Hasmonean era, they would have been dispersed in the rural countryside or living in self-contained Essene communities, or otherwise largely invisible to history.[58]

Who then are the Sadducees who appear in rabbinic writings as interlocutors of the Pharisees in the first century,[59] and who are portrayed in the gospel accounts as members of the senior priesthood?[60] These can only be representatives of the small group of families imported into the priesthood by Herod, who constituted "a new aristocracy....from families that had never previously supplied high priests."[61] These latter-day "Sadducees" of the first century C.E. may have taken that name to legitimize their claims to the high priesthood, but apart from that self-identification, they have no discernible connection to the Sadducees introduced by Josephus in the second century B.C.E. Moreover, even though Josephus provides the barest of information about the Sadducees, it seems likely that the little he does say about their beliefs and practices (e.g., *Ant.* 18.16–17) is based on his personal experience with the so-called Sadducees of his own era.

We now turn to the Essenes. Although these sectarians were ostensibly living lives as pacifists, scholars have detected a "growing apocalyptic mood" that accompanied the isolationism of the scroll community.[62] From their beginnings as a group alienated by the impurity (as they saw it) of the Temple and the legitimacy of those then serving as priests, the broader Essene movement had metamorphosed into one that zealously awaited a utopian future in which God would visit the world and redress the iniquities of the present age. This expectation of a better future was likely the result of witnessing the repeated victories of Roman power and the perpetuation of a regime they considered evil. How else could they explain God allowing this to happen in the face of their determined efforts to follow his commandments? Here is their rationale in their own words,

"In his mysterious wisdom, God has countenanced an era in which perversity triumphs, but at the time appointed for (his) visitation, he shall destroy such forever" (1QS 4.18).

The *Yahad* was a very secretive group. Their literature strictly proscribes communication with outsiders. It is then entirely possible that their vision of a violent end to the established order eluded the scrutiny of even Herod's many spies. This would account for Josephus's statement that Herod viewed the Essenes as benign (*Ant.* 15.378). However, as Shaye Cohen has noted,[63] they envisioned a final bloody conflict at the time of God's visitation, in which they themselves would participate as "sons of light" alongside angelic forces. That alliance would triumph over the "sons of darkness," who included not only Romans and their Jewish clients but also (perhaps primarily) "those other Jews who did not adhere to the group's legal interpretations."

By the first century C.E., the total population of Essenes numbered some 4,000, according to Josephus. They lived distributed throughout Judea in largely self-sufficient settlements within many villages and towns. Estimates of the number of residents that could be supported at Qumran vary,[64] but that relatively small group could not have represented more than a tiny fraction of the total Essene sect. What then was the relationship between Qumran and the larger Essene population? A number of scholars have noted that the term *Yahad*—often translated "community"—does not apply narrowly to only the residents of Qumran but rather the entire population of individuals unified by shared beliefs and practices.[65] If, as many suppose, Qumran was a center for the production and/or safekeeping of the sect's written material, it may have served as a sort of intellectual hub that preserved and refined the sect's beliefs, as well as providing indoctrination for new initiates.[66] This understanding of Qumran is supported by the fact that Pliny the Elder singled it out for special attention, and emphasized that it was a destination for newcomers to the sect.

A further matter of curiosity regarding the Essenes is that while their writings contain at least 35 allusions to identifiable historical persons or events prior to 30 B.C.E, the contents of the scrolls make no mention of anything of a later date.[67] This is remarkable, if the scroll authors were Essenes, as the sect continued to exist well into the first century, according to both literary and archaeological sources.[68] The silence is all the more remarkable because many distinctive ideas found in the scrolls appear in early Christianity.

The one sect that seems to have transitioned into the first century more or less intact is the Pharisees, who appear to have gained the upper hand over the other sects.[69] This should not come as a surprise. Following Salome Alexandra's installation of Pharisees into positions of authority, they appeared in the highest councils of both Hyrcanus II and Herod.[70] And later, when war with Rome breaks out, leading Pharisees are specifically identified as part of the ruling coalition. Although some scholars have pointed to a paucity of information about the historical role of the Pharisees, these scattered glimpses should nevertheless be sufficient to support a conclusion that the Pharisees exercised considerable authority more or less continuously from the time of Alexandra through to the Jewish Revolt.

Josephus assesses their influence as follows: "...they are extremely influential among the townsfolk; and all prayers and sacred rites of divine worship are performed according to their exposition..." (*Ant.* 18.15).

It is understandable that individual Jews wishing to comply with God's commandments would want assurance that they were conforming precisely to the rules, and who better to provide that assurance than the recognized expert interpreters of the law? Josephus goes on to note that even the aristocratic Sadducees, although nominally in charge of Temple operations, had to conduct public rituals in accordance with protocols established by the Pharisees.

The gospel accounts, notably Matthew 23, as well as rabbinic literature add to the impression created by Josephus[71] of the influential role of the Pharisees in first-century Judean society. Some scholars have objected that these texts were written after the fact; however, in the case of Josephus, even though he was writing after the destruction of the Temple, he was surely basing his observations on earlier personal experience.

Despite these indications, questions remain about the extent of actual authority wielded by the Pharisees. One possible interpretation is that, "No one group and no one institution—neither the Pharisees, nor the high priests, nor the regular priests, nor the (mysterious) Sanhedrin, nor the (mysterious) scribes, nor the (mysterious) elders—seem to have been in charge."[72] It is true that the removal of hereditary rulers—king, high priest, or both—resulted in a rather unstructured system of government in Jerusalem, and it is not easy from a distance of two millennia to discern exactly who was "in charge." A good guess, however, is that the Sanhedrin had considerable say in local matters. We saw in the case of Herod's trial, for example, that this body apparently was able to impose capital punishment. Equally, when Herod wanted to rid himself of Hyrcanus II, he used a verdict from the Sanhedrin to provide justification (*Ant.* 15.173). There are numerous other instances when Josephus refers to "elders" or "leading men of the Jews," that he is likely referring to an established body rather than to some ad hoc assemblage. Judicial decisions would have needed to be consistent with Mosaic Law, and, as recognized expert interpreters of that law, the Pharisees who were Sanhedrin members would have carried significant weight in that body's deliberations.

In connection with the imposition of the Census of Quirinius[73] (6 C.E.), Josephus introduces yet another, unnamed sect that has come to be known to historians as "the fourth philosophy," because Josephus seems to place it alongside the other three. The new movement was announced publicly by a certain "Galilean named

Judas" (*J.W.*), who in *Antiquities* is further identified as a resident of Gamala, a city on the eastern shore of the Sea of Galilee.[74] In *War*, Josephus provides only a brief outline of Judas's proclamation. Judas, he says, "incited his countrymen to revolt, upbraiding them as cowards for consenting to pay tribute to the Romans and tolerating mortal masters after having God for their lord" (*J.W.* 2.118). Josephus goes on to say that the new sect was of Judas's own invention, having nothing in common with the other three.

In *Antiquities*, by contrast, Josephus elaborates on this new movement, saying that Judas formulated his call to revolution in concert with a certain "Saddok, a Pharisee," and, moreover, this "fourth philosophy" agreed in all other respects with the opinions of the Pharisees, except that its adherents had "a passion for liberty that is almost unconquerable, since they are convinced that God alone is their leader and master" (*Ant.* 18.23). Scholars have struggled to reconcile these seemingly contradictory positions—that is, was the fourth philosophy an autonomous sect or was it somehow connected to the Pharisees? The latter notion is quite contrary to the position of leading Pharisees, who even after war broke out hoped for reconciliation. In addition, Acts 5:37 describes a prominent Pharisee of the mid-first century, Gamaliel, declaring that the movement initiated by Judas failed because God did not support it. Readers are left with one of Josephus's many contradictions that have not been satisfactorily resolved.

A distinguishing feature of Judas's call for rebellion is his expectation not only that God would favor their cause, but, importantly, that such heavenly support would be in direct proportion to the strength of their own commitment, including especially such "high devotion... that they did not shrink from bloodshed that might be necessary" (*Ant.* 18.5–6). This view is in sharp contrast to that of other apocalyptic visionaries—notably the Essenes—who expected the overthrow of the present age to be initiated by divine agency rather than human force of arms.

The belief that the revolutionaries would receive divine assistance (if they showed enough determination) had far-reaching consequences. The movement attracted many adherents, and even though Judas himself was destroyed along with his early followers (Acts 5:37), it carried on under the leadership of his descendants.[75] Eventually, it led to a full scale war against Rome, as will be described shortly.

Christians

Arguably, Christians are today the most famous of the groups that emerged in first-century Judea.[76] The earliest Christian community, as described in the Book of Acts, shared many features with certain other Jewish groups, in particular the Essenes. For example, for both Christians and Essenes, property was held in common, the respective groups dined together and prayed together. The organizations were strictly hierarchical, and disobedience to superiors was not tolerated (Acts 5:1–11). Both groups exhibited a sense of alienation from the rest of society and shared a remarkably similar eschatological expectations. New members were required to repent of their past sinful lives, vow to change their behavior, and they were initiated by baptism. Indeed, early Christianity exhibited so many features in common with what we know about the Essenes that one is tempted to suppose a connection between the two groups. Yet, that notion has been widely rejected by scholars. Instead, Christianity is thought to have emerged out of a broader matrix of Jewish ideas.[77]

The religion that would become Christianity first gained a public face with the emergence of John the Baptist. According to the Gospel of Luke, John appeared "in the wilderness" during the fifteenth year of Emperor Tiberius, that is in 29. John's message contained an insight that had not previously been expressed in other apocalyptic views. Instead of being a future event whose timing was known only to God, the anticipated "end of time" was imminent. Since only those who repented of their sins and vowed to live righteous lives would be saved, John and his disciples set out to save as many souls as possible in the short time they thought remained.

John's urgent calls for repentance were echoing through the same countryside as the calls for rebellion being voiced by the followers of the "fourth philosophy." Both appeals envisioned the imminent overthrow of the established order. John and his disciples, much like the Essenes, thought the event would be brought about by divine forces, with perhaps some human help once the process started.[78] The movement started by Judas the Galilean, for its part, wanted to up-end the world by force of arms, although they too envisioned heavenly assistance once the ball got rolling. To those being targeted for overthrowing—the senior priests, the leading Pharisees, other members of the ruling elite—it would have been nearly impossible to distinguish between these two groups. One such authority figure was Herod Antipas, the tetrarch of Galilee and Perea, where John's outreach had been particularly active. Although the proximate cause of the dispute between John and Antipas was the latter's marriage to Herodias, that John had proclaimed unlawful, both Josephus and the Gospels make it clear that Antipas's real concern was that John's eschatological message would spark a rebellion.[79] That was a risk Antipas was not prepared to take, so he ordered John beheaded.

Many scholars have noted that the "fourth philosophy" would not have gained much traction in a society that was otherwise content. Rebellion in the ancient world was very much a life-risking undertaking, requiring strong provocation to initiate it. In the case of first century Judea, the combination of economic distress and the perceived trampling on religious traditions would have made for a volatile tinder that only needed a spark to burst into flame. Antipas must have been well aware of such conditions among his subject population, hence his decision to remove John the Baptist.

Following John's arrest, leadership of his movement was assumed by one of his disciples, a charismatic figure who has become known to history as Jesus of Nazareth. Among his many teachings, some of which may well be authentic, but others are likely the work of later editors, Jesus evidently carried on John's message[80] that the end of time was imminent and only the repentant would be saved. If, as the Gospels suggest, crowds were responding enthusiastically to the forecast of a soon-to-come demise of the established order, it stands to reason that those at the pinnacle of that same order would have been alarmed, just as Antipas had been. In due course, Jesus led his tiny entourage to Jerusalem, where thousands of pilgrims would be converging for the Passover festival. Such events had a well-established potential for volatility, and the Jerusalem authorities, including the high priest Caiaphas (18–37) and his father-in-law Ananus,[81] would have been on high alert. Possibly matters came to a head when Jesus assaulted the Temple money changers, but whatever the cause, he was arrested, tried, and crucified alongside two "bandits."[82] Notably, the execution was carried out by Roman soldiers under the direction of the then Roman prefect Pontius Pilate (26?–37), and crucifixion was the traditional form of punishment for rebels.[83]

The loss of their leader only strengthened the early Christian movement, as his disciples and many other followers believed that God had resurrected him from death. Inspired by this understanding, these early "Christians" (as they would come to be known)[84] stepped up their outreach efforts and soon began extending their appeal to gentiles. Over time, what had emerged as a Jewish religion began to take on a distinctly un-Jewish character, as certain traditional Jewish practices, such as circumcision and food restrictions, were abandoned. Moreover, the figure of Jesus himself was elevated to a higher theological position than any angel or other intermediary figure in Judaism. By the end of the first century C.E., the migration of Christianity away from its Jewish roots was largely complete.[85]

The rift between Judaism and Christianity was not stress free. Proselytism had always been a feature of Judaism, but in a mostly passive form. That is, if an individual was attracted to the concept of a single, all-powerful God who protected his chosen people, he or she was permitted (but not necessarily encouraged) to participate in certain Jewish activities such as synagogue scripture readings and prayers. These "godfearers," as they were known, would not become full-fledged Jews, unless they also committed to the more stringent covenantal requirements, notably circumcision.[86] By contrast, the early Christian movement, fired by the imminence of the coming "day of wrath" as well as the miracle of Jesus's resurrection, took a much more active approach to seeking out new initiates, while simultaneously relaxing the requirements for membership. This was bound to provoke an angry response among traditional-minded Jews. Moreover, the more aggressive outreach of Christian missionaries in the Diaspora would soon become a threat to Roman authorities, with local Jewish populations often caught up in the confusion. These disturbances would add to the already volatile mix of social and economic discord, and eschatological and revolutionary fervor of the first century.

Agrippa I

Agrippa I was born in 10 B.C.E, the son of Aristobulus—Herod's son by his wife Mariamme I—who had been executed by Herod when Agrippa was barely three years old. He was brought up in Rome, and his young adulthood was characterized by an extravagant, debt-fueled lifestyle that led to his banishment from the imperial household in 23 C.E., to which he was reinstated ten years later. During this later period, he befriended the emperor's great nephew Gaius, nick-named Caligula. Upon the death of Tiberius, in 37, Caligula became emperor and rewarded his friend Agrippa with the vacant tetrarchy of Philip along with the title of king, and later the tetrarchy of Antipas.

As Caligula's megalomania progressed, he demanded to be worshiped as a God and ordered statues of himself installed in every temple in the empire, including in Jerusalem. This was a dramatic departure from past Roman practice that, since the days of Julius Caesar, had recognized the special status of Jews, not only in Judea but also in the Diaspora. It was understood, for example, that Jews refused to worship any god (including divine emperors) but their own, that they refused to work or make court appearances on the Sabbath, and would not tolerate images in public places or on coins circulated in Judea. In many cities in the East, including especially Alexandria, Jews were authorized to create autonomous ethnic communities called *politeumata.* Not surprisingly, these perceived "special privileges" came to provoke resentment among gentile neighbors. At about the same time that Caligula ordered his statue installed in the Jerusalem Temple, he also instructed his legate in Egypt to withdraw the special privileges of the Jewish population in Alexandria. Crises were thus precipitated in both cities.[87]

In Alexandria, violence erupted between gentile and Jewish residents. In Jerusalem, the protestors assembled *en masse* before the Roman governor, Petronius, and declared that he must kill every one of them before they would allow their temple to be violated.[88] The crises in both cities were averted with the assassination of Caligula, in 41.[89] According to Josephus, Agrippa then acted as an intermediary between Caligula's uncle Claudius and the Roman senate,[90] leading to Claudius's ascension as the next Roman emperor. Two of Claudius's early acts were to write sternly to the citizens of Alexandria,[91] warning both Jews and gentiles to cease hostilities, and to declare Agrippa king of Judea.

The replacement of Roman prefects with a Jewish king with at least partial Hasmonean credentials[92] seems to have soothed tensions in Judea at least temporarily, although perhaps less decisively than is sometimes supposed. Josephus describes a certain resident of Jerusalem named Simon who was openly critical of the new king (*Ant.* 19.332–34). Agrippa summoned Simon to appear before him at his base in Caesarea, and when Simon begged forgiveness, Agrippa sent him on his way. Josephus emphatically characterizes Agrippa's disposition of the matter as illustrative of his compassionate nature.

The Book of Acts (12:1–11) tells a parallel story involving Agrippa I and Simon—in this case the Simon nick-named Peter, the former disciple of Jesus and now a ranking apostle in the emergent Christian movement. In this version of the story, Agrippa was anything but compassionate. He "laid violent hands" on some members of the Church, executed another former disciple, James (the son of Zebedee), and imprisoned Simon. Acts and Josephus are transparently telling different versions of the same episode, and the impression that emerges is that Christians were becoming more outspoken and provocative to authority figures in Judea. This phenomenon would be yet another element of social tension in the years to come.

The Road to War (44–66 C.E.)

Agrippa I died unexpectedly in 44. Because his 17-year-old son Agrippa II was deemed too young to succeed him, Judea was returned to the regime of Roman procurators.[93] Unfortunately for Judea, the procurators who followed were incompetent, insensitive, corrupt, or all of these.[94] Over the next two decades, there would be a seemingly endless series of complaints against procurators, mixed with clashes between Jewish and gentile populations (both within and outside Judea), riots, assassinations, banditry, prophets promising miracles, and growing tension between traditional Jews and the increasingly active Christian apostles.

The first procurator of this new regime, Cuspius Fadus (44–46), began his term by attempting to take control of the high priest's vestments that had most recently been under Agrippa's care. One of Herod the Great's more cunning insights had been to sequester these special clothes—that were essential to the performance of the high priest's ritual functions—as a way of controlling the office of high priest. The new Syrian legate arrived with "a great army ... out of fear that the injunctions of Fadus should force the Jews to rebel" (*Ant.* 20.7).

Roman Rulers of Judea

Coponius	Roman prefect of Judea, 6–9 C.E.
Marcus Ambiblius	Roman prefect of Judea, 9–12
Annius Rufus	Roman prefect of Judea, 12–15
Valerius Gratus	Roman prefect of Judea, 15–26 (or 18)
Pontius Pilate	Roman prefect of Judea, 26 (or 18)–36
Marcellus	Roman prefect of Judea, 36–37
Marullus	Roman prefect of Judea, 37–41
Cuspius Fadus	Roman procurator of Judea, 44–c. 46
Tiberius Julius Alexander	Roman procurator of Judea, c. 46–48
Ventidius Cumanus	Roman procurator of Judea, 48–c. 52
Marcus Antonius Felix	Roman procurator of Judea, c. 52–60
Porcius Festus	Roman procurator of Judea, 60–62
Albinus	Roman procurator of Judea, 62–64
Gessius Florus	Roman procurator of Judea, 64–66

A compromise that staved off violence was reached, the Jerusalem authorities were allowed to appeal to Claudius, and the emperor conferred the right to appoint high priests to Herod of Chalcis (Agrippa I's brother). When the latter died, in 48, the appointment of high priests reverted to Agrippa II. The episode, though seemingly of minor importance in some accounts, nevertheless indicates the intense sensitivity of Jews to the notion of a Roman controlling their most sacred office.

Fadus was succeeded by Tiberius Alexander (46–48), son of a wealthy Alexandrian who had rescued Agrippa I from debt. Under his procuratorship, two of the sons of Judas the Galilean were apprehended and crucified, indicating that the revolutionary "fourth philosophy" was still an active movement some 40 years after its inception.

The year 49 brought indications of trouble in Rome itself. The Roman historian Suetonius reports that Claudius "expelled the Jews from Rome on account of their continuous rioting at the instigation of Chrestus" (*Divus Claudius* 25). As Margaret Williams has observed, these public disturbances are best interpreted as analogues to those attested in several diaspora locations during the same time period, caused by apostles like Paul preaching a doctrine to which traditional Jews strenuously objected.[95]

During the procuratorship of Ventidius Cumanus (48–52), the pace of disturbances in Judea accelerated. Roman soldiers were routinely stationed above the Temple cloisters to guard against potential violence at major festivals. At the Passover of 49, a soldier exposed himself in a vulgar way to the assembled pilgrims, precipitating a riot in which great numbers perished (*Ant.* 20.112). Likely in response, a band of rebels robbed a Roman courier barely 12 miles from Jerusalem, and Cumanus ordered the surrounding villages plundered. When Samaritans murdered "a great many" Galilean pilgrims,[96] Cumanus was thought to have accepted bribes to overlook the crime. Outraged by this perceived injustice, a collection of Judeans that apparently included known rebels[97] attacked Samaritan villages. Cumanus ordered Roman soldiers to repel the attackers, and the violence intensified to the point where the Syrian governor Quadratus was forced to intervene. Cumanus was eventually disciplined, but the episode was further confirmation to Judeans that they could not expect justice from a Roman procurator.

Cumanus was replaced in 52 by Felix, whom Tacitus describes as "brutal and licentious" (*Annals* 12.54.1). Josephus supports this characterization by reporting that when the former high priest Jonathan was outspokenly critical of Felix, the procurator bribed a gang of rebels to assassinate him.[98] The collusion between a Roman procurator and insurgent elements is a further symptom of the disintegration of law and order.

Probably dated to the late 50s, there is yet more evidence of friction between traditional Jews and the increasingly aggressive Christian movement. The Book of Acts reports an incident in which a mob of angry Jews attacked the apostle Paul in the precincts of the Temple. While the exact historicity of this event is open to question, the basic charge that Paul was "teaching against our people and our law" (Acts 21:28) supports the notion of growing hostility of Jews to (in their view) heretical Christian teachings. Curiously as well, when Paul was taken into custody, the tribune in charge reportedly mistook him for "the Egyptian," a self-styled prophet who according to Josephus had led a mob to attack Jerusalem (*J.W.* 2.261–63; *Ant.* 20.169). If there is any truth to this mistaken identity, it would be further confirmation that Roman authorities had difficulty distinguishing between apocalyptic visionaries and political insurrectionists.

The terms of the next two procurators, Porcius Festus (60–62) and Albinus (62–64), provided additional examples of the growing chaos in Judea: violent clashes between the gentile and Jewish residents of Caesarea, false prophets promising salvation to hordes of people desperate for it, "bandits" and "robbers" conducting kidnappings and assassinations, and bribery and extortion by the procurators. Then, in the interregnum between Festus's departure and Albinus's arrival—in 62—, the high priest Ananus[99] convened the Sanhedrin and brought unspecified charges[100] against James brother of Jesus, who was the acknowledged leader of the Christian church in Jerusalem. The Sanhedrin rendered a guilty verdict, and James was stoned to death (*Ant.* 20.199–200). The enmity between Christians and the Jerusalem establishment had evidently reached a boiling point.

Jewish leaders were not the only authority figures threatened by prophecies about the imminent end of time and overthrow of the established order. In 64, a great fire swept through Rome and, according to Tacitus, Emperor Nero needed a scapegoat to dispel gossip that he had ordered the conflagration himself. Tacitus reports as follows:

> Nero therefore found culprits on whom he inflicted the most exotic punishments. These were people hated for their shameful offenses whom the (Roman) commoners called Christians. The man who gave them their name, Christus, had been executed during the rule of Tiberius by the procurator Pontius Pilatus. The pernicious superstition had been temporarily suppressed, but it was starting to break out again, not just in Judea, the origin of the curse, but in Rome as well, where all that is abominable and shameful in the world flows together and gains popularity.
> (ANNALS 15.44)

It is unclear what aspect of Christian beliefs Tacitus found abhorrent, but their eschatological expectations are likely candidates, especially if they foresaw that the end would be accomplished in an all-consuming fire.[101]

As Shaye Cohen has pointed out, the revolutionaries in Judea may have held similar eschatological views,[102] such that those in authority would have had difficulty distinguishing between multiple factions with messianic claims. The history of the first century is filled with executions of both insurrectionists, such as the sons of Judas the Galilean and Eleazar son of Dineus, and leaders of the Church, such as James son of Zebedee and James brother of Jesus.

To the volatile mix of social discord, wealth disparity, revolutionary fervor, and prophets (Christian and otherwise) promising salvation at the end of time, would now be added discord within the ranks of the Judean priesthood. Josephus records that the chief priests—that is, members of the few families who monopolized[103] the senior priesthood—forcefully deprived the junior priests of the tithes to which they would normally have been entitled (*Ant.* 20.206–207). This latter group would have been comprised of rural priests who served on a rotating basis and no doubt included descendants of the Sadducean priesthood of the Hasmonean era. This priestly cadre would be in the vanguard of the uprising soon to follow.

A Violent Crescendo

The growing unrest in Judea under the Roman procurators reached a violent crescendo during the term of Gessius Florus (64–66). The proximate cause of trouble, according to Josephus, was that Florus had accepted a payment from the Jews of Caesarea to protect them from the persecution of the city's gentile residents. Florus failed to deliver on his promise, then jailed the Caesarean Jews who complained. News of this perfidy sparked protests in Jerusalem, and Florus responded by confiscating 17 talents from the Temple treasury. This was deemed an outrage (although we later learn that scheduled tribute had been withheld), and when Florus arrived in Jerusalem with a military escort, he was greeted by insults from the crowd, to which he responded by deploying his soldiers, with deadly effect.

Both parties appealed to the Syrian governor, Cestius Gallus, and the latter sent a representative, one Neapolitanus, to mediate. He arrived accompanied by Agrippa II, who made a lengthy speech (transparently a rhetorical flourish of Josephus) on the folly of opposing Rome and was greeted by jeers and rocks thrown from the crowd. In the history of popular uprisings, it is often observed that those whose lives are comfortable are most desirous of preserving the status quo, while those whose lives have become intolerable lead the way in agitating for change. Josephus drives this point home in his description of the frenzied negotiations that took place during Neapolitanus's visit, when he characterizes the chief priests of the Jews and leading citizens of the council (i.e., the Sanhedrin) as "men of position and owners of property and (therefore) desirous of peace" (*J.W.* 2.338). By contrast, the actual outbreak of hostilities would in due course be initiated by the same cadre of rank-and-file priests who recently had been driven to starvation when deprived of their customary tithes by the chief priests.

Having failed to convince the crowd, Agrippa withdrew to his own territory, leaving the Jerusalem peace party—that is, the chief priests and Sanhedrin members who consistently include leading Pharisees[104]— with the responsibility of collecting unpaid tribute. During the brief interregnum that followed, word came to Jerusalem that a band of insurgents had captured the fortress at Masada, after slaughtering the Roman garrison and taking possession of their weapons. Possibly inspired by this news, the Temple captain, Eleazer son of Ananias,[105] announced a suspension of sacrifices on behalf of the Roman emperor. This was tantamount to a declaration of war and emphasizes the rift between the aristocratic peace faction and the junior priests, as the latter "remained obdurate as their numbers gave them great confidence" when "the chief priests and notables earnestly besought them not to abandon the customary offering" (*J.W.* 2.410).

The peace party in alarm sent emissaries to Florus and Agrippa II. According to Josephus, Florus[106] was delighted at the prospect of rebellion and did nothing, while Agrippa dispatched 2,000 mounted soldiers to support the aristocrats. Their arrival provoked open hostilities, and the insurgents, now led by Eleazar, drove the royal troops and the aristocrats (conspicuously including Eleazar's father and uncle) to the palace in the upper city,[107] where the Roman garrison was stationed. Days of fierce fighting ensued, resulting in a stalemate of sorts between the exhausted combatants. During that lull in the fighting, the insurgents set fire to the public archives in order, Josephus says, to destroy the records of indebtedness. In this report, we have a clear indication that wealth disparity was an underlying cause of the revolt.

Then in mid-August 66 the insurgents were reinforced by the arrival of one Menachem, the son (or, more likely, the grandson) of Judas the Galilean, with a well-armed contingent of followers identified by Josephus as "Zealots" (*J.W.* 2,244). The introduction of a descendant of Judas the Galilean into the thick of the fighting shows that the "fourth philosophy," initiated by Judas in 6 C.E., remained intact after some two generations, although it is unclear whether this was a coherent movement or simply a label for individuals desiring rebellion.[108] Describing the followers of Menachem as "Zealots" does, however, reveal the underlying religious aspect of the insurgency, which Josephus throughout his two histories does his utmost to conceal. The last thing he would have wanted his Roman readers to understand was that the rebellion was rooted in the Jewish religion. However, he scarcely could have omitted the term "Zealot" altogether, as the Romans would have known from captives and informers that this is how their opponents described themselves.[109]

There has been considerable scholarly debate—indeed, entire books[110]—on the meaning of the term *Zealot*, but it essentially describes a person or group willing to take violent action to punish disobedience to God's commandments. This sense of the term must have been widely understood in the first century C.E., as Philo explains it clearly writing at least a generation before the revolt.[111] Josephus, however, takes pains to conceal the religious significance of "zeal" from his readers. For example, when he tells the story of Phinehas (in *Ant.* 4.150–55), the terms "zeal" and "zealous" that are so central to the biblical account (Numbers 25:10) are nowhere to be found. Josephus also omits the "zeal" of Elijah from his retelling of 1 Kings 19:10, 14. And whereas 1 Maccabees invokes the "zeal" of Phinehas half a dozen times, Josephus uses it only once, and then only in the generic sense of "commitment"—without reference to religious principles or Phinehas. Finally, when Josephus characterizes the Zealots, he says only that they were "zealous for the cause of virtue" (*J.W.* 4.161), without explaining to his readers the specific religious nature of that virtue. Thus, while there may have been diverse groups who shared a willingness to fight the Romans, but differed from one another in other respects,[112] they likely shared a desire to reinstate Jewish religious traditions, which they viewed as being subverted by Roman domination.

Josephus elsewhere describes certain elements of the insurrection—including those who captured and later died in the defense of Masada—as *sicarii*, a Latin word denoting dagger-wielding criminals. Unlike the term Zealot, which was a self-designation used by insurgents who saw themselves inspired by religious principles, the term *Sicarii* was probably a label used by the Romans to describe the most violent of their opponents. Thus, it seems entirely possible that the same group of insurgents could refer themselves as Zealots, while being labeled Sicarii by their enemies (Jewish or Roman).

Seeing the insurgents thus reinforced by Menachem's Zealots, Agrippa's soldiers surrendered and were allowed to depart, leaving the aristocrats and the Roman garrison to their own devices. The Romans retreated to the defensive towers of the palace, while Menachem's forces swarmed into the palace grounds where, among their other victims, Ananias the aristocratic father of Eleazer was killed. This provoked a strong reaction from Eleazar's partisans, who now attacked Menachem and his followers. Menachem was killed, and the others retreated to Masada under the leadership of Menachem's relative Eleazar son of Jairus (*J.W.* 2.448).

The surviving Romans trapped in the palace towers now asked for terms, and the besiegers pledged to allow them to depart if they disarm themselves. However, when the Romans complied and gave up their arms, Eleazer's partisans attacked and massacred the defenseless victims. Only the commander, one Metillus, was spared on condition that he be circumcised and become a Jew (*J.W.* 2.454). If authentic, this story reinforces the underlying religious character of the revolt.

Word of the Jerusalem uprising and the destruction of the Roman garrison[113] prompted fighting between Jews and gentiles throughout the Syrian province, and it even spread to Alexandria (*J.W.* 2.487–98). Cestius Gallus was forced to mobilize, and in September 66, he departed Antioch at the head of the Twelfth Legion, some 5,000 soldiers and as many auxiliaries. Cestius made his way south, encountering growing resistance as he approached Jerusalem. Pausing at Mt. Scopus, overlooking the city from the north, he proceeded to the suburbs, where he received a message from "the leading citizens"[114] promising to open the city gates to him (*J.W.* 2.532). Cestius, however, must have deemed his single legion overmatched, because he decided to withdraw instead.

The sight of the retreating legion gave courage to Eleazar's insurgents. They poured out of the city in great numbers and launched a furious attack on the Romans' rear guard. Their line of retreat required the Romans to cross a narrow defile between two rows of hills and the village of Beth Horon. From the days of Joshua, Jewish forces had trapped many an unwary foe in this treacherous passage. Legion 12 was not to be an exception. Cestius himself managed to escape with a small group of survivors, but on November 8, 66, the rest of the legion perished to the last man[115] (*J.W.* 2.555).

The Great War

The annihilation of a Roman legion was an exhilarating victory for Eleazar and the insurgents, but an equally unsettling outcome for the chief priests and Pharisees who had consistently advocated compromise and acceptance of Roman hegemony. Many of the pro-Roman faction fled the city, "as swimmers desert a sinking ship" (*J.W.* 2.556). Those who remained realized that the loss of Legion 12 would not go unpunished and (however reluctantly) they had to prepare for war. Moreover, they knew they had to keep silent about any hopes they might still harbor for a negotiated settlement, as such ideas were now viewed as apostasy and subject to severe punishment.

Accordingly, a new ruling council was formed out of the remains of the former Sanhedrin, and generals were elected to prosecute the coming conflict. Josephus was designated governor of Galilee, which would bear the brunt of the Romans' advance. Meanwhile, in early 67, Nero appointed the most experienced commander available, the 58-year-old Titus Flavius Vespasian to reclaim Judea. Vespasian organized three legions and in the spring of that year assaulted Galilee. Josephus's makeshift army scattered at the Roman advance, and Josephus retreated to Jotapata, a well-fortified hilltop town, to join the remnant of his forces still willing to fight. Josephus provides page after page of vivid prose[116] about the stubborn defense of Jotapata with emphasis on his own heroics. After seven weeks, Jotapata fell, Josephus was captured and, according to his account, won Vespasian's favor by prophesying that the general would soon become Roman emperor.

By the end of 67, all of Galilee had been subdued, and one of Galilee's rebel leaders, John of Gischala (who had been Josephus's nemesis), fled to Jerusalem with a band of followers. In due course, John inserted himself into the leadership of the insurgency, which by then included other remnant groups from the countryside and, of course, Eleazar's partisans. Together, these cadres formed the dominant faction in the city that Josephus labels collectively "Zealots." Josephus treats the Zealots with contempt, labeling them "brigands," "bandits," and "robbers." Of course, in the minds of Josephus's Roman readers, this is what any group hostile to Rome would appear to be. However, as we have seen, the term "Zealot" had a religious significance that Josephus was anxious to conceal. Experience shows, as well, that groups inspired by religious zeal often fight as strenuously against one another as they do against their common foe. And if Josephus's reporting is at all authentic, that is exactly what would happen in Jerusalem while waiting for Vespasian's advance.

ARCH OF TITUS RELIEF. The golden menorah, a pair of trumpets, the golden table and other booty from the Jerusalem Temple are carried aloft in a Roman victory procession, depicted in this marble relief from the Arch of Titus. Erected in Rome in 80 C.E., the arch celebrates the Roman victory over the Jews and conquest of Jerusalem.

By the summer of 68, Vespasian had pacified all of Galilee and most of the remaining Judean countryside and was preparing to attack Jerusalem. However, news arrived that Nero had committed suicide,[117] so Vespasian suspended operations and dispatched his son Titus to determine the wishes of the new emperor, Galba. This hiatus should have been a boon to the revolutionaries, allowing them time to organize and fortify the city.[118] Instead, however, the city was overcome by internecine strife, first between the aristocratic and more proletarian elements, and, once the aristocrats were beaten, among the more radical revolutionaries themselves. Meanwhile, Rome was experiencing internecine conflict of its own, as Galba was executed by Otho, who in turn was deposed by Vitellius. At that point the patience of the legions had run out; the empire could not survive without a level-headed ruler, and one after another the legions declared their allegiance to Vespasian. In December 69, Josephus's prophecy was fulfilled, and Vespasian hastened to Rome to take control, leaving the Judean campaign in Titus's hands, with Josephus as a valued advisor.

In the spring of 70, the Romans surrounded Jerusalem and cut off all means of supply. This was a disaster for the defenders since large stocks of grain within the city had already been destroyed during the sectarian fighting. The city's multiple walls, towers, and fortified palaces, as well as the seemingly impregnable Temple Mount, made Jerusalem one of the most defensible capitals in the ancient world. However, Roman siege craft, with its missile launchers, battering rams, and assault towers, would ultimately prove equal to the task. As the battle for the city raged, Josephus toured the walls urging the insurgents in their own language to surrender; in reply, they mocked him as a traitor. The defenders put aside their factional differences and repelled assault after assault; meanwhile noncombatant residents starved by the thousands. Even as the fighting raged, the priests maintained the customary rituals, although the "continual sacrifice" offered every morning and evening eventually had to be suspended as there were no lambs remaining to be sacrificed.[119]

The Romans methodically broke through the outer city walls and then the inner, until by mid-summer only the Temple itself remained in the hands of the defenders. Besides being a sacred place, the Temple was also a formidable fortress, with massive walls and defensive towers, from which the Jews continued to hurl missiles at the attackers. When battering rams proved ineffective, Titus ordered the gates of the outer court be set on fire. Romans dashed through the openings thus created, past bodies of slain defenders, and into the sanctuary itself. Soon the entire Temple was engulfed in flames, the result reportedly of a soldier tossing a burning brand without orders. Whether by Titus's command or not, the holiest place of the Jews was destroyed by an imperial power for the second time in history.[120]

On September 26, 70, Jerusalem's resistance ended. The once magnificent Temple as well as the surrounding cloisters were now a smoking ruin. Titus ordered the city destroyed first by fire[121] and then razed stone by stone to the ground. The few defenders still alive were summarily executed or taken as prisoners to be sacrificed in gladiatorial events. The wealth confiscated from the Temple was said to be enormous, enough in fact to enable the Flavians to finance the construction of the Roman Colosseum.[122] The triumphal Arch of Titus may be viewed by visitors to modern Rome, where a number of the Temple's artifacts are pictured in the carved stone.[123]

Masada

Masada is the name of the remote hilltop fortress near the southwest corner of the Dead Sea that had been captured by a group of insurgents during the early stages of the revolt. Rebel elements led by Eleazar ben Jair, including their wives and children, as well as possibly other refugees, continued to occupy the site following the fall of Jerusalem in 70 C.E. Josephus consistently refers to these occupants of Masada as Sicarii, although, as discussed above, Eleazar and his comrades may well have thought of themselves as Zealots. Perhaps these survivors considered themselves secure, as Masada was thought to be impregnable. The fortress stood on a plateau some 1,400 feet above ground level, surrounded on all sides by sheer rock cliffs, and accessible by only a single, winding, narrow path. Herod the Great had designed it as a place of refuge for himself and his family, carving enormous cisterns to provide plentiful water and stocking storehouses with extensive food supplies.

Herod's Temple Mount Meets the Fury of Rome

Among the many architectural marvels that Herod built in Jerusalem was the magnificent Royal Stoa, an expansive colonnaded basilica that extended across the southern end of the Temple Mount. The basilica included four long rows of towering Corinthian columns that created three majestic halls, the central one with an especially high roof. On the Temple Mount side, the stoa was unwalled, providing a view of the Temple itself in the center of the mount. The structure's grandeur was apparently so awe-inspiring that the Jewish historian Josephus thought the Royal Stoa "more worthy of description than any other under the sun."

When the Romans burned Jerusalem's Temple Mount in 70 C.E., marble architectural fragments from Herod's Royal Stoa fell to the street below. As reported by archaeologist Orit-Peleg Barkat and geologist Aryeh Shimron in the pages of *BAR* ("New Evidence of the Royal Stoa and Roman Flames," March/April 2010), hundreds of limestone fragments from the stoa, many beautifully preserved and decorated with floral and geometric motifs, were uncovered by Professor Benjamin Mazar during his excavations along the southern wall of the Temple Mount. These elegantly crafted architectural elements, which include column bases and drums, Corinthian capitals, Doric friezes, and modillion cornices, provide archaeological confirmation of the Royal Stoa's magnificence as described by Josephus.

But as Shimron explains, the recovered pieces from the Royal Stoa also help tell the story of Rome's destruction of the Temple Mount. Many of the marble fragments were covered with a fine white crust, originally thought to be a layer of decorative plaster. The crust, however, is not plaster, but rather the mineralogical residue left on the marble from an intense conflagration whose flames often exceeded a thousand degrees centigrade. –ED.

LOTS CAST BY MASADA'S DEFENDERS? THE FIRST-CENTURY C.E. Jewish historian Josephus tells us that three years after the Roman destruction of Jerusalem in 70 C.E., the remaining Jewish rebels, besieged at Masada, decided to commit suicide rather than succumb to the Roman army. With defeat just hours away, the Jewish commander Eleazar Ben Yair convinced his fighters to die with their families rather than become Roman slaves. By lot, the rebels selected ten men who would slay the rest of the community.

The late Israeli archaeologist Yigael Yadin, who excavated Masada in the 1960s, speculated that these sherds, each inscribed with a different name, were the very lots used by the defenders. The sherd at lower left bears the name "Ben Yair." However, some scholars question whether Ben Yair ever made such a speech and even whether a mass suicide occurred.

By 73, however, the Roman general Flavius Silva led the Tenth Legion into the Judean wilderness with the goal of eliminating the last vestige of insurrection. Soon after arriving at the base of the hill, the legionnaires constructed a wall—10 to 12 feet high and approximately 4,000 yards long—that surrounded Masada, cutting off all possibility of escape or reinforcement.[124] The legion's estimated 8,000 combat-hardened soldiers[125] plus auxiliaries arrayed themselves in eight separate camps, whose remains are still in evidence to modern visitors to the site. Using a low hill at the western base of the site as a starting point, the Romans ordered slaves to begin construction of an enormous ramp. Day by day the ramp progressed upward under a hail of missiles from the defenders above, until it reached the base of Masada's defensive wall. Then Roman engineers brought up siege engines to batter that wall down.

According to Josephus, when the legionnaires stormed through the gap in the wall, they discovered the defenders and their families (some 960 souls in all) lying dead. Josephus explains that as certain defeat by the Romans was at hand, the surviving insurgents (either Sicarii or Zealots, readers may take their choice) opted for suicide rather than capture. The men drew lots to determine who would kill whom until only one would remain. This last survivor took his own life.

Scholars have raised many questions about the credibility of Josephus's reporting of this episode. Some of these concerns are rather easily explained, others are more troubling. Moreover, the factual basis for the suicide story is mixed with political coloration—that is, were these terrorists or freedom fighters? This question is largely a matter of opinion, as throughout the history of insurrection one person's terrorist is as often as not another person's freedom fighter.

Scholars note that a mass suicide was a common theme in ancient history, and Josephus has used it elsewhere; moreover, when he writes of his own supposed shipwreck (another common theme), the story is wildly inflated (*Life* 15), as are many of his numerical facts. Unfortunately, archaeology has not (so far) been able to resolve the question. Where, for example, are the remains of 960 bodies? When the Romans left a garrison on Masada after its capture, they likely had either burned any bodies or taken them off the site. In the final analysis, Shaye Cohen offered probably the most realistic assessment of the story: Some of the defenders of Masada likely did take their own lives in preference to being captured by the Romans, and Josephus has dramatized that fact by turning it into a story that all the defenders did so.[126] Whatever the truth, the fall of Masada closed the final chapter on the era of Roman domination.

Retrospective

The causes of the war with Rome were many and varied: tension between rich and poor, city and country, and Jewish and gentile; religious speculation about the imminent end of time and a messianic redeemer; nationalist stirrings against a foreign ruler; resentment caused by incompetent and insensitive procurators.[127] Embedded in this list, and intensifying all the other factors, was the impetus for insurrection that Josephus worked hard to conceal—that is, the nature of the Judeans' religion itself. The beliefs and practices of the Judeans were both ancient and deeply rooted, and the concept of a *covenant* between a people and their creator was in many ways unique. Certain traditions, such as the profound holiness of the Temple and the requirement of absolute purity and probity of its priests, were deeply ingrained in the Jewish psyche. When these traditions were perceived to be violated, they inflamed resentment due to other causes so as to infect large segments of Judean society with an almost suicidal fervor.

It does not seem accidental that Josephus begins his account of the "Jewish War" with the Maccabean revolt some 250 years earlier, because the two episodes have much in common. The Maccabean uprising (chap. 7) was as much a civil conflict between Jews eager or at least willing to live according to Hellenistic cultural norms and those committed to preserving their traditional way of life. The Maccabees invoked the *zeal* of Phinehas in punishing those they viewed as apostates, just as the first-century self-identified Zealots took out their enmity on other Judeans who accepted or, worse, were perceived to be benefiting from Roman rule. The vanguard of the Maccabean forces were the priests and Levites of the countryside; the precipitating factor in the war with Rome was the cessation of sacrifices on behalf of the emperor, instigated by the junior priests and Levites, who then led the attack on the Twelfth Legion.

In many respects, it could be argued that the Romans brought this war upon themselves by violating their customary practice of governing vassal states through native dynasties. Herod was never accepted by large segments of the Jewish population. Neither he nor his successors, therefore, could function as a proper native dynasty. He repeatedly offended Jewish traditions, martyring those who protested and precipitating uprisings upon his death. His appointed high priests were from unfamiliar families, who offered Judeans neither the purity nor the probity that tradition demanded of their office. Moreover, these latter-day "Sadducees"—both under Herod and, later, under the Roman procurators—were obviously enriching themselves at the expense of the junior priests and Levites.

Rome compounded its error by converting Judea to a Roman province and subjecting Judeans to direct Roman control. The presence of Romans (with their forbidden icons and offensive behavior), especially in the precincts of the Temple, served to further inflame Jewish sensibilities. The Romans (if they could respond to this analysis) would likely argue that a proper local dynast (Antigonus) had disqualified himself by his alliance with the Parthians. However, compromise in the interest of stability goes both ways, as Augustus demonstrated when he retained Herod after the latter had backed Antony. By not making a similar compromise with respect to Antigonus, the Romans arguably set in motion a chain of events that were ultimately destructive to both sides.

Notes

1. The Ancestral Narratives

1 With two tweaks, though: First, Levi is not a proper tribe, but rather is distinguished for sacerdotal service. Second, Joseph subdivides into two tribes, Ephraim and Manasseh, based on the names of his two sons.

2 The listing of the three patriarchs as "Abraham, Isaac, and Jacob" occurs 20 times in the Bible, mostly in the Torah (Genesis 50:24 through Deuteronomy 34:4), with two additional passages in 2 Kings 13:23 and Jeremiah 33:26. See also Psalm 105:9–10. The listing of the three patriarchs as "Abraham, Isaac, and Israel" occurs in Exodus 32:13; 1 Kings 18:36; 1 Chronicles 29:18; and 2 Chronicles 30:6.

3 To quote the phrase used seven times in the Book of Qohelet (or Ecclesiastes): 1:14; 2:11; 2:17; 2:26; 4:4; 4:6; 6:9.

4 At this point in the narrative, the first patriarch is still called Abram. His name is changed to Abraham in Genesis 17:5 (see also Nehemiah 9:7). To avoid confusion, we use the latter name throughout this chapter, unless quoting a biblical passage in which the former name occurs.

5 The Hebrew word *'eber,* "beyond," may serve as the source of the word *'ibri,* "Hebrew," which thus would mean (in the plural) "those who came from beyond" (the River Euphrates), though various other etymologies have been proposed. The origins of the names of peoples and countries often are lost in the mists of time, as in the cases of France, España (Spain), Sverige (Sweden), etc. Even when we know the source, sometimes the connection is very tenuous: America—simply because the cartographer Martin Waldseemüller produced a world map, in 1507, on which he named the new continent using the Latin feminine form of Amerigo Vespucci's first name; Canada—from the St. Lawrence Iroquoian word *kanata,* "settlement," first recorded in a European language by Jacques Cartier in 1545; California—used by Spanish explorers due to the appearance of the name in a popular 16th-century novel for a distant island (which in turn probably is based on the word *caliph*).

6 This was commonly accepted in 19th-century biblical scholarship; see, for example, George Bush, *Notes Critical and Practical on the Book of Genesis* (New York: Gould, Newman & Saxton, 1839), 189, whose author is distantly related to the presidential family of the same name. For a lively discourse on the scholar's life, see Shalom Goldman, *God's Sacred Tongue: Hebrew and the American Imagination* (Chapel Hill: Univ. of North Carolina Press, 2004), 199–207, 314–15.

7 See Cyrus H. Gordon, "Abraham and the Merchants of Ura," *JNES* 17 (1958), 28–31; and Gordon, "Where Is Abraham's Ur?" *BAR,* June 1977, 20–21, 52.

8 The location of Harran in southern Turkey, just north of the Syrian border, is accepted by all. The city name is retained until the present day.

9 Even the Vatican erred when Pope John Paul II visited Ur in southern Iraq, believing it to be the birthplace of Abraham. See Hershel Shanks, "Abraham's Ur—Is the Pope Going to the Wrong Place?" *BAR,* March/April 2000, 62–63.

10 However, the identification was made earlier, beginning with Henry C. Rawlinson, "Biblical Geography," *The Athenaeum,* no. 1799 (April 19, 1862), 529–31.

11 The same is true also with any attempt to date the Slavery and the Exodus in the Book of Exodus 1–15; see further chap. 2.

12 Nahum M. Sarna, *Understanding Genesis* (New York: Schocken, 1966), 83–84.

13 See Gary A. Rendsburg, "The Internal Consistency and Historical Reliability of the Biblical Genealogies," *VT* 40 (1990), 185–206; and Rendsburg, "The Date of the Exodus and the Conquest/Settlement: The Case for the 1100s," *VT* 42 (1992), 510–27.

14 Based on the research of David P. Henige, *The Chronology of Oral Tradition: The Quest for a Chimera* (Oxford: Clarendon Press, 1974), 121–44, much of which is summarized in Henige, "Generation-counting and Late

New Kingdom Chronology," *JEA* 67 (1981), 182–84.

15 Other biblical lineages cohere with this overall picture; see Rendsburg, "The Internal Consistency" (see n. 13), 186–89 (esp. the summary chart and family trees on 189).

16 Nabonidus, Sippar Cylinder Inscription, col. 2, line 58, for which see Paul-Alain Beaulieu, "The Sippar Cylinder of Nabonidus," in *COS* 2: 312.

17 On reflections of modern Bedouin culture in the Bible, see Clinton Bailey, "How Desert Culture Helps Us Understand the Bible," *BR*, August 1991, 14–21, 38; and Bailey, *Bedouin Culture in the Bible* (New Haven: Yale Univ. Press, 2018), with genealogies discussed on 169–72.

18 See Jack M. Sasson, "About 'Mari and the Bible'," *RA* 92 (1998), 97–123; Daniel E. Fleming, "Mari and the Possibilities of Biblical Memory," *RA* 92 (1998), 41–78; and Abraham Malamat, *Mari and the Bible*, Studies in the History and Culture of the Ancient Near East, 12 (Leiden: Brill, 1998).

19 See Genesis 33:18–19, where Jacob purchases land from the local people of Shechem on which he pitched his tent (and presumably pastured his flocks).

20 King Arthur is similarly a historical figure for some and a purely legendary character for others. For the Welsh, he serves as a "symbol of national renewal and linguistic revival" (Geraint Evans, "Modernist Arthur: The Welsh Revival," in H. Fulton, ed., *A Companion to Arthurian Literature*, Blackwell Companions to Literature and Culture, 58 [Chichester: Blackwell, 2012], 447).

21 See Gary A. Rendsburg, *How the Bible Is Written* (Peabody, MA: Hendrickson, 2019), 568–92, for a literary analysis of the story of Jacob and Rachel meeting at the well and of their subsequent marriage as narrated in Genesis 29.

22 For detailed analyses of these two epics, with comparisons to the biblical material, see Simon B. Parker, *The Pre-Biblical Narrative Tradition*, SBL Resources for Biblical Study, 24 (Atlanta: Scholars Press, 1989).

23 See Gary A. Rendsburg, "Unlikely Heroes: Women as Israel," *BR*, February 2003, 16, 18–21, 23, 52–53.

24 These interconnections and many others were posited more than 60 years ago by Cyrus H. Gordon, in his path-breaking article "Homer and Bible: The Origin and Character of East Mediterranean Literature," *Hebrew Union College Annual* 26 (1955), 43–108; reprinted by Ventnor Publishers in 1967. See also Gordon, *The Common Background of Greek and Hebrew Civilizations* (New York: W. W. Norton, 1965).

25 See Martha T. Roth, *Law Collections from Mesopotamia and Asia Minor*, Writings from the Ancient World, 6 (Atlanta: Scholars Press, 1995).

26 For general introduction and a sampling of documents, see Maynard P. Maidman, *Nuzi Texts and Their Uses as Historical Evidence*, Writings from the Ancient World, 18 (Atlanta: SBL, 2010).

27 The official designation of this text is HSS V 67 = Edward Chiera, *Texts of Varied Contents*, Harvard Semitic Studies, 5 = Excavations at Nuzi, 1 (Cambridge, MA: Harvard Univ. Press, 1931), text no. 67 (plates lxi–lxiii). For a complete transcription and translation, see E. A. Speiser, "New Kirkuk Documents Relating to Family Law," Annual of the American Schools of Oriental Research 10 (1928–1929), 31–33. See also Theophile J. Meek, "Mesopotamian Legal Documents," in *ANET*, 220.

28 Though there may be a difference in the two systems: in the Nuzi legal custom, the adopted son is reduced to second position, so that he still would inherit something; while Genesis 15:4 implies that Eliezer would inherit naught.

29 See Jonathan Paradise, "Marriage Contracts of Free Persons at Nuzi," *JCS* 39 (1987), 28–29.

30 All things being equal, if a couple was unable to produce a child, the ancients assumed that the problem lay with the woman; hence her responsibility to act in order to ensure the continuation of the family lineage. The term "Lullu" derives from the term "Lullubi," a mountainous area to the east of Nuzi, in the general vicinity of modern-day northeastern Iraq / northwestern Iran. Apparently, women from this region were used as servants, hence the origin of the term.

31 For some potential parallels, see John Van Seters, "The Problem of Childlessness in Near Eastern Law and the Patriarchs of Israel," *JBL* 87.4 (1968), 401–408, though to my mind the Nuzi document HSS V 67 remains the most informative vis-à-vis Genesis 15–16.

32 For a general survey, see Barry L. Eichler, "Nuzi and the Bible: A Retrospective," in H. Behrens, D. Loding, and M.T. Roth, eds., *Dumu-e2-dub-ba-a: Studies in Honor of Åke W. Sjöberg* (Philadelphia: Samuel Noah Kramer Fund, University Museum, 1989), 107–19. See also M.J. Selman, "Comparative Customs and the Patriarchal Age," in A.R. Millard and D.J. Wiseman, eds., *Essays on the Patriarchal Narratives* (Leicester: Inter-Varsity Press, 1980 / Winona Lake, IN: Eisenbrauns, 1983), 91–139. As both authors note, in the early years of Nuzi studies (1920s and 1930s),

major scholars of the documents, such as E. A. Speiser and Cyrus H. Gordon, were wont to see numerous parallels with the Genesis narratives. Scholars are less inclined to do so today, but the relevance of HSS V 67 to the Book of Genesis has stood the test of time.

33 For further discussion, see Edward L. Greenstein, "The Formation of the Biblical Narrative Corpus," *AJS Review* 15.2 (1990), 151–78, esp. 165–67.

34 For a more developed statement, see Rendsburg, *How the Bible Is Written* (see n. 21), 443–67.

35 The approach taken here views the ancestral narratives as a unified literary construct. Most scholars subdivide the Book of Genesis into three separate sources: Yahwist (J), Elohist (E), and Priestly (P), of varying dates, though J is typically dated to the tenth century B.C.E. (see the Learn More box).

2. Egypt and the Exodus

1 Much of what we present herein is based on our earlier treatments: Manfred Bietak, "On the Historicity of the Exodus: What Egyptology Today Can Contribute to Assessing the Sojourn in Egypt," in Thomas E. Levy, Thomas Schneider, and William H.C. Propp, eds., *Israel's Exodus in Transdisciplinary Perspective: Text, Archaeology, Culture, and Geoscience* (Cham: Springer, 2015), 17–36; and Gary A. Rendsburg, "The Early History of Israel," in Gordon D. Young, Mark W. Chavalas, and Richard E. Averbeck, eds., *Crossing Boundaries and Linking Horizons: Studies in Honor of Michael C. Astour on His 80th Birthday* (Bethesda, MD: CDL Press, 1997), 433–53.

2 See in general Donald B. Redford, *Egypt, Canaan, and Israel in Ancient Times* (Princeton: Princeton Univ. Press, 1992). This book contains much valuable information on the interconnections between Egypt and Canaan, but the present authors part company with Redford on issues relating to the Exodus and associated topics discussed in the present chapter. See also Thomas Schneider, "Foreigners in Egypt: Archaeological Evidence and Cultural Context," in Willeke Wendrich, ed., *Egyptian Archaeology*, Blackwell Studies in Global Archaeology (Oxford: Blackwell, 2010), 143–63; and Anna-Latifa Mourad, *The*

Rise of the Hyksos: Egypt and the Levant from the Middle Kingdom to the Early Second Intermediate Period (Oxford: Archaeopress, 2015).

3 Percy E. Newberry, *Beni Hasan*, Part I, Archaeological Survey of Egypt 1 (London: Egypt Exploration Fund, 1893), 69, pl. XXX. See more recently: Susan Cohen, "Interpretative Uses and Abuses of the Beni Hasan Tomb Painting," *JNES* 74 (2015), 19–38, esp. 36; Janice Kamrin, *The Cosmos of Khnumhotep II at Beni Hasan* (London: Kegan Paul, 1999 / London: Routledge, 2016), 93–96; and Mourad, *Rise of the Hyksos* (see n. 2), 86–90.

4 See also the meaning "lineage, ancestor(s)," etc., in Ugaritic, Safaitic, etc. For the Egyptian evidence, see Adolf Erman, *Wörterbuch der Aegyptischen Sprache*, vol. 1 (Berlin: Akademie-Verlag, 1926), 167. For a discussion on the problematics of this term, see Thomas Schneider, *Ausländer in Ägypten während des Mittleren Reiches und der Hyksoszeit*, Teil 2: *Die Ausländische Bevölkerung*, Ägypten und Altes Testament 42 (Wiesbaden: Harrassowitz, 2003), 5–7; and Mourad, *Rise of the Hyksos* (see n. 2), 14 nn. 14–15.

5 See the classic treatment by J. M. A. Janssen, "On the Ideal Lifetime of the Egyptians,"

Oudheidkundige Mededelingenesis uit het Rijksmuseum van Oudheden 31 (1950), 33–43.

6 Though we also should note that Joseph's father, Jacob/Israel, was similarly embalmed/mummified (Genesis 50:2).

7 Throughout this chapter, we have used the ancient Egyptian chronology reconstructed by Thomas Schneider, "Contributions to the Chronology of the New Kingdom and the Third Intermediate Period," *Egypt and the Levant* 20 (2010), 373–409. To keep matters simple, we have dispensed with the "circa" (c.) that would be required before each date.

8 For the Egyptian text, see Alan H. Gardiner, *Late Egyptian Miscellanies* (Brussels: Fondation égyptologique Reine Élisabeth, 1937), 76–77. For standard translations, see Ricardo A. Caminos, *Late-Egyptian Miscellanies* (London: Oxford Univ. Press, 1954), 293; and John A. Wilson, "The Report of a Frontier Official," in *ANET*, 259.

9 For literature on the Shasu Bedouin, see Raphael Giveon, *Les bédouins Shosou des documents égyptiens,* Documenta et Monumenta Orientis Antiqui 18 (Leiden: Brill, 1971), 131–34; Manfred Weipert, "Semitische Nomaden des zweiten Jahrtausends: Über die Šꜣśw der ägyptischen Quellen," *Biblica* 55 (1974), 265–80; William A. Ward, "The Shasu 'Bedouin', Notes on a Recent Publication," *Journal of Economic and Social History of the Orient* 15 (1972), 35–60; and Shmuel Aḥituv, "Nodedim ba-Negev bi-Mqorot Miṣrayim" [Nomads in the Desert in Egyptian Sources], in Robert Chazan, William W. Hallo, and Lawrence H. Schiffman, eds., *Ki Baruch Hu: Ancient Near Eastern, Biblical, and Judaic Studies in Honor of Baruch A. Levine* (Winona Lake, IN: Eisenbrauns, 1999), 21*–27*.

10 See James E. Hoch, *Semitic Words in Egyptian Texts of the New Kingdom and Third Intermediate Period* (Princeton: Princeton Univ. Press, 1994), 106–107.

11 Hoch, *Semitic Words* (see n. 10), 270–71. As Hoch observes, in this instance the phonetic correspondence is atypical, but the lexical correspondence seems secure. The word shows two very fitting classifiers: wall and building .

12 Gardiner, *Miscellanies* (see n. 8), 35; and Caminos, *Miscellanies* (see n. 8), 126, 128.

13 Sarah I. Groll, "The Egyptian Background of the Exodus and the Crossing of the Reed Sea: A New Reading of Papyrus Anastasi VIII," in Irene Shirun-Grumach, ed., *Jerusalem Studies in Egyptology*, Ägypten und Altes Testament 40 (Wiesbaden: Harrassowitz, 1998), 190. The word has a more complicated history, though. First it was borrowed from Semitic *gašm*, "rain, storm," into Egyptian (for which see Hoch, *Semitic Words* [see n. 10], 354); it then became the name of the region; and then the term (re-)entered Hebrew as *gošen* (though see the Greek form in the Septuagint that retained the final /m/, thus Γεσεμ (Gesem). For the paleolake in the Wadi Tumilat, see Manfred Bietak, *Tell el-Dab'a II* (Vienna: Österreichische Akademie der Wissenschaften, 1975), 88–90, plan 4.

14 Bietak, "Historicity of the Exodus" (see n. 1), 22–23.

15 For discussion, see James K. Hoffmeier, *Ancient Israel in Sinai* (Oxford: Oxford Univ. Press, 2005), 242–43. See also chap. 3 herein. The identification of *śa-ʿ-r-ir* with Seʿir is not accepted by everybody: see Michael C. Astour, "Yahweh in Egyptian Topographic Lists," in Manfred Görg and Edgar Pusch, eds., *Festschrift Elmar Edel 12. März 1979*, Ägypten und Altes Testament 1 (Bamberg: [n. publ.], 1979), 17–34; and Faried Adrom and Matthias Müller, "The Tetragrammaton in Egyptian Sources – Facts and Fiction," in Jürgen van Oorschot and Markus Witte, eds., *The Origins of Yahwism*, BZAW 484 (Berlin: De Gruyter, 2017), 93–113.

16 If the former option is followed, then the form "Yahweh" most likely derives from the Semitic verbal root *h-y-h* / *h-w-h*, "to be, exist," and the divine name means either simply "He is" or "He exists," or with the derived meaning "He causes things to be" or "He causes things to exist." If the latter option is followed, the meaning of "Yahweh" as a place name would be lost in the mists of time, though once adopted as a divine name, the devotees of the deity, that is, the Israelites, came to etymologize and understand the form per the above, as "He is," "He exists," etc. On the overlap between the names of deities and places, we may note Athena goddess of Athens; the Celtic goddess Arduinna, associated with the Ardennes Forest (modern-day Belgium); or Bethel, the city in Canaan, which morphs into

a deity in Hebrew, Phoenician, and Aramaic texts (see, e.g., Jeremiah 48:13).

17 Modern parallels abound: Americans may not be able to distinguish between Dutch and (Flemish-speaking) Belgians, French and (French-speaking) Belgians, Czechs and Slovaks, Germans (esp. Bavarians) and Austrians, and so on; while Europeans may not be able to distinguish between Aussies and Kiwis, Americans and Canadians (Québécois excepted), and so on. Consider, e.g., how Hercule Poirot would be miffed when referred to as French, rather than Belgian.

18 See Eric H. Cline, *1177 B.C.: The Year Civilization Collapsed* (Princeton: Princeton Univ. Press, 2014), 142–47.

19 The two texts are discussed by Itamar Singer, "A Political History of Ugarit," in W. G. E. Watson and n. Wyatt, eds., *Handbook of Ugaritic Studies*, Handbuch der Orientalistik 39 (Leiden: Brill, 1999), 715. See also Harry Hoffner, *Letters from the Hittite Kingdom*, ed. Gary M. Beckman, SBL WAW 15 (Atlanta: SBL, 2009), 281–83.

20 Colleen Manassa, *The Great Karnak Inscription of Merneptah* (New Haven: Yale Egyptological Seminar, 2003), 34, 100–101 (for the hieroglyphic transcription, see Plate 6, line 24); and Kenneth A. Kitchen, *Rameside Inscriptions, Translated and Annotated*, vol. IV, *Merenptah and the Late Nineteenth Dynasty* (Oxford: Blackwell, 2003), 5.

21 Dafna Langgut, Israel Finkelstein, and Thomas Litt, "Climate and the Late Bronze Collapse: New Evidence from the Southern Levant," *TA* 40 (2013), 149–75.

22 See Aidan M. Dodson, "Fade to Grey: The Chancellor Bay, *Éminence Grise* of the Late Nineteenth Dynasty," in Mark Collier and Steven S. Snape, eds., *Ramesside Studies in Honour of K. A. Kitchen* (Bolton, BC: Rutherford Press, 2011), 145–58.

23 Pierre Grandet, "L'exécution du chancelier Bay: O. IFAO 1864," *Bulletin de l'Institut français d'archéologie orientale* 100 (2000), 339–56.

24 See Ernst Axel Knauf and Philippe Guillaume, *A History of Biblical Israel: The Fate of the Tribes and Kingdoms from Merenptah to Bar Kochba* (Sheffield: Equinox, 2016), 36. For a detailed study, see Israel Knohl, "Joseph and the Famine: The Story's Origins in Egyptian

History," online at https://www.thetorah.com/article/joseph-and-the-famine-the-storys-origins-in-egyptian-history (2019). Knohl further speculates that the name Bay, which he reads as Baya, means "in Yah," that is, the name of Yahweh in shortened form.

25 See Abd el-Mohsen Bakir, *Slavery in Pharaonic Egypt*, Supplement des Annales du Service des Antiquités de l'Égypte 18 (Cairo: Institut français d'archéologie orientale, 1952); Shafik Allam, "Slaves," in Donald B. Redford, ed., *The Oxford Encyclopedia of Ancient Egypt* (Oxford: Oxford Univ. Press, 2001), vol. 3, 293–96; and Antonio Loprieno, "Slavery and Servitude," in Elisabeth Frood and Willeke Wendrich, eds., *UCLA Encyclopedia of Egyptology* (Los Angeles: UCLA, 2012), online at: https://uee.cdh.ucla.edu/articles/slavery_and_servitude.

26 D.J.A. Clines, ed., The *Dictionary of Classical Hebrew*, 6.215–25.

27 See, in general, Ann Macy Roth, "Work Force," in *Oxford Encyclopedia* (see n. 25), vol. 3, 519–24; and Loprieno, "Slavery and Servitude" (see n. 25).

28 Note that in Late Egyptian, in use during the New Kingdom, final /r/ sounds often were dropped. Hence, the identification of Egyptian Per-Atum with Hebrew *pitom* (Pithom) is secure. For the phonology, see Antonio Loprieno, *Ancient Egyptian: A Linguistic Introduction* (Cambridge: Cambridge Univ. Press, 1995), 38.

29 Though the Israelites also engaged in field work (see Exodus 1:14), presumably with reference to agricultural labor.

30 Some studies located Pithom at Tell el-Maskhuta, but this identification no longer is tenable. See Donald B. Redford, "Pithom," in Wolfgang Helck and Wolfhart Westendorf, eds., *Lexikon der Ägyptologie* (Wiesbaden: Harrassowitz, 1982), cols. 1054–58; and John S. Holladay, "Pithom," in *Oxford Encyclopedia* (see n. 25), vol. 3, 50–53.

31 Alan H. Gardiner, "The Delta Residence of the Ramessides," *JEA* 5 (1918), 267–69; Henri Cazelles and Jean Leclant, "Pithom", in Louis Pirot, et al., ed., *Supplément au Dictionnaire de la Bible*, vol. VIII, fasc. 42 (Paris: Letouzey / Ané, 1967), cols. 1–6; Kenneth A. Kitchen, *On the Reliability of the Old Testament* (Grand Rapids: Eerdmans, 2003), 256–59, 555; Manfred Bietak, "Review of John S. Holladay,

Cities of the Delta III, Tell el-Maskhuta," *Bibliotheca Orientalis* 41 (1984), cols. 619–22; James K. Hoffmeier, *Israel in Egypt* (New York: Oxford Univ. Press, 1996), 119–21; and Bietak, "Historicity of the Exodus" (see n. 1), 26.

32 Note that while the Bible calls the latter city simply Raʾamses, its fuller name in Egyptian is Pi-Ramesse (or Per-Ramesse), i.e., "the house of Ramesses."

33 Tell ed-Dabʿa, 1 mile south of Qantir, is the location of Avaris, the Hyksos capital during the Second Intermediate Period, and constitutes the southern part of Pi-Ramesse. See Labib Habachi, "Khataʿna-Qantir: Importance," *Annales du Service des Antiquités de l'Égypte* 52 (1954), 443–559; Habachi, *Tell el-Dabʿa I: Tell el-Dabʿa and Qantir: The Site and its Connection with Avaris and Piramesse*, ed. Eva-Maria Engel et al. (Vienna: Österreichische Akademie der Wissenschaften, 2001), 69–75; and John van Seters, *The Hyksos: A New Investigation* (New Haven: Yale Univ. Press 1966). For the firmest evidence, based on the more recent excavations of the site, see Manfred Bietak, *Tell el-Dabʿa II* (Vienna: Österreichische Akademie der Wissenschaften, 1975); Bietak, *Avaris and Piramesse: Archaeological Exploration in the Eastern Nile Delta*, Ninth Mortimer Wheeler Archaeological Lecture (Oxford: Oxford Univ. Press, 1981); and Manfred Bietak and Edgar B. Pusch, "Piramesse/Qantir," in Roger S. Bagnall, ed., *The Encyclopedia of Ancient History* (New York: Oxford Univ. Press, 2013), vol. 9, 5333–36.

34 For another evocation of Tanis in the Bible, see Numbers 13:22. Incidentally, just as Pi-Ramesse "moved" from Qantir to Tanis, so did Per-Atum (Pithom)—from Tell er-Retaba to Tell el-Maskhuta (see nn. 30–31), which is to say, the Temple to Atum was relocated from the former to the latter sometime during the late Saite period (second part of the 26th Dynasty / c. 600–525 B.C.E.) or afterward.

35 In general, see K. A. Kitchen, "From the Brickfields of Egypt," *TynB* 27 (1976), 137–47.

36 For the text, see Gardiner, *Miscellanies* (see n. 8), 30–31. For the translation, see Caminos, *Miscellanies* (see n. 8), 105–106.

37 For the text, see Gardiner, *Miscellanies* (see n. 8), 48–49, 57. For the translation, see Caminos, *Miscellanies* (see n. 8), 188–89, 225.

38 Ellen F. Morris, *The Architecture of Imperialism: Military Bases and the Evolution of Foreign Policy in Egypt's New Kingdom*, Probleme der Ägyptologie 22 (Leiden: Brill, 2005), 740–42. On the former, see also Jozef Hudec et al., "Formation of an Empire: Results of the Season 2017 in Tell el-Retaba; Part 3: Defensive Constructions of the Nineteenth and Twentieth Dynasties—Phases E, D4 and D3," *Egypt and the Levant* 29 (2019), 40–49. Note that the fortress at Kom Qulzoum, while smaller, has exceptionally thick walls. Other such fortresses in the Isthmus of Suez may await discovery and/or may have been destroyed during the construction of the Suez Canal during the 19th century.

39 Kitchen, "From the Brickfields of Egypt" (see n. 35), 141–42.

40 For the text, see Gardiner, *Miscellanies* (see n. 8), 134. For the translation, see Caminos, *Miscellanies* (see n. 8), 91.

41 For secondary literature, see John A. Wilson, "The ʿEperu of the Egyptian Inscriptions," *American Journal of Semetic Languages* 49 (1933), 275–80; Moshe Greenberg, *The Ḫab/piru*, American Oriental Series 39 (New Haven: American Oriental Society, 1955); Rafael Giveon, "Hapiru," in Wolfgang Helck and Wolfhart Westendorf, eds., *Lexikon der Ägyptologie*, vol. II (Wiesbaden: Harrassowitz, 1977), col. 952–55; Oswald Loretz: *Habiru-Hebräer: Eine sozio-linguistische Studie über die Herkunft des Gentiliziums ʿibrî vom Appellativum Ḫabiru* (Berlin: Walter de Gruyter, 1984); Nadav Naʾaman, "Ḫabiru and Hebrews: The Transfer of a Social Term to the Literary Sphere," *JNES* 45 (1986), 271–88; and Anson F. Rainey, "Shasu or Habiru: Who Were the Early Israelites?" *BAR*, November/December 2008, 51–55.

42 Rainey, "Shasu or Habiru" (see n. 41), 51–55.

43 See further David A. Falk, "Brick by Brick: What Did the Israelites Build in Egypt?" *BAR*, Spring 2020, 54–57.

44 Uvo Hölscher, *The Excavation of Medinet Habu*, vol. 2: *The Temples of the Eighteenth Dynasty*, Oriental Institute Publications 41 (Chicago: Univ. of Chicago Press, 1939), 68–72, fig. 59.

45 Manfred Bietak, "An Iron Age Four Room House in Ramesside Egypt," *Eretz-Israel*

(Avraham Biran Volume) 23 (1991), 10*-12*; and Bietak, "Historicity of the Exodus" (see n. 1), 18-20.

46 The literature is vast; see especially the following: Israel Finkelstein, *The Archaeology of the Israelite Settlement* (Jerusalem: IES, 1988), 236-59; Ehud Netzer, "Domestic Architecture in the Iron Age," in Aharon Kempinski and Ronny Reich, eds., *The Architecture of Ancient Israel, From the Prehistoric to the Persian Period* (Jerusalem: IES, 1992), 193-201; John S. Holladay, "Four-Room House," in Eric M. Meyers, ed., *The Oxford Encyclopedia of the Archaeology in the Near East* (Oxford: Oxford Univ. Press, 1997), 337-42; Shlomo Bunimovitz and Avraham Faust, "Ideology in Stone: Understanding the Four-Room House," *BAR*, July/August 2002, 32-41, 59-60; Bunimovitz and Faust, "Building Identity: The Four Room House and the Israelite Mind," in W. G. Dever and S. Gitin, eds., *Symbiosis, Symbolism, and the Power of the Past: Canaan, Ancient Israel, and Their Neighbors from the Late Bronze Age Through Roman Palaestina* (Winona Lake, IN: Eisenbrauns, 2003), 411-23; and Faust, *Israel's Ethnogenesis* (London: Equinox, 2006), 71-84. See also chap. 3 herein.

47 Translation based on John A. Wilson, "From the Lists of Ramses III," in *ANET*, 262. For the hieroglyphic transcription, see Wolja Erichsen, *Papyrus Harris I, Hieroglyphische Transkription*, Bibliotheca Aegyptiaca V (Brussels: Fondation égyptologique Reine Élisabeth, 1933), 93; and Pierre Grandet, *Le papyrus Harris I*, Bibliothèque d'Étude 109/i-ii (Cairo: IFAO, 1994), 202-207.

Point of general interest: P.Harris I is the longest Egyptian papyrus roll ever found, measuring 41 meters. It was purchased in Egypt by Anthony Charles Harris (1790-1869) in 1855 and then sold by his daughter to the British Museum in 1872 (along with other documents).

48 The Egyptian scribe uses the Semitic word for tents here, namely *ihr*, which corresponds to the Hebrew *'ohel*, for which see Hoch, *Semitic Words* (see n. 10), 31.

49 See conveniently the map in Faust, *Israel's Ethnogenesis* (see n. 46), 76.

50 A surface reading of Genesis 47 may suggest that Goshen and the "land of Ra'amses" are one and the same location—and many commentaries on the Book of Genesis state this explicitly. However, based on our ever-increasing knowledge of the eastern Delta and the Wadi Tumilat, the two should be distinguished, as indicated here.

51 On this aspect of the Exodus account, see Ronald Hendel, "The Exodus in Biblical Memory," *JBL* 120 (2001), 601-22; and Ronald Hendel, "The Exodus as Cultural Memory: Egyptian Bondage and the Song of the Sea," in *Israel's Exodus* (see n. 1), 65-77.

52 On the dating of biblical texts, see in general Ronald Hendel and Jan Joosten, *How Old Is the Hebrew Bible?* (New Haven: Yale Univ. Press, 2019). For Archaic Biblical Hebrew specifically, with attention to Exodus 15 and Judges 5, see the early study by David A. Robertson, *Linguistic Evidence in Dating Early Hebrew Poetry* (Missoula, MT: SBL, 1972). For a more recent concise survey, see Alice Mandell, "Biblical Hebrew, Archaic," in Geoffrey Khan, ed., *Encyclopedia of Hebrew Language and Linguistics* (Leiden: Brill, 2013), vol. 1, 314-18. For further insights into the antiquity of Judges 5, see Hendel and Joosten, *How Old Is the Hebrew Bible?* 101-104.

53 W. M. Flinders Petrie, *Six Temples at Thebes, 1896* (London: Bernard Quaritch, 1897), with the mention of Israel, in the translation of the stele by Wilhelm Spiegelberg, on p. 28.

54 Translation after Kitchen, *Ramesside Inscriptions*, vol. IV (see n. 20), 15, lines 19:2-10.

55 The Egyptian scribe here uses the Semitic word *shalom*, "peace," for which see Hoch, *Semitic Words* (see n. 10), 285-86.

56 Shmuel Ahituv, *Canaanite Toponyms in Ancient Egyptian Documents* (Jerusalem: Magnes / Leiden: Brill, 1984), 198-200.

57 For discussion, see Robert A. Mullins, "The Emergence of Israel in Retrospect," in *Israel's Exodus* (see n. 1), 523-24. For a more wide-ranging discussion, see Anson F. Rainey, "Israel in Merenptah's Inscription and Reliefs," *IEJ* 51 (2001), 57-75.

58 For the original publication, see Alan H. Gardiner, *Egyptian Hieratic Texts* (Leipzig: J. C. Hinrichs, 1911), 25*. For translations, see John A. Wilson, "A Satirical Letter," in *ANET*, 477; Edward F. Wente, *Letters from Ancient Egypt*, ed. Edmund S. Meltzer, SBL WAW 1 (Atlanta: Scholars Press, 1990), 108; and James

P. Allen, "The Craft of the Scribe," in *COS*, vol. 3, 13. We hasten to add here: not that all Shasu are Israelites, nor are all Israelites to be classified as Shasu—but as we suggest above, concerning the Shasu of Edom in P.Anastasi VI, possibly here in P.Anastasi I the Shasu in the area may be (proto)-Israelites.

59 For bibliography on this text, see n.58. There are numerous alternative interpretations of *Isr* in this passage, for which see Hans-Werner Fischer-Elfert, *Die satirische Streitschrift des Papyrus Anastasi I: Übersetzung und Kommentar*, Ägyptologische Abhandlungen 44 (Wiesbaden: Harrassowitz, 1986), 199–200. See also Aḥituv, *Canaanite Toponms* (see n.56), 73. To our mind, though, the connection between *Isr* and Asher remains secure; such is also implied by Rainey, "Israel in Merenptah's Inscription and Reliefs" (see n.57), 75. For an extensive discussion, including possible other mentions of *Isr* in Egyptian texts, see Alan H. Gardiner, *Ancient Egyptian Onomastica* (Oxford: Oxford Univ. Press, 1947), vol. 1, 191*–193*. See further chap. 3 herein.

60 To this day, the Galilee is populated by Bedouin Arabs. Although they live in small villages, they retain their Bedouin ways and Bedouin identity.

61 Finkelstein, *Archaeology of the Israelite Settlement* (see n.46), 336–41; and Erez Ben-Yosef, "The Architectural Bias in Current Biblical Archaeology," *VT* 69 (2019), 361–387.

62 Zeev Herzog, "The Beer-Sheba Valley: From Nomadism to Monarchy," in Israel Finkelstein and Nadav Na'man, eds., *From Nomadism to Monarchy: Archaeological and Historical Aspects of Early Israel* (Jerusalem: IES, 1994), 146–49. Herzog points out that the material culture may allow us to identify more different population groups involved than just the Canaanites: Israelites, Amalekites, Kenites, Calebites, and others.

63 Gary A. Rendsburg, "Moses as Equal to Pharaoh," in Gary M. Beckman and Theodore J. Lewis, eds., *Text, Artifact, and Image: Revealing Ancient Israelite Religion*, Brown Judaic Studies 346 (Providence: Brown Judaic Studies, 2006), 201–19; and Rendsburg, "Moses the Magician," in *Israel's Exodus* (see n.1), 243–58. For yet another (potential) indication of how conversant the Israelites were with Egyptian culture and religion, note the

copy of the Book of the Dead, dated to the 19th Dynasty, owned by one Adoni-ro'eh-yah ("My Lord is the shepherd of Yah," where Yah is the shortened form of the name of the God of Israel)—at least according to the reading and interpretation in Thomas Schneider, "The First Documented Occurrence of the God Yahweh? (Book of the Dead Princeton 'Roll 5')," *JANER* 7 (2008), 113–20.

64 See further Gary A. Rendsburg, "Reading the Plagues in Their Ancient Egyptian Context" (2015), at https://www.thetorah.com/article/reading-the-plagues-in-their-ancient-egyptian-context; and Rendsburg, "YHWH's War Against the Egyptian Sun-God Ra" (2016), at: https://www.thetorah.com/article/yhwhs-war-against-the-egyptian-sun-god-ra.

65 *CAT* 1.14 col. III, line 55–col. IV, line 18. For the Ugaritic text and an English translation, see Edward L. Greenstein, "Kirta," in Simon B. Parker, ed., *Ugaritic Narrative Poetry*, SBL WAW 9 (n.p.: Scholars Press, 1997), 18–19. There are many more parallels to the larger Exodus narrative and the Epic of Kirta, for which see Cyrus H. Gordon, "Notes on the Legend of Keret," *JNES* (1952), 212–13; Gregorio del Olmo Lete, "La conquista de Jericó y la leyenda ugaritica de KRT," *Sefarad* 25 (1965), 1–15; and Gary A. Rendsburg, "The Epic Tradition in Ancient Israel—and What Happened to It?" in Isaac Kalimi, ed., *Writing and Rewriting History in Ancient Israel and Near Eastern Cultures* (Wiesbaden: Harrassowitz, 2020), 17–30, esp. 19–21.

For a study which places the Moses narrative into an even larger cultural context, see Edward L. Greenstein, "The Fugitive Hero Narrative Pattern in Mesopotamia," in John J. Collins, T. M. Lemos, and Saul M. Olyan, eds., *Worship, Women, and War: Essays in Honor of Susan Niditch*, Brown Judaic Studies (Providence: Brown Univ., 2015), 17–35.

66 For something very specific, albeit with a separate geography and a separate chronology from our present concern, see Manfred Bietak, "Gedanken zur Ursache der ägyptisierenden Einflüsse in Nordsyrien in der Zweiten Zwischenzeit," in Heike Guksch and Daniel Polz, eds., *Stationen: Beiträge zur Kulturgeschichte Ägyptens Rainer Stadelmann gewidmet* (Mainz: Philip von Zabern, 1998), 165–76.

67 Translation based on John A. Wilson, "The Pursuit of Runaway Slaves," in *ANET*, 259.

68 The word appears not only in P.Anastasi V 20.2 but also elsewhere in Egyptian texts; see further Hoch, *Semitic Words* (see n. 10), 169–70.

69 James K. Hoffmeier, "The Search for Migdol of the New Kingdom and Exodus 14:2: An Update," *Buried History* 44 (2008), 3–12.

70 For reasons still largely unknown, almost 2,300 years ago the Jews of Alexandria rendered this term into Greek as *erythra thalassa*, "Red Sea" (thus the Septuagint, c. 250 B.C.E.), from which the sense passed into Latin as *mare rubrum*, "Red Sea" (thus the Vulgate, c. 400 C.E.). These renderings yielded English "Red Sea" in older English translations, a tradition which persisted into the 20th century, until scholars realized that the Hebrew term *yam suf* really means "Sea of Reeds." The picture is actually more complicated, since in other passages (e.g., 1 Kings 9:26), the term *yam suf* is used to refer to the Gulf of Eilat/Aqaba, one of the northern arms of the Red Sea.

71 P.Sallier I 4.9; P.Anastasi III 2.11–12; P.Anastasi IV 15.6 (written without the definite article pꜣ); P.Anastasi VIII recto 3.4; etc.

72 For the localization and geographical position, see Bietak, *Tell el-Dabʿa II* (see n. 33), 117–21 (fig. 23); 136–37, 139, 221 (fig. 45); Manfred Bietak, "Comments on the 'Exodus'," in *Egypt, Israel, Sinai: Archaeological and Historical Relationships in the Biblical Period* (Tel-Aviv: Tel-Aviv Univ. Press, 1987), 163–71, esp. 167; Sarah Israelit-Groll, "pꜣ-ṯwf," in Eliezer D. Oren and Shmuel Aḥituv, eds., *Aharon Kempinski Memorial Volume: Studies in Archaeology and Related Disciplines* (Beer-sheva: Ben-Gurion Univ. Press, 2002) = *Beer-sheva* 15 (2002), 138–42, esp. 139; Hoffmeier, *Israel in Egypt* (see n. 31), 199–222; Hoffmeier, *Ancient Israel in Sinai* (see n. 15), 75–109; James K. Hoffmeier and Stephen O. Moshier, "New Paleo-Environmental Evidence from North Sinai to Complement Manfred Bietak's Map of the Eastern Delta and Some Historical Implications," in Ernst Czerny et al., *Timelines: Studies in Honour of Manfred Bietak*, Orientalia Lovaniensia Analecta 149 (Leuven: Peeters, 2006), vol. 2, 167–76; and Bietak, "Historicity of the Exodus" (see n. 1), 27–29, esp. figs. 2.3–4.

73 See Rendsburg, "Moses the Magician" (see n. 63), 251–52.

74 Translation of Miriam Lichtheim, *Ancient Egyptian Literature*, vol. 3 (Berkeley: Univ. of California Press, 1980), 130.

75 See Verena M. Lepper, *Untersuchungen zu pWestcar: Eine philologische und literaturwissenschaftliche (Neu-) Analyse*, Ägyptologische Abhandlungen 70 (Wiesbaden: Harrassowitz, 2008).

76 Translation of Miriam Lichtheim, *Ancient Egyptian Literature*, vol. 1 (Berkeley: Univ. of California Press, 1973), 217.

77 See further Rendsburg, "Moses the Magician" (see n. 63), 252–53. See also F. Ll. Griffith, "Herodotus II, 90: Apotheosis by Drowning," *Zeitschrift für Ägyptische Sprache und Altertumskunde* 46 (1909–1910), 132–34.

78 Translation by A. D. Godley, *Herodotus: The Persian Wars*, vol. 1, Loeb Classical Library 117 (London: William Heinemann, 1921), 375.

79 For a survey, see James M. Weinstein, "Egypt and the Levant in the Reign of Ramesses III," in Eric H. Cline and David O'Connor, eds., *Ramesses III: The Life and Times of Egypt's Last Hero* (Ann Arbor: Univ. of Michigan Press, 2012), 164–71. See also James M. Weinstein, "The Egyptian Empire in Palestine: A Reassessment," *BASOR* (1981), 1–28. Even with new data from new excavations during the last 40 years, the picture described by Weinstein remains more or less valid. See recently Nadav Naʾaman, "Egyptian Centres and the Distribution of the Alphabet in the Levant," *TA* 47.1 (2020), 29–54.

80 Beno Rothenberg, ed., *Researches in the Arabah 1959–1984*, vol. 1: *The Egyptian Mining Temple at Timna* (London: Institute for Archaeo-Metallurgical Studies, 1988), 270–78.

81 The mention of the Egyptians in Judges 10:11, in the mouth of God, presumably refers back to the Exodus narrative.

82 David Ussishkin, *The Renewed Archaeological Excavations at Lachish (1973–1994)*, vol. 1 (Tel Aviv: Emery and Claire Yass Publications in Archaeology, 2004), 1626–28; and Ussishkin, *Biblical Lachish: A Tale of Construction, Destruction, Excavation and Restoration* (Jerusalem: IES / Washington: BAS, 2014), 194–96, figs. 10.5–6. A leading expert on scarabs, Baruch

Brandl, rejects the identification of the Lachish scarab with the name of Ramesses IV, but the seal seems to date to the 20th Dynasty; see "Scarabs and Plaques Bearing Royal Names of the Early 20th Egyptian Dynasty Excavated in Canaan – From Sethnakht to Ramesses IV," *Egypt and the Levant* 14 (2004), 60.

83 David Ussishkin, "Lachish," *NEAEHL* (1993), vol. 3, 900–904. For further details, see Ussishkin, "Levels VII and VI at Tel Lachish and the End of the Late Bronze Age in Canaan," in Jonathan n. Tubb, ed., *Palestine in the Bronze and Iron Ages: Papers in Honour of Olga Tufnell* (London: Univ. College London Institute of Archaeology, 1985), 213–30; Ussishkin, *Renewed Archaeological Excavations*, vol. 1 (see n. 82), 352–61; and Ussishkin, *Biblical Lachish* (see n. 82), 191–98. On the Egyptian objects, see also Cline, *1177 B.C.* (see n. 18), 120–21.

84 Given the short distance to the Philistine towns of Gath (9 mi) and Ekron (14 mi), David Ussishkin, the excavator of Lachish, is of the opinion that more likely the Sea Peoples destroyed the town, though he does not rule out an Israelite destruction; see Ussishkin, *Biblical Lachish* (see n. 82), 196–201. The explicit statement in Joshua 10:31–32, however, that the town was taken by the Israelites because Lachish was in a coalition of enemies, along with the archaeological evidence, which reveals a total destruction (as stated in the biblical text), speaks in favor of an Israelite destruction. There are also no traces of any Philistine material culture at the site.

85 Ussishkin, *Biblical Lachish* (see n. 82), 191–94.

86 For translations, see Kenneth A. Kitchen, *Ramesside Inscriptions, Translated and Annotated*, vol. V: *Sethnakht, Ramesses III & Contemporaries* (Oxford: Blackwell, 2008), 8; and Rosemarie Drenkhahn, *Die Elephantine-Stele des Sethnachts und ihr historischer Hintergrund*, Ägyptologische Abhandlungen 36 (Wiesbaden: Harrassowitz, 1980), 64.

87 Translation based on John A. Wilson, "A Syrian Interregnum," in *ANET*, 260. For the original, see Erichsen, *Papyrus Harris I* (see n. 47), 91; P. Grandet, *Le papyrus Harris I* (see n. 47), 335–36 (75,6–76.2).

88 Interestingly, the Hebrew lexical-semantic approximation of this Egyptian phrase (*s nb m'k3-f*) occurs in Judges 17:6; 21:25, "each man did what was right in his own eyes," to describe the chaos that the biblical authors sensed in the lead-up to the establishment of the monarchy.

89 That is, with no king or central authority.

90 The name means literally "he made himself" (compare English "self-made man"), so it is unclear if Irsu is his proper name or a sobriquet of some sort.

91 For scholars who have looked to the turmoil of c. 1198 B.C.E. as the backdrop of the Exodus, see Abraham Malamat, "The Exodus: Egyptian Analogies," in Ernest S. Frerichs and Leonard H. Lesko, eds., *Exodus – The Egyptian Evidence* (Winona Lake, IN: Eisenbrauns, 1997), 22–25; Johannes C. de Moor, *The Rise of Yahwism: The Roots of Israelite Monotheism*, 2nd ed. (Leuven: Leuven Univ. Press & Peeters, 1997), 227–40 (with the more specific identification of Irsu = Moses); Knauf and Guillaume, *History of Biblical Israel* (see n. 24), 36; and Israel Knohl, "Pinpointing the Exodus from Egypt," *Harvard Divinity Bulletin* (Autumn/Winter 2018), at: https://bulletin.hds.harvard.edu/pinpointing-the-exodus-from-egypt/.

92 For the former text, see K. A. Kitchen, *Ramesside Inscriptions Historical and Biographical*, vol. V (Oxford: Blackwell, 1983), 27–35. For the translation, see K. A. Kitchen, "The 'Sea Peoples' Records of Ramesses III," in *COS* 4.11–14. For further details, see Eric H. Cline and David O'Connor, "The Sea Peoples," in *Ramesses III* (see n. 79), 180–208.

93 Incidentally, most scholars believe that the Sea Peoples first tried to invade Egypt by land and by sea, and then, once defeated by Ramesses III, they moved northward along the Mediterranean coast and settled the coastal plain of southern Canaan or were even settled there by Ramesses III. In reality, the opposite occurred. First the Sea Peoples took from the Egyptian province Canaan a part of the coastal strip and settled there. Afterward they attacked Egypt, both by sea and by land (i.e., by marching across the Sinai). In general, the attempt of an invasion by land and its logistics were largely overlooked by scholars. After all, in order to invade Egypt by land, one first would need a land base. For details, see Rainer Stadelmann, "Die Abwehr der Seevölker unter Ramses III," *Saeculum* 19 (1968), 156–71; and Manfred Bietak, "The Sea Peoples and the End of the Egyptian Administration in Canaan," in Avraham Biran and Joseph Aviram, ed., *Biblical Archaeology Today II: Proceedings of the Second International Congress on Biblical Archaeology, Jerusalem, June–July 1990* (Jerusalem: IES, 1993), 299–306.

94 See references above, n. 38.

95 For the most recent treatment, with a new suggestion, see Yoel Elitzur, "Qīr of the Aramaeans: A New Approach" (in Hebrew), *Shnaton* 21 (2012), 141–52, with English abstract on pp. ix–x.

96 Gary A. Rendsburg, "The Internal Consistency and Historical Reliability of the Biblical Genealogies," *VT* 40 (1990), 185–206.

97 Abraham Malamat, "Tribal Societies: Biblical Genealogies and African Lineage Systems," *European Journal of Sociology / Archives Européennes de Sociologie* 14 (1973), 126–36, esp. 136.

98 A key factor in fixing the date of David to c. 1000 is the synchrony between Sheshonq I (r. 962–941), founder of the 22nd Dynasty, with Solomon and Rehoboam (David's two successors). Said pharaoh is referred to as Shishaq (in English translations: Shishak) in 1 Kings 11:40; 14:25, referring to Solomon and Rehoboam, respectively. See chaps. 4 and 5.

99 David P. Henige, *The Chronology of Oral Tradition: Quest for a Chimera* (Oxford: Clarendon Press, 1974), 121–44. Much of this research is summarized in concise form in David P. Henige, "Generation-counting and Late New Kingdom Chronology," *JEA* 67 (1981), 182–84. For a similar calculation, see Martha T. Roth, "Age at Marriage and the Household: A Study of Neo-Babylonian and Neo-Assyrian Forms," *Comparative Studies in Society and History* 29 (1987), 715–47; and Karl Jansen Winkeln, "The Relevance of Genealogical Information for Egyptian Chronology," *Egypt and the Levant* 16 (2006) 257–73.

To mention just two lineages, one from antiquity with direct relevance to the Bible, and one of more recent vintage but with some resonance in the field of biblical studies, note

the following: a) the Achaemenid dynasty, during the years 522–338, from Darius I through Artaxerxes III, spanning six generations, for an average of 30.8 years per generation; and b) the so-called Solomon dynasty of Ethiopia, which includes 17 generations spanning the years 1270–1851 (from Yekuno Amlak through Yohannes III), or 582 years, for an average of 34.2 years per generation.

100 Note that the genealogies of Samuel and Zadok in the Book of Chronicles link them to the tribal ancestor Levi, but these lineages clearly have been doctored to establish a Levite heritage for these two key figures. The registry in 1 Chronicles 6:18–23 places Samuel 19 generations removed from Levi, while the parallel lineage in 1 Chronicles 6:7–13 is garbled and too difficult to reconstruct. The genealogy of Zadok also occurs twice in Chronicles (1 Chronicles 5:30–34; 6:35–38), though without variation, with David's priest appearing 13 generations removed from Levi. Both lists reflect "lineage growth," a common phenomenon in the transmission of genealogies, for which see Henige, *Chronology of Oral Tradition* (see n. 99), 38. To be sure, the genealogies of Samuel and Zadok should not and cannot be used in the current enterprise; see in detail Rendsburg, "Internal Consistency" (see n. 96), 195–97.

101 See above, n. 98; and see further herein, chap. 4.

102 On the internal chronology of the Book of Judges, see chap. 3, pp. 89–90.

103 For an additional round number, though not one which is a multiple of 40, see Jephthah's use of 300 years in Judges 11:26.

104 Nabonidus, Sippar Cylinder Inscription, col. 2, line 58, for which see Paul-Alain Beaulieu, "The Sippar Cylinder of Nabonidus," in *COS* 2.312.

105 We do, however, admit that 400 years of the 400-Year Stele (see the excursus on the Hyksos below) appears to be an accurate representation of the passage of time—from Horemheb back to Nehesy, the 14th Dynasty pharaoh and the first to use the epithet "beloved of Seth."

106 See chap. 5 herein.

107 On the shift from the epic storytelling tradition (mainly Genesis through Samuel) to the style of the Book of Kings and elsewhere, see Rendsburg, "Epic Tradition" (see n. 65), 26–27.

108 Israelit-Groll, "*pȝ-ṯwf*" (see n. 72), 139. See also Bietak, "Historicity of the Exodus" (see n. 1), 29–30.

109 See chap. 3 herein.

110 For additional related lineages, see Rendsburg, "Internal Consistency" (see n. 96), 186–89, esp. the chart on p. 189.

111 The question of possible separate sources aside, the different numbers (400 and 430) may reflect an unstated inner-biblical tradition of 30 years of free and prosperous living while Joseph was yet alive and in charge.

112 A different approach is offered by Nadav Na'aman, who assumes that the Israelites originated from the local Canaanite population, with the suggestion that the burden of the Egyptian occupation during the Late Bronze Age in Canaan might have added later to the popularity of the Exodus story and to its establishment as the national myth. Nadav Na'aman, "The Exodus Story: Between Historical Memory and Historical Composition," *JANER* 11 (2011), 39–69.

113 Others have used the same analogy; see, e.g., William G. Dever, *Who Were the Early Israelites and Where Did They Come From?* (Grand Rapids, MI: Eerdmans, 2003), 234.

114 See the earlier statement in Bietak, "Historicity of the Exodus" (see n. 1), 28 and map here on p. 22.

115 Abraham Malamat, "Let My People Go and Go and Go and Go," *BAR*, January/February 1998, 62–66.

116 The Hebrew term lives on in the name of the Christian holiday of Easter in various languages: Spanish *Pascua*, Italian *Pasqua*, Portuguese *Páscoa*, French *Pâques*, Dutch *Pasen*, Swedish *Påsk*, Greek *Páscha*, Russian *Pascha*, etc.

117 For example, Hershel Shanks, ed., *Ancient Israel*, 3rd ed., 51–52.

118 See already Bietak, "Historicity of the Exodus" (see n. 1), 31–32; and with much greater detail, Bietak, "From Where Came the Hyksos and Where Did They Go?" in Marcel Marée, ed., *The Second Intermediate Period (Thirteenth–Seventeenth Dynasties): Current Research, Future Prospects*, Orientalia Lovaniensia Analecta 192 (Leuven: Peeters, 2010), 139–81 + plates 11–26.

119 Burnt acorns found on an altar in front of the Broad-Room Temple and the Bent-Axis Temple are an indication that the goddess Asherah, who is synonymous with the oak tree, was venerated here. A tree pit beside the altar may have been for such a tree, which is not native to Egypt and must have been introduced by the Canaanites.

120 The name Baal Zephon is attested in the Ugaritic ritual texts, meaning "Baal of Mt. Zaphon (= modern-day Jebel Aqra' in northern Syria). But see also the appearance of this term as a place name in Exodus 14:2; 14:9, in the lead-up to the Sea of Reeds crossing—even if its precise location cannot be established.

121 Labib Habachi, "Sethos I's Devotion to Seth and Avaris," *Zeitschrift für ägyptische Sprache und Altertumskunde* 100 (1974), 95–102 + plates V–VI.

122 For more on Josephus, see chaps. 7–8.

123 Strictly speaking, the Hyksos were the rulers (see above, for the etymology of the word), and thus we use the term "Hyksos-people" to refer to the general population of Avaris and environs during the 15th Dynasty.

124 See also Numbers 11:4, though a different term, *'asafsuf*, is used there.

3. The Emergence of Israel in the Land of Canaan

1 Israel Finkelstein et al., "Reconstructing Ancient Israel: Integrating Macro- and Micro-archaeology," *Hebrew Bible and Ancient Israel* 1 (2012), 141. For the most sustained exposition, see Israel Finkelstein, *The Archaeology of the Israelite Settlement* (Jerusalem: IES, 1988). Over the years, the author has retreated from some of his statements in the book, though I consider them valid still, especially as the evidence remains unchanged.

2 For a wide-ranging survey on sedentarization, with modern parallels, see Thomas E.

Levy and Augustin F. C. Holl, "Migrations, Ethnogenesis, and Settlement Dynamics: Israelites in Iron Age Canaan and Shuwa-Arabs in the Chad Basin," *JAA* 21 (2002), 83–118.

3 Michael M. Homan, *To Your Tents, O Israel! The Terminology, Function, Form, and Symbolism of Tents in the Hebrew Bible and the Ancient Near East*, CHANE 12 (Leiden: Brill, 2002), 17–19.

4 B. S. J. Isserlin, *The Israelites* (London: Thames and Hudson, 1998), 122–24; and Philip J. King and Lawrence E. Stager, *Life in Biblical Israel* (Louisville: Westminster John Knox Press, 2001), 21–23. For detailed information on more than two dozen sites, see Avraham Faust, *The Archaeology of Israelite Society in Iron Age II* (Winona Lake, IN: Eisenbrauns, 2002), 207–12, even if the data derive mainly from the eighth–seventh centuries B.C.E., due to the nature of the evidence.

5 Many of these expressions have a good English pedigree: Lucas Reilly, "The Origins of 12 Horse-Related Idioms," *Mental Floss*, May 22, 2014 (http://mentalfloss.com/article/56850/origins-12-horse-related-idioms). For more detailed analysis, see *Oxford English Dictionary*, s.v. 'horse'.

6 Both sites are in Nubia, in present-day northern Sudan.

7 For much of what follows, see Avraham Faust, "The Emergence of Israel and Theories of Ethnogenesis," in S. Niditch, ed., *The Wiley Blackwell Companion to Ancient Israel* (Chichester: John Wiley & Sons, 2016), 155–73.

8 See Avraham Faust, "Pigs in Space (and Time): Pork Consumption and Identity Negotiations in the Late Bronze and Iron Ages of Ancient Israel," *NEA* 81 (2018), 276–99.

9 For possible explanations regarding the origins of the pig prohibition, see Joseph A. Callaway and Hershel Shanks, "The Settlement in Canaan: The Period of the Judges," in H. Shanks, ed., *Ancient Israel*, 3rd ed. (Washington: BAS, 2011), 73–74; and Gary A. Rendsburg, "The Vegetarian Ideal in the Bible," in L. J. Greenspoon, R. A. Simkins, and G. Shapiro, eds., *Food and Judaism*, Studies in Jewish Civilization 15 (Omaha: Creighton Univ. Press, 2005), 319–34.

10 While it started as the basic domicile, in time the four-room house was adapted to larger structures as well (see plan no. 1 on p. 69).

11 The lack of clear evidence notwithstanding, some scholars have proposed that the four-room house was modeled after individual Bedouin tent structures. See, e.g., Volkmar Fritz, "Conquest or Settlement?: The Early Iron Age in Palestine," *Biblical Archaeologist* 50 (1987), 84–100, esp. 97, with the following comment: "These types of houses may have developed from tent constructions, although what type of tent was used in the second millennium is not known." For additional information on the Bedouin tent, with some historical considerations, see Benjamin A. Saidel, "Coffee, Gender, and Tobacco: Observations on the History of the Bedouin Tent," *Anthropos* 104 (2009), 179–86.

12 Elizabeth Bloch-Smith and Beth Alpert Nakhai, "A Landscape Comes to Life: The Iron Age I," *NEA* 62 (1999), 62–92, 101–27, esp. 75.

13 Gary A. Rendsburg and Jeremy D. Smoak, "Kinship Terms," in Geoffrey Khan, ed., *Encyclopedia of Hebrew Language and Linguistics*, vol. 2 (Leiden: Brill, 2013), 471–77, esp. 471.

14 Elizabeth Lang, "The Daily Grind: Women's Experience of Bread-Making in Non-elite Households of New Kingdom Egypt," Ph.D. Dissertation (New Haven: Yale University, 2017).

15 See Carol Meyers, "Having Their Space and Eating There Too: Bread Production and Female Power in Ancient Israelite Households," *Nashim: A Journal of Jewish Women's Studies and Gender Issues* 5 (2002), 14–44, esp. 21–22; and Carol Meyers, *Rediscovering Eve: Ancient Israelite Women in Context* (New York: Oxford Univ. Press, 2013), 129–30. For a delightful re-creation of the scene, see Jennie R. Ebeling, *Women's Lives in Biblical Times* (London: T. & T. Clark, 2010), 43–44.

16 Meyers, *Rediscovering Eve* (see n. 15), 32, 133; and Ebeling, *Women's Lives* (see n. 15), 57–58.

17 Harry Hoffner, "Symbols for Masculinity and Femininity," *JBL* 85 (1966), 326–34.

18 On these features, see William G. Dever, *Who Were the Early Israelites and Where Did*

They Come From? (Grand Rapids: Eerdmans, 2003), 113–17.

19 Avraham Faust, *Israel's Ethnogenesis: Settlement, Interaction, Expansion and Resistance* (London: Equinox, 2006), 191–205.

20 Faust, *Israel's Ethnogenesis* (see n. 19), 92–107; and Faust, "Emergence of Israel" (see n. 7). For a summary statement, see Avraham Faust, "Early Israel: An Egalitarian Society," *BAR*, July/August 2013.

21 Joshua A. Berman, *Created Equal: How the Bible Broke with Ancient Political Thought* (New York: Oxford Univ. Press, 2008).

22 For a fuller treatment, see Callaway and Shanks, "Settlement in Canaan" (see n. 9), 62–74.

23 Relevant publications include W. F. Albright, "Archaeology and the Date of the Hebrew Conquest of Palestine," *BASOR* 58 (1935), 10–18; and W. F. Albright, "The Israelite Conquest of Canaan in the Light of Archaeology," *BASOR* 74 (1939), 11–23. Many of Albright's students, such as John Bright and G. Ernest Wright, continued along the same path. Another major contributor to this school was Yigael Yadin, excavator of Hazor; see his essay "Is the Biblical Account of the Israelite Conquest of Canaan Historically Reliable?" *BAR*, March/April 1982.

24 Albrecht Alt, "The Settlement of the Israelites in Palestine," in *Essays on Old Testament History and Religion*, trans. R. A. Wilson (Garden City, NY: Doubleday, 1968), 175–221; originally published in German, in 1925.

25 A generation or so later, Alt was followed by Yohanan Aharoni; see his essay "The Israelite Occupation of Canaan: An Account of the Archaeological Evidence," *BAR*, May/June 1982.

26 Dever, *Who Were the Early Israelites?* (see n. 18), 121.

27 Finkelstein, *Archaeology of the Israelite Settlement* (see n. 1), 274. It is important to note, however, that Finkelstein wrote these words in 1988, 15 years before Dever's book. Moreover, less than a decade later, Finkelstein's position apparently had changed, as expressed in his "Pots and Peoples Revisited: Ethnic Boundaries in the Iron Age," in n. A. Silberman and D. Small, eds., *The Archaeology*

of Israel: Constructing the Past, Interpreting the Present (Sheffield: Sheffield Academic Press, 1997), 226: "[Pottery forms] on both sides of the Jordan reflect environmental, social, and economic traits of the settlers. They tell us nothing about ethnicity."

28 Frank H. Polak, "The Oral and the Written: Syntax, Stylistics and the Development of Biblical Prose Narrative," *JANES* 26 (1998), 59–105.

29 For the original text and an English translation, see Alan H. Gardiner, *Egyptian Hieratic Texts* (Leipzig: J. C. Hinrichs, 1911), with the passage to be discussed herein on pp. 25*, 70. A more recent edition is H. W. Fischer-Elfert, *Die satirische Streitschrift des Papyrus Anastasi I*, vol. 1 (Wiesbaden: Harrassowitz, 1983), with our passage discussed on 139.

30 A few comments on the translation offered here: a) the foreign terms written in Egyptian hieroglyphs are presented here in italics with hyphens between the consonantal sounds; b) the precise identity of the *ḥtmt*-animal is unknown, and thus we content ourselves with (bear?/hyena?), the two possibilities proposed by scholars; c) the precise identity of the *b-k-l*-tree also is unknown, with pear and balsam the two possibilities proposed by scholars. For a translation of P.Anastasi I, see Edward Wente, *Letters from Ancient Egypt*, SBL Writings from the Ancient World (Atlanta: Scholars Press, 1990), 98–110, with our passage on 108.

31 For a survey of opinions on this passage, see Fischer-Elfert, *Satirische Streitschrift* (see n. 29), vol. 2, 199–200.

32 For the text, see C. R. Lepsius, *Denkmaeler der Aegypten und Aethiopien*, Dritte Abtheilung, Band VI (Berlin: Nicolai, 1849), plate 140a, at http://edoc3.bibliothek.uni-halle.de/lepsius/tafelwa3.html.

33 For a translation of this important historical text, with parallel material in P.Harris I, see K. A. Kitchen, "The 'Sea Peoples' Records of Ramesses III," in *COS* 4.11–14.

34 See K. A. Kitchen, *Ramesside Inscriptions*, vol. 5 (Oxford: Blackwell, 1981), 40, lines 3–4.

35 See Sara Japhet, *I and II Chronicles* (Louisville: Westminster John Knox Press, 1993), 174.

36 The first person to propose the identity of biblical Dan with the Dan(an)u of the Sea Peoples was Cyrus H. Gordon, "The Mediterranean Factor in the Old Testament," in *Congress Volume Bonn 1962*, VTSup 9 (Leiden: Brill, 1963), 19–31, esp. 21. The proposal was developed further by Yigael Yadin, "And Dan, Why Did He Remain in Ships?" *Australian Journal of Biblical Archaeology* 1 (1968), 9–23.

37 On the Mesha Stele, see chap. 5.

38 On such alignments and re-alignments, see Emanuel Marx, *Bedouin of the Negev* (Manchester: Manchester Univ. Press, 1967), 137–38. For general treatment of the Bedouin, with an eye to the Bible, see Clinton Bailey, *Bedouin Culture in the Bible* (New Haven: Yale Univ. Press, 2018).

39 The terms "Amorite" and "Hittite" here appear to be general synonyms for "Canaanite." Alternatively, they may refer to some remnants of the former Amorites and Hittites known from second-millennium B.C.E. sources.

40 True, the same word *mišpətayim* (sheepfolds) occurs in Genesis 49:14, with reference to Issachar, but the usage there is metaphorical, as the son/tribe is compared to a donkey.

41 This is clear from a reading of Joshua 13–19, though one must assume that 16:9 refers to both Ephraim and Manasseh.

42 Most translations, such as the New Revised Standard Version used in the other chapters of this book, render *ḥaṣerim* as "villages," but I prefer "settlements," with specific reference to unwalled settlements.

43 The same is true for the northern kingdom, based on the literary remains thereof that are preserved in the Bible, with the focus on Dan, Bethel, Shechem, and Samaria.

44 Chaps. 11–12 provide summary information regarding the rest of the land of Canaan.

45 See Abraham Malamat, "Israelite Conduct of War in the Conquest of Canaan, According to the Biblical Tradition," in F. M. Cross, ed., *Symposia Celebrating the Seventy-Fifth Anniversary of the Founding of the American Schools of Oriental Research, 1900–1975* (Cambridge, MA: ASOR, 1979), 35–55. For a popular version, see Abraham Malamat, "How Inferior Israelite Forces Conquered Fortified Canaanite Cities," *BAR*, March/April 1982.

46 Amnon Ben-Tor, "Who Destroyed Canaanite Hazor?" *BAR*, July/August 2013.

47 The different versions of the defeat of Hazor in Joshua and in Judges is just one more instance of the conflicting information in the two books.

48 While an overall conquest of Canaan remains most unlikely (as argued above), for some food for thought, see B. S. J. Isserlin, "The Israelite Conquest of Canaan: A Comparative Review of the Arguments Applicable," *PEQ* 115 (1983), 85–94, where the author rightly observes that there is also little archaeological evidence for some known historical events, such as the Norman conquest of England, the Anglo-Saxon invasion of England, and the Muslim Arab conquest of the Levant.

49 While the former three animals are commonly sacrificed according to the priestly legislation in Leviticus and Numbers, deer are permitted to be eaten but are never mentioned in the sacrificial texts. So either the deer were sacrificed at Mt. Ebal (which would be an example of extra-Torah traditions attested in the archaeological record), or they were consumed but not offered on the altar.

50 For the original publication, see Adam Zertal, "An Early Iron Age Cultic Site on Mount Ebal: Excavation Seasons 1982–1987: Preliminary Report," *TA* 14 (1987), 105–65. For a recent treatment, see Ralph K. Hawkins, *The Iron Age I Structure on Mt. Ebal: Excavation and Interpretation* (Winona Lake, IN: Eisenbrauns, 2015).

51 Amihai Mazar, "Bronze Bull Found in Israelite 'High Place' from the Time of the Judges," *BAR*, September/October 1983.

52 Except for 1 Kings 14:2, 4, with reference to the home of the prophet Ahijah in Shiloh.

53 Israel Finkelstein, "Shiloh Yields Some, but Not All, of Its Secrets," *BAR*, January/February 1986. For the discovery of an altar about 2 km from Shiloh, which would seem not to be related to the Tabernacle at Shiloh, but which remains a curiosity, nonetheless, see Yoel Elitzur and Doron Nir-Zevi, "Four-Horned Altar Discovered in Judean Hills," *BAR*, May/June 2004.

54 See Antonio Loprieno, *Ancient Egyptian: A Linguistic Introduction* (Cambridge: Cambridge Univ. Press, 1995), 38.

55 The same stela mentions Israel, for which see above, chap. 2.

56 Regarding Dan, see Judges 18, the story of the migration of the tribe from the coastal plain to the far north of Israel—apparently due to pressure caused by the expanding Philistines. With this process, the Danites evidently left their Sea Peoples origins (and culture too?) behind, as they established themselves at the headwaters of the Jordan River. Later biblical writers henceforth would refer to the extent of Israel as "from Dan to Beersheba" (1 Samuel 3:20, etc.).

57 Not that all of these elements appear in each of the accounts, but the schematic pattern is noticeable, nonetheless.

58 The relatively short time span for all the events enumerated in Joshua-Judges also is indicated by the mention of Moses's grandson Jonathan and Aaron's grandson Pinḥas (English: Phinehas) in the closing chapters of the Book of Judges (18:30; 20:28, respectively). If the grandsons of the two leaders of the Exodus generation were yet alive at this point, the period narrated by Joshua-Judges must be shorter than is usually assumed. For the former passage, note that the text originally read "Moses" (as is reflected in the Septuagint recension of Codex Alexandrinus), which was later changed to "Manasseh"—for pietistic reasons.

59 For the linguistic profile, see Tania Notarius, *The Verb in Archaic Biblical Poetry: A Discursive, Typological, and Historical Investigation of the Tense System* (Leiden: Brill, 2013), 125–50; and Ronald Hendel and Jan Joosten, *How Old Is the Hebrew Bible?* (New Haven: Yale Univ. Press, 2018), 101–104. For some

literary features, see Edward L. Greenstein, "Signs of Poetry Past: Literariness in Pre-Biblical Hebrew Literature," in M. L. Satlow, ed., *Strength to Strength: Essays in Appreciation of Shaye J. D. Cohen* (Providence: Brown Judaic Studies, 2018), 5–25, esp. 17–18.

60 See Robert S. Kawashima, "From Song to Story: The Genesis of Narrative in Judges 4 and 5," *Prooftexts* 21 (2001), 151–78; reprinted as Robert S. Kawashima, *Biblical Narrative and the Death of the Rhapsode* (Bloomington: Indiana Univ. Press, 2004), 17–32.

61 For the shift to narrative prose storytelling in ancient Israel, see Gary A. Rendsburg, *How the Bible Is Written* (Peabody, MA: Hendrickson, 2019), 443–67 (i.e., chap. 21).

62 For reading Judges as a political statement, see Marc Z. Brettler, "The Book of Judges: Literature as Politics," *JBL* 108 (1989), 395–418.

63 See Marc Z. Brettler, *God Is King: Understanding an Israelite Metaphor* (Sheffield: Sheffield Academic Press, 1989).

64 Technically, the terms "king," "kingship," and the verb "reign" are not used in Judges 8:22, but dynastic succession is implied in the people's words to Gideon: "Rule over us, you and your son and your grandson; for you have saved us from the hand of Midian."

65 See also the parable of the trees which follows closely in chap. 9: beautiful trees—the olive tree, the fig tree, and the grape vine—prefer not to reign over the arboreal world, so that kingship is then offered to and accepted by the lowly bramble.

66 See also Judges 18:1; 19:1, with the first half of the statement: "In those days there was no king in Israel" (albeit in slightly different formulations in the two passages).

4. The Early Monarchy

1 William E. Evans, "An Historical Reconstruction of the Emergence of Israelite Kingship and the Reign of Saul," in W.W. Hallo et al., eds., *Scripture in Context II* (Winona Lake, IN: Eisenbrauns, 1983), 61–78, esp. 77.

2 Israel Finkelstein, "The Emergence of the Monarchy in Israel: The Environmental and

Socio-Economic Aspects," *JSOT* 44 (1989), 43–74.

3 J. Maxwell Miller, "Is It Possible to Write a History of Israel Without Relying on the Hebrew Bible?" in *The Fabric of History*, D.V. Edelman, ed., JSOTSup 127 (Sheffield: Sheffield Academic, 1991), 93–102, esp. 101; Rainer

Albertz, "Secondary Sources Also Deserved to Be Historically Evaluated: The Case of the United Monarchy," in *The Historian and the Bible: Essays in Honor of Lester L. Grabbe*, P.R. Davies and D.V. Edelman, eds., LHBOTS 530 (New York: T&T Clark, 2010), 31–45; E. Blum, "Solomon and the United Monarchy: Some Textual Evidence," in R.G. Kratz and H. Spieckermann, eds., *One God—One Cult—One Nation: Archaeological and Biblical Perspectives*, BZAW 405 (Berlin: de Gruyter, 2010), 59–78.

4 See, e.g., Walter Dietrich, *The Early Monarchy in Israel: The Tenth Century*, Biblical Encyclopedia 3 (Atlanta: SBL, 2007), esp. 99–226; Avraham Faust and Yair Sapir, "The 'Governor's Residency' at Tel Eton, the United Monarchy and the Impact of the Old-House Effect on Large-Scale Archaeological Reconstructions," *Radiocarbon* 60.3 (2018), 801–20; Zachary Thomas, "A Matter of Interpretation: On Methdology and the Archaeology of the United Monarchy," *Archaeology and Text* 2 (2018), 25–52; Erez Ben-Yosef, "The Architectural Bias in Current Biblical Archaeology," *VT* 69 (2019), 261–87.

5 See, e.g., Israel Finkelstein, "The Archaeology of the United Monarchy: An Alternative View," *Levant* 28 (1996), 177–87; Amihai Mazar, "Iron Age Chronology: A Reply to I. Finkelstein," *Levant* 29 (1997), 157–67; Lawrence E. Stager, "The Patrimonial Kingdom of Solomon," in W.G. Dever and S. Gitin, eds., *Symbiosis, Symbolism, and the Power of the Past: Canaan, Ancient Israel, and Their Neighbors from the Late Bronze Age Through Roman Palaestina* (Winona Lake, IN: Eisenbrauns, 2003), 63–73; Israel Finkelstein, "City-States to States: Polity Dynamics in the 10th–9th Centuries B.C.E.," in *Symbiosis, Symbolism, and the Power* (see above), 76–83; Raz Kletter, "Chronology and United Monarchy: A Methodological Review," *ZDPV* 120 (2004), 13–54; Steven M. Ortiz, "Deconstructing and Reconstructing the United Monarchy: House of David or Tent of David (Current Trends in Iron Age Chronology)," in J.K. Hoffmeier and A. Millard, eds., *The Future of Biblical Archaeology* (Grand Rapids: Eerdmans, 2004), 121–47; Amihai Mazar, "The Debate over the Chronology of the Iron Age in the Southern Levant: Its History, the Current Situation, and a Suggested Resolution," in

T.E. Levy and T. Higham, eds., *The Bible and Radiocarbon Dating: Archaeology, Text and Science* (London: Equinox, 2005), 15–30; Steven M. Ortiz, "Does the 'Low Chronology' Work?: A Case Study of Tel Qasile X, Tel Gezer X, and Lachish V," in A.M. Maeir and P. de Miroschedji, eds., *"I Will Speak the Riddles of Ancient Times": Archaeological and Historical Studies in Honor of Amihai Mazar* (Winona Lake, IN: Eisenbrauns, 2006), 587–611; Israel Finkelstein and Eliazer Piasetzky, "The Iron I–IIA in the Highlands and Beyond: 14C Anchors, Pottery Phases and the Sheshonq I Campaign," *Levant* 38 (2006), 45–61; see also "Radiocarbon Dating and Philistine Chronology," Ägypten *und Levante* 17 (2007), 73–82; Amihai Mazar, "The Spade and the Text: The Interaction between Archaeology and Israelite History Relating to the Tenth-Ninth Centuries BCE," in H.G.M. Williamson, ed., *Understanding the History of Ancient Israel*, Proceedings of the British Academy 143 (Oxford: Oxford Univ. Press, 2007), 143–71; Israel Finkelstein and Amihai Mazar, *The Quest for the Historical Israel: Debating Archaeology and the History of Early Israel*, SBL Archaeological and Biblical Studies 17 (Atlanta: SBL, 2007); Brad E. Kelle, "The Early Monarchy and the Stories of Saul, David and Solomon," in S. Niditch, ed., *The Wiley-Blackwell Companion to Ancient Israel* (Malden, MA: Wiley-Blackwell, 2016), 177–96.

For a popular treatment, see Hershel Shanks, "Where Is the Tenth Century?" *BAR*, March/April 1998; Hershel Shanks, "A 'Centrist' at the Center of Controversy: BAR Interviews Israel Finkelstein," *BAR*, November/December 2002; Amihai Mazar, "Does Amihai Mazar Agree with Finkelstein's 'Low Chronology'?" *BAR*, March/April 2003; Hershel Shanks, "The Devil Is Not So Black as He Is Painted," *BAR*, May/June 2010; Yosef Garfinkel, "The Birth and Death of Biblical Minimalism," *BAR*, May/June 2011; Hershel Shanks, "Did the Kingdoms of Saul, David and Solomon Actually Exist?" *BAR*, September/October 2017; William G. Dever, "For King and Country: Chronology and Minimalism," *BAR*, March/April/May/June 2018.

6 See, e.g., Amihai Mazar, "Archaeology and the Biblical Narrative: The Case of the United Monarchy," in *One God—One Cult—One Nation* (see n. 3), 29–58.

7 See, e.g., Margaret M. Gelinas, "United Monarchy—Divided Monarchy: Fact or Fiction," in *The Pitcher Is Broken: Memorial Essays for Gösta W. Ahlström*, JSOTSup 190 (Sheffield: Sheffield Academic, 1995), 227–37; Israel Finkelstein and Neil Asher Silberman, *David and Solomon: In Search of the Bible's Sacred Kings and the Roots of Western Tradition* (New York: Free Press, 2006); Finkelstein and Mazar, *The Quest for the Historical Israel* (see n. 5); Israel Finkelstein, "A Great United Monarchy? Archaeological and Historical Perspectives," in *One God—One Cult—One Nation* (see n. 3), 3–28.

For a popular treatment, see Hershel Shanks, "The Biblical Minimalists," *BR*, June 1997; and Shanks, "Biblical Minimalists Meet Their Challengers," *BAR*, July/August 1997.

8 Finkelstein, "A Great United Monarchy?" (see n. 7), 21; Finkelstein, "Geographical and Historical Realities Behind the Earliest Layer in the David Story," *SJOT* 27 (2013), 131–50, at 135. This a priori is repeated or supposed in several recent papers, e.g., Nadav Na'aman, "Saul, Benjamin and the Emergence of 'Biblical Israel,'" *ZAW* 121 (2009), 211–24, 335–49; Israel Finkelstein, "The Date of the List of Towns That Received the Spoil of Amalek (1 Sam 30:26–31)," *TA* 37 (2010), 175–87; Nadav Na'aman, "Game of Thrones: Solomon's 'Succession Narrative' and Esarhaddon's Accession to the Throne," *TA* 45 (2018), 89–113.

9 Manfred Weippert, "The Balaam Text from Deir 'Alla and the Study of the Old Testament," in J. Hoftijzer and G. van der Kooij, eds., *The Balaam Text from Deir 'Alla Re-evaluated* (Leiden: Brill, 1991), 100–105, at 105; André Lemaire, "Review of D.W. Jamieson-Drake, *Scribes and Schools*, JSOTS 109 (Sheffield: Almond Press, 1991)," *JAOS* 112 (1992), 707–708; Alan Millard, "Scripts and Their Uses in the 12th–10th Centuries B.C.E.," in G. Galil et al., eds., *The Ancient Near East in the 12th–10th Centuries B.C.E.: Culture and History*, AOAT 392 (Münster: Ugarit-Verlag, 2012), 405–12; André Lemaire, "Levantine Literacy ca. 1000–750 B.C.E.," in *Contextualizing Israel's Sacred Writings: Ancient Literacy, Orality, and Literary Production*, Ancient Israel and Its Literature 22 (Atlanta: SBL Press, 2015), 11–46, esp. 14; Matthieu Richelle, "Elusive Scrolls: Could Any Hebrew Literature Have Been Written Prior to the Eighth Century B.C.E.?" *VT* 66 (2016), 556–94; Alan Millard, "Ancient Hebrew Inscriptions: Their Distribution and Significance," in I. Finkelstein et al., eds., *Alphabet, Text, and Artifacts in the Ancient Near East, Studies Presented to Benjamin Sass* (Paris: Van Dieben, 2016), 270–78, esp. 274–77; Christopher A. Rollston, "Inscriptional Evidence for the Writing of the Earliest Texts of the Bible: Intellectual Infrastructure in Tenth- and Ninth-Century Israel, Judah, and the Southern Levant," in J.C. Gertz et al., eds., *The Formation of the Pentateuch: Bridging the Academic Cultures of Europe, Israel, and North America* (Tübingen: Mohr Siebeck, 2016), 15–45; Rollston, "Epigraphic Evidence from Jerusalem and Its Environs at the Dawn of Biblical History: Methodologies and the Long-Durée Perspective," in *New Studies in the Archaeology of Jerusalem and Its Region, Collected Papers*, vol. 11 (Jerusalem: 2017), 7*–20*, at https://lisa.biu.ac.il/files/lisa/shared/maeir_jerusalem_mb_nsajr_11_2017.pdf.

For a popular treatment, see Christopher A. Rollston, "What's the Oldest Hebrew Inscription?" *BAR*, May/June 2012; Gérard Leval, "Ancient Inscription Refers to Birth of Israelite Monarchy," *BAR*, May/June 2012; Alan Millard, "The New Jerusalem Inscription—So What?" *BAR*, May/June 2014.

10 Yardenna Alexandre, "A Canaanite Early Phoenician Inscribed Bronze Bowl in an Iron Age IIA-B Burial Cave at Kefar Veradim, Northern Israel," *Maarav* 13 (2006), 7–41; R.E. Tappy et al., "An Abecedary from the Mid-Tenth Century B.C.E. from the Judean Shephelah," *BASOR* 344 (2006), 5–46; Aren M. Maeir et al., "A Late Iron Age I/Early Iron Age II Old Canaanite Inscription from Tell eṣ-Ṣafi/Gat, Israel: Palaeography, Dating and Historical-Cultural Significance," *BASOR* 351 (2008), 39–71; H. Misgav et al., "The Ostracon," in Y. Garfinkel and S. Ganor, eds., *Khirbet Qeiyafa I. Excavation Report 2007–2008* (Jerusalem: IES, 2009), 243–57; P. Kyle McCarter et al., "An Archaic Baal Inscription from Tel Beth-Shemesh," *TA* 28 (2011), 179–83; Eilat Mazar et al., "An Inscribed Pithos from the Ophel, Jerusalem," *IEJ* 63 (2013), 39–49; Shmuel Aḥituv and Amihai Mazar, "The Inscriptions from Tel Reḥov and Their Contribution to the Study of Script and Writing from Iron Age IIA," in E. Eshel and

Y. Levin, eds., *I Will Bring a Scroll Recounting What Befell Me* (Ps 40:8): *Epigraphy and Daily Life from the Bible to the Talmud Dedicated to the Memory of Professor Ḥanan Eshel* (Göttingen: Vandenhoeck & Ruprecht, 2014), 39–68; Aren M. Maeir and Esther Eshel, "Four Short Alphabetic Inscriptions from Late Iron IIA Philistia and Environs," in *I Will Bring a Scroll*, 69–88; David Hamidović, "L'inscription du pithos de l'Ophel à Jérusalem," *Semitica* 56 (2014), 137–49; Y. Garfinkel et al., "The 'IshBaal Inscription from Khirbet Qeiyafa," *BASOR* 373 (2015), 217–33; Matthieu Richelle, "Quelques nouvelles lectures sur l'ostracon de Khirbet Qeiyafa," *Semitica* 57 (2015), 147–62; P. Zilberg, "chap. 9: The Debate on Writing and Language, in Y. Garfinkel et al., eds., *Debating Khirbet Qeiyafa: A Fortified City in Judah from the Time of King David* (Jerusalem: IES, The Hebrew Univ., 2016), 157–72; Benjamin Sass and Israel Finkelstein, "The Swan-Song of Proto-Canaanite in the Ninth Century B.C.E. in Light of an Alphabet Inscription from Megiddo," *Semitica et Classica* 9 (2016), 19–42. The divergent dating of Benjamin Sass ("The Khirbet Qeiyafa Ostracon in Its Setting," in S. Schroer and S. Münger, eds., *Khirbet Qeiyafa in the Shephelah*, OBO 282 [New York; Göttingen: Academic Press, Vandenhoeck & Rupecht, 2017], 87–111; Benjamin Sass, "The Emergence of Monumental, West Semitic Alphabetic Writing with an Emphasis on Byblos," *Semitica* 59 [2017], 109–42) does not take into account the historical argument for dating the Byblos inscriptions of Abibaal and Elibaal (André Lemaire, "La datation des rois de Byblos Abibaal et Elibaal et les relations entre l'Égypte et le Levant au Xᵉ siècle av. notre ère," *Comptes rendus de l'Académie des Inscriptions et Belles-Lettres* [2006], 1,697–1,716) and has been generally rejected (Christopher A. Rollston, *Writing and Literacy in the World of Ancient Israel*, Archaeology and Biblical Studies 11 [Atlanta: SBL, 2010], 24–27; Millard, "Ancient Hebrew Inscriptions" [see n. 9], 275; David S. Vanderhooft, "The Final Phase of the Common 'Proto-Semitic' Alphabet in the Southern Levant: A Rejoinder to Sass and Finkelstein," in O. Lipschits et al., eds., *Rethinking Israel: Studies in the History and Archaeology of Ancient Israel in Honor of Israel Finkelstein* [Winona Lake, IN: Eisenbrauns, 2017], 441–50); Raz Kletter, "The First Melchizedek Bottle? Notes on the Jerusalem Iron IIA Pithos Inscription," *PEQ* 150 (2018), 265–70.

11 See Steven L. McKenzie, "Saul in the Deuteronomistic History," in C.S. Ehrlich and M.C. White, eds., *Saul in Story and Tradition*, FAT 47 (Tübingen: Mohr Siebeck, 2006), 59–70; Yairah Amit, "The Delicate Balance in the Image of Saul and Its Place in the Deuteronomistic History," in *Saul in Story and Tradition* (see above), 70–79; Gregory Mobley, "Glimpses of the Heroic Saul," in *Saul in Story and Tradition* (see above), 80–87. See also Klaus-Peter Adam, *Saul und David in der judäischen Geschichts-schreibung*, FAT 51 (Tübingen: Mohr Siebeck, 2007).

12 See Trude Dothan, "The Philistines Reconsidered," in *Biblical Archaeology Today 1984* (Jerusalem: IES, 1985), 165–76; "The Philistines and the Dothans: An Archaeological Romance, Part I," *BAR*, January/February 1990, 26–36; Trude Dothan and Moshe Dothan, *People of the Sea: The Search for the Philistines* (New York: Macmillan, 1992); Ed Noort, *Die Seevölker in Palästina* (Kampen, Netherlands: Pharos, 1994); Ann E. Killebrew, *Biblical Peoples and Ethnicity: An Archaeological Study of Egyptian, Canaanites, Philistines, and Early Israel, 1300–1100 B.C.E.* (Leiden: Brill, 2005); Seymour Gitin, "Philistines in the Books of Kings," in A. Lemaire and B. Halpern, eds., *The Books of Kings: Sources, Composition, Historiography and Reception*, VTSup 129 (Leiden: Brill, 2010), 301–64.

13 For the migrations of the Sea Peoples, see the contrasting views of Tristan Barako and Assaf Yassar-Landau in "One if by Sea ... Two if by Land: How Did the Philistines Get to Canaan?" *BAR*, March/April 2003.

14 *ANET*, 262–63; Thomas L. Gertzen, "Profiling the Philistines: Further Remarks on the Egyptian Depiction of Philistine Warriors at Medinet Habu," *Ancient Near Eastern Studies* 45 (2008), 85–101; K.A. Kitchen, "The 'Sea Peoples' Records of Ramses III," in *COS* 4: 11–14.

15 Franco Pintore, "Sérèn, tarwanis, tyrannos," in O. Carruba et al., eds., *Studi orientalistici in ricordo di F. Pintore*, Studia mediterranea 4 (Padua, Italy: GJES, 1983), 285–322.

16 Itamar Singer, "Egyptians, Canaanites, and Philistines in the Period of the Emergence of

Israel," in I. Finkelstein and n. Na'aman, eds., *From Nomadism to Monarchy: Archaeological and Historical Aspects of Early Israel* (Jerusalem: IES, 1994), 282–338.

17 In the 12th to 11th centuries B.C.E., iron technology developed in the Aegean, on Cyprus, and in Canaan; this development apparently had an Aegean origin. See James D. Muhly, "How Iron Technology Changed the Ancient World and Gave the Philistines a Military Edge," *BAR*, November/December 1982; Aren M. Maeir, "The Philistines be upon thee, Samson (Jud. 16:20): Reassessing the Martial Nature of the Philistines—Archaeological Evidence vs. Ideological Image," in L. Niesiolowski-Spano and M. Wecowski, eds., *Change, Continuity and Connectivity: North-Eastern Mediterranean at the Turn of the Bronze Age and in the Early Iron Age* (Wiesbaden: Harrassowitz, 2018), 158–68; Alla Rabinowitz et al., "The Metal Assemblage from Early Iron Age IIA Khirbet Qeiyafa and Its Implications for the Inception of Iron Production and Use," *BASOR* 382 (2019), 89–110.

18 The Iron Age I site of Izbet Sartah is generally identified with biblical Ebenezer. See Aaron Demsky and Moshe Kochavi, "An Israelite Village from the Days of the Judges," *BAR*, September/October 1978.

19 According to the Bible, the Ark did the Philistines no good and was ultimately returned. See Aren M. Maeir, "Did Captured Ark Afflict Philistines with E.D.?" *BAR*, May/June 2008; and Thomas Römer, "L'arche de YHWH: de la guerre à l'alliance," *Études Théologiques et Religieuses* 94 (2019), 95–108.

20 See A.D.H. Mayes, "The Period of Judges and the Rise of the Monarchy," in J.H. Hayes and J.M. Miller, eds., *Israelite and Judaean History* (Philadelphia: Westminster, 1977), 285–331, esp. 325; Nadav Na'aman, "The Pre-Deuteronomistic Story of King Saul and Its Historical Significance," *CBQ* 54 (1992), 638–58; Walter Dietrich, "David, Amnon und Absalom (2 Samuel 13): Literarische, textliche und historische Erwägungen zu den ambivalenten Beziehungen eines Vaters zu seinen Söhnen," *Textus* 23 (2007), 115–43. Nahash's way of treating the Israelites (see Frank Moore Cross, "The Ammonite Oppression of the Tribes of Gad and Ruben," in H. Tadmor and M. Weinfeld, eds., *History, Historiography,*

and Interpretation [Jerusalem: Magnes Press, 1983], 148–58) is attested in Assyria (see Albert Kirk Grayson, *Assyrian Royal Inscriptions I* [Wiesbaden: Harrassowitz, 1972], sec. 530 [esp. n.177]; vol. 2 [1976], sec. 549).

21 See Volkmar Fritz, "Die Deutungen des Königtums Sauls in den Überlieferungen von seiner Enstehung, I Sam 9–11," *ZAW* 88 (1976), 346–62.

22 This number seems to be accepted by J. Alberto Soggin, see *A History of Ancient Israel* (Philadelphia: Westminster, 1984), 49–50.

23 See Joseph Blenkinsopp, "The Quest of the Historical Saul," in J.W. Flanagan and A.W. Robinson, eds., *No Famine in the Land: Studies in Honor of John L. McKenzie* (Missoula, MT: Scholars Press, 1975), 75–79; Na'aman, "Pre-Deuteronomistic Story," (see n.20), 638–58; V. Philips Long, "How Did Saul Become King? Literary Reading and Historical Reconstruction," in A.R. Millard, ed., *Faith, Tradition, and History: Old Testament Historiography in Its Near Eastern Context* (Winona Lake, IN: Eisenbrauns, 1994), 271–84; Siegfried Kreuzer, "Saul—Not Always—at War: A New Perspective on the Rise of Kingship in Israel," in *Saul in Story and Tradition* (see n.11), 39–58; Israel Finkelstein, *The Forgotten Kingdom: The Archaeology and History of Northern Israel* (Atlanta: SBL Press, 2013), with good remarks about the geography but without any serious basis for the historical interpretation of a connection between Saul and Sheshonq.

24 See David M. Gunn, *The Fate of King Saul*, JSOTSup 14 (Sheffield: Sheffield Academic, 1980); Diana Vikander Edelman, *King Saul in the Historiography of Judah*, JSOTSup 121 (Sheffield: Sheffield Academic, 1991); Sara J. Milstein, *Tracking the Master Scribe* (Oxford, Oxford Univ. Press, 2016), 174–206.

25 See André Caquot and Philippe de Robert, *Les livres de Samuel* (Geneva: Labor et fides, 1994), 19–20; Robert P. Gordon, "In Search of David: The David Tradition in Recent Study," in *Faith, Tradition, and History* (see n.23), 285–98, esp. 298.

26 See W. Lee Humphreys, "The Rise and Fall of King Saul," *JSOT* 18 (1980), 74–90; Humphreys, "From Tragic Hero to Villain: A Study of the Figure of Saul and the Development of 1 Samuel," *JSOT* 22 (1982), 95–117.

27 See P. Kyle McCarter Jr., "The Apology of David," *JBL* 99 (1980), 485–504. On this literary genre in Assyria, see Hayim Tadmor, "Autobiographical Apology in the Royal Assyrian Literature," in Tadmor and Weinfeld, eds., *History, Historiography, and Interpretation* (see n. 20), 36–57; Andrew Knapp, *Royal Apologetic in the Ancient Near East*, WAWSup 4 (Atlanta: SBL Press, 2015), 161–276.

28 André Lemaire, "La montagne de Juda (XIII–XIe siècle av. J.-C.)," in E.-M. Laperrousaz, ed., *La protohistoire d'Israël* (Paris: Cerf, 1990), 293–98.

29 Walter Dietrich and Stefan Münger, "Die Herrschaft Sauls und der Norden Israel," in C.G. den Hertog et al., eds., *Saxa Loquentur: Studien zur Archäologie Palästinas/Israels. Festschrift für Volkmar Fritz*, AOAT 302 (Münster: Ugarit-Verlag, 2003), 39–59.

30 One may be skeptical of the idea that Saul was "initially … a petty king of Gibeon," as proposed by Diana Vikander Edelman, in "Saul Ben Kish in History and Tradition," in V. Fritz and P.R. Davies, eds., *The Origins of the Ancient Israelite States*, JSOTSup 228 (Sheffield: Sheffield Academic, 1996), 142–59, esp. 156. One may, however, compare Saul to Labayu, the Late Bronze Age king of Shechem. See Israel Finkelstein, "The Last Labayu: King Saul and the Expansion of the First North Israelite Territorial Entity," in Y. Amit et al., eds., *Essays on Ancient Israel in Its Near Eastern Context: A Tribute to Nadav Na'aman* (Winona Lake, IN: Eisenbrauns, 2006), 171–87.

31 Adam Zertal, *The Manasseh Hill Country Survey I–II*, CHANE 21 (Leiden: Brill, 2004, 2008); see also "'To the Land of the Perizzites and the Giants': On the Israelite Settlement in the Hill Country of Manasseh," in *From Nomadism to Monarchy* (see n. 16), 47–69, esp. 57–60.

32 See Israel Finkelstein, *The Archaeology of the Israelite Settlement* (Jerusalem: IES, 1988), esp. 260–69.

33 Israel Finkelstein and Yitzhak Magen, eds., *Archaeological Survey of the Hill Country of Benjamin* (Jerusalem: IAA, 1993); Amihai Mazar, "Jerusalem and Its Vicinity in Iron Age

I," in *From Nomadism to Monarchy* (see n. 16), 70–91, esp. 70–78.

34 See Moshe Kochavi, "An Ostracon of the Period of the Judges from 'Izbet Sartah," *TA* 4 (1977), 1–13; Israel Finkelstein, *'Izbet Sartah: An Early Iron Age Site near Rosh Ha'ayin, Israel*, British Archaeological Reports, International Series 299 (Oxford: Oxford Univ. Press, 1986).

35 Mazar, "Jerusalem and Its Vicinity" (see n. 33), 75.

36 Israel Finkelstein, "Excavations at Khirbet ed-Dawwara: An Iron Age I Site Northeast of Jerusalem," *TA* 17 (1990), 163–208; Avraham Faust, "Settlement Patterns and State Formation in Southern Samaria and the Archaeology of (a) Saul," in *Saul in Story and Tradition* (see n. 11), 14–38, esp. 26–27.

37 See Nadav Na'aman, "Hirbet ed-Dawara: a Philistine Stronghold on the Benjamin Desert Fringe," *ZDPV* 128 (2012), 1–9.

38 André Lemaire, "Aux origines d'Israël: la montagne d'Ephraïm et le territoire de Manassé," in *La protohistoire d'Israël* (see n. 28), 183–292, esp. 251–55, 284–86.

39 Israel Finkelstein and Zvi Lederman, "Shiloh, 1983," *IEJ* 33 (1983), 267–68; Finkelstein, *Archaeology of the Israelite Settlement* (see n. 32), 225–26, 322–23.

For a popular treatment, see, on the destruction of Ai, Joseph A. Callaway, "A Visit with Ahilud," *BAR*, September/October 1983, 42–53. See Israel Finkelstein, "Shiloh Yields Some, but Not All, of Its Secrets," *BAR*, January/February 1986; "Did the Philistines Destroy the Israelite Sanctuary at Shiloh? The Archaeological Evidence," *BAR*, June 1975.

40 Baruch Rosen, "Subsistence Economy in Iron Age I," in *From Nomadism to Monarchy* (see n. 16), 339–51.

41 Finkelstein, *Archaeology of the Israelite Settlement* (see n. 32), 82; comment in *Biblical Archaeology Today 1984* (see n. 12); "The Emergence of the Monarchy in Israel: The Environmental and Socio-Economic Aspects," *JSOT* 44 (1989), 43–74, esp. 59.

42 Trude Dothan, "What We Know About the Philistines," *BAR*, July/August 1982.

43 Seymour Gitin, "Excavating Ekron," *BAR*, November/December 2005; Trude

Dothan and Seymour Gitin, "Ekron of the Philistines," *BAR*, January/February 1990.

44 See "Philistine Temple Discovered Within Tel Aviv City Limits," *BAR*, June 1975, 1, 6–9; Amihai Mazar, *Excavations at Tell Qasile I, The Philistine Sanctuary*, Qedem 12 (Jerusalem: Hebrew Univ. Press, 1980); *Excavations at Tell Qasile II*, Qedem 20 (1985); Trude Dothan, *The Philistines and Their Material Culture* (New Haven: Yale Univ. Press, 1982); Ze'ev Herzog, "Tel Gerisa," *IEJ* 33 (1983), 121–23; see also "Tel Miqne/Ekron—The Rise and Fall of a Philistine City," *Qadmoniot* 27 (1994), 2–28; Trude Dothan, "Tell Miqne Ekron: The Aegean Affinities of the 'Sea Peoples' ('Philistines') Settlement in Canaan in the Iron Age I," in S. Gitin, ed., *Recent Excavations in Israel: A View to the West: Reports on Kabri, Nami, Miqne-Ekron, Dor, and Ashkelon* (Dubuque, IA: Kendall, Hunt, 1995), 41–59; Lawrence E. Stager, *Ashkelon: Seaport of the Canaanites and the Philistines*, Schweich Lectures on Biblical Archaeology (London, 2004); Moshe Dothan and David Ben-Shlomo, *Ashdod VI: Excavations of Areas H and K (1968–1969)*, IAA Reports 24 (Jerusalem: IAA, 2005); Lawrence E. Stager, "New Discoveries in the Excavations of Ashkelon in the Bronze and Iron Ages," *Qadmoniot* 39 (2006), 2–19; "Ashkelon," *NEAEHL*, vol. 5 (2008), 1,577–1,586; Lawrence E. Stager et al., *Ashkelon I. Introduction and Overview (1985–2006)* (Winona Lake, IN: Eisenbrauns, 2008); Trude Dothan, Yosef Garfinkel, and Seymour Gitin, *Tel Miqne-Ekron Excavations 1985–1988, 1990, 1992–1995: Field IV Lower—The Elite Zone. Part 1: The Iron Age I Early Philistine City* (Winona Lake, IN: Eisenbrauns, 2016).

For a popular treatment, see Lawrence Stager, "When Canaanites and Philistines Ruled Ashkelon," *BAR*, March/April 1991.

45 Aren M. Maeir, "Tell es-Safi/Gath, 1996–2002," *IEJ* 53 (2003), 237–46; "Ten Years of Excavations at Biblical Gat Plishtim," *Qadmoniot* 40, no. 133 (2007), 15–24; Maeir, ed., *Tell es-Safi/Gath I. Report of the 1996–2005 Seasons*, Ägypten und Altes Testament 69 (Wiesbaden: Harrassowitz, 2012); Maeir, "Insights on the Philistine Culture and Related Issues: An Overview of 15 Years of Work at Tell es-Safi/Gath," in *The Ancient Near East in the 12th–10th Centuries B.C.E.* (see n. 9), 345–404; Louise A. Hitchcock and Aren M. Maeir, "New Insights

into the Philistines in Light of Excavations at Tell es-Sâfi/Gath," *NEA* 81 (2018), 6–14; Maeir, "Philistine and Israelite Identities: Some Comparative Thoughts," *Die Welt des Orients* 49 (2019), 151–60; Maeir et al., "Technological Insights on Philistine Culture: Perspectives from Tell es-Safi/Gath," *Journal of Eastern Mediterranean Archaeology and Heritage Studies* 7 (2019), 76–118.

For a popular treatment, see Carl S. Ehrlich and Aren M. Maeir, "Excavating Philistine Gath: Have We Found Goliath's Hometown?" *BAR*, November/December 2001.

46 This *lament* could well not be from David himself but from saulide circles. See, e.g., Eben Scheffler, "Saving Saul from the Deuteronomist," in J.C. de Moor and H.F. Van Rooy, eds., *Past, Present, Future*, Oudtestamentische Studiën 44 (Leiden; Boston: Brill, 2000), 263–71, esp. 266.

47 Mario Liverani, "Le 'origini' d'Israele projetto irrealizzable di ricerca etnogenetica," *Rivista biblica* 28 (1980), 9–31.

48 J. Alberto Soggin, "The Davidic-Solomonic Kingdom," in *Israelite and Judaean History* (see n. 20), 332–80; Soggin, "The History of Israel—A Study in Some Questions of Method," *Eretz-Israel* 14 (Jerusalem: IES, 1978), 44–51; Soggin, *History of Ancient Israel* (see n. 22), 19–40.

49 Soggin, "Davidic-Solomonic Kingdom" (see n. 48), 332.

50 See Philip R. Davies, *In Search of 'Ancient Israel,'* JSOTSup 148 (Sheffield: Sheffield Academic, 1992), 68–69; Giovanno Garbini, *History and Ideology in Ancient Israel* (New York: Crossroad, 1988), 21–32; Ernst A. Knauf, "From History to Interpretation," in *The Fabric of History* (see n. 3), 26–64, esp. 39. See also David W. Jamieson-Drake, *Scribes and Schools in Monarchic Judah: A Socio-Archaeological Approach*, JSOTSup 109 (Sheffield: Almond Press, 1991) and my critical review, "Review of D.W. Jamieson-Drake," in *JAOS* 112 (see n. 9).

51 Knauf, "From History to Interpretation," (see n. 50), 26–64, esp. 39.

52 See also André Lemaire, "La dynastie davidique (*byt dwd*) dans deux inscriptions ouest-sémitiques du IXe s. av. J.-C.," *Studi epigrafici e linguistici* 11 (1994), 17–19; Lemaire,

"The Mesha Stele and the Omri Dynasty," in *Ahab Agonistes: The Rise and Fall of the Omri Dynasty*, LHBOTS 421 (New York: T&T Clark, 2007), 135–44; esp. 141; Lemaire, "La stèle de Mésha: problèmes épigraphiques, philologiques et chronologiques," in H. Niehr and Th. Römer, eds., *Nouvelles recherches autour de la stèle de Mésha*, ADPV (Wiesbaden: Harrassowitz, forthcoming). A few scholars did not accept this reading and interpretation (see lately Erasmus Gass, *Die Moabiter: Geschichte und Kultur eines ostjordanischen Volkes im 1. Jahrtausend v. Chr.*, ADPV 38 [Wiesbaden: Harrassowitz, 2009], 48; Christian Frevel, *Geschichte Israels* [Stuttgart: Kohlhammer, 2016], 110; Israel Finkelstein, Nadav Na'aman, and Thomas Römer, "Restoring Line 31 in the Mesha Stele: The 'House of David' or Biblical Balak?" *TA* 46 [2019], 3–11; and Na'aman, "The Alleged 'Beth David' in the Mesha Stele: The Case Against it," *TA* 46 [2019], 192–97), but without any serious epigraphical argument (Michael Langlois, "The Kings, the City and the House of David in the Mesha Stele in Light of New Imaging Techniques," *Semitica* 61 [2019], 23–47)."

For a popular treatment on Mesha, see André Lemaire, "'House of David' Restored in Moabite Inscription," *BAR*, May/June 1994.

53 See also André Lemaire, "Épigraphie palestinienne: nouveaux documents I. Fragments de stèle araméenne de Tell Dan (IXᵉ s. av. J.-C.)," *Henoch* 16 (1994), 87–93; Avraham Biran and Joseph Naveh, "The Tel Dan Inscription: A New Fragment," *IEJ* 45 (1995), 1–18; William M. Schniedewind, "Tel Dan Stela: New Light on Aramaic and Jehu's Revolt," *BASOR* 302 (1996), 75–90; André Lemaire, "The Tel Dan Stela as a Piece of Royal Historiography," *JSOT* 81 (1998), 3–15; "'Maison de David,' 'maison de Mopsos', et les Hivvites," in C. Cohen et al., eds., *Sefer Moshe: The Moshe Weinfeld Jubilee Volume* (Winona Lake, IN: Eisenbrauns, 2004), 303–12; Hallvard Hagelia, *The Tel Dan Inscription*, Studia Semitica Upsaliensia 22 (Uppsala: Uppsala Univ. Library, 2006), 165–67; Shuichi Hasegawa, *Aram and Israel During the Jehuite Dynasty*, BZAW 434 (Berlin: de Gruyter, 2012), 35–46; K. Lawson Younger Jr., *A Political History of the Arameans: From Their Origins to the End of Their Polities*, Archaeology and Biblical Studies 123 (Atlanta: SBL Press, 2016), 592–613.

For a popular treatment on Hazael and the Dan inscription, see "'David' Found at Dan," *BAR*, March/April 1994.

54 See, e.g., Gary n. Knoppers, "The Vanishing Solomon: The Disappearance of the United Monarchy from Recent Histories of Ancient Israel," *JBL* 116 (1997), 19–44.

55 See Nadav Na'aman, "David's Sojourn in Keilah in Light of the Amarna Letters," *VT* 60 (2010), 87–97.

56 Ziklag is generally located at Tell esh-Shari'a. See Eliezer D. Oren, "Ziklag—A Biblical City on the Edge of the Negev," *BA* 45 (1982), 155–66, esp. 163. For a divergent identification at Tell es-Seba', see Volkmar Fritz, "Der Beitrag der Archäologie zur historischen Topographie Palästinas am Beispiel von Ziklag," *ZDPV* 106 (1990), 78–85; see also "Where Is David's Ziklag?" *BAR*, May/June 1993. Yosef Garfinkel and Saar Ganor, "Was Khirbet al-Ra'i Ancient Ziklag?" *Strata: Bulletin of the Anglo-Israel Archaeological Society* 37 (2019), 51–59.

57 For the location of Mahanaim at Tulul edh-Dhahab, see André Lemaire, "Galaad et Makir," *VT* 31 (1981), 39–61, esp. 53–54.

58 See Nadav Na'aman, "The Kingdom of Ishbaal," *BN* 54 (1990), 33–37 (= *Ancient Israel's History and Historiography: The First Temple Period*, Collected Essays, vol. 3 [Winona Lake, IN: Eisenbrauns, 2006], 18–22).

59 On the problem of David's possible responsibility, see James C. VanderKam, "Davidic Complicity in the Deaths of Abner and Eshbaal: A Historical and Redactional Study," *JBL* 99 (1980), 521–39; Jean-Claude Haelewyck, "La mort d'Abner: 2 Sam 3, 1–39," *RB* 102 (1995), 161–92.

60 N.L. Tidwell, "The Philistine Incursions into the Valley of Rephaim," in J. A. Emerton, ed., *Studies in the Historical Books of the O.T.*, VTSup 30 (Leiden; Boston: Brill, 1980), 190–212.

61 The identity of the Jebusites remains enigmatic despite the suggestion of Nadav Na'aman, "Jebusites and Jabeshites in the Saul and David Story-Cycles," *Biblica* 95 (2014), 481–97.

62 See R. Rezetko, *Source and Revision in the Narratives of David's Transfer of the Ark: Text, Language, and Story in 2 Samuel 6 and 1 Chronicles 13, 15–16*, LHBOTS 470 (New York: T&T Clark, 2007); Walter Dietrich, "Die Überlieferung der Lade nach Jerusalem (2 Sam 6): Geschichten und Geschichte," in A.A. Graeme and E. Eynikel, eds., *For and Against David: Story and History in the Books of Samuel*, BETL 232 (Leuven: Peeters, 2010), 235–53; Nadav Na'aman, "A Hidden Anti-David Polemic in 2 Samuel 6:2," in D.S. Vanderhooft and A. Wintzer, eds., *Literature as Politics, Politics as Literature: Essays on the Ancient Near East in Honor of Peter Machinist* (Winona Lake, IN: Eisenbrauns, 2013), 321–28; Daniel E. Fleming, "David and the Ark: A Jerusalem Festival Reflected in Royal Narrative," in *Literature as Politics* (see above), 75–95; Nadav Na'aman, "The Judahite Temple at Tel Moza near Jerusalem: The House of Obed-Edom?" *TA* 44 (2017), 3–13.

63 See Israel Finkelstein et al., "Excavations at Kiriath-Jearim near Jerusalem, 2017: A Preliminary Report," *Semitica* 60 (2018), 31–84, esp. 32–38; Finkelstein et al., "Les fouilles archéologiques de Qiryat Yéarim et le récit de l'arche d'alliance," *Comptes rendus de l'Académie des inscriptions et belles-lettres* (2018), 983–1,000.

64 Jon D. Levenson and Baruch Halpern, "The Political Import of David's Marriages," *JBL* 99 (1980), 507–18.

65 See Nadav Na'aman, "The List of David's Officers (*šālîšim*)," *VT* 38 (1988), 71–79 (= *Ancient Israel's History and Historiography* [see n. 58], 62–70).

66 See Edward Lipiński, "Aram et Israel du Xᵉ au VIIIᵉ siècle av. n. è.," *Acta Antiqua* 27 (1979), 49–102; P.E. Dion, *Les Araméens à l'âge du Fer: histoire politique et structures sociales*, Études bibliques NS 34 (Paris: Gabalda, 1997), 79–84.

67 On this kingdom, see Edward Lipiński, *The Aramaeans: Their Ancient History, Culture, Religion*, OLA 100 (Leuven: Peeters, 2000), 331–41; Younger, *A Political History of the Arameans* (see n. 53), 192–204.

68 Christa Schäfer-Lichtenberger describes this period as the "inchoate early state," see "Sociological and Biblical Views of the Early State," in *Origins of the Ancient Israelite States* (see n. 30), 78–105, esp. 92. For the social and

political evolution, see also F.S. Frick, *The Formation of the State in Ancient Israel*, SWBAS 4 (Sheffield: Almond Press, 1985); Robert B. Coote and Keith W. Whitelam, *The Emergence of Early Israel in Historical Perspective of the Davidic State*, SWBAS 5 (Sheffield: Almond Press, 1987), 139–66; Juval Portugali, "Theoretical Speculations on the Transition from Nomadism to Monarchy," in *From Nomadism to Monarchy* (see n. 16), 203–17, esp. 212–17.

69 See Sophia Katharina Bietenhard, *Des Königs General: Die Heerführertraditionen in den vorstaatlichen und frühen staatlichen Zeit und die Joabgestalt in 2 Sam 2–20; 1 Kön 1–2*, OBO 163 (Göttingen: Universitätsverlag, Vandenhoeck & Ruprecht, 1998); Michael A. Eschelbach, *Has Joab Foiled David?: A Literary Study of the Importance of Joab's Character in Relation to David*, Studies in Biblical Literature 76 (New York: P. Lang, 2005); David Janzen, "'What He Did for Me': David's Warning About Joab in 1 Kings 2.5," *JSOT* 39 (2015), 265–79.

70 However, Gordon J. Wenham ("Were David's Sons Priests?" *ZAW* 87 [1975], 79–82) proposed to read *sknym* instead of *khnym*.

71 See Stefan Seiler, *Die Geschichte von der Thronfolge Davids (2 Sam 9–20; 1 Kön 1–2)*, BZAW 267 (Berlin: de Gruyter, 1998); John Barton, "Dating the 'Succession Narrative,'" in J. Day, ed., *In Search of Pre-Exilic Israel* (New York: T&T Clark, 2004), 95–106; Joseph Blenkinsopp, "Another Contribution to the Succession Narrative Debate (2 Samuel 11–20; 1 Kings 1–2)," *JSOT* 38 (2014), 35–58; Nadav Na'aman, "Source and Composition in the Story of Sheba's Revolt (2 Samuel 20)," *RB* 125 (2018), 340–52 (with a late dating).

72 For a literary analysis of these traditions, see François Langlamet, "David et la maison de Saül," *RB* 86 (1979), 194–213, 385–436, 481–513.

73 See Daniel Bodi, *The Michal Affair: From Zimri-Lim to the Rabbis* (Sheffield: Phoenix Press, 2005).

74 Henri Cazelles, "David's Monarchy and the Gibeonite Claim," *PEQ* 87 (1955), 165–75.

75 See also the hypothetical essays of Omer Sergi, "The United Monarchy and the Kingdom of Jeroboam II in the Story of Absalom and Sheba's Revolts (2 Samuel 15–20)," *Hebrew Bible and Ancient Israel (HBAI)* 6

(2017), 329–53; Nadav Na'aman, "Sources and Composition in the Story of Sheba's Revolt (2 Samuel 20)," *RB* 125 (2018), 340–52; Matthiew J. Suriano, "Remembering Absalom's Death in 2 Samuel 18–19: History, Memory and Inscriptions," *HBAI* 7 (2017), 172–200.

76 Such is the presentation of 1 Kings 2. See J. Vermeylen, "David a-t-il été assassiné?" *RB* 107 (2000), 481–94; Baruch Halpern and Regine Hunziker-Rudewall, in Ch. Schäfer-Lichtenberger, ed., *Die Samuelbücher und die Deutronomisten*, BWA(N)T 188 (Stuttgart: Kohlhammer, 2010), 76–107.

77 See Daniel Bodi, "The Story of Samuel, Saul, and David," in B.T. Arnold and R.S. Hess, eds., *Ancient Israel's History: An Introduction to Issues and Sources*, (Grand Rapids: Baker, 2014), 190–226; Steven M. Ortiz, "United Monarchy, Archaeology, and Literary Sources," *Ancient Israel's History* (see above), 227–61.

78 Nadav Na'aman, "Sources and Composition in the History of David," in *Origins of the Ancient Israelite States,* (see n. 30), 170–86 (= *Ancient Israel's History and Historiography* [see n. 58], 23–37). His argumentation, however, in "In Search of Reality Behind the Account of David's Wars with Israel's Neighbors," *IEJ* 52 (2002), 200–24 (= *Ancient Israel's History and Historiography* [see n. 58], 38–61) is not convincing.

79 André Lemaire, "Vers l'histoire de la rédaction des livres des Rois," *ZAW* 98 (1986), 221–36 (= "Toward a Redactional History of the Book of Kings," in Gary n. Knoppers and J. Gordon McConville, eds., *Reconsidering Israel and Judah: Recent Studies on the Deuteronomistic History* [Winona Lake, IN: Eisenbrauns, 2000], 446–61); Caquot and de Robert, *Les livres de Samuel* (see n. 25), 19–20; see also Erik Eynikel, *The Reform of Kings Josiah and the Composition of the Deuteronomistic History*, Old Testament Studies 33 (Leiden: Brill, 1996); Baruch Halpern, "The Construction of the Davidic State: An Exercise in Historiography," in *The Origins of the Ancient Israelite States* (see n. 30), 44–75. For a divergent view with a late writing, see Omer Sergi et al., "Memories of the Early Israelite Monarchy in the Books of Samuel and Kings," in I. Koch et al., eds., *Writing, Rewriting and Overwriting in the Books of Deuteronomy and the Former Prophets: Essays in Honour of Cynthia Edenburg*, BETL 304 (London, Peeters, 2019), 173–94

80 Niels P. Lemche, "David's Rise," *JSOT* 10 (1978), 2–25. For a detailed historical interpretation, see Baruch Halpern, *David's Secret Demons: Messiah, Murderer, Traitor, King* (Grand Rapids: Eerdmans, 2001), 73–103.

81 See J.D. Levinson and Baruch Halpern, "The Political Import of David's Marriages," *JBL* 99 (1980), 507–28; Daniel Bodi and Brigitte Donnet-Guez, *The Michal Affair: From Zimri-Lim to the Rabbis*, Hebrew Bible Monographs 3 (Sheffield: Phoenix Press, 2005); A. Wénin, "Bethsabée, épouse de David et mère de Salomon," in C. Lichtert and D. Nocquet, eds., *Le roi Salomon: Un héritage en question. Hommage à Jacques Vermeylen* (Brussels: Lessius, 2008), 207–28; André Lemaire, "The Residence of Abigail in 1 Samuel 25," in *Abigail, Wife of David and Other Ancient Oriental Women*, Hebrew Bible Monographs 60 (Sheffield: Phoenix Press, 2013), 7 11.

82 See A. Knapp, *Royal Apologetics in the Ancient Near East*, WAWSup 4 (Atlanta: SBL Press, 2015), at 275.

83 On Bathsheba, see Wénin, "Bethsabée," in *Le roi Salomon* (see n. 81), 207–28. On the problem of Nathan's personality, see Ilse von Loewenclau, "Der Prophet Nathan im Zweilicht von theologischer Deutung und Historie," in E. Albertz et al., eds., *Werden und Wirken des Alten Testaments: Festschrift C. Westermann* (Neukirchen; Göttingen: Neukirchener Verlag; Vandenhoeck & Ruprecht, 1980), 202–15.

84 See Tomoo Ishida, "Solomon's Succession to the Throne of David—Political Analysis," in T. Ishida, ed., *Studies in the Period of David and Solomon* (Tokyo: Yamakawa-Shuppansha, 1982), 175–87.

85 For a tentative interpretation, see Nadav Na'aman, "Memories of Monarchical Israel in the Narratives of David's Wars with Israel's Neighbours," *HBAI* 6 (2017), 308–28.

86 See Walter Dietrich, "David and the Philistines: Literature and History," in *The Ancient Near East in the 12th–10th Centuries B.C.E.* (see n. 9), 79–98, at 96.

87 See Herbert Donner, "The Interdependence of Internal Affairs and Foreign Policy During the Davidic-Solomonic Period (With

Special Regard to the Phoenician Coast)," in *Studies in the Period of David and Solomon* (see n. 84), 205–14.

88 In 2 Samuel 8:13–14, there was probably a confusion between "Edom" and "Aram," which were written in the same way in the fifth–third centuries B.C.E. Second Samuel 8:14a seems to be a doublet of 2 Samuel 8:6a.

89 See G. Galil, "A Concise History of Palistin/Patin/Unqi/ʿmq in the 11th–9th Centuries B.C.," *Semitica* 56 (2014), 75–104, esp. 78, 84; Younger, *A Political History of the Arameans* (see n. 53), 146, 446.

90 See J.D. Hawkins, "Cilicia, the Amuq, and Aleppo: New Light on a Dark Age," *NEA* 72 (2009), 164–73; Hawkins, "The Inscriptions of the Aleppo Temple," *Anatolian Studies* 61 (2011), 35–54; I. Singer, "The Philistines in the North and the Kingdom of Taita," in *Ancient Near East in the 12th–10th Centuries B.C.E.* (see n. 9), 451–71.

91 The identification is proposed and argued by C. Steitler, "The Biblical King Toi of Hamath and the Late Hittite State P/Walas(a) tina," *BN* 46 (2010), 81–99. It is disputed by Nadav Naʾaman, see "Memories of Monarchical Israel in the Narratives of David's Wars with Israel's Neighbours," *HBAI* 6 (2017), 308–28, at 323, n. 50.

92 See Abraham Malamat, "A Political Look at the Kingdom of David and Solomon and Its Relations with Egypt," in *Studies in the Period of David and Solomon* (see n. 84), 189–205; "The Monarchy of David and Solomon," in H. Shanks and B. Mazar, eds., *Recent Archaeology in the Land of Israel* (Washington, DC; Jerusalem: BAS; IES, 1984), 161–72.

93 See Ziony Zevit, "The Davidic-Solomonic Empire from the Perspective of Archaeological Bibliology," in C. Cohen et al., eds., *Birkat Shalom: Studies in the Bible, Ancient Near Eastern Literature, and Postbiblical Judaism Presented to Shalom M. Paul* (Winona Lake, IN: Eisenbrauns, 2008), 201–24.

94 These possibly include Megiddo (Stratum VIA), Beth-Shean (Stratum V), and Yoqneam. See Amihai Mazar, "The Excavations at Tel Beth-Shean in 1989–1990," in A. Biran and J. Aviram, eds., *Biblical Archaeology Today 1990* (Jerusalem: IES, 1993), 607–19, esp. 617.

95 Yohanan Aharoni, "The Building Activities of David and Solomon," *IEJ* 24 (1974), 13–16; see also Hershel Shanks, "King David as Builder," *BAR*, March 1975, 13.

96 Eilat Mazar, "Excavate King David's Palace!" *BAR*, January/February 1997; "Did I Find King David's Palace?" *BAR*, January/February 2006; Avraham Faust, "Did Eilat Find David's Palace?" *BAR*, September/October 2012.

97 See also Israel Finkelstein, Zeev Herzog, and David Ussishkin, "Has King David's Palace in Jerusalem Been Found?" *TA* 34 (2007), 142–64; Ronny Reich and Eli Shukron, "The Date of City-Wall 501 in Jerusalem," *TA* 35 (2008), 114–22. For a popular treatment, see Hershel Shanks, "The Devil Is Not So Black as He Is Painted," *BAR*, May/June 2010.

98 See Amihai Mazar, "Archaeology and the Biblical Narrative: The Case of the United Monarchy," in *One God—One Cult—One Nation* (see n. 3), 29–58; Avraham Faust, "The Large Stone Structure in the City of David," *ZDPV* 126 (2010), 116–30; Nadav Naʾaman, "Biblical and Historical Jerusalem," *Biblica* 93 (2012), 21–42; William G. Dever, *Beyond the Texts: An Archaeological Portrait of Ancient Israel and Judah* (Atlanta: SBL Press, 2017), 276–83; Matthieu Richelle, *The Bible and Archaeology* (Peabody, MA: Hendrickson, 2018), chap. 5.

99 See, e.g., Israel Finkelstein, "The 'Large Stone Structure' in Jerusalem: Reality Versus Yearning," *ZDPV* 127 (2011), 1–10.

100 That is part of the truth; see Margreet Steiner, "David's Jerusalem: Fiction or Reality? It's Not There: Archaeology Proves a Negative," *BAR*, July/August 1998, 26–33, 62–63. However, such a small town may still have been the capital of a strong chiefdom. See Nadav Naʾaman, "The Contribution of the Amarna Letters to the Debate on Jerusalem's Political Position in the Tenth Century B.C.E.," *BASOR* 304 (1996), 17–27; Naʾaman, "Cow Town or Royal Capital? Evidence for Iron Age Jerusalem," *BAR*, July/August 1997, 43–47, 67; and Naʾaman, "David's Jerusalem: Fiction or Reality? It Is There: Ancient Texts Prove It," *BAR*, July/August 1998, 42–44. See also Jane Cahill, "David's Jerusalem: Fiction or Reality? It Is There: The Archaeological Evidence Proves It," *BAR*, July/August 1998, 34–41, 63; David D. Pioske, *David's Jerusalem*

Between Memory and History, Routledge Studies in Religion 45 (New York: Routledge, 2015), 177–259; Hermann Michael Niemann, "Judah and Jerusalem: Reflections on the Relationship Between Tribe and City and the Role of Jerusalem in Judah," *ZDPV* 135 (2019), 1–31.

101 Avi Ofer, "'All the Hill Country of Judah': From a Settlement Fringe to a Prosperous Monarchy," in *From Nomadism to Monarchy*, (see n. 16), 92–121, esp. 104, 119–21; Avi Ofer, "Hebron," in *NEAEHL*, 606–609; Avi Ofer, "The Monarchic Period in the Judaean Highland: A Spatial Overview," in A. Mazar, ed., *Studies in the Archaeology of the Iron Age in Israel and Jordan*, JSOTSup 331 (Sheffield: Sheffield Academic, 2001), 14–37.

102 Jeffery Chadwick, "Discovering Hebron," *BAR*, September/October 2005.

103 Yosef Garfinkel and Saar Ganor, *Khirbet Qeiyafa*, vol. 1: *Excavation Report 2007–2008* (Jerusalem: IES, 2009), vii, 3–18; Garfinkel, Igor Kreinerman, and Peter Zilberg, *Debating Khirbet Qeiyafa: A Fortified City in Judah from the Time of King David* (Jerusalem: IES, 2015). See also Dever, *Beyond the Texts* (see n. 98), 285–88.

104 Hershel Shanks, "Newly Discovered: A Fortified City from King David's Time," *BAR*, January/February 2009; Yosef Garfinkel, Michael Hasel, and Martin Klingbeil, "An Ending and a Beginning: Why We're Leaving Qeiyafa and Going to Lachish," *BAR*, November/December 2013.

105 Nadav Na'aman, "Khirbet Qeiyafa in Context," *UF* 42 (2010), 497–526; Na'aman, "Was Khirbet Qeiyafa a Judahite City? The Case Against It," *Journal of Hebrew Scriptures* 17 (2017), article 7 (40 pp.). See also Silvia Schroer and Stefan Munger, eds., *Khirbet Qeiyafa in the Shephelah: Papers Presented at a Colloquium of the Swiss Society for Ancient Near Eastern Studies Held at the University of Bern, September 6, 2014*, OBO 282 (Fribourg; Göttingen: Academic Press; Vandenhoeck & Ruprecht, 2017).

106 Egypt was then practically divided between the kingdoms of Tanis and Thebes.

107 Siegfried Herrmann, "King David's State," in W.B. Barrick and J.R. Spencer, eds., *In the Shelter of Elyon: Essays on Ancient*

Palestinian Life and Literature in Honor of G.W. Ahlström, JSOTSup 31 (Sheffield: Sheffield Academic, 1984), 261–75.

108 See André Lemaire, *The Birth of Monotheism: The Rise and Disappearance of Yahwism* (Washington, DC: BAS, 2007), 36–41.

109 See above n. 52.

110 Malamat, "A Political Look," in *Studies in the Period of David and Solomon* (see n. 84), esp. 197–201; Kenneth A. Kitchen, *The Third Intermediate Period in Egypt (1100–650 B.C.)*, 2nd ed. (Warminster, UK: Aris & Phillips, 1986), 280–83.

For a popular treatment, see Abraham Malamat, "The First Peace Treaty Between Israel and Egypt," *BAR*, September/October 1979.

111 William G. Dever, "Further Excavations at Gezer, 1967–1971," *BA* 34 (1971), 110; Dever, "Gezer," *NEAEHL*, 496–506.

112 See also 1 Kings 11:1, 5, 7. If Rehoboam was 41 years old when he became king, the marriage of Solomon with Naamah must have taken place toward the end of David's reign. See Abraham Malamat, "Naamah, the Ammonite Princess, King Solomon's Wife," *RB* 106 (1999), 35–40.

113 See D. Noël, "Le surdimensionnement du royaume de Salomon en 1 R 5,1.4," *Transeuphratène* 29 (2005), 155–70.

114 E.W. Heaton, *Solomon's New Men: The Emergence of Ancient Israel as a National State* (London: Thames & Hudson, 1974).

115 This mention of Zadok and Abiathar is probably a later addition taken from 2 Samuel 8:17.

116 Trygve N.D. Mettinger, *Solomonic State Officials* (Lund, Sweden: Gleerup, 1971).

117 Yohanan Aharoni, "The Solomonic Districts," *TA* 3 (1976); Hartmut n. Rösel, "Zu den 'Gauen' Salomons," *ZDPV* 100 (1986), 84–90; Volkmar Fritz, "Die Verwaltungsgebiete Salomos nach 1 Kön. 4,7–19," in *Meilenstein: Festgabe für Herbert Donner*, Ägypten und Altes Testament 30 (Wiesbaden: Harrassowitz, 1995), 19–26. However, there is some confusion about the land of Hepher. André Lemaire, "Le 'pays de Hepher' et les 'filles de Zelophehad' à la lumière des ostraca de Samarie," *Semitica* 22 (1972), 13–20; Lemaire,

Inscriptions hébraïques I, Les ostraca (Paris: Cerf, 1977), 287–89; J. Kamlah, "Die Liste der Regionalfürsten in 1 Kön 4,7–19 als historische Quelle für die Zeit Salomos," *BN* 106 (2001), 57–78; Thomas Römer, "Salomon d'après les Deutéronomistes: un roi ambigu," in *Le roi Salomon* (see n. 81), 98–130, esp. 104–105 (nuanced); Koert van Bekkum, "'The Situation Is More Complicated,' Archaeology and Text in the Historical Reconstruction of the Iron Age IIA Southern Levant," in E. van der Steen et al., eds., *Exploring the Narrative: Jerusalem and Jordan in the Bronze and Iron Ages*, LHBOTS 583 (London: Bloomsbury, 2014), 215–44, esp. 226–36. For a divergent historical appreciation, see Herrmann M. Niemann, *Herrschaft, Königtum, und Staat*, FAT 6 (Tübingen: Mohr Siebeck, 1993), 17–41, 246–51; Paul S. Ash, "Solomon's? District? List," *JSOT* 67 (1995), 67–86; Nadav Na'aman, "Solomon's District List (1 Kings 4:7–19) and the Assyrian Province System in Palestine," in Na'aman, *Ancient Israel's History and Historiography* (see n. 58), 102–19.

118 See Richard S. Hess, "The Form and Structure of the Solomonic District List in 1 Kings 4:7–19," in G.D. Young et al., eds., *Crossing Boundaries and Linking Horizons, Studies in Honor of M.C. Astour* (Bethesda, MD: CDL Press, 1997), 279–92.

119 Moshe Elat, "The Monarchy and the Development of Trade in Ancient Israel," in E. Lipiński, ed., *State and Temple Economy in the Ancient Near East II* (Leuven: Dept Oriëntalistiek, 1979), 527–46.

120 On the problem of the identification of Ophir, see Vassilios Christidès, "L'énigme d'Ophir," *RB* 77 (1970), 240–46; Lois Berkowitz, "Has the U.S. Geological Survey Found King Solomon's Gold Mines?" *BAR*, September 1977, 1, 28–33; Manfred Görg, "Ofir und Punt," *BN* 82 (1996), 5–8; Edward Lipiński, *Itineraria Phoenicia*, Studia Phoenicia XVII / OLA 127 (Leuven: Peeters, 2004), 189–223. By comparison with the ancient Egyptian texts, the most probable solution still seems Somalia-Ethiopia.

121 See André Lemaire, "Les Phéniciens et le commerce entre la Mer Rouge et la Mer Méditerranée," in Edward Lipiński, ed., *Phoenicia and the East Mediterranean in the First Millennium B.C.*, Studia Phoenicia 5/OLA

22 (Leuven: Peeters, 1987), 49–60; Avner Raban, "Phoenician Harbours in the Levant," *Michmanim* 11 (1997), 7*–27*, esp. 13*–15*; Maria E. Aubet, "Aspects of Tyrian Trade and Colonization in the Eastern Mediterranean," *Münstersche Beiträge zur antiken Handelsgeschichte* 19 (2000), 70–120, esp. 84–90.

122 On the change of defense strategy under Solomon, see Chris Hauer, "Economics of National Security in Solomonic Israel," *JSOT* 18 (1980), 63–73.

123 See Yukata Ikeda, "Solomon's Trade in Horses and Chariots in Its International Setting," in *Studies in the Period of David and Solomon* (see n. 84), 215–38; André Lemaire, "Chars et cavaliers dans l'ancien Israël," *Transeuphratène* 15 (1998), 165–82.

124 See Sarah Japhet, "The Wall of Jerusalem from a Double Perspective: Kings Versus Chronicles," in *Essays on Ancient Israel in Its Near Eastern Context* (see n. 30), 205–19.

125 See Gösta W. Ahlström, *Royal Administration and National Religion* (Leiden: Brill, 1982). For this motive in Assyria, see Sylvie Lackenbacher, *Le roi bâtisseur, les récits de construction assyriens des origines à Téglatphalazar III* (Paris: Ed. Recherche sur les civilisations, A.D.P.F., 1982).

126 See Eilat Mazar, "Royal Gateway to Ancient Jerusalem Uncovered," *BAR*, May/June 1989; Eilat Mazar, "King David's Palace," *BAR*, January/February 1997.

127 See Nili Lipschitz, "Cedar of Lebanon: Exploring the Roots," *BAR*, May/June 2013.

128 Cabul is probably to be identified with Ras Abu Zeitun. See Zvi Gal, "Cabul, Jiphtah-El, and the Boundary Between Asher and Zebulun in the Light of Archaeological Evidence," *ZDPV* 101 (1985), 114–27.

129 Victor Hurowitz, "Inside Solomon's Temple," *BR*, April 1994; Hurowitz, "Solomon's Temple in Context," *BAR*, March/April 2011; see also Madeleine Mumcuoglu and Yosef Garfinkel, "The Puzzling Doorways of Solomon's Temple," *BAR*, July/August 2015.

130 See David Ussishkin, "The Temple Mount in Jerusalem During the First Temple Period: An Archaeologist's View," in D. Schloen, ed., *Exploring the Longue Durée: Essays in Honor of Lawrence E. Stager* (Winona Lake, IN:

Eisenbrauns, 2009), 473–83; André Lemaire, "The Evolution of the 8th Century B.C.E. Jerusalem Temple," in I. Finkelstein and n. Na'aman, eds., *The Fire Signals of Lachish: Studies in the Archaeology and History of Israel in the Late Bronze Age, Iron Age, and Persian Period in Honor of David Ussishkin* (Winona Lake, IN: Eisenbrauns, 2011), 195–202; P. Dubovský, *The Building of the First Temple: A Study in Redactional, Text-Critical, and Historical Perspective*, FAT 103 (Tübingen: Mohr Siebeck, 2015); W. Zwickel, "Die Beziehungen zwischen Tempel und Palast im Eisenzeitlichen Israel," in *Kings, Gods, and People: Establishing Monarchies in the Ancient World*, Acta Antiqua Mediterranea et Orientalia 4, AOAT 390/4 (Münster: Ugarit-Verlag, 2016), 187–207.

131 J. Monson, "The 'Ain Dara Temple and the Jerusalem Temple," in G.M. Beckman and Th.J. Lewis, eds., *Text, Artifact, and Image Revealing Ancient Israelite Religion*, Brown Judaic Studies 366 (Providence, RI: Brown Judaic Studies, 2006), 273–99.

132 Z. Greenhut and A. De Groot, *Salvage Excavations at Tel Moẓa: The Bronze and Iron Age Settlement and Later Occupations*, IAA Reports 39 (Jerusalem: IAA, 2009); S. Kilevitz, "The Iron IIA Judahite Temple at Tel Moẓa," *TA* 42 (2015), 147–64. See also Nadav Na'aman, "The Judahite Temple at Tel Moẓa near Jerusalem: The House of Obed-Edom?" *TA* 44 (2017), 3–13.

133 Keith W. Whitelam, "The Symbols of Power: Aspects of Royal Propaganda in the United Monarchy," *BA* 49 (1986), 166–73.

134 See J. Alberto Soggin, "Compulsory Labor Under David and Solomon," in *Studies in the Period of David and Solomon* (see n. 84), 259–67.

135 Julio C. Trebolle Barrera, *Salomon y Jeroboan* (Valencia, Spain: Institucion San Jeronimo, 1980), esp. 364–66.

136 Actually "Hadad" sounds more like an Aramean name, and Hadad originally was probably an Aramean. In the Hebrew text of the Bible, there are several confusions between "Aram" and "Edom." The Edomites seem to have been independent, with their own king, only about the year 845 B.C.E. (see 2 Kings 8:20–22). So Solomon's political power over Aramean countries was very short, if it ever existed. See André Lemaire, "Hadad l'édomite ou Hadad l'araméen?" *BN* 43 (1987), 14–18; Lemaire, "D'Édom à l'Idumée et à Rome," in A. Sérandour, ed., *Des Sumériens aux Romains d'Orient: La perception géographique du monde*, Antiquités sémitiques 2 (Paris: Maisonneuve, 1997), 81–103, esp. 85; Lemaire, "Les premiers rois araméens dans la tradition biblique," in P.M. Michèle Daviau et al., ed., *The World of the Aramaeans I: Biblical Studies in Honour of Paul-Eugène Dion*, JSOT-Sup 324 (Sheffield: Sheffield Academic, 2001), 113–43, esp. 129–34. For a divergent view, see Nadav Na'aman, "Israel, Edom, and Egypt in the 10th Century B.C.E.," *TA* 19 (1992), 71–93, esp. 75; Younger, *A Political History of the Arameans* (see n. 53), 566–71.

137 For a literary criticism of these texts, see Helga Weippert, "Die Ätiologie des Nordreiches und seines Königshauses (1 Reg 11:29–40)," *ZAW* 95 (1983), 344–75; A. Schenker, "Jéroboam et la division du royaume dans la Septante ancienne LXX 1 R 12,24 a-z, TM 11–12; 14 et l'histoire deutéronomiste," in A. de Pury, T. Römer, and J.-D. Macchi, eds., *Israël construit son histoire, l'historiographie deutéronomiste à la lumière des recherches récentes* (Geneva: Labor et fides, 1995), 194–236.

138 The Masoretic text has "Molech," but the context indicates that we must read "Milcom."

139 Probably the Mount of Scandal or Mount of Perdition (*har hammashit*).

140 J. Maxwell Miller, "Separating the Solomon of History from the Solomon of Legend," in L.K. Handy, ed., *The Age of Solomon: Scholarship at the Turn of the Millennium*, Studies in the History and Culture of the Ancient Near East 11 (Leiden: Brill, 1997), 1–24, esp. 24; J. Alberto Soggin, "King Solomon," in *Birkat Shalom* (see n. 93), 169–74; and Martin A. Sweeney, "Synchronic and Diachronic Considerations in the DtrH Portrayal of the Demise of Solomon's Kingdom," in *Birkat Shalom* (see above), 175–89.

141 André Lemaire, "Wisdom in Solomonic Historiography," in J. Day, R.P. Gordon, and H.G.M. Williamson, eds., *Wisdom in Ancient Israel: Essays in Honour of J.A. Emerton*, (Cambridge: Cambridge Univ. Press, 1995), 106–18. For a different view of "vor-Dtr Weisheitsquelle," see Pekka Särkiö, *Die*

Weisheit und Macht Salomos in der israelitischen Historiographie, Schriften der Finnischen Exegetischen Gesellschaft 60 (Helsinki; Göttingen, 1994); "Die Struktur der Salomogeschichte (1 Kön 1-11) und die Stellung der Weisheit in ihr," *BN* 83 (1996), 83-106; Nadav Na'aman, "Sources and Composition in the History of Solomon," in *The Age of Solomon* (see n. 140), 57-80 (= *Ancient Israel's History and Historiography, First Temple, Essays, vol. 3* [see n. 58], 79-101); Anne E. Gardner, "The Narratives of Solomon's Reign in the Light of the Historiography of Other Ancient Civilizations," *ABR* 56 (2008), 1-18; D.S. Holland, "The Form and Function of the Sources Citations in 1-2 Kings," *ZAW* 130 (2018), 559-70, esp. 561.

142 For a general history of redaction of the Books of Kings, see Lemaire, "Vers l'histoire de la rédaction des livres des Rois," (see n. 79), 221-36; Gary n. Knoppers, "Theories of the Redaction(s) of Kings," in *The Books of Kings: Sources, Composition, Historiography, and Reception* (see n. 12), 69-88; Baruch Halpern and André Lemaire, "The Composition of Kings," in *The Books of King* (see above) 123-53.

143 See Ronald S. Hendel, "The Archaeology of Memory: King Solomon Chronology, and Biblical Representation," in S. Gitin et al., eds., *Confronting the Past: Archaeological and Historical Essays on Ancient Israel in Honor of William G. Dever* (Winona Lake, IN: Eisenbrauns, 2006), 219-30.

144 Hugh G.M. Williamson, *1 and 2 Chronicles*, New Century Bible Commentary (Grand Rapids: Eerdmans, 1982), 229-30.

145 See, e.g., Alan R. Millard, "Texts and Archaeology: Weighing the Evidence: The Case for King Solomon," *PEQ* 123 (1991), 19-27; "Solomon: Text and Archaeology," *PEQ* 123 (1991), 117-18; J. Maxwell Miller, "Solomon: International Potentate or Local King?" *PEQ* 123 (1991), 28-31; Alan R. Millard, "King Solomon's Shields," in M.D. Coogan, J.C. Exum, and L.E. Stager, eds., *Scripture and Other Artifacts: Essays in Honor of Philip J. King* (Louisville: Westminster John Knox, 1994), 286-95; A. Millard, "King Solomon in His Ancient Context," in *The Age of Solomon* (see n. 140), 30-53; W.M. Schniedewind, "Excavating the Text of 1 Kings 9," in T. E. Levy, ed., *Historical Biblical Archaeology and the Future:*

The New Pragmatism (London: Oakville, 2010), 241-49.

146 See Donald B. Redford, "The Relations Between Egypt and Israel from El-Amarna to the Babylonian Conquest," in *Biblical Archaeology Today 1984* (see n. 12), 192-205; Kenneth A. Kitchen, "Egypt and East Africa," in *The Age of Solomon* (see n. 140), 107-25; Jacques Briend, "Les relations du roi Salomon avec les pays voisins," in *Le roi Salomon* (see n. 81), 27-35.

147 Kenneth A. Kitchen, "Sheba and Arabia," in *The Age of Solomon* (see n. 140), 126-53.

148 See Dever, *Beyond the Texts* (see n. 98), esp. 363.

149 See Albert R. Green, "Solomon and Siamun: A Synchronism Between Early Dynastic Israel and the Twenty-First Dynasty of Egypt," *JBL* 97 (1978), 353-67; Kenneth A. Kitchen, *On the Reliability of the Old Testament* (Grand Rapids: Eerdmans, 2003), 107-12.

150 Compare Abdi-Heba in EA 286:10-15: "... neither my father nor my mother put me in this place, but the strong arm of the king brought me into my father's house ..." See William L. Moran, "Tell el-Amarna," in *COS* 3: 237-42, esp. 237.

151 See André Lemaire, "Salomon et la fille de Pharaon: un problème d'interprétation historique," in *"I Will Speak the Riddles of Ancient Times"* (see n. 5), 699-710. For a divergent interpretation, see Volkmar Fritz, "Solomon and Gezer," in *Confronting the Past* (see n. 143), 303-307.

152 See more generally Shirly Ben-Dor Evian, "Egypt and the Levant in the Iron Age I-IIA: The Ceramic Evidence," *TA* 38 (2011), 94-119; Ben-Dor Evian, "Sheshonq I and the Levant: synchronizing chronologies," in P. James and P.G. van der Veen, eds., *Solomon and Shishak: Current Perspectives from Archaeology, Epigraphy, History and Chronology*, BAR International Series (Oxford: Hadrian Books, 2015), 17-19; Meindert Dijkstra, "Canaan in the Transition from the Late Bronze to the Early Iron Age from an Egyptian Perspective," in L.L. Grabbe, ed., *The Land of Canaan in the Late Bronze Age*, LHBOTS 636 (London; New York: Bloomsbury; T&T Clark, 2016), 59-89; Ben-Dor Evian, "Egypt and Israel: The Never-Ending Story," *NEA* 80 (2017),

30–39; J.F. Quack, "Ägyptische Einflüsse auf nordwestsemitisch Königspresentationen?" in C. Levin and R. Müller, eds., *Herrschaftlegitimation in vorderorientalischen Reichen der Eisenzeit*, Oriental Religions in Antiquity 21 (Tübingen: Mohr Siebeck, 2017), 1–65. Note that Egyptian influence extended to North Arabia (Gunner Sperverslage, "Ägyptische Einflüsse auf der Arabischen Halbinsel in vorislamischer Zeit am Beispiel der Oase von Tayma," *Zeitschrift für Orient-Archäologie* 6 [2013], 234–52) and to Red Sea (P. Tallet, "Les Égyptiens et le littoral de la mer Rouge à l'époque pharaonique," *Comptes rendus de l'Académie des Inscriptions et Belles-Lettres* [2009], 687–719).

153 Henri Cazelles, "Administration salomonienne et terminologie administrative égyptienne," *Comptes Rendus du GLECS* 17 (1973), 23–25; Mettinger, *Solomonic State Officials* (see n.116).

154 Donald B. Redford, "Studies in Relations Between Palestine and Egypt During the First Millennium B.C., Part I: The Taxation System of Solomon," in J.W. Wevers and D. Redford, eds., *Studies on the Ancient Palestinian World Presented to F.V. Winnett* (Toronto: Univ. of Toronto Press, 1972), 141–56. Most of the commentators agree that this list is ancient; see Hess, "The Form and Structure of Solomonic District List" (see n.118); Martin J. Mulder, *1 Kings 1–11*, Historical Commentary on the Old Testament (Leuven: Peeters, 1998), 171–86; Jens Kamlah, "Die Liste der Regionalfürsten in 1 Kön 4,7–19 als historische Quelle für die Zeit Salomos," *BN* 106 (2001), 57–78. The hypothesis of Nadav Na'aman ("Solomon's District List [1 Kings 4:7–19] and the Assyrian Province System in Palestine," *Ugarit-Forschungen* 33 [2001], 419–35 = *Ancient Israel's History and Historiography* [see n.58], 102–19; see also R.D. Nelson, "Solomon's Administrative Districts: A Scholarly Illusion," in I.D. Wilson and D.V. Edelman, eds., *History, Memory, Hebrew Scriptures: A Festschrift für Ehud Ben Zvi* [Winona Lake, IN: Eisenbrauns, 2015], 103–15) is not convincing.

155 Albert R. Green, "Israelite Influence at Shishak's Court," *BASOR* 233 (1979), 59–62.

156 Ahlström, *Royal Administration* (see n.125), 33.

157 This identification has been doubted by several articles in James and van der Veen, *Solomon and Shishak* (see n.152) but without convincing arguments.

158 For the Egyptian list of towns, see *ANET*, 263–64; Benjamin Mazar, "The Campaign of Pharaoh Shishak to Palestine," in *Congrès de Strasbourg*, VTSup 4 (Leiden; Boston: Brill, 1957), 57–66; Yohanan Aharoni, *The Land of the Bible: A Historical Geography*, rev. and enlarged, trans. and ed. Anson F. Rainey (Philadelphia: Westminster, 1979), 323–30; Na'aman, "Israel, Edom, and Egypt in the 10th Century B.C.E." (see n.136); David M. Rohl, "Some Chronological Conundrums of the 21st Dynasty," *Ägypten und Levante* 3 (1992), 133–41, esp. 134–36; Gösta W. Ahlström, "Pharaoh Sheshonq's Campaign to Palestine," in A. Lemaire and B. Otzen, eds., *History and Traditions of Early Israel: Studies Presented to Eduard Nielsen*, VTSup 50 (Leiden: Brill, 1993), 1–16; Israel Finkelstein, "The Campaign of Shoshenk I to Palestine: A Guide to the 10th-Century B.C.E. Polity," *ZDPV* 118 (2002), 109–35; Kevin A. Wilson, *The Campaign of Pharaoh Sheshonq I into Palestine*, FAT 2, Reihe 9 (Tübingen: Mohr Siebeck, 2005); K.A. Kitchen, "The Levant Campaign of Sheshonq (945–924 BCE), Karnak: Temple of Amon-Re, Bubastis Gate," in *COS* 4: 14–18. This list of towns is generally interpreted as a list of towns *destroyed* by Sheshonq; however Jeroboam was patronized by Sheshonq and the Israelite towns could have welcomed the pharaoh.

159 See Herbert Donner, "Israel und Tyrus im Zeitalter Davids und Salomos," *JNSL* 10 (1982), 43–52; Alberto R. Green, "David's Relations with Hiram: Biblical and Josephan Evidence for Tyrian Chronology," in C.L. Meyers and M. O'Connor, eds., *The Word of the Lord Shall Go Forth: Essays in Honor of D.N. Freedman* (Winona Lake, IN: Eisenbrauns, 1983), 373–97; Kitchen, *Third Intermediate Period* (see n.110), 432–47; Edward Lipiński, *On the Skirts of Canaan in the Iron Age*, OLA 153 (Leuven: Peeters, 2006), 166–76. See also, with the a priori of "no Hebrew historiography before the 8th century," Nadav Na'aman, "Hiram of Tyre in the Book of Kings and in the Tyrian Records," *JNES* 78 (2019), 75–85.

160 See Giovanno Garbini, "Gli 'Annali di Tiro' et la storiogafia fenicia," in *I Fenici,* *storia e religione* (Naples: Instituto Universita-rio Orientale, 1980), 71–86; André Lemaire, "Les écrits phéniciens," in A. Barucq et al., eds., *Écrits de l'Orient ancien et sources Bibliques*, Petite Bibliothèque des Sciences Bibliques, Ancien Testament 2 (Paris: Desclée, 1986), 213–39, esp. 217–19; Josette Elayi, *Histoire de la Phénicie* (Paris: Perrin, 2013), 128–34.

161 For Phoenician royal tenth-century B.C.E. inscriptions, see André Lemaire, "La datation des rois de Byblos Abibaal et Élibaal et les relations entre l'Égypte et le Levant au Xᵉ s. av. n.è.," *Comptes rendus de l'Académie des Inscriptions et Belles-Lettres* (2006), 1,697–1,716; Christopher A. Rollston, "The Dating of the Early Royal Byblos Phoenician Inscriptions: A Response to Benjamin Sass," *Maarav* 15 (2008), 57–93; Rollston, *Writing and Literacy in the World of Ancient Israel*, Archaeology and Biblical Studies 11 (Atlanta: SBL, 2010), 20–27; Rollston, "The Iron Age Phoenician Script," in J.H. Hackett and W.E. Aufrecht, eds., *"An Eye for Form": Epigraphic Essays in Honor of Frank Moore Cross* (Winona Lake: Eisenbrauns, 2014), 72–99.

162 *Ag. Ap.* 1.113; see *Josephus I: The Life Against Apion*, Loeb, 209.

163 *Ag. Ap.* 1.117–119; *Josephus I* (see n. 162), 211.

164 Lemaire, "Phéniciens et le commerce" (see n. 121).

165 See André Lemaire, "Asher et le royaume de Tyr," in E. Lipiński, ed., *Phoenicia and the Bible*, Studia Phoenicia 11 (Leuven: Peeters, 1991), 135–52; Gunnar Lehmann, "Das Land Kabul: Archäologische und historisch-geographische Erwägungen," in M. Witte and J.F. Diehl, eds., *Israeliten und Phönizier*, OBO 235 (Fribourg; Göttingen: Academic Press; Vandenhoeck & Ruprecht, 2008), 39–94, esp. 40–41. See also, from the archaeological viewpoint, Meir Edrey et al., "The Iron Age IIA Tombs of Area E, Tel Achzib: Between Local Traditions and the Consolidation of the Tyrian Polity," *IEJ* 68 (2018), 150–81, esp. 173–74 with bibliography.

166 See Israel Eph'al, *The Ancient Arabs* (Jerusalem: Magnes Press, 1984), 28ff.; Giovanno Garbini, "I Sabei del Nord come problema storico," in R. Traini, ed., *Studi in onore F. Gabrieli* (Rome: Univ. di Roma, 1984), 373–80.

167 See Mario Liverani, "Early Caravan Trade Between South-Arabia and Mesopotamia," *Yemen* 1 (1992), 111–15.

168 See Abraham J. Drewes et al., "Some Absolute Dates for the Development of Ancient South Arabian Minuscule Scripts," *Arabian Archaeology and Epigraphy* 24 (2013), 196–207; Abraham J. Drewes and Jacques Ryckmans, *Les inscriptions sudarabes sur bois* (Wiesbaden: Harrassovitz, 2016), esp. xiii, 14–15; Norbert Nebes, *Der Tatenbericht des Yiṯaʿamar Watar bin Yakrubmalik aus Ṣirwāḥ (Jemen): Zur Geschichte Südarabiens im frühen 1. Jahrtausend vor Christus*, Deutsches Archäologisches Institut Orient-Abteilung, Epigraphische Forschungen auf der Arabischen Halbinsel Band 7 (Berlin: Deutsches Archäologisches Institut, 2016), esp. 51, 57 with nn. 219, 72; Peter Stein, "Sabäer in Juda, Juden in Saba, Sprach- und Kulturkontakt zwischen Südarabien und Palästina in der Antique," in U. Hübner and H. Niehr, eds., *Sprachen in Palästina im 2. und 1. Jahrtausend v. Chr*, Abhandlungen des Deutschen Palästina-vereins 43 (Wiesbaden: Harrassovitz, 2017), 91–120, esp. 113 with n. 71; François Bron, "Rev. of Nebes, Der Tatenbricht..." *Orientalia* 87 (2018), 258–61, esp. 261.

169 See André Lemaire, "Queen or Delegation of Saba to Solomon?" in R.I. Thelle et al., eds., *New Perspectives on Old Testament Prophecy and History: Essays in Honour of Hans M. Barstad*, VTSup 168 (Leiden; Boston: Brill, 2015), 191–96. For the possible confusion *mlk/mlʾk*, see also Noam Mizrahi, "Kings or Messengers? The Text of 2 Samuel 11:1 in the Light of Hebrew Historical Phonology," *Zeitschrift für Althebräistik* 25–28 (2012–2015), 57–83.

170 See André Lemaire, "La reine de Saba à Jérusalem: la tradition ancienne reconsidérée," in *Kein Land für sich allein, Studien zum Kulturkontakt in Kanaan, Israel/Palästina und Ebirnâri für Manfred Weippert*, OBO 186 (Göttingen: Universitätsverlag; Vandenhoeck & Ruprecht, 2002), 43–55; Lemaire, "The Queen of Sheba and the Trade Between South Arabia and Judah," in A.A. Hussein and A. Oettinger, eds., *A Collection of Studies Dedicated to Prof. Yosef Tobi. Ben 'Ever La'arav* 6 (Haifa, 2014), xi–xxxiv. A newly discovered South Arabian inscription dating to the sixth century B.C.E. confirms the trading partnership between Sheba and Judah. See Lemaire,

"Solomon & Sheba, Inc.," *BAR*, January/February 2010.

171 See, e.g., Nadav Na'aman, "Sources and Composition in the Biblical History of Edom," in *Sefer Moshe* (see n. 53), 313–20, esp. 316.

172 See Lemaire, "Les premiers rois araméens dans la tradition biblique" (see n. 136), 129–34.

173 See, e.g., Amihai Mazar, "Three 10th–9th century B.C.E. inscriptions from Tel Rehov," in *Saxa Loquentur* (see n. 29), 171–84.

174 Philip J. King and Lawrence E. Stager, "Of Fathers, Kings, and the Deity," *BAR*, March/April 2002; Jane Cahill, "Jerusalem in David and Solomon's Time: It Really Was a Major City in the Tenth Century B.C.E.," *BAR*, November/December 2004.

175 See André Lemaire, "Phénicien et philistien: paléographie et dialectologie," in M.E. Aubet and M. Barthélemy, eds., *Actas del IV Congreso Internacional de Estudios Fenicios y Punicos, Cadiz, 2–6 Octubre 1995* (Cadiz: Publicaciones, Universidad de Cadiz, 2000), 243–49.

176 For the Tel Zayit abecedary, see Ron E. Tappy et al., "An Abecedary of the Mid-Tenth Century B.C.E. from the Judaean Shephelah," *BASOR* 344 (2006), 5–45. This inscription could be connected with the kingdom of Gath and date to around 900 B.C.E. See Christopher A. Rollston, "The Phoenician Script of the Tel Zayit Abecedary and Putative Evidence for Israelite Literacy," in Tappy and P.K. McCarter, eds., *Literate Culture and Tenth-Century Canaan: The Tel Zayit Abecedary in Context* (Winona Lake, IN: Eisenbrauns, 2008), 89. For the Khirbet Qeiyafa ostracon, see Garfinkel and Ganor, *Khirbet Qeiyafa* Vol. 1 (see n. 103), 243–70. See also Gershon Galil, "The Hebrew Inscription from Khirbet Qeiyafa/Neṭa'im," *UF* 41 (2009), 193–242; Émile Puech, "L'ostracon de Khirbet Qeiyafa et les débuts de la Royauté en Israël," *RB* 117 (2010), 162–84; Bob Becking and Paul Sanders, "Plead for the Poor and the Widow: The Ostracon from Khirbet Qeiyafa as Expression of Social Consciousness," *ZABR* 17 (2011), 133–48; Alan R. Millard, "The Ostracon from the Days of David Found at Khirbet Qeiyafa," *TynB* 62 (2011), 1–13; Christopher Rollston, "The Khirbet Qeiyafa Ostracon: Methodological

Musings and Caveats," *TA* 38 (2011), 79–80; R. Achenbach, "The Protection of *Personae miserae* in Ancient Israelite Law and Wisdom and in the Ostracon from Khirbet Qeiyafa," *Semitica* 54 (2012), 93–125; Matthieu Richelle, "Quelques nouvelles lectures sur l'ostracon de Khirbet Qeiyafa," *Semitica* 57 (2015), 147–62.

177 See "Prize Find: Oldest Hebrew Inscription Discovered," *BAR*, March/April 2010.

178 See Hannalis Schulte, *Die Entstehung der Geschichtsschreibung im Alten Israel*, BZAW 128 (Berlin: de Gruyter, 1972); Baruch Halpern, *The First Historians: The Hebrew Bible and History* (San Francisco: Harper & Row, 1988). According to John Van Seters ("Histories and Historians of the Ancient Near East," *Orientalia* 50 [1981], 137–85, esp. 185), "Dtr [Deuteronomist] stands at the beginning of historiography," but this is probably too simplistic a view; see Lemaire, "Vers l'histoire de la rédaction" (see n. 79).

179 See Caquot and de Robert, *Les livres de Samuel* (see n. 25), 20, "un Ebyataride ... le premier historien de l'antiquité israélite."

180 On Hebron, see André Lemaire, "Cycle primitif d'Abraham et contexte géographico-historique," in *History and Traditions of Early Israel* (see n. 158), 62–75.

181 See Werner H. Schmidt, "A Theologian of the Solomonic Era? A Plea for the Yahwist," in *Studies in the Period of David and Solomon* (see n. 84), 55–73; Richard E. Friedman, "Solomon and the Great Histories," in Andrew G. Vaughn and Ann E. Killebrew, eds., *Jerusalem in Bible and Archaeology: The First Temple Period*, SBL Symposium Series 18 (Atlanta: SBL, 2003), 171–80.

182 Nili Fox, "Royal Officials and Court Families: A New Look at the *YLDYM* (*yelâdîm*) in 1 Kings 12," *BA* 59 (1996), 225–32; Na'aman, "Cow Town or Royal Capital?" (see n. 100).

183 André Lemaire, *Les écoles et la formation de la Bible dans l'ancien Israël*, OBO 39 (Fribourg; Göttingen: Editions Universitaires; Vandenhoeck & Ruprecht, 1981), 46–50; Nili Shupak, *Where Can Wisdom Be Found? The Sage's Language in the Bible and in Ancient Egyptian Literature*, OBO 130 (Fribourg: Editions Universitaires, 1993), esp. 349–54. The contrary opinion of Jamieson-Drake, in *Scribes and Schools in Monarchic Judah* (see n. 50) is ill-founded methodologically and has an incomplete archaeological basis. See Lemaire, "Review of D. W. Jamieson-Drake" (see n. 9).

184 Stefan Wimmer, *Palästinisches Hieratisch: Die Zahl- und Sonderzeichen in der althebräischen Schrift*. Ägypten und Altes Testament 75 (Wiesbaden: Harrassovitz, 2008). See also Anson F. Rainey, "The Saga of Eliashib," *BAR*, March/April 1987.

185 William G. Dever, "Monumental Architecture in Ancient Israel in the Period of the United Monarchy," in *Studies in the Period of David and Solomon* (see n. 84), 269–306; Dever, "Archaeology and the 'Age of Solomon': A Case-Study in Archaeology and Historiography," in *Age of Solomon* (see n. 140), 217–51; see also Volkmar Fritz, "Salomo," *Mitteilungen der Deutschen Orient-Gesellschaft* 117 (1985), 47–67. For provisory syntheses of Iron IIA (tenth century B.C.E.), see Larry G. Herr, "The Iron Age II Period: Emerging Nations," *BA* 60 (1997), 114–83, esp. 120–29; William G. Dever, "Histories and Non-Histories of Ancient Israel: The Question of the United Monarchy," in *In Search of Pre-Exilic Israel* (see n. 71), 65–94; Shlomo Bunimovitz and Zvi Lederman, "The Early Israelite Monarchy in the Sorek Valley: Tel Beth-Shemesh and Tel Batash (Timnah) in the 10th and 9th Centuries BCE," in *"I Will Speak the Riddles of Ancient Times"* (see n. 5), 407–27; Steven M. Ortiz, "United Monarchy, Archaeology, and Literary Sources," in B. T. Arnold and R. S. Hess, eds., *Ancient Israel's History* (Grand Rapids: Baker Academic, 2014), 227–62, esp. 237–61.

186 For a general presentation, see Wolfgang Zwickel, *Der salomonische Tempel,* Kulturgeschichte der antiken Welt 83 (Mainz: Philipp von Zabern, 1999); Yosef Garfinkel and Madeleine Mumcuoglu, "The Temple of Solomon in Iron Age Context," *Religions* 10/198 (2019), 1–17. For a nearly identical temple dating to the same period, see John Monson, "The New Ain Dara Temple, Closest Solomonic Parallel," *BAR*, May/June 2000.

187 Ernest-Marie Laperrousaz, "A-t-on dégagé l'angle sud-est du 'temple de Salomon'?" *Syria* 50 (1973), 355–99; Laperrousaz, "Angle sud-est du 'temple de Salomon' ou vestiges de l'Accra des Séleucides'? Un faux problème," *Syria* 52

(1975), 241–59; Laperrousaz, "Après le 'temple de Salomon,' la *bamah* de Tel Dan: l'utilisation de pierres à bossage phénicien dans la Palestine pré-exilique," *Syria* 59 (1982), 223–37; Laperrousaz, "À propos des murs d'enceinte antiques de la colline occidentale et du temple de Jérusalem," *Revue des études juives* 141 (1982), 443–58.

For a popular treatment, see Laperrousaz, "King Solomon's Wall Still Supports the Temple Mount," *BAR*, May/June 1987. More recently, archaeologist Eilat Mazar has discovered additional walls south of the Temple Mount that she believes date to the reign of Solomon. Eilat Mazar, "The Royal Quarter Constructed by King Solomon in the Ophel of Jerusalem in Light of Recent Excavations," *Qadmoniot* 48/149 (2015), 20–27.

188 Israel Finkelstein et al., "The Mound on the Mount: A Possible Solution to the Problem of Jerusalem," *Journal of Hebrew Scriptures* 11 (2009), article 12.

189 Dever, *Beyond the Texts* (see n. 98), 279.

190 Margreet Steiner, "David's Jerusalem: Fiction or Reality? It's Not There: Archaeology Proves a Negative," *BAR*, July/August 1998; Jane Cahill, "David's Jerusalem: Fiction or Reality? It Is There: The Archaeological Evidence Proves It," *BAR*, July/August 1998.

191 See also Yigal Shiloh, *Excavations at the City of David I, 1978–1982*, Qedem 19 (Jerusalem: Hebrew Univ. Press, 1984), esp. 27 ("Stratum 14"); Shiloh, "Jérusalem, la Ville de David (1978–1981)," *RB* 91 (1984), 420–31, esp. 428–29; Margreet Steiner, "The Jebusite Ramp of Jerusalem: The Evidence from the Macalister, Kenyon, and Shiloh Excavations," in *Biblical Archaeology Today 1990* (see n. 94), 585–88; Steiner, "Re-dating the Terraces of Jerusalem," *IEJ* 44 (1994), 13–20; Steiner, "David's Jerusalem," (see n. 100); Eilat Mazar, "The Solomonic Wall in Jerusalem," in *"I Will Speak the Riddles of the Time"* (see n. 5), 775–86. For a date c. 1200, see Jane Cahill and David Tarler, "Respondents," in *Biblical Archaeology Today 1990* (see n. 94), 625–26; Cahill and Tarler, "Excavations Directed by Yigal Shiloh at the City of David, 1978–1985," in *Ancient Jerusalem Revealed*, ed. Hillel Geva (Jerusalem: IES, 1994), 30–45, esp. 34–35. See also Cahill, "David's Jerusalem" (see n. 100), 50. For different tentative syntheses, see

Cahill, "Jerusalem at the Time of the United Monarchy: The Archaeological Evidence," in *Jerusalem in Bible and Archaeology* (see n. 181), 13–80; Israel Finkelstein, "The Rise of Jerusalem and Judah: The Missing Link," in *Jerusalem in Bible and Archaeology* (see n. 181), 81–101; David Ussishkin, "Solomon's Jerusalem: The Text and the Facts on the Ground," in *Jerusalem in Bible and Archaeology* (see n. 181), 103–15; Amihai Mazar, "Jerusalem in the 10th Century B.C.E.: The Glass Half Full," in *Essays on Ancient Israel in Its Near Eastern Context* (see n. 30), 255–72; A. Mazar, "Archaeology and the Biblical Narrative," in *One God—One Cult—One Nation* (see n. 3), 29–57, esp. 34–49; H.M. Niemann, "Juda und Jerusalem: Überlegungen zum Verhältnis von Stamm und Stadt und sur Rolle Jerusalems in Juda," *UF* 47 (2016), 147–90, esp. 169–72.

192 Yigael Yadin, "Solomon's City Wall and Gate at Gezer," *IEJ* 8 (1958), 82–86; "Yadin's Popular Book on Hazor Now Available," *BAR*, September 1975, 14–17, 32; "A Rejoinder," *BASOR* 239 (1980), 19–23.

193 "Monarchy at Work? The Evidence of Three Gates," sidebar to "Face to Face," *BAR*, July/August 1997; Valerie M. Fargo, "Is the Solomonic City Gate at Megiddo Really Solomonic?" *BAR*, September/October 1983.

194 A casemate wall consists of two parallel walls, crossed by short perpendicular walls that form internal rooms for storage, etc.

195 For a divergent view, see David Milson, "The Design of the Royal Gates at Megiddo, Hazor, and Gezer," *ZDPV* 102 (1986), 87–92.

196 William G. Dever, "Late Bronze Age and Solomonic Defenses: New Evidence," *BASOR* 262 (1986), 9–34, esp. 18–20; Dever, "Gezer," *NEAEHL*, vol. 2, 504–505.

197 Amnon Ben-Tor, "Tel Hazor," *IEJ* 45 (1995), 66–68; Amnon Ben-Tor and Doron Ben-Ami, "Hazor and the Archaeology of the Tenth Century B.C.E.," *IEJ* 48 (1998), 1–37; André Lemaire, "Hazor in the Second Half of the Tenth Century B.C.E.: Historiography, Archaeology, and History," in *The Historian and the Bible* (see n. 3), 55–72; Amnon Ben-Tor, Doron Ben-Ami, and Debora Sandhaus, *Hazor VI: The 1990–2009 Excavations: The Iron Age* (Jerusalem: IES, 2012), 2–3; Amnon Ben-Tor, "Hazor in the Tenth Century B.C.E.,"

NEA 76 (2013), 105–109; Amnon Ben-Tor, *Hazor: Canaanite Metropolis, Israelite City: "The Head of All Those Kingdoms" (Joshua 11:10)* (Jerusalem: IES, 2016), 132–46. For a different view, see Israel Finkelstein, "Hazor and the North in the Iron Age: A Low Chronology Perspective," *BASOR* 314 (1999), 55–66.

198 See the following articles in *BASOR* 277/278 (1990): G.J. Wightman, "The Myth of Solomon"; John S. Holladay Jr., "Red Slip, Burnish, and the Solomonic Gateway at Gezer"; David Ussishkin, "Notes on Megiddo, Gezer, Ashdod, and Tel Batash in the Tenth to Ninth Centuries B.C."; Israel Finkelstein, "On Archaeological Methods and Historical Considerations"; and William Dever, "Of Myths and Methods." See also Hershel Shanks, "Where Is the Tenth Century?" *BAR*, March/April 1998, 56–60; Shanks, "San Francisco Tremors," *BAR*, March/April 1998, 54–56, 60–61.

199 P.L.O. Guy, *New Light from Armageddon,* Oriental Institute Communications 9 (Chicago: Univ. of Chicago, 1931), 37–47.

200 Yigael Yadin, "The Megiddo Stables," in Frank Moore Cross et al., eds., *Magnalia Dei, The Mighty Acts of God: in Memory of G.E. Wright* (New York: Doubleday, 1976), 249–52.

201 See, e.g., John S. Holladay Jr., "The Stables of Ancient Israel: Functional Determinants of Stable Construction and the Interpretation of Pillared Building Remains of the Palestinian Iron Age," in Lawrence T. Geraty and Larry G. Herr, eds., *The Archaeology of Jordan and Other Studies Presented to S. Horn* (Berrien Springs, MI: Andrews Univ., 1986), 103–65; Ze'ev Herzog, "Administrative Structures in the Iron Age," in Aharon Kempinski and Ronny Reich, eds., *The Architecture of Ancient Israel from the Prehistoric to the Persian Periods* (Jerusalem: IES, 1992), 223–30; Deborah Cantrell, "Horse Troughs at Megiddo?" *Revelations from Megiddo* 5 (2000), 1–2. See also Moshe Kochavi, "Divided Structures Divide Scholars," *BAR*, May/June 1999.

202 Graham I. Davies, "Solomonic Stables at Megiddo After All?" *PEQ* 120 (1988), 130–41.

203 See, e.g., Aharon Kempinski, *Megiddo: A City-State and Royal Centre in North Israel* (Munich: C.H. Beck, 1989), 90–95; Baruch Halpern, "The Gate of Megiddo and the

Debate on the 10th Century," in André Lemaire and Magne Saebo, eds., *Congress Volume, Oslo 1998*, VTSup 80 (Leiden: Brill, 2000), 79–121; Dever, *Beyond the Texts* (see n. 98), 273–75.

204 David Ussishkin, "Was the 'Solomonic' City Gate at Megiddo Built by King Solomon?" *BASOR* 239 (1980), 1–18; Ussishkin, "Fresh Examination of Old Excavations: Sanctuaries in the First Temple Period," in *Biblical Archaeology Today 1990* (see n. 94), 67–85; Ussishkin, "Notes on Megiddo, Gezer, Ashdod, and Tel Batash" (see n. 198), 71–91; Ussishkin, "Jezreel, Samaria, and Megiddo: Royal Centres of Omri and Ahab," in John A. Emerton, ed., *Congress Volume, Cambridge 1995*, VTSup 66 (Leiden: Brill, 1997), 351–64, esp. 359–61.

205 Wightman, "The Myth of Solomon" (see n. 198), 5–22.

206 See A. Mazar, "Iron Age Chronology" (see n. 5), 157–67.

207 Israel Finkelstein, "The Archaeology of the United Monarchy: An Alternative View," *Levant* 28 (1996), 177–87; Israel Finkelstein and Neil Asher Silberman, *The Bible Unearthed* (New York: Free Press, 2001); Finkelstein and Silberman, *David and Solomon* (see n. 7). See also Shanks, "Where Is the Tenth Century?" (see n. 198); Shanks, "San Francisco Tremors" (see n. 198).

208 See Israel Finkelstein, "The Iron Age Chronology Debate: Is the Gap Narrowing?" *NEA* 74 (2011), 50–54; Amihai Mazar, "The Iron Age Chronology Debate: Is the Gap Narrowing? Another Viewpoint," *NEA* 74 (2011), 105–11.

209 See Israel Finkelstein and Benjamin Sass, "The West Semitic Alphabetic Inscriptions, Late Bronze II to Iron IIA—Archaeological Context, Distribution, and Chronology," *HBAI* 2 (2003), 149–220, esp. 180: "Early Iron IIA: mid 10th to early 9th century"; see also Benjamin Sass, "The Khirbet Qeiyafa Ostracon in Its Setting," in *Khirbet Qeiyafa in the Shephelah: Papers Presented at a Colloquium of the Swiss Society for Ancient Near Eastern Studies Held at the University of Bern September 6, 2011*, ed. D. Schroer and S. Munger, OBO 282 (Fribourg; Göttingen: Academic Press;

Vandenhoeck & Ruprecht, 2017), 87–111, esp. 98.

210 Rudolph Cohen and Yigal Yisrael, "The Iron Age Fortresses at 'En Haseva," *BA* 58 (1995), 223–35; Cohen and Yisrael, *On the Road to Edom: Discoveries from 'En Hazeva*, Israel Museum Catalogue 370 (Jerusalem: Israel Museum, 1995), esp. 17. For a divergent dating, see Israel Finkelstein and Lily Singer-Avitz, "The Pottery of Edom: A Correction," *Antiguo Oriente* 6 (2008), 13–24.

211 For a provisory list, see Herr, "The Iron Age II Period" (see n. 185), 114–83, esp. 121; Yosef Garfinkel et al., "Lachish Fortifications and State Formation in the Biblical Kingdom of Judah in Light of Radiometric Datings," *Rediocarbon* (2019.5), 1–18.

212 Rudolph Cohen, "The Iron Age Fortresses in the Central Negev," *BASOR* 236 (1980), 61–79; "Excavations at Kadesh-Barnea 1976–1978," *BA* 44 (1981), 93–107; Cohen, "Did I Excavate Kadesh-Barnea?" *BAR*, May/June 1981, 20–33; Zeev Herzog et al., "The Israelite Fortress at Arad," *BASOR* 254 (1984), 1–34, esp. 6–8. For a different dating and interpretation, see Israel Finkelstein, "The Iron Age 'Fortresses' of the Negev—Sedentarization of Desert Nomads," *TA* 11 (1984), 189–209; Alexander Fantalkin and Israel Finkelstein, "The Sheshonq I Campaign and the 8th-Century-B.C.E. Earthquake—More on the Archaeology and History of the South in the Iron I–IIA," *TA* 33 (2006), 18–42; Rudolph Cohen and Rebecca Cohen-Amin, *Ancient Settlement of the Negev Highlands: The Iron Age and the Persian Period*, IAA Reports 20 (Jerusalem: IAA, 2004); Rudolph Cohen and Hannah Bernick-Greenberg, *Excavations at Kadesh Barnea (Tell el-Qudeirat) 1976–1982*, IAA Reports 34 (Jerusalem: IAA, 2007); and Lily Singer-Avitz, "The Earliest Settlement at Kadesh Barnea," *TA* 35 (2008), 73–81; Amihai Mazar, "Discoveries from the Early Monarchic Period at Tel Rehov," in Amihai Mazar, *It Is the Land of Honey: Discoveries from Tel Rehov, the Early Days of the Israelite Monarchy* (Tel Aviv: Musa Eretz Israel Museum, 2016), 9e–59e.

For a popular treatment, see Rudolph Cohen, "The Fortresses King Solomon Built to Protect His Southern Border," *BAR*, May/June 1985.

213 See Zeev Herzog and Lily Singer-Avitz, "Redefining the Centre: The Emergence of State in Judah," *TA* 31 (2004), 209–44, esp. 232–35. For a divergent interpretation, see Elisabetta Boaretto, Israel Finkelstein, and Ruth Shahack-Gross, "Radiocarbon Results from the Iron IIA Site of Atar Haroa in the Negev Highlands and Their Archaeological and Historical Implications," *Radiocarbon* 52 (2010), 1–12.

214 Thomas E. Levy et al., "Reassessing the Chronology of Biblical Edom: New Excavations and 14C Dates from Khirbet en-Nahas (Jordan)," *Antiquity* 78 (2004), 865–79, esp. 867; G. Weisberger, "The Mineral Wealth of Ancient Arabia and Its Use I: Copper Mining and Smelting at Feinan and Timna—Comparison and Evaluation of Techniques, Production, and Strategies," *Arabian Archaeology and Epigraphy* 17 (2006), 1–30; Andreas Hauptmann, *The Archaeometallurgy of Copper: Evidence from Faynan, Jordan* (Berlin: Springer-Verlag, 2007), 127.

See also Thomas E. Levy and Mohammad Najjar, "Edom and Copper—The Emergence of Ancient Israel's Rival," *BAR*, July/August 2006; Levy and Najjar, "Condemned to the Mines," *BAR*, November/December 2011.

215 Thomas E. Levy and Mohammad Najjar, "Some Thoughts on Khirbet en-Nahas, Edom, Biblical History and Anthropology—A Response to Israel Finkelstein," *TA* 33 (2006), 3–17; Israel Finkelstein and Eli Piasetzky, "Radiocarbon and the History of Copper Production at Khirbet en-Nahas," *TA* 35 (2008), 82–96; Israel Finkelstein and Lily Singer-Avitz, "The Pottery of Edom: A Correction," *Antiguo Oriente* 6 (2008), 13–24.

216 See Erez Ben-Yosef et al., "The Beginning of Iron Age Copper Production in the Southern Levant: New Evidence from Khirbet al-Jariya, Faynan, Jordan," *Antiquity* 84 (2010), 724–46; Thomas E. Levy et al., "Ancient Texts and Archaeology Revisited—Radiocarbon and Biblical Dating in the Southern Levant," *Antiquity* 84 (2010), 834–47; Bradly Liss et al., "Up the Wadi: Development of an Iron Age Industrial Landscape in Faynan, Jordan," *Journal of Field Archaeology*, DOI 10.1080/00934690.2020.1767792, 1–15, esp. 1.

217 See G. Weisgerber, "The Mineral Wealth of Ancient Arabia and Its Use I: Copper Min-

ing and Smelting at Feinan and Timna—Comparison and Evaluation of Techniques, Production, and Strategies," *Arabian Archaeology and Epigraphy* 17 (2006), 1–30; Hauptmann, *Archaeometallurgy of Copper* (see n. 214); Erez Ben-Yosef, "Back to Solomon's Era: Results of the First Excavations at the Slaves' Hill (Timna, Israel)," *BASOR* 374 (2016), 169–98; S. Kleinman, A. Kleinman, and Erez Ben-Yosef, "The Ceramic Assemblage from Site 34 (Slaves' Hill) in the Timna Valley," *TA* 44 (2017), 232–64.

218 See Thomas E. Levy, M. Najjar, and T. Higham, "Iron Age Complex Societies, Radiocarbon Dates, and Edom: Working with the Data and Debates," *Antiguo Oriente* 5 (2007), 13–34, esp. 19–20; Israel Finkelstein, "The Archaeology of Tell el-Kheleifeh and the History of Ezyon-Geber/Elath," *Semitica* 56 (2014), 106–36, esp. 130 with a later dating (eighth century); Thomas E. Levy et al., "Intensive Surveys, Large-Scale Excavations Strategies and Iron Age Industrial Metallurgy in Faynan, Jordan: Fairly Tales Don't Come True," in Erez Ben-Yosef, ed., *Mining for Ancient Copper: Essays in Memory of Beno Rothenberg* (Tel Aviv, 2018), 245–58.

219 See Volkmar Fritz, "Monarchy and Re-urbanization: A New Look at Solomon's Kingdom," in *Origins of the Ancient Israelite States* (see n. 30), 187–95.

220 See David Ussishkin, "King Solomon's Palaces," *Biblical Archaeologist Reader IV* (Sheffield: Almond Press, 1983), 227–47; Yigal Shiloh, *The Proto-Aeolic Capital and Israelite Ashlar Masonry*, Qedem 11 (Jerusalem: Hebrew Univ. Press, 1979); B. Gregori, "Considerazioni sui palazzi 'hilani' del periodo salomonico a Megiddo," *Vicino Oriente* 5 (1982), 85–101.

221 Yohanan Aharoni, *The Archaeology of the Land of Israel* (Philadelphia: Westminster, 1982), esp. 239; see also John S. Holladay Jr., "The Use of Pottery and the Other Diagnostic Criteria from the Solomonic Era to the Divided Kingdom," in *Biblical Archaeology Today 1990* (see n. 94), 86–101, esp. 95: "Red burnish is only introduced well into Solomon's reign, probably around 950 B.C.E. or so." See also Holladay, "Red Slip, Burnish, and the Solomonic Gateway at Gezer" (see n. 198), 23–70.

222 John Bright, *A History of Israel*, 3rd ed. (Philadelphia: Westminster, 1982), 217.

223 Israel Finkelstein, "Environmental Archaeology and Social History: Demographic and Economic Aspects of the Monarchic Period," in *Biblical Archaeology Today 1990* (see n. 94), 56–66, esp. 62–63; see also Gunnar Lehmann, "The United Monarchy in the Countryside: Jerusalem, Judah, and the Shephelah During the Tenth Century B.C.E.," in *Jerusalem in Bible and Archaeology* (see n. 181), 117–62.

224 See Winfried Theil, "Soziale Wandlungen in der frühen Königszeit Alt-Israels," in H.

Klengel, ed., *Gesellschaft und Kultur in alten Vorderasien* (Berlin: Akademie Verlag, 1982), 235–46.

225 See Hayim Tadmor, "Traditional Institutions and the Monarchy: Social and Political Tensions in the Time of David and Solomon," in *Studies in the Period of David and Solomon* (see n. 84), 239–57.

226 On the distinction between Israel and Judah, see Edward Lipiński, "Judah et 'Tout Israël': Analogies et contrastes," in Lipiński, ed., *The Land of Israel: Cross-Roads of Civilizations*, OLA 19 (Leuven: Peeters, 1985), 93–112.

5. Israel and Judah in Iron Age II

1 Israel Finkelstein and Eli Piasetzky, "The Iron Age Chronology Debate: Is the Gap Narrowing?" *NEA* 74:1 (2011), 50–54; and Amihai Mazar, "The Iron Age Chronology Debate: Is the Gap Narrowing? Another Viewpoint," *NEA* 74:2 (2011), 105–11. For additional analysis, see David Ussishkin, "Archaeology of the Biblical Period: On Some Questions of Methodology and Chronology of the Iron Age," in H. G. M. Williamson, ed., *Understanding the History of Ancient Israel* (Oxford: Oxford Univ. Press, 2007), 131–41; and Daniel A. Frese and Thomas E. Levy, "The Four Pillars of the Iron Age Low Chronology," in T. E. Levy, ed., *Historical Biblical Archaeology and the Future: The New Pragmatism* (London: Equinox, 2010), 187–202.

2 For more discussion, see Aren Maeir, "Stones, Bones, Texts and Relevance: Or, How I Lost My Fear of Biblical Archaeology and Started Enjoying It," in *Historical Biblical Archaeology* (see n. 1), 295–303; Thomas W. Davis, "Theory and Method in Biblical Archaeology," in J. K. Hoffmeier and A. Millard, eds., *The Future of Biblical Archaeology: Reassessing Methodologies and Assumptions* (Grand Rapids: Eerdmans, 2004), 20–28.

3 The relation of this corpus to Josiah's time stems from the tradition that a "Book of the Law" was found during the temple restoration project during his reign (2 Kings 22:8). For a sustained analysis of its compositional history, see Steven L. McKenzie, *1 Kings 16–2 Kings 16*, International Exegetical Commentary on the

Old Testament (Stuttgart: W. Kohlhammer, 2019), 23–45. See also n. 179 herein.

4 For an overview, see Nadav Na'aman, "The 'Discovered Book' and the Legitimation of Josiah's Reform," *JBL* 130 (2011), 47–62; Hermann Spieckermann, "The Former Prophets: The Deuteronomistic History," in L. G. Perdue, ed., *The Blackwell Companion to the Hebrew Bible* (Oxford: Blackwell, 2001), 337–52; Thomas Römer, "Deuteronomy: In Search of Origins," in G. n. Knoppers and J. G. McConville, eds., *Rediscovering Israel and Judah: Recent Studies on the Deuteronomistic History* (Winona Lake, IN: Eisenbrauns, 2000), 112–38.

5 Isaac Kalimi, *The Reshaping of Ancient Israelite History in Chronicles* (Winona Lake, IN: Eisenbrauns, 2005); Ehud Ben Zvi, "The House of Omri/Ahab in Chronicles," in L. L. Grabbe, ed., *Ahab Agonistes: The Rise and Fall of the Omri Dynasty* (London: T & T Clark, 2007), 41–53; Melody D. Knowles, "1 and 2 Chronicles," in G. R. O'Day and D. L. Petersen, eds., *Theological Bible Commentary* (Louisville, KY: Westminster John Knox Press, 2009), 145–54.

6 Volkmar Fritz, "Copper Mining and Smelting in the Area of Feinan at the End of Iron Age I," in E. D. Oren and S. Ahituv, eds., *Aharon Kempinski Memorial Volume: Studies in Archaeology and Related Disciplines* (Beer-sheba: Ben-Gurion Univ. of the Negev Press, 2002), 93–102; Erez Ben-Yosef, "Back to Solomon's Era: Results of the First Excavations at 'Slaves'

Hill' (Site 34, Timna, Israel)," *BASOR* 376 (2016), 169–98.

7 Yigal Levin, "Did Pharaoh Sheshonq Attack Jerusalem?" *BAR*, July/August 2012.

8 Amihai Mazar, "The Spade and the Text: The Interaction Between Archaeology and Israelite History Relating to the Tenth-Ninth Centuries BCE," in *Understanding the History of Ancient Israel* (see n.1), 143–71; Kevin A. Wilson, *The Campaign of Pharaoh Sheshonq I into Palestine* (Tübingen: Mohr Siebeck, 2005); Andrew D. H. Mayes, "Pharaoh Shishak's Invasion of Palestine and the Exodus from Egypt," in B. Becking and L. L. Grabbe, eds., *Between Evidence and Ideology: Essays on the History of Ancient Israel Read at the Joint Meeting of the Society for Old Testament Study and the Oud Testamentisch Werkgezelschap* (Leiden: Brill, 2011), 129–44; Israel Finkelstein and David Ussishkin, "Archaeological and Historical Conclusions," in I. Finkelstein, D. Ussishkin, and B. Halpern, eds., *Megiddo III: The 1992–1996 Seasons* (Tel Aviv: Emery and Claire Yass Publications in Archaeology, 2000), 576–605, esp. 599 and n.19; and Ernst Axel Knauf, "Who Destroyed Megiddo VIA?" *BN* 103 (2000), 30–35.

9 Baruch Halpern, "Archaeology, the Bible and History: The Fall of the House of Omri—and the Origins of the Israelite State," in *Historical Biblical Archaeology* (see n.1), 262–84 (276).

10 For a description of several areas that look like cultic sites in Dan, see Avraham Biran, "Sacred Spaces: Of Standing Stones, High Places and Cult Objects at Tel Dan," *BAR*, September/October 1998; and A. Biran, "The High Places of Biblical Dan," in A. Mazar, ed., *Studies in the Archaeology of the Iron Age in Israel and Jordan* (London: Sheffield Academic Press, 2001), 148–55.

11 But see 2 Chronicles 11:13–18, which relates (perhaps optimistically?) that priests and people came from Israel to worship in Jerusalem and live in Judah.

12 Amihai Mazar, *Archaeology of the Land of the Bible 10,000–586 B.C.E.*, Anchor Bible Reference Library (New York: Doubleday, 1990), 350–51; and A. Mazar, "Bronze Bull Found in Israelite 'High Place' from the Time of the Judges," *BAR*, September/October 1983.

13 *COS* 2: 171; Ze'ev Meshel, "Did Yahweh Have a Consort?" *BAR*, March/April 1979; Ze'ev Meshel, *Kuntillet 'Ajrud (Horvat Teman): An Iron Age II Religious Site on the Judah-Sinai Boarder*, Liora Freud, ed. (Jerusalem: IES, 2012). Note also that Yaho is called "our Bull" and equated with the god Bethel in a version of Psalm 20 from Papyrus Amherst 63 (fourth century B.C.E.); see Karel van der Toorn, "Egyptian Papyrus Sheds New Light on Jewish History," *BAR*, July/August 2018; Karel van der Toorn, *Papyrus Amherst 63* (Münster: Ugarit-Verlag, 2018).

14 For a discussion, see David Ussishkin, *The Renewed Archaeological Excavations at Lachish (1973-1994)* (Tel Aviv: Institute of Archaeology of Tel Aviv Univ., 2004), 75–6, 79–82.

15 Avraham Biran and Joseph Naveh, "An Aramaic Stele Fragment from Tel Dan," *IEJ* 43 (1993), 81–98; [N.A.], "'David' Found at Dan," *BAR*, March/April 1994; Avraham Biran and Joseph Naveh, "The Tel Dan Inscription. A New Fragment," *IEJ* 45 (1995), 1–18.

16 Ben-hadad was the name of more than one king of Damascus. Here he is further identified as the son of Tabrimmon son of Hezion. Attempts have been made to identify his grandfather, Hezion, with Solomon's contemporary Rezon son of Eliyada (1 Kings 11:23–24). The identification of Hezion with Rezon is unlikely on philological grounds; however, Hezion might well have been Rezon's successor. See Wayne T. Pitard, *Ancient Damascus: A Historical Study of the Syrian City-State from Earliest Times until its Fall to the Assyrians in 732 B.C.E* (Winona Lake, IN: Eisenbrauns, 1987), 100–104.

17 A massive, 15-foot-thick wall constructed at this time has been found at Tell en-Nasbeh, ancient Mizpah. See Jeffrey R. Zorn, "Mizpah: Newly Discovered Stratum Reveals Judah's Other Capital," *BAR*, September/October 1997. For an alternative proposal for the location of Mizpah, see Yitzhak Magen, "Nebi Samwil: Where Samuel Crowned Israel's First King," *BAR*, May/June 2008.

18 Norma Franklin, "Samaria: From the Bedrock to the Omride Palace," *Levant* 36:1 (2004), 189–202; "Lost Tombs of the Israelite Kings," *BAR*, July/August 2007. See also Ron E. Tappy, *The Archaeology of Israelite Samaria*, vol. 2: *The Eighth Century BCE* (Winona Lake,

IN: Eisenbrauns, 2001); David Ussishkin, "The Disappearance of Two Royal Burials," *BAR*, November/December 2007; Norma Franklin, "Don't Be So Quick to Be Disappointed, David Ussishkin," *BAR*, March/April 2008; David Ussishkin, "Samaria, Jezreel and Megiddo: Royal Centres of Omri and Ahab," in *Ahab Agonistes* (see n.5), 293–309; Rupert Chapman, "Samaria—Capital of Israel," *BAR*, September/October 2017. For an argument that Samaria was more a royal residence than a capital city, see Hermann Michael Niemann, "Royal Samaria – Capital or Residence? Or: The Foundation of the City of Samaria by Sargon II," in *Ahab Agonistes* (see n.5), 184–207.

19 Ephraim Stern, "Phoenicia and its Special Relationship with Israel," *BAR*, November/December 2017.

20 Marjo C.A. Korpel, "Fit for a Queen: Jezebel's Royal Seal," *BAR*, March/April 2008. See also Queries and Comments, "Jezebel Post-Postscript," *BAR*, May/June 2008; Queries and Comments, "Seal Scholar Defends Her Position," *BAR*, July/August 2008. For an argument that the seal is not that of Queen Jezebel, see Christopher A. Rollston, "Prosopography and the YZBL Seal," *IEJ* 59 (2009), 86–91.

21 Ashlars are precisely square-cut stones smoothed on all sides to fit together tightly without mortar. See Franklin, "Samaria" (see n.18), 189–202. For more on Omride building projects and architecture, see Israel Finkelstein, *The Forgotten Kingdom: The Archaeology and History of Northern Israel* (Atlanta: SBL, 2013), 85–105. Note the response of Hermann Michael Niemann, "Observations on the Layout of Iron Age Samaria—A Reply to Israel Finkelstein," in M. Gerhards, ed., *History of Ancient Israel, Archaeology, and Bible: Collected Essays* (Münster: Ugarit, 2015), 79–90.

22 Tappy, *Archaeology of Israelite Samaria* (see n.18), 351–441; J. W. Crowfoot, G. M. Crowfoot, and Kathleen M. Kenyon, *The Objects from Samaria* (London: Palestine Exploration Fund, 1957); J. W. Crowfoot and G. M. Crowfoot, *Early Ivories from Samaria* (London: Palestine Exploration Fund, 1938).

23 Ronny Reich, Eli Shukron, and Omri Lernau, "Recent Discoveries in the City of David, Jerusalem," *IEJ* 57 (2007), 153–69.

24 Avraham Biran, *Biblical Dan* (Jerusalem: Hebrew Union College—Jewish Institute of Religion, 1994), 235–54; Amnon Ben-Tor, "Excavating Hazor, Part One: Solomon's City Rises from the Ashes," *BAR*, March/April 1999; Amnon Ben-Tor, "Hazor and the Chronology of Northern Israel: A Reply to Israel Finkelstein," *BASOR* 317 (2000), 9–15.

25 For surface surveys indicating the minor settlements throughout the Galilee and Samaria hills, see Adam Zertal, "The Heart of the Monarchy: Pattern of Settlement and Historical Considerations of the Israelite Kingdom of Samaria," in *Studies in the Archaeology of the Iron Age* (see n.10), 38–64. Ussishkin, "Samaria, Jezreel and Megiddo" (see n.18); Nadav Na'aman, "The Northern Kingdom in the Late Tenth-Ninth Centuries BCE," in *Understanding the History of Ancient Israel* (see n.1), 406–407.

26 1 Kings 20 describes a two-phase assault on Israel near the end of Ahab's reign by "King Ben-hadad of Aram." The first phase was a siege of Samaria that was broken when the much stronger Aramean force was defeated by Ahab's army after the intervention of an anonymous prophet; the second phase included an Aramean assault at Aphek the following spring, when the Arameans were again defeated, and Ben-hadad sued for peace, agreeing to return "the towns that [his] father took from [Ahab's] father." 1 Kings 22 indicates that three years later, Ahab marched with Jehoshaphat of Judah to Ramoth-gilead to try to wrest its control from "the king of Aram." The Israelite army was defeated, and Ahab died in battle.

Serious problems arise if we accept these passages as accounts of historical events late in Ahab's reign. There is, in the first place, a series of discrepancies with information found in contemporary Assyrian inscriptions, which represent Ahab as an ally of Damascus—at least in 853, at the end of his reign—while the biblical passages indicate that Samaria and Damascus had been at war for more than three years at the time of Ahab's death. Moreover, though the biblical account depicts Israel as militarily inferior to Damascus, the Assyrian inscriptions describing the battle of Qarqar in 853 indicate that Ahab was very strong, especially in chariots. Also, the Assyrian inscriptions show that the king of Damascus in 853 B.C.E. was Hadadezer, whereas 1 Kings 20 and 22 call him Ben-hadad. The references to the towns that Ben-hadad's father took from Ahab's father are also a problem, since, as already noted, it seems that Omri rather gained than lost territory to the Arameans. The final problem contains a hint of the solution: The name Ahab sits very loosely in the biblical text; most often, "the king of Israel" is not named, and the places where he is named vary considerably in the ancient witnesses to the texts in Hebrew.

For all of these reasons, many historians believe that 1 Kings 20 and 22 derive from accounts of the Aramean campaigns of a later king of Israel, a member of the Jehu dynasty and most probably Joash, who is known to have had victories over Ben-hadad son of Hazael. If this is correct, 1 Kings 20 reflects the historical situation described in 2 Kings 13:22–25, and Ahab is not likely to have been killed by a random arrow at Ramoth-gilead, as indicated by 1 Kings 22:34–35, but to have died a natural death, as implied by the language of the notice in 1 Kings 22:40 that "Ahab slept with his ancestors."

For a fuller discussion, see McKenzie, *1 Kings 16–2 Kings 16* (see n. 3), 169–77.

27 See n. 18.

28 Biran, "Sacred Spaces" (see n. 10); and Biran, "High Places" (see n. 10).

29 Amnon Ben-Tor and Doron Ben-Ami, "Hazor and the Archaeology of the Tenth Century B.C.E." *IEJ* 48 (1998), 1–37; Ben-Tor, "Excavating Hazor" (see n. 24); Ben-Tor, "Hazor and the Chronology" (see n. 24); Danny Rosenberg and Jennie Ebeling, "Romancing the Stones: The Canaanite Artistic Tradition at Israelite Hazor," *BAR,* January/February 2018.

30 Finkelstein and Ussishkin, "Archaeological and Historical Conclusions" (see n. 8), 596–97.

31 See the evidence for a winery (but no traces of a royal palace) in Norma Franklin, Jennie Ebeling, Philippe Guillaume, and Deborah Appler, "Have We Found Naboth's Vineyard at Jezreel?" *BAR,* November/December 2017. See also Norma Franklin, "Jezreel: Before and After Jezebel," in Lester L. Grabbe, ed., *Israel in Transition: From the Late Bronze II to Iron IIa (c. 1250–850 B.C.E.),* vol. 1: *The Archaeology*

(New York: T&T Clark, 2008), 45–53, and the publications in note 20.

32 André Lemaire, "La dynastie Davidique (*byt dwd*) dans deux inscription ouest-sémitiques du IXᵉ S. av. J.-C." *Studi epigraphici e linguistici* 11 (1994), 17–19; André Lemaire, "'House of David' Restored in Moabite Inscription," *BAR,* May/June 1994, with the reading "And he [i.e., Omri] dwelt in it [i.e., the land of Medeba] in his days and the sum of the days of his sons: 40 years." Nadav Na'aman raises the possibility that "his son" might not refer to Ahab but rather a descendant such as Joram. Nadav Na'aman, "Royal Inscription Versus Prophetic Story: Mesha's Rebellion According to Biblical and Moabite Historiography," in *Ahab Agonistes* (see n. 5), 145–83; André Lemaire, "The Mesha Stele and the Omride Dynasty," in *Ahab Agonistes* (see n. 5), 135–44.

33 For the rise of Assyria, see Peter R. Bedford, "The Neo-Assyrian Empire," in Ian Morris and Walter Scheidel, eds., *The Dynamics of Ancient Empires: State Power from Assyria to Byzantium* (Oxford: Oxford Univ. Press, 2009), 30–65; Christopher B. Hays, "Who Were the Assyrians?" *BAR,* May/June 2019.

34 *COS* 2:261–64. Note that Hadadezer is called Adad-idri in this text. The Aramean form of his name was Hadad-'idr, and the Hebrew was Hadad-'ēzer—Hadadezer in English (see 2 Samuel 8:3)—though this Hadadezer, the contemporary of Ahab, is not mentioned in the Bible. Many historians have identified Hadadezer of Damascus with the Ben-hadad mentioned in 1 Kings 20 and 22, but this no longer seems likely—see n. 26. For the reference to the Ben-hadad of 2 Kings 8:7–15, see below.

35 The last reference to Hadadezer in the Assyrian records is in 845 B.C.E., and the records from 841 identify the ruler of Damascus as Hazael. Hazael's status as a usurper is shown by the Assyrian inscription on an undated basalt statue of Shalmaneser from ancient Ashur (*COS* 2:268–69. See also Pitard, *Ancient Damascus* (see n. 16), 132–38; and Finkelstein, *Forgotten Kingdom* (see n. 21), 119–28.

36 *COS* 2:266–67.

37 Jehoram of Judah and Joram of Israel have variants of the same name. In the ninth century B.C.E., this name was pronounced *Yāhū-rām* in Judah and *Yaw-rām* in Israel, both of which mean "Yahweh is exalted." These spellings are not consistent in the Hebrew Bible, and the variations are preserved in most English translations, in which the king of Judah is most often called Jehoram, but frequently Joram, and the king of Israel is called Jehoram and Joram in roughly equal proportion. To minimize the confusion, and for convenience, the king of Judah is always called Jehoram in our discussion, and the king of Israel is called Joram.

38 This seems likely even if we assume that the prophetic narratives in 2 Kings 6 and 7 belong in a later historical context, so that Joram was not the unnamed "king of Israel" in the parts of those chapters that describe war with Damascus.

39 David Ussishkin, "Jezreel—Where Jezebel Was Thrown to the Dogs," *BAR*, July/August 2010.

40 Biran and Naveh, "Aramaic Stele Fragment" (see n. 15); "'David' Found at Dan" (see n. 15); Biran and Naveh, "Tel Dan Inscription" (see n. 15).

41 Ingo Kottsieper, "The Tel Dan Inscription (KAI 310) and the Political Relations Between Aram-Damascus and Israel in the First Half of the First Millennium BCE," in *Ahab Agonistes* (see n. 5), 104–34; Na'aman, "Northern Kingdom" (see n. 25), 414–15.

42 The location is given in Shalmaneser's annalistic texts on monumental bulls from Calah (*COS* 2:266–67) and on a marble slab from Ashur (*COS* 2:267–68). The Ashur text describes the spot as "opposite Tyre," and this better suits Ras en-Naqura than Mt. Carmel, which is otherwise an attractive alternative.

43 *COS* 2:269–70.

44 Like the names Jehoram and Joram, Jehoash and Joash are variants of the same name, which in the ninth century was pronounced *Yāhū-āš* in Judah and *Yaw-āš* in Israel, both meaning "Yahweh has given." English bibles use both names for Jehoash son of Ahaziah, king of Judah (r. c. 835–801), and for his northern namesake, Joash or Jehoash of Israel (r. c. 802–787). The variation arises from inconsistencies in the spelling of the names in the Hebrew Bible. To minimize the confusion, and for convenience, the king of Judah is always called Jehoash in our discussion, and the king of Israel is called Joash.

45 According to the version in 2 Chronicles 22:11, Jehosheba was Jehoiada's wife.

46 Pierre Bordreuil, Felice Israel, and Dennis Pardee, "Deux ostraca paléo-hébraux de la collection Sh. Moussaïeff," *Semitica* 46 (1996), 49–76; Pierre Bordreuil, Felix Israel, and Dennis Pardee, "King's Command and Widow's Plea: Two New Hebrew Ostraca of the Biblical Period," *NEA* 61 (1998), 2–13. Although these scholars assign the text to the late seventh century B.C.E., the script largely belongs to the Hebrew cursive tradition of the late ninth century B.C.E., the time of Jehoash of Judah. Since the ostracon was not found in a controlled archaeological excavation, its authenticity has been questioned. Nevertheless, the ostracon and its ink have been subjected to a series of scientific tests in leading laboratories (see the sidebar "Are They Genuine" in Christopher A. Rollston, "King's Command and Widow's Plea," *NEA* 61 [1988], 8–9) and none of the results has cast doubt on its antiquity.

47 The name appears as *šyhw*, that is, *āšyāhû* (Ashyahu), instead of *yāhūāš*, the ninth-century form of Jehoash. In other words, the divine name (*yāhū*, "Yahu, Yahweh") and verbal element (*āš*, "has given") are reversed in relation to the biblical form. This phenomenon is well known in Hebrew personal names, including royal names, in both the Bible and the epigraphic record.

48 Aren M. Maeir, "The Historical Background and Dating of Amos VI 2: An Archaeological Perspective from Tell es-Safi/Gath," *VT* 54:3 (2004), 319–34.

49 Second Kings 12:20–21 indicates that Jehoash was murdered by members of his own government, a crime later avenged by his son and successor, Amaziah (2 Kings 14:5). The Chronicler's account of the assassination plot (2 Chronicles 24:25–26) sets it in the immediate aftermath of Jehoash's capitulation to Hazael and attributes the motive of the conspirators to retribution for the death of Zechariah.

50 For more, see D. Matthew Smith, *The Coups of Hazael and Jehu: Building an Historical Narrative* (Piscataway, NJ: Gorgias, 2008); and Hadi Ghantous, *The Elisha-Hazael Paradigm and the Kingdom of Israel: The Politics of God in Ancient Syria-Palestine* (Durham: Acumen, 2013).

51 Since he had the same name as Ben-hadad son of Tabrimmon, the nemesis of Baasha of Israel in the early ninth century B.C.E., we will call him Ben-hadad II. If Hadadezer was succeeded briefly by a son named Ben-hadad, a possibility strongly supported by 2 Kings 8:7–15, then we should call Hazael's son Ben-hadad III.

52 *COS* 2:275–76.

53 Amaziah survived the debacle with Joash, but his subsequent death may have been an indirect result of the humiliation he had brought on his kingdom. Like his father, Jehoash, he was the victim of a conspiracy in Jerusalem, which obliged him to flee to Lachish, where he was overtaken and killed (2 Kings 14:19 = 2 Chronicles 25:27).

54 The text of a stela found in 1982 at Pazarcik, Turkey (*COS* 2:283–84), shows that in that year the Assyrian king received tribute from a king of Damascus named Hadiani—possibly the same name as that of the grandfather of Ben-hadad (1 Kings 15:18).

55 Second Samuel 8:1–14; 1 Kings 4:21 [Old Testament] = 1 Kings 5:1 [Hebrew Bible]; and 1 Kings 8:65.

56 The superscription of the book that preserves his oracles (Amos 1:1) describes Amos as prophesying during the reigns of Jeroboam II of Israel and Uzziah (also called Azariah) of Judah. Most think that his brief career as a prophet took place in the mid-eighth century B.C.E., sometime late in Jeroboam II's reign. For an argument that the book dates to this period, see Hans M. Barstad, "Can Prophetic Texts Be Dated? Amos 1–2 as an Example," in *Ahab Agonistes* (see n. 5), 21–40.

57 For Dan, see Biran, *Biblical Dan* (see n. 24); Biran, "Sacred Spaces" (see n. 10); and Biran, "High Places" (see n. 10). For Megiddo, see Finkelstein and Ussishkin, "Archaeological and Historical Conclusions" (see n. 8), 597–602. For Hazor, see Ben-Tor, "Excavating Hazor" (see n. 24); and Ben-Tor, "Hazor and

the Chronology" (see n. 24). For an overview of other sites, see Ann E. Killebrew, "Israel During the Iron Age II period," in M. L. Steiner and A. E. Killebrew, eds., *The Oxford Handbook of the Archaeology of the Levant c. 8000–332 BCE* (Oxford: Oxford Univ. Press, 2014), 730–42.

58 Finkelstein, *Forgotten Kingdom* (see n. 21), 135–38; Ze'ev Meshel, *Kuntillet 'Ajrud (Horvat Teman): An Iron Age II Religious Site on the Judah-Sinai Boarder*, Liora Freud, ed. (Jerusalem: IES, 2012).

59 Crowfoot, Crowfoot, and Kenyon, *Objects from Samaria* (see n. 22); Crowfoot and Crowfoot, *Early Ivories* (see n. 22).

60 The ivories were found in the debris of the 722/721 B.C.E. Assyrian destruction of Samaria, so that they are technically eighth-century artifacts, and many must have come from the time of Jeroboam II; but dating ivories stratigraphically is precarious since not only is the archaeological context complicated, but they were probably preserved and reused from generation to generation (the heirloom factor). Thus it is possible—and usually assumed—that some number of the Samaria ivories were also of ninth-century manufacture. See also Tappy, *Archaeology of Israelite Samaria* (see n. 18), 443–95.

61 Unfortunately, this magnificent seal, which features an elegantly engraved roaring lion, disappeared soon after its discovery, and we have only a bronze cast.

62 Ron E. Tappy, *The Archaeology of the Ostraca House at Israelite Samaria: Epigraphic Discoveries in Complicated Contexts* (Boston: ASOR, 2016); G. A. Reisner, C. S. Fisher, and D. G. Lyon, *Harvard Excavations at Samaria 1908–10.* (Cambridge: Harvard Univ. Press, 1924).

63 Richard Hess, "Aspects of Israelite Personal Names and Pre-Exilic Israelite Religion," in Meir Lubetski, ed., *New Seals and Inscriptions: Hebrew, Idumean, and Cuneiform* (Sheffield: Sheffield Phoenix Press, 2007), 301–13 (307).

64 Hermann Michael Niemann, "A New Look at the Samaria Ostraca: The King-Clan Relationship," *TA* 35:2 (2008), 249–66.

65 On the other hand, Azariah is said to have greatly strengthened the defensive position of Jerusalem, erecting fortification towers at strategic points and installing ingenious anti-siege devices on the walls (2 Chronicles 26:9, 15). This could be seen as an attempt to protect the city from invasion by Israel. Indeed, one of the gates Azariah fortified, the Corner Gate at the city's northwestern angle, was located in the area where Joash had breached the wall in an earlier generation (2 Kings 14:13). The later notice in 2 Kings 15:37 indicates that Israel, now in league with Damascus, began incursions into Judah in the reign of Jotham, Azariah's son and coregent.

66 The original homeland of the Meunites was evidently in the vicinity of Ma'an, about 12 miles southeast of Petra. They are first mentioned in the Bible as participants in a raid into Judah conducted by the Moabites and Ammonites in the time of Jehoshaphat (2 Chronicles 20:1, where the second occurrence of "Ammonites" in the Hebrew text should be corrected to "Meunites," following the Greek).

67 Reading "Meunites" with the Greek text of 26:8 in preference to the Hebrew "Ammonites." The Meunites not only remained in southern Judah but eventually became kin, having been incorporated into the Judahite genealogy (see Ezra 2:50; Nehemiah 7:52).

68 Ancient Elath is sometimes identified with modern Aqaba, which, however, lacks evidence of occupation at this period or at any other time in the Iron Age. Tell el-Kheleifeh, between Aqaba and modern Elath, is usually said to have been biblical Ezion-Geber, though this, too, is disputed. It may also be that Ezion-Geber and Elath were two names for the same site.

69 If Elath was another name for Ezion-Geber, it had been controlled by Judah since the time of Solomon (1 Kings 9:26; 22:48). It was probably lost in the Edomite revolt against Jehoram, in the mid-ninth century (2 Kings 8:20–22). Azariah "restored it to Judah" (2 Kings 14:22), but only temporarily. It was lost again to Edom in the time of Ahaz, when Jerusalem was threatened by the alliance of Samaria and Damascus (2 Kings 16:6).

70 The biblical term *ṣāra'at,* conventionally translated "leprosy," refers to a variety of skin ailments and conditions, ranging from the benign to the virulent. It does not necessarily connote true leprosy or Hansen's disease.

See Kenneth V. Mull and Carolyn Sandquist Mull, "Biblical Leprosy—Is It Really?" *BR,* April 1992, 32–39, 62.

71 McKenzie is right to point out that the text does not use the root *mlk* ("to rule, to be king") in the description of Jotham's "co-regency," perhaps indicating that his role was more of a royal steward. McKenzie, *1 Kings 16–2 Kings 16* (see n.3), 508.

72 This likelihood is enhanced by the description in 2 Chronicles 26:16–21 of a conflict between Azariah and the priesthood. As the Chronicler presents it, the high priest, whose name was also Azariah—the king is called Uzziah in this account—and 80 of his colleagues accused the king of usurping priestly prerogatives by making offerings on the altar of incense in the Temple. When the king became angry, his forehead broke out with "leprosy," which the priests immediately diagnosed. They then rushed him into quarantine.

73 The original location of the plaque and the circumstances of its discovery are unknown, but it was deposited and preserved in the Russian Orthodox Convent on the Mount of Olives. It bears an Aramaic inscription of late Herodian date that reads "To this place have been brought the bones of Uzziah, the king of Judah—do not open!" See Kyle P. McCarter, *Ancient Inscriptions: Voices from the Biblical World* (Washington DC: BAS, 1996), 132–33.

74 See also Philip J. King and Lawrence E. Stager, *Life in Biblical Israel* (Louisville: Westminster/John Knox, 2001), 85–112; William G. Dever, *The Lives of Ordinary People in Ancient Israel: Where Archaeology and the Bible Intersect* (Grand Rapids: Eerdmans, 2012); Cynthia Shafer-Elliott, *Food in Ancient Judah: Domestic Cooking in the Time of the Hebrew Bible* (Sheffield: Equinox, 2012); Avraham Faust, "Society and Culture in the Kingdom of Judah during the Eighth Century," in Z. I. Farber and J. Wright, eds., *Archaeology and History of Eighth-Century Judah* (Atlanta: SBL Press, 2018), 179–203; Jenny Ebeling, "Daily Life," in *Archaeology and History of Eighth-Century Judah* (see above), 267–77; and Cynthia Shafer Elliott, "'He Shall Eat Curds and Honey' (Isa 7:15): Food and Feasting in Late Eighth Century Judah," in *Archaeology and History of Eighth-Century Judah* (see above), 279–98.

75 Carol Meyers, *Rediscovering Eve: Ancient Israelite Women in Context* (Oxford: Oxford Univ. Press, 2013), 103–24.

76 James W. Hardin, *Lahav II: Households and the Use of Domestic Space at Iron II Tell Halif: An Archaeology of Destruction*, Vol. 2 (Winona Lake: Eisenbrauns, 2010); Cynthia Shafer-Elliott, "Baking Bread in Ancient Judah," *BAR*, July/August/September/October 2019.

77 Meyers, *Rediscovering Eve* (see n. 75), 125–47; Jennie R. Ebeling, *Women's Lives in Biblical Times* (London: T&T Clark, 2001).

78 Nahman Avigad and Benjamin Sass, *Corpus of West Semitic Stamp Seals* (Jerusalem: Israel Academy of Sciences and Humanities, 1997), 60–65. See also the references in n. 20.

79 Robert Deutsch and Michael Heltzer, *New Epigraphic Evidence from the Biblical Period* (Tel Aviv: Archaeological Center Publications, 1995), 83–88.

80 Rainer Albertz, Beth Alpert Nakhai, Saul M. Olyan, and Rüdiger Schmitt, eds., *Family and Household Religion: Toward a Synthesis of Old Testament Studies, Archaeology, Epigraphy, and Cultural Studies* (Winona Lake, IN: Eisenbrauns, 2014); Rainer Albertz and Rüdiger Schmitt, *Family and Household Religion in Ancient Israel and the Levant* (Winona Lake, IN: Eisenbrauns, 2012); John Bodel and Saul M. Olyan, eds., *Household and Family Religion in Antiquity* (Oxford: Blackwell, 2008); Aaron Brody, "Materiality of Religion in Judean Households: A Contextual Analysis of Ritual Objects from Iron II Tell en-Nasbeh," *NEA* 81.3 (2018), 212–21; Zev I. Farber, "Religion in Eighth-Century Judah: An Overview," in *Archaeology and History of Eighth-Century Judah* (see n. 74), 431–53.

81 Ze'ev Meshel, *Kuntillet Ajrud (Horvat Teman): An Iron Age II Religious Site on the Judah-Sinai Border*, ed. Liora Freud (Jerusalem, IES, 2012); Brent A. Strawn and Joel M. LeMon, "Religion in Eighth-Century Judah: The Case of Quntillet 'Ajrud (and Beyond)," in *Archaeology and History of Eighth-Century Judah* (see n. 74), 379–400.

82 The name appears in the form *ꜣyw ḥmlk*, "'Ashyaw the king," that is, "Yaw'ash," or Joash/Jehoash. The theophoric and verbal elements are transposed in the name, exactly as in the case of Joash/Jehoash of Judah in the ostracon described above.

83 On this and other aspects of the religious characteristics of the Kuntillet 'Ajrud texts, see P. K. McCarter, "Aspects of the Religion of the Israelite Monarchy: Biblical and Epigraphic Data," in P. D. Hanson, S. D. McBride, and P. D. Miller Jr., eds., *Ancient Israelite Religion: Essays in Honor of Frank Moore Cross* (Philadelphia: Fortress Press, 1987), 137–55.

84 Erin D. Darby, "Judean Pillar Figurines and the Making of Female Piety in Ancient Israelite Religion," in Sandra Blakely, ed., *Gods, Objects, and Ritual Practice* (Atlanta: Lockwood, 2017), 193–214; Erin D. Darby, *Interpreting Judean Pillar Figurines: Gender and Empire in Judean Apotropaic Ritual*, FAT (Tübingen: Mohr Siebeck, 2014); William G. Dever, "A Temple Built for Two," *BAR*, March/April 2008; William G. Dever, *Did God Have a Wife? Archaeology and Folk Religion in Ancient Israel* (Grand Rapids: Eerdmans, 2005); Raz Kletter, "Between Archaeology and Theology: The Pillar Figurines from Judah and the Asherah," in *Studies in the Archaeology of the Iron Age* (see n. 10), 179–216; Erin Darby, "Judean Pillar Figurines (JPFs)," in *Archaeology and History of Eighth-Century Judah* (see n. 74), 401–14; Tallay Ornan, "Ištar as Depicted on Finds from Israel," in *Studies in the Archaeology of the Iron Age* (see n. 10), 235–56.

85 Ze'ev Herzog, "The Date of the Temple of Arad: Reassessment of the Stratigraphy and the Implications for the History of Religion in Judah," in *Studies in the Archaeology of the Iron Age* (see n. 10), 156–78; Ze'ev Herzog, "The Fortress Mound at Tel Arad: An Interim Report," *TA* 29 (2002), 3–109.

86 Uzi Avner, "Sacred Stones in the Desert," *BAR*, May/June 2001.

87 Nava Panitz-Cohen and Naama Yahalom-Mack, "The Wise Woman of Abel Beth Maacah," *BAR*, July/August/September/October 2019; Naama Yahalom-Mack, Nava Panitz-Cohen, and Robert Mullins, "From a Fortified Canaanite City-State to 'a City and a Mother' in Israel: Five Seasons of Excavation at Tel Abel Beth Maacah," *NEA* 81.2 (2018), 145–56. See also I Kings 15 and 2 Kings 15.

88 Finkelstein, *Forgotten Kingdom* (see n. 21), 138–39.

89 For more, see K. Lawson Younger Jr., "Assyria's Expansion West of the Euphrates (ca. 870–701 BCE)," in *Archaeology and History of Eighth-Century Judah* (see n. 74), 17–33.

90 *COS* 2:284–86. Menahem's payment consisted of 1,000 talents of silver according to 2 Kings 15:19, where Tiglath-pileser is called "Pul." This shortened form of his name is often said to have been Tiglath-pileser's throne name as king of Babylon, a position he claimed in his first regnal year. This name has not been found in contemporary sources, however, though Tiglath-pileser was referred to as Pulu in much later cuneiform sources.

91 For an overview, see Steven L. McKenzie, "The Last Days of Israel: Chronological Considerations," in S. Hasegawa, C. Levin, K. Radner, eds., *The Last Days of the Kingdom of Israel* (Berlin: Walter de Gruyter, 2019), 289–99; and McKenzie, *1 Kings 16–2 Kings 16* (see n. 3), 507–508, 514–20.

92 According to McKenzie, the designation "Gileadiates" may indicate that they are relatives of Shallum the son of Jabash (2 Kings 15:13), and thus working out of revenge. McKenzie, *1 Kings 16–2 Kings 16* (see n. 3), 506.

93 This likelihood is increased by the fact that the revolt came out of Gilead, Transjordanian Israel, where the influence of Damascus would be strongest.

94 McKenzie notes that the absence of the root *mlk* ("to rule, to be king") in the description of Jotham's "coregency" may indicate that he was more of a royal steward (see n. 71).

95 The Medes were an Indo-Iranian people who lived on a plateau corresponding to the northwestern part of modern Iran. Traditional enemies of Assyria, they would eventually become the principal ally of the Babylonians in the overthrow of the Assyrian Empire.

96 For an unprovenanced clay bulla, or impression, of the personal seal of Ahaz, see Robert Deutsch, "First Impression: What We Learn from King Ahaz's Seal," *BAR*, May/June 1998.

97 Joachim Begrich, "Der syrisch-ephraimitische Krieg und seine weltpolitischen Zusammenhänge," *Zeitschrift der deutschen morgenländischen Gesellschaft* 83 (1929), 213–37.

98 The change in historical interpretation was stimulated especially by the influential study of Bustenay Oded, "The Historical Background of the Syro-Ephraimite War Reconsidered," *CBQ* 34 (1972), 153–65.

99 See Isaiah 7:1–2. In response to Ahaz's anxiety, the prophet does two things in Yahweh's name: he assures Ahaz that Rezin and "the son of Remaliah," as he calls Pekah, will never conquer Jerusalem, and he gives a sign to certify the doom of the two nations that have attacked Jerusalem. This is the well-known Immanuel sign, according to which a child by that name will be born and "before the child knows how to refuse the evil and choose the good"—that is, before the child grows up—"the land before whose two kings you are in dread will be deserted" (Isaiah 7:16).

100 Alan R. Millard, *The Eponyms of the Assyrian Empire 910–612 BC* (Helsinki: The Neo-Assyrian Text Corpus Project, 1994), 44.

101 *COS* 2:289. The spelling in the Assyrian annals corresponds to the long form of the king's name, "Jehoahaz," of which the biblical "Ahaz" is an abbreviated form.

102 Millard, *Eponyms* (see n. 100), 45.

103 Evidence of Tiglath-pileser's destructive campaign through the Galilee region has been documented at the site of Bethsaida (et-Tell). See Rami Arav, Richard A. Freund, and John F. Schroder Jr., "Bethsaida: Lost and Rediscovered," *BAR*, January/February 2000; Rami Arav, "Beth Saida: The Capital City of the Kingdom of Geshur," in *Archaeology and History of Eighth-Century Judah* (see n. 74), 79–98.

104 *COS* 2:286.

105 According to Tiglath-pileser's annals, after Pekah was destroyed, Tiglath-pileser "installed Hoshea [as king] over them" (*COS* 2:288, see also pp. 291 and 292).

106 The region north of Ramoth-gilead, long disputed between Samaria and Damascus, became the Assyrian province of Qarnini (Karnaim). For a description of the roles of both the city of Megiddo and Jezreel under Assyrian rule, see Norma Franklin, "Megiddo and Jezreel Reflected in the Dying Embers of the Northern Kingdom of Israel," in *Last Days* (see n. 91), 189–208.

107 *COS* 2:286.

108 *COS* 2:286.

109 André Lemaire, "Solomon & Sheba, Inc.," *BAR*, January/February 2010.

110 *COS* 2:289.

111 *COS* 2:288, 290–91, 291–92.

112 For Assyrian interests in Israel specifically, see Frederick Mario Fales, "Why Israel? Reflections on Shalmaneser V's and Sargon II's Grand Strategy for the Levant," in *Last Days* (see n. 91), 87–99.

113 For a fuller overview of Israel in the eighth century B.C.E., see Gilad Itach, "The Kingdom of Israel in the Eighth Century: From a Regional Power to Assyrian Provinces," in *Archaeology and History of Eighth-Century Judah* (see n. 74), 57–77.

114 Nothing of the Tyrian annals survives in the original Phoenician, but they were translated into Greek by Menander of Ephesus or Pergamon and are cited in the writings of the Jewish historian Flavius Josephus. For the background to the fall of Samaria, the relevant passage in Josephus is *Ant.* 9.283–87.

115 The Babylonian Chronicles is a record of annual events begun in the mid-eighth century B.C.E. For the text, see A. K. Grayson, *Assyrian and Babylonian Chronicles* (Winona Lake, IN: Eisenbrauns, 2000).

116 See, e.g., the large "summary" inscription, in *COS* 2:296–97. For a helpful discussion of the relevant texts from the reign of Sargon, see Eckart Frahm, "Samaria, Hamath, and Assyria's Conquests in the Levant in the Last 720s," in *Last Days* (see n. 91), 55–86. For an overview of the various proposals to make sense of the text, see Ron E. Tappy, "The Annals of Sargon II and the Archaeology of Samaria: Rhetorical Claims, Empirical Evidence," in *Last Days* (see n. 91), 147–87; Bob Becking, "How to Encounter an Historical Problem? '722–720 BCE' as a Case Study," in *Last Days* (see n. 91), 17–32. For an overview of Sargon's military campaigns, see S. C. Melville, *The Campaigns of Sargon II, King of Assyria, 721–705 BC* (Norman: Univ. of Oklahoma Press, 2016).

117 Merodachbaladan was from Bit-Yakin, the most southerly of the three Chaldean tribes in Babylonia. The Chaldeans, who were closely related to the Arameans, begin to appear in extant cuneiform sources in the ninth century B.C.E., and by the eighth century they were vying for leadership in Babylonia. Eventually their name became synonymous with Babylonians (see Genesis 11:28). The nationalistic movement that Merodachbaladan led for more than 20 years during the reigns of Sargon and Sennacherib was fired in part by resentment of the Assyrian kings' practice (beginning with Tiglath-pileser III) of claiming the Babylonian throne for themselves.

118 Ilu-bi'di's revolt is well documented in Sargon II's records, including the annals (*COS* 2:293) and other inscriptions (i.e., *COS* 2:295).

119 These included Queen Samsi of Arabia, who had also paid tribute to Tiglath-pileser, and It'amar the Sabaean, chieftain of the powerful trading people of southwestern Arabia from whom the fabled Queen of Sheba of Solomonic lore also came. Their tribute came in the form of gold, horses, and camels. When Sargon returned west in his seventh year (715 B.C.E.) to resettle captive peoples in the provinces, Samsi and It'amar brought tribute again (*COS* 2:296).

120 *COS* 2:295–96.

121 *COS* 2:295–96.

122 The list in 2 Kings 17:24 is part of the peroration on the fall of Samaria by the Exilic Deuteronomist (see below). It may contain the names of peoples transported to former Israelite territories at different times, thus collapsing several resettlements into a single statement. From Sargon's own records, we know only that he brought captives from a number of Arabian tribes and settled them in Samaria in 715 B.C.E. He may well have resettled additional peoples in Samaria in 711, when he made his final visit to Palestine to suppress a revolt in Ashdod, and there were probably still other resettlements of which we have no record.

123 Reading "mountain country" or "highlands" with the Greek of 2 Kings 17:6 in preference to the Hebrew reading "cities."

124 On the resettlement of Israelites (and Judahites) in Mesopotamia generally, see

Bustenay Oded, "The Settlement of the Israelites and the Judean Exiles in Mesopotamia in the 8th and 6th Centuries B.C.E.," in G. Galil and M. Weinfeld, eds., *Studies in Historical Geography and Biblical Historiography Presented to Zecharia Kallai*, VT Supplement 81 (Leiden: Brill, 2000), 91–103. For the inscriptional evidence, see Ran Zadok, "Israelites and Judaeans in the Neo-Assyrian Documentation (732–602 BCE): An Overview of the Sources and a Socio-Historical Assessment," *BASOR* 374 (2015), 159–86; and Karen Radner, "The 'Lost Tribes of Israel' in the Context of the Resettlement Programme of the Assyrian Empire," in *Last Days* (see n. 91), 101–23.

125 Israelite-Assyrian pottery indicates that the site remained occupied after the assault. See Tappy, *Archaeology of Israelite Samaria* (see n. 18), 351–441; Tappy, "Annals of Sargon II" (see n. 116); William G. Dever, "Archaeology and the Fall of the Northern Kingdom: What Really Happened," in S. White-Crawford, A. Ben-Tor, and W. G. Dever, eds., *Up to the Gates of Ekron: Essays on the Archaeology and History of the Eastern Mediterranean in Honor of Seymour Gitin* (Jerusalem: Albright Institute, 2007), 78–92; and Chapman, "Samaria" (see n. 18).

126 Agricultural terraces remained largely undisturbed in Israel, perhaps indicating that the Assyrians were interested in ongoing food production. See Becking, "How to Encounter An Historical Problem?" (see n. 116), 24.

Although Tell Qudadi (Tell esh-Shuna) on the northern bank of the Yarkon River was previously considered a fortress, ceramic assemblage indicates that the site was not established before the second half of the eighth century B.C.E. It is thus more likely an Assyrian establishment to secure the Assyrian trade along the Via Maris. See Alexander Fantalkin and Olen Tal, "Re-Discovering the Iron Age Fortress at Tell Qudadi in the context of Neo-Assyrian Imperialistic Policies," *PEQ* 141 (2009), 188–206; Yifat Thareani, "The Empire and the 'Upper Sea': Assyrian Control Strategies along the Southern Levantine Coast," *BASOR* 375 (2016), 77–102. For more on Assyrian control of trade routes, see Avraham Faust, "The Interests of the Assyrian Empire in the West: Olive Oil Production as a Test-Case," *JESHO* 54 (2011), 62–86.

127 *COS* 2:145–46. A bulla bearing the impression of Hezekiah's seal was found in the excavation of Ophel in Jerusalem along with 33 other stamped bullae, and other non-provenanced bullae bearing Hezekiah's seal have come to light. See Frank Moore Cross, "A Bulla of Hezekiah, King of Judah," in P. H. Williams Jr. and T. Hiebert, eds., *Realia Dei: Essays in Archaeology and Biblical Interpretation in Honor of Edward F. Campbell Jr. at His Retirement* (Atlanta: Scholars Press, 1999), 62–66; Frank Moore Cross, "King Hezekiah's Seal Bears Phoenician Imagery," *BAR*, March/April 1999; Robert Deutsch, "Lasting Impressions: New Bullae Reveal Egyptian-Style Emblems on Judah's Royal Seals," *BAR*, July/August 2002; Robert Deutsch, *Biblical Period Hebrew Bullae: The Josef Chaim Kaufman Collection* (Tel Aviv: Archaeological Center Publication, 2003), 13–18; Eilat Mazar, *The Ophel Excavations to the South of the Temple Mount: 2009–2013* (Jerusalem: Hebrew Univ. of Jerusalem, 2015).

128 Hershel Shanks, "The Mystery of the Nechushtan," *BAR*, March/April 2007.

129 In fact, this very point was part of the rhetoric of Sennacherib's spokesman, the Rabshakeh, in his attempt to intimidate Hezekiah's delegation at the beginning of the siege of Jerusalem (2 Kings 18:22).

130 The Chronicler's account of Hezekiah's reforms, which constitutes the bulk of three chapters (2 Chronicles 29–31), is much more extensive than the three verses assigned to the subject in the Kings account (2 Kings 18:4–6). This is explainable in part as the Chronicler's expansion of subjects in which he had a particular interest (note, e.g., the emphasis on role of the Levites in the purification of the Temple in chap. 30). But we must also allow for a tendency on the part of the Deuteronomistic historian, who was responsible for the Kings account, to diminish the extent of Hezekiah's reform. To be sure, the historian admired Hezekiah and praised him highly, asserting that in his trust in Yahweh "... there was no one like him among all the kings of Judah after him, or among those who were before him" (2 Kings 18:5). But if the author was working in the time of Josiah—indeed, under the patronage of Josiah—it is not surprising that he would minimize Hezekiah's role in the reform movement in order to reserve the primary credit for Josiah.

131 After Ze'ev Herzog (2001; 2002: 58–72), who assigns Stratum IX to the eighth century B.C.E. See Ze'ev Herzog, "The Date of the Temple of Arad: Reassessment of the Stratigraphy and the Implications for the History of Religion in Judah," in *Studies in the Archaeology of the Iron Age* (see n. 10), 156–78; Herzog, "Fortress Mound at Tel Arad (see n. 85); Ze'ev Herzog, "Perspectives on Southern Israel's Cult Centralization: Arad and Beer-sheba," in R. G. Kratz and H. Spieckermann, eds., *One God – One Cult – One Nation: Archaeological and Biblical Perspectives* (Berlin: de Gruyter, 2010), 169–99. For a dissenting view, see Diana Edelman, "Hezekiah's Alleged Cultic Centralization," *JSOT* 32 (2008), 395–434. See also the discussion in David Rafael Moulis, "Hezekiah's Cultic Reforms according to the Archaeological Evidence," in F. Čapek and O. Lipschits, eds., *The Last Century in the History of Judah: The Seventh Century BCE in Archaeological, Historical, and Biblical Perspectives* (Atlanta. SBL Press, 2019), 167–80.

132 Sargon's boastful self-designation in his Nimrud Inscription (*COS* 2:298–99) as "the subduer of Judah [?] which lies far away" remains enigmatic.

133 Azuri's revolt is mentioned in Sargon II's annals and other inscriptions. See *COS* 2:293–94 and 296–97.

134 After Sargon had suppressed the revolt, Ashdod was turned into an Assyrian city-state and provincial center. See Hershel Shanks, "Assyrian Palace Discovered in Ashdod," *BAR*, January/February 2007.

135 See also Donald Redford, "Egypt and Judah in the Eighth Century BCE," in *Archaeology and History of Eighth-Century Judah* (see n. 74), 161–75.

136 Second Kings 20:12–13 (see also Isaiah 39:1–2; 2 Chronicles 32:31) describes a visit of Merodachbaladan's envoys to Jerusalem, where Hezekiah showed them the Temple treasury. This visit is typically placed after Sennacherib's invasion, but it must have occurred earlier, since in 701 Merodachbaladan was no longer in power. It fits nicely into the events of 704–703, when it would have been very much in Merodachbaladan's interest to cultivate alliances with other Assyrian vassal states and to encourage them to rebel. Some place the visit during Merodachbaladan's first term

as king of Babylon (722–710). See Mordechai Cogan and Hayim Tadmor, *II Kings,* Anchor Bible Commentary (New York: Doubleday, 1988), 260–61.

137 This was the third of the eight campaigns of Sennacherib recorded in the final edition of his annals, preserved in the Taylor and Oriental Institute prisms, both of which are dependent, for this campaign, on the slightly fuller account in the so-called Rassam Cylinder, which was composed shortly after the campaign itself (*COS* 2:302–303). When the Assyrian records are complemented with biblical accounts (2 Kings 18:13–19:8; Isaiah 36:1–37:8; 2 Chronicles 32:1–22) and the ample archaeological testimony from sites like Lachish and Jerusalem, the story is one of the most complete in the history of the Assyrian Empire.

138 Presumably this huge force ("a countless force," *COS* 2:303) had been dispatched by Shebitku (r. 706–690), king of Egypt. The reference in 2 Kings 19:9 (= Isaiah 37:9) to "King Tirhakah of Ethiopia" is evidently a mistake, since in 701 Taharqa (r. 690–664 B.C.E., the biblical Tirhakah) was still a child living in Nubia and would not come to the throne of Egypt for another decade. This lapse on the part of the Israelite historian has helped give rise to the hypothesis of a second, later campaign by Sennacherib against Judah.

139 Padi's name also appears in a five-line inscription found in the ruins of a temple at Tel Miqne, ancient Ekron (*COS* 2:164).

140 At certain points, the correspondences are remarkably close. At the beginning of the account of the advance against Hezekiah in the Assyrian annals, Sennacherib says, "I besieged forty-six of his fortified walled cities and surrounding smaller towns ... I conquered [them] ..." (*COS* 2:303), while the biblical account opens with the statement that "King Sennacherib of Assyria came up against all the fortified cities of Judah and captured them" (2 Kings 18:13). In the Assyrian account, the amount of precious metal in the tribute Hezekiah paid is given as "30 talents of gold, 800 talents of silver" (*COS* 2:303), while the biblical account specifies the amount as "three hundred talents of silver and thirty talents of gold" (2 Kings 18:14).

141 For a seal of the prophet, see Eilat Mazar, "Is This the Prophet's Isaiah's Signature?" *BAR*, March/April/May/June 2018.

142 See Ehud Ben Zvi, "Who Wrote the Speech of Rabshakeh and When?" *JBL* 109 (1990), 79–92; Dominic Rudman, "Is the Rabshakeh also Among the Prophets? A Rhetorical Study of 2 Kings xviii 17–35," *VT* 50 (2000), 111–10; Nadav Na'aman, "Updating the Messages: Hezekiah's Second Prophetic Story [2 Kings 19:9b–35] and the Community of Babylonian Deportees," in L. L. Grabbe, ed., *'Like a Bird in a Cage': The Invasion of Sennacherib in 701 BCE* (Sheffield: Sheffield Academic Press, 2003), 201–20. For a more conservative position, see William R. Gallagher, *Sennacherib's Campaign to Judah: New Studies* (Leiden: Brill, 1999).

143 Extensive archaeological evidence of Sennacherib's Judahite campaign has recently been uncovered at Tel Halif, south of Jerusalem. See Oded Borowski, "Tel Halif: In the Path of Sennacherib," *BAR*, May/June 2005.

144 See David Ussishkin, *The Conquest of Lachish by Sennacherib* (Tel-Aviv: Tel Aviv Univ., 1982); David Ussishkin and Miriam Feinberg Vamosh. *Biblical Lachish: A Tale of Construction, Destruction, Excavation and Restoration* (Jerusalem: IES, 2015); for a re-evaluation of the reliefs, see Christoph Uehlinger, "Clio in a World of Pictures—Another Look at the Lachish Reliefs from Sennacherib's Southwest Palace at Nineveh," in *'Like a Bird in a Cage'* (see n.142), 221–305.

145 *COS* 2:303.

146 David Ussishkin has argued "that Sennacherib, given the choice, did not intend to conquer Jerusalem by force," preferring instead to reduce Hezekiah to Assyrian vassalage by a strategy of attrition and intimidation, holding up the fate of Lachish as a terrifying example; see "Sennacherib's Campaign to Philistia and Judah: Ekron, Lachish, and Jerusalem," in Y. Amrit et al., *Essays on Ancient Israel in Its Near Eastern Context: A Tribute to Nadav Na'aman* (Winona Lake, IN: Eisenbrauns, 2006), 339–57 (353–54).

147 The enigmatic *millo* is first mentioned in connection with the rebuilding of the city after David's conquest (2 Samuel 5:9). It was evidently some kind of fortification, perhaps a filled-earth rampart.

148 For more on a well-constructed, 20-foot thick wall attributed to Hezekiah by the excavator, see Nahman Avigad, *Discovering Jerusalem* (Nashville: Abingdon, 1980), 46–57. Pointing out that some of the pottery types thought to be diagnostic of the time of Hezekiah were already in use in the early eighth century, Na'aman argues that the wall was built in connection with a Jerusalem population crest at the end of the eighth century, the result of a gradual increase that began in the early eighth century or earlier and culminated with the arrival of refugees from the events of 701. Nadav Na'aman, "When and How Did Jerusalem Become a Great City? The Rise of Jerusalem as Judah's Premier City in the Eighth–Seventh Centuries B.C.E.," *BASOR* 347 (2007), 21–56 (24–27). For a critique of this view by Israel Finkelstein, who strongly doubts an expansion of Jerusalem before the late eighth century, see "Concerning Disappearing Potsherds and Invented Population Growth: A Reply to Nadav Na'aman Regarding Jerusalem's Growth in the 8th Century B.C.E. [Hebrew]," *Zion* 72 (2007), 325–37. The archaeological evidence strongly points to a re-emergence of an urban fortified Jerusalem (last in evidence only in the Middle Bronze IIC) in the Iron IIC period (c. 720–586 B.C.E.). For an overview, see Ann E. Killebrew, "Biblical Jerusalem: An Archaeological Assessment," in L.L. Grabbe, ed., *The Hebrew Bible and History: Critical Readings* (London: T&T Clark, 2019), 352–66.

149 Hezekiah's tunnel is commonly known as the Siloam Tunnel, a name derived from the Shiloah or Siloam Channel, an aqueduct that transported the waters of the Gihon along the southeastern slope of the Ophel to agricultural terraces in the Kidron basin. For theories on how the tunnel was constructed, see Hershel Shanks, "Sound Proof: How Hezekiah's Tunnelers Met," *BAR*, September/October 2008; Dan Gill, "How They Met: Geology Solves Long-Standing Mystery of Hezekiah's Tunnelers," *BAR*, July/August 1994. For the inscription, see *COS* 2:145–46. For arguments that the tunnel dates to later periods, see John Rogerson and Philip R. Davies, "Was the Siloam Tunnel Built by Hezekiah?" *BA* 59 (1996), 138–49; Stig

Norin, "The Age of the Siloam Inscription and Hezekiah's Tunnel," *VT* 48 (1998), 37–48; E. Axel Knauf, "Hezekiah or Manasseh? A Reconsideration of the Siloam Tunnel and Inscription," *TA* 28 (2001), 281–87.

150 Hershel Shanks, "A Tiny Piece of the Puzzle," *BAR*, March/April 2009.

151 Further evidence that the *lmlk* stamps were part of a centralized administrative program comes from the determination that they were all manufactured in a single site in the Judean Shephelah, as revealed by analysis of the clay. See further Hans Mommsen, Isadore Perlman, and Joseph Yellin, "The Provenience of the *lmlk* Jars," *IEJ* 34 (1984), 89–113.

152 See the discussion in Andrew G. Vaughn, *Theology, History, and Archaeology in the Chronicler's Account of Hezekiah* (Atlanta: Scholars Press, 1999), 152–57; Oded Lipschits, "Judah Under Assyrian Rule and the Early Phase of Stamping Jar Handles," in *Archaeology and History of Eighth-Century Judah* (see n. 74), 337–55; Andrew G. Vaughn, "Should All of the *LMLK* Jars Still Be Attributed to Hezekiah? Yes!" in *Archaeology and History of Eighth-Century Judah* (see n. 74), 357–62.

153 The overall structure of the biblical narrative is designed to show that the survival of the city was the result of divine deliverance in fulfillment of the oracles of Isaiah, especially the oracle in 2 Kings 19:32–34 announcing that Yahweh would defend the city. The night after this prophecy was uttered, we are told (2 Kings 19:35), "The angel of the Lord ... struck down one hundred eighty-five thousand in the camp of the Assyrians ..." This is the biblical language of plague, as correctly interpreted in Ben Sira 48:21, and it might preserve a historical memory of one of the factors leading to the Assyrian withdrawal, namely, the spread of disease among the siege troops. Herodotus (*History* 2.141) relates the story of a similar deliverance of Egypt from "Sennacherib, king of the Arabs [!] and Assyrians," when mice gnawed the weapons of the Assyrians while they were encamped at Pelusium in the eastern Nile Delta. This story has been associated with Sennacherib's siege of Jerusalem by some historians, who regard the reference to mice as an indirect confirmation of an outbreak of plague in the Assyrian camp. But the Herodotus story

is not historical in anything like its present form—Sennacherib never invaded Egypt—and, in any case, it makes no mention of Judah or Jerusalem. At best it might be regarded as a distorted recollection of an event in the reign of Esarhaddon, Sennacherib's successor, who did invade Egypt and was assisted in doing so by Arab guides.

154 For an overview of various sites in Judah during this period, see Lester L. Grabbe, "Introduction," in *'Like a Bird in a Cage'* (see n. 142), 2–43 (11–18). For a brief description of a single site (Tel Beth Shemesh), see "Highway Through History," *BAR*, July/August/September/October 2019.

155 The Hezekiah's tribute list (*COS* 2:303) is the longest in any of Sennacherib's extant inscriptions.

156 Some have argued that Sennacherib conducted a second campaign against Judah, sometime after the accession of Taharqa, in 690. The two-campaign hypothesis is an attempt to solve the problems created by the reference to "King Tirhakah of Ethiopia" in 2 Kings 19:9 and especially the contradiction regarding the outcome of the siege between the Assyrian account, which says that Hezekiah capitulated and accepted vassal status, and the biblical account, which concludes with Sennacherib's army retreating from Judah after having been severely punished by the hand of Yahweh. According to the two-campaign theory, Sennacherib's surviving inscriptions refer to the 701 B.C.E. campaign, which ended in the reduction of Judah to vassalage, while the biblical references to the failure and withdrawal of the Assyrian army and to the involvement of Taharqa refer to a campaign not mentioned in extant Assyrian sources. The occasion for this second campaign would have been a rebellion in the West, led by Hezekiah and supported by Taharqa, that broke out after the Assyrian army was defeated by the Babylonians and Elamites in 691 B.C.E., and Sennacherib would have launched it after his capture of Babylon, in 689. Though ingenious, the two-campaign theory does not inspire confidence, since the problems being addressed arise only in the final part of the biblical account of the siege, which, as noted earlier, is widely regarded as late in origin, while the opening summary of the biblical account (2 Kings 18:13–16), usually

regarded as early, is in close agreement with the Assyrian account.

157 *ANET*, 291a, 294a.

158 The rest of the list of practices for which he is condemned in 2 Kings 21:3–6 corresponds very closely to the cultic sins listed in 2 Kings 17:16–17, amid the long Deuteronomistic sermon on the fall of Samaria in 2 Kings 17:7–23. Thus, he erected altars to a foreign god (Baal; 2 Kings 21:3) and "the host of heaven," astral deities whose rooftop worship was condemned by prophets like Zephaniah (1:5) and Jeremiah (19:13); he reinstituted the "sacred pole" or *asherah* (2 Kings 21:3); and he made "his son pass through fire" and practiced soothsaying and augury (2 Kings 21:6). In 2 Kings 17:16–18, these are the very sins that the author believes led to the downfall of the northern kingdom, and it seems clear that the purpose of the Exilic Deuteronomist in composing the present list was to accuse Manasseh of bringing similar judgment on Judah. This is surely the point of the comparison of Manasseh to "King Ahab of Israel" in 2 Kings 21:3.

159 The Medes were Indo-Iranian people living on the plateau corresponding to the northwestern part of modern Iran. Traditional enemies of Assyria, they eventually became the principal ally of Babylonia in the overthrow of the Assyrian Empire.

160 The Cimmerians—called *Gōmer* in the Bible (Ezekiel 38:6; see also Genesis 10:2–3)—were Indo-Aryan nomads, originally from southern Russia. In the eighth century B.C.E., they had been driven south across the Caucasus under pressure from the Scythians and Assyrians into Asia Minor. Sargon II was fighting the Cimmerians in Asia Minor when he was killed in 705 B.C.E.

161 The Scythians—called *'ašûkênaz,* "Ashkenaz," in the Bible (Jeremiah 51:27; see also Genesis 10:3)—were a nomadic people who spoke an Indo-Iranian language. In the eighth century B.C.E., they had moved from their homeland in southern Russia (north and northeast of Black Sea) through the Caucasus into the Near East. Originally enemies of Assyria, they became allies briefly, then enemies again.

162 Anthony Spalinger, "Esarhaddon and Egypt: An Analysis of the First Invasion of Egypt," *Orientalia* 43 (1974), 299.

163 *ANET*, 302b.

164 *ANET*, 292b. Earlier (c. 677), Esarhaddon had pacified Arab tribes in the vicinity of the Wadi of Egypt (*ANET*, 291b–92a), guaranteeing their neutrality and learning from them the value of the camel and waterskin.

165 This is according to the Babylonian Chronicle (*ANET*, 302b–303a); for the narrative account in the so-called Zinjirli stela from southeastern Turkey (ancient Sam'al), see *ANET*, 293a.

166 In a stela carved on the rock wall of the Dog River near Beirut, he boasts, "I entered Memphis ... amidst (general) jubilation and rejoicing" (*ANET*, 292a).

167 According to the Babylonian Chronicle, *ANET*, 303b.

168 According to the so-called Rassam Cylinder from Kuyunjik, ancient Nineveh (*ANET*, 294–96a), Assurbanipal led this expedition himself, but other inscriptions indicate that he stayed home and entrusted the task to his second-in-command, the *turtānu*.

169 *ANET*, 294a.

170 This was the period of the Saite Renaissance in Egypt, so called because of the revival of the ancient Memphite traditions of Lower Egypt, which was now ruled from Sais in the north rather than from Thebes in Upper Egypt.

171 The enigmatic biblical tradition of Manasseh's arrest by the Assyrians (2 Chronicles 33:11) is sometimes thought to belong in the context of the Shamash-shum-ukin revolt. Manasseh is said to have been dragged in chains to Babylon, then released and restored to power. Apart from the defection just noted of some of Assyria's Arabian allies, we have only scant evidence to indicate that the revolt spread into the western provinces. But if there was more unrest there than our surviving records indicate, it would not be surprising to find that Manasseh had become involved, especially in view of the biblical and archaeological evidence cited below, which suggests he was moving toward independence later in his reign. Certainly, there is nothing implausible about the story of his arrest and restoration to power, since it would parallel the experiences of others in the hands of Assurbanipal. In their overextended empire, Assurbanipal and Esarhaddon before him had little choice other than to try, with the help of intimidation and promises, to find native rulers who would be loyal to Assyria. The experience of Manasseh, as described in 2 Chronicles 33:11, e.g., parallels that of Necho in Egypt and the Arab leader Uate' in Transjordan, both of whom rebelled, were captured and brought before the Assyrian king, then sent home to rule again.

172 For Esarhaddon's campaign against the Arabs, which is also described on the so-called Rassam Cylinder, see *ANET*, 297b–301a.

173 In 2 Kings 21:16, Manasseh is accused of "shedding innocent blood." The basis of this charge was supplied in postbiblical tradition: According to a variety of Jewish and Christian sources, Manasseh, again like Ahab (2 Kings 21:3), persecuted the prophets and even had Isaiah sawed in two (Josephus, *J.A.* 10.38; BT Sanhedrin 103b; Ascension of Isaiah 5:1–7; Justin, *Dialogue with Trypho* 120; Jerome, *Comment on Isaiah* 57:2; see also Hebrews 11:37).

174 For the principal suggestions, see Dan Bahat, "The Wall of Manasseh in Jerusalem," *IEJ* 31 (1981), 235–36. On the difficulties in the archaeological interpretation of the walls of Jerusalem during the last part of the Judean monarchy, see Avigad, *Discovering Jerusalem* (see n. 148), 46–60 and n. 140.

175 For a proposal that Josiah aimed to reunite Judah with Israel and reign as anointed king from Jerusalem (with the Temple as the kingdom's center), see Marvin Sweeney, *King Josiah of Judah: The Lost Messiah of Judah* (Oxford: Oxford Univ. Press, 2001).

176 For a brief overview of this period, see Oded Lipschits, *The Fall and Rise of Jerusalem: Judah Under Babylonian Rule* (Winona Lake, IN: Eisenbrauns, 2005), 11–20.

177 For an overview of the urban fortified Jerusalem in the Iron IIC period (c. 720–586), see Killebrew, "Biblical Jerusalem" (see n. 148).

178 Na'aman, "'Discovered Book'" (see n. 4). For an argument that the account of Josiah's reform is a later development and that the Book of Deuteronomy could be dated to a much later period, see Philip R. Davies, "Josiah and the Law Book," in *Hebrew Bible and History* (see n. 148), 391–403. For a rebuttal, see Rainer Albertz, "Why a Reform Like Josiah's Must Have Happened," in *Hebrew Bible and History* (see n. 148), 404–24.

179 According to Uelinger, the waning power of Assyria is partially indicated in the account of Josiah's reform. The meaning of images tied to the Assyro-Aramean astral cult, such as the horses and chariots of the sun (2 Kings 23:11), had been lost by the time of Josiah, and their destruction indicates a new cultic orientation to remove obsolete rituals rather than an anti-Assyrian impulse. Christoph Uehlinger, "Was There a Cult Reform under King Josiah? The Case for a Well-Grounded Minimum," in *Hebrew Bible and History* (see n. 148), 425–66.

180 For a discussion of the borders of Judah during the time of Josiah, see Lipschits, *Fall and Rise of Jerusalem* (see n. 176), 135–46; and Nadav Na'aman, "Josiah and the Kingdom of Judah," in L.L. Grabbe, ed., *Good Kings and Bad Kings* (London: T&T Clark, 2005), 189–247 (217–26). For a synopsis of Egypt's political and military situation during this period, see Lipschits, *Fall and Rise of Jerusalem* (see n. 176), 20–29.

181 An inscription of Psammetichus, dated 612 B.C.E., boasts of Egyptian control of Phoenicia and its timber trade.

182 Herodotus, *History* 2.157.

183 Herodotus, *History* 1.105.

184 For a brief description of the struggles between the Babylonians and Egyptians in 609–605 B.C.E., see Lipschits, *Fall and Rise of Jerusalem* (see n. 176), 32–35.

185 Riblah had been an Assyrian administrative and military center earlier, and shortly after this it became a Babylonian military center.

186 See 1 Chronicles 3:15: "The sons of Josiah: Johanan the firstborn, the second Jehoiakim, the third Zedekiah, the fourth Shallum." That Jehoahaz was Shallum is shown by Jeremiah 22:11–12. The reason "the people of the land" chose the youngest of Josiah's sons is not given. The firstborn, Johanan, is not mentioned earlier and may have died before his father. Jehoiakim, with whom Necho supplanted Jehoahaz, may have been passed over by "the people of his land" because of his pro-Egyptian leanings.

187 Babylonian Chronicle 5 in Grayson, *Assyrian and Babylonian Chronicles* (see n. 115), 99–100.

188 Babylonian Chronicle 5 in Grayson, *Assyrian and Babylonian Chronicles* (see n. 115), 100. On the Babylonian destruction of Ashkelon, see Lawrence E. Stager, "The Fury of Babylon: Ashkelon and the Archaeology of Destruction," *BAR*, January/February 1996.

189 Babylonian Chronicle 5 in Grayson, *Assyrian and Babylonian Chronicles* (see n. 115),

101–102; Herodotus names the site as Magdolos, in *History* 2.159.

190 Babylonian Chronicle 5 in Grayson, *Assyrian and Babylonian Chronicles* (see n. 115), 101–102; cf. Jeremiah 49:28–33.

191 For a presentation of the effects of the Babylonian conquest in the archaeological evidence for Jerusalem and surrounding countryside, see Lipschits, *Fall and Rise of Jerusalem* (see n. 176), 210–58.

192 For more on Gedaliah, see Lipschits, *Fall and Rise of Jerusalem* (see n. 176), 84–97.

6. Exile and Return

1 For an argument that Gedaliah was installed as a king, see J. Maxwell Miller and John H. Hayes, *A History of Ancient Israel and Judah*, 2nd ed. (Louisville: Westminster John Knox, 2006), 482–85.

2 See Jill Middlemas, *The Templeless Age: An Introduction to the History, Literature, and Theology of the "Exile"* (Louisville: Westminster John Knox, 2007); Robert P. Carroll, "Exile! What Exile? Deportation and the Discourses of Diaspora," in Lester L. Grabbe, ed., *Leading Captivity Captive: The Exile as History and Ideology*, JSOTSup 278 (Sheffield: Sheffield Academic, 1998). See also Laurie E. Pierce, "New Evidence for Judeans in Babylonia," in Oded Lipschits, Gary n. Knoppers, and Manfred Oeming, ed., *Judah and the Judeans in the Achaemenid Period: Negotiating Identity in an International Context* (Winona Lake, IN: Eisenbrauns, 2006), 399–411.

3 All quotations of biblical texts come from the NRSV.

4 See Hans Barstad, *The Myth of the Empty Land: A Study in the History and Archaeology of Judah During the "Exilic" Period* (Oslo: Scandinavian Univ. Press, 1996); Robert P. Carroll, "The Myth of the Empty Land," *Semeia* 59 (1993), 79–93. For an up-to-date review of the archaeological material and one that is critical of Barstad and Carroll, see William G. Dever, "Archaeology and the Fall of Judah," in *Eretz Israel* 29, volume in honor of Ephraim Stern (2009), 29–35.

5 From Oded Lipschits, *The Fall and Rise of Jerusalem* (Winona Lake, IN: Eisenbrauns,

2005). Lipschits's figures represent an upward revision of the numbers found in Charles Carter, *The Emergence of Yehud in the Persian Period*, JSOTSup 294 (Sheffield: Sheffield Academic, 1999). See also my essay, "The Babylonian Exile Revisited: Demographics and the Emergence of the Canon of Scripture," in Armin Lange, K.F. Diethard Römheld, and Matthias Weigold, ed., *Judaism and Crisis: Crisis as a Catalyst in Jewish Cultural History*, Schriften des Institutum Judaicum Delitzschianum (Göttingen: Vandenhoeck & Ruprecht, 2011), 1–13.

6 Lipschits, *Fall and Rise* (see n. 5), 262 (table 4.1), notes an 89 percent decrease in settled dunams for Jerusalem environs and 83 percent for the Shephelah. To this discussion, we may add Charles Carter's most recent study, "(Re) Defining 'Israel': The Legacy of the Neo-Babylonian and Persian Periods," in Susan Niditch, ed., *The Wiley-Blackwell Companion to Ancient Israel* (Malden, MA: Wiley-Blackwell, 2016), 215–40. See also Eric M. Meyers, "Haggai and Zechariah: A Maximalist View of the Return in a Minimalist Social Context," in Christopher A. Rollston, ed., *Enemies and Friends of the State: Ancient Prophecy in Context* (Winona Lake, IN: Eisenbrauns, 2017), 433–48.

7 See, e.g., F.W. Dobbs-Alsopp, *Weep, O Daughter of Zion: A Study of the City-Lament Genre in the Hebrew Bible* (Rome: Editrice Pontificio Istituto Biblico, 1993); and Meyers, "Haggai and Zechariah" (see n. 6), 438–40.

8 David Jamieson-Drake, *Scribes and Schools in Monarchic Judah: A Socio-Archeological Approach* (Sheffield: Almond Press, 1991).

9 See Rainer Albertz, *Israel in Exile: The History and Literature of the Sixth Century B.C.E.* (Atlanta: SBL, 2003), 96.

10 See the two views of Joseph Blenkinsopp and Ephraim Stern in "The Babylonian Gap Revisited," *BAR*, May/June 2002.

11 Literally, "chief cook."

12 We reject the suggestion, by Yitzhak Magen, that Nebi Samuel is Mizpah. See Yitzhak Magen, "Nebi Samuel—Where Samuel Crowned Israel's First King," *BAR*, May/June 2008.

13 Jeffrey R. Zorn, "Tell en-Nasbeh and the Problem of the Material Culture of the Sixth Century," in Oded Lipschits and Joseph Blenkinsopp, eds., *Judah and the Judeans in the Neo-Babylonian Period* (Winona Lake, IN: Eisenbrauns, 2003), 437. Though decimated, Jerusalem was not uninhabited. See Gabriel Barkay's discovery of tombs in use in the sixth century at Ketef Hinnom. Barkay, "The Riches of Ketef Hinnom," *BAR*, July/August/September/October 2009; Barkay, "The Priestly Benediction on Silver Plaques from Ketef Hinnom in Jerusalem," *TA* 19 (1992), 139–92. See also Lipschits, *Fall and Rise* (see n. 5), 210–13. The silver amulet texts have been republished using high-quality imaging techniques in Gabriel Barkay, Andrew G. Vaughn, Marilyn J. Lundberg, and Bruce Zuckerman, "The Amulets from Ketef Hinnom: A New Edition and Evaluation," *BASOR* 334 (2004), 41–71. On the importance of Ramat Raḥel in this period, see Oded Lipschits, Yuval Gadot, and Dafna Langgut, "The Riddle of Ramat Raḥel: The Archaeology of a Royal Persian Period Edifice," *Transeuphratène* 21 (2012), 57–79.

14 Lipschits, *Fall and Rise* (see n. 5), 187.

15 David Vanderhooft, *The Neo-Babylonian Empire and Babylon in the Latter Prophets* (Atlanta: Scholars Press, 1999).

16 See Middlemas, *Templeless Age* (see n. 2); Joseph Blenkinsopp, "Bethel in the Neo-Babylonian Period" in *Judah and the Judeans in the Neo-Babylonian Period* (see n. 13). There, Blenkinsopp (p. 100) adduces Zechariah 7:2 as further evidence of this idea, but his reading

of this difficult text ("Sar-eser, Regemmelech, and his men had sent to Bethel to placate YHVH") is unlikely, because "Bethel" reads much more naturally as the subject of the sentence. See Carol L. Meyers and Eric M. Meyers, *Haggai, Zechariah 1–8*, AB (New York: Doubleday, 1987), 382.

17 Albertz (*Israel in Exile* [see n. 9], 94–95) connects the 582 B.C.E. deportation to Gedaliah's assassination, an interpretation that Lipschits (*Fall and Rise* [see n. 5]) rejects.

18 On this literature, see Erich S. Gruen, *Diaspora: Jews Amidst Greeks and Romans* (Cambridge, MA: Harvard Univ. Press, 2002); W. Lee Humphreys, "A Life-Style for Diaspora: A Study of the Tales of Esther and Daniel," *JBL* 92 (1973), 211–23; Lawrence Wills, *The Jew in the Court of the Foreign King* (Minneapolis: Fortress, 1990).

19 See Laurie Pearce, "New Evidence for Judeans in Babylonia," in Oded Lipschits and Manfred Oeming, ed., *Judah and the Judeans in the Persian Period* (Winona Lake, IN: Eisenbrauns, 2006), 399–412. Naming a settlement for the place of origin of the inhabitants was common in Babylonia.

20 Pearce, "New Evidence for Judeans" (see n. 19).

21 *ANET*, 308.

22 Albertz, *Israel in Exile* (see n. 9), 99.

23 Albertz, *Israel in Exile* (see n. 9), 101; and Michael D. Coogan, *West Semitic Names in the Murašu Documents* (Missoula, MT: Scholars Press, 1976).

24 Albertz, *Israel in Exile* (see n. 9), 102. Albertz proposes that some of the dislike of Exile was due to the social humiliation of former political and religious elites being reduced to having to farm.

25 For this approach, see Daniel Smith-Christopher, *A Biblical Theology of Exile* (Minneapolis: Fortress, 2002).

26 See Mark S. Smith, *The Origins of Biblical Monotheism: Israel's Polytheistic Background and the Ugaritic Texts* (New York: Oxford Univ. Press, 2001); André Lemaire, *The Birth of Monotheism: The Rise and Disappearance of Yahwism* (Washington, DC: BAS, 2007).

27 Carol Meyers and Eric Meyers, *Zechariah 9–14*, AB (New York: Doubleday, 1993); see also Stephen L. Cook, *Prophecy and Apocalypticism: The Post-Exilic Social Setting* (Minneapolis: Fortress, 1995).

28 See Lee I. Levine, "The Nature and Origin of the Palestinian Synagogue Reconsidered," *JBL* 115, no. 3 (1996), 425–48.

29 Paul-Alain Beaulieu, "King Nabonidus and the Neo-Babylonian Empire," in Jack Sasson, ed., *Civilizations of the Ancient Near East* (Peabody, MA: Hendrickson, 2000), 969–79.

30 Pierre Briant, *From Cyrus to Alexander: A History of the Persian Empire*, trans. Peter T. Daniels (Winona Lake, IN: Eisenbrauns, 2002), 40–43. Taking into account the diversity of ethnicities of the partisan empire, we may also assess Persians' policies of "toleration" from a more pragmatic perspective; see Jennifer Gates-Foster, "Achaemenids, Royal Power, and Persian Ethnicity," in Jeremy McInerney, ed., *A Companion to Ethnicity in the Ancient Mediterranean* (New York: Wiley & Sons, 2014), 175–93.

31 *COS* 2: 124.

32 Amelie Kuhrt, "The Cyrus Cylinder and Achaemenid Imperial Policy," *JSOT* 25 (1983), 83–97. See also Touraj Daryaee, ed., *Cyrus the Great: An Ancient Iranian King* (Santa Monica, CA: Afshar, 2013).

33 Miller and Hayes (*History of Ancient Israel and Judah* [see n. 1], 510) suggest two possibilities: that it indicates Sheshbazzar's royal status or that it is a Judean translation or reuse of a Babylonian title.

34 Isaiah 52:11–12 may also be a reference to the Sheshbazzar, or at least to a return of the Temple vessels at the outset of the Persian period.

35 The notice that many chose to send material support rather than, one would assume, return themselves might indicate that even the author of Ezra 1–6 knew of a tradition of a small initial return.

36 Lipschits, *Fall and Rise* (see n. 5), 267–71.

37 Based on analyses of comparable Aramaic letters, serious doubts have been raised about the authenticity of the documents in the Book of Ezra. See the discussion in Lester L. Grabbe, *A History of the Jews and Judaism in the Second Temple Period, vol. 1* (London: T&T Clark, 2004), 76–77.

38 Diana Edelman, *The Origins of the "Second" Temple: Persian Imperial Policy and the Rebuilding of Jerusalem* (London: Equinox, 2005). See also the critique by Ralph Klein, "Were Joshua, Zerubbabel, and Nehemiah Contemporaries? A Response to Diana Edelman's Proposed Late Date for the Second Temple," *JBL* 127 (2008), 697–701.

39 See Robert P. Carroll, "So What Do We *Know* About the Temple? The Temple in the Prophets," in *Second Temple Studies 2: Temple Community in the Persian Period* (Sheffield: JSOT Press, 1994), 34–51.

40 Carol L. Meyers, "Temple, Jerusalem," in *ABD*, vol. 6, 363.

41 Meyers and Meyers, *Zechariah 9–14* (see n. 27); Antti Laato, "Zechariah 4:6b–10a and the Akkadian Royal Building Inscriptions," *ZAW* 106 (1994), 53–69. On building inscriptions in general, see Victor Hurowitz, *"I Have Built You an Exalted House": Temple Building in the Bible in the Light of Mesopotamian and North-West Semitic Writings* (Sheffield: Sheffield Academic, 1991).

42 See, however, the skepticism regarding the status of the high priesthood as a clearly defined role in the early Persian period, in Benjamin Scolnic, *Chronology and Papponymy: A List of the Judean High Priests of the Persian Period* (Atlanta: Scholars Press, 1999).

43 See Maria Brosius, *The Persians: An Introduction* (London: Routledge, 2006), esp. 72–76.

44 See the evidence of the Persepolis Fortification Tablets. On this topic, however, note the cautions of Briant, *From Cyrus to Alexander* (see n. 30), 447–48.

45 Briant, *From Cyrus to Alexander* (see n. 30), 586.

46 Lipschits, *Fall and Rise* (see n. 5), 179–81. More recently see Oded Lipschits and David S. Vanderhooft, *The Yehud Stamp Impressions: A Corpus of Inscribed Impressions from the Persian and Hellenistic Periods in Judah* (Winona Lake, IN: Eisenbrauns, 2011); Lipschits and Vanderhooft, "Continuity and Change in the Persian Period Judahite Stamped Jar Handles," in C. Frevel and I. Cornelius, eds., *Jewish "Material"*

Otherness? Studies in the Formation of Persian Period Judaism(s), OBO 264 (Fribourg: Academic Press Fribourg, 2014), 43–66.

47 Christoph Uehlinger, "'Powerful Persianisms' in Glyptic Iconography of Persian Period Palestine," in B. Becking and M.C.A. Korpel, eds., *The Crisis of Israelite Religion: Transformation of Religious Tradition in Exilic and Post-Exilic Times* (Leiden; Boston: Brill, 1999), 134–82.

48 See Kenneth Hoglund, *Achaemenid Imperial Administration in Syria-Palestine and the Missions of Ezra and Nehemiah* (Atlanta: Scholars Press, 1992).

49 Grabbe, *History of the Jews and Judaism* (see n. 37), 292–94.

50 Some scholars of Ezra-Nehemiah have expressed doubts concerning the idea that Nehemiah was originally a governor, suggesting that the notices that refer to him as governor (Nehemiah 5.14, 18; 12:26) are part of later additions to the narrative. See H.G.M. Williamson, *Ezra, Nehemiah* (Waco, TX: Word Books, 1985); Jacob L. Wright, *Rebuilding Identity: The Nehemiah-Memoir and Its Earliest Readers*, BZAW 348 (Berlin: de Gruyter, 2004).

51 The size and extent of Jerusalem during this period are debated. See David Ussishkin, "Big City, Few People," *BAR*, July/August 2005; Hillel Geva, Another View, "Small City, Few People," *BAR*, May/June 2006.

52 Eilat Mazar, "The Wall That Nehemiah Built," *BAR*, March/April 2009.

53 See John R. Bartlett, "Editorial," *PEQ* 140 (2008), 77–78.

54 Briant, *From Cyrus to Alexander* (see n. 30), 584–86.

55 Joachim Schaper, "The Jerusalem Temple as an Instrument of the Achaemenid Fiscal Administration," *VT* 45 (1995), 528–39.

56 One document from Elephantine from the mid-fifth century mentions Shelemiah and Delaiah as the "sons of Sanballat governor of Samaria"; in another, that same Delaiah works in tandem with the governor of Yehud. Also, one of the Wadi Daliyeh seal impressions from the fourth century refers to another "son of Sanballat, governor of Samaria."

57 Gary Knoppers, "Nehemiah and Sanballat: The Enemy Without or Within?" in Oded Lipschits, Gary Knoppers, and Rainer Albertz, ed., *Judah and the Judeans in the Fourth Century B.C.E.* (Winona Lake, IN: Eisenbrauns, 2007), 305–31.

58 The Tobiad line is outlined in Meyers and Meyers, *Haggai, Zechariah 1–8* (see n. 16), 340–43. For the magnificent and unique archaeological site, see Fawzi Zayadine, "'Iraq el-Amir," in *The Oxford Encyclopedia of Archaeology in the Near East*, vol. 3, 177–81.

59 Lisbeth Fried, *The Priest and the Great King: Temple-Palace Relations in the Persian Empire* (Winona Lake, IN: Eisenbrauns, 2004).

60 Conceding Grabbe's point in *A History of the Jews and Judaism* (see n. 37).

61 Most recently, see Miller and Hayes, *History of Ancient Israel and Judah* (see n. 1), 528–30.

62 See the essays in James W. Watts, ed., *Persia and Torah: The Theory of Imperial Authorization of the Pentateuch* (Atlanta: SBL, 2001).

63 Jean Louis Ska, *Introduction to Reading the Pentateuch* (Winona Lake, IN: Eisenbrauns, 2007).

64 Briant, *From Cyrus to Alexander* (see n. 30), 510–11.

65 See Joseph Blenkinsopp, *Ezra-Nehemiah: A Commentary*, Old Testament Library (Philadelphia: Westminster, 1988), esp. 57–59. See also my article, "The Rise of Scripture in a Minimalist Demographic Context," in Peter Dubovský and Federico Giuntoli, eds., *Stones, Tablets, and Scrolls: Periods of the Formation of the Bible* (Tübingen: Mohr Siebeck, 2020), 379–94. It is my contention there and in other places that a good portion of the Tanakh was edited and promulgated by the time of Ezra (mid-fifth century B.C.E.) and constituted perhaps the greatest achievement of the post-Exilic period.

66 Bezalel Porten believes that the *Letter of Aristeas* refers to an earlier pharaoh, Psammetichus I. See "Settlement of the Jews at Elephantine and the Arameans at Syene," in *Judah and the Judeans in the Neo-Babylonian Period* (see n. 13), 451–70.

67 *Textbook of Aramaic Documents from Ancient Egypt*, trans. Bezalel Porten and Ada Yardeni (Winona Lake, IN: Eisenbrauns, 1986), A4.10.

68 Bezalel Porten, "Did the Ark Stop at Elephantine?" *BAR*, May/June 1995.

69 *Textbook of Aramaic Documents from Ancient Egypt* (see n. 67), A4.1.

70 Bezalel Porten, *The Elephantine Papyri in English: Three Millennia of Cross-Cultural Continuity and Change* (Leiden; Boston: Brill, 1996), 18.

71 Notes that copies were also sent to Shelemiah and Delaiah, sons of the Samarian governor Sanballat. On the letter to Bagavahya in particular and on Elephantine in general, see Gard Granerod, *Dimensions of Yahwism in the Persian Period: Studies in the Religion and Society of the Judaean Community at Elephantine* (Berlin: de Gruyter, 2016), 153–60. On marriage and divorce, see sections 6.3.4.1,2 esp. concerning Mibtahiah.

72 A non-Jewish source, Hermopolis (letter 4:1), mentions a temple to the Queen of Heaven in Syene. See C. Houtman, "Queen of Heaven," in *Dictionary of Deities and Demons in the Bible*, 2nd ed. (Leiden; Boston: Brill, 1999), 1,281.

73 See esp. Ziony Zevit, *The Religions of Ancient Israel: A Parallactic Synthesis* (New York: Continuum, 2001).

74 Yitzhak Magen, "Bells, Pendants, Snakes & Stones," *BAR*, November/December 2010, 24–36.

75 See Izchak Magen, Haggai Misgav, and Levana Tsfania, *Mount Gerizim Excavations, vol. 1: The Aramaic, Hebrew, and Samaritan Inscriptions* (Jerusalem: IAA, 2004), passim.

76 Parts of the Nehemiah Memorial may very well be speaking to tensions in later periods. See Diana Edelman, "Seeing Double: Tobiah the Ammonite as an Encrypted Character," *RB* 113 (2006), 570–84; Jacob Wright, *Rebuilding Identity: The Nehemiah-Memoir and Its Earliest Readers* (Berlin: de Gruyter, 2004); and more recently Sean Burt, *The Courtier and the Governor: Transformations of Genre in the Nehemiah Memoir*, Journal of Ancient Judaism Supplements 17 (Göttingen: Vandenhoeck & Ruprecht, 2014).

77 See, e.g., Sara Japhet, "Can the Persian Period Bear the Burden? Reflections on the Origins of Biblical History," in *From the Rivers of Babylon to the Highlands of Judah: Collected Studies on the Restoration Period* (Winona Lake, IN: Eisenbrauns, 2006); William Schniedewind, *How the Bible Became a Book* (New York: Cambridge Univ. Press, 2004).

78 Israel Finkelstein, "Jerusalem and Judah 600–200 BCE: Implications for Understanding Pentateuchal Texts," in Peter Dubovský, Dominik Markl, and Jean-Pierre Sonnet, eds., *The Fall of Jerusalem and the Rise of Torah*, FAT 107 (Tübingen: Mohr Siebeck, 2016), 6–18, has suggested that the lack of inscriptional evidence in Aramaic or Hebrew for the early Second Temple period is so great that the dating of most biblical books should be lowered to the Hellenistic period. My critique of this point of view is in "The Rise of Scripture in a Minimalist Demographic Context" (see n. 65).

79 Several of these are written in Standard Biblical Hebrew (SBH) and not, as one might expect, in Late Biblical Hebrew (LBH). For the issues and problems surrounding the chronological distinction between SBH and LBH, see the essays in Ian Young, ed., *Biblical Hebrew: Studies in Chronology and Typology* (London; New York: T&T Clark, 2003).

80 See Carter, *The Emergence of Yehud* (see n. 5), 287–88—an idea he has taken from Gerhard Lenski, *Power and Privilege: A Theory of Social Stratification* (New York: McGraw Hill, 1966).

81 See Grabbe, *A History of the Jews and Judaism* (see n. 37), 319–21; James C. VanderKam, *From Joshua to Caiaphas: High Priests After the Exile* (Minneapolis: Fortress, 2004), 54–63.

82 Briant, *From Cyrus to Alexander* (see n. 30), 674–75.

83 Ephraim Stern, "The Religious Revolution in Persian-Period Judah," in *Judah and the Judeans in the Persian Period* (see n. 19), 199–206.

84 See Oded Lipschits and David Vanderhooft, "Yehud Stamp Impressions in the Fourth Century B.C.E.: A Time of Administrative Consolidation?" in *Judah and the Judeans in the Fourth Century B.C.E.* (see n. 57), 75–94, esp. 89–90.

85 André Lemaire, "Administration of Fourth-Century B.C.E. Judah in Light of

Epigraphy and Numismatics," in *Judah and the Judeans in the Fourth Century B.C.E.* (see n. 57), 53–74. See also Bezalel Porten and Ada Yardeni, "Social, Economic, and Onomastic Issues in the Aramaic Ostraca of the Fourth Century B.C.E.," in *Judah and the Judeans in the Persian Period* (see n. 19), 457–90.

86 Josef Wiesehofer, "The Achaemenid Empire in the Fourth Century B.C.E.: A Period of Decline?" in *Judah and the Judeans in the Fourth Century B.C.E.* (see n. 57), 11–32, esp. 28.

87 Pierre Briant in fact calls Alexander "the last Achaemenid." Quoted in Wiesehofer, "Achaemenid Empire" (see n. 87), 28.

88 Mary Joan Winn Leith, *Wadi Daliyeh I: The Wadi Daliyeh Seal Impressions, Discoveries in the Judaean Desert* 24 (Oxford: Clarendon Press, 1997), 39–94, 107–34, 209–28, 231–41.

89 Einat Ambar-Armon and Amos Kloner, "Archaeological Evidence of Links Between the Aegean World and the Land of Israel in the Persian Period," in Yigal Levin, ed., *A Time of Change: Judah and Its Neighbours in the Persian and Early Hellenistic Periods* (London; New York: T&T Clark, 2007), 1–22, at 4–5. This subject is also treated in Eric M. Meyers and Mark A. Chancey, *Alexander to Constantine: Archaeology of the Land of the Bible, vol. 3* (New Haven: Yale Univ. Press, 2012), 3–7.

7. Judea in the Hellenistic Period

1 Ptolemy I had been one of a small group of Alexander's elite companions who, in their youth, had studied under Aristotle, who, in turn, had been trained by Plato, a disciple of Socrates. Ptolemy took Greek culture seriously, and his now-lost history of Alexander was used as a principal source by Arrian of Nicomedia for his own biography of Alexander.

2 The limits of Coele Syria are unclear, but likely included Judea, Gaulanitis, Galilee, Samaria, Idumea, Perea, and Ammon, all of which were ultimately incorporated into the Hasmonean realm (see map on p. 247).

3 See Lee I. Levine, "The Age of Hellenism: From Alexander the Great Through the Hasmonean Kingdom (332–63 B.C.E.)," in H. Shanks, ed., *Ancient Israel*, 3rd ed. (Washington, DC: BAS, 2011), 243.

4 Much of the historical material in this chapter is based on the histories of Flavius Josephus (37–105 C.E.). See the preface to chap. 8 for comments on the reliability of Josephus.

5 Levine, "Age of Hellenism" (see n. 3), 242–43.

6 Tobiah had married the (unnamed) sister of Onias II (*Ant.* 12.160).

7 The letter was composed after the death of Antiochus IV (164 B.C.E.) and before the death of Judas (160 B.C.E.).

8 The interaction between Judeans and prominent Alexandrian Jews that began in the Ptolemaic era continued in the era of Roman domination (see chap. 8), and included such figures as Simon Boethus, who became Herod's father-in-law and high priest, Nicholas of Damascus, former tutor to Cleopatra's children who became Herod's trusted advisor, and Alexander Lysimachus (Philo's brother), who made substantial donations to Herod's reconstructed Temple, and financed Agrippa I's repayment of debt, paving the way for his kingship.

9 Andrea Berlin, "Manifest Identity: From *Ioudaios* to Jew. Household Judaism as anti-Hellenization in the Late Hasmonean Era," in R. Albertz and J. Wöhrle, eds., *Between Cooperation and Hostility: Multiple Identities in Ancient Judaism and the Interaction with Foreign Powers*, Journal of Ancient Judaism Supplements (Göttingen: Vandenhoeck & Ruprecht, 2013), 151–75 [157–58].

10 The exact function of the building is unknown and has been variously described as a palace, fortress, or temple. Most likely, it was a mausoleum; see Stephen Rosenberg, "Castle of the Slave—Mystery Solved," *BAR*, May/June 2012.

11 The building can confidently be attributed to Hyrcanus because it matches precisely details of such a structure that Josephus says was erected by Hyrcanus at this location (Josephus calls it a "fortress"; *Ant.* 12.230–33).

12 Levine, "Age of Hellenism" (see n. 3), 242.

13 While the book ends with a more traditional admonition to "fear God and keep his commandments," many scholars attribute this to a later editor.

14 Ben Sira's treatise was translated from Hebrew into Greek by his grandson, who had migrated to Egypt in 132 B.C.E. He was another in the long list of prominent Judeans with Egyptian connections.

15 The so-called Forth Syrian War, 219–217 B.C.E.

16 Peter Green, *Alexander to Actium* (Berkeley, CA: Univ. of California Press, 1993), 290–91.

17 Or by an Egyptian actress, depending on which version of Josephus's report one believes (*Ant.* 12.186–90).

18 Josephus's chronology of the Tobiad story contains several anomalies.

19 Interpolated from analysis in Magen Broshi, "Estimating the Population of Ancient Jerusalem," *BAR*, June 1978.

20 During the preceding Persian period, there were apparently at various times "governors" who served alongside or perhaps in superior relation to the high priest. However, the exact nature of the authority of such "governors" vis a vis the high priest is unclear. By the end of the Persian period, moreover, the last high priest, Jaddua, is portrayed as having both military and financial authority (based on *Ant.* 11.317). See James C. VanderKam, *From Joshua to Caiaphas: High Priests after the Exile* (Minneapolis: Fortress Press, 2004), 84.

21 Victor Tcherikover, *Hellenistic Civilization and the Jews* (Philadelphia: Jewish Publication Society of America, 1959), 59.

22 Apparently, this oligarchical form of governance had been in effect since the Persian era (*Ant.* 11.111).

23 While there is no scholarly consensus, a supposed genealogical connection to David and Solomon's high priest Zadok is the most widely accepted source of the name Sadducee.

24 Josephus introduced the Sadducees in *J.W.* 2.119; in *Ant.* 13.171, he says that the Sadducees, along with the Essenes and Pharisees were active sects in c. 144–143. See discussion below.

25 It is generally understood that both priests and Levites were divided into 24 "courses," each of which served for two weeks per year. See discussion in Emil Schurer, *A History of the Jewish People in the Time of Jesus Christ*, vol. II.1 (Peabody, MA: Hendrickson, 1998), 218–29.

26 VanderKam, *From Joshua to Caiaphas* (see n. 20), 192.

27 Both Josephus and 2 Maccabees agree that there was a dispute at the highest level involving civic authority, and that the losers—whom Josephus identifies as "Sons of Tobias" (*J.W.* 1.31)—were forced out of Jerusalem. It seems clear that both sources are reporting on the same dispute, the same disputants, and the same outcome, with Josephus labeling the loser(s) sons of Tobias, and 2 Maccabees identifying Simon in that role.

28 This is the plain meaning of "to carry out the king's purpose" (2 Maccabees 3:8).

29 In 2008, archaeologists discovered a stela that provides documentary evidence of Heliodorus's mission. See Hershel Shanks, "Inscription Reveals Roots of Maccabean Revolt," *BAR*, November/December 2008.

30 The message of 2 Maccabees seems to be that while women themselves were unable to offer resistance to the impending sacrilege, their anguish served to encourage those who were better equipped to take action.

31 2 Maccabees 4:5. Some authorities take this to mean that Onias traveled to Antioch to make his appeal personally. However, an alternative interpretation is that he sent his brother Jason to appeal on his behalf, and that is how Jason came to obtain the high priesthood. This seems to be the import of 2 Maccabees 4:8, which says that Jason met personally with Antiochus.

32 Assassinated, in fact, by none other than Heliodorus!

33 The terms of Seleucus's will left the kingdom to his infant son, with Antiochus as regent, but Antiochus arranged to have the child murdered, and declared himself king instead.

34 Levine, "Age of Hellenism" (see n. 3), 244.

35 Tcherikover, *Hellenistic Civilization* (see n. 21), 162.

36 The composition of this group probably did not differ greatly from the former *gerousia*, as both groups included leading citizens; but under the structure of the *polis*, civic authority was no longer in the hands of the high priest.

37 Levine ("Age of Hellenism" [see n. 3], 245) calls attention to the fact that no religious reforms were reported and that when a Jerusalem delegation was sent to participate in the athletic games at Tyre, they were careful to contribute gifts to the Tyrean navy rather than to the local god, as was customary.

38 Simon and Menelaus appear to be the same as the "sons of Tobias" who, according to Josephus, had been "cast out of the city" (*J.W.* 1.31).

39 We know from Roman sources that Antiochus invaded Egypt once in 169 but withdrew without conquering Alexandria and that he invaded again in 168 and was on the verge of over-running Alexandria when he was deterred by the Roman ambassador Gaius Popillius Laenas. 1 Maccabees says Antiochus returned from Egypt in the 143rd year—i.e., between the spring of 169 and the spring of 168—when he proceeded to loot the Temple and shed much blood (1 Maccabees 20–24). The episode being described seems to echo the looting and massacre described in 2 Maccabees 5:11–14, which clearly occurred following Antiochus's second invasion, in 168. Further, 1 Maccabees knows nothing of Jason's rebellion, while 2 Maccabees apparently knows nothing of Antiochus's supposed first looting (in 169). Other than his need for money, Antiochus had no reason to loot the Temple in 169, and in particular no reason to massacre the inhabitants of Jerusalem. One can therefore reasonably argue that 1 and 2 Maccabees are reporting a single episode of looting and massacre and that 1 Maccabees is mistaken about the date. Josephus for his part knows of only one assault on the city in his *J.W.*, and only one in *Ant.*, which he dates (apparently following 1 Maccabees) to 169. However, Josephus seems to be conflating the two invasions of Egypt, because he attributes Antiochus's withdrawal to "fear of the Romans" (*Ant.* 12.246), which would seem to describe the second invasion, in 168.

40 Josephus specifies, in *J.W.* 1.32, that Antiochus targeted "those that favored Ptolemy," while in *Ant.* 12.247 he uses the more ambiguous expression "those of the other party," which nevertheless implies the pro-Ptolemaic faction.

41 In 167 B.C.E., according to 1 Maccabees 1:29.

42 First postulated by Bezalel Bar-Kochva in an appendix to his *Judas Maccabaeus: Jewish Struggle Against the Seleucids* (New York: Cambridge Univ. Press, 1989). An identification based on preliminary excavation results is here: Doron Ben-Ami and Yana Tchekhanovets, "'Then They Built up the City of David with a High, Strong Wall and Strong Towers, and It Became Their Citadel' (1 Maccabees 1:33)," in E. Meiron, ed., *City of David Studies of Ancient Jerusalem* 11 (2016), 19*–29*.

43 Levine, "Age of Hellenism" (see n. 3), 247.

44 For a summary, see Levine, "Age of Hellenism" (see n. 3), 248.

45 Tcherikover, *Hellenistic Civilization* (see n. 21), 191.

46 2 Maccabees 5:17–20 hints at this when it attempts to explain why Antiochus had not been repulsed in the same fashion as Heliodorus (see above, pp. 257–59).

47 1 Chronicles 9:25 suggests a weekly rotation, although other sources have Levites rotating every two weeks. For the dating of Chronicles to the Hasmonean era, see below, p. 270.

48 From which, the descendants of Matthias and his sons are called by historians "Hasmoneans."

49 Compare Deuteronomy 5:22.

50 The military significance of the terms used to describe Gatekeepers is explained in John Wesley Wright, "Guarding the Gates: 1 Chronicles 26:1-19 and the Roles of Gatekeepers in Chronicles," *JSOT* 48 (1990), 69–81. Wright shows that the Greek term *ischyroi dynamei* (Hebrew: *gibbore hayil*)— used to describe Levite Gatekeepers in, e.g., 1 Chronicles 26:6—is almost always used in a military context when it appears elsewhere, and therefore the common translation as "men of great ability" overlooks the military significance of the Gatekeepers.

51 Meaning the "hammer" or possibly "hammerhead."

52 It is perhaps significant that Judas is also called a "mighty warrior" in 1 Maccabees 2:66. On the surface, this would place him among the Levite Gatekeepers. However, 1 Chronicles 9:20 states that none other than the legendary Phinehas was commander of the Gatekeepers. If Israel Finkelstein is correct in dating 1 Chronicles and 1 Maccabees as roughly contemporary, then Judas is being portrayed as the new Phinehas, i.e., a high-ranking priest rather than an ordinary Levite.

53 Some scholars suppose that Ptolemy may have had an expectation, or even a clandestine understanding, that Antiochus VII would favor him with the high priesthood if he disposed of Simon.

54 See Renee Sivan and Giora Solar, "Excavations in the Jerusalem Citadel, 1980–1988," in H. Geva, ed., *Ancient Jerusalem Revealed* (Jerusalem: IES, 2000), 168–76.

55 The passage is inserted into the narrative after Jonathan has allied himself with Trypho, but before being betrayed and executed by the latter.

56 Levine, "Age of Hellenism" (see n. 3), 270.

57 Levine, "Age of Hellenism" (see n. 3), 272.

58 Levine, "Age of Hellenism" (see n. 3), 274.

59 Jesus ben Sira, who wrote in the era just before the revolt, also comes to mind as a precursor of the Pharisees.

60 Josephus originally composed *J.W.* in Aramaic, and it was later translated into Greek with the assistance of helpers; since *Essenoi* is used as a proper name, it must have been rendered into Greek phonetically.

61 See *ABD* 2, 620.

62 *Good Person* 12.75; 13.91; *Hypothetica* 11.1.

63 See above, p. 263.

64 *Good Person* 12.78.

65 Levine, "Age of Hellenism" (see n. 3), 269.

66 The French, American, and Bolshevik revolutions all come to mind.

67 Levine, "Age of Hellenism" (see n. 3), 254.

68 See Magen Broshi, "Estimating the Population of Jerusalem," *BAR*, September

1978. For further details, see Levine, "Age of Hellenism" (see n. 3), 262–63.

69 See Levine, "Age of Hellenism" (see n. 3), 265–67.

70 Josephus claims in both his histories that Hyrcanus became wealthy by opening the sepulcher of King David and from it extracting 3,000 talents (*Ant.* 13.249; *J.W.* 1.61). However, this report is surely metaphorical, as it seems highly unlikely that such wealth would have survived the predations of Nebuchadnezzar and Antiochus Epiphanes. Instead, the metaphor suggests that Hyrcanus, like David, became wealthy as ruler of a prosperous state.

71 Levine notes ("Age of Hellenism" [see n. 3], 255) that although Hyrcanus destroyed the Samaritan Temple on Mt. Gerizim, he apparently left the Samaritan population alone, perhaps because their way of life was so similar to that of the Jews.

72 Israel Finkelstein, *Hasmonean Realities behind Ezra, Nehemiah, and Chronicles* (Atlanta: SBL Press, 2018).

73 See Levine, "Age of Hellenism" (see n. 3), 255.

74 Even without Finkelstein's conclusions, the narratives in Ezra and Nehemiah describe numerous events that have remarkable parallels to events during the early years of John Hyrcanus's high priesthood. These include celebrating the Festival of Booths; the rebuilding of Jerusalem's walls; conflicts with Samaria and Idumea; removal of a Tobiad from the Temple; and emphasis on ethnic purity.

75 Andrea Berlin, "Jewish Life Before the Revolt: The Archaeological Evidence, *JSJ* 36 (2005), 429–34.

76 The discovery of large numbers of stone vessels was once, too, thought to reflect a newly awakened concern for purity during the Hasmonean period (Levine, "Age of Hellenism" [see n. 3], 282), but current consensus dates them to the later, Herodian era.

77 Levine, "Age of Hellenism" (see n. 3), 283.

78 Andrea Berlin, "Power and Its Afterlife: Tombs in Hellenistic Palestine," *NEA* 65 (2002), 143–47.

79 Levine, "Age of Hellenism" (see n. 3), 260.

80 The particular hostility of the Judeans toward the Seleucid regime was apparently reciprocated, as reflected in the exhortation of Antiochus VII's advisors during the siege of Jerusalem that the king, "take the city by storm and wipe out completely the race of Jews...." (Diodorus, *Library of World History* 34.1).

81 *Ant.* 13.354.

82 Both the Essene and Pharisaic (rabbinic) literature support the emergence of these sects at roughly the same time. See Levine, "Age of Hellenism" (see n. 3), 270.

83 As Levine observed, "the Essene role in public affairs was not even remotely comparable to that of the Sadducees or Pharisees..." (Levine, "Age of Hellenism" [see n. 3], 277).

84 Levine, "Age of Hellenism" (see n. 3), 271.

85 For details, see the section *Common Judaism Under the Hasmoneans*, in Levine, "Age of Hellenism" (see n. 3), 280–81.

86 As Matthias declared at the onset of the revolt (1 Maccabees 1:22, cf. Deuteronomy 5:22).

87 It is unclear, however, whether this characterization by Josephus refers to Pharisees in an earlier era or to those in his own experience. See chap. 8, p. 317.

88 Levine, "Age of Hellenism" (see n. 3), 277.

89 Levine, "Age of Hellenism" (see n. 3), 277.

90 For details, see Levine, "Age of Hellenism" (see n. 3), 274–75.

91 The Greek *syngeneus* could also be construed as "fellow Jew," so it could be argued that Ananias was not suggesting that Jannaeus was a blood relative. However, the fact that Jannaeus was a fellow Jew would scarcely have been a compelling argument for not attacking him. Further, the notion that his authority (as king and high priest) "belonged to him" seems to imply a strong endorsement of his credentials to hold those offices, especially coming from a descendant of the last true Zadokite, Onias III.

92 When the Pharisees exhorted John Hyrcanus to relinquish the high priesthood, they did not cite lack of Zadokite qualifications, which as legal experts they could easily have

done if such qualifications were lacking. See below.

93 Levine, "Age of Hellenism" (see n. 3), 274.

94 See above, pp. 266–67.

95 The descriptions of Philo and Josephus suggest that members of the Essene sect were skilled in these areas.

96 *Good Person* 12.75.

97 *J.W.* II.124; Philo, *Good Person* 12.76.

98 Leviticus 21:7, 14 forbid priests from marrying a "woman who has been defiled," and Josephus (*Ag. Ap.* 1.35–36) advises that female prisoners were assumed to be defiled.

99 As Levine points out (Levine, "Age of Hellenism" [see n. 3], 275), this was perhaps the only discernible point of difference between the two sects. The Sadducees considered the Written Law to be divine, and all other regulations to be man-made, hence carrying no imperative for later generations.

100 Some scholars have opined that the Pharisees were more popular because their interpretations were more liberal, but there is no information on what the specific differences were between the sects. Rabbinic literature may hint at few but was composed centuries after the fact. See Levine, "Age of Hellenism" (see n. 3), 275 n. 119.

101 In *Ant.* 13.320, the wife of Aristobulus I is called Salina Alexandra. It was she who made Jannaeus king (*Ant.* 13.320). Although Josephus never uses the name Salome Alexandra, rabbinic sources and the Dead Sea Scrolls (4Q 322) reveal that the wife of Alexander Jannaeus was Shelamzion (i.e., Salome) Alexandra. This has prompted vigorous debate as whether there was one Alexandra who as the widow of Aristobulus I released Jannaeus from confinement and married him, or whether Salina Alexandra and Salome Alexandra were two different women. The majority opinion supports the one-Alexandra theory, and with good reason. First, the Hasmoneans typically employed both a Hebrew and a Greek name. For the queen of Aristobulus I to have *two* Greek names would have been quite improper. Second, it was common for Jewish aristocrats, including Hasmoneans, to practice papponymy—that is, naming a child after its grandfather. In the case of a ruling family, this would have been particularly relevant to the first-born son of the heir apparent. Thus, the firstborn son of Aristobulus I would have been named after John Hyrcanus I. It is inconceivable that Hyrcanus I would have countenanced the name Hyrcanus being given to the son of his third-born, exiled and out-of-favor Jannaeus. And third, it is quite implausible that the Pharisees would have sanctioned a marriage between one of their highest-ranking daughters to the same out-of-favor and exiled prince, who at the time would have been no older than 14 and at least 15 years her junior in any event. As for the occurrence of Salina in *Ant.* 13.20, this is easily explained as either a scribal error, of which the texts of Josephus are replete when it comes to proper names, or a deliberate change to provide Greek-speaking readers with a more familiar name.

102 *Ant.* 13.308: "The queen and those who were plotting with her...".

103 See Kenneth Atkinson, *Queen Salome* (Jefferson, NC: McFarland, 2012), 100.

104 Jannaeus died in 76 B.C.E. at the age of 49 (*Ant.* 13.404), making his birth year 125 B.C.E. Alexandra died in 67 B.C.E. at the age of 73, making her birth year 140 B.C.E., (*Ant.* 13. 430), or 15 years older than Jannaeus.

105 If Josephus has accurately reported the age of Hyrcanus II, in *Ant.* 15.178, as "above fourscore years old" when he died in 31 or at the latest 30 B.C.E., then his latest birthdate would have been 110 B.C.E., and possibly earlier. This would have made him at least 7 years old when Salome Alexandra and Jannaeus were married. Further, if he were the eldest son of Aristobulus I, he would have been given his grandfather's name (see n. 101).

106 Josephus does not provide a date for the event, but in his narrative, it occurs after the death of Antiochus Tryphon, which occurred in 96 B.C.E. (*Ant.* 13.365).

107 Celebrants of Tabernacles traditionally carried palm fronds and citrons.

108 Josephus's reported figure of 6,000 (*Ant.* 13.375) is undoubtedly an exaggeration, but even a tenth of that number would be significant, given the size of Jerusalem's population.

109 Called here "seekers after smooth things."

110 If authentic, this advice would have been redundant, since that was most likely the queen's goal all along.

111 M.O. Wise, M.G. Abegg, and E.M. Cook, *The Dead Sea Scrolls* (San Francisco: HarperCollins 1996), 31.

112 Levine persuasively argues (Levine, "Age of Hellenism" [see n.3], 269) that the dialogue accompanying this episode reveals that the Sadducean priests in question were potent military men.

113 They were allowed in all citadels except Hyrcania, Alexandrium, and Machaerus, where the queen's treasure was held (*Ant.* 13.417). There apparently were at least 22 such "strong places" (*Ant.* 13.427), a fact that will become relevant to our later consideration of the location and function of Qumran (see p. 287).

114 *J.W.* 1.120 relates that Alexandra also appointed Hyrcanus II as king just before her death. This event does not appear in *Ant.*, but *Ant.* 14.4 implies that Hyrcanus II has assumed "royal power."

115 See Steve Mason, "Josephus's Pharisees," in J. Neusner and B. Chilton, eds., *In Quest of the Historical Pharisees* (Waco, TX: Baylor Univ. Press, 2007), 32.

116 This experience may account for some of the skeptical tone one finds in some of his comments about the Pharisees—e.g., that they "appear" more religious than the others, and "seem" to interpret the laws more accurately (*J.W.* 1.110).

117 Nabatea had earlier been at war with Jannaeus; Antipater was married to Cypros, a high-ranking Nabatean woman, a relative or possibly even the daughter of King Aretas (*J.W.* 1.181).

118 In this passage (and many others that follow), Aristobulus and his successors never fail to attract widespread support.

119 For a discussion of the divisions of priests and Levites and the distribution of their residence, see Schurer, *History* (see n.25), 216ff.

120 Rabbinic tradition appears to identify this same figure as "Honi the circle-drawer," because in times of draught he would draw a circle around himself and stay within it until his prayers for rain were answered.

121 The precise nature of relationship between Judea and Rome is not specified, but the most reasonable presumption is that there were defined tribute obligations. Josephus says that Pompey "made Jerusalem a tributary to the Romans" (*Ant.* 14.74) and that the Romans extracted from Judea more than 10,000 talents "in a little time" (*Ant.* 14.78).

122 A *genizah* is a storage room for worn-out manuscripts that, although no longer usable, are considered too sacred to be destroyed.

123 For the intriguing details of this complicated process, see Hershel Shanks, *The Mystery and Meaning of the Dead Sea Scrolls* (New York: Random House, 1999).

124 Philo was based in Alexandria and did not have first-hand knowledge of Palestine. One can also infer from Josephus's autobiography that he had scant personal experience with the Essenes. Since the Josephus material shares many elements in common with Philo, it seems likely that he used Philo as a source or that both authors used a common source.

125 Its original title is *Serekh ha-Yahad*.

126 The celibacy of the Essenes is emphasized by Josephus and Philo, but it is unclear exactly what proportion of the sect practiced it.

127 Although surely not the only reason.

128 The Hebrew root *zdk* could signify a proper name (Zadok) or a quality (righteousness).

129 Especially 1Q28a and, of course, 1QM.

130 Levine, "The Age of Hellenism" (see n. 3), 280.

131 Cf. Otto Betz, "Was John the Baptist an Essene?" *Bible Review*, December 1990.

132 Some scholars have objected that Pliny's reference to the Essene site as being "above" Ein Gedi refers to its higher altitude rather than to its more northern location.

133 As thoroughly documented in Robert R. Cargill, "The Fortress at Qumran: A History of Interpretation," *The Bible and Interpretation*, May 2009, at https://bibleinterp.arizona.edu/articles/qumfort.

134 These features would be recognized by anyone with military training as those of a FOP, or forward observation post. The forti-

fied building was not intended to withstand assault by a large army but rather to observe such a force approaching and to fend off any scouting parties or "skirmishers" long enough to warn the main base.

135 And indeed, is summarized in Levine, "Age of Hellenism" (see n. 3), 257.

136 See Jodi Magness, *The Archaeology of Qumran and the Dead Sea Scrolls* (Grand Rapids: Eerdmans, 2002), 65.

137 Magness, *Archaeology of Qumran* (see n. 136), 65. See also Michael Wise, "Dating the Teacher of Righteousness and the Floruit of His Movement," *JBL* 122 (2003), 53–87.

138 Assuming that the Hasmoneans were not themselves Sadducees, for which there is significant contrary evidence (see above, p. 274).

139 An extensive discussion of the tentative identifications of the Wicked Priest and Man of the Lie may be found in John J. Collins, *Beyond the Qumran Community* (Grand Rapids: Eerdmans, 2010), 88–121.

140 Michael O. Wise, "The Origins and History of the Teacher's Movement," in J.J. Collins and T.H. Lim, eds., *The Oxford Handbook of the Dead Sea Scrolls* (Oxford: Oxford Univ. Press, 2010), 103.

141 Michael Wise ("Origins and History," [see n. 140], 111) points out that the Hebrew word *nadah*, found in the Teacher hymns, typically means "to expel" or "drive away."

142 CD 3.21; 4.2; 14.3.

143 Michael Wise ("Origins and History," [see n. 140], 112) argues that the Teacher's original place of exile was the steppe desert southeast of the kingdom of Damascus.

144 For example, Shaye J.D. Cohen, "Roman Domination: The Jewish Revolt and the Destruction of the Second Temple," in H. Shanks, ed., *Ancient Israel*, 3rd ed. (Washington, DC: BAS, 2011), 288.

145 As Shaye Cohen has pointed out ("Roman Domination" [see n. 144], 297), the Romans were quite happy to incorporate local ethnic rulers into their empire, provided they stayed loyal, kept the peace, and paid the appropriate tribute.

146 Notwithstanding Peter Richardson's defense of Herod's credentials, his father was Idumean, an Arabic race that had only recently converted to Judaism under duress

(*Ant.* 14.8–10, 121, 403), and his mother, Cypros, was a Nabatean Arab. See chap. 8, n. 23.

147 According to, e.g., Exodus 29:29.

8. The Era of Roman Domination

1 Aristobulus (even though in Roman custody) was still both king and high priest at that time.

2 Including, evidently, Aristobulus's uncle Absalom (*Ant.* 14.71).

3 See chap. 7, p. 282.

4 Josephus enumerates the following: Hippos, Sythopolis, Pella, Dios, Samaria, Marissa, Ashdod, Jamnia, Arethusa, Gaza, Joppa, Dor, and Strato's Tower (*Ant.* 14.74–76).

5 Presumably including what was left of Judea after the foregoing transfers of authority.

6 This logical conclusion is seemingly confirmed when, some 15 years later, a certain Sameas, whom rabbinic sources identify as either Simon ben Shetah or Shemaiah (both leading Pharisees) is discovered to be a prominent member of the Sanhedrin at the time of Herod's trial. See below, p. 299.

7 Soon after Pompey's departure, Antipater brokered a peace between the new Roman governor (Aemilius Scaurus) and the Nabateans that included a 300-talent bribe for Scaurus.

8 Antipater aided the Roman effort with weapons and supplies—another step in establishing his *bona fides* with the Romans.

9 See chap. 7, pp. 257–59.

10 Josephus for all parts of his account regarding Antipater and Herod is relying heavily on a history composed by Nicholas of Damascus, who was Herod's close advisor. Even allowing for some amplification of the exploits of father and son, the basic outlines of the story, including the successful dealings of the two with Romans, seem authentic.

11 Ironically, a position Josephus himself would hold more than a century later.

12 Galilee seems to have been a hotbed of insurgent activity. The last two battles—at Taricheae (against Pitholaus) and Mt. Tabor (against Alexander)—had been fought there.

13 One of many examples where women influence the course of history. One wonders how the wives of these notorious bandits received such a receptive hearing in Jerusalem.

14 They also complained vehemently to Hyrcanus that Antipater had usurped his own authority.

15 Josephus does not identify them further, except by name—Malichus and his brother Felix. However, their complaint—that they were attempting to "preserve Hyrcanus's government" echoes that made earlier by members of the ruling council, necessarily including leading Pharisees.

16 Mariamme was the child of a marriage between Hyrcanus's daughter Alexandra and Aristobulus's son Alexander, who in 49 B.C.E. was executed by the Pompeians. That marriage likely occurred in c. 66 B.C.E., during the short-lived reconciliation between Hyrcanus and Aristobulus.

17 In *Ant.* 14.366, Josephus modifies this to say Antigonus "cut off" his uncle's ears, perhaps in deference to the sensibilities of his Roman readers.

18 Josephus reports that Herod had not expected to be appointed king due to his lack of genealogical credentials (*Ant.* 14.386–87).

19 Josephus says that the combined force amounted to 11 legions; those numbers may be exaggerated, but the besieging army was apparently considerably larger than that employed by Pompey in 63.

20 Dio Cassius reports that Antigonus was flogged and crucified, the traditional form of punishment for rebels (*Roman History* XLIX 22.3–6). If accurate, this would prefigure in a dramatic way the execution two generations later of another "king of the Jews," Jesus of Nazareth.

21 Herod also executed "forty-five of the principal men of Antigonus's party" who apparently had managed to survive the earlier massacre (*Ant.* 15.4).

22 Antigonus had made this charge explicit during the siege of Jerusalem (*Ant.* 14.403).

23 Peter Richardson (*Herod*, Minneapolis: Fortress Press, 1999) argues strenuously in favor of Herod's Jewish credentials. He cites, e.g., the argument of Caesarean Jews in the late 50s C.E. that their rights were superior to those of the city's Syrian residents because Herod, the founder of the city, had been of Jewish descent. However, this self-serving legal argument assumes facts not in evidence. Richardson also cites the fact that two of Herod's siblings (Joseph and Salome) had Jewish names. However, he omits the fact that another brother, Phasael, had a distinctly Arabic name. Shaye J.D. Cohen, "Roman Domination: The Jewish Revolt and the Destruction of the Second Temple," in H. Shanks, ed., *Ancient Israel*, 3rd ed. (Washington, DC: BAS, 2011), 382 n. 11, makes the valid point that Herod's "Jewishness" depended on whether the observer liked him or not. Josephus's descriptions of the end of Herod's career and the accompanying epitaph would suggest that the majority of Herod's subjects hated him.

24 *J.W.* 1.181 says that Antipater "had married a lady named Cypros, of an *illustrious Arabian family*...and through this matrimonial alliance he had won the friendship of the king of Arabia" (emphasis added). This statement is supported by multiple episodes that illustrate the close link between Antipater and Aretas the king of Nabatea (i.e., Arabia). *Ant.* 14.121, however, seems to contradict Josephus's earlier remark, saying that Antipater was "in great repute with *the Idumeans* out of which nation he married a wife, who was the daughter of one of their eminent men, and her name was Cypros." The substitution of Idumea for Arabia seems to make little sense in context. We already know Antipater is a leading Idumean, as his father had been appointed *strategos* of that territory, so Antipater did not need to marry an Idumean wife to gain "repute." The appearance of Idumea in place of Arabia is one of those contradictions in Josephus's reporting that is difficult to explain; however, Arabia, makes considerably more sense in context.

25 The exact nature of Ananel's background has provoked much scholarly debate, owing to the seeming contradictions in Josephus's reporting. See James VanderKam, *From Joshua to Caiaphas* (Minneapolis: Fortress Press, 2004), 394–98.

26 Curiously, Josephus also identifies Pollio as the Sanhedrin member who had spoken favorably at Herod's trial ten years earlier (see above, p. 299); however, in the reporting of that event, Josephus says the speaker was Sameas (*Ant.* 14.172).

27 Mariamme was the daughter of Alexandra and thereby granddaughter of Hyrcanus II, and Alexander, thereby granddaughter of Aristobulus II.

28 That is, of Hyrcanus II and his Pharisee-dominated Sanhedrin.

29 See Cohen, "Roman Domination" (see n. 23), 292.

30 E.g., Exodus 29:29.

31 Josephus says Hyrcanus II was past 80 at the time (*Ant.* 15.178). If so, he had to be born around 110 B.C.E., which would suggest that he and his brother may have been adopted by Alexander Jannaeus (see chap. 7, p. 277).

32 While it is impossible to confirm or deny Herod's suspicions, it is also difficult to think that Mariamme retained much affection for her husband after he had executed her brother and grandfather.

33 Costobarus was the husband of Herod's sister Salome.

34 Cohen, "Roman Domination" (see n. 23), 295.

35 Whether Herod's sarcophagus has been discovered is much debated. See Hershel Shanks, "Was Herod's Tomb Really Found?" *BAR*, May/June 2014.

36 Kathleen Ritmeyer and Leen Ritmeyer, "Reconstructing Herod's Temple Mount in Jerusalem," *BAR*, November/December 1989.

37 One such notice has been recovered by archaeologists. See Erich Lessing, "A Temple's Golden Anniversary," *BAR*, January/February 2016.

38 The exact location of the gate is unclear—was it the main gate giving access to the

Temple or one of the gates to the Temple Mount?

39 The events during the latter part of Herod's career would have been remembered by the parents and grandparents of Josephus's contemporaries; it seems unlikely that he would have exaggerated Herod's depredations excessively.

40 These were the charges brought by Archelaus's cousin Antipater at the hearing before Augustus. Antipater was scarcely an unbiased witness, but he produced significant corroborating testimony. Moreover, when Augustus dispatched an emissary to summon Archelaus to Rome ten years later, the emissary arrived to discover Archelaus "feasting with his friends" (*Ant.* 17.344).

41 One group pleaded that the kingship of Judea be eliminated entirely and its territory become a Roman province under the jurisdiction of the Roman governor at Antioch.

42 The principal difference between ethnarch and king is that the former does not have the right to name a successor.

43 He also gave some additional northern territories to Antipas's half-brother Philip.

44 And for which Herod had been brought to trial, see the above p. 299.

45 Cohen, "Roman Domination" (see n. 23), 297.

46 Indeed, when a similar delegation had made almost identical or even more strongly worded complaints against Herod, they had been ignored (*Ant.* 17.299–315).

47 This logic is suggested by a discussion in VanderKam, *From Joshua to Caiaphas* (see n. 25), 416.

48 Or, possibly, four sons and a grandson.

49 We learn much later that the office of high priest could be bought and paid for (see n. 103). A reasonable inference is that this was common practice throughout the provincial period.

50 See chap. 7, p. 272.

51 Cohen, "Roman Domination" (see n. 23), 302.

52 See n. 21 in chap. 8 of the 3rd edition for references to books about ancient synagogues,

such as Hershel Shanks, *Judaism in Stone* (Washington, DC: BAS, 1978).

53 A good example of this rationalization can be found in 1 Thessalonians 4:13–18.

54 Cohen, "Roman Domination" (see n. 23), 304.

55 Cohen, "Roman Domination" (see n. 23), 305.

56 See Lee I. Levine, "The Age of Hellenism: From Alexander the Great through the Hasmonean Kingdom (332–63 B.C.E.)," in H. Shanks, ed., *Ancient Israel*, 3rd ed. (Washington, DC: BAS, 2011), 274; see also chap. 7, p. 275.

57 See chap. 7, p. 289.

58 A conspicuous exception to this identification would have been Josephus, who in his autobiography traces his ancestry from a daughter of the Hasmonean Jonathan.

59 For a complete inventory of these exchanges between Pharisees and Sadducees as contained in Tannaitic sources, see Ellis Rivkin, *Defining the Pharisees: The Tannaitic Sources* (Cincinnati: Hebrew Union College, 1970).

60 Not all scholars accept the identification of the senior priests as Sadducees. See discussion in VanderKam, *From Joshua to Caiaphas* (see n. 25), 477–78.

61 Cohen, "Roman Domination" (see n. 23), 292.

62 Cohen, "Roman Domination" (see n. 23), 306.

63 Cohen, "Roman Domination" (see n. 26), 306.

64 From as few as 10–15 to as many as 50–70. See Jodi Magness, *The Archaeology of Qumran* (Grand Rapids: Eerdmans, 2002), 69.

65 In fact, some would prefer "union" as a translation of *Yahad.*

66 The analogy of Harvard College in 17th-century New England comes to mind. The Puritan colonists lived in scattered, self-sufficient communities, led pious lives, were devoted to scripture, and sent their sons for training at the only institution then available. Michael Wise also points out that hundreds of individual hands are represented in the

931 separate documents within the Dead Sea Scrolls. See Michael O. Wise, "The Origins and History of the Teacher's Movement," in T. H. Lim and J. J. Collins, eds., *The Oxford Handbook of the Dead Sea Scrolls* (Oxford: Oxford Univ. Press, 2010), 97. This would be consistent with a small indoctrination center with, say, 20 proselytes (10 in each of two classes), each practicing their hand on one manuscript per year. Over the site's more than century of operation, this would result in many hundreds of different practice documents in different hands with those being deemed surplus or deficient (but nevertheless of sacred character) being deposited in Cave 4 as a *genizah*, as some scholars have suggested was its function.

67 Wise, "Origins and History" (see n. 66), 117.

68 According to Magness (*Archaeology of Qumran* [see n. 64], 66–69), the Qumran may have been abandoned briefly in 31 B.C.E due to an earthquake, and again in 4 B.C.E. (or a bit earlier), but was otherwise continually occupied until destroyed by the Romans in c. 68 C.E. Josephus has the Essenes as an active sect (whether at Qumran or not) until the Great Revolt, when he describes their cruel treatment at the hands of the Romans (*J.W.* 2.152–53).

69 Cohen, "Roman Domination" (see n. 23), 306.

70 See Steve Mason, "*Josephus's Pharisees: The Narratives*," in J. Neusner and B.D. Chilton, eds., *In Quest of the Historical Pharisees* (Waco, TX: Baylor Univ. Press, 2007), 33.

71 In *J.W.* 2.163, Josephus explicitly states that the Pharisees "hold the position of the leading sect."

72 Cohen, "Roman Domination" (see n. 23), 308.

73 Quirinius was the Roman governor of the Syrian province to which Judea was attached; Coponius was the prefect (or procurator) in charge of local affairs in Judea at the time the census was initiated.

74 Gamala would become a center of the revolutionary movement in the eventual war with Rome (*J.W.* 4.1).

75 Two sons of Judas, James and Simon, were executed during the procuratorship of Tiberius Alexander (46–48).

76 Cohen, "Roman Domination" (see n. 23), 309.

77 For a summary of this enduring view, see James Charlesworth, *Jesus and the Dead Sea Scrolls* (New York: Doubleday, 1991), 37–40: "Jesus was certainly not an Essene...He was also not taught by or significantly influenced by the Essenes...."

78 See, e.g., the Essene *War Scroll*.

79 *Ant.*18.118; Matthew 14:5.

80 Compare, e.g., Matthew 3:2 and Matthew 4:17.

81 Both Caiaphas and Ananus are referred to as "high priests" in the Gospel accounts, even though Ananus had not served since approximately 15 C.E. A reasonable assumption is that the title "high priest," much like modern governmental titles, stay attached to individuals even after they have left office.

82 Matthew 27:28. Translated from the Greek term *lestai* that is the same word Josephus repeatedly uses to describe revolutionaries.

83 Readers will recall that according to Dio Cassius, this is how Antigonus was executed— see n. 20

84 Notwithstanding Acts 11:26, some scholars opine that the term "Christian" does not appear until the second century, while the movement in the first century was most likely known as "the sect of the Nazoreans" (cf. Acts 24:5). See J.D.G. Dunn, "From the Crucifixion to the End of the First Century," in H. Shanks, ed., *Partings: How Judaism and Christianity Became Two* (Washington, DC: BAS, 2013), 28.

85 This process is described in Shaye J.D. Cohen, *From the Maccabees to the Mishnah* (Louisville, KY: Westminster John Knox Press, 2006), 159–62.

86 For further discussion, see Bruce Chilton, "The Godfearers: From the Gospels to Aphrodisias," in *Partings* (see n. 84), 55–71.

87 The relationship between these two episodes is difficult to determine because the chronology has not been adequately established. See Cohen, "Roman Domination" (see n. 23), 299 and n. 16.

88 Although the Judeans expressed their willingness to die, Josephus advises that Petronius delayed enforcing the emperor's edict because he feared "a war," and apparently had assembled an army in preparation for that eventuality (*Ant.* 18.269, 301, 302).

89 Although Josephus says that Agrippa, who was in Rome at the time, had already persuaded Caligula to relent.

90 Agrippa's role in these negotiations is sometimes questioned because it is not reported by any Roman source.

91 A copy of Claudius's letter to the embassy in Alexandria survived on a papyrus roll known today as *P.Lond.* 6.1912.

92 Agrippa's mother, Berenice, was the Idumean daughter of Herod's sister Salome; his father, Aristobulus, was the son of Herod and his Hasmonean wife Mariamme I. By this reckoning, Agrippa I was one-quarter Hasmonean.

93 The title "prefect" was apparently used in the era before Agrippa I and "procurator" afterward.

94 Cohen, "Roman Domination" (see n. 23), 302.

95 Margaret H. Williams, "Jews and Christians at Rome," in *Partings* (see n. 84), 155.

96 So Josephus reports in *Ant.* 20.118, although his *J.W.* 2.232 states only one.

97 Such as Eleazar son of Dineus (*Ant.* 20.121).

98 It is curious that Josephus reveals the connection between Felix and the assassins only in *Ant.* One suspects that in *J.W.* former procurators or friends and relatives still had enough influence in Rome to cause Josephus to pull his punches.

99 The fifth son of Ananus or perhaps his grandson. See above p. 313.

100 Josephus does not say what the charges were, but it must have been something akin to blasphemy to warrant punishment by stoning.

101 See Williams, "Jews and Christians" (see n. 95), 158.

102 Cohen, "Roman Domination" (see n. 23), 311.

103 In 63, Agrippa II deposed Jesus son of Damneus and appointed in his place Jesus son of Gamaliel. According to rabbinic sources (*b. Yebam:* 61a), Jesus b. Gamaliel was married to a Boethusan woman who bribed Agrippa II with (figuratively) "a bucket of silver." Although the historical accuracy of this passage may be suspect, it tends to confirm the belief (if not the fact) that the high priests were linked by marriage and that the office was being obtained by bribery. See discussion in VanderKam, *From Joshua to Caiaphas* (see n. 25), 483–87.

104 Cf. *J.W.* 2.411.

105 Ananias had served as high priest from 48 to 59 and was one of the wealthiest men in Jerusalem.

106 Josephus does not report on the ultimate fate of Florus, but Suetonius in his biography of Vespasian says that "the rebellious Jews … murdered their governor," presumably meaning Florus (*Vespasianus* 4).

107 Herod the Great's former palace that was well protected by defensive walls and towers.

108 As Shaye Cohen observed (Cohen, "Roman Domination" [see n. 23], 314), "… diverse groups shared a common willingness to fight the Romans, but differed from each other in many other respects."

109 "…the *Zealots*, for so these miscreants *called themselves*" (*J.W.* 4.161).

110 For example, Martin Hengel, *The Zealots* (Edinburgh: T&T Clark, 1989).

111 "And he (who swears falsely before God) will never escape punishment, for there are thousands who have their eyes upon him, zealots (*zelotai*) for the law and strictest guardians of ancestral traditions, merciless to those who subvert them" (*On the Special Laws* 2.253).

112 As described in Cohen, "Roman Domination" (see n. 23), 314.

113 The garrison was described earlier as a cohort, i.e., a unit of about 500 soldiers.

114 Evidently, the "peace party," this time led by one Ananus son of Jonathan (presumably the former high priest who had been assassinated during the procuratorship of Felix).

115 Josephus puts the casualties at 5,300 legionnaires and 480 members of cavalry. This is likely one of the rare cases where Josephus's numbers are not inflated.

116 The Classic Greek is reminiscent of well-known Greek epic tales, such as the *Iliad* or the war chronicles of Thucydides, and almost certainly is the work of Josephus's "helpers."

117 Presumably to avoid assassination by his own guards.

118 Cohen, "Roman Domination" (see n. 23), 316.

119 Cohen, "Roman Domination" (see n. 23), 317.

120 For the details of the final battle, see Eric H. Cline, *Jerusalem Besieged: From Ancient Canaan to Modern Israel* (Ann Arbor: Univ. of Michigan Press, 2004), 125–27.

121 Vivid evidence of the fiery destruction has been unearthed by archaeologists. See Nahman Avigad, "Jerusalem in Flames—The Burn House Captures a Moment in Time," *BAR*, November/December 1983.

122 Louis H. Feldman, "Financing the Colosseum," *BAR*, July/August 2001.

123 Steven Fine, "The Temple Menorah—Where Is It?" *BAR*, July/August 2005; for the color reconstruction, see Steven Fine, Peter J. Schertz, and Donald H. Sanders, "True Colors: Digital Reconstruction Restores Original Brilliance to the Arch of Titus," *BAR*, May/June 2017, 28–35, 60–61.

124 For these and other archaeological details, see Jodi Magness, *Masada: From Jewish Revolt to Modern Myth* (Princeton: Princeton Univ. Press, 2019); and Gwyn Davies, "The Masada Siege—From the Roman Viewpoint," *BAR*, July/August 2014, 28–36, 70.

125 The Tenth Legion had led the attack on two other extremely well defended sites, Gamla and Machaerus.

126 Cohen, "Roman Domination" (see n. 23), 321.

127 Cohen, "Roman Domination" (see n. 23), 321.

Index

Ahaz, king of Judah
anxiety, 385n99; Assyrian vassalage, 178, 180; bulla of, *177;* death, 188; Israel and Damascus's assaults on, 177–78; loss of Elath, 383n69; name forms, 385n101; reign, *147;* successor, 188

Ahaziah, king of Israel, *147,* 150, 155

Ahaziah, king of Judah, *147,* 155–57, 159, *plate 7*

Aḥer, 80

Ahijah (prophet), 121, 138–39, 146, 354n52

Ahijah (son of Shisha), 118

Ahimelech, 107, 111

Ahinoam (daughter of Ahimaaz, wife of Saul), 102

Ahinoam of Jezreel (wife of David), 108, 109

Ahishar, 118

Ahitub (priest of Nob), 107, 111

Ahlström, Gösta, 123

Ahmose, pharaoh, 56

Ahuzzath, 8

Ai, 67, 84

'Ain Dara (Syria), 120

'Ajrud *see* Kuntillet 'Ajrud

Akkad, 8, 49

Akra (citadel), 261

al-Yahudu, 218

Albertz, Rainer, 394n17, 394n24

Albinus (Roman procurator), *324,* 326

Albright, William F., 13, 73

Alexander (Herod's son), 307, *308*

Alexander (son of Aristobulus II), 296–97, 405n12, 405n16

Alexander Dius Polyhistor, 124

Alexander Jannaeus, Hasmonean king
adopted children, 406n31; civil war, 278–79; Cleopatra and, 272, 274, 277–78, 402n91; death, 279, 403n104; Feast of Tabern acles, 278; as high priest, 277, 278; as "Lion of Wrath," 277–79, 288; map of conquests, *268;* marriage, 277, 402n101, 403n105; Pharisees and, 278–79; reign, *263,* 277–79; territorial expansion, 270, 277–78; war with Nabatea, 403n117

Alexander the Great
conquest of Persia, 241–42, 245–46; conquest of Tyre, 247; control of Egypt, 245; death and aftermath,

246; education, 398n1; Ptolemy I and, 398n1; as respectful of local deities, 261; tax system, 241; as "the last Achaemenid," 398n87

Alexandra (Hyrcanus II's daughter), 303, 405n16, 406n27

Alexandria, Egypt
Caligula and, 322; Claudius and, 322, 409n91; Jerusalem revolt (64–66) and, 330; Jewish community, 246, 249–50, 272–73, 322, 398n8; Ptolemaic era, 246, 249–50, 398n8

Alexandrium, 403n113

Alt, Albrecht, 73, 74

Amalekites, 101, 103, 107

Amara, 64

Amaziah, king of Judah
death, 382n53; defeated by Joash, 162, 382n53; Edomite campaign, 162, 168; father's death avenged by, 381n49; reign, *147;* "to your tents" phrase, *62*

Ambiblius, Marcus, *324*

Amduat 10th Hour, *42*

Amenemopet (scribe), 78

American history analogies, 52–53, 77, 407n66

American Schools of Oriental Research, 242

Amman, Jordan, *98*

Ammon, 191, 210, 211, 398n2

Ammonites
David's wars against, 109, 110, 114; deities, 121, 139; as Israel's adversaries, 98, 99, 100, 101, 110; Jephthah's battle with, 90; Judah, raid of, 383n66; Judah's ceding of territory to, 215; king, *98;* Meunites and, 383nn67–68; Saul's wars against, 99, 100, 101; threat to early monarchy, 93

Amnon (son of David), 112

Amon, king of Judah, *147,* 201

Amorites, 82, 354n39

Amos (prophet), 163, 164, 382n56

Amos, Book of, 46

Amram, 7, 51

Amraphel of Shinar, 6

Amun temple, Karnak, *137,* 139

Ananel (high priest), 302, 303, 330, 406n25

176–201; Assyrian King Shalmaneser III and rise of imperial Assyria, 151–54, 157; in biblical texts, 135–36; "charismatic" kingship, 146; Damascene hegemony, 155–61; Damascus alliance, 177–78, 383n65, 383n69; Damascus conflicts, 149, 379n26; early years, 136–46; eighth-century prosperity, 161–74; everyday life, 166–68; extent of territory, 163; fall of, 133, 142; fall of Jerusalem, 207–11; fall of Samaria, 183–88; Hazael's ascendancy, 157–61; Jehu's revolt, 155–57; Jeroboam's reign, 141–43; list of kings, 147; map, 145; Omri's dynasty, 146–54; Phoenicia, relations with, 148–49, 150, 164; political turmoil, 146; popular religion, 173, 175; prosperity under Jeroboam II, 163–65; reign of Jeroboam II, 162–66; reign of Josiah and end of the Assyrian Empire, 201–7; reign of Manasseh and Assyrian conquest of Egypt, 196–201; reigns of Rehoboa m and Jeroboam, 141–43; religion, 168–74; restoration as trading power under Omri, 146–49; resurgence, 161–62; royal assassinations, 144–46, 155, 176; schism from Judah, 93, 132, 133, 136–39; separation from Davidic-Solomonic dynasty, 88; Shechem as capital, 88; Sheshonq's invasion, 139–41, 140; sources of evidence for reconstructing the period, 133–36; tensions with Judah, 132; Tiglath-pileser III, 176–83; wars of early Divided Monarchy, 143–46

Israelites
Canaanite peasant revolt model, 73–74; Canaanites, battle with, 90; characteristic features of early Israelites in central hill country, 64–71; four-room houses, 30–32, 31, 33, 66–68, 67; historiography, beginnings of, 126–27; Hyksos connection, 56–58; Iron Age I, 104; origins, 75; Philistines as archenemy, 80, 101–2; proto-Israelites, 24–27, 32; religion, 188; symbols of divinity, plate 6; worship of Canaanite deities, 88, 89

Issachar, 354n40
Issachar, tribe of, 81, 143
Isserlin, B. S. J., 354n48
Ištar (goddess), 173
It'amar the Sabaean, 386n119

Ittobaal, king of Sidon, 191
Ittobaal, king of Tyre, 148
Itureans, 269, 270
ivory, 148, 164, 382n60, plate 5, plate 8
'Izbet Sartah, 60, 67, 70, 103, 359n18

J

J (Jahwist) source, 13, 127
Jabesh-Gilead, 99, 100
Jabin, 89, 90
Jabneh, 165
Jacob (Israel)
age, symbolism of, 7; all of Israel descended from, 1; ancestral narratives, 1–2, 52; burying jewelry near Shechem, 8; dating of, 7; in Egypt, 52; embalmed/mummified, 343n6; as eponymous ancestor, 1, 9; family's migration to Egypt, 21; genealogy, 7, 127; in J source, 127; literary tradition, 123; as progenitor of Israel, 25; purchasing land in Shechem, 341n19; sons of, 1, 2; younger son motif, 9, 10

Jaddua (Judean high priest), 245, 247, 399n20
Jair, 89
James (brother of Jesus), 326, 327
James (son of Judas), 327, 408n75
James, P., 370n157
James son of Zebedee, 323, 327
Jamieson-Drake, David W., 373n183
Jamnia, 405n4
Jason (high priest), 258–61, 399n31, 400n39
Jason of Cyrene, 255
Jebusites, 82, 109, 362n61
Jedaniah, 236–37
Jedaniah archive, 236
Jehoahaz, king of Judah (609), 147, 205–6, 392n186
Jehoahaz, king of Judah (735–727) see Ahaz, king of Judah
Jehoash, king of Judah
childhood, 159; conflict with priesthood, 166; Hazael, capitulation to, 161, 381n49; murder of, 381n49; name forms, 381n44, 381n47, 384n82; reign, 147, 159–60; Temple repairs, 159–61

Jehohanan (high priest), 269

ANCIENT ISRAEL

Jehoiachin, king of Judah
ascension to throne, 209; Exilic
period, 209, 215, 219; loyalty to
Nebuchadnezzar, 210; reign, *147*

Jehoiada (high priest), 159, 381n45

Jehoiakim, king of Judah, *147,* 206, 209, 215, 392n186

Jehoram, king of Judah, *147,* 151, 155, 381n37, 383n69

Jehoshaphat (son of Ahilud), 111, 118

Jehoshaphat, king of Judah, *147,* 151, 155, 379n26, 383n66

Jehosheba, 159, 381n45

Jehu, king of Israel
Black Obelisk, *158;* reign, *147;* relations
with Assyria, 157; relations with
Damascus, 157, 158–59; revolt, 155–57

Jehu son of Hanani, 146

Jephthah, 89, 90

Jeremiah (prophet)
on Babylonian deportations from
Jerusalem, 209, 211; bulla of scribe,
210; condemnation of worship of
astral deities, 391n158; on Exile,
221–22, 231; Exilic period, 218, 219; fall
of Jerusalem, 211; on Judeans in Egypt,
235, 238; on life after fall of Jerusalem,
214; prophesies about Babylonian
incursion into Judah, 208; on Shiloh's
destruction by Philistines, 87

Jericho, 84, 216, *228,* 305, 310

Jeroboam I, king of Israel
Ahijah's prophecy, 138–39; bull statue,
plate 6; capital at Penuel, 141, 147;
capital at Tirzah, 141, 147; death, 143;
Rehoboam's conflict with, 141; reign,
141–43, 146, *147;* religious centers at
Dan and Bethel, 141, 203; revolt against
Solomon, 121; Shechem as capital, 88;
Shishak/Sheshonq as ally, 121, 123, 138,
139, 141, 370n158; Shishak/Sheshonq
as enemy, 139–41; successor, 143; wars
of the early Divided Monarchy, 143

Jeroboam II, king of Israel, *147,* 162–66, 176

Jerusalem
Alexander the Great and, 245, 247;
American Schools of Oriental Research,
242; Ark of the Covenant in, 109;
Assyrian control of, 389n146; Assyrian
siege of, 192, 194, 196, 207, 387n129,

390n153; Babylonian deportations,
209, 211, 213; Babylonian siege, 209;
centrality of, 109, 203, 241; civil war
under Alexander Jannaeus, 278–79;
Corner Gate, 383n65; Damascus-Israel
siege of, 178; as David's capital, 111,
116, 365n100; David's conquest of, 82,
109, 127; David's palace, 115; David's
temple plans, 111; defenses, 195, 287,
333, 382n65, 389nn147–48, 404n134;
Divided Monarchy, 88, 141–42, 144, 162,
177, 378n11, 382n65; divine deliverance,
390n153; Exilic period, 214–18, 394n13;
fall of, 197, 207–11, 213; fall of, aftermath,
214–18; First Jewish Revolt, 327–35, *332,*
410nn113–15, 410n121; Gihon Spring,
148–49; as Greek *polis,* 258–60,
400n36; under Hasmonean rule,
269; Hellenistic period, 246, 250, 251,
264–65; Hellenistic reform movement,
255–62; Herod's building projects,
335; Herod's death, aftermath of, 310;
Herod's reconquest of, 300–301, 314,
405n19; internecine strife, 333; Jesus
in, 320; Jotham's building projects,
177; Maccabean Revolt, 263; *millo,* 195,
389n147; Ophel, 115, 119, 177, 387n127,
389n149; Persian period, 231, 232, 241;
Pompey's conquest, 280–83, 291,
404n121; Pompey's conquest, aftermath
of, 295–96; population after Exile, 215,
393nn5–6; population growth, 389n148;
as Rehoboam's seat of government, 88;
Roman destruction of (70 C.E.), *332,*
333–35, 410n121; as Roman tributary,
295; Royal Stoa, 335, *335;* sacrifices, 142;
Seleucid siege of, 402n80; Sennacherib's
invasion, 193–95, 389n146; Shishak/
Sheshonq's invasion, 140–41; Solomon's
building projects, 119, 128, 373n187;
Stepped-Stone Structure, 115, *127,*
128–29; walls, 119, 128, 195, 201, 228,
232, 265, 373n187, 389n148; Yahweh
associated with, 64; see also Salem

Jerusalem Studies in Egyptology (Shirun-Grumach, ed.), 20

Jerusalem Temple (Solomonic Temple)
Babylonian destruction of, 128,
211, 213, 220, 226; centrality of, 15;
construction date, 48; construction of,
119–20; decorations, 119–20, 131, *plate 8;*
Hezekiah and, 189, 388n136; Jehoash's

428

K

R

INDEX

Sadducees

aftermath of Pompey's conquest of Jerusalem, 295, 314; differences from Pharisees, 276, 402n99; Essenes and, 289; etymology of word, 274, 314, 399n23; first century C.E., 314–15; Hasmonean era, 274, 275, 279–80, 289, 314, 404n138; Josephus on, 255, 265, 273, 315, 399n24; Maccabean Revolt, 265, 267; as military leaders, 265, 403n112; role in public affairs, 317, 402n83; sectarian rivalry, 276, 278, 281–82, 289–90; Written Law as divine, 276, 402n99

Sais, Egypt, 391n170

Saite Renaissance, 204, 391n170

Salamanu of Moab, 180

Salamis, Battle of, 247

Salem, 6, 15; *see also* Jerusalem

Salina Alexandra *see* Salome Alexandra, Hasmonean queen

Salmon, 47

Salome (Herod's descendant), *308*

Salome (Herod's sister), 406n23, 406n33, 409n92

Salome Alexandra, Hasmonean queen
death, 280, 403n104; Judea in Hellenistic period, 279–80; marriages, 276, 277, 402n101, 403n105; Pharisees and, 276, 277, 279–80, 289, 290, 314, 316; reign, *263,* 277; Sadducees and, 279–80, 314; successor, 403n104; treasure, 403n113

Samaria/Samaritans
acropolis, 150; anti-Assyrian alliance, 185; Aramean siege of, 379n26; architecture, 149; Assyria, revolts against, 185–86; under Assyrian control, 185–87, 386n122; Assyrian destruction of, 382n60; as Assyrian province, 186, 188; Assyrian siege of, 184, 185; bronze bull, 142; in Coele Syria, 398n2; fall of, 183–88, 386n114; Hasmonean territorial expansion, 269; Hellenism in, 242, 243; Herod's family in, 301; ivories, 164, 382n60; John Hyrcanus I and, 401n71; Mt. Gilboa, 85, *86;* Mt. Gerizim temple, 401n71; murder of Galilean pilgrims, 325; as northern kingdom capital, 88; Omri's founding of, 141, 146, 147–48; ostraca, 164; pottery, 387n125; Roman jurisdiction,

405n4; Sebaste, 305; tensions with Jews, 238–39; in Wadi Daliyeh papyri, 242

Sameas (Pharisee), 299, 302, 405n6, 406n26

Samsi, queen of Arabia, 178, 183, 386n119

Samson, 80, 88, 89, 90

Samuel
David and, 106; denunciation of kingship proposal, 72, 90; genealogy, 350n100; leadership, 99; Saul and, 99, 101

Samuel, Books of
central hill country locations, 65; David, 106, 113; Deuteronomistic history, 135; early monarchy, 94, 101; "Edom" and "Aram" confusion, 365n88; Genesis parallels, 14–15; literary motifs, 14–15; Philistines, 103–4; Saul-David contrast, 102–3

Sanballat of Samaria, 232, 233, 238, 242, 396n56, 397n71

Sanhedrin
authority, 317; Christians, trials of, 326; compliance with Herod, 302, 304, 317; Herod Archelaus and, 311; Herod's trial, 299, 317, 405n6, 406n26; Jerusalem revolt and, 328; priesthood and, 311; *see also* Council of Elders

Sanipu of Bit-Ammon, 180

sara'at (leprosy), 383n70

Sarah/Sarai
Abraham's origins, 3–4; ancestral narratives as family affair, 2; dating of, 14; monarchy associated with, 15; Nuzi parallels, 12; Ugaritic parallels, 9, 10, 11

Sargon II, king of Assyria
campaign map, *181;* death, 189, 190, 391n160; Judah and, 189, 388n132; Nimrud Inscription, 388n132; revolts against, 185–86, 189, 388nn133–34; tributes to, 186, 386n119; two-way relocations, 185, 186, 386n122

Satirical Letter *see* P.Anastasi I

Saul, king of Israel
archaeological evidence, 103–4; choice of, as king, 99–100; contrasted with David, 102–3; David as adversary of, 102–3, 106–7; death, 100–101, 104; early monarchy, 93–132; evaluation of his reign, 101–4; expedition against

Image Credits

Numbers refer to pages.

Adam Zertal: 85

Alain Guilleux/Alamy Stock Photo: 54

Amihai Mazar: 86

André Lemaire: 184

Avraham Faust: 66 (redrawn); 69 (redrawn)

Baron Wolman: plate 10

Collection Israel Antiquities Authority; exhibited Israel Museum Jerusalem: 171; 208; plate 3

Daniel Frese/Bibleplaces.com. 129

David Harris/Bible Lands Museum Jerusalem: plate 5

David Harris/Collection Israel Antiquities Authority; exhibited Israel Museum Jerusalem: 228, top; 336

Erich Lessing/Art Resource, NY: 97; 137; 158; 192; 194; 332

Garo Nalbandian: 70, top; plate 9

Hershel Shanks: 195; plate 2

Israel Finkelstein: 60; 61; 67; 69; 70, bottom; 71

Israel Museum Jerusalem: plate 4

J. Liepe: 65

James K. Hoffmeier: 23

Leen Ritmeyer: 306

Linda G. Meiberg: 72

Manfred Bietak: 22; 24; 40; 46 (redrawn)

Metropolitan Museum of Art, Rogers Fund, painting by Norman de Garis Davies: 19

Nahman Avigad: 217

Nahum Slapak/Israel Museum Jerusalem: plate 8

NASA Johnson Space Center, Image Science & Analysis Laboratory: plate 1

Penn Museum, Gift of the American Exploration Society, 1906: 28

Peter Lanyi/Israel Museum Jerusalem: 257

Robert Deutsch: 177, right; 187, bottom right; 210, right

Shai Halevi/Israel Antiquities Authority: 284

Tatsiana Salauyova/Alamy Stock Photo: 42

The Brooklyn Museum: 236

The Shlomo Moussaieff Collection, London: 160; 177; 187, top; 210, left

The Trustees of the British Museum/Art Resource, NY: 225

Vladimir Naikhin: 335

Werner Braun: 172

Yosef Garfinkel: 115 (photo by Skyview); 125 (photo taken at the MegaVision Lab)

Ze'ev Meshel and Avraham Hai: 169; 170

Zev Radovan/BibleLandPictures.com: 98; 127; 152; 173; 187, bottom left; 228, bottom; 269; 286; plate 6; plate 7

Carl R. Lepsius, *Denkmäler aus Ägypten und Äthiopien* (Leipzig: J. C. Hinrichs, 1913): 18, bottom

Percy E. Newberry, *Beni Hasan*, part I: *Archaeological Survey of Egypt 1* (London: Egypt Exploration Fund, 1893), plate XXX: 18, top

Uvo Hölscher, *The Temples of the Eighteenth Dynasty* (Chicago: Oriental Institute, 1939): 31